SQL Server MVP
Deep Dives

SQL Server MVP
Deep Dives

Edited by Paul Nielsen ▪ Kalen Delaney ▪ Greg Low
Adam Machanic ▪ Paul S. Randal ▪ Kimberly L. Tripp

MANNING

Greenwich
(74° w. long.)

For online information and ordering of this and other Manning books, please visit www.manning.com. The publisher offers discounts on this book when ordered in quantity. For more information, please contact

Special Sales Department
Manning Publications Co.
Sound View Court 3B
Greenwich, CT 06830
Email: orders@manning.com

Manning Publications Co.
Sound View Court 3B
Greenwich, CT 06830

Development editor: Jeff Bleiel
Lead copyeditor: Andy Carroll
Typesetter: Dottie Marsico
Cover designer: Marija Tudor

ISBN 978-1-935182-04-7
Printed in the United States of America

1 2 3 4 5 6 7 8 9 10 – MAL – 14 13 12 11 10 09

MVP contributors and their chapters

Technical Editor
Rod Colledge

To all children traumatized by the horrors of war
and War Child's efforts to help children be children again

brief contents

contents

6 Error handling in SQL Server and applications 73
BILL GRAZIANO

7 Pulling apart the FROM clause 86
ROB FARLEY

preface

Each year Microsoft invites all the MVPs from every technology and country to Redmond for an MVP Summit—all top secret—"don't tweet what you see!" During the MVP Summit, each product team holds a series of presentations where they explain their technologies, share their vision, and listen to some honest feedback.

At the 2007 MVP Summit in Seattle, Bill Gates presented his vision of the future of computing to the MVPs and then took questions for about an hour. I really enjoy these dialogues. I get the sense that if BillG wasn't the founder of Microsoft, he'd make a great MVP. You can tell he likes us as fellow Geeks, and he's rather candid in the MVP Q&A time. It's one of my favorite parts of the MVP Summit.

During the Q&A, the lines at the microphones are far too long to bother to join, so I daydream a few questions I'd ask BillG:

- As the world's wealthiest Geek, what can you tell me about your PC?
- Even with all your accomplishments, do you still find the most happiness and satisfaction with your family?
- Do you play Age of Empires 2, and if so, want to join me in a game?
- Kirk or Picard?
- Can I buy you lunch?

And then I thought of a good, deep, Charlie Rose-type of question: "Centuries from now, would you rather be remembered as the guy who put a computer on every desk, or as the guy who ended malaria and fought the good fight against poverty?"

As I try to guess what BillG might say, the answer is obvious. I'm glad that BillG's intellect and resources are being directed at improving the human condition, and as an original Windows fan I'm proud of BillG. But the answer to my question is both—Windows has already done as much to fight poverty as will the Bill and Melinda Gates Foundation.

Toward the end of the Q&A time, which was mostly taken up with technical questions, I was thrilled to hear one of the MVPs ask for his advice as a philanthropist. BillG said that we should all be involved in our communities and give of ourselves in creative ways: at the library, at schools, and with charities. "Do philanthropy where you are." This idea of giving of ourselves is central to the MVP community.

I'd been noodling for a while with the idea of an MVP charity book to help children, and I discussed it with my friend, Kalen Delaney, who liked the idea. The next step was to float the idea past the other SQL Server MVPs and see if it resonated with any of them. The response was overwhelming—within a couple of days, about 50 MVPs had signed on to the project. The question was, would a publisher bite?

My agent, David Fugate of Launch Books, offered to help us for free. As David worked out how to assemble a contract with 50 authors, with all the author proceeds going to charity, Kalen and I pitched the idea to those we know in publishing. When Michael Stephens of Manning Publications heard about it, he told me that Manning wanted in—that this was exactly the type of project that Manning wanted to publish. Mike liked both the community aspect of the project and the charity goals of the project. Manning also offered us a higher than usual author royalty, because we're giving it all to charity.

With a book contract under way, Kalen and I recruited Adam Machanic, Greg Low, Paul Randal, and Kimberly Tripp to help us with the editing. The book was divided into five sections aligned with the five job roles around SQL Server—database architecture and design, database development, database administration, performance tuning and optimization, and business intelligence. There was no rigid organization to the outline—MVPs were simply asked to submit abstracts for chapters that they wanted to write, and those abstracts were directed to the appropriate section editor. This would be a book driven by the MVPs' individual passions, not by a comprehensive feature list. The section editors selected the best abstracts, but we committed to the idea that every MVP who wanted to contribute to the book could contribute.

To select the charity, the MVPs nominated their choice with the restriction that it had to be a non-sectarian group that benefited children. And we wanted to give to a smaller charity—we didn't just want our contribution to be added to a billion-dollar fund. Hugo Kornelis had heard good things about War Child in the Netherlands, and his nomination was selected in the first round of voting.

I'm still amazed that this project came together. The 53 MVPs who contributed to this book did so for numerous personal reasons—a desire to make a difference in children's lives, wanting to share knowledge, wanting to participate in a group effort for change. For some of us, it was an expression of our faith. Several MVPs told me they were glad to be a part of a project that reached beyond their typical circles and helped children.

If you are reading this book, then you are "rich." Considering your place in human history, you're wealthier than most kings of centuries past—you are well educated, your grocery store shelves are full, you have a family doctor. For too many in the

Some (not all!) of the SQL Server MVPs contributing to this book were photographed by Bill Vaughn at the 2009 MVP Summit.

world, that is not the case. There are communities without clean water, children hurting from war, and AIDS orphans who have no family or place to sleep. When one ponders the immense need and poverty in the world, it's easy to become overwhelmed with hopelessness. How can a single drop of ink change the color of an ocean? But we have no other option than to do what we can. My philosophy is that of Confucius: "It is better to light one small candle than to curse the darkness."

Even BillG can't heal the world, but we can each make a difference. By buying this book, you've supported War Child. I echo BillG's words, that we should all find ways to do philanthropy where we are. I encourage you to find the best way you can to make a difference.

So, welcome to SQL Server MVP Deep Dives—a collaborative work by 53 passionate MVPs.

PAUL NIELSEN

acknowledgments

The first thank you has to go to the 53 MVPs who penned this book, and to their families for supporting them in the effort.

To my fellow editors, Adam Machanic, Paul S. Randal, Kimberly L. Tripp, Kalen Delaney, and Greg Low, who went beyond the call to pull together their sections and ensure that this is a quality book: thank you.

To Marjan Bace, our publisher, thank you for helping us refine the concept, supporting the project, and partnering with us.

To Michael Stephens, Jeff Bleiel, Andy Carroll, Deepak Vohra, Katie Tennant, Dottie Marsico, Todd Green, Mary Piergies, and the rest of the team at Manning Publications, thanks for believing in this project and enduring with it to the end.

Thanks to Bill Vaughn for taking the group photo at the 2009 MVP Summit.

A hearty thanks to Rod Colledge (SQL guru from Down Under, of www.sql-crunch.com fame) for contributing his time as the technical editor. Well done!

A thank you to David Fugate of Launch Books for helping us develop the idea and work out the contract.

Many thanks to Ed Lehman, our SQL Server product team MVP Liaison, for his support, the many good times, and all the great swag.

To our MVP leads through the years, Shawn Aebi, Paul Wehland, Stephen Dybing, Ben Miller, Alison Brooks, and Suzanna Moran, and others internationally, thank you for supporting our community efforts.

To everyone in the Microsoft SQL Server product team, our enthusiastic thanks for developing a product worthy of our passion.

A heartfelt thank you to War Child for all you do for the children.

And finally, thank you, readers, for supporting our project and helping us support War Child.

PAUL NIELSEN

about War Child

War Child International is an award-winning charity that provides opportunities and long-term solutions for war-affected children, focusing on education, strengthening children's rights, reducing poverty, and fostering self-reliance. War Child works in partnership with local people and organizations to build sustainable programming that empowers children and their communities. War Child Canada currently provides support to communities in Afghanistan, Darfur, Sudan, Uganda, Sierra Leone, Democratic Republic of Congo, Ethiopia, Sri Lanka, and Georgia. Working closely with the entertainment and tech industries, War Child provides awareness, support, and action for children's rights everywhere.

Learn more at www.warchild.org and www.warchild.ca.

A letter from the director of War Child follows on the next page.

November 4, 2009

To Paul, Kalen, Greg, Adam, Paul, Kimberly, and all the SQL Server MVPs,

On behalf of War Child, I would like to thank the SQL Server MVPs who worked so hard on this project for selecting War Child and for your contribution. It greatly encourages me to see your concern for children who have been traumatized by war.

War Child was launched in North America in 1999. Since that time, much has changed, but one thing has not. Conflicts continue to rage around the world and children, increasingly, are its victims.

Like all charities, our ultimate goal is to become unnecessary. Unfortunately, a decade in, our work is now more vital than ever. And that is why your support is so greatly appreciated.

Once again, thanks to everyone who has contributed to this book.

James Topham
Director of Communications
War Child

about this book

In this book, the world's leading practitioners of SQL Server present a collection of articles on techniques and best practices for SQL Server development and administration based on many years of combined experience. The 53 MVPs who contributed to the book each picked an area of special interest to them and shared their insights and practical know-how with you. The topics covered will appeal to a broad range of readers with varied levels of SQL Server experience, from beginner to advanced.

How the book is organized

This book has 59 chapters divided into five parts that correspond to the five job roles around SQL Server:

Part 1   Database architecture and design
Part 2   Database development
Part 3   Database administration
Part 4   Performance tuning and optimization
Part 5   Business intelligence

There is no rigid construction to the book, no list of SQL Server features that needed to be covered. The contributors to the book submitted abstracts on their topics of expertise and these were added to the appropriate sections. The parts editors reviewed the abstracts and chose the ones that best fit into their grouping of chapters.

Source code

All source code in listings or in text is in a `fixed-width font like this` to separate it from ordinary text. Code annotations accompany some of the listings, highlighting important concepts. In some cases, numbered bullets link to explanations that follow the listings.

The source code for the examples in this book is available online from the publisher's website at www.manning.com/SQLServerMVPDeepDives. The source code is organized by chapter, but please note that not all chapters have code listings in them.

Author Online

The purchase of *SQL Server MVP Deep Dives* includes free access to a private web forum run by Manning Publications, where you can make comments about the book, ask technical questions, and receive help from the authors and from other users. To access the forum and subscribe to it, point your web browser to http://www.manning.com/SQLServerMVPDeepDives.

This page provides information about how to get on the forum once you're registered, what kind of help is available, and the rules of conduct on the forum. Manning's commitment to our readers is to provide a venue where a meaningful dialogue between individual readers and between readers and the authors can take place. It's not a commitment to any specific amount of participation on the part of the authors, whose contribution to the book's forum remains voluntary (and unpaid). We suggest you try asking them some challenging questions, lest their interest stray!

The Author Online forum and the archives of previous discussions will be accessible from the publisher's website as long as the book is in print.

about SQL Server MVPs

The Microsoft Most Valuable Professional (MVP) award is given in recognition of contributions to the community and is renewed yearly. Contributions can take many forms, and those forms are constantly evolving.

MVPs are simply the top influencers in many different kinds of communities. They all give their time to the community in one or more significant ways. They may be forum or newsgroup moderators, authors, bloggers, trainers, speakers, user group or SQL PASS leaders, and I'm sure I'm leaving some activities out. MVPs are also the most highly skilled individuals on Microsoft's technology outside of Microsoft. In recognition of their place as the best aggregators of customer feedback and the broadest channel of communications out to customers, MVPs are given more access to dev teams than any group of customers in order to maximize both inbound and outbound communications with the community.

Most MVPs work across a number of SQL Server areas. Having a single broad category allows MVPs more access to the breadth of the product. Earlier this year some of us started a customer profile initiative on http://connect.microsoft.com/sqlserver that enables us to better identify all the interests of MVPs and other customers to help our dev teams engage more effectively with the MVPs who specialize in their areas of the product.

Microsoft invests a lot in the SQL Server MVP program, and in the following short interview, MVP Liaison Ed Lehman explains why this investment is worthwhile.

Interview with Ed Lehman,
SQL Server Product Team MVP Liaison

Q: How have the MVPs influenced SQL Server—any anecdotes from Katmai or Yukon?

Ed: MVPs have influence on the product from two different perspectives. We look to our MVPs as an aggregated voice of the community as well as a rallying force within the community.

Q: When did the SQL Server MVP program get started?

Ed: I don't know exactly how long the SQL Server MVP program has been around, but I do know that it has grown significantly in the last few years, and I believe that our culture has grown over that same period of time to value customer feedback more and be much more transparent with MVPs on our future directions.

Q: Any funny stories about the SQL Server MVP program?

Ed: Not really a funny story, but one of my favorite memories is when I first starting getting more involved with the MVPs. Stephen Dybing was moving on to a new role after a number of years working with the SQL Server MVPs. At his last summit meeting, all the MVPs presented him with a special award and gave him a standing ovation for all his hard work over the years. I knew then that this was a special family that I was privileged to be involved with. Of course, that was about 15 minutes before I got my first personal taste of passionate feedback from the MVPs. I think it was over the ever-popular question of newsgroups versus forums.

Another one of my favorite times is the end of each of our summits over the last couple of years where I get to hear feedback from the MVPs and dev teams about the value of the time they have spent together and how re-energized the MVPs are to go back out into the community.

Q: How does Microsoft engage with MVPs?

Ed: Once each year, the Microsoft campus is overrun by an event to which all MVPs are invited. In recent years, this has been the largest event hosted on campus. The focus of the event is multiple days of deep-dive sessions where dev teams explain future plans and spend a lot of time getting feedback on those plans. For the past few years, we have started a tradition of having an additional MVP summit for data platform and related MVPs as a track of private sessions during the SQL PASS summit covering the same kinds of feedback discussions. This additional event gives us two great opportunities each year for concentrated face-to-face interactions between the MVPs and dev teams.

PART 1

Database design and architecture

Edited by Paul Nielsen

Any database can be evaluated on six basic criteria: usability, data integrity, scalability, extensibility, availability, and security. Of these database objectives, the first four are primarily driven by the design and development of the database. One of the best practices that serves as a root cause for each of the four design-driven goals is the elegance of the database design itself.

The trouble is that elegance of design can be an elusive creature—difficult to define, difficult to achieve, and difficult to teach. But we do know that at the core of every well-designed database are the principles of normalization. In the application development world, technologies are annual trends, but not so in the database world. Even after nearly 40 years, normalization—one grouping of things is one entity, one thing is one tuple, one fact is one attribute, and every attribute must describe the tuple—is still the foundation of database technology. In the quest for elegance of design, the concepts of generalization and data-driven design augment, but don't negate, normalization. The war cry of the data architect is still, "The key, the whole key, and nothing but the key!"

I am concerned, however, that database development skills—database design, normalization, and T-SQL—seem to be a dying art. In many shops, the lone data architect is outnumbered 50 to 1 by developers who don't respect the importance of data integrity. Managers listen to the crowd, and systems are designed for today rather than for next year, much less the next decade. The design methods and development tools used to encapsulate data should be at least as stable and live as long as the data. And data lasts a long, long time. Ask around, and see how many DBAs manage data that's 10, 20, or 50 years old. Most do.

The average lifecycle of a popular application development language is 3 to 5 years; a stored procedure written 20 years ago still runs (with maybe a slight tweak to the JOIN syntax). I picture the database as a granite rock that will last for an eon. Occasionally a UI developer comes along and paints a pretty chalk picture on the rock; it washes off and a few more UI developers add their pictures. They all wash off with time, but the rock remains. OK, it's a stretch, and I do like a great UI, but the point is that any IT architecture should be founded on data integrity.

This part of the book has three chapters focused on improving your skills in gathering data requirements and designing the database.

About the editor

Paul Nielsen is a SQL Server data architect who has enjoyed playing with data for three decades. He's the author of the *SQL Server Bible series* (Wiley), is convinced that SSMS is the ultimate UI, and dreams in E/R diagrams and T-SQL. Paul is the founder of NordicDB—a software startup company that offers a specialized SaaS CRM solution for non-profits. Paul lives in Colorado Springs with a wife who is far more beautiful than he deserves and his three children (ages 22, 21, and 5). He speaks at most conferences and offers seminars in database design. His website is http://www.SQLServerBible.com.

1 Louis and Paul's 10 key relational database design ideas

Paul Nielsen and Louis Davidson

Even though the database world is more stable than the app dev world, which seems to have a hot new language every other week (our procs written in SQL Server T-SQL 4.21 still run, for the most part), there are still controversies and key ideas that are worth examining. For the 24 Hours of PASS, we presented a session on Ten Big Ideas in Database Design:

1 Denormalization is for wimps
2 Keys are key
3 Generalize, man!
4 Class <> table
5 Data drives design
6 Sets good, cursors bad
7 Properly type data
8 Extensibility through encapsulation
9 Spaghetti is food, not code
10 NOLOCK = no consistency

1. Denormalization is for wimps

A common database development phrase is "Normalize 'till it hurts, then denormalize 'till it works." Poppycock! Although denormalization may have yielded better results for OLTP databases using SQL Server 6.5 and earlier, it is only rarely the case in modern times.

For OLTP or operational databases (not reporting databases or BI) a correctly indexed normalized schema will nearly always perform better than a denormalized one. The extra work required to double insert, double update, or pivot denormalized data when reading will almost always cost more than the perceived benefit of reading from a single denormalized location. Unless you do performance testing and know your application's profile, it is likely that when you denormalize, you're introducing performance problems that would have been easy to avoid by learning better SQL practices. But the root cause of most less-than-normalized databases isn't an effort to improve performance; it's the incompetence of the person designing the database and the programmers writing the queries.

In specific cases it's good to denormalize even in an OLTP database. For example, within an inventory system, it might make sense to precalculate the inventory transactions and store the quantity on hand for parts per location. Read/write ratios should be carefully considered, and you should never assume that denormalization is required without testing it both ways under load—properly normalized and denormalized. (And consider asking an MVP in the newsgroups if there is a better way to do things—helping people is what the MVP program is all about.)

First normal form is critical: first normal form means not duplicating columns, but it also means one fact per attribute with plain, human-readable data, as well as not having unique rows. Violating first normal form is more common than you might think: smart keys such as product codes that embed data within the product code violate first normal form. If it takes combining multiple attributes to deduce a fact, that violates first normal form. Bitmasked attributes that embed data within a binary column (bit 1 means this, bit 2 means that) is an extreme violation of first normal form because anyone who can figure out binary encoding should know better. Remember, good index utilization is very specifically tied to first normal form. Embedded meaning inside a column (for example, the middle three characters of a five-character string), is not so easily indexed, particularly when it is not the first part of the value.

2. Keys are key

It's downright scary how many production databases have no primary and foreign key constraints, and even more use identity integers or GUIDs as the only uniqueness constraints on their tables. I guess the idea is that the front-end application is ensuring only good data is passed to the database.

I wonder if those developers have ever flown internationally. In 2007, I (Paul) made three trips to Russia (and had a great time). At the Delta ticket check-in counter, they check your passport. When boarding the plane, they check your ticket and your passport. But in Moscow, the passport control officers don't just assume that everything must be okay. They scan your passport, do a quick computer check on your identity, and verify your Russian visa. In the UK, everyone entering is photographed. The U.S. takes fingerprints. These are folks who understand the concept of database enforced keys.

There are two true things about every database I've ever worked with that had no keys. First, the IT manager thought the data was good. Second, the database was full of bad data.

There are some database developers who don't use keys. Don't be that guy.

While we're on the subject of primary keys, composite primary keys lead to composite foreign keys, which eventually lead to joining on nine columns and clustered indexes as wide as the Grand Canyon. Although this is technically not incorrect, it is annoying, it causes poor performance, and it's one of the reasons the concept of surrogate keys was introduced.

Surrogate keys (`INT IDENTITY` columns) are small, fast, and popular, but don't forget to add a unique constraint to the candidate key columns or you'll end up with duplicates and bad data. That's just one more guy you don't want to be.

3. Generalize, man!

Some so-called "normalized" databases are overly complicated, which causes some developers to feel that the more normalized a database is, the more tables it will have. This leads them to say weird things like, "I only normalize to third normal form; otherwise there are too many tables."

A typical cause of an overly complicated database is that the data modeler was overly specific in determining what types of things should be grouped together into an entity. This extreme bloats out the number of tables, makes development both expensive and frustrating, and gives normalization a bad name.

On the other extreme, some database designers merge too many types of things into a single huge gelatinous blob. These database designs appear simple and easy to work with but in fact tend to exhibit integrity issues over time.

The technique that many database developers naturally use but don't name is *generalization*—combining similar types of things to make the databases simpler. A well-generalized database is still perfectly normalized—the difference is that the scope of things in an entity has been explicitly designed. This reduces development time, makes the database more flexible, and increases the life of the database.

The art of database design—moving from the extreme to an elegant design—is all about learning how to generalize entities so you have a database that's both normalized (has integrity) and usable (meets requirements but is not overly complex).

4. Class <> table

There's both a technical and cultural impedance mismatch between the object world and the database world. Relational databases don't readily represent inheritance. The .NET-heads treat the database as nothing more than a data dump, and the database geeks don't care to understand classes, inheritance, and objects. Since most shops have a .NET to database developer or data modeler ratio of about 50 to 1, the database voices are drowned out. In addition, application programming languages are like ear candy to managers just dying to get the job done faster, and we just have T-SQL (good old faithful works-like-a-charm T-SQL, but face it, not the most exciting language). The result is that management is losing any respect it had for the database discipline. The database is under attack and losing the war.

Too often the solution is to use an application layer object-relational mapper, such as NHibernate or the Entity Framework. This provides a poor abstraction for the database. The response is all too often to create a table for every class and a row for every object. This fails to properly represent the classes.

The solution is not something that can be bottled as a magic potion. The object layer needs to be designed for the .NET needs, and the database for the database's needs (that part is easy!).

Part of the solution is to model the object world in the database using supertypes, subtypes, and views that join the tables to present all the objects in a class. But some things are tables in a relational database and multivalued properties in the object. Some classes will expand to many tables. What is required to make this work?

Teamwork. Architects from the relational and object-oriented disciplines need to work together and build an intermediate layer that works. Then we can build tools to make that process easier.

5. Data drives design

According to common wisdom, business logic has no business in the database. If the point is to keep messy hard-coded logic out of T-SQL code, I agree, but business logic is most flexible when it's pushed down from the application front end, down past the data access layer, down deeper than the stored procedure layer, down past the database schema, all the way into the data.

The best place for business logic is in the data. Every variable in the business formula should be stored in the database rather than coded in any programming language. The behavior of the application is then determined not by .NET code, or T-SQL case expressions, but by the data. Joining from the current data set to the business-rules data sets can dynamically plug the correct values into the business formula for the appropriate row. An admin application can modify the business-rule data at any time without code changes. This is the freedom and elegance that a data-driven database adds to the application.

6. Sets good, cursors bad

Perhaps the most egregious error in SQL Server development is the T-SQL cursor. Nearly everyone has heard how evil cursors are. Writing a database cursor is like going to the bank and depositing a million dollars, one dollar at a time, using a million tiny deposits. In the set-based solution, you just hand over a million one dollar bills at once. The same work is done (the money is counted and deposited) but the teller will not have to have a separate conversation with you for each piece of paper. The performance difference is obvious, and you are saving 999,999 deposit slips to boot. Typically a set-based solution will perform a magnitude better than an iterative solution and will scale significantly better.

There are times when writing a cursor is the best technique—when the logic depends on the order of the rows, or when the code is iterating though DDL code generations, for example. But claiming that "it's really hard to figure out the set-based way to handle this problem" is not a legitimate reason to write a cursor. Unfortunately, cursors are sometimes written because the database design is so horrid that set-based code is nearly impossible.

The key point concerning cursors and database design is that a well-normalized database schema will encourage set-based queries, whereas a denormalized (or never normalized) database schema will discourage set-based code. That's one more reason to normalize that database schema.

7. Properly type data

Don't make every string column VARCHAR(255). Don't make every column that holds money values MONEY. You wouldn't serve pigs from a teacup, nor would you serve tea from a pig's trough. Use the right-sized data type; this is the first line of defense in ensuring the integrity of your data. It is amazing how many databases use VAR-CHAR(255) when the front-end application only allows 30 characters and report definitions only allow 20.

TIP   Obfuscated database schemas are another real pain, and they serve no purpose. J12K98D is not a reasonable table name.

8. Extensibility through encapsulation

Architects recognize the value of separation of concerns, and encapsulation is the heart of service-oriented architecture. Why isn't encapsulation for the database respected?

Of all the possible SQL Server practices, one of the very worst is application-based ad hoc SQL: any SQL statement that is passed directly from the object layer directly referencing SQL Server tables. Why? Because the tightly-coupled database becomes brittle—a slight change to the database breaks hundreds to thousands of objects throughout the application code, reports, and ETL processes. An abstraction layer lets the database developer modify the database and, so long as the database API isn't changed, the outside world is not affected.

Every individual computing component should be wrapped in a protective layer, encapsulated to hide the complexities of what's inside.

9. Spaghetti is food, not code

Spaghetti coding was very much the norm back in the "good old days" (which weren't all that good, if you ask me). We had BASIC or COBOL, and when you wanted to change the next line that you were executing, you said GOTO 1000, which took you to line 1000 of the source code. It was cool at the time, but as programming became more complex, this got out of hand, and people were using GOTOs like crazy. The term *spaghetti code* referred to how the control jumped all over the place like a strand of spaghetti.

So you are probably thinking, "We don't even use GOTOs in our code." That's true, but what we do is often much worse. Sometimes we write messy code that does unnecessary dynamic SQL calls that cannot be readily interpreted by the support person, and in other cases we create blocks of code like the following that are difficult to support:

```
IF condition
        QUERY
ELSE IF condition
      QUERY
ELSE
      EXECUTE procedure --which in turn has another IF block like this
END
```

This kind of spaghetti coding pattern is bad enough, but it really gets messy when it is difficult to discern where a problem is coming from because it is happening "somewhere" in the code—not in an easily located call. Consider these examples:

- An UPDATE fires a trigger that calls a procedure that inserts data in a table that then fires a trigger that calls a procedure that contains complex business logic.
- A stored procedure uses a temp table created in a different stored procedure, which is then modified in another stored procedure.
- A global temporary table is created in a procedure, and then is used in a different connection.
- A global cursor is opened in a procedure and is used by other procedures that may or may not be called or closed.

One of the reasons things like triggers get a bad name is that there is so much overuse of triggers that fire other triggers and procedures, and programmers don't like unexpected results from the "magic" that triggers can do. And can you blame them? Getting predictable results is very important to the process, and a mess of triggers calling procedures calling triggers with cursors (and so on) makes getting correct results difficult and support nearly impossible.

10. NOLOCK = no consistency

Locks are a very important part of SQL Server to understand. They allow multiple users to use the same resources without stomping on each other, and if you don't understand them, your job of tuning the server is going to be a lot harder.

For many people, the seemingly logical way to get around the problem of locks is to ignore them by using one of these methods:

- Using SET TRANSACTION ISOLATION LEVEL READ UNCOMMITTED to have all following code neither set nor respect locks
- Using locking hints of NOLOCK or READUNCOMMITTED on tables in queries

But both of these methods open up more complicated problems for your support status. By ignoring locks, you will get rows that are in the middle of being processed, and they may not be in their final resting place. This means that you may be getting data that was never committed to the database, or data that is in an intermediate state.

What is the solution? Consider how long the locks are held and how much is being locked. The default isolation level for SQL Server, READ COMMITTED, will generally only lock one row at a time when it fetches rows. Even inside a transaction, you can get different results for the same query depending on the transaction isolation level. (Only the highest transaction isolation level, serializable, will prevent other users from changing or adding rows that your query has viewed; snapshot isolation level will let your results stay constant by saving changes temporarily for your queries.) However, transaction isolation assumes that the server can discern your actions from the structure of your database. For example, consider the following:

```
UPDATE tableName
  SET  column = 'Test'
  WHERE tableNameKey = 1
```

If I asked you how many rows needed to be locked, you would immediately assume one, right? That depends on the indexing of tableNameKey. If there is no index, an update will scan every row, and the lock taken could lock all readers out of the table. Many locking issues fall into this category, where the query processor has to lock many more rows than would be necessary if it knew that only one row would be affected by this query.

In SQL Server 2005, Microsoft added in something called SNAPSHOT isolation level. In SNAPSHOT isolation level, when you start a transaction, all the data you read will look exactly as it did when you started the transaction. Currently executing processes don't lock you out; they maintain the previous version for anyone who wants to see it. This is a nifty way to implement a system, but it presents some difficulties for modifying data—you really have to consider how the SNAPSHOT isolation level will affect your queries and applications. SNAPSHOT transaction isolation uses row versioning to store the before image of the data in tempdb, so fully understanding the impact on your hardware is very important.

All of this leads us to a database setting called READ_COMMITTED_SNAPSHOT that will change the way the default READ COMMITTED isolation behaves. This setting uses SNAPSHOT isolation level at a statement level, so the results you get for a query will only include rows that have been committed; but if someone changes the data after you start getting results, you won't see that. This is generally good enough locking, and it is certainly enough if you are using optimistic locking techniques to protect users from overwriting other users' changes.

One thing that is clear is that concurrency is not an easy problem to solve. In this chapter, we are pointing out that ignoring locks is not the same as tuning your database system because you are sacrificing consistency for speed. If your data really does need to be heavily locked, perhaps it's better to let it be.

Summary

This list of ten key database ideas offers a quick taste of the challenges you'll face when designing and developing database applications. It's not always easy, but unlike many other computer-related challenges, the theory and practices for designing and implementing a relational database have remained relatively stable for many years. The main reason for this is that when Codd developed the initial relational database system, he took into consideration the kind of stuff we talked about in our eighth point: encapsulation.

Whereas SQL has remained reasonably stable, the engines that run the database servers have become more and more powerful. If you follow the rules, normalize your data schema, and write set-based queries, that SQL statement you write on a small dataset on your own machine will be far easier to optimize when you get to the reality of millions of rows on a SQL Server machine in the cloud, where you don't have access to the hardware, only the SQL engine.

About the authors

Paul Nielsen is a SQL Server data architect who has enjoyed playing with data for three decades. He's the author of the *SQL Server Bible series* (Wiley), is convinced that SSMS is the ultimate UI, and dreams in E/R diagrams and T-SQL. Paul is the founder of NordicDB—a software startup company that offers a specialized SaaS CRM solution for non-profits. Paul lives in Colorado Springs with a wife who is far more beautiful than he deserves and his three children (ages 22, 21, and 5). He speaks at most conferences and offers seminars in database design. His website is http://www.SQLServerBible.com.

Louis Davidson has over 15 years of experience as a corporate database developer and architect. Currently he is the Data Architect for the Christian Broadcasting Network. Nearly all of Louis' professional experience has been with Microsoft SQL Server from the early days to the latest version currently in beta. Louis has been the principal author of four editions of a book on database design, including one for SQL Server 2008. Louis' primary areas of interest are database architecture and coding in T-SQL, and he has experience designing many databases and writing thousands of stored procedures and triggers through the years.

2 SQL Server tools for maintaining data integrity

Louis Davidson

You've probably seen it before: a client has called the help desk and reported that a couple of queries have seemingly inconsistent results. You're called in to test the queries, so you start digging. You run two queries, and the results for one query don't seem right, considering the other query's results. So you start to wonder, "Is it my understanding of the schema?" You then start looking at the data model and the tables seem wonderfully designed. Your query should work. Dang, now what?

You dig deeper, and realize... the only objects you find in the database are tables. No constraints, no relationships, no nothing. A quick query later and you find that orphaned rows in a child table show up in one query but not another. At this point it's clear that almost all of the data in these tables is suspect because if you can't trust that a simple relationship works, can you trust that the child rows that exist are for the proper parent? Sadly, the answer is no, because the software may have created a new parent row that reused a key value. Now ideally you'll test the consistency of the data every time you use the data, to verify that it's correct. It doesn't take a genius to determine how long before that gets old.

So how do you avoid this calamity? Protect the data using all of the tools you have available. In this chapter, I'll present many of the tools that SQL Server gives you to help protect your data from corruption, usually in a behind-the-scenes manner that the client doesn't really have to worry about. I'll also present guidance on how to decide what type of protection and where, and give examples of each type of protection. I'll break down the topic into the following two sections:

- *Protection tools*—Introducing the tools that SQL Server gives us and techniques for using them
- *When and why to use what tool*—Examining the different types of protection tools and discussing when and where they should be used

The goal will be to protect the data such that it's guaranteed to be fundamentally correct, meaning that completely illogical or impossible data isn't allowed. For example, consider a column that holds an employee's salary. Logically, it'll be a number value, and should probably have a reasonable upper and lower bound. What those bounds are is up to the individual situation, but the minimal goal is to make sure completely illogical data is never stored. Without any real concern, you can set a lower bound of 0 on a salary, as by definition a salary is pay, not a fee to come to work (that is what timesheets and staff meetings are for). You might use a `numeric(15,2)` data type to establish an upper bound of `999,999,999,999.99` for the salary value (even the CEO of Enron never made that kind of money).

The application code will be used to warn users that the average salary for a data architect is less than 200 million dollars... but if you want to pay that much, I'll take it. The final result is that there's no way that the value *too freaking little* will show up in the salary column.

Protection tools

In this section I'll introduce the different tools available for you to protect the quality of your data. Understanding the tools at your disposal for protecting data quality is the second most important thing to know and know well (the third being how to write set-based queries, and the first being normalization). This chapter is about automatic data protection, meaning tools that can be used to seamlessly protect the integrity of the data without any further coding effort or user action to make sure that they work, and no method of overriding the protection without cheating (you can disable some protections, and you can get around them using bulk copy methods).

You can also take manual steps to protect your data; they generally require the client to adhere to a given API to work. This could include stored procedures, client code, defaults, and so forth. I won't discuss manual protection in this chapter, but the point of using manual data protection techniques is that they enforce rules that can be overridden or applied situationally, or that are frequently changed. These rules are generally apt to change, so you wouldn't be able to easily write a query to find data that didn't meet the rules over a long period of time.

We'll discuss the following types of protection that allow you to design integrity into the base structure:

- *Data types*—Defining the storage of values of the proper base type and size
- *NULL specifications*—Making sure that only columns where you might have a NULL value are defined to allow NULLs
- *Uniqueness constraints*—Preventing duplicate values for a column or set of columns
- *Filtered unique indexes*—Preventing duplicate values for a column or set of columns for a subset of rows in the table
- *Foreign key constraints*—Making sure every foreign key value has a corresponding primary key value in the related table

- *Check constraints*—Checking that values in the row meet the minimum standards
- *Triggers*—The catch-all of data protection, which allows you to execute a batch of code for any DML operation to validate data and even introduce side effects to the DML operation that happen without the knowledge of the client

As you'll see in the following subsections, this list is loosely ordered from the most desirable to the least desirable, particularly where there's overlap.

Data types

The most fundamental thing you can do to ensure the quality of your data is to choose a reasonable container for the value being stored. Want to store an integer value? Use an integer type. Want to store an image? Use a varbinary(max). Could you use a varchar(50) or varchar(max) to store every value? In almost every situation, you sure could. You could also stick your tongue in a lamp socket, but I guarantee you it's a bad idea unless you want to say hi to your cat that your mother told you was "sent off to live on the farm."

Way too often, I see designs where every column is nvarchar(50), unless they want to store something larger; then it's an nvarchar(max). Storagewise, unless you expect that some values will have special characters, using a Unicode-enabled type just costs you space, and even worse is absolutely horrible for data integrity.

It's perfectly possible to do this and get by, as all values can be represented as a textual value in a T-SQL DML statement. So why bother? First, consider performance. As an example, consider storing a GUID value in a varchar column. Using the uniqueidentifier data type, you can store the 36-character value in 16 bytes. Put it in a varchar column and you'll need 36 bytes, or 72 if the column is nvarchar.

The second, more important problem is data integrity. A uniqueidentifier column requires a properly formatted GUID to be stored, whereas a varchar column is happy to take *Your data integrity blows* as a value.

NULL specification

Setting the NULL specification of a column to allow or disallow NULLs is an important step in getting correct data. It's quite common to see that someone has created a perfectly acceptable design, but left each column nullable. Part of this is probably laziness, as not specifying a column's NULL specification will by default allow the column to allow NULL values.

NULLs greatly increase the complexity of using a column, because NULL isn't equal to anything, including itself. But NULL = NULL isn't false; rather it evaluates to NULL. Then consider the expression NOT(NULL) which also evaluates to NULL, but really looks like it should be true, right? You might be thinking that it's silly, that you'd never need to care about this type of thing, right? Well, consider the following:

```
SELECT *
FROM   table
WHERE NOT(nullableColumn = @value)
```

If all values for nullableColumn were NULL, then that statement would return the same rows as the following:

```
SELECT *
FROM  table
WHERE (nullableColumn = @value)
```

Because the expression nullableColumn = @value evaluates to a Boolean value, in the case where nullableColumn is NULL, nothing is returned. Only rows where the expression evaluates to TRUE are returned.

If you need to allow a value to have no known value, then having nullable columns is acceptable. But, in many cases, columns allow NULLs because the implementer didn't think or care if it mattered and let some other code manage whether data is optional. The problem here is twofold:

- The SQL Server engine uses all information it has to make your queries faster. The fact that all values *must* be filled in helps the optimizer to not worry about the case where a value is NULL.
- You have to write code that validates this over and over. Placing it in the definition of the data makes sure that it's always adhered to, regardless of whether the UI has checked to make sure that the user entered a value.

So the fact is, there's no reason not to disallow nulls where they should never occur; it can only help your system, and never hurt it. I'm not going to get any deeper into the NULL discussion than this, and I leave it to you to find all of the ways that NULL makes comparisons more interesting. The point of this section is to show that although NULL can be a useful tool, it behooves you to protect against unnecessary NULL values, as unhandled NULLs in comparisons will mess up your query results in ways that won't be obvious to you without some thought.

Uniqueness constraints

One of the most common newbie questions is how to remove duplicate data from a table. After demonstrating the requisite query to remove the duplicated data (removing what might actually be a row of important data that the user updated instead of the kept copy), a nice but stern rant follows on why you must protect your data against duplicated data. In SQL Server, uniqueness is enforced using either a primary key or a unique constraint. The primary key is used for the main value that each row will be referenced as. Unique constraints are then applied to all other candidate keys, which are frequently other sets of columns that a user will want to reference a row as.

Every table should have a primary key to make sure that you have some way to distinguish one row from other rows. In addition, it's important to make sure that you have either the primary key or a unique key on a value in the table that has some meaning. An identity value in the table doesn't have any actual meaning, as you could have two rows with exactly the same value other than the identity key, and the two rows would be technically indistinguishable from one another. This isn't always completely possible, as there are some tables where a key that has full meaning can't be created, such as a table that logs events that have occurred, where multiple events of the same type could occur at the same instance. For logging situations, adding a sequence number is an acceptable trade-off, though that shouldn't be the only value in the key.

As an example, if you had a customer table with an identity value `customerId` for a surrogate key (the name given a key that's generated without regard to any meaningful data to stand in for a more complex key value) and a `customerNumber`, which the user enters, the table would be defined as the following:

```
CREATE TABLE customer
(
    customerId int identity NOT NULL CONSTRAINT PKcustomer PRIMARY KEY,
    customerNumber char(10) NOT NULL
            CONSTRAINT AKcustomer_customerNumber UNIQUE
)
```

You can also use `ALTER TABLE` syntax to add a `PRIMARY KEY` or `UNIQUE` constraint once the table has been created:

```
ALTER TABLE customer
    ADD CONSTRAINT PKcustomer PRIMARY KEY (customerId)
ALTER TABLE customer
    ADD CONSTRAINT AKcustomer_customerNumber UNIQUE (customerNumber)
```

Internally, `PRIMARY KEYS` and `UNIQUE` constraints are actually hybrid objects—they're constraints, but physically they're implemented internally by creating a unique index. The syntax for creating a `PRIMARY KEY` or `UNIQUE` constraint includes several of the different settings for an index, such as whether the index to create is clustered, what partition to place it on, and so on.

Semantically, the distinction between a unique index and a constraint should be considered as part of your design. A constraint declares that some factor must be true, and for key constraints, this is declaring that the values in the selected columns must be unique. An index is a physical construct used specifically to speed up some operation; in this case, SQL Server is applying a unique index to speed up checking for duplicate values. I generally think of an index as something that can be created or dropped by the production staff without helping or harming anything other than performance.

Filtered unique indexes

As mentioned in the previous section, indexes are, in general, only to be used to improve performance, not for data protection. For SQL Server 2008, Microsoft has given us a `WHERE` clause on the `CREATE INDEX` syntax that also has data protection capabilities not found in `UNIQUE` constraints. If you want to protect for unique values except for when the value is some given value (most commonly, the use is unique values when not `NULL`), you can use a unique index with a `WHERE` clause. For example, if you have a table that holds persons, and you want to associate a unique customer number with the user if she becomes a customer, but not until, you could define an index such as the following:

```
CREATE INDEX AKSperson_customerNumber on person(customerNumber)
                WHERE customerNumber is not null
```

If you're using a previous version of SQL Server, there are other methods to use, such as an indexed view where you define the view to exclude data like you did with the WHERE clause on the CREATE INDEX statement. Then you add a clustered unique index on the view. Either method is acceptable, and implements the same sort of constructs with the same overhead.

Foreign key constraints

A foreign key constraint is used to make sure that columns involved in a relationship contain only correct data. I started out the chapter with an example that contained a foreign key reference. The reason for this is because it's probably the most frustrating of errors; it's rarely a problem in most databases, so it's not the first thing that will pop to mind.

For example, say you have an invoice table and a table to represent what's on the invoice. The keys for these tables might look like the following:

```
CREATE TABLE invoice
(
    invoiceNumber char(10) CONSTRAINT PKinvoice PRIMARY KEY,
    invoiceStatus varchar(10) CONSTRAINT invoice$invoiceStatus
)
CHECK (invoiceStatus in ('Open','Closed'))
CREATE TABLE invoiceItem
(
    invoiceNumber char(10),
    invoiceItemNumber int,
    CONSTRAINT PKinvoiceItem PRIMARY KEY (invoiceNumber, invoiceItemNumber)
)
```

If you don't take the time to add the foreign key constraint, then the value for order-Number in the orderItem table isn't bound to any domain of values. It could be "Hello!" for all that matters, even if that value didn't get created in the order table. The problem is that no matter the intentions of the non–data tier implementers, it's difficult to test for all possible scenarios, and impossible to stop a DBA from messing up the data by accident.

A good example of the kinds of problems you can run into is a query against a child, such as an invoice line item. A query against this table should give consistent results whether or not you include the invoice in the query. So executing a query like the following

```
SELECT sum(invoiceLineItem.amount)
FROM   invoiceLineItem
```

should give the same result as this:

```
SELECT sum(invoiceLineItem.amount)
FROM   invoiceLineItem
    JOIN invoice
      ON invoiceLineItem.invoiceId = invoice.invoiceId
```

On the surface, this seems a safe bet, as why would you put data in invoiceLineItem without a matching value in invoice? But unless you've created a constraint between invoice and invoiceLineItem, you could have values for invoiceLineItem.invoiceId that aren't in the invoice table. These values would be excluded in the second query, causing the user to have to think about why this is true. Simply adding

```
ALTER TABLE invoiceLineItem
    ADD CONSTRAINT invoice$has$invoiceLineItems
        FOREIGN KEY (invoiceId) REFERENCES invoice (invoiceId)
```

could prevent a lot of heartache trying to decipher the random bits and bytes from the meaningful data. Even worse, note that you'd also be required to check for bad data like this in any program that uses this data (such as ETL for your warehouse), or you'd corrupt the sources of data that use this data, requiring even more data cleanup.

Check constraints

Check constraints allow you to define, for an individual column or row, a condition of the data that must occur. You use them to constrict the set of values to a certain domain. For example, if you want to make sure that the values could only be entered into the status column of the invoice table, you'd define a condition that said status in ('active','inactive'). The following is the syntax for adding a constraint to an existing table:

```
ALTER TABLE <tableName>
    ADD [CONSTRAINT <constraintName>] CHECK <BooleanCondition>
```

For the invoice table example, you could code the following:

```
ALTER TABLE invoice
  ADD CONSTRAINT invoice$statusDomain
        CHECK (invoiceStatus in ('active','inactive'))
```

No matter how many rows you modify in a statement, the condition specified by a constraint is checked one row at a time, and can't see which other rows are modified. You can access the columns in a table by name with no alias, or you can access data in other rows, or even tables using user-defined functions. As another example, consider the employee.salary example we used previously in the chapter. If you wanted to make sure it's greater than 0, you might define the following:

```
ALTER TABLE employee
    ADD CONSTRAINT employee$salaryNonNegative CHECK (salary > 0)
```

The Boolean expression can't directly reference another table, but you can use a function to access the data in the table. Note that I said you can't see which other rows were modified, but the data is already in the table, so you can access it in the function's query.

One example of using a function is limiting the cardinality of a value in a database (or the count of the times a value can appear). Using a unique constraint, you can easily limit the cardinality to 1, but if you want to allow a number different than 1, there isn't an easy way to do this declaratively. So we can use a function and a check constraint. Take the following table:

```
create table cardinalityLimit
(
  value varchar(10)
)
```

If we want no more than two of the same values for the value column, you can build a simple function like this:

```
CREATE FUNCTION dbo.cardinalityLimit$countValue
(
  @value varchar(10)
)
RETURNS INT
AS
 BEGIN
  RETURN (SELECT count(*)
      FROM  cardinalityLimit
      WHERE value = @value)
  END
```

It counts the number of values in the table that match the @value parameter. In the following constraint, you'll check to see if the count is 2 or less:

```
ALTER TABLE cardinalityLimit
   ADD CONSTRAINT cardinalityLimit$valueCardinality2
      CHECK (dbo.cardinalityLimit$countValue(value) <= 2)
```

Constraints see the data in the table from the current DDL statement. Now you should be careful to test the statements. First, insert rows one at a time:

```
INSERT INTO cardinalityLimit
VALUES ('one')
INSERT INTO cardinalityLimit
VALUES ('one')
INSERT INTO cardinalityLimit
VALUES ('one')
```

After the third one, you'll get an error. After creating a constraint that accesses other tables, you should test all of the possible types of combinations of rows you may get. For example, we tested the case of sending one row at a time, but in this case you should test modifying multiple rows in a single DML statement to make sure that it behaves correctly. In the next statement, I'll check to make sure that it works for a set of two rows:

```
INSERT INTO cardinalityLimit
VALUES ('two'),('two')
Which it does. Then try three at a time:
INSERT INTO cardinalityLimit
VALUES ('three'),('three'),('three')
```

This again fails with the same error message. (I'll leave it to you to test the UPDATE scenarios.) This leads to the most difficult problem with check constraints: terrible error messages. The following are the errors you get from our cardinality example:

```
Msg 547, Level 16, State 0, Line 1
The INSERT statement conflicted with the CHECK constraint
➡ "cardinalityLimit$valueCardinality2". The conflict occurred in database
➡ "tempdb", table "dbo.cardinalityLimit", column 'value'.
```

Proper naming conventions help, and in my database design book, *Pro SQL Server 2008 Relational Database Design and Implementation* (Apress, 2008), I present a method of mapping these messages by parsing the message and creating a table of constraint names, but it's a cumbersome process at the least.

Check constraints have a downside, but they're important to the process of keeping the data clean of illogical data. Done right, your reporting and ETL process won't have to check for out-of-range values that can trip up calculations (and as mentioned, make users wary of trusting "your" numbers). Just like we did with the salary example, you should make judicious use of check constraints to prevent data from being fouled up in an unreasonable manner. For example, I generally put a constraint on all varchar columns to make sure that the empty string isn't inserted. If the employee table had a lastName column, I'd add the following:

```
ALTER TABLE employee
   ADD CONSTRAINT employee$nameNotEmpty CHECK (LEN(RTRIM(lastName)) > 0)
```

This isn't to say that I always enforce this sort of constraint, as sometimes allowing an empty string is a good thing, because it allows you to differentiate between no value and a NULL value. But, when a column value is required, it's usually not the best plan of attack to allow the user to enter a single space character in lieu of a "real" value. And for unique indexing purposes, I really don't want strings containing different numbers of spaces to be treated as different values; users sometimes use this technique to get around putting in reasonable data values (though you can't stop them from putting in gibberish for values, at least not easily).

One last note: when you create a CHECK constraint, you can specify WITH NOCHECK to tell SQL Server to not test existing data against the constraint. This can be a faster way to add a constraint, but generally speaking, it's not a good idea. Two problems often come up. First, the constraint can't be used by the optimizer to know what data could exist in the column(s). Second, if there's invalid data, it'll fail if it's updated to the same value. UPDATE table SET column = column is something that should never fail, but untrusted constraints can leave you open to these kinds of spurious errors that the user interface probably couldn't even help prevent. You can determine whether your constraints are tested by looking at the is_not_trusted column in sys.check_constraints.

Triggers

Triggers are stored batches of T-SQL, much like stored procedures. But instead of being called directly, they execute indirectly when you execute an INSERT, UPDATE, or DELETE operation. You can do almost anything in them that you can do in T-SQL, with only a few caveats (check Books Online for more information). In capable hands—particularly the hands of those who understand the caveats of triggers—they can fill gaps left by constraints by allowing you to handle problems that constraints are incapable of and have the solution automatically occur without user or programmer involvement. On the other hand, in the wrong hands, they can drag down the performance of your system faster than you can kiss a duck.

Some people feel that triggers are more evil than cursors (and putting a cursor in a trigger is a capital offense in some locales). Others use them for just about everything, often to do the sorts of simple checks that you could use a CHECK constraint for. The truth is somewhere in between. There's an overhead in using the inserted and updated virtual tables to access the modified rows inside the trigger, and this overhead needs to be considered before using triggers.

There are two different types of triggers. First there are AFTER triggers, which execute after the rows are in the table and after constraints have been applied. These triggers are most often used to validate some condition or to cause some cascading operation that can't be done declaratively using a CHECK constraint.

The second type is called INSTEAD OF triggers, and they fire as the first operation before any other actions, even before the row is in the table. Instead of a trigger, you'll have to manually execute the operation you want to occur. For example, if you have an INSTEAD OF INSERT trigger, you have to code the INSERT statement in the trigger to do the INSERT that the trigger fired for. INSTEAD OF triggers can be useful for formatting data, or possibly redirecting data to a different table. An easy example is directing data that's unusual to a holding table, such as taking all data from a data entry clerk but putting out-of-normal-range data into a table for more validation. In this scenario, the user doesn't know there was anything wrong, his job is just to key in data (and yes, no doubt a slap on the wrist will come to users who enter too much out-of-range data, but we can't govern the social aspects of our software, now can we?). INSTEAD OF triggers can also be placed on views as well as tables to allow DML on a view to modify more than one table at a time.

Triggers are useful as a last resort when you can't use one of the previously mentioned tools to do the same thing. They have the benefit that you can't "forget" to invoke them, particularly if you don't have coding practices that require all modifications to an object to use a common object that knows how to protect. The following list represents the main types of uses I have for triggers, and even this list is apt to start a minor argument between T-SQL experts:

- *Cross-database referential integrity (RI)*—SQL Server doesn't allow declarative constraints across database boundaries, so triggers can be written to validate that data exists in a different database. Databases are independent containers, so this method isn't nearly as good as having constraints in the same database, but as long as you understand that you have to be careful with cross-database references, it's definitely usable.

- *Intra-table, inter-row constraints*—These are used when you need to see that the sum of a column value over multiple rows is less than some value (possibly in another table). You can use a constraint with a function, but the query will be executed once per row modified, whereas a trigger need only run the query a single time.

- *Inter-table constraints*—When a value in one table relies on the value in another, triggers are useful for checking for correct values. This might also be written as a functions-based CHECK constraint, but it's often more maintainable to use a trigger.

- *Introducing desired side effects to your queries*—Constraints support cascading operations on UPDATE, but it's possible to come up with many different side effects that might be desired. For example, cascading inserts, maintaining denormalized data, logging who modified a row, and so on.

Triggers come at a price, and the biggest concern is performance. Triggers fire once per DML operation, so whether you modify 1 or 1,000 rows, the trigger fires only once. During trigger execution, SQL Server sets up two tables, one called *inserted*, which contains all rows that are to be created (or are to be used instead of triggers), and another for removed rows called *deleted*. You have to be very careful that your code considers the number of rows involved in the operation and the trigger can handle multiple rows being modified.

The inserted and deleted tables aren't indexed, and are reflections of the changes that have been made to the table and are captured in tempdb. Hence, you need to be careful with the queries in the trigger to make sure that you're ready for 1 or 1,000 rows to be updated. In some cases, you won't be able to optimize a trigger for large numbers of rows, so you might have to set a cutoff point and fail the operation for large numbers of changed rows. To start the examples, I present the template shown in listing 1. It's the basic form I use for all triggers I write.

Listing 1   Basic template for triggers

```
CREATE TRIGGER <schema>.<tablename>$<actions>[<purpose>]Trigger
ON <schema>.<tablename>
INSTEAD OF <comma delimited actions> AS
--or
AFTER <comma delimited actions> AS
BEGIN

  DECLARE @rowsAffected int,  --stores the number of rows affected
      @msg varchar(2000)  --used to hold the error message

  SET @rowsAffected = @@rowcount

  --no need to continue on if no rows affected
```

```
      IF @rowsAffected = 0 return

      SET NOCOUNT ON --to avoid the rowcount messages
      SET ROWCOUNT 0 --in case the client has modified the rowcount

      BEGIN TRY
         --[validation section]
         --[modification section]
      END TRY
      BEGIN CATCH
           IF @@trancount > 0
             ROLLBACK TRANSACTION

           --[log errors section]

           DECLARE @ERROR_MESSAGE nvarchar(4000)
           SET @ERROR_MESSAGE = ERROR_MESSAGE()
           RAISERROR (@ERROR_MESSAGE,16,1)

        END CATCH
   END
```

Each of the values such as <name> is something to replace, and there are three sections where code is placed. The validation section is where to put code that's used to validate the data that has been updated. I rarely use this section in an INSTEAD OF trigger because any validation you can do in an INSTEAD OF trigger you should do in a constraint. The modification section is where to update data in this or another table, or for an INSTEAD OF trigger, to perform the action that the trigger fired for. And the log errors section is used to log errors after the transaction has been rolled back.

For example, if you had an invoiceLineItem table and you wanted to make sure that the total of items was > 0, and then create a row in the invoiceLog table, you might build the trigger shown in listing 2 for the UPDATE action. New code is shown in bold.

> **Listing 2   Trigger to ensure line item total > 0**

```
CREATE TRIGGER dbo.invoiceLineItem$UPDATETrigger
ON dbo.invoiceLineItem
AFTER UPDATE AS
BEGIN

  DECLARE @rowsAffected int,  --stores the number of rows affected
     @msg varchar(2000)  --used to hold the error message

  SET @rowsAffected = @@rowcount

  --no need to continue on if no rows affected
  IF @rowsAffected = 0 return

  SET NOCOUNT ON --to avoid the rowcount messages
  SET ROWCOUNT 0 --in case the client has modified the rowcount

  BEGIN TRY
     --[validation section]
     IF EXISTS(    SELECT *
        FROM  (   SELECT sum(amount) as total
                  FROM  invoiceLineItem
```

```
                        WHERE invoiceId in (SELECT invoiceId
                                 FROM  inserted
                                 UNION ALL
                                  SELECT invoiceId
                                  FROM  deleted)
                          GROUP BY invoiceId) as totals
                          WHERE totals.total < 0)
         RAISERROR ('The sum of amounts for the item must be > 0',16,1)

      --[modification section]
      INSERT INTO invoiceLog(invoiceNumber, action, changedByLoginId)
      SELECT invoice.invoiceNumber, 'Added LineItems',original_login_id
      FROM  inserted
            JOIN invoice
              ON inserted.invoiceId = invoice.invoiceId
  END TRY
  BEGIN CATCH
      IF @@trancount > 0
        ROLLBACK TRANSACTION

      --[log errors if desired]

      DECLARE @ERROR_MESSAGE nvarchar(4000)
      SET @ERROR_MESSAGE = ERROR_MESSAGE()
      RAISERROR (@ERROR_MESSAGE,16,1)

   END CATCH
END
```

The query is built in three layers, the first of which is almost always a join or a correlated subquery to the inserted or deleted table to get the rows to check. For the INSERT and DELETE triggers you'd need to complete the solution, you could vary the subquery to reference only the inserted or deleted tables respectively. In this particular example, you could use the same trigger (because the inserted and deleted tables are available in every trigger), but I usually try to have a trigger per action, which makes it easier to add additional code and easier to test. Admittedly, I use tools to create triggers that allow parts of the code to be built in a macro, which allows coding modularity while producing specific code. I do this because in most cases it's better for T-SQL code to be as specific as possible, even if that means writing hundreds of similar procedures or triggers. No, it doesn't seem like a good idea for code reuse, but it's much better for performance.

If you want to stop the trigger because of invalid conditions, you raise an error and the TRY...CATCH block handles the rest. If you use the trigger to make modifications to other tables, you don't really need to do anything else; the error handler will capture any errors that occur, meaning that you don't have to check the error level after each statement. If an error occurs, it'll take you to the CATCH block immediately.

NOTE Something I won't cover is that you can also build triggers using the CLR. I haven't heard of any valuable reason to use the CLR for triggers, but it can be done, and all of the same caveats are still a consideration.

When and why to use what tool

It's important to consider how to apply all of these tools to common situations. Bear in mind that for the most part, most of the situations we protect against and the errors that will be sent to the client should rarely if ever occur. The UI and application layer should prevent them. Our goal in placing these protections is twofold.

First, without a guarantee, mistakes will often be made. There are too many clients and too many situations to guarantee perfection in the object layers that are created. Having this impenetrable layer of protection protects us from any mistakes being made.

Second, there are performance benefits as well. Many of the objects that we've looked at will improve performance:

- Using proper data types can reduce storage overhead and prevent comparisons between unlike types eliminating index utilization.
- Limiting NULLs can help the optimizer not consider NULL as a possibility, and make comparisons easier.
- Uniqueness constraints can help the optimizer know that only one value can match for a query.
- Using proper indexes (including unique indexes) generally helps performance unless grossly overused, even ones on a view or filtered index (with a WHERE clause).
- Using foreign key constraints helps the optimizer to know whether related values exist.
- Using check constraints (when trusted) lets the optimizer know what sorts of values can be in a table, so searching for an illegal value is a known fail.

In general, the major problem with all of these objects is that they take work. So unless you have an advocate for the process, it's often quite hard to make the case for database protection that duplicates some of the protection that's in the application code. The goal of this section is to give you a succinct overview of the different types of objects in terms of types of things you're trying to protect against.

Independent of performance, there's a tremendous amount of overlap in which tools you use to solve any problem. Triggers could be written to do all data validation, and in the early (dark) ages of SQL Server, triggers, NULL specifications, and unique indexes were all we had for implementation. There were no constraints whatsoever and we made do. Clearly a trigger-only approach isn't the best practice today; rather, the best practice is to use the tools in the order we first discussed, considering whether you can use the technique mentioned to cover your particular need:

- Data types to constrain data to a basic physical structure that best matches the need.
- NULL specifications to keep NULL data out of columns that shouldn't have NULLs (this is one of the worst offences that people do: letting values be NULL so that the UI can send multiple updates).

- Uniqueness constraints to make sure that the set of values for some column or columns only have unique values.
- Filtered indexes to implement selective uniqueness (and performance, but this isn't a performance-tuning chapter).
- Foreign key constraints to make certain that related values have matches.
- Check constraints to implement checks on the same row, as well as checks on other tables when you want them to happen row by row.
- Triggers for everything else you need to validate in the table, as well as introducing side effects to a query. They're seldom used as they're rarely needed, but they're tools that you can use on occasion.

Sadly this topic also becomes a polarizing political topic as well. There are many application developers who'll be annoyed that you want to use constraints to manage anything. They'll become incensed at the errors that are sent to their client by your constraints, and will demand their removal. Even though your goal is to only use constraints to manage "never-occurring" errors, the fact is that they weren't prepared for bugs in the application code that allow errors to occur. This is a defining point in your career when you can, while making them feel good about themselves, explain why this is spurious reasoning.

There are two reasons why this reasoning is less than sound. First, if the errors are not supposed to occur, nobody should notice your constraints in the first place. Second, you can't stop *all* errors from happening. SQL Server could encounter a hardware glitch and an error might occur. More importantly, deadlocks aren't 100 percent preventable, so your application code needs to be aware that a deadlock might occur and be able to handle it. Knowing what changes were running during a transaction (which you need for a deadlock handler to retry the transaction) is the same thing you need to know for an error handler.

Taking this knowledge that you need to protect against errors already, and noting that it's rare if ever that you should see an error from a constraint raised to even the application code (usually the only reason you should ever see an error occur is a bug or some trouble with your database), it should be clear why you need to protect your data in SQL Server.

Now the onus is on you to carefully consider how enforceable and permanent each rule you are attempting to enforce is. It doesn't behoove you to build a lot of constraints and triggers that have to be frequently changed, and it's best if you can use some client code or stored values to data-drive as many of the variables to your systems as you can. For example, if you can give a customer a variable amount of discount, based on external settings, don't hard-code the settings: build a table and let the client code look it up.

As a final example, consider the salary example from the previous section. You, being the intrepid reader, probably noted that salaries are bound by position, and a new DBA's salary might be bound by the current year's salary bounds. You may even want to create a table that contains the minimum and maximum salary that can be offered. Although this might sound like a rigid rule that could easily be built into a constraint or trigger, this isn't a likely candidate for rigid database constraints, because no matter what the database says, we all know that if you had a shot to get Kalen Delaney to come work for your company as a regular employee, you'd quickly break the salary rules and give her what she wanted (and perhaps a tad more than she wanted to make sure she stayed happy). Having rules be optional like this prevents the user from needing to make a new phony position with its own salary rules to handle fringe cases. A simple piece of data indicating who chose to override the common rules is more than enough. On the other hand, you definitely want to make sure that you use a proper data type to store the salary amount (possibly a data type such as numeric(12,2)) and a check constraint to make sure only positive values are inserted. In some cases, you might add a column that indicates who overrode the rules and then ignore checking the rules, but again, it can end up like spaghetti code if you start to build a web of enforcement rules that allow too much overriding.

Summary

SQL Server provides quite a few ways to implement data protection using methods that can help you take your well-designed database from being simple data storage that has to be constantly validated on use and turn it into a trustable source of information. Every tool we presented can be coded in a manner that the database user needn't have any idea that it's running.

We can't stop the user who wants to spell the name Michael as Micheal (or even F-R-E-D, for that matter), but we can stop someone from putting in a salary of -100, or entering NULL for required data, and we can do our best to avoid the most basic issues that take tons of time to code around when data is used. SQL Server provides tools such as data types to define the reasonable storage of values, NULL specifications to require data when it must be available, uniqueness constraints to prevent duplicate values, filtered unique indexes to prevent duplicate values on a subset of rows, foreign key constraints to ensure related data is correct, check constraints to make sure that values in the row meet the minimum standards, and finally, as a last resort, triggers to catch all other needs.

None of this is all that hard to do. Even triggers are straightforward to code once you get the concept of multi-row handling. The hardest part is gaining the acceptance of the programmer community. During the development process, they're likely to get pinged with errors that they don't expect because they haven't written their code to cover all of the cases that might occur. Remind them that you're building an application for the future, not just to get done faster.

About the author

 Louis Davidson has more than 15 years of experience as a corporate database developer and architect. Currently he's the data architect for the Christian Broadcasting Network. Nearly all of Louis's professional experience has been with Microsoft SQL Server, from the early days to the latest version he can get access to legitimately. Louis has been the principal author of four editions of a book on database design, including one for SQL Server 2008 entitled *Pro SQL Server 2008 Relational Database Design and Implementation* (Apress, 2008). Louis's primary areas of interest are database architecture and coding in T-SQL; he's had experience designing many databases and writing thousands of stored procedures and triggers through the years.

3 Finding functional dependencies

Hugo Kornelis

Some people will tell you that properly normalizing your tables is hard. It's not. The normalization rules are clear, and once you know all the functional dependencies in your data, you merely have to follow the rules carefully, taking care not to forget anything, and you'll always end up with a properly normalized design.

The hard part comes before you can start normalizing—when you try to find all the functional dependencies. Considering how exact and well laid down the rules of normalization are, it's surprising to find that there are no similar rules for finding the functional dependencies. For what use is a set of rules that guarantees a correct model from a correct set of functional dependencies if there's no way to *find* that correct set of functional dependencies?

In this chapter, I'll present a method to find all the functional dependencies. The only thing left for you to do is to find a domain expert who's willing to answer your questions.

Interview method

Communication between domain experts and data modelers can be prone to misunderstandings. Once the interview gets beyond the basics, the domain expert can go into details that are far too advanced and complicated for the data modeler to understand, unless he's a domain expert himself. And questions asked by the data modeler are often so abstract that the domain expert might misunderstand them, unless she has lots of experience with data modeling herself. To minimize the chance of misunderstandings, I use a technique that's not used often in interviews, but has proven its worth many times: I use concrete examples (preferably in a notation familiar to the domain expert) instead of asking abstract questions.

To illustrate the benefits of this interview technique, let's briefly assume that you, as a domain expert in the field of relational databases, are being interviewed by someone who has to make a data model for relational databases. At one point, this data modeler might ask you, "Can a table with a composite primary key be referenced by a foreign key constraint from more than a single table?" Before reading on, think about this question. Try to interpret what the data modeler wants, then answer the question.

Now what if the data modeler had instead asked you this: "Suppose I have TableA with a composite primary key made up of the columns Foo and Bar, TableB with a column Foo among others, and TableC with a column Bar among others. Is it allowed to define a foreign key constraint from the columns Foo and Bar in TableB and TableC, referencing Foo and Bar in TableA?" Would your answer still be the same? Or did you interpret the original question as being about two separate foreign key relationships, one from each of the referencing tables? I expect the latter, for after having worked with databases for some time, you've grown so accustomed to thinking in the patterns that make sense in the context of a database that you're bound to interpret an ambiguous question in those patterns.

Although this illustrates the difference between an abstract question and a question asked by using a concrete example, it doesn't show you the benefit of using a notation that's familiar to the subject matter. But if you compare the data modeler's second question to the exact same scenario depicted as a database diagram, as shown in figure 1, you'll probably agree that this example makes the intention of the data modeler even easier to understand than either of the questions using words only.

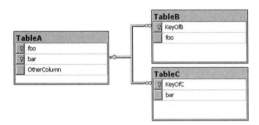

Figure 1   A mocked-up database diagram makes it immediately obvious that this foreign key isn't allowed.

Figure 1 demonstrates that you can reduce the chance of misunderstandings by using concrete examples, preferably in a notation that the domain expert is familiar with. But it doesn't help you to find functional dependencies. For that, you also need to know *which questions* to ask, and *what conclusions* to draw from the possible answers. I'll cover that in the rest of the chapter, where I take on the role of the data modeler, trying to find the correct model for a sales order database.

Modeling the sales order

The sales order has to be one of the most standard and most downtrodden examples in the history of data modeling textbooks. Surely you don't need any advanced techniques to find the functional dependencies for this example; you've seen it so often that you could build the relevant tables in your sleep. And that makes this an ideal example scenario for this chapter. Using a simple and recognizable example enables you to check my questions and the answers provided by the fictitious domain expert, and to see for yourself that the procedure of asking questions and drawing conclusions outlined in this chapter will indeed result in the correct data model—a statement you'd have to take for granted if I'd chosen to use a more complex example.

In real life, you won't follow all steps exactly as I outline them here, but instead immediately conclude functional dependencies in case you feel confident that you're sufficiently familiar with the domain, and use the detailed procedure in situations where you're in doubt or have no idea at all. But for illustration purposes, I'll presume that I (as the data modeler) am completely unfamiliar with the domain of sales orders, so I can't assume anything, but have to ask the domain expert everything I need to know.

So let's focus on WeTrade, Inc., a fictitious trading company, where I'm supposed to model the database for their sales orders. I've already acquired a sample order confirmation form (figure 2), which I used to determine that the data model would include the attributes OrderNo, CustomerName, CustomerID, Product, Qty, Price, TotalPrice, and OrderTotal.

The procedure for finding all functional dependencies is easier to perform if you first lay out all attributes in a simple tabular format, with the attribute names as column headers and some sample data below them. You need to start with at least one row of data, and you're well advised to keep the number of rows low. I chose to use the contents of figure 2 as my starting data, so this table will look like table 1.

You'll probably have noted that this table is already in first normal form. That should be the starting point. If at this stage there are multivalued attributes (for instance, an attribute Customer with contents of `Northwind/12` and `AdventureWorks/ 15`) or repeating groups (for instance, attributes Product1, Product2, Product3, Qty1, Qty2, Qty3, TotalPrice1, TotalPrice2, and TotalPrice3), get rid of those first before you start the procedure to find functional dependencies.

WeTrade, Inc.			Order confirmation form	
Order number: 7001		Customer name: Northwind		
		Customer ID: 12		
Product	**Quantity**	**Price ($)**	**Total Price ($)**	
Gizmo	10	12.50	125.00	
Dooble	10	10.00	100.00	
Order Total			**225.00**	

Figure 2   A sample order confirmation form

Table 1   Sample data in tabular format

OrderNo	CustomerName	CustomerID	Product	Qty	Price	TotalPrice	OrderTotal
7001	Northwind	12	Gizmo	10	12.50	125.00	225.00
7001	Northwind	12	Dooble	10	10.00	100.00	225.00

First step: finding single-attribute dependencies

A functional dependency can be single-attribute (when a single attribute determines the dependent attribute) or multiattribute (when two or more attributes have to be combined to determine the dependent attribute). In the first step of the procedure, you'll only search for single-attribute dependencies.

The definition of *functional dependency* implies that it's never allowed to have two rows of data with the same value for the determining attribute but different values for the dependent attribute. I'll leverage that knowledge by changing the sample data to include exactly those patterns and then asking the domain expert if the changed data would still be allowed.

FIRST ATTRIBUTE: ORDERNO

Finding single-attribute functional dependencies is done on an attribute-by-attribute basis. I'll start with OrderNo. I now have to either add a row or modify some existing data in my table so that I get a combination of two rows with the same value in the OrderNo column and different values in all other columns. I'll modify some data, resulting in the data in table 2.

Table 2   Changing the data in the second row to find what attributes depend on OrderNo

OrderNo	CustomerName	CustomerID	Product	Qty	Price	TotalPrice	OrderTotal
7001	Northwind	12	Gizmo	10	12.50	125.00	250.00
7001	AdventureWorks	15	Dooble	12	10.00	100.00	200.00

We've already established that the best way to ask questions of the domain expert is to use concrete examples in a notation she's familiar with. I have the concrete example, so all I need to do now is to transform it back into the familiar notation—that of an order confirmation form. The result is shown in figure 3.

Note that there are sometimes different ways to represent the information from your table in a familiar format. For instance, in this case I used a single form with two customer names, two customer IDs, and two order totals. I could also have chosen to use two separate forms, one for each row in table 2. In fact, because I'm completely unfamiliar with the domain of sales orders, I should try both versions to make sure that I won't conclude that the data isn't allowed if the domain expert rejects an example that's correct but incorrectly represented. To save space, I won't include the two extra order confirmation forms I have to make to test the alternative representation.

```
┌─────────────────────────────────────────────────────────────────────┐
│  ┌───────────────────────────────────────────────────────────────┐  │
│  │                                                                 │  │
│  │  WeTrade, Inc.                    Order confirmation form      │  │
│  │                                                                 │  │
│  │    Order number: 7001          Customer name: Northwind / AdventureWorks │
│  │                                Customer ID:    12 / 15          │  │
│  │                                                                 │  │
│  │  ┌────────────────────┬──────────┬──────────┬────────────────┐ │  │
│  │  │      Product       │ Quantity │ Price ($)│ Total Price ($) │ │  │
│  │  ├────────────────────┼──────────┼──────────┼────────────────┤ │  │
│  │  │ Gizmo              │       10 │    12.50 │         125.00  │ │  │
│  │  │ Dooble             │       12 │    10.00 │         100.00  │ │  │
│  │  │                    │          │          │                │ │  │
│  │  ├────────────────────┴──────────┴──────────┼────────────────┤ │  │
│  │  │  Order Total                             │ 225.00/200.00  │ │  │
│  │  └──────────────────────────────────────────┴────────────────┘ │  │
│  └───────────────────────────────────────────────────────────────┘  │
└─────────────────────────────────────────────────────────────────────┘
```

Figure 3   Sample order confirmation modified to find which attributes depend on OrderNo

When I showed my altered examples to the domain expert and asked her if these could be valid order confirmations, she told me that there were many problems. It's not allowed to have two separate orders with the same order number, so this rules out the alternate representation I just described. But it's also not allowed to have more than a single customer name or more than a single customer number on an order confirmation form. And finally, the total price of the order for 12 doobles doesn't match the quantity and price, and neither of the order totals matches the sum of the individual total price values; all these numbers should match.

The last statement illustrates an important pitfall when using examples to find functional dependencies (or other constraints). A domain expert could reject an example for reasons other than what you're trying to test. In this case, I wanted to know if more than one total price is allowed for a single order, but the domain expert rejects the example because a different business rule (total price = price * quantity) was violated. It's important that you always verify *why* the domain expert rejects your example before jumping to conclusions.

Normally, the next step would be to correct the errors in the calculation of total price and order total and then consult the domain expert again. After all, the fact that she rejected the total price of the doobles because of a calculation error doesn't imply that she'd also reject it if the calculation were correct—so far I've failed to create a proper test to check whether a single order can encompass more than a single total price. But in this case I can already see from the original example (figure 2), which is a correct example, that there can be multiple total prices for a single order, so there's no need to test this column. This doesn't fly for the order total, though. And no matter how hard I try, I quickly find that there's no way to create an example with two order totals on a single order confirmation form that both match the sum of the individual total prices and yet are different. This shows that it's impossible to have more than a single order total on a single order confirmation form, which is what I needed to know. I can already deduct this myself, so there's no need to bother the domain expert with this.

Because the domain expert objected to associating multiple customer names or multiple customer IDs to a single order number and I could deduct that it's impossible to associate multiple order totals with a single order number, I can now conclude that I've found three functional dependencies: CustomerName, CustomerID, and OrderTotal all are dependent on OrderNo.

SECOND ATTRIBUTE: CUSTOMERNAME

I obviously have to repeat the previous step for all attributes in the table. But I can save myself (and the domain expert) a lot of work if I take already-discovered functional dependencies into account.

In this case, because I already know that CustomerName is dependent on OrderNo, I also know that it's impossible for attributes that don't depend on OrderNo to depend on CustomerName. After all, if for instance Product depended on CustomerName, then it would as a result of the OrderNo → CustomerName dependency also transitively depend on OrderNo. And because I already established that Product doesn't depend on OrderNo, there's no way that it can depend on OrderNo. For this reason, I can exclude product, quantity, price, and total price from this round of testing.

I do still need to test the other columns, though. So I once more change the data from the original example to make sure that I get two rows with the same customer name, but different order number, customer ID, and order total. The result is shown in table 3.

Table 3   Another set of changed data, this time to test dependencies for CustomerName

OrderNo	CustomerName	CustomerID	Product	Qty	Price	TotalPrice	OrderTotal
7001	Northwind	12	Gizmo	10	12.50	125.00	125.00
7002	Northwind	15					200.00

You'll have noted that I left some cells empty. This is done deliberately, to draw your focus to the value combinations that I need to test for. I'll next add in some values for the missing cells, taking particular care not to violate any of the already-identified functional dependencies or other business rules, and then I'll once more transform this to the familiar notation of an order confirmation form before consulting the domain expert. I won't include these steps here (nor for any of the following examples), to save space.

The domain expert informed me that there was nothing wrong with this new example. This shows that it's great that I don't have any knowledge about this domain, for I might otherwise have assumed that the combination of two customer IDs with the same customer name wouldn't be allowed. Obviously, WeTrade, Inc., does business with different customers that share the same name.

Because the modified example wasn't rejected, I can conclude that none of the attributes are functionally dependent on CustomerName.

THIRD ATTRIBUTE: CUSTOMERID

CustomerID is also functionally dependent on OrderNo, so I can again omit testing if any of the attributes Product, Qty, Price, or TotalPrice depend on CustomerID. This leaves the attributes OrderNo, CustomerName, and OrderTotal to be tested. For this, I create a new example order form based on the population in table 4.

Table 4   Testing functional dependencies for CustomerID

OrderNo	CustomerName	CustomerID	Product	Qty	Price	TotalPrice	OrderTotal
7001	Northwind	12	Gizmo	10	12.50	125.00	125.00
7002	AdventureWorks	12					200.00

This time, the domain expert rejects the example. She tells me that it's incorrect to have orders for the same customer ID but with different names—same customer ID should always imply same customer name. This leads me to the conclusion that CustomerName is functionally dependent on CustomerID. I already know that both CustomerName and CustomerID depend on OrderNo, which means I can deduct that OrderNo → CustomerName is a transitive dependency. Because third normal form disallows transitive dependencies in a table, I now know that I'll end up with a separate table for CustomerID and CustomerName, and the latter removed from this table. I can choose to remove the column later and continue testing first (in which case I'll have a complete set of dependencies when I'm done testing), or I can choose to remove this column now and continue my tests with the remaining attributes only (in which case I must take care not to forget testing the extra table just created, unless all possible dependencies have already been examined). I choose the latter—because the number of tests to perform increases more than linearly with the number of attributes in each table, I prefer to do the tests on several narrow tables rather than on one single wide table.

NEXT ATTRIBUTE: PRODUCT

I haven't yet found any attribute that Product depends on, so I can't use the same argument used previously to exclude attributes without unknown dependency from the test. In this case, though, I can exclude the attributes that *are* already known to depend on some attribute. The reason for this is explained in the sidebar "Why can't an attribute depend on two independent attributes?"

After having removed the transitively dependent attribute CustomerName and after modifying the remainder of the second row to test OrderNo, Qty, Price, and TotalPrice for dependency on Product, I got the data as shown in table 5.

The domain expert rejected this modified example; she claimed that the same product would always have the same price. Obviously, price is functionally dependent on product, and this means that according to third normal form, we have to create a new

Table 5 Testing functional dependencies for Product

OrderNo	CustomerID	Product	Qty	Price	TotalPrice	OrderTotal
7001	12	Gizmo	10	12.50	125.00	125.00
7002		Gizmo	20	15	300.00	

table, with the product as the candidate key and including all attributes that depend on product (in this case, only price), which are then removed from the orders table. Once more, I choose to do this immediately. In this case, I need to make sure that I also create a test case to check whether there's a functional dependency from Price to Product as well, but I won't cover that in this chapter.

Why can't an attribute depend on two independent attributes?

In the main text, I claim that it's not required to test whether an attribute that depends on OrderNo (such as OrderTotal) also depends on an attribute that doesn't depend on OrderNo (such as Product). The reason for this is because it's impossible for an attribute to depend on two other attributes unless there's at least one dependency between those two attributes. I already know that Product doesn't depend on OrderNo, and I test for the reverse dependency in this step. If OrderNo depends on Product, then the transitive dependency from Product to OrderTotal is automatically implied and there's no need to test for it. And if OrderNo doesn't depend on Product, then there's no way that OrderTotal could depend on it.

The reason for this impossibility is hard to explain in abstract terms, but obvious to explain by using a concrete example. Suppose we have two orders, one with order ID 1, product Gizmo, and an order total of $100.00, and the other with order ID 2, product Dooble, and an order total of $200.00. Because order total depends on order ID, order ID 1 can only be associated with an order total of $100.00. And if order total also depended on product, than the product Dooble should always be associated with an order total of $200.00. The absence of any functional dependency between order ID and product implies that it's allowed to add a row with order ID 1 and product Dooble. But what should the order total of that row be? Product ID 1 implies it should be $100.00, but product Dooble implies it has to $ 200.00. The only possible conclusion is that this particular set of functional dependencies can't exist.

THE REMAINING ATTRIBUTES

After removing Price from the table, I still have three attributes left to test for single-attribute dependencies: Qty, TotalPrice, and OrderTotal. The first two are exactly like Product: I haven't yet found any dependency for them. And OrderTotal is exactly like CustomerName and CustomerID, because it also depends on OrderNo. So the same rules apply when testing the functional dependencies for these three attributes. The modified data I used to test these attributes is represented in tables 6, 7, and 8.

Table 6   Testing functional dependencies for Qty

OrderNo	CustomerID	Product	Qty	TotalPrice	OrderTotal
7001	12	Gizmo	10	125.00	125.00
7002		Dooble	10	170.00	

Table 7   Testing functional dependencies for TotalPrice

OrderNo	CustomerID	Product	Qty	TotalPrice	OrderTotal
7001	12	Gizmo	10	125.00	125.00
7002		Dooble	20	125.00	

Table 8   Testing functional dependencies for OrderTotal

OrderNo	CustomerID	Product	Qty	TotalPrice	OrderTotal
7001	12	Gizmo	10	125.00	125.00
7002	15				125.00

None of these examples were rejected by the domain expert, so I was able to conclude that there are no more single-column dependencies in this table.

Note that I didn't produce these three examples at the same time. I created them one by one, for if there had been more functional dependencies I could've further reduced the number of tests still needed. But because there turned out to be no more dependencies, I decided to combine them in this description, to save space and reduce the repetitiveness.

Second step: finding two-attribute dependencies

After following the preceding steps, I can now be sure that I've found all the cases where an attribute depends on one of the other attributes. But there can also be attributes that depend on two, or even more, attributes. In fact, I hope there are, because I'm still left with a few attributes that don't depend on any other attribute. If you ever run into this, it's a sure sign of one or more missing attributes on your shortlist—one of the hardest problems to overcome in data modeling.

The method for finding multiattribute dependencies is the same as that for single-attribute dependencies—for every possible combination, create a sample with two rows that duplicate the columns to test and don't duplicate any other column. If at this point I hadn't found any dependency yet, I'd be facing an awful lot of combinations to test. Fortunately, I've already found some dependencies (which you'll find is almost always the case if you start using this method for your modeling), so I can rule out most of these combinations.

At this point, if you haven't already done so, you should remove attributes that don't depend on the candidate key or that transitively depend on the primary key. You'll have noticed that I already did so. Not moving these attributes to their own tables now will make this step unnecessarily complex.

The key to reducing the number of possible combinations is to observe that at this point, you can only have three kinds of attributes in the table: a single-attribute candidate key (or more in the case of a mutual dependency), one or more attributes that depend on the candidate key, and one or more attributes that don't depend on the candidate key, or on any other attribute (as we tested all single-attribute dependencies). Because we already moved attributes that depend on an attribute other than the candidate key, these are the only three kinds of attributes we have to deal with. And that means that there are six possible kinds of combinations to consider: a candidate key and a dependent attribute; a candidate key and an independent attribute; a dependent attribute and an independent attribute; two independent attributes; two dependent attributes; or two candidate keys. Because alternate keys always have a mutual dependency, the last category is a special case of the one before it, so I won't cover it explicitly. Each of the remaining five possibilities will be covered below.

CANDIDATE KEY AND DEPENDENT ATTRIBUTE

This combination (as well as the combination of two candidate keys, as I already mentioned) can be omitted completely. I won't bother you with the mathematical proof, but instead will try to explain in language intended for mere mortals.

Given three attributes (A, B, and C), if there's a dependency from the combination of A and B to C, that would imply that for each possible combination of values for A and B, there can be at most one value of C. But if there's also a dependency of A to B, this means that for every value of A, there can be at most one value of B—in other words, there can be only one combination of A and B for every value of A; hence there can be only one value of C for every value of A. So it naturally follows that if B depends on A, then every attribute that depends on A will also depend on the combination of A and B, and every attribute that doesn't depend on A can't depend on the combination of A and B.

CANDIDATE KEY AND INDEPENDENT ATTRIBUTE

For this combination, some testing is required. In fact, I'll test combination first, because it's the most common—and the sooner I find extra dependencies, the sooner I can start removing attributes from the table, cutting down on the number of other combinations to test.

But, as before, it's not required to test all other attributes for dependency on a given combination of a candidate key and an independent attribute. Every attribute that depends on the candidate key will also appear to depend on any combination of the candidate key with any other attribute. This isn't a real dependency, so there's no need to test for it, or to conclude the existence of such a dependency.

This means that in my example, I need to test the combinations of OrderNo and Product, OrderNo and Qty, and OrderNo and TotalPrice. And when testing the first combination (OrderNo and Product), I can omit the attributes CustomerID and OrderTotal, but I do need to test whether Qty or TotalPrice depend on the combination of OrderNo and Price, as shown in table 9. (Also note how in this case I was able to observe the previously-discovered business rule that TotalPrice = Qty x Price—even though Price is no longer included in the table, it is still part of the total collection of data, and still included in the domain expert's familiar notation.)

Table 9   Testing functional dependencies for the combination of OrderNo and Product

OrderNo	CustomerID	Product	Qty	TotalPrice	OrderTotal
7001	12	Gizmo	10	125.00	225.00
7001		Gizmo	12	150.00	

The domain expert rejected the sample order confirmation I based on this data. As reason for this rejection, she told me that obviously, the orders for 10 and 12 units of Gizmo should've been combined on a single line, as an order for 22 units of Gizmo, at a total price of $375.00. This proves that Qty and TotalPrice both depend on the combination of OrderNo and Product. Second normal form requires me to create a new table with the attributes OrderNo and Product as key attributes, and Qty and Total-Price as dependent attributes. I'll have to continue testing in this new table for two-attribute dependencies for all remaining combinations of two attributes, but I don't have to repeat the single-attribute dependencies, because they've already been tested before the attributes were moved to their own table. For the orders table, I now have only the OrderNo, CustomerID, and OrderTotal as remaining attributes.

TWO DEPENDENT ATTRIBUTES

This is another combination that should be included in the tests. Just as with a single dependent attribute, you'll have to test the key attribute (which will be dependent on the combination in case of a mutual dependency, in which case the combination is an alternate key) and the other dependent attributes (which will be dependent on the combination in case of a transitive dependency).

In the case of my sample Orders table, I only have two dependent attributes left (CustomerID and OrderTotal), so there's only one combination to test. And the only other attribute is OrderID, the key. So I create the test population of table 10 to check for a possible alternate key.

Table 10   Testing functional dependencies for the combination of CustomerID and OrderTotal

OrderNo	CustomerID	OrderTotal
7001	12	125.00
7002	12	125.00

The domain expert saw no reason to reject this example (after I populated the related tables with data that observes all rules discovered so far), so there's obviously no dependency from CustomerID and OrderTotal to OrderNo.

TWO INDEPENDENT ATTRIBUTES

Because the Orders table used in my example has no independent columns anymore, I can obviously skip this combination. But if there still were two or more independent columns left, then I'd have to test each combination for a possible dependency of a candidate key or any other independent attribute upon this combination.

DEPENDENT AND INDEPENDENT ATTRIBUTES

This last possible combination is probably the least common—but there are cases where an attribute turns out to depend on a combination of a dependent and an independent attribute. Attributes that depend on the key attribute can't also depend on a combination of a dependent and an independent column (see the sidebar a few pages back for an explanation), so only candidate keys and other independent attributes need to be tested.

Further steps: three-and-more-attribute dependencies

It won't come as a surprise that you'll also have to test for dependencies on three or more attributes. But these are increasingly rare as the number of attributes increases, so you should make a trade-off between the amount of work involved in testing all possible combinations on one hand, and the risk of missing a dependency on the other. The amount of work involved is often fairly limited, because in the previous steps you'll often already have changed the model from a single many-attribute relation to a collection of relations with only a limited number of attributes each, and hence with a limited number of possible three-or-more-attribute combinations.

For space reasons, I can't cover all possible combinations of three or more attributes here. But the same logic applies as for the two-attribute dependencies, so if you decide to go ahead and test all combinations you should be able to figure out for yourself which combinations to test and which to skip.

What if I have some independent attributes left?

At the end of the procedure, you shouldn't have any independent attributes left—except when the original collection of attributes was incomplete. Let's for instance consider the order confirmation form used earlier—but this time, there may be multiple products with the same product name but a different product ID. In this case, unless we add the product ID to the table before starting the procedure, we'll end up with the attributes Product, Qty, and Price as completely independent columns in the final result (go ahead, try it for yourself—it's a great exercise!).

So if you ever happen to finish the procedure with one or more independent columns left, you'll know that either you or the domain expert made a mistake when producing and assessing the collections of test sample data, or you've failed to identify at least one of the candidate key attributes.

Summary

I've shown you a method to find all functional dependencies between attributes. If you've just read this chapter, or if you've already tried the method once or twice, it may seem like a lot of work for little gain. But once you get used to it, you'll find that this is very useful, and that the amount of work is less than it appears at first sight.

For starters, in a real situation, many dependencies will be immediately obvious if you know a bit about the subject matter, and it'll be equally obvious that there are no dependencies between many attributes. There's no need to verify those with the domain expert. (Though you should keep in mind that some companies may have a specific situation that deviates from the ordinary.)

Second, you'll find that if you start by testing the dependencies you suspect to be there, you'll quickly be able to divide the data over multiple relations with relatively few attributes each, thereby limiting the number of combinations to be tested.

And finally, by cleverly combining multiple tests into a single example, you can limit the number of examples you have to run by the domain expert. This may not reduce the amount of work you have to do, but it does reduce the number of examples your domain expert has to assess—and she'll love you for it!

As a bonus, this method can be used to develop sample data for unit testing, which can improve the quality of the database schema and stored procedures.

A final note of warning—there are some situations where, depending on the order you choose to do your tests, you might miss a dependency. You can find them too, but they're beyond the scope of this chapter. Fortunately this will only happen in cases where rare combinations of dependencies between attributes exist, so it's probably best not to worry too much about it.

About the author

Hugo is cofounder and R&D lead of perFact BV, a Dutch company that strives to improve analysis methods and to develop computer-aided tools that will generate completely functional applications from the analysis deliverable. The chosen platform for this development is SQL Server.

In his spare time, Hugo likes to share and enhance his knowledge of SQL Server by frequenting newsgroups and forums, reading and writing books and blogs, and attending and speaking at conferences.

PART 2

Database Development

Edited by Adam Machanic

It can be argued that database development, as an engineering discipline, was born along with the relational model in 1970. It has been almost 40 years (as I write these words), yet the field continues to grow and evolve—seemingly at a faster rate every year. This tremendous growth can easily be seen in the many facets of the Microsoft database platform. SQL Server is no longer just a simple SQL database system; it has become an application platform, a vehicle for the creation of complex and multifaceted data solutions.

Today's database developer is expected to understand not only the Transact-SQL dialect spoken by SQL Server, but also the intricacies of the many components that must be controlled in order to make the database system do their bidding. This variety can be seen in the many topics discussed in the pages ahead: indexing, full-text search, SQL CLR integration, XML, external interfaces such as ADO.NET, and even mobile device development are all subjects within the realm of database development.

The sheer volume of knowledge both required and available for consumption can seem daunting, and giving up is not an option. The most important thing we can do is understand that while no one can know everything, we can strive to continually learn and enhance our skill sets, and that is where this book comes in. The chapters in this section—as well as those in the rest of the book—were written by some of the top minds in the SQL Server world, and whether you're just beginning your journey into the world of database development or have several years of experience, you will undoubtedly learn something new from these experts.

It has been a pleasure and an honor working on this unique project with such an amazing group of writers, and I sincerely hope that you will thoroughly enjoy the results of our labor. I wish you the best of luck in all of your database development endeavors. Here's to the next 40 years.

About the editor

Adam Machanic is a Boston-based independent database consultant, writer, and speaker. He has written for numerous websites and magazines, including SQLblog, Simple Talk, Search SQL Server, SQL Server Professional, *CODE,* and *VSJ.* He has also contributed to several books on SQL Server, including *SQL Server 2008 Internals* (Microsoft Press, 2009) and *Expert SQL Server 2005 Development* (Apress, 2007). Adam regularly speaks at user groups, community events, and conferences on a variety of SQL Server and .NET-related topics. He is a Microsoft Most Valuable Professional (MVP) for SQL Server, Microsoft Certified IT Professional (MCITP), and a member of the INETA North American Speakers Bureau.

4 Set-based iteration, the third alternative

Hugo Kornelis

When reading SQL Server newsgroups or blogs, you could easily get the impression that there are two ways to manipulate data: declarative (set-based) or iterative (cursor-based). And that iterative code is always bad and should be avoided like the plague.

Those impressions are both wrong.

Iterative code isn't *always* bad (though, in all honesty, it *usually* is). And there's more to SQL Server than declarative or iterative—there are ways to combine them, adding their strengths and avoiding their weaknesses. This article is about one such method: *set-based iteration*.

The technique of set-based iteration can lead to efficient solutions for problems that don't lend themselves to declarative solutions, because those would result in an amount of work that grows exponentially with the amount of data. In those cases, the trick is to find a declarative query that solves a part of the problem (as much as feasible), and that doesn't have the exponential performance problem—then repeat that query until all work has been done. So instead of attempting a single set-based leap, or taking millions of single-row-sized miniature steps in a cursor, set-based iteration arrives at the destination by taking a few seven-mile leaps.

In this chapter, I'll first explain the need for an extra alternative by discussing the weaknesses and limitations of purely iterative and purely declarative coding. I'll then explain the technique of set-based iteration by presenting two examples: first a fairly simple one, and then a more advanced case.

The common methods and their shortcomings

Developing SQL Server code can be challenging. You have so many ways to achieve the same result that the challenge isn't coming up with working code, but picking the "best" working code from a bunch of alternatives. So what's the point of adding yet another technique, other than making an already tough choice even harder?

The answer is that there are cases (admittedly, not many) where none of the existing options yield acceptable performance, and set-based iteration does.

Declarative (set-based) code

Declarative coding is, without any doubt, the most-used way to manipulate data in SQL Server. And for good reason, because in most cases it's the fastest possible code.

The basic principle of declarative code is that you don't tell the computer *how to process the data* in order to create the required results, but instead *declare the results you want* and leave it to the DBMS to figure out how to get those results. Declarative code is also called *set-based code* because the declared required results aren't based on individual rows of data, but on the entire set of data.

For example, if you need to find out which employees earn more than their manager, the declarative answer would involve one single query, specifying all the tables that hold the source data in its FROM clause, all the required output columns in its SELECT clause, and using a WHERE clause to filter out only those employees that meet the salary requirement.

BENEFITS

The main benefit of declarative coding is its raw performance. For one thing, SQL Server has been heavily optimized toward processing declarative code. But also, the query optimizer—the SQL Server component that selects how to process each query—can use all the elements in your database (including indexes, constraints, and statistics on data distribution) to find the most efficient way to process your request, and even adapt the execution plan when indexes are added or statistics indicate a major change in data distribution.

Another benefit is that declarative code is often much shorter and (once you get the hang of it) easier to read and maintain than iterative code. Shorter, easier-to-read code directly translates into a reduction of development cost, and an even larger reduction of future maintenance cost.

DRAWBACKS

Aside from the learning curve for people with a background in iterative coding, there's only one problem with the set-based approach. Because you have to declare the results in terms of the original input, you can't take shortcuts by specifying end results in terms of intermediate results. In some cases, this results in queries that are awkward to write and hard to read. In other cases, it may result in queries that force SQL Server to do more work than would otherwise be required.

Running totals is an example of this. There's no way to tell SQL Server to calculate the running total of each row as the total of the previous row plus the value of the current row, because the running total of the previous row isn't available in the input, and partial query results (even though SQL Server does know them) can't be specified in the language.

The only way to calculate running totals in a set-based fashion is to specify each running total as the sum of the values in all preceding rows. That implies that a lot more summation is done than would be required if intermediate results were available. This results in performance that degrades exponentially with the amount of data, so even if you have no problems in your test environment, you *will* have problems in your 100-million-row production database!

> **Running totals in the OVER clause**
>
> The full ANSI standard specification of the OVER clause includes windowing extensions that allow for simple specification of running totals. This would result in short queries with probably very good performance—if SQL Server had implemented them. Unfortunately, these extensions aren't available in any current version of SQL Server, so we still have to code the running totals ourselves.

Iterative (cursor-based) code

The base principle of iterative coding is to write T-SQL as if it were just another third-generation programming language, like C#, VB.NET, Cobol, and Pascal. In those languages, the only way to process a set of data (such as a sequentially organized file) is to iterate over the data, reading one record at a time, processing that record, and then moving to the next record until the end of the file has been reached. SQL Server has cursors as a built-in mechanism for this iteration, hence the term *cursor-based code* as an alternative to the more generic *iterative code.*

Most iterative code encountered "in the wild" is written for one of two reasons: either because the developer was used to this way of coding and didn't know how (or why!) to write set-based code instead; or because the developer was unable to find a good-performing set-based approach and had to fall back to iterative code to get acceptable performance.

BENEFITS

A perceived benefit of iterative code might be that developers with a background in third-generation languages can start coding right away, instead of having to learn a radically different way to do their work. But that argument would be like someone from the last century suggesting that we hitch horses to our cars so that drivers don't have to learn how to start the engine and operate the steering wheel.

Iterative code also has a real benefit—but only in a few cases. Because the coder has to specify each step SQL Server has to take to get to the end result, it's easy to store an intermediate result and reuse it later. In some cases (such as the running totals already mentioned), this can result in faster-running code.

DRAWBACKS

By writing iterative code, you're crippling SQL Server's performance in two ways at the same time. You not only work around all the optimizations SQL Server has for fast set-based processing, you also effectively prevent the query optimizer from coming up with a faster way to achieve the same results. Tell SQL Server to read employees, and for each employee read the details of his or her department, and that's exactly what'll happen. But tell SQL Server that you want results of employees and departments combined, and that's only one of the options for the query optimizer to consider.

Set-based iteration

An aspect that's often overlooked in the "set-based or cursor" discussion is that they represent two extremes, and there's plenty of room for alternate solutions in between. Iterative algorithms typically use one iteration for each row in the table or query that the iteration is based on, so the number of iterations is always equal to the number of rows, and the amount of work done by a single execution of the body of the iteration equates to processing a single row. Set-based code goes to the other extreme: processing all rows at once, in a single execution of the code. Why limit ourselves to choosing either one execution that processes N rows, or N executions that process one row each?

The most basic form

The most basic form of set-based iteration isn't used to prevent exponential performance scaling, but to keep locking short and to prevent the transaction log from overflowing. This technique is often recommended in newsgroups when UPDATE or DELETE statements that affect a large number of rows have to be run. To prevent long-lasting locks, lock escalation, and transaction log overflow, the TOP clause is used (or SET ROWCOUNT on versions older than SQL Server 2005) to limit the number of rows processed in a single iteration, and the statement is repeated until no more rows are affected. An example is shown in listing 1, where transaction history predating the year 2005 is removed in chunks of 10,000 rows. (Note that this example, like all other examples in this chapter, should run on all versions from SQL Server 2005 upward.)

Listing 1   Set-based iteration with the TOP clause

```
SET NOCOUNT ON;
DECLARE @BatchSize int, @RowCnt int;

SET @BatchSize = 10000;
SET @RowCnt = @BatchSize;

WHILE @RowCnt = @BatchSize
BEGIN;
  DELETE TOP (@BatchSize)
  FROM   TransactionHistory
  WHERE  TranDate < '20050101';

  SET @RowCnt = @@ROWCOUNT;
END;
```

This form of set-based iteration won't increase performance of the code. It's used to limit the impact of code on concurrency, but may make the code run slower.

This form of set-based iteration isn't sophisticated enough to warrant much discussion. I merely wanted to include it for the sake of completeness. Using set-based iteration to increase performance of problematic code takes, unfortunately, more than just adding a TOP clause to the query.

Running totals

Adding running totals to a report is a common business requirement. It's also one of the few situations where declarative code often (though not always) results in poor performance.

In this example, I'll use the AdventureWorks sample database to report all sales, arranged by customer, ordered by date, and with a running total of all order amounts for a customer up to and including that date. Note that the Microsoft-supplied sample database is populated with more than 31,000 orders for over 19,000 customers, and that the highest number of orders for a single customer is 28.

DECLARATIVE CODE

In current versions of SQL Server, the only way to calculate running totals in declarative code is to join each row from the table to all preceding rows for the same customer from itself, adding all those joined rows together to calculate the running total. The code for this is shown in listing 2.

Listing 2   Declarative code for calculating running totals

```
USE AdventureWorks;
SET NOCOUNT ON;

SELECT          s.CustomerID, s.OrderDate, s.SalesOrderID, s.TotalDue,
                SUM(s2.TotalDue) AS RunningTotal
FROM            Sales.SalesOrderHeader AS s
INNER JOIN      Sales.SalesOrderHeader AS s2
      ON        s2.CustomerID = s.CustomerID
      AND(      s2.OrderDate < s.OrderDate            SalesOrderID used
          OR(   s2.OrderDate = s.OrderDate            as tie breaker
            AND s2.SalesOrderID <= s.SalesOrderID))
GROUP BY        s.CustomerID, s.OrderDate, s.SalesOrderID, s.TotalDue
ORDER BY        s.CustomerID, s.OrderDate, s.SalesOrderID;
```

The performance of this query depends on the average number of rows in the self-join. In this case, the average is less than 2, resulting in great performance: approximately 0.2 seconds on my laptop. But if you adapt the code to produce running totals per sales territory instead of per customer (by replacing all occurrences of the column name CustomerID with TerritoryID), you're in for a nasty surprise: with only 10 different territories in the database, the average number of rows in the self-join is much higher. And because performance in this case degrades exponentially, not linearly, the running time on my laptop went up to over 10 minutes (638 seconds, to be exact)!

ITERATIVE CODE

Because the declarative running totals code usually performs poorly, this problem is commonly solved with iterative code, using a server-side cursor. Listing 3 shows the code typically used for this.

Listing 3   Iterative code for calculating running totals

```
USE AdventureWorks;
SET NOCOUNT ON;

DECLARE @Results TABLE
        (CustomerID int NOT NULL,
         OrderDate datetime NOT NULL,
         SalesOrderID int NOT NULL,
         TotalDue money NOT NULL,
         RunningTotal money NULL,
         PRIMARY KEY (CustomerID, OrderDate, SalesOrderID));

INSERT INTO @Results(CustomerID, OrderDate, SalesOrderID, TotalDue)
SELECT CustomerID, OrderDate, SalesOrderID, TotalDue
FROM    Sales.SalesOrderHeader;

DECLARE @CustomerID int,            @OrderDate datetime,
        @SalesOrderID int,          @TotalDue money,
        @CurrCustomerID int,        @RunningTotal money;
SET     @CurrCustomerID = 0;
SET     @RunningTotal = 0;
```

❶

STATIC cursor here faster than FAST_FORWARD

```
DECLARE SalesCursor CURSOR STATIC READ_ONLY
FOR SELECT   CustomerID, OrderDate, SalesOrderID, TotalDue
    FROM       @Results
    ORDER BY CustomerID, OrderDate, SalesOrderID;
OPEN SalesCursor;

FETCH NEXT FROM SalesCursor
      INTO @CustomerID, @OrderDate, @SalesOrderID, @TotalDue;
WHILE @@FETCH_STATUS = 0
BEGIN;
  IF @CustomerID <> @CurrCustomerID
  BEGIN;
    SET @CurrCustomerID = @CustomerID;
    SET @RunningTotal = 0;
  END;

  SET @RunningTotal = @RunningTotal + @TotalDue;
  UPDATE @Results
  SET     RunningTotal = @RunningTotal
  WHERE   CustomerID = @CustomerID
  AND     OrderDate = @OrderDate
  AND     SalesOrderID = @SalesOrderID;

  FETCH NEXT FROM SalesCursor
        INTO @CustomerID, @OrderDate, @SalesOrderID, @TotalDue;
END;

CLOSE SalesCursor;
DEALLOCATE SalesCursor;

SELECT   CustomerID, OrderDate, SalesOrderID, TotalDue, RunningTotal
FROM       @Results
ORDER BY CustomerID, OrderDate, SalesOrderID;
```

❷ ❸ ❹

The code is pretty straightforward. In order to get all results as one result set, a table variable ❶ is used to store the base data and the calculated running totals. The primary key on the table variable is there primarily to create a good clustered index for the iteration, which explains why it includes more columns than the key (which is on SalesOrderID only). The only way to index a table variable is to add PRIMARY KEY or UNIQUE constraints to it.

A T-SQL cursor is then used to iterate over the rows. For each row, the variable holding the running total is incremented with the total of that order and then stored in the results table ❹, after resetting the running total to 0 when the customer changes ❸. The ORDER BY of the cursor ❷ ensures that the data is processed in the proper order, so that the calculated running totals will be correct.

On my laptop, this code takes 1.9 seconds. That's slower than the declarative version presented earlier. But if I change the code to calculate running totals per territory, the running time remains stable at 1.9 seconds. This shows that, even though the declarative solution is faster when the average number of rows in the self-join is low, the iterative solution is faster at all other times, with the added benefit of stable and predictable performance. Almost all processing time is for fetching the order rows, so the performance will grow linearly with the amount of data.

SET-BASED ITERATION

For each customer, the running total of her first order is equal to the order total. The running total of the second order is then equal to the order total plus the first running total, and so on. This is the key to a solution that uses set-based iteration to determine the running total for the first orders of all customers, then calculate all second running totals, and so forth.

This algorithm, for which the code is shown in listing 4, needs as many iterations as the highest number of orders for a single customer—28 in this case. Each individual iteration will probably be slower than a single iteration of the iterative solution, but because the number of iterations is reduced from more than 30,000 to 28, the total execution time is faster.

Listing 4 Set-based iteration for calculating running totals

```
USE AdventureWorks;
SET NOCOUNT ON;

DECLARE @Results TABLE
        (CustomerID int NOT NULL,
         OrderDate datetime NOT NULL,
         SalesOrderID int NOT NULL,
         TotalDue money NOT NULL,              ❶
         RunningTotal money NULL,
         Rnk int NOT NULL,
         PRIMARY KEY (Rnk, CustomerID));

INSERT INTO @Results
       (CustomerID, OrderDate, SalesOrderID,   ❷
        TotalDue, RunningTotal, Rnk)
```

```
SELECT CustomerID, OrderDate, SalesOrderID,
       TotalDue, TotalDue,
       RANK() OVER (PARTITION BY CustomerID
                    ORDER BY    OrderDate,
                                SalesOrderID)
FROM   Sales.SalesOrderHeader;

DECLARE @Rank int,
        @RowCount int;
SET     @Rank = 1;
SET     @RowCount = 1;

WHILE @RowCount > 0
BEGIN;
  SET @Rank = @Rank + 1;

  UPDATE      nxt
  SET         RunningTotal    = prv.RunningTotal
                              + nxt.TotalDue
     FROM     @Results    AS nxt
  INNER JOIN @Results     AS prv
       ON     prv.CustomerID  = nxt.CustomerID
      AND     prv.Rnk         = @Rank- 1
  WHERE       nxt.Rnk         = @Rank;

  SET @RowCount = @@ROWCOUNT;
END;

SELECT   CustomerID, OrderDate, SalesOrderID, TotalDue, RunningTotal
FROM     @Results
ORDER BY CustomerID, OrderDate, SalesOrderID;
```

Just as in the iterative code, a table variable **❶** is used to store the base data and the calculated running totals. In this case, that's not only to enable all results to be returned at once and in the expected order, but also because we need to store intermediate results and reuse them later.

During the initial population **❷** of the results table, I calculate and store the rank of each order. This is more efficient than calculating it in each iteration, because this also allows me to base the clustered index on this rank. It's possible to code this algorithm without materializing the rank in this table, but that makes the rest of the code more complex, and (most important) hurts performance in a big way!

While populating the table variable, I also set the running total for each order equal to its order total. This is, of course, incorrect for all except the first orders, but it saves the need for a separate UPDATE statement for the first orders, and the running totals for all other orders will eventually be replaced later in the code.

The core of this algorithm is the UPDATE statement **❸** that joins a selection of all orders with the next rank to those of the previous rank, so that the next running total can be set to the sum of the previous running total and the next order total.

On my laptop, this code runs in 0.4 seconds. This speed depends not only on the amount of data, but also on the required number of iterations. If I change the code to calculate running totals per territory rather than per customer, the number of iterations goes up to almost 7,000, causing the execution time to rise to approximately 0.9 seconds. And if I change the code to calculate overall running totals (forcing the number of iterations to be equal to the number of rows), the clock stops at 2 seconds.

The bottom line is that, even though declarative code runs slightly faster in cases with a very low iteration count and iterative code is slightly better for very high iteration counts, set-based iteration presents a good algorithm that's the fastest in many situations and only slightly slower in the other cases.

Bin packing

The *bin-packing problem* describes a category of related problems. In its shortest form, it can be expressed as "given an unlimited supply of bins, all having the same capacity, and a collection of packages, find a way to combine all packages in the least number of bins."

The bin-packing problem is sometimes thought to be mainly academic, of interest for mathematicians only. That's a misconception, as there are many business situations that are a variation on the bin-packing problem:

- *Transport*—You have to transport five packages from Amsterdam to Paris. The packages weigh two, three, four, five, and six tons. The maximum capacity of a single truck is 10 tons. You can, of course, place the first three packages in a single truck without exceeding the maximum weight, but than you'd need two extra trucks for the last two packages. With this small amount of data, it's obvious that you can get them transported in two trucks if you place the packages of four and six tons in one truck and the other three in the second. But if there are 400 packages, it becomes too hard for a human to see how to spare one or two trucks, and computerized assistance becomes crucial.

- *Seating groups*—Imagine a theatre with 40 rows of 30 seats each. If a group makes a reservation, they'll expect to get adjacent seats on a single row. But if you randomly assign groups to rows, you have a high chance that you'll end up with two or three empty seats in each row and a group of eight people who can't get adjacent seats anymore. If you can find a more efficient way to assign seats to groups, you might free up eight adjacent seats on one row and sell an extra eight tickets.

- *Minimizing cut loss*—Materials such as cable and fabric are usually produced on rolls of a given length. If a builder needs to use various lengths of cable, or a store gets orders for various lengths of fabric, they don't want to be left with one or two meters from each roll and still have to use a new roll for the last required length of six meters.

According to mathematicians, you can only be 100 percent sure that you get the absolute minimum number of bins by trying every possible permutation. It's obvious that, however you implement this, it'll never scale, as the number of possible permutations grows exponentially with the number of packages. Most businesses will prefer an algorithm that produces a "very good" distribution in a few seconds over one that might save two or three bins by finding the "perfect" solution after running for a few days.

DECLARATIVE CODE

I've never found a set-based approach to finding a "good enough" solution for the bin-packing problem. But I've found set-based code that finds the "perfect" solution. This code was originally posted by John Gilson; I've corrected and optimized this code and then published it to my blog (http://sqlblog.com/blogs/hugo_kornelis/archive/2008/10/27/bin-packing-part-4-the-set-based-disaster.aspx), but it's too large to reproduce here. There's no reason to, either, because this code can never be used in practice—not only because it couples already-bad performance with the ugliest exponential growth curve I've ever seen, but also because it requires extra columns in intermediate result sets and many extra lines of code as the bin size and the number of packages increases, such that for real-world problems, you'd need millions of lines of code (and a version of SQL Server that allows more than 4,096 columns per SELECT statement). And then you'll still get execution times measured in days, if not years.

ITERATIVE CODE

Because a set-based solution for the bin-packing problem is way too slow, even in cases that are limited enough that such a solution is even possible, we need to investigate other options. And the most obvious alternative is an iterative solution. Of all the possible strategies I investigated (see my blog for the details), I found that the best combination of speed and packing efficiency is attained by an algorithm that stays close to how I'd pack a bunch of physical packages into physical bins: take a bin, keep adding packages to it until it overflows, then start with a new bin unless the overflowing package fits into one of the other already filled bins. Listing 5 shows the code to set up the tables and fill them with some randomly generated data, and listing 6 shows the T-SQL version of this algorithm.

Listing 5   Set up tables and generate random data for bin packing

```
SET NOCOUNT ON;

IF OBJECT_ID('dbo.Packages', 'U') IS NOT NULL
  BEGIN;
  DROP TABLE dbo.Packages;
  END;

CREATE TABLE dbo.Packages
            (PackageNo int NOT NULL IDENTITY PRIMARY KEY,
             Size smallint NOT NULL,
             BinNo int DEFAULT NULL);

DECLARE @NumPackages int,
        @Loop int;
SET @NumPackages = 100000;          ⟵┘ Number of packages
SET @Loop = 1;                           to generate
```

```
WHILE @Loop <= @NumPackages
BEGIN;
  INSERT INTO dbo.Packages(Size)
  VALUES (CEILING(RAND() * 30) + CEILING(RAND() * 30));
  SET @Loop = @Loop + 1;
END;
```

Generates random
number between
2 and 60

Listing 6 Iterative code for bin packing

```
SET NOCOUNT ON;

DECLARE @BinSize       smallint
       ,@PackageNo     int
       ,@Size          smallint
       ,@CurBinNo      int
       ,@CurSpaceLeft  smallint
       ,@BinNo         int;
SET      @BinSize     = 100

IF OBJECT_ID('dbo.Bins', 'U') IS NOT NULL
  BEGIN;
  DROP TABLE dbo.Bins;
  END;
CREATE TABLE dbo.Bins
  (BinNo int NOT NULL PRIMARY KEY
  ,SpaceLeft smallint NOT NULL);
CREATE INDEX ix_Bins ON dbo.Bins(SpaceLeft);

SET @CurBinNo = 1;
SET @CurSpaceLeft = @BinSize;
INSERT INTO dbo.Bins (BinNo, SpaceLeft)
VALUES (@CurBinNo, @CurSpaceLeft);

DECLARE PackageCursor CURSOR STATIC
FOR SELECT    PackageNo, Size
    FROM      dbo.Packages;

OPEN PackageCursor;

FETCH NEXT
FROM   PackageCursor
INTO   @PackageNo, @Size;

WHILE @@FETCH_STATUS = 0
BEGIN;

  IF @CurSpaceLeft >= @Size
  BEGIN;
    SET @BinNo = @CurBinNo;
  END;
  ELSE
  BEGIN;
    SET @BinNo =
      (SELECT   TOP (1) BinNo
       FROM     dbo.Bins
       WHERE    SpaceLeft >= @Size
       AND      BinNo      <> @CurBinNo
       ORDER BY SpaceLeft);
```

Variables for cursor data

Variables for current bin

Stored for
extra performance

Start with empty
current bin

①

②

③

```
      IF @BinNo IS NULL                              ❹
      BEGIN;
        UPDATE dbo.Bins                         ❺
        SET    SpaceLeft = @CurSpaceLeft
        WHERE  BinNo     = @CurBinNo;

        SET @CurBinNo = @CurBinNo + 1;               ❹
        SET @CurSpaceLeft = @BinSize;
        INSERT INTO dbo.Bins (BinNo, SpaceLeft)
        VALUES (@CurBinNo, @CurSpaceLeft);

        SET @BinNo = @CurBinNo;
      END;
    END;

    UPDATE dbo.Packages
    SET    BinNo     = @BinNo
    WHERE  PackageNo = @PackageNo;

    IF @BinNo = @CurBinNo                Current bin not yet
    BEGIN;                               on disc, so no need
      SET @CurSpaceLeft = @CurSpaceLeft - @Size;   to update space left
    END;
    ELSE
    BEGIN;
      UPDATE dbo.Bins
      SET    SpaceLeft = SpaceLeft - @Size
      WHERE  BinNo     = @BinNo;
    END;

    FETCH NEXT
    FROM  PackageCursor
    INTO  @PackageNo, @Size;
  END;

  IF @CurBinNo IS NOT NULL
  BEGIN;
    UPDATE dbo.Bins                       ❺
    SET    SpaceLeft = @CurSpaceLeft
    WHERE  BinNo     = @CurBinNo;
  END;

  CLOSE       PackageCursor;
  DEALLOCATE PackageCursor;

  SELECT COUNT(*) AS NumPackages,
         SUM(SpaceLeft) AS WastedSpace
  FROM   dbo.Bins;
```

The main logic is coded in the WHILE loop. For every package, I first check whether the current bin has enough room left ❷. If not, I check whether the package would fit one of the other already partly filled bins ❸ before creating a new bin for it ❹. To save time, I don't write the data for the current bin to disc after each package, but I pay for this by having to write it at two slightly less logical locations in the code ❺—when a new bin is started, or (for the last bin) after the last package has been assigned.

This algorithm is fast, because adding several packages to the same bin right after each other saves on the overhead of switching between bins. It's also efficient because, even if a large package forces me to start a new bin when the previous one is still half empty, that half-empty bin will still be reconsidered every time a package would overflow the current bin, so it should eventually fill up. There's no ORDER BY specified in the cursor definition ❶. Adding ORDER BY BinSize DESC will improve the packing efficiency by about 4 percent, but at the cost of a performance hit that starts at 5–10 percent for small amounts of test data (10,000–50,000 packages), but grows to more than 20 percent for 500,000 packages.

When I tested this code on my laptop, it was able to pack 100,000 packages in bins in approximately 143 seconds. The running time went up to 311 seconds for 200,000 packages, and to 769 seconds for 500,000 packages. The growth is much better than exponential, but worse than linear, probably due to the increasing cost of checking an ever-increasing number of partly filled bins when a package would overflow the current bin.

Some extrapolation of my test results indicates that a run with a million packages will probably take half an hour, and maybe 6 or 7 hours are needed to pack ten million packages. This sure beats packing the bins by hand, but it might not be fast enough in all situations.

SET-BASED ITERATION

In those situations where the iterative solution isn't fast enough, we need to find something faster. The key here is that it's easy to calculate an absolute minimum number of bins—if, for example, the combined size of all packages is 21,317 and the bin size is 100, then we can be sure that there will never be a solution with less than 214 bins—so why not start off with packing 214 bins at once?

I start by finding the 214 largest packages and putting one in each of the 214 available bins. After that, I rank the bins by space remaining, rank the packages (excluding those that are already too large for any bin) by size, match bins and packages by rank, and add packages that will still fit into their matching bins. I then repeat this step until there are no packages left that fit in the remaining space of an available bin (either because all packages are packed, or they're all larger than the largest free space).

Ideally, all packages have now been catered for. In reality, there will often be cases where not all packages can be handled in a single pass—so I then repeat this process, by summing the total size of the remaining packages, dividing by the bin size, assigning that number of bins and repeatedly putting packages into bins until no more packages that fit in a bin are left. This second pass is often the last. Sometimes a third pass can be required.

The code in listing 8 shows a SQL Server 2005–compatible implementation of this algorithm. (On SQL Server 2008, the UPDATE FROM statement can be replaced with MERGE for better ANSI compatibility, though at the cost of slightly slower performance.) This code uses a numbers table—a table I believe should exist in every database, as it can be used in many situations. Listing 7 shows how to make such a table and fill it with numbers 1 through 1,000,000. Note that creating and filling the numbers table is a one-time operation!

Listing 7   Creating the numbers table for use in the set-based bin-packing code

```
SET NOCOUNT ON;

CREATE TABLE dbo.Numbers
             (Num int NOT NULL PRIMARY KEY);

WITH Digits(d) AS
  (SELECT 0 UNION ALL SELECT 1 UNION ALL SELECT 2 UNION ALL
   SELECT 3 UNION ALL SELECT 4 UNION ALL SELECT 5 UNION ALL
   SELECT 6 UNION ALL SELECT 7 UNION ALL SELECT 8 UNION ALL SELECT 9)
INSERT INTO dbo.Numbers(Num)
SELECT a.d + b.d * 10 + c.d * 100 + d.d * 1000
     + e.d * 10000 + f.d * 100000 + 1
FROM   Digits a, Digits b, Digits c, Digits d, Digits e, Digits f;
```

Listing 8   Set-based iteration for bin packing

```
SET NOCOUNT ON;

DECLARE @BinSize        smallint
       ,@MinBin         int
       ,@MaxBin         int
       ,@BinsNeeded     int
       ,@Threshold      smallint;
SET     @BinSize     = 100;
SET     @MaxBin      = 0;

IF OBJECT_ID('dbo.Bins', 'U') IS NOT NULL
  BEGIN;
  DROP TABLE dbo.Bins;
  END;
CREATE TABLE dbo.Bins
  (BinNo int NOT NULL PRIMARY KEY
  ,SpaceLeft smallint NOT NULL);

WHILE 1 = 1
BEGIN;

  SET @BinsNeeded =
   (SELECT CEILING(1.0 * SUM(Size) / @BinSize) AS Needed
    FROM   dbo.Packages
    WHERE  BinNo IS NULL)
  IF @BinsNeeded IS NULL
    BREAK;

  SET @MinBin = @MaxBin + 1;
  SET @MaxBin = @MaxBin + @BinsNeeded;

  INSERT INTO dbo.Bins (BinNo, SpaceLeft)
  SELECT     Num, @BinSize
  FROM       dbo.Numbers
  WHERE      Num BETWEEN @MinBin AND @MaxBin;

  WHILE 1 = 1
  BEGIN;

    SET @Threshold =
     (SELECT MAX(SpaceLeft)
```

Range of bins
currently being filled

❶

All packages done?

Range of bins
currently being filled

❶

❷

```
      FROM    dbo.Bins
      WHERE   BinNo BETWEEN @MinBin AND @MaxBin);        ❷

   WITH
      RankedBins AS
        (SELECT BinNo, SpaceLeft,                         ❸
           ROW_NUMBER() OVER (ORDER BY SpaceLeft DESC) AS Ranking
         FROM    dbo.Bins
         WHERE   BinNo BETWEEN @MinBin AND @MaxBin
         AND     SpaceLeft > 0)
      ,RankedPackages AS
        (SELECT Size, BinNo,                              ❹
               ROW_NUMBER() OVER (ORDER BY Size DESC) AS Ranking
         FROM    dbo.Packages
         WHERE   BinNo IS NULL
         AND     Size <= @Threshold)
   UPDATE      p
   SET         BinNo          = b.BinNo                   ❺
   FROM        RankedPackages AS p
   INNER JOIN RankedBins      AS b
         ON   b.Ranking       = p.Ranking
   WHERE       b.SpaceLeft    >= p.Size;

   IF @@ROWCOUNT = 0              │ All bins full?
     BREAK;                       │

   UPDATE dbo.Bins
   SET    SpaceLeft = @BinSize -
       (SELECT SUM(p.Size)                                ❻
        FROM   dbo.Packages AS p
        WHERE  p.BinNo = Bins.BinNo)
   WHERE  BinNo BETWEEN @MinBin AND @MaxBin;

   END;

END;

SELECT COUNT(*) AS NumPackages,
       SUM(SpaceLeft) AS WastedSpace
FROM   dbo.Bins;
```

This code uses two nested WHILE loops. The outer loop generates as many rows in the Bins table as the minimum number of bins required for the packages that aren't already in a bin ❶ and then hands control over to the inner loop for filling these bins. This inner loop first finds the largest available space in any of the current batch of bins, to avoid wasting time on packages that are larger than that ❷. It then ranks the bins by available space ❸, ranks the packages by size ❹, and assigns packages to bins that have the same ranking, but only if they fit ❺. After that, the remaining space is recalculated for each bin in the current batch ❻.

The queries in the inner loop of this algorithm are quite complex and are bound to take some time. But, as the number of iterations of these loops is low (28 executions of the inner loop for the 100,000 row test set and 29 for the 200,000 row test set), the total execution time is very fast: only 12.5 seconds on my laptop for 100,000 rows, 25.8 seconds for 200,000 rows, and 47.5 seconds for 500,000 rows. These numbers also indicate that this algorithm scales better than the iterative algorithm. I expect that packing 10 million packages should take less than 15 minutes. And if that's still too slow for you, then you can always use a real server instead of a laptop.

My tests also showed that the solution that uses set-based iteration tends to be slightly more efficient. The number of bins used varies from less than 0.5 percent more to almost 2 percent less, with an average of 0.8 percent less. If you recall that the iterative version can be improved by about 4 percent (at the cost of a big performance hit) by adding an ORDER BY clause, you'll also understand that this modified iterative version will need about 3 percent fewer bins than the version based on set-based iteration. So if you need to find a solution with as few bins as possible and you can afford to wait long enough for the iterative version (with ORDER BY) to finish, use that one. Otherwise, save yourself lots of time by using set-based iteration.

Summary

In this article, I've shown that iterative code and set-based code aren't the only options for T-SQL developers, but rather two extremes. Set-based iteration is a technique that sits in between these two extremes, combining a low number of iterations with a set-based query that doesn't affect all rows at once, but does attempt to affect as many rows as possible without incurring exponential performance loss.

The technique of set-based iteration is neither easy to use, nor a panacea for all performance problems. There's no simple recipe that you can follow to find an algorithm using set-based iteration for a problem. It requires creativity, fantasy, out-of-the-box thinking, and lots of experience to see a promising approach, and then a lot of hard work to implement and test it. Even then it's still possible that the set-based iteration may turn out not to perform as well as expected.

I've attempted to use set-based iteration in more cases than described here. In many cases, the only result was a performance *decrease*, or a performance gain that was too small to warrant the extra complexity in the code. But there were also situations where the performance gain was impressive. For those situations, the technique of set-based iteration can be an invaluable tool in the T-SQL developer's toolbox.

About the author

Hugo Kornelis is co-founder and R&D lead of perFact BV, a Dutch company that strives to improve analysis methods and develop computer-aided tools that will generate completely functional applications from the analysis deliverable. The chosen platform for this development is SQL Server.

In his spare time, Hugo likes to share and enhance his knowledge of SQL Server by frequenting newsgroups and forums, reading and writing books and blogs, and attending and speaking at conferences.

5 Gaps and islands

Itzik Ben-Gan

This chapter describes problems known as gaps and islands and their solutions. I start out with a description of gaps and islands problems, describe the common variations on the problems, and provide sample data and desired results. Then I move on to ways of handling gaps and islands problems, covering multiple solutions to each problem and discussing both their logic and performance. The chapter concludes with a summary of the solutions.

Description of gaps and islands problems

Gaps and islands problems involve missing values in a sequence. Solving the gaps problem requires finding the ranges of missing values, whereas solving the islands problem involves finding the ranges of existing values.

The sequences of values in gaps and islands problems can be numeric, such as a sequence of order IDs, some of which were deleted. An example of the gaps problem in this case would be finding the ranges of deleted order IDs. An example of the islands problem would be finding the ranges of existing IDs.

The sequences involved can also be temporal, such as order dates, some of which are missing due to inactive periods (weekends, holidays). Finding periods of inactivity is an example of the gaps problem, and finding periods of activity is an example of the islands problem. Another example of a temporal sequence is a process that needs to report every fixed interval of time that it is online (for example, every 4 hours). Finding unavailability and availability periods is another example of gaps and islands problems.

Besides varying in terms of the data type of the values (numeric and temporal), sequences can also vary in terms of the uniqueness of values. For example, the sequence can have unique values, that is, unique keys, or non-unique values, that is, order dates. When discussing solutions, for simplicity's sake I'll present them against a numeric sequence with unique values. I'll explain the changes you need to make to apply the solution to the variants.

Sample data and desired results

To demonstrate the logical aspects of the solutions to the gaps and islands problems, I'll use a table called NumSeq. Run the code in listing 1 to create the table NumSeq and populate it with sample data.

Listing 1   Code creating and populating table NumSeq

```
SET NOCOUNT ON;
USE tempdb;

-- dbo.NumSeq (numeric sequence with unique values, interval: 1)
IF OBJECT_ID('dbo.NumSeq', 'U') IS NOT NULL
  DROP TABLE dbo.NumSeq;

CREATE TABLE dbo.NumSeq
(
  seqval INT NOT NULL CONSTRAINT PK_NumSeq PRIMARY KEY
);

INSERT INTO dbo.NumSeq(seqval) VALUES(2);
INSERT INTO dbo.NumSeq(seqval) VALUES(3);

INSERT INTO dbo.NumSeq(seqval) VALUES(11);
INSERT INTO dbo.NumSeq(seqval) VALUES(12);
INSERT INTO dbo.NumSeq(seqval) VALUES(13);

INSERT INTO dbo.NumSeq(seqval) VALUES(31);

INSERT INTO dbo.NumSeq(seqval) VALUES(33);
INSERT INTO dbo.NumSeq(seqval) VALUES(34);
INSERT INTO dbo.NumSeq(seqval) VALUES(35);

INSERT INTO dbo.NumSeq(seqval) VALUES(42);
```

The column `seqval` is a unique column that holds the sequence values. The sample data represents a sequence with ten unique values with four gaps and five islands. The solutions to the gaps problem should return the ranges of missing values, as table 1 shows.

start_range	end_range
4	10
14	30
32	32
36	41

Table 1   Desired result for gaps problem

The solutions to the islands problem should return the ranges of existing values, as table 2 shows.

When discussing performance, I'll provide information based on tests I did against a table called BigNumSeq with close to 10,000,000 rows, representing a numeric sequence with unique values, with 10,000 gaps. Run the code in listing 2 to create the

start_range	end_range
2	3
11	13
31	31
33	35
42	42

Table 2   Desired result for islands problem

BigNumSeq table and populate it with sample data. Note that it may take a few minutes for this code to finish.

Listing 2   Code creating and populating the BigNumSeq table

```
-- dbo.BigNumSeq (big numeric sequence with unique values, interval: 1)
IF OBJECT_ID('dbo.BigNumSeq', 'U') IS NOT NULL
  DROP TABLE dbo.BigNumSeq;

CREATE TABLE dbo.BigNumSeq
(
  seqval INT NOT NULL CONSTRAINT PK_BigNumSeq PRIMARY KEY
);

-- Populate table with values in the range 1 through to 10,000,000
-- with a gap every 1000 (total 10,000 gaps)
WITH
L0   AS(SELECT 1 AS c UNION ALL SELECT 1),
L1   AS(SELECT 1 AS c FROM L0 AS A, L0 AS B),
L2   AS(SELECT 1 AS c FROM L1 AS A, L1 AS B),
L3   AS(SELECT 1 AS c FROM L2 AS A, L2 AS B),
L4   AS(SELECT 1 AS c FROM L3 AS A, L3 AS B),
L5   AS(SELECT 1 AS c FROM L4 AS A, L4 AS B),
Nums AS(SELECT ROW_NUMBER() OVER(ORDER BY (SELECT 0)) AS n FROM L5)
INSERT INTO dbo.BigNumSeq WITH(TABLOCK) (seqval)
  SELECT n
  FROM Nums
  WHERE n <= 10000000
    AND n % 1000 <> 0;
```

Now that you understand the problems and the desired results and have created and populated the sample tables, you are ready to start working on solutions. I encourage you to come up with your own solutions and test and tune them against the big table before you look at my solutions.

Solutions to gaps problem

I'll present four solutions to the gaps problem: two using subqueries, one using ranking calculations, and (how can I not?) one using the notorious cursors. I'll conclude this section with a performance summary.

Gaps—solution 1 using subqueries

Listing 3 shows the first solution to the gaps problem.

> **Listing 3   Gaps—solution 1 using subqueries**

```
SELECT
  seqval + 1 AS start_range,
  (SELECT MIN(B.seqval)
   FROM dbo.NumSeq AS B
   WHERE B.seqval > A.seqval) - 1 AS end_range
FROM dbo.NumSeq AS A
WHERE NOT EXISTS
  (SELECT *
   FROM dbo.NumSeq AS B
   WHERE B.seqval = A.seqval + 1)
  AND seqval < (SELECT MAX(seqval) FROM dbo.NumSeq);
```

This solution is based on subqueries. In order to understand it you should first focus on the filtering activity in the WHERE clause and then proceed to the activity in the SELECT list. The purpose of the NOT EXISTS predicate in the WHERE clause is to filter only points that are a point before a gap. You can identify a point before a gap when you see that for such a point, the value plus 1 doesn't exist in the sequence. The purpose of the second predicate in the WHERE clause is to filter out the maximum value from the sequence because it represents the point before infinity, which does not concern us.

That filter left only points that are a point before a gap. What remains is to relate to each such point the next point that exists in the sequence. A subquery in the SELECT list is used to return for each point the minimum value that is greater than the current point. This is one way to implement the concept of *next* in SQL.

Each pair is made of a point before a gap, and the next point that exists in the sequence represents a pair of values bounding a gap. To get the start and end points of the gap, add 1 to the point before the gap, and subtract 1 from the point after the gap.

This solution performs well, and I must say that I'm a bit surprised by the efficiency of the execution plan for this query. Against the BigNumSeq table, this solution ran for only about 8 seconds on my system, and incurred 62,262 logical reads. To filter points before gaps, I expected that the optimizer would apply an index seek per each of the 10,000,000 rows, which could have meant over 30 million random reads. Instead, it performed two ordered scans of the index, costing a bit over 30,000 sequential reads, and applying a merge join between the two inputs for this purpose. For each of the 10,000 rows that remain (for the 10,000 points before gaps), an index seek is used to return the next existing point. Each such seek costs 3 random reads for the three levels in the index b-tree, amounting in total to about 30,000 random reads. The total number of logical reads is 62,262 as mentioned earlier. If the number of gaps is fairly small, as in our case, this solution performs well.

To apply the solution to a temporal sequence, instead of using +1 or -1 to add or subtract the interval 1 from the integer sequence value, use the DATEADD function to add or subtract the applicable temporal interval from the temporal sequence.

To apply the solution to a sequence with duplicates, you have several options. One option is to substitute the reference to the table that is aliased as A with a derived table based on a query that removes duplicates: (SELECT DISTINCT seqval FROM dbo.TempSeq) AS A. Another option is to add a DISTINCT clause to the SELECT list.

Gaps—solution 2 using subqueries

Listing 4 shows the second solution for the gaps problem.

Listing 4   Gaps—solution 2 using subqueries

```
SELECT cur + 1 AS start_range, nxt - 1 AS end_range
   FROM (SELECT
            seqval AS cur,
            (SELECT MIN(B.seqval)
              FROM dbo.NumSeq AS B
             WHERE B.seqval > A.seqval) AS nxt
         FROM dbo.NumSeq AS A) AS D
WHERE nxt - cur > 1;
```

As with solution 1, this solution is also based on subqueries. The logic of this solution is straightforward. The query that defines the derived table D uses a subquery in the SELECT list to produce current-next pairs. That is, for each current value, the subquery returns the minimum value that is greater than the current. The current value is aliased as cur, and the next value is aliased as nxt. The outer query filters the pairs in which the difference is greater than 1, because those pairs bound gaps. By adding 1 to cur and subtracting 1 from nxt, you get the gap starting and ending points. Note that the maximum value in the table (the point before infinity) will get a NULL back from the subquery, the difference between cur and nxt will yield a NULL, the predicate NULL > 1 will yield UNKNOWN, and the row will be filtered out. That's the behavior we want for the point before infinity. It is important to always think about the three-valued logic and ensure that you get desired behavior; and if you don't, you need to add logic to get the behavior you are after.

The performance measures for this solution are not as good as solution 1. The plan for this query shows that the index is fully scanned to retrieve the current values, amounting to about 16,000 sequential reads. Per each of the 10,000,000 current values, an index seek operation is used to return the next value to produce the current-next pairs. Those seeks are the main contributor to the cost of this plan, as they amount to about 30,000,000 random reads. This query ran for about 48 seconds on my system, and incurred 31,875,478 logical reads.

To apply the solution to a temporal sequence, use the DATEADD function instead of using +1 and -1 and the DATEDIFF function to calculate the difference between cur and nxt.

To apply the solution to a sequence with duplicates, use guidelines similar to those in the previous solution.

Gaps—solution 3 using ranking functions

Listing 5 shows the third solution to the gaps problem.

Listing 5   Gaps—solution 3 using ranking functions

```
WITH C AS
(
  SELECT seqval, ROW_NUMBER() OVER(ORDER BY seqval) AS rownum
  FROM dbo.NumSeq
)
SELECT Cur.seqval + 1 AS start_range, Nxt.seqval - 1 AS end_range
FROM C AS Cur
  JOIN C AS Nxt
    ON Nxt.rownum = Cur.rownum + 1
WHERE Nxt.seqval - Cur.seqval > 1;
```

This solution implements the same logic as the previous solution, but it uses a different technique to produce current-next pairs. This solution defines a common table expression (CTE) called *C* that calculates row numbers to position sequence values. The outer query joins two instances of the CTE, one representing current values, and the other representing next values. The join condition matches current-next values based on an offset of 1 between their row numbers. The filter in the outer query then keeps only those pairs with a difference greater than 1.

The plan for this solution shows that the optimizer does two ordered scans of the index to produce row numbers for current and next values. The optimizer then uses a merge join to match current-next values. The two ordered scans of the index are not expensive compared to the seek operations done in the previous solution. However, the merge join appears to be many-to-many and is a bit expensive. This solution ran for 24 seconds on my system, and incurred 32,246 logical reads.

To apply the solution to a temporal sequence, use the DATEADD function instead of using +1 and -1, and the DATEDIFF function to calculate the difference between Nxt.seqval and Cur.seqval.

To apply the solution to a sequence with duplicates, use the DENSE_RANK function instead of ROW_NUMBER, and add DISTINCT to the SELECT clause of the inner query.

Gaps—solution 4 using cursors

Listing 6 shows the fourth solution to the gaps problem.

Listing 6   Gaps—solution 4 using cursors

```
SET NOCOUNT ON;

DECLARE @seqval AS INT, @prvseqval AS INT;
DECLARE @Gaps TABLE(start_range INT, end_range INT);
```

```
DECLARE C CURSOR FAST_FORWARD FOR
  SELECT seqval FROM dbo.NumSeq ORDER BY seqval;

OPEN C;

FETCH NEXT FROM C INTO @prvseqval;
IF @@FETCH_STATUS = 0 FETCH NEXT FROM C INTO @seqval;

WHILE @@FETCH_STATUS = 0
BEGIN
  IF @seqval - @prvseqval > 1
    INSERT INTO @Gaps(start_range, end_range)
      VALUES(@prvseqval + 1, @seqval - 1);

  SET @prvseqval = @seqval;
  FETCH NEXT FROM C INTO @seqval;
END

CLOSE C;

DEALLOCATE C;

SELECT start_range, end_range FROM @Gaps;
```

This solution is based on cursors, which represent the ordered sequence values. The code fetches the ordered sequence values from the cursor one at a time, and identifies a gap whenever the difference between the previous and current values is greater than one. When a gap is found, the gap information is stored in a table variable. When finished with the cursor, the code queries the table variable to return the gaps.

This solution is a good example of the overhead involved with using cursors. The I/O work involved here is a single ordered scan of the index, amounting to 16,123 logical reads. However, there's overhead involved with each record manipulation that is multiplied by the 10,000,000 records involved. This code ran for 250 seconds on my system and is the slowest of the solutions I tested for the gaps problem.

To apply the solution to a temporal sequence, use the DATEADD function instead of using +1 and -1 and the DATEDIFF function to calculate the difference between @seqval and @prvseqval.

Nothing must be added to handle a sequence with duplicates.

Performance summary for gaps solutions

Table 3 shows a summary of the performance measures I got for the four solutions presented.

Table 3   Performance summary of solutions to gaps problem

Solution	Runtime in seconds	Logical reads
Solution 1—using subqueries	8	62,262
Solution 2—using subqueries	48	31,875,478
Solution 3—using ranking functions	24	32,246
Solution 4—using cursors	250	16,123

As you can see, the first solution using subqueries is by far the fastest, whereas the fourth solution using cursors is by far the slowest.

Solutions to islands problem

I'll present four solutions to the islands problem: using subqueries and ranking calculations; using a group identifier based on subqueries; using a group identifier based on ranking calculations; and using cursors. I'll also present a variation on the islands problem, and then conclude this section with a performance summary.

Islands—solution 1 using subqueries and ranking calculations

Listing 7 shows the first solution to the islands problem.

Listing 7   Islands—solution 1 using subqueries and ranking calculations

```
WITH StartingPoints AS
(
  SELECT seqval, ROW_NUMBER() OVER(ORDER BY seqval) AS rownum
  FROM dbo.NumSeq AS A
  WHERE NOT EXISTS
    (SELECT *
     FROM dbo.NumSeq AS B
     WHERE B.seqval = A.seqval - 1)
),
EndingPoints AS
(
  SELECT seqval, ROW_NUMBER() OVER(ORDER BY seqval) AS rownum
  FROM dbo.NumSeq AS A
  WHERE NOT EXISTS
    (SELECT *
     FROM dbo.NumSeq AS B
     WHERE B.seqval = A.seqval + 1)
)
SELECT S.seqval AS start_range, E.seqval AS end_range
FROM StartingPoints AS S
  JOIN EndingPoints AS E
    ON E.rownum = S.rownum;
```

This solution defines two CTEs—one called StartingPoints, representing starting points of islands, and one called EndingPoints, representing ending points of islands. A point is identified as a starting point if the value minus 1 doesn't exist in the sequence. A point is identified as an ending point if the value plus 1 doesn't exist in the sequence. Each CTE also assigns row numbers to position the starting/ending points. The outer query joins the CTEs by matching starting and ending points based on equality between their row numbers.

This solution is straightforward, and also has reasonable performance when the sequence has a fairly small number of islands. The plan for this solution shows that the index is scanned four times in order—two ordered scans and a merge join are used to identify starting points and calculate their row numbers, and similar activity to identify ending points. A merge join is then used to match starting and ending points.

This query ran for 17 seconds against the BigNumSeq table, and incurred 64,492 logical reads.

To apply the solution to a temporal sequence, use DATEADD to add or subtract the appropriate interval instead of using +1 and -1.

As for a sequence with duplicates, the existing solution works as is; no changes are needed.

Islands—solution 2 using group identifier based on subqueries

Listing 8 shows the second solution to the islands problem.

Listing 8   Islands—solution 2 using group identifier based on subqueries

```
SELECT MIN(seqval) AS start_range, MAX(seqval) AS end_range
FROM (SELECT seqval,
        (SELECT MIN(B.seqval)
         FROM dbo.NumSeq AS B
         WHERE B.seqval >= A.seqval
           AND NOT EXISTS
             (SELECT *
              FROM dbo.NumSeq AS C
              WHERE C.seqval = B.seqval + 1)) AS grp
      FROM dbo.NumSeq AS A) AS D
GROUP BY grp;
```

This solution uses subqueries to produce, for each point, a group identifier (grp). The group identifier is a value that uniquely identifies the island. Such a value must be the same for all members of the island, and different than the value produced for other islands. When a group identifier is assigned to each member of the island, you can group the data by this identifier, and return for each group the minimum and maximum values.

The logic used to calculate the group identifier for each current point is this: return the next point (inclusive) that is also a point before a gap. Try to apply this logic and figure out the group identifier that will be produced for each point in the NumSeq table. For the values 2, 3 the grp value that will be produced will be 3, because for both values the next point (inclusive) before a gap is 3. For the values 11, 12, 13, the next point before a gap is 13, and so on. Recall the techniques used previously to identify the next point—the minimum value that is greater than the current. In our case, the next point should be inclusive; therefore you should use the >= operator instead of the > operator. To identify a point before a gap, use a NOT EXISTS predicate that ensures that the value plus 1 doesn't exist. Now combine the two techniques and you get the next point before a gap. The query defining the derived table D does all the work of producing the group identifiers. The outer query against D is then left to group the data by grp, and return for each island the first and last sequence values.

If you think that the logic of this solution is complex, I'm afraid its performance will not comfort you. The plan for this query is horrible—it scans the 10,000,000 sequence values, and for each of those values it does expensive work that involves a merge join between two inputs that identifies the next point before a gap. I aborted the execution of this query after letting it run for about 10 minutes.

Islands—solution 3 using group identifier based on ranking calculations

Listing 9 shows the third solution.

Listing 9   Islands—solution 3 using group identifier based on ranking calculations

```
SELECT MIN(seqval) AS start_range, MAX(seqval) AS end_range
FROM (SELECT seqval, seqval - ROW_NUMBER() OVER(ORDER BY seqval) AS grp
      FROM dbo.NumSeq) AS D
GROUP BY grp;
```

This solution is similar to solution 2 in the sense that it also calculates a group identifier that uniquely identifies the island; however this solution is dramatically simpler and more efficient. The group identifier is calculated as the difference between the sequence value and a row number that represents the position of the sequence value. Within an island, both the sequence values and the row numbers keep incrementing by the fixed interval of 1. Therefore, the difference between the two is constant. When moving on to the next island, the sequence value increases by more than 1, while the row number increases by 1. Therefore, the difference becomes higher than the previous island. Each island will have a higher difference than the previous island. Note that the last two characteristics that I described of this difference (constant within an island, and different for different islands) are the exact requirements we had for the group identifier. Hence, you can use this difference as the group identifier. As in solution 2, after the group identifier is calculated, you group the data by this identifier, and for each group, return the minimum and maximum values.

For performance, this solution is efficient because it required a single ordered scan of the index to calculate the row numbers, and an aggregate operator for the grouping activity. It ran for 10 seconds against the BigNumSeq table on my system and incurred 16,123 logical reads.

To apply this solution to a temporal sequence, subtract from the sequence value as many temporal intervals as the row number representing the position of the sequence value. The logic is similar to the integer sequence, but instead of getting a unique integer per island, you will get a unique time stamp for each island. For example, if the interval of the temporal sequence is 4 hours, substitute the expression `seqval - ROW_NUMBER() OVER(ORDER BY seqval) AS grp` in listing 9 with the expression `DATEADD(hour, -4 * ROW_NUMBER() OVER(ORDER BY seqval), seqval) AS grp`.

For a numeric sequence with duplicates, the trick is to have the same rank for all duplicate occurrences. This can be achieved by using the `DENSE_RANK` function instead of `ROW_NUMBER`. Simply substitute the expression `seqval - ROW_NUMBER() OVER(ORDER BY seqval) AS grp` in listing 9 with the expression `seqval - DENSE_RANK() OVER(ORDER BY seqval) AS grp`.

Islands—solution 4 using cursors

For kicks, and for the sake of completeness, listing 10 shows the fourth solution, which is based on cursors.

Listing 10   Islands—solution 4 using cursors

```
SET NOCOUNT ON;

DECLARE @seqval AS INT, @prvseqval AS INT, @first AS INT;
DECLARE @Islands TABLE(start_range INT, end_range INT);

DECLARE C CURSOR FAST_FORWARD FOR
  SELECT seqval FROM dbo.NumSeq ORDER BY seqval;

OPEN C;

FETCH NEXT FROM C INTO @seqval;
SET @first = @seqval;
SET @prvseqval = @seqval;

WHILE @@FETCH_STATUS = 0
BEGIN
  IF @seqval - @prvseqval > 1
  BEGIN
    INSERT INTO @Islands(start_range, end_range)
      VALUES(@first, @prvseqval);
    SET @first = @seqval;
  END

  SET @prvseqval = @seqval;
  FETCH NEXT FROM C INTO @seqval;
END

IF @first IS NOT NULL
  INSERT INTO @Islands(start_range, end_range)
    VALUES(@first, @prvseqval);

CLOSE C;

DEALLOCATE C;

SELECT start_range, end_range FROM @Islands;
```

The logic of this solution is to scan the sequence values in order, and at each point, check if the difference between the previous value and the current is greater than 1. If it is, you know that the last island ended with the previous value closed, and a new one just started with the current value. As expected, the performance of this solution is not good—it ran for 217 seconds on my system.

Variation on the islands problem

Before I present a performance summary for the different solutions, I want to show a variation on the islands problem, and a solution based on the fast technique with the ranking calculation. I'll use a table called *T1* with new sample data to discuss this problem. Run the code in listing 11 to create the table T1 and populate it with sample data.

Listing 11   Code creating and populating table T1

```
SET NOCOUNT ON;
USE tempdb;

IF OBJECT_ID('dbo.T1') IS NOT NULL
  DROP TABLE dbo.T1;

CREATE TABLE dbo.T1
(
  id  INT        NOT NULL PRIMARY KEY,
  val VARCHAR(10) NOT NULL
);
GO

INSERT INTO dbo.T1(id, val) VALUES(2, 'a');
INSERT INTO dbo.T1(id, val) VALUES(3, 'a');
INSERT INTO dbo.T1(id, val) VALUES(5, 'a');
INSERT INTO dbo.T1(id, val) VALUES(7, 'b');
INSERT INTO dbo.T1(id, val) VALUES(11, 'b');
INSERT INTO dbo.T1(id, val) VALUES(13, 'a');
INSERT INTO dbo.T1(id, val) VALUES(17, 'a');
INSERT INTO dbo.T1(id, val) VALUES(19, 'a');
INSERT INTO dbo.T1(id, val) VALUES(23, 'c');
INSERT INTO dbo.T1(id, val) VALUES(29, 'c');
INSERT INTO dbo.T1(id, val) VALUES(31, 'a');
INSERT INTO dbo.T1(id, val) VALUES(37, 'a');
INSERT INTO dbo.T1(id, val) VALUES(41, 'a');
INSERT INTO dbo.T1(id, val) VALUES(43, 'a');
INSERT INTO dbo.T1(id, val) VALUES(47, 'c');
INSERT INTO dbo.T1(id, val) VALUES(53, 'c');
INSERT INTO dbo.T1(id, val) VALUES(59, 'c');
```

This variation involves two attributes: one represents a sequence (id in our case), and the other represents a kind of status (val in our case). The task at hand is to identify the starting and ending sequence point (id) of each consecutive status (val) segment. Table 4 shows the desired output.

This is a variation on the islands problem. Listing 12 shows the solution to this problem.

mn	mx	val
2	5	A
7	11	B
13	19	A
23	29	C
31	43	A
47	59	C

Table 4   Desired result for variation on the islands problem

Listing 12   Solution to variation on the islands problem

```
WITH C AS
(
  SELECT id, val,
    ROW_NUMBER() OVER(ORDER BY id)
      - ROW_NUMBER() OVER(ORDER BY val, id) AS grp
  FROM dbo.T1
)
SELECT MIN(id) AS mn, MAX(id) AS mx, val
FROM C
GROUP BY val, grp
ORDER BY mn;
```

The query defining the CTE C calculates the difference between a row number representing id ordering and a row number representing val, id ordering, and calls that difference grp. Within each consecutive status segment, the difference will be constant, and smaller than the difference that will be produced for the next consecutive status segment. In short, the combination of status (val) and that difference uniquely identifies a consecutive status segment. What's left for the outer query is to group the data by val and grp, and return for each group the status (val), and the minimum and maximum ids.

Performance summary for islands solutions

Table 5 shows a summary of the performance measures I got for the four solutions presented.

Table 5   Performance summary of solutions to islands problem

Solution	Runtime in seconds	Logical reads
Solution 1—using subqueries and ranking calculations	17	64,492
Solution 2—using group identifier based on subqueries	Aborted after 10 minutes	
Solution 3—using group identifier based on ranking calculations	10	16,123
Solution 4—using cursors	217	16,123

As you can see, solution 3 that uses the row number function to calculate a group identifier is the fastest. Solution 4 using a cursor is slow, but not the slowest. Solution 2 that uses subqueries to calculate a group identifier is the slowest.

Summary

In this chapter I explained gaps and islands problems and provided different solutions to those problems. I compared the performance of the different solutions and as you could see, the performance of the solutions varied widely. The common theme was that the cursors performed badly, and the solutions that were based on ranking calculations performed either reasonably or very well. Some of the solutions based on subqueries performed well, whereas some not so well.

One of my goals in this chapter was to cover the specifics of the gaps and islands problems and identify good performing solutions. However, I also had an additional goal. It is common to find that for any given querying problem there are several possible solutions that will vary in complexity and performance. I wanted to emphasize the importance of producing multiple solutions, and analyzing and comparing their logic and performance.

About the author

Itzik Ben-Gan is a Mentor and Co-Founder of Solid Quality Mentors. A SQL Server Microsoft MVP (Most Valuable Professional) since 1999, Itzik has delivered numerous training events around the world focused on T-SQL Querying, Query Tuning, and Programming. Itzik is the author of several books, including *Microsoft SQL Server 2008: T-SQL Fundamentals, Inside Microsoft SQL Server 2008: T-SQL Querying,* and *Inside Microsoft SQL Server 2008: T-SQL Programming.* He has written many articles for SQL Server Magazine as well as articles and white papers for MSDN. Itzik's speaking activities include TechEd, DevWeek, SQLPASS, SQL Server Magazine Connections, various user groups around the world, and Solid Quality Mentors' events, to name a few. Itzik is the author of Solid Quality Mentors' Advanced T-SQL Querying, Programming and Tuning and T-SQL Fundamentals courses along with being a primary resource within the company for their T-SQL related activities.

6 Error handling in SQL Server and applications

Bill Graziano

Prior to SQL Server 2005, error handling was limited to testing @@ERROR after each statement. This required users to write lots of similar code to do error handling. The introduction of TRY...CATCH blocks in Transact-SQL (T-SQL) gives the developer more options to detect and handle errors. It is now possible to completely consume errors on the server. Or if you'd like, you can return specific errors back to the client.

The .NET development languages also have a series of classes for SQL Server error handling. These can be used to process errors and capture informational messages from SQL Server. The combination of TRY...CATCH on the server and the SQL Server–specific error handling on the client give developers many options to capture errors and handle them appropriately.

Handling errors inside SQL Server

Consider the following T-SQL statements that generate an error:

Listing 1   Error sent to SQL Server Management Studio

```
SELECT [First] = 1
SELECT [Second] = 1/0
SELECT [Third] = 3
```

This returns the following result to SQL Server Management Studio:

```
First
-----------
1

Second
-----------
Msg 8134, Level 16, State 1, Line 4
Divide by zero error encountered.
```

```
Third
-----------
3
```

The error message from the second SELECT statement is displayed and then the third SELECT statement executes. This error would've been returned to a client application.

Now consider the same three SELECT statements inside a TRY...CATCH block, as shown in listing 2.

Listing 2   T-SQL statements in a TRY...CATCH block

```
BEGIN TRY
    SELECT [First] = 1
    SELECT [Second] = 1/0
    SELECT [Third] = 3
END TRY
BEGIN CATCH
    PRINT 'An error occurred'
END CATCH
```

This will produce the following result:

```
First
-----------
1

Second
-----------

An error occurred
```

The T-SQL statements inside the TRY block will execute until an error is encountered, and then execution will transfer to the code inside the CATCH block. The first SELECT statement executes properly. The second statement generates an error. You can see that it returned the column header but not any resultset. The third SELECT statement didn't execute because control had been passed to the CATCH block. Inside the CATCH block, the PRINT statement is executed.

The use of a TRY...CATCH block also prevents the error from being returned to a client. In effect, the CATCH block consumed the error and no error was returned to a client application.

A TRY...CATCH block has some limitations:

- A TRY...CATCH block can't span batches.
- Severity levels of 20 or higher will not be caught because the connection is closed. We will cover severity levels in more detail shortly.
- Compile errors will not be caught because the batch never executes.
- Statement recompilation errors will not be caught.

Returning information about the error

Each error that's captured in a CATCH block has properties that we can examine using system-provided functions. These functions only return values inside a CATCH block. If they're called outside a CATCH block, they return NULL. A stored procedure called from within a CATCH block will have access to the functions. These functions are illustrated in listing 3.

Listing 3   Outputting error properties with system-provided functions

```
BEGIN TRY
    SELECT [Second] = 1/0
END TRY
BEGIN CATCH
    SELECT [Error_Line] = ERROR_LINE(),
           [Error_Number] = ERROR_NUMBER(),
           [Error_Severity] = ERROR_SEVERITY(),
           [Error_State] = ERROR_STATE()

    SELECT [Error_Message] = ERROR_MESSAGE()
END CATCH
```

This returns the following result:

```
Second
-----------

Error_Line  Error_Number  Error_Severity Error_State
----------- ------------- -------------- -----------
4           8134          16             1

Error_Message
------------------------------------
Divide by zero error encountered.
```

NOTE   Any line number is this chapter is dependent on the amount of whitespace in the batch. Your results may vary.

The ERROR_NUMBER() function returns the error number that caused the code to jump into this CATCH block. This value will not change for the duration of the CATCH block. You can see a list of system messages and errors in sys.messages.

The ERROR_MESSAGE() function returns the text of the error that caused the code to jump into the CATCH block. For system errors this value can also be found in sys.messages. The ERROR_MESSAGE() function will return the message with any parameters expanded.

You can return the severity of the error using the ERROR_SEVERITY() function. TRY...CATCH blocks behave differently depending on the severity of the error. Errors (or messages) with a severity of 10 or less don't cause the CATCH block to fire. These are typically informational messages. Error severities of 11 or higher will cause the CATCH block to fire unless the error terminates the connection. Error severities from 11 to 16 are typically user or code errors. Severity levels from 17 to 25 usually indicate a software or hardware problem, where processing may be unable to continue. Books Online has a detailed description of each severity under the heading "Database Engine Error Severities."

The ERROR_STATE() function can be used to determine the error state. Some system error messages can be raised at different points in the SQL Server engine. SQL Server uses the error state to differentiate when these errors are raised.

The last two properties of an error are the line number and the name of the stored procedure where the error occurred. These can be returned using the ERROR_LINE() function and the ERROR_PROCEDURE() function, respectively. The ERROR_PROCEDURE() function will return NULL if the error occurs outside a stored procedure. Listing 4 is an example of these last two functions inside a stored procedure.

Listing 4   ERROR_LINE and ERROR_PROCEDURE functions in a stored procedure

```
CREATE PROCEDURE ChildError
AS
  BEGIN
    RAISERROR('My Error', 11, 1)
  END
GO
CREATE PROCEDURE ParentError
AS
  BEGIN
    EXEC ChildError
  END
GO

BEGIN TRY
    EXEC ParentError
END TRY
BEGIN CATCH
    SELECT Error_Line = ERROR_LINE(),
           Error_Proc = ERROR_PROCEDURE()
END CATCH
```

This returns the following result:

```
Error_Line  Error_Proc
----------- -------------
4           ChildError
```

Let's look now at how we can generate our own custom error messages.

Generate your own errors using RAISERROR

The RAISERROR function can be used to generate SQL Server errors and initiate any error processing. The basic use of RAISERROR for a dynamic error looks like this:

```
RAISERROR('Invalid Customer', 11, 1)
```

This returns the following when run in SQL Server Management Studio:

```
Msg 50000, Level 11, State 1, Line 1
Invalid Customer
```

The first parameter is the custom error message. The second is the severity (or level). Remember that 11 is the minimum severity that will cause a CATCH block to fire. The last parameter is the error state.

RAISERROR can also be used to return user-created error messages. The code in listing 5 illustrates this.

Listing 5   Returning user-created error messages with RAISERROR

```
EXEC sp_addmessage
    @msgnum = 50001,
    @severity = 11,
    @msgtext = 'My custom error',
    @replace = 'replace';
GO
RAISERROR(50001, 11, 1);
GO
```

This returns the following result:

```
Msg 50001, Level 11, State 1, Line 1
My custom error
```

The @REPLACE parameter of sp_addmessage says to replace the error if it already exists. When RAISERROR is called with a message description rather than an error number, it returns an error number 50000.

Ordinary users can specify RAISERROR with severity levels up to 18. To specify severity levels greater than 18, you must be in the sysadmin fixed server role or have been granted ALTER TRACE permissions. You must also use the WITH LOG option. This option logs the messages to the SQL Server log and the Windows Application Event Log. WITH LOG may be used with any severity level. Using a severity level of 20 or higher in a RAISERROR statement will cause the connection to close.

Nesting TRY...CATCH blocks

TRY...CATCH blocks can be nested inside either TRY or CATCH blocks. Nesting inside a TRY block looks like listing 6.

Listing 6   Nesting TRY...CATCH blocks

```
BEGIN TRY
    PRINT 'One'

    BEGIN TRY
        PRINT 1/0
    END TRY
    BEGIN CATCH
        PRINT 'Caught by the inner catch'
    END CATCH

    PRINT 'Two'
END TRY
BEGIN CATCH
    PRINT 'Caught by the outer catch'
END CATCH
```

This batch returns the following result:

```
One
Caught by the inner catch
Two
```

This allows specific statements inside a larger TRY...CATCH to have their own error handling. A construct like this can be used to selectively handle certain errors and pass any other errors further up the chain. Here's an example in listing 7.

> **Listing 7   Error handling with nested TRY...CATCH statements**

```
BEGIN TRY
    PRINT 'One'

    BEGIN TRY
        PRINT CAST('Hello' AS DATETIME)
    END TRY
    BEGIN CATCH
        IF ERROR_NUMBER() = 8134
            PRINT 'Divide by zero.  Again.'
        ELSE
          BEGIN
            DECLARE @ErrorNumber INT;
            DECLARE @ErrorMessage NVARCHAR(4000)
            DECLARE @ErrorSeverity INT;
            DECLARE @ErrorState INT;

            SELECT
              @ErrorNumber = ERROR_NUMBER(),
              @ErrorMessage = ERROR_MESSAGE() + ' (%d)',
              @ErrorSeverity = ERROR_SEVERITY(),
              @ErrorState = ERROR_STATE();

            RAISERROR( @ErrorMessage,
                       @ErrorSeverity,
                       @ErrorState,
                       @ErrorNumber )
          END
    END CATCH

    PRINT 'Two'
END TRY
BEGIN CATCH
    PRINT 'Error: ' + ERROR_MESSAGE()
END CATCH
```

This returns the following result:

```
One
Error: Conversion failed when converting datetime from character string.
    (241)
```

In the inner CATCH block I'm checking whether we generated error number 8134 (divide by zero) and if so, I print a message. For every other error message, I "reraise" or "rethrow" the error to the outer catch block. Note the text string that's added to the error message variable. The `%d` is a placeholder that's replaced by the first additional parameter passed to RAISERROR, which is `@ErrorNumber` in my example. Books Online has more information on the different types of replace variables that can be used in RAISERROR.

The error functions can be used in any stored procedure called from inside the CATCH block. This allows you to create standardized error-handling modules such as the one in listing 8.

Listing 8   An error-handling module

```
CREATE PROCEDURE ErrorHandler
AS
BEGIN
    PRINT 'I should log this error:'
    PRINT ERROR_MESSAGE()
END
GO

BEGIN TRY
    SELECT 1/0
END TRY
BEGIN CATCH
    EXEC ErrorHandler
END CATCH
```

This block of code will return the following results:

```
I should log this error:
Divide by zero error encountered.
```

This is typically used to handle any errors in the code that logs the error information to a custom error table.

TRY...CATCH and transactions

A common use for a TRY...CATCH block is to handle transaction processing. A common pattern for this is shown in listing 9.

Listing 9   Transaction processing in a `TRY...CATCH` block

```
BEGIN TRY
    BEGIN TRANSACTION

    INSERT INTO dbo.invoice_header
        (invoice_number, client_number)
    VALUES (2367, 19)

    INSERT INTO dbo.invoice_detail
        (invoice_number, line_number, part_number)
    VALUES (2367, 1, 84367)

    COMMIT TRANSACTION
END TRY
BEGIN CATCH
```

```
    IF @@TRANCOUNT > 0 ROLLBACK TRANSACTION
    -- And rethrow the error
END CATCH
```

Remember that the CATCH block completely consumes the error; therefore it is important to return some type of error or message back to the calling program.

Handling SQL Server errors on the client

The examples in this section use C# as the client application. Any .NET client application that supports try...catch constructs will behave in a similar fashion. The key points to learn here are which .NET classes are involved in error handling and what methods and properties they expose.

When a .NET application executes a SQL statement that causes an error, it throws a SqlException. This can be caught using a try...catch block like we saw previously. The SQL Server exception could also be caught by catching a plain Exception, but the SqlException class provides additional SQL Server–specific properties. A simple example of this in C# is shown in listing 10.

Listing 10   Outputting SQL Server–specific error properties with `SqlException`

```
using System.Data;
using System.Data.SqlClient;

class Program
{
    SqlConnection conn = new SqlConnection("...");
    SqlCommand cmd = new SqlCommand("RAISERROR('My Error', 11, 1)", conn);

    try
    {
        cmd.Connection.Open();
        cmd.ExecuteNonQuery();
        Console.WriteLine("No error returned");
    }
    catch (SqlException sqlex)
    {
        Console.WriteLine("Error Message: " + sqlex.Message);
        Console.WriteLine("Error Severity: {0}", sqlex.Class.ToString());
        Console.WriteLine("Line Number: {0}", sqlex.LineNumber.ToString());
    }
}
```

This returns the following result:

```
Error Message: My Error
Error Severity: 11
Line Number: 1
```

Exceptions with a severity of 10 or less don't trigger the catch block on the client. The connection is closed if the severity level is 20 or higher; it normally remains open if the severity level is 19 or less. You can use RAISERROR to generate severities of 20 or higher and it'll close the connection and fire the try...catch block on the client.

The error returned typically indicates that the connection was closed rather than the error text you specified.

The SqlException class inherits from the System.SystemException and includes many properties that are specific to .NET. Some key SQL Server–specific properties of the SqlException class are shown in table 1.

Table 1 SQLException **class properties**

Property	Description
Class	Error severity level
LineNumber	Line number in the batch or stored procedure where the error occurred
Message	Description of the error
Number	SQL Server error number
Procedure	Stored procedure name where the error occurred
Server	SQL Server instance that generated the error
Source	Provider that generated the error (for example, .Net SqlClient Data Provider)
State	SQL Server error state (the third parameter of RAISERROR)

Another interesting property of the SqlException class is the Errors property. This is a collection of SqlError objects. The SqlError class includes only the SQL Server–specific properties from the SqlException object that are listed in table 1. Because a batch of SQL can generate multiple SQL Server errors, an application needs to check whether multiple errors have occurred. The first error in the Errors property will always match the error in the SqlExcpetion's properties. Listing 11 is an example.

Listing 11 Handling multiple errors with the Errors property

```
using System.Data;
using System.Data.SqlClient;

class Program
{
    static void Main(string[] args)
    {
        SqlConnection conn = new SqlConnection(@"Server=L60\YUKON;
        ➥Integrated Security=SSPI");
        SqlCommand cmd = new SqlCommand(
          @"RAISERROR('My Error', 11, 17)
            SELECT 1/0
            SELECT * FROM dbo.BadTable", conn);

        try
        {
            cmd.Connection.Open();
            cmd.ExecuteReader();
```

```
            Console.WriteLine("No error returned");
        }
        catch (SqlException sqlex)
        {
            for (int i = 0; i < sqlex.Errors.Count; i++)
            {
                Console.WriteLine("Error #{0}: {1}",
                    i.ToString(), sqlex.Errors[i].Message);
            }
        }

    }
}
```

This returns the following result:

```
Error #0: My Error
Error #1: Divide by zero error encountered.
Error #2: Invalid object name 'dbo.BadTable'.
```

In closing, let's look at how we can handle SQL Server messages inside our application code.

Handling SQL Server messages on the client

When a message is sent from SQL Server via a PRINT statement or a RAISERROR with a severity level of 10 or less, it generates an event on the .NET side. You can capture this event by writing a handler for the SqlConnection class's InfoMessage event. The handler for the InfoMessage event takes two parameters: the sender and an instance of SqlInfoMessageEventArgs. This class contains three properties. The first is the Message that was printed or generated by the RAISERROR statement. The second is the Source, which is usually the .Net SqlClient Data Provider. The third is the Errors property, which is a collection of SqlError objects and behaves just like it did when we saw it earlier. Listing 12 is an example.

Listing 12   Outputting SQL Server messages

```
using System.Data;
using System.Data.SqlClient;

class Program
{
    static void Main(string[] args)
    {
        SqlConnection conn = new SqlConnection(@"Server=L60\YUKON;
        ➥Integrated Security=SSPI");
        SqlCommand cmd = new SqlCommand("PRINT 'Hello'", conn);
        conn.InfoMessage += new
        ➥SqlInfoMessageEventHandler(conn_InfoMessage);

        try
        {
            cmd.Connection.Open();
```

```
            cmd.ExecuteNonQuery();
            cmd.CommandText ="RAISERROR('An error as message', 5, 12)";
            cmd.ExecuteNonQuery();
            Console.WriteLine("No error returned");
        }
        catch (SqlException sqlex)
        {
            Console.WriteLine("First Error Message: " + sqlex.Message);
            Console.WriteLine("Error Count: {0}",
            ➥sqlex.Errors.Count.ToString());
        }

    }

    static void conn_InfoMessage(object sender, SqlInfoMessageEventArgs e)
    {
        Console.WriteLine("SQL Server Message: {0}", e.Message);
        Console.WriteLine("Message Source: {0}", e.Source);
        Console.WriteLine("Message Count: {0}", e.Errors.Count.ToString());
    }
}
```

This returns the following result:

```
SQL Server Message: Hello
Message Source: .Net SqlClient Data Provider
Message Count: 1
SQL Server Message: An error as message
Message Source: .Net SqlClient Data Provider
Message Count: 1
No error returned
```

Another interesting characteristic of this approach is that you can capture informational RAISERROR statements as they're executed rather than when a batch ends. Listing 13 shows an example.

Listing 13   Capturing RAISERROR statements

```
using System.Data;
using System.Data.SqlClient;

class Program
{
    static void Main(string[] args)
    {
        SqlConnection conn = new SqlConnection(@"Server=L60\YUKON;
        ➥Integrated Security=SSPI");
        SqlCommand cmd = new SqlCommand(
            @"PRINT 'Printed at buffer flush'
              RAISERROR('Starting', 0, 1) WITH NOWAIT;
              WAITFOR DELAY '00:00:03';
              RAISERROR('Status', 0, 1) WITH NOWAIT;
              WAITFOR DELAY '00:00:03';
              PRINT 'Done';", conn);
        conn.InfoMessage += new
        ➥SqlInfoMessageEventHandler(conn_ShortMessage);
```

```
        try
        {
            cmd.Connection.Open();
            cmd.ExecuteReader();
            Console.WriteLine("No error returned");
        }
        catch (SqlException sqlex)
        {
            Console.WriteLine("First Error Message: " + sqlex.Message);
            Console.WriteLine("Error Count: {0}",
            ➥sqlex.Errors.Count.ToString());
        }
    }
    static void conn_ShortMessage(object sender, SqlInfoMessageEventArgs e)
    {
        Console.WriteLine("[{0}] SQL Server Message: {1}",
            System.DateTime.Now.ToLongTimeString(), e.Message);
    }
}
```

This returns the following result:

```
[3:39:26 PM] SQL Server Message: Printed at buffer flush
[3:39:26 PM] SQL Server Message: Starting
[3:39:29 PM] SQL Server Message: Status
[3:39:32 PM] SQL Server Message: Done
No error returned
```

Normally, when you do a series of PRINT statements inside a SQL Server batch or stored procedure, the results are all returned at the end. A RAISERROR WITH NOWAIT is sent immediately to the client, as is any previous PRINT statement. If you remove the WITH NOWAIT from the first RAISERROR, the first three lines are all printed at the same time when the RAISERROR WITH NOWAIT pushes them all to the client. This approach can provide a convenient way to return status information for long-running tasks that contain multiple SQL statements.

Summary

SQL Server error handling doesn't need to be an afterthought. SQL Server 2005 provides powerful tools that allow developers to selectively handle, capture, and consume errors inside SQL Server. Errors that can't be handled on the server can be passed back to the application. .NET has specialized classes that allow applications to capture detailed information about SQL Server exceptions.

About the author

Bill Graziano has been a SQL Server consultant for 10 years, doing production support, performance tuning, and application development. He serves on the board of directors for the Professional Association for SQL Server (PASS), where he serves as the vice president of marketing and sits on the executive committee. He's a regular speaker at conferences and user groups across the country. Bill runs the popular web site http://SQLTeam.com and is currently a SQL Server MVP.

7 Pulling apart the FROM clause

Rob Farley

When can you ever have a serious query that doesn't involve more than one table? Normalization is a wonderful thing and helps ensure that our databases have important characteristics such as integrity. But it also means using JOINs, because it's unlikely that all the data we need to solve our problem occurs in a single table. Almost always, our FROM clause contains several tables.

In this chapter, I'll explain some of the deeper, less understood aspects of the FROM clause. I'll start with some of the basics, to make sure we're all on the same page. You're welcome to skip ahead if you're familiar with the finer points of INNER, OUTER, and CROSS. I'm often amazed by the fact that developers the world over understand how to write a multi-table query, and yet few understand what they're asking with such a query.

JOIN basics

Without JOINs, our FROM clause is incredibly simple. Assuming that we're using only tables (rather than other constructs such as subqueries or functions), JOINs are one of the few ways that we can make our query more complicated. JOINs are part of day one in most database courses, and every day that follows is full of them. They are the simplest mechanism to allow access to data within other tables. We'll cover the three types of JOINs in the sections that follow.

The INNER JOIN

The most common style of JOIN is the INNER JOIN. I'm writing that in capitals because it's the keyword expression used to indicate the type of JOIN being used, but the word INNER is completely optional. It's so much the most common style of JOIN that when we write only JOIN, we're referring to an INNER JOIN.

An INNER JOIN looks at the two tables involved in the JOIN and identifies matching rows according to the criteria in the ON clause. Every INNER JOIN requires an ON clause—it's not optional. Aliases are optional, and can make the ON clause much shorter and simpler to read (and the rest of the query too). I've made my life easier by specifying p and s after the table names in the query shown below (to indicate Product and ProductSubcategory respectively). In this particular example, the match condition is that the value in one column in the first table must be the same as the column in the second table. It so happens that the columns have the same name; therefore, to distinguish between them, I've specified one to be from the table p, and the other from the table s. It wouldn't have mattered if I specified these two columns in the other order—equality operations are generally commutative, and it doesn't matter whether I write a=b or b=a.

The query in listing 1 returns a set of rows from the two tables, containing all the rows that have matching values in their ProductSubcategoryID columns. This query, as with most of the queries in this chapter, will run on the AdventureWorks database, which is available as a sample database for SQL Server 2005 or SQL Server 2008.

Listing 1   Query to return rows with matching product subcategories

```
SELECT p.Name, s.Name
FROM Production.Product p
    JOIN
    Production.ProductSubcategory s
    ON p.ProductSubcategoryID = s.ProductSubcategoryID;
```

This query could return more rows than there are in the Product table, fewer rows, or the same number of rows. We'll look at this phenomenon later in the chapter, as well as what can affect this number.

The OUTER JOIN

An OUTER JOIN is like an INNER JOIN except that rows that do not have matching values in the other table are not excluded from the result set. Instead, the rows appear with NULL entries in place of the columns from the other table. Remembering that a JOIN is always performed between two tables, these are the variations of OUTER JOIN:

- LEFT—Keeps all rows from the first table (inserting NULLs for the second table's columns)
- RIGHT—Keeps all rows from the second table (inserting NULLs for the first table's columns)
- FULL—Keeps all rows from both tables (inserting NULLs on the left or the right, as appropriate)

Because we must specify whether the OUTER JOIN is LEFT, RIGHT, or FULL, note that the keyword OUTER is optional—inferred by the fact that we have specified its variation. As in listing 2, I generally omit it, but you're welcome to use it if you like.

Listing 2   A LEFT OUTER JOIN

```
SELECT p.Name, s.Name
FROM Production.Product p
    LEFT JOIN
    Production.ProductSubcategory s
    ON p.ProductSubcategoryID = s.ProductSubcategoryID;
```

The query in listing 2 produces results similar to the results of the last query, except that products that are not assigned to a subcategory are still included. They have NULL listed for the second column. The smallest number of rows that could be returned by this query is the number of rows in the Product table, as none can be eliminated.

Had we used a RIGHT JOIN, subcategories that contained no products would have been included. Take care when dealing with OUTER JOINs, because counting the rows for each subcategory would return 1 for an empty subcategory, rather than 0. If you intend to count the products in each subcategory, it would be better to count the occurrences of a non-NULL ProductID or Name instead of using COUNT(*). The queries in listing 3 demonstrate this potential issue.

Listing 3   Beware of COUNT(*) with OUTER JOINs

```
/* First ensure there is a subcategory with no corresponding products */
INSERT Production.ProductSubcategory (Name) VALUES ('Empty Subcategory');

SELECT s.Name, COUNT(*) AS NumRows
FROM Production.ProductSubcategory s
    LEFT JOIN
    Production.Product p
    ON s.ProductSubcategoryID = p.ProductSubcategoryID
GROUP BY s.Name;

SELECT s.Name, COUNT(p.ProductID) AS NumProducts
FROM Production.ProductSubcategory s
    LEFT JOIN
    Production.Product p
    ON s.ProductSubcategoryID = p.ProductSubcategoryID
GROUP BY s.Name;
```

Although LEFT and RIGHT JOINs can be made equivalent by listing the tables in the opposite order, FULL is slightly different, and will return at least as many rows as the largest table (as no rows can be eliminated from either side).

The CROSS JOIN

A CROSS JOIN returns every possible combination of rows from the two tables. It's like an INNER JOIN with an ON clause that evaluates to true for every possible combination of rows. The CROSS JOIN doesn't use an ON clause at all. This type of JOIN is relatively rare, but it can effectively solve some problems, such as for a report that must include every combination of SalesPerson and SalesTerritory (showing zero or NULL where appropriate). The query in listing 4 demonstrates this by first performing a CROSS JOIN, and then a LEFT JOIN to find sales that match the criteria.

Listing 4   Using a CROSS JOIN to cover all combinations

```
SELECT p.SalesPersonID, t.TerritoryID, SUM(s.TotalDue) AS TotalSales
FROM Sales.SalesPerson p
    CROSS JOIN
    Sales.SalesTerritory t
    LEFT JOIN
    Sales.SalesOrderHeader s
    ON p.SalesPersonID = s.SalesPersonID
    AND t.TerritoryID = s.TerritoryID
GROUP BY p.SalesPersonID, t.TerritoryID;
```

Formatting your FROM clause

I recently heard someone say that formatting shouldn't be a measure of good or bad practice when coding. He was talking about writing C# code and was largely taking exception to being told where to place braces. I'm inclined to agree with him to a certain extent. I do think that formatting guidelines should form a part of company coding standards so that people aren't put off by the layout of code written by a colleague, but I think the most important thing is consistency, and Best Practices guides that you find around the internet should generally stay away from formatting. When it comes to the FROM clause, though, I think formatting can be important.

A sample query

The Microsoft Project Server Report Pack is a valuable resource for people who use Microsoft Project Server. One of the reports in the pack is a Timesheet Audit Report, which you can find at http://msdn.microsoft.com/en-us/library/bb428822.aspx. I sometimes use this when teaching T-SQL.

The main query for this report has a FROM clause which is hard to understand. I've included it in listing 5, keeping the formatting exactly as it is on the website. In the following sections, we'll demystify it by using a method for reading FROM clauses, and consider ways that this query could have retained the same functionality without being so confusing.

Listing 5   A FROM clause from the Timesheet Audit Report

```
FROM      MSP_EpmResource
            LEFT OUTER JOIN MSP_TimesheetResource

            INNER JOIN MSP_TimesheetActual
              ON MSP_TimesheetResource.ResourceNameUID
                = MSP_TimesheetActual.LastChangedResourceNameUID
              ON MSP_EpmResource.ResourceUID
                = MSP_TimesheetResource.ResourceUID

            LEFT OUTER JOIN MSP_TimesheetPeriod

            INNER JOIN MSP_Timesheet
              ON MSP_TimesheetPeriod.PeriodUID
                = MSP_Timesheet.PeriodUID
```

```
INNER JOIN MSP_TimesheetPeriodStatus
    ON MSP_TimesheetPeriod.PeriodStatusID
        = MSP_TimesheetPeriodStatus.PeriodStatusID

INNER JOIN MSP_TimesheetStatus
    ON MSP_Timesheet.TimesheetStatusID
        = MSP_TimesheetStatus.TimesheetStatusID
    ON MSP_TimesheetResource.ResourceNameUID
        = MSP_Timesheet.OwnerResourceNameUID
```

The appearance of most queries

In the western world, our languages tend to read from left to right. Because of this, people tend to approach their FROM clauses from left to right as well.

For example, they start with one table:

```
FROM    MSP_EpmResource
```

Then they JOIN to another table:

```
FROM    MSP_EpmResource
            LEFT OUTER JOIN MSP_TimesheetResource
                ON MSP_EpmResource.ResourceUID
                    = MSP_TimesheetResource.ResourceUID
```

And they keep repeating the pattern:

```
FROM    MSP_EpmResource
            LEFT OUTER JOIN MSP_TimesheetResource
                ON MSP_EpmResource.ResourceUID
                    = MSP_TimesheetResource.ResourceUID
            INNER JOIN MSP_TimesheetActual
                ON MSP_TimesheetResource.ResourceNameUID
                    = MSP_TimesheetActual.LastChangedResourceNameUID
```

They continue by adding on the construct JOIN table_X ON table_X.col = table_Y.col.

Effectively, everything is done from the perspective of the first table in the FROM clause. Some of the JOINs may be OUTER JOINs, some may be INNER, but the principle remains the same—that each table is brought into the mix by itself.

When the pattern doesn't apply

In our sample query, this pattern doesn't apply. We start with two JOINs, followed by two ONs. That doesn't fit the way we like to think of our FROM clauses. If we try to rearrange the FROM clause to fit, we find that we can't. But that doesn't stop me from trying to get my students to try; it's good for them to appreciate that not all queries can be written as they prefer. I get them to start with the first section (before the second LEFT JOIN):

```
FROM    MSP_EpmResource
            LEFT OUTER JOIN MSP_TimesheetResource

            INNER JOIN MSP_TimesheetActual
```

```
ON MSP_TimesheetResource.ResourceNameUID
   = MSP_TimesheetActual.LastChangedResourceNameUID
ON MSP_EpmResource.ResourceUID
   = MSP_TimesheetResource.ResourceUID
```

Many of my students look at this part and immediately pull the second ON clause (between MSP_EpmResource and MSP_TimesheetResource) and move it to before the INNER JOIN. But because we have an INNER JOIN applying to MSP_TimesheetResource, this would remove any NULLs that are the result of the OUTER JOIN. Clearly the logic has changed. Some try to fix this by making the INNER JOIN into a LEFT JOIN, but this changes the logic as well. Some move the tables around, listing MSP_EpmResource last, but the problem always comes down to the fact that people don't understand this query. This part of the FROM clause can be fixed by using a RIGHT JOIN, but even this has problems, as you may find if you try to continue the pattern with the other four tables in the FROM clause.

How to read a FROM clause

A FROM clause is easy to read, but you have to understand the method. When I ask my students what the first JOIN is, they almost all say "the LEFT JOIN," but they're wrong. The first JOIN is the INNER JOIN, and this is easy to find because it's the JOIN that matches the first ON. To find the first JOIN, you have to find the first ON. Having found it, you work backwards to find its JOIN (which is the JOIN that immediately precedes the ON, skipping past any JOINs that have already been allocated to an ON clause). The right side of the JOIN is anything that comes between an ON and its corresponding JOIN. To find the left side, you keep going backwards until you find an unmatched JOIN or the FROM keyword. You read a FROM clause that you can't immediately understand this way:

1 Find the first (or next) ON keyword.
2 Work backwards from the ON, looking for an unmatched JOIN.
3 Everything between the ON and the JOIN is the right side.
4 Keep going backwards from the JOIN to find the left side.
5 Repeat until all the ONs have been found.

Using this method, we can clearly see that the first JOIN in our sample query is the INNER JOIN, between MSP_TimesheetResource and MSP_TimesheetActual. This forms the right side of the LEFT OUTER JOIN, with MSP_EpmResource being the left side.

When the pattern can't apply

Unfortunately for our pattern, the next JOIN is the INNER JOIN between MSP_TimesheetPeriod and MSP_Timesheet. It doesn't involve any of the tables we've already brought into our query. When we continue reading our FROM clause, we eventually see that the query involves two LEFT JOINs, for which the right sides are a series of nested INNER JOINs. This provides logic to make sure that the NULLs are introduced only to the combination of MSP_TimesheetResource and MSP_TimesheetActual, not just one of them individually, and similarly for the combination of MSP_Time-sheetPeriod through MSP_TimesheetStatus.

And this is where the formatting becomes important. The layout of the query in its initial form (the form in which it appears on the website) doesn't suggest that anything is nested. I would much rather have seen the query laid out as in listing 6. The only thing I have changed about the query is the whitespace and aliases, and yet you can see that it's far easier to read.

> **Listing 6   A reformatted version of the FROM clause in listing 5**

```
FROM
    MSP_EpmResource r
    LEFT OUTER JOIN
        MSP_TimesheetResource tr
        INNER JOIN
        MSP_TimesheetActual ta
        ON tr.ResourceNameUID = ta.LastChangedResourceNameUID
    ON r.ResourceUID = tr.ResourceUID
    LEFT OUTER JOIN
        MSP_TimesheetPeriod tp
        INNER JOIN
        MSP_Timesheet t
        ON tp.PeriodUID = t.PeriodUID
        INNER JOIN
        MSP_TimesheetPeriodStatus tps
        ON tp.PeriodStatusID = tps.PeriodStatusID
        INNER JOIN
        MSP_TimesheetStatus ts
        ON t.TimesheetStatusID = ts.TimesheetStatusID
    ON tr.ResourceNameUID = t.OwnerResourceNameUID
```

Laying out the query like this doesn't change the importance of knowing how to read a query when you follow the steps I described earlier, but it helps the less experienced people who need to read the queries you write. Bracketing the nested sections may help make the query even clearer, but I find that bracketing can sometimes make people confuse these nested JOINs with derived tables.

Writing the FROM clause clearly the first time

In explaining the Timesheet Audit Report query, I'm not suggesting that it's wise to nest JOINs as I just described. However, being able to read and understand a complex FROM clause is a useful skill that all query writers should have. They should also write queries that less skilled readers can easily understand.

Filtering with the ON clause

When dealing with INNER JOINs, people rarely have a problem thinking of the ON clause as a filter. Perhaps this comes from earlier days of databases, when we listed tables using comma notation and then put the ON clause predicates in the WHERE clause. From this link with the WHERE clause, we can draw parallels between the ON and

WHERE clauses, but the ON clause is a different kind of filter, as I'll demonstrate in the following sections.

The different filters of the SELECT statement

The most obvious filter in a SELECT statement is the WHERE clause. It filters out the rows that the FROM clause has produced. The database engine controls entirely the order in which the various aspects of a SELECT statement are applied, but logically the WHERE clause is applied after the FROM clause has been completed.

People also understand that the HAVING clause is a filter, but they believe mistakenly that the HAVING clause is used when the filter must involve an aggregate function. In actuality (but still only logically), the HAVING clause is applied to the groups that have been formed through the introduction of aggregates or a GROUP BY clause. It could therefore be suggested that the ON clause isn't a filter, but rather a mechanism to describe the JOIN context. But it is a filter.

Filtering out the matches

Whereas the WHERE clause filters out rows, and the HAVING clause filters out groups, the ON clause filters out matches.

In an INNER JOIN, only the matches persist into the final results. Given all possible combinations of rows, only those that have successful matches are kept. Filtering out a match is the same as filtering out a row. For OUTER JOINs, we keep all the matches and then introduce NULLs to avoid eliminating rows that would have otherwise been filtered out. Now the concept of filtering out a match differs a little from filtering out a row.

When a predicate in the ON clause involves columns from both sides of the JOIN, it feels quite natural to be filtering matches this way. We can even justify the behavior of an OUTER JOIN by arguing that OUTER means that we're putting rows back in after they've been filtered out. But when we have a predicate that involves only one side of the JOIN, things feel a bit different.

Now the success of the match has a different kind of dependency on one side than on the other. Suppose a LEFT JOIN has an ON clause like the one in listing 7.

Listing 7 Placing a predicate in the ON clause of an outer join

```
SELECT p.SalesPersonID, o.SalesOrderID, o.OrderDate
FROM
    Sales.SalesPerson p
    LEFT JOIN
    Sales.SalesOrderHeader o
    ON o.SalesPersonID = p.SalesPersonID
    AND o.OrderDate < '20020101';
```

For an INNER JOIN, this would be simple, and we'd probably have put the OrderDate predicate in the WHERE clause. But for an OUTER JOIN, this is different.

Often when we write an OUTER JOIN, we start with an INNER JOIN and then change the keyword to use LEFT instead of INNER (in fact, we probably leave out the word INNER). Making an OUTER JOIN from an INNER JOIN is done so that, for example, the salespeople who haven't made sales don't get filtered out. If that OrderDate predicate was in the WHERE clause, merely changing INNER JOIN to LEFT JOIN wouldn't have done the job.

Consider the case of AdventureWorks' SalesPerson 290, whose first sale was in 2003. A LEFT JOIN without the OrderDate predicate would include this salesperson, but then all the rows for that salesperson would be filtered out by the WHERE clause. This wouldn't be correct if we were intending to keep all the salespeople.

Consider also the case of a salesperson with no sales. That person would be included in the results of the FROM clause (with NULL for the Sales.SalesOrderHeader columns), but then would also be filtered out by the WHERE clause.

The answer is to use ON clause predicates to define what constitutes a valid match, as we have in our code segment above. This means that the filtering is done before the NULLs are inserted for salespeople without matches, and our result is correct. I understand that it may seem strange to have a predicate in an ON clause that involves only one side of the JOIN, but when you understand what's being filtered (rows with WHERE, groups with HAVING, and matches with ON), it should feel comfortable.

JOIN uses and simplification

To understand the FROM clause, it's worth appreciating the power of the query optimizer. In this final part of the chapter, we'll examine four uses of JOINs. We'll then see how your query can be impacted if all these uses are made redundant.

The four uses of JOINs

Suppose a query involves a single table. For our example, we'll use Production.Product from the AdventureWorks sample database. Let's imagine that this table is joined to another table, say Production.ProductSubcategory. A foreign key relationship is defined between the two tables, and our ON clause refers to the ProductSubcategoryID column in each table. Listing 8 shows a view that reflects this query.

> **Listing 8   View to return products and their subcategories**

```
CREATE VIEW dbo.ProductsPlus AS
SELECT p.*, s.Name as SubcatName
FROM
  Production.Product p
  JOIN
  Production.ProductSubcategory s
  ON p.ProductSubcategoryID = s.ProductSubcategoryID;
```

This simple view provides us with the columns of the Product table, with the name of the ProductSubcategory to which each product belongs. The query used is a standard lookup query, one that query writers often create.

Comparing the contents of this view to the Product table alone (I say *contents* loosely, as a view doesn't store data unless it is an indexed view; it is simply a stored subquery), there are two obvious differences.

First, we see that we have an extra column. We could have made our view contain as many of the columns from the second table as we like, but for now I'm using only one. This is the first of the four uses. It seems a little trivial, but nevertheless, we have use #1: additional columns.

Secondly, we have fewer rows in the view than in the Product table. A little investigation shows that the ProductSubcategoryID column in Production.Product allows NULL values, with no matching row in the Production.ProductSubcategory table. As we're using an INNER JOIN, these rows without matches are eliminated from our results. This could have been our intention, and therefore we have use #2: eliminated rows.

We can counteract this side effect quite easily. To avoid rows from Production. Product being eliminated, we need to convert our INNER JOIN to an OUTER JOIN. I have made this change and encapsulated it in a second view in listing 9, named dbo.ProductsPlus2 to avoid confusion.

Listing 9　View to return all products and their subcategories (if they exist)

```
CREATE VIEW dbo.ProductsPlus2 AS
SELECT p.*, s.Name AS SubcatName
FROM
  Production.Product p
  LEFT JOIN
  Production.ProductSubcategory s
  ON p.ProductSubcategoryID = s.ProductSubcategoryID;
```

Now when we query our view, we see that it gives us the same number of rows as in the Production.Product table.

JOINs have two other uses that we don't see in our view.

As this is a foreign-key relationship, the column in Production.ProductSubcategory is the primary key, and therefore unique. There must be at most one matching row for each row in Production.Product—thereby not duplicating any of the rows from Production.Product. If Production.ProductSubcategory.ProductSubcategoryID weren't unique, though, we could find ourselves using a JOIN for use #3: duplicated rows.

Please understand I am considering this only from the perspective of the first table, and the lack of duplications here is completely expected and desired. If we consider the query from the perspective of the second table, we are indeed seeing the duplication of rows. I am focusing on one table in order to demonstrate when the JOIN serves no direct purpose.

The fourth use is more obscure. When an OUTER JOIN is performed, rows that don't have matches are persisted using NULL values for columns from the other table. In our second view above, we are using a LEFT JOIN, and NULL appears instead of the Name column from the Production.ProductSubcategory table. This has no effect on the fields from the table of products, but if we were using a RIGHT JOIN or FULL JOIN, and we had subcategories that contained no products allocated, we would find additional rows amongst our list of Products. That's use #4: added NULL rows.

These four uses make up the entire functionality and purpose of JOINs: (1) gaining additional columns, (2) eliminating rows, (3) duplicating rows, and (4) adding NULL rows. The most commonly desired function would be the first one listed, but the other functions are just as valid. Perhaps we're counting the number of times an event has occurred, and we take advantage of the duplication effect. Perhaps we want to consider only those records that have a match in another table, or perhaps we are using the added NULLs to find the *empty* subcategories. Whatever the business reason for performing the JOIN, everything comes back to these four uses.

Simplification using views

If listing the name of the ProductSubcategory with the product is often required, then a lookup similar to the one in the views created earlier could be functionality that is repeated frequently. Although a developer may consider this trivial and happily write out this JOIN notation as often as needed, there may be a temptation to use a view to simplify the query.

Consider the query in listing 10.

Listing 10   Query to return products and their subcategory

```
SELECT p.ProductID, p.Name, p.Color, s.Name as SubcatName
FROM
   Production.Product p
   LEFT JOIN
   Production.ProductSubcategory s
   ON p.ProductSubcategoryID = s.ProductSubcategoryID;
```

For every product in the Production.Product table, we are selecting the ProductID, Name, and Color, with the name of the subcategory to which it belongs. From our earlier discussion, we can see that the JOIN is not eliminating or duplicating rows, nor adding NULL rows, because of the LEFT JOIN, the uniqueness of s.ProductSubcategory-ID, and the absence of a RIGHT/FULL JOIN, respectively.

Whereas it may seem useful to see that the SubcatName column is coming from a different table, the query could seem much simpler if it took advantage of our view dbo.ProductsPlus2, as created earlier:

```
SELECT ProductID, Name, Color, SubcatName
FROM dbo.ProductsPlus2;
```

Again, a view doesn't store any data unless it is indexed. In its non-indexed form, a view is just a stored subquery. You can compare the execution plans of these two queries, as shown in figure 1, to see that they are executed in exactly the same way.

The powerful aspect of this view occurs if we're not interested in the SubcatName column:

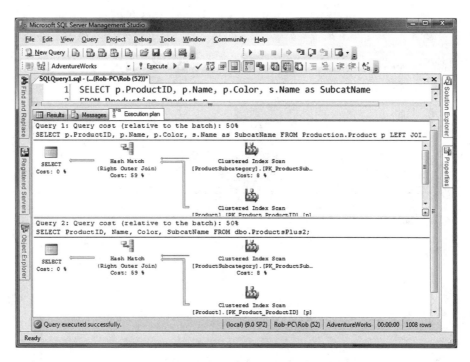

Figure 1   Identical query plans demonstrating the breakdown of the view

```
SELECT ProductID, Name, Color
FROM dbo.ProductsPlus2;
```

Look at the execution plan for this query, as shown in figure 2, and you'll see a vast difference from the previous one. Despite the fact that our view definition involves a second table, this table is not being accessed at all.

The reason for this is straightforward. The query optimizer examines the effects that the JOIN might have. When it sees that none apply (the only one that had applied was additional columns; ignoring the SubcatName column removes that one too), it realizes that the JOIN is not being used and treats the query as if the JOIN were not there at all. Furthermore, if we were not querying the Color column (as shown in figure 3), the query could take advantage of one of the nonclustered indexes on the Product table, as if we were querying the table directly.

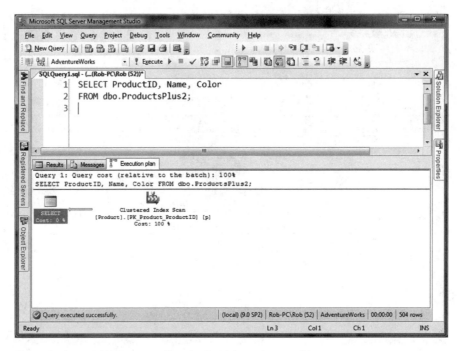

Figure 2   A much simpler execution plan involving only one table

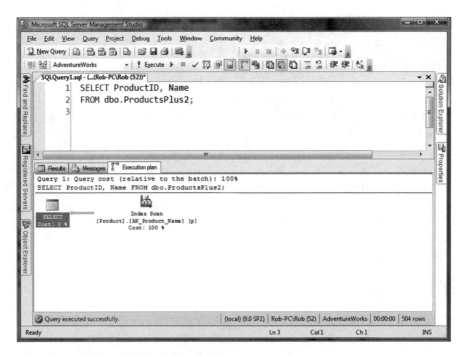

Figure 3   A nonclustered index being used

As an academic exercise, I'm going to introduce a third view in listing 11—one that uses a FULL JOIN.

Listing 11 Using a FULL JOIN

```
CREATE VIEW dbo.ProductsPlus3 AS
SELECT p.*, s.Name as SubcatName
FROM
  Production.Product p
  FULL JOIN
  Production.ProductSubcategory s
  ON p.ProductSubcategoryID = s.ProductSubcategoryID;
```

This is far less useful, but I want to demonstrate the power of the query optimizer, so that you can better appreciate it and design your queries accordingly. In figure 4, notice the query plan that is being used when querying dbo.ProductsPlus3.

This time, when we query only the Name and ProductID fields, the query optimizer does not simplify out the Production.ProductSubcategory table. To find out why, let's look at the four JOIN uses. No additional columns are being used from that table. The FULL JOIN prevents any elimination.No duplication is being created as the ProductSubcategoryID field is still unique in the second table. But the other use of a JOIN—the potential addition of NULL rows—could apply. In this particular case we have no empty subcategories and no rows are added, but the system must still perform the JOIN to satisfy this scenario.

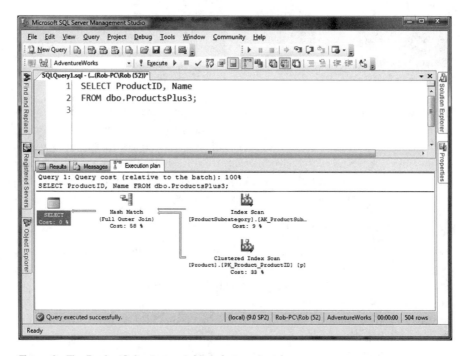

Figure 4 The ProductSubcategory table being used again

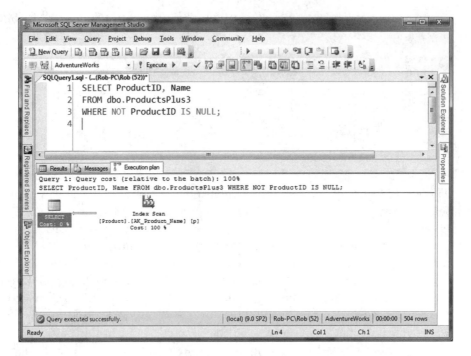

Figure 5   This execution plan is simpler because NULLs are not being introduced.

Another way to ensure that NULL rows do not appear in the results of a query would be to use a WHERE clause:

```
SELECT ProductID, Name
FROM dbo.ProductsPlus3
WHERE NOT ProductID IS NULL;
```

And now once more our execution plan has been simplified into a single-table query as shown in figure 5. The system detects that this particular use for a JOIN is made redundant regardless of whether it is being negated within the view or within the outer query. After all, we've already seen that the system treats a view as a subquery.

Regardless of what mechanism is stopping the JOIN from being used, the optimizer will be able to remove it from the execution plan if it is redundant.

How JOIN uses affect you

Although this may all seem like an academic exercise, there are important takeaways.

If the optimizer can eliminate tables from your queries, then you may see significant performance improvement. Recently I spent some time with a client who had a view that involved many tables, each with many columns. The view used OUTER JOINs, but investigation showed that the underlying tables did not have unique constraints on the columns involved in the JOINs. Changing this meant that the system could eliminate many more tables from the queries, and performance increased by orders of magnitude.

It is useful to be able to write queries that can be simplified by the optimizer, but if you can also make your queries simpler to understand, they're probably quicker to write and easier to maintain. Why not consider using views that contain lookup information? Views that can be simplified can still wrap up useful functionality to make life easier for all the query writers, providing a much richer database to everyone.

Summary

We all need to be able to read and understand the FROM clause. In this chapter we've looked at the basics of JOINs, but also considered a methodology for reading more complex FROM clauses, and considered the ways that JOINs can be made redundant in queries.

I hope that after reading this chapter, you reexamine some of your FROM clauses, and have a new appreciation for the power of JOINs. In particular, I hope that part of your standard query writing process will include considering ways to allow JOINs to become redundant, using LEFT JOINs and uniqueness as demonstrated in the second half of this chapter.

About the author

Rob Farley is a Microsoft MVP (SQL) based in Adelaide, Australia, where he runs a SQL and BI consultancy called LobsterPot Solutions. He also runs the Adelaide SQL Server User Group, and regularly trains and presents at user groups around Australia. He holds many certifications and has made several trips to Microsoft in Redmond to help create exams for Microsoft Learning in SQL and .NET. His passions include Arsenal Football Club, his church, and his wife and three amazing children. The address of his blog is http://msmvps.com/blogs/robfarley, and his company website is at http://www.lobsterpot.com.au.

8 What makes a bulk insert a minimally logged operation?

Denis Gobo

By using a *minimally logged operation*, SQL Server doesn't have to work as hard as if the operation was fully logged. The result is that your import will be much faster, and also that your log file could be a fraction of the size of a fully logged operation.

Before we start, we first need to understand what a minimally logged operation is. A minimally logged operation logs only the pages and extents that are affected; a fully logged operation will log all the individual insert, update, and delete statements. If you have 100 insert statements in a fully logged operation, you'd have 100 entries in the log file, whereas if it were minimally logged, you'd only have one entry.

A minimally logged bulk copy can be performed if all of these conditions are met:

- The recovery model is simple or bulk-logged.
- The target table isn't being replicated.
- The target table doesn't have any triggers.
- The target table either has zero rows or doesn't have indexes.
- The TABLOCK hint is specified.

In this chapter, I'm going to concentrate on the TABLOCK hint (used to obtain a shared lock on a table which is held until the end of a T-SQL statement) and how it can be used to increase performance. I'll show you that performance will greatly increase when you specify the TABLOCK hint.

Recovery and locking

Three kinds of locks can be acquired on a table. The lowest-level lock is a row lock: this will only lock one row. A coarser-grain lock is the page lock, which will lock all the data on a page. Finally, a table lock will lock the whole table. Only when you specify a table lock in your bulk insert statement can you have a minimally logged operation.

SQL Server has three recovery models: Full, Simple, and Bulk-Logged.

- *Simple Recovery*—Simple Recovery uses the least amount of log space, and you can only restore to the most recent full database or differential backup.
- *Full Recovery*—Full Recovery uses the most log space and gives you full recoverability of data, because you can use backups as well as transaction logs to restore to a point in time.
- *Bulk-Logged Recovery*—Bulk Logged Recovery is similar to the Full Recovery model, but offers no point-in-time recovery for bulk operations. Bulk operations would have to be redone.

To show you how the recovery model and the TABLOCK hint affect the size of the log, we will create six databases: two databases per recovery level. For each recovery level, we will run the bulk insert with and without the TABLOCK hint.

Start by executing the scripts in listing 1, which will create our six databases.

Listing 1 SQL scripts to create databases

```
CREATE DATABASE TestRecoverySimple
GO

ALTER DATABASE TestRecoverySimple
SET RECOVERY SIMPLE
GO

CREATE DATABASE TestRecoverySimpleLock
GO

ALTER DATABASE TestRecoverySimpleLock
SET RECOVERY SIMPLE
GO

CREATE DATABASE TestRecoveryBulk
GO

ALTER DATABASE TestRecoveryBulk
SET RECOVERY BULK_LOGGED
GO

CREATE DATABASE TestRecoveryBulkLock
GO

ALTER DATABASE TestRecoveryBulkLock
SET RECOVERY BULK_LOGGED
GO

CREATE DATABASE TestRecoveryFull
GO

ALTER DATABASE TestRecoveryFull
SET RECOVERY FULL
GO
```

```
CREATE DATABASE TestRecoveryFullLock
GO

ALTER DATABASE TestRecoveryFullLock
SET RECOVERY FULL
GO
```

Now that the databases have been created, we can continue by creating our bulk import file.

Creating the file to import

Next, we need to create a file to use for our bulk import; the easiest way to create a file is to use the bcp utility. The bcp utility is a program that accepts a variety of arguments, making it ideal for importing and exporting a wide range of file formats. You can run the bcp utility in two ways: from the command line or from a query window by using xp_cmdshell.

In order to create our import file, we need some data; we will use the sysobjects table to generate this data. The sysobjects table is a system table that exists in each database; this table contains one row for each object created in the database. We will create a file with 500,000 rows by cross-joining the sysobjects table with itself. Here's what the query looks like:

```
SELECT top 500000 s.name,s.id,s.userstat,s2.name,newid()
FROM master..sysobjects s
CROSS JOIN master..sysobjects s2
```

To use bcp from the command line, copy the following line and paste it into a command window:

```
bcp "select top 500000 s.name,s.id,s.userstat,s2.name,newid() from
    ➥ master..sysobjects s cross join master..sysobjects s2" queryout
    ➥ c:\BulkTestData.txt -c -S(local)\sql2008 -T
```

To use bcp from a query window, you need to do the following:

```
master..xp_cmdshell 'bcp "select top 500000
    ➥ s.name,s.id,s.userstat,s2.name,newid() from master..
sysobjects s cross
    ➥ join master..sysobjects s2" queryout c:\BulkTestData.txt -c -
    ➥ S(local)\sql2008 -T'
```

NOTE I have a named instance on my machine named sql2008; if you don't have a named instance, just use (local), or if you do have a named instance, use (local)\InstanceName.

You might get the error in listing 2, because SQL Server ships with xp_cmdshell disabled by default as of SQL Server 2005.

Listing 2   Error message on running bcp utility from a query window

```
Server: Msg 15281, Level 16, State 1, Procedure xp_cmdshell, Line 1

SQL Server blocked access to procedure 'sys.xp_cmdshell' of component
    'xp_cmdshell' because this component is turned off as part of the
    security configuration for this server. A system administrator can
    enable the use of 'xp_cmdshell' by using sp_configure. For more
    information about enabling 'xp_cmdshell', see "Surface Area
    Configuration" in SQL Server Books Online.
```

To enable xp_cmdshell, execute the code in listing 3.

Listing 3   Script to enable xp_cmdshell

```
EXECUTE SP_CONFIGURE 'show advanced options', 1
RECONFIGURE WITH OVERRIDE
GO

EXECUTE SP_CONFIGURE 'xp_cmdshell', '1'
RECONFIGURE WITH OVERRIDE
GO

EXECUTE SP_CONFIGURE 'show advanced options', 0
RECONFIGURE WITH OVERRIDE
GO
```

Creating the tables to store the data

After we create the file, we need to create tables to store the data in. We will create the same table in all six databases with the code in listing 4.

Listing 4   Script to create a database table in six different databases

```
USE TestRecoveryBulk
GO

CREATE TABLE BulkImport (
    name1 varchar(500) not null,
    id int not null,
    userstat int not null,
    name2 varchar(500) not null,
    SomeVal uniqueidentifier not null
)

USE TestRecoverySimple
GO

CREATE TABLE BulkImport (
    name1 varchar(500) not null,
    id int not null,
    userstat int not null,
    name2 varchar(500) not null,
    SomeVal uniqueidentifier not null
)

USE TestRecoveryFull
GO
```

```
CREATE TABLE BulkImport (
    name1 varchar(500) not null,
    id int not null,
    userstat int not null,
    name2 varchar(500) not null,
    SomeVal uniqueidentifier not null
)

USE TestRecoveryBulkLock
GO

CREATE TABLE BulkImport (
    name1 varchar(500) not null,
    id int not null,
    userstat  int not null,
    name2 varchar(500) not null,
    SomeVal uniqueidentifier not null
)

USE TestRecoverySimpleLock
GO

CREATE TABLE BulkImport (
    name1 varchar(500) not null,
    id int not null,
    userstat  int not null,
    name2 varchar(500) not null,
    SomeVal uniqueidentifier not null
)

USE TestRecoveryFullLock
GO

CREATE TABLE BulkImport (
    name1 varchar(500) not null,
    id int not null,
    userstat  int not null,
    name2 varchar(500) not null,
    SomeVal uniqueidentifier not null
)
```

Importing the data

Here's where the import starts. First we will do the imports without the TABLOCK hint by executing the three BULK INSERT statements in listing 5.

Listing 5   BULK INSERT statements to import data without the TABLOCK hint

```
BULK INSERT TestRecoveryFull..BulkImport
FROM 'c:\BulkTestData.txt'
WITH (DATAFILETYPE = 'char',
    FIELDTERMINATOR = '\t',
    ROWTERMINATOR = '\n')

BULK INSERT TestRecoverySimple..BulkImport
FROM 'c:\BulkTestData.txt'
WITH (DATAFILETYPE = 'char',
```

```
        FIELDTERMINATOR = '\t',
        ROWTERMINATOR = '\n')
BULK INSERT TestRecoveryBulk..BulkImport
FROM 'c:\BulkTestData.txt'
WITH (DATAFILETYPE = 'char',
        FIELDTERMINATOR = '\t',
        ROWTERMINATOR = '\n')
```

Next we will do the import with the TABLOCK hint by executing the block of code in listing 6.

Listing 6   BULK INSERT statement to import data with TABLOCK hint

```
BULK INSERT TestRecoveryFullLock..BulkImport
FROM 'c:\BulkTestData.txt'
WITH (DATAFILETYPE = 'char',
        FIELDTERMINATOR = '\t',
        ROWTERMINATOR = '\n',
        TABLOCK)

BULK INSERT TestRecoverySimpleLock..BulkImport
FROM 'c:\BulkTestData.txt'
WITH (DATAFILETYPE = 'char',
        FIELDTERMINATOR = '\t',
        ROWTERMINATOR = '\n',
        TABLOCK)

BULK INSERT TestRecoveryBulkLock..BulkImport
FROM 'c:\BulkTestData.txt'
WITH (DATAFILETYPE = 'char',
        FIELDTERMINATOR = '\t',
        ROWTERMINATOR = '\n',
        TABLOCK)
```

Now that we've imported all the files, let's find out how big the log files are for all six databases. Execute the query in listing 7.

Listing 7   Query to determine the size of log files

```
SELECT size,name
FROM TestRecoveryBulk.sys.sysfiles
WHERE name LIKE '%log'

UNION ALL

SELECT size,name
FROM TestRecoveryBulkLock.sys.sysfiles
WHERE name LIKE '%log'

UNION ALL

SELECT size,name
FROM TestRecoverySimple.sys.sysfiles
WHERE name LIKE '%log'

UNION ALL
```

```
SELECT size,name
FROM TestRecoverySimpleLock.sys.sysfiles
WHERE name LIKE '%log'

UNION ALL

SELECT size,name
FROM TestRecoveryFull.sys.sysfiles
WHERE name LIKE '%log'

UNION ALL

SELECT size,name
FROM TestRecoveryFullLock.sys.sysfiles
WHERE name LIKE '%log'
```

The result set should look like table 1.

Table 1   Resultant log file sizes

Size in KB	Database name
24912	TestRecoveryBulk_log
160	TestRecoveryBulkLock_log
24912	TestRecoverySimple_log
160	TestRecoverySimpleLock_log
24912	TestRecoveryFull_log
5408	TestRecoveryFullLock_log

As you can see, when using simple or bulk-logged recovery with the TABLOCK hint, the size of the log file is much smaller than when you aren't using the TABLOCK hint.

If you are using SQL Server Integration Services and the BULK INSERT task, you must also lock the table for minimal logging. You can enable this in two ways. The first way is to right-click on the Bulk Insert Task icon and select Properties, or double-click on the Bulk Insert Task icon. This will bring up the dialog box shown in figure 1; click on the drop-down box next to Options and select Table Lock.

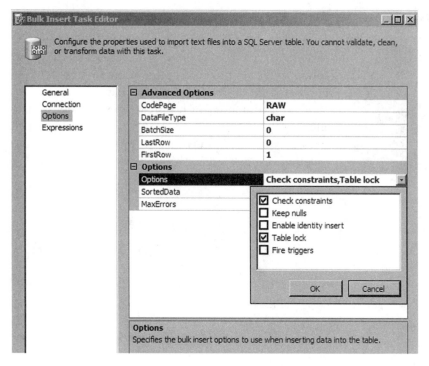

Figure 1   Bulk Insert Task Editor

Another way is to scroll down to Table Lock in the Properties pane on the right side of Business Intelligence Development Studio and set TableLock to True, as shown in figure 2.

Summary

As you've seen in this chapter, choosing the correct recovery model isn't enough to make a bulk insert a minimally logged operation; you also need to make sure that you lock the table.

Figure 2   Properties window

About the author

Denis Gobo resides in Princeton, New Jersey, with his wife and three kids. For the last four years, Denis has worked for Dow Jones, where his task is to optimize the storage and retrieval of a good amount of data; most of this data is stored in SQL Server. Denis is a cofounder of http://www.lessthandot.com, a community site for tech professionals, where he also blogs and answers questions in the forums. In his free time, Denis likes to read, watch horror movies, and spend time with his family.

9 Avoiding three common query mistakes

Kathi Kellenberger

Writing correct and well-performing queries is both an art and a science. The query must return the expected results and execute in a reasonable time. Many blogs and articles have been written about improving query performance, but this chapter will focus on common mistakes that ultimately cause incorrect or incomplete data to be returned. These are problems I have frequently been asked to help solve or have encountered myself.

The examples in this chapter use SQL Server 2008 and the Adventure-Works2008 database that is available for download at http://www.codeplex.com. Search for "SQL Server 2008 code samples" on the site to find the latest release of the database. The queries will also work with the SQL Server 2005 version of the AdventureWorks database.

NULL comparisons

The NULL value means *unknown*; no value has been assigned. This is not the same as an empty string or zero. As long as the ANSI_NULLS setting is turned on, which is the default, comparing a value to NULL returns unknown. One usually expects a value of TRUE or FALSE when making comparisons, but unknown complicates matters under certain conditions.

When comparing a known value to NULL and unknown is returned, it effectively works the same as FALSE, and no results are returned. The AdventureWorks2008 database has a Production.Product table with a Color column that can contain NULLs. If you are trying to find all the products with the color *red*, you most likely do not want to see the products with no color assigned; therefore, this is not a problem. But if you would like a list of the products where the color *does not equal red*, you must decide whether or not the values with no assigned color belong in the results. If you intend for the NULL rows to be included, the criteria WHERE color <> 'red' will be incorrect.

Why is this the case? The expression value <> 'red' is the same as NOT(value = 'red'). If the value happens to be NULL, then unknown is the result of comparing the value to red within the parentheses. When applying NOT to unknown, the expression still returns unknown. Not FALSE is equal to TRUE, but not unknown is still unknown.

Listing 1 shows three ways to write a query to produce the partial results shown in figure 1. The second and third queries each use a function, ISNULL or COALESCE, to replace NULL with an empty string. This allows the color to be compared to the empty string instead of NULL.

Results	Messages
ProductID	Color
1	NULL
2	NULL
3	NULL
4	NULL
316	NULL
317	Black
318	Black
319	Black

Figure 1 NULL values are included along with the colors that have data.

Listing 1 Three queries to include NULL

```
SELECT ProductID, Color
FROM Production.Product
WHERE Color <> 'red' OR Color IS NULL

SELECT ProductID, Color
FROM Production.Product
WHERE ISNULL(Color,'') <> 'red'

SELECT ProductID, Color
FROM Production.Product
WHERE COALESCE(Color,'') <> 'red'
```

You also need to be careful when your expression contains the less-than operator (<). Again, the expression will return unknown when comparing a value to NULL.

Another query type that will leave T-SQL developers scratching their heads when NULLs are involved is using a subquery in the WHERE clause with NOT IN. If there is a NULL value returned in the subquery results, no rows will be returned from the outer query.

Suppose you have a table listing possible colors that could be used to populate the Color column in the Production.Product table, and you need to find out if any of the colors from the list are not used. A table of colors doesn't exist in the Adventure-Works2008 database; therefore, let's create our own. Run the code in listing 2 to create and populate the ColorList table.

Listing 2 The code to create the Production.ColorList table

```
CREATE TABLE Production.ColorList(
    Color nvarchar(15) NOT NULL PRIMARY KEY)
GO

INSERT INTO Production.ColorList(Color)
SELECT Color FROM Production.Product
WHERE Color IS NOT NULL
GROUP BY Color

INSERT INTO Production.ColorList(Color)
VALUES('Purple'),('Orange'),('Lemon'),('Gold')
```

The Production.ColorList table contains all of the colors used in the Production.Product table and a few additional colors. To find the colors that haven't been used in Production.Product, you might write the query in listing 3, but it will not return any results (see figure 2).

Figure 2 No results returned

Listing 3   Query returns no rows because of NULL values in the subquery

```
SELECT Color
FROM Production.ColorList
WHERE Color NOT IN (SELECT Color FROM Production.Product)
```

When the database engine processes the WHERE clause, each color in the Production.ColorList table is compared to the color values in the Production.Product table. Think of the subquery as a list of values that the Color column in the outer query will be compared to; for example, 'red', 'blue', 'green',NULL. When a color value from the Production.Product table is compared to the NULL value in the list, unknown is returned. Recall that unknown is not the same as False. When the NOT operator is applied, the answer is still unknown, and nothing shows up in the results.

Here is an example that illustrates this concept a bit more. Suppose you tried to compare the value "orange" to the list. This is equivalent to the following:

- 'orange' <> 'red'—True
- 'orange' <> 'blue'—True
- 'orange' <> 'green'—True
- 'orange' <> NULL—Unknown

Because unknown is returned, we don't know if orange is in the list or not; therefore, orange does not show up in the results.

Listing 4 demonstrates how to write the query so that you get the correct results by filtering out the NULL values from the subquery. You can see the results in figure 3.

Figure 3 The list of colors not used in the Production.Product table

---

Listing 4   The correct code to find the list of unused colors

```
SELECT Color
FROM Production.ColorList
WHERE Color NOT IN (SELECT Color FROM Production.Product
WHERE Color IS NOT NULL)
```

Multiple OUTER JOINS

When you need to retrieve all the rows from one table in a join, even when there is not a matching row in the second table for every row in the first table, you must use an OUTER JOIN instead of an INNER JOIN. The query will return NULL values in the columns from non-matching rows in the second table.

Listing 5 is an example that shows the rows from Production.ColorList along with Production.Product data even when there are no rows in Production.Product that match. The results will contain `NULL` in the ProductID column when there isn't a match. Figure 4 shows the results.

Listing 5   How to return all rows even if there isn't a match

```
SELECT c.Color, p.ProductID
FROM Production.ColorList AS c
LEFT OUTER JOIN Production.Product AS p ON c.Color = p.Color
ORDER BY p.Color
```

	Color	ProductID
1	Purple	NULL
2	Gold	NULL
3	Lemon	NULL
4	Orange	NULL
5	Black	989
6	Black	990
7	Black	991
8	Black	992
9	Black	993

Figure 4   All rows from the Production.ColorList and the Production.Product rows that match. Non-matching rows return NULL in the ProductID column.

Notice that the keyword `LEFT` is used in listing 5. That designates the position of the table that will return all rows. I prefer to use `LEFT OUTER JOIN` so that the main table is listed first. The query in listing 6 will produce the same results using a `RIGHT OUTER JOIN`.

Listing 6   The same results are returned when using a `RIGHT OUTER JOIN`.

```
SELECT c.Color, p.ProductID
FROM Production.Product AS p
RIGHT OUTER JOIN Production.ColorList AS c ON c.Color = p.Color
ORDER BY p.Color
```

If another table must be added to the query in listing 5, should you add it with an `INNER JOIN`, a `RIGHT OUTER JOIN`, or a `LEFT OUTER JOIN`? Well, that depends. If the new table joins the Production.Product table, it must be a `LEFT OUTER JOIN` because the columns of any of the non-matched rows from Production.Product will contain `NULL` values. The `NULL` values will be unable to join to the third table. In addition, any rows from Production.Product that do not appear in the Sales.OrderDetail table will drop out. When you use an `INNER JOIN` to join the third table, the non-matching rows from the main table will be eliminated.

	Color	ProductID	SalesOrderID
1	Red	707	43665
2	Red	707	43668
3	Red	707	43673
4	Red	707	43677
5	Red	707	43678
6	Red	707	43680
7	Red	707	43681
8	Red	707	43683
9	Red	707	43692

The query in listing 7, joining the Sales.SalesOrderDetail table to the query from listing 5, is written incorrectly. The query eliminates the non-matching rows because rows with a `NULL` ProductID cannot match the Sales.SalesOrderDetail table (see figure 5).

Figure 5   The non-matching rows are lost.

Listing 7 Non-matching rows lost when `INNER JOIN` follows `LEFT OUTER JOIN`.

```
SELECT c.Color, p.ProductID, d.SalesOrderID
FROM Production.ColorList AS c
LEFT OUTER JOIN Production.Product AS p ON c.Color = p.Color
INNER JOIN Sales.SalesOrderDetail AS d
    ON p.ProductID = d.ProductID
ORDER BY p.ProductID
```

The correct way to write the query continues using `LEFT OUTER JOIN` down the `LEFT OUTER JOIN` path. The query in listing 8 does not eliminate the non-matching rows. Figure 6 shows that the rows with `NULL` ProductID values continue to show up in the results.

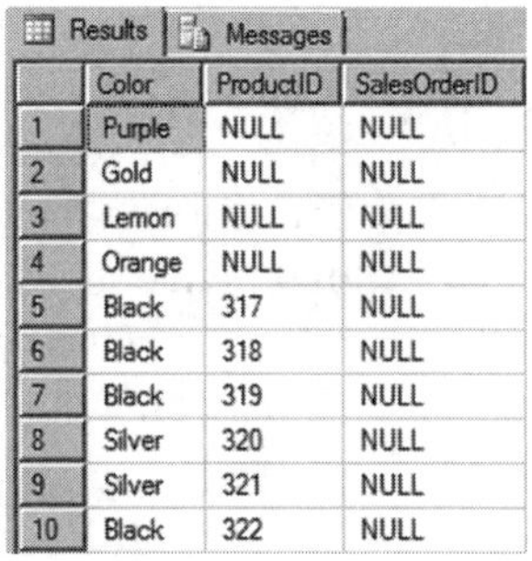

	Color	ProductID	SalesOrderID
1	Purple	NULL	NULL
2	Gold	NULL	NULL
3	Lemon	NULL	NULL
4	Orange	NULL	NULL
5	Black	317	NULL
6	Black	318	NULL
7	Black	319	NULL
8	Silver	320	NULL
9	Silver	321	NULL
10	Black	322	NULL

Figure 6 The correct results when the `LEFT OUTER JOIN` is continued

Listing 8 Using `LEFT OUTER JOIN` down the `OUTER JOIN` path

```
SELECT c.Color, p.ProductID, d.SalesOrderID
FROM Production.ColorList AS c
LEFT OUTER JOIN Production.Product AS p ON c.Color = p.Color
LEFT OUTER JOIN Sales.SalesOrderDetail AS d
    ON p.ProductID = d.ProductID
ORDER BY p.ProductID
```

Another reason, besides listing the main table first, that I prefer to use `LEFT` instead of `RIGHT`, is that starting out with `LEFT` allows you to continue to use `LEFT`. When you start out with a `RIGHT OUTER JOIN`, you must switch to `LEFT` when adding the third table, which is confusing in my opinion. Listing 9 returns the same results and demonstrates how you must switch to `LEFT` when starting out with `RIGHT`.

Listing 9 Using a `RIGHT OUTER JOIN` followed by a `LEFT OUTER JOIN`

```
SELECT c.Color, p.ProductID, d.SalesOrderID
FROM Production.Product AS p
RIGHT OUTER JOIN Production.ColorList AS c ON c.Color = p.Color
LEFT OUTER JOIN Sales.SalesOrderDetail AS d ON p.ProductID = d.ProductID
ORDER BY p.ProductID
```

If you start out with `LEFT`, you can continue to use `LEFT` along that path as more tables are added.

If another table must be joined to the Production.ColorList table, the type of join to use depends on whether there will be any rows that don't match. Whether to use an `OUTER` or `INNER JOIN` down a new path is not dependent on the previous join.

Incorrect GROUP BY clauses

Figuring out which columns belong in the GROUP BY clause in an aggregate query often aggravates T-SQL developers. The rule is that any column that is not part of an aggregate expression in the SELECT or ORDER BY clauses must be listed in the GROUP BY clause. That rule seems pretty simple, but I have seen many questions on forums about this very point.

If a required column is missing from the GROUP BY clause, you will not get incorrect results—you will get no results at all except for an error message. If extra columns are listed in the GROUP BY clause, no warning message will appear, but the results will probably not be what you intended. The results will be grouped at a more granular level than expected. I have even seen code that incorrectly included the aggregated column in the GROUP BY clause.

The query in listing 10 is missing the GROUP BY clause.

Listing 10   Missing the GROUP BY clause

```
SELECT COUNT(*), CustomerID
FROM Sales.SalesOrderHeader

Msg 8120, Level 16, State 1, Line 1
Column 'Sales.SalesOrderHeader.CustomerID' is invalid in the select list
    because it is not contained in either an aggregate function or the GROUP
    BY clause.
```

Listing 11 contains a query that lists the count of orders by CustomerID. The query includes the order date in the GROUP BY clause so that the results do not make sense. Figure 7 shows that there are multiple rows for each CustomerID value.

Listing 11   An extra column in the GROUP BY clause

```
SELECT COUNT(*) AS CountOfOrders, CustomerID
FROM Sales.SalesOrderHeader
GROUP BY CustomerID, OrderDate
ORDER BY CustomerID
```

Another issue to watch out for is including only the column in the GROUP BY clause when the column is used in an expression in the SELECT list. Say you want the results grouped by the year in which the orders were placed. If you leave the order date out of the GROUP BY clause, an error will result. If you add the column, the error goes away, but the results are not grouped as expected.

	CountOfOrders	CustomerID
1	1	11000
2	1	11000
3	1	11000
4	1	11001
5	1	11001
6	1	11001
7	1	11002
8	1	11002
9	1	11002
10	1	11003
11	1	11003
12	1	11003

Figure 7   An extra column in the GROUP BY clause causes unexpected results.

	CountOfOrders	OrderYear
1	7	2001
2	1	2001
3	11	2001
4	4	2001
5	2	2001
6	7	2001
7	8	2001
8	4	2001

Figure 8 Invalid results because `OrderDate` was included instead of the expression

	CountOfOrders	OrderYear
1	1379	2001
2	3692	2002
3	12443	2003
4	13951	2004

Figure 9 The results when the expression is included in the `GROUP BY` clause

The query in listing 12 will not produce an error, but the results will not be as intended. We want a total for each year; therefore, there should only be one row per year. Figure 8 shows multiple rows for 2001 because the results are grouped by the order date.

Listing 12 This query runs, but the results are invalid.

```
SELECT COUNT(*) AS CountOfOrders,
    YEAR(OrderDate) AS OrderYear
FROM Sales.SalesOrderHeader
GROUP BY OrderDate
ORDER BY YEAR(OrderDate)
```

The way to correct the query is to include the exact expression in the `GROUP BY` clause, not only the column. Listing 13 shows the corrected query with only four rows returned this time, one for each year (see figure 9).

Listing 13 Writing the query so that the expression is used in the `GROUP BY` clause

```
SELECT COUNT(*) AS CountOfOrders,
    YEAR(OrderDate) AS OrderYear
FROM Sales.SalesOrderHeader
GROUP BY YEAR(OrderDate)
ORDER BY YEAR(OrderDate)
```

Summary

Learning to write T-SQL queries is not a skill you gain overnight. You must overcome many challenges along the way in order to write queries that return the expected results. Hopefully, this chapter will help you avoid three common mistakes.

Make sure you always think about `NULL`, especially when `NOT`, not equal to, or less than (<>, `!=`, or <) is part of the `WHERE` clause. Remember to continue `LEFT OUTER JOIN` down the `OUTER JOIN` path. And always check your `GROUP BY` clause to make sure that it contains the exact non-aggregate expressions and columns from the `SELECT` list and `ORDER BY` clause.

About the author

Kathi Kellenberger is a database administrator for Bryan Cave LLP, an international law firm headquartered in St. Louis, Missouri. She is coauthor of *Professional SQL Server 2005 Integration Services* (Wrox, 2006) and author of *Beginning T-SQL 2008* (Apress, 2009). Kathi speaks about SQL Server for user groups and local events and has presented at PASS, DevTeach/SQLTeach, and SSWUG Virtual Conference. She has written over 25 articles, including her first one for *SQL Server Magazine* in July 2009. Kathi has been a volunteer for PASS since 2005, winning the PASSion award for her contributions to the organization in 2008.

10 Introduction to XQuery on SQL Server

Michael Coles

Starting with SQL Server 2005, Microsoft added built-in support for XML Query Language (XQuery). XQuery allows you to query your XML (Extensible Markup Language) data using a simple, yet powerful, path-style syntax. XQuery support makes it easy to

- Retrieve XML elements from XML content
- Extract scalar values from XML data
- Check for the existence of elements or values in XML data
- Modify your XML data via XML Data Manipulation Language (XML DML) extensions

SQL Server 2008 includes XQuery support with some slight improvements over the SQL Server 2005 release. This chapter is designed as an introduction to the XQuery functionality available in SQL Server. In this chapter we will assume little or no knowledge of XQuery in general.

What is XQuery?

XQuery is the XML Query Language, as defined by the World Wide Web Consortium (W3C) Recommendation at http://www.w3.org/TR/xquery/. The XQuery recommendation provides the syntax and semantics for a language for querying XML data. XML is a markup language that allows the creation of custom markup languages. SQL Server provides support for XQuery via the xml data type methods, listed in table 1.

The primary means of querying XML data using XQuery is with a path-style syntax inherited directly from another W3C recommendation, the XML Path Language (XPath). XQuery and XPath path expressions look similar to an operating system file path you might enter at a command-line prompt. In fact, if you look at

Table 1   XML data type methods summary

xml data type method	Description
.exist()	Checks for the existence of a node in your XML data
.modify()	Modifies the content of an XML document
.nodes()	Shreds XML content into relational data
.query()	Queries XML content using XQuery syntax
.value()	Extracts scalar values from XML content

your XML data as similar to an operating system directory structure, you can immediately see the similarities. Consider the simple XML document in listing 1.

Listing 1   Simple XML document

```
<Math>
  <Constants>
    <e>2.71828183</e>
    <pi>3.14159265</pi>
    <square-root-2>1.41421356</square-root-2>
  </Constants>
</Math>
```

If you were to view this XML document as a filesystem, it might look something like figure 1.

Like your filesystem, XML is structured hierarchically. If you wanted to access the contents of the pi file in your filesystem, you could use a file path like this:

```
\Math\Constants\pi
```

Similarly, to access the contents of the <pi> element in the previous XML document, you'd use an XQuery path expression like this:

```
/Math/Constants/pi
```

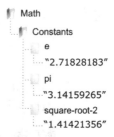

Figure 1   XML document viewed as a filesystem hierarchy

XQuery paths come with several options that allow you to create more complex path expressions to query your XML. For instance, you can use the // axis step to locate any matching elements below the current element. Using // at the front of your path expression locates matching elements anywhere they occur in your XML document. For instance, the following path expression returns <Constants> elements anywhere they occur in your XML content:

```
//Constants
```

You can also use the wildcard character (*) in your path expression to match any node. The following path expression matches all elements under every <Constants> element wherever they occur in your XML content:

```
//Constants/*
```

The comparison of XML data to a hierarchical filesystem only goes so far. XML data can be much more complex in structure than a standard hierarchical filesystem. For example, you can have multiple elements with the same name in an XML document at the same level. Consider the XML data in listing 2, which has multiple <Colonel> elements at the same level.

> **Listing 2   XML with multiple instances of the same element at the same level**

```
<Officers>
  <Colonel id = "1">Harland Sanders</Colonel>
  <Colonel id = "2">Tom Parker</Colonel>
  <Colonel id = "3">Henry Knox</Colonel>
</Officers>
```

In order to query a specific <Colonel> element from the XML document, you need a method of differentiating them. XQuery provides *predicates* to fulfill this need. A predicate follows a path expression step and is enclosed in square brackets ([]). The predicate determines which element you want to retrieve. Only elements where the predicate evaluates to true are returned. As an example, consider a situation in which you want to return Colonel Tom Parker. Using the XML in listing 2, you could apply a path expression like the following:

```
/Officers/Colonel[. = "Tom Parker"]
```

In this case, the predicate compares the content of the <Colonel> elements to the string literal "Tom Parker". When it finds one that matches, the matching element is returned. In this example, it doesn't make much sense to search for the string literal "Tom Parker", unless you are just checking to see if the name exists in your <Colonel> elements.

Using a different predicate, you can retrieve elements by their attributes. Note that each of the <Colonel> elements in the example has a related id attribute. You can retrieve Colonel Tom Parker from your XML data by using the id in the attribute, as shown in the following path expression:

```
/Officers/Colonel[@id = "2"]
```

This path expression returns Colonel Tom Parker because his <Colonel> element's id attribute is set to 2.

NOTE   In XQuery, you differentiate attribute names from element names by prefixing attribute names with an at sign (@). In the previous example, the attribute id is specified as @id in the path expression.

XQuery predicates also provide access to a special function known as `position()`. You can use the `position()` function to return an element at a specific position in your XML data. You can also retrieve `Colonel Tom Parker` from the sample XML data using the `position()` function, as shown in the following path expression:

```
/Officers/Colonel[position() = 2]
```

You can also use a special type of predicate, known as a *numeric predicate*, which consists of a single integer number, as shown in the following path expression:

```
/Officers/Colonel[2]
```

The numeric predicate is functionally equivalent to using the `position()` function. It acts similarly to a 1-based array index. The numeric predicate in the example returns the second instance of a `<Colonel>` element that it encounters in the path expression—in this case the path expression retrieves the `Colonel Tom Parker` element.

How XQuery sees your XML

XQuery doesn't process your XML in its textual form. Querying the text of your XML documents would have negative results, including the following:

- Storing the plain text of your XML documents would be inefficient.
- Querying the textual content of your XML documents would degrade performance, in many cases severely.
- Querying that relies on the raw textual representation of your XML documents would be inflexible, because you couldn't assign data types to your XML document content.

In order to accommodate more efficient storage and querying, and to increase flexibility, XQuery converts your raw textual XML data to a format known as the *XQuery/XPath Data Model* (XDM). XDM relies on a tree-like representation of your textual XML document. Consider the XML content in listing 3.

Listing 3 Sample employee XML content

```
<employee id = "109">
  <name>Ken J. Sánchez</name>
  <title>CEO</title>
  <date-of-hire>2002-10-12</date-of-hire>
</employee>
<employee id = "6">
  <name>David Bradley</name>
  <title>Marketing Mgr</title>
  <date-of-hire>2003-01-04</date-of-hire>
</employee>
```

NOTE   The full W3C XDM recommendation is available at http://www.w3.org/TR/xpath-datamodel/.

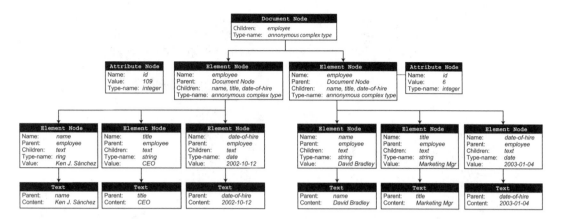

Figure 2 XDM representation of an XML document

This XML content is logically represented in XDM in a hierarchical form similar to that shown in figure 2.

XDM provides an efficient hierarchical representation of raw XML textual data. XDM also allows you to type your XML data, so that you can manipulate XML content using numeric, date, or other type-specific operations.

NOTE Creating typed XML instances in SQL Server requires the use of XML schemas, which are beyond the scope of this chapter.

Also keep in mind that when you store XML data in a SQL Server xml data type instance, it is automatically converted to XDM form internally. During the conversion process, SQL Server strips document type definitions (DTDs) and insignificant whitespace from your XML data. It also converts your XML character data content to typed binary representations.

The first thing to notice about the sample XDM representation is that, like your XML data, it's hierarchical in structure. XDM converts XML elements and other markup structures (such as attributes and processing instructions) into logical nodes within the hierarchical tree structure.

Another interesting feature of XDM is that it can handle both well-formed XML (having a single root node) and XML content with multiple root nodes. The XML content in listing 3 has two <employee> root elements, meaning the content isn't well-formed. XDM creates a single *conceptual root node* at the top of every XDM node hierarchy. This conceptual root node is indicated by the leading forward slash (/) in a path expression. The conceptual root node allows XQuery to easily query both non–well-formed XML fragments and well-formed XML documents.

NOTE You can use the keyword DOCUMENT when declaring SQL Server xml data type columns or variables to restrict their contents to well-formed XML documents. Alternatively you can use the keyword CONTENT when your column or variable will contain XML data that has more than one root node, but is otherwise well-formed. I want to stress that although XML content can have more than one root node, it must follow all other rules for well-formed XML. In SQL Server terminology, the DOCUMENT and CONTENT keywords indicate *facets* that constrain your xml data. The default facet is CONTENT. More information is available in Books Online at http://msdn.microsoft.com/en-us/library/ms187339.aspx.

Querying XML

As we discussed in the section "What is XQuery?" SQL Server's xml data type exposes several methods that allow you to query and manipulate XML data using XQuery. The .query() method is the most basic xml data type method. It accepts an XQuery expression and returns an XML result. Consider listing 4, which creates an xml data type variable, assigns an XML document to it, and then queries the document using the xml data type .query() method. The result is shown in figure 3.

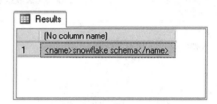

Figure 3   Retrieving XML via the .query() method

Listing 4   Querying XML data

```
DECLARE @x xml;

SET @x = N'<?xml version = "1.0"?>
<definitions category = "Business Intelligence">
  <concept>
    <name>star schema</name>
    <definition>
      The star schema (sometimes referenced as star join schema) is the
      simplest style of data warehouse schema. The star schema consists of
      a few &quot;fact tables&quot; (possibly only one, justifying the
      name) referencing any number of &quot;dimension tables&quot;. The
      star schema is considered an important special case of the snowflake
      schema.
    </definition>
    <source>Wikipedia</source>
  </concept>
  <concept>
    <name>snowflake schema</name>
    <definition>
      A snowflake schema is a logical arrangement of tables in a relational
      database such that the entity relationship diagram resembles a
      snowflake in shape. Closely related to the star schema, the snowflake
      schema is represented by centralized fact tables which are connected
      to multiple dimensions. In the snowflake schema, however, dimensions
      are normalized into multiple related tables whereas the star
      schema&apos;s dimensions are denormalized with each dimension being
      represented by a single table.
    </definition>
```

```
    <source>Wikipedia</source>
  </concept>
</definitions>';
SELECT @x.query(N'/definitions/concept[2]/name');
```

As you can see, the XQuery path expression follows the hierarchical structure of the XML document. The first step of the path expression starts at the root of the XML document and then looks below to the <definitions> element. The second step uses a numeric predicate [2], indicating that the second occurrence of the <concept> element should be selected. Finally, the last step of the path expression indicates that the <name> element under the <concept> element should be retrieved.

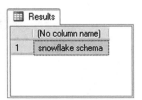

Figure 4   Single scalar value returned by the `.value()` method

The `.value()` method accepts both a path expression and a SQL Server data type. It returns a single scalar value from the XML data, cast to the appropriate data type. The SELECT query in listing 5 uses the `.value()` method on the xml data type variable defined in listing 4. The result is shown in figure 4.

Listing 5   Retrieving a single scalar value

```
SELECT @x.value(N'(/definitions/concept[2]/name)[1]', N'nvarchar(100)');
```

The entire path expression is wrapped in parentheses in this example, and a numeric predicate of [1] is used on the entire path expression. This ensures that only a single scalar value is returned. The `.value()` method will not accept any path expression that isn't guaranteed, during the pre-execution *static analysis phase* of processing, to return a single scalar value.

NOTE   XQuery uses two-phase processing. Initially there's a static analysis phase, during which XQuery checks syntax, data typing, and conformance to any special requirements (such as returning only a single node or single scalar value when necessary). XQuery performs *pessimistic* static type checking, meaning that it'll throw errors during the static analysis phase whenever the path expression could potentially generate a static type error. After the static analysis phase, XQuery goes into the *execution phase*, where your path expression is evaluated against your data.

The xml data type also provides the `.exist()` method, which accepts a path expression and returns 1 if the query returns any nodes, and alternatively returns 0 if the query doesn't return any nodes. Consider listing 6, which tells you whether the word *dimensions* appears in the character data of any of the <definition> elements in the XML data. This sample relies on the sample data used in listing 4. Results are shown in figure 5.

Listing 6   Confirming existence of a node

```
SELECT CASE @x.exist
  (
    N'/definitions/concept/definition[contains(., "dimensions")]'
  )
  WHEN 1 THEN N'The word "dimensions" exists in a definition'
  WHEN 0 THEN N'The word "dimensions" doesn''t exist in a definition'
END;
```

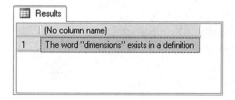

Figure 5   Results of using the `.exist()`
method to check for node existence

TIP   Listing 6 introduces a new XQuery function, `contains()`, which works
similarly to (but not exactly like) the SQL Server `CHARINDEX()` function to
determine whether a given string is contained within your data. The full
list of XQuery functions and operators (often referred to with the abbreviation *F&O*) available to SQL Server XQuery is available in Books Online
at http://msdn.microsoft.com/en-us/library/ms189254.aspx.

In this example, we used a different predicate that uses the XQuery `contains` function. This function accepts a node and a string value. In this example, we used the
period character (`.`), which indicates the *current context node*. The predicate returns
`true` for every node that matches the predicate criteria. In this case, every node that
contains the word *dimensions* returns `true`. The `contains` function (like XML in general, and by extension XQuery) is case sensitive. The `.exist()` method is most commonly used in the `WHERE` clause of SQL statements.

The `.nodes()` method allows you to shred your XML data or convert it into relational form. This method accepts a path expression and returns a relational result set
of matching nodes as an `xml` data type column. The `.nodes()` method requires you to
alias the result set and column name that will be returned. In listing 7, we used the
alias `Result` for the returned result set and `Col` for the single `xml` data type column in
that set. Again, this sample relies on the XML data introduced in listing 4. Partial
results are shown in figure 6.

Listing 7   Shredding XML with the `.nodes()` **method**

```
SELECT Col.value(N'(./name)[1]', N'nvarchar(100)') AS [Name],
  Col.value(N'(./definition)[1]', N'nvarchar(1000)') AS [Definition]
FROM @x.nodes(N'//concept') Result(Col);
```

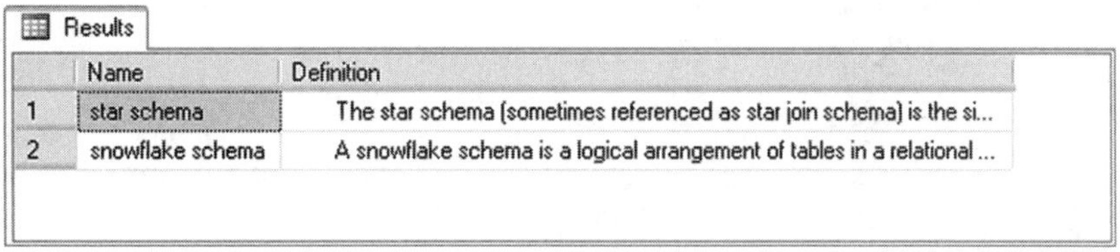

	Name	Definition
1	star schema	The star schema (sometimes referenced as star join schema) is the si...
2	snowflake schema	A snowflake schema is a logical arrangement of tables in a relational ...

Figure 6   Shredding XML data with the `.nodes()` **method**

Querying `.nodes()` results

Although the `.nodes()` method returns a result set of `xml` data type, it is a functionally limited version of the `xml` data type. You can't query the result set instances directly. The only way to access the contents of the result set are through the use of the other `xml` data type methods, such as `.value()` or `.query()`. If you do try to query the contents directly, you'll get an extremely verbose error message similar to the following:

```
Msg 493, Level 16, State 1, Line 35
The column 'Col' that was returned from the nodes() method cannot be
used directly. It can only be used with one of the four XML data type
methods, exist(), nodes(), query(), and value(), or in IS NULL and IS
NOT NULL checks.
```

FLWOR expressions

You can take advantage of powerful XQuery FLWOR expressions (an acronym for the XQuery keywords `for-let-where-order by-return`) in SQL Server. FLWOR expressions let you act on *tuple streams* as they're generated by your path expression.

NOTE   In terms of XQuery, a tuple stream is a stream of nodes returned by a path expression. FLWOR expressions act on a tuple stream that's generated by the `for` clause. The `return` clause returns the result of the tuple stream.

The FLWOR expression, at a minimum, requires a `for` clause and a `return` clause, as shown in listing 8. As in previous examples, listing 8 relies on the XML data introduced in listing 4. Results are shown in figure 7.

Listing 8   Querying XML with a FLWOR expression

```
SELECT @x.query
(
  N'for $i in //name
  return <topic>{$i/text()[1]}</topic>'
);
```

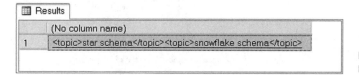

Figure 7   Result of a simple FLWOR expression

In this example, the `for` clause generates a tuple stream from the `//name` path expression and binds each tuple to the `$i` variable in turn. The tuple stream consists of the stream of tuples returned by each iteration of the `for` clause. The `return` clause returns the concatenated results generated by the tuple stream.

This simple FLWOR expression demonstrates an interesting feature of XQuery: *XML construction*. XML construction allows you to generate new XML content from source XML content. In this case, we've taken the content of every <name> element in the source XML document and reformatted that content as <topic> elements.

The `let` keyword allows you to bind tuples generated by the `for` clause tuple stream to variables. Consider listing 9, where we use the `let` clause to assign the character content of each <name> element to a variable named `$j`. The results are the same as those generated by listing 8.

Listing 9   Binding tuples to variables with the `let` clause

```
SELECT @x.query
(
  N'for $i in //name
  let $j := $i/text()[1]
  return <topic>{$j}</topic>'
);
```

NOTE   The `let` clause wasn't implemented in SQL Server 2005 XQuery, but is available in SQL Server 2008.

The `order by` clause allows you to sort your results. The FLWOR expression in listing 10 sorts the results in ascending order by the character content of the <name> elements. The results, shown in figure 8, are the reverse of those shown in figure 7.

Listing 10   Sorting tuples with the order by clause

```
SELECT @x.query
(
  N'for $i in //name
  let $j := $i/text()[1]
  order by $j ascending
  return <topic>{$j}</topic>'
);
```

Figure 8   Results of a FLWOR expression with the `order by` clause

The order by clause can accept the ascending or descending keywords to indicate sort direction. Ascending is the default if you don't explicitly specify a sort order. If you don't use an order by clause in your FLWOR expressions, results are always returned in *document order*. Document order is the default order in which elements occur in your XML document or data. The FLWOR expression order by clause is functionally similar to the T-SQL ORDER BY clause.

Finally, the FLWOR expression where clause allows you to limit the results returned with a predicate. The FLWOR expression's where clause is analogous to the T-SQL WHERE clause. Listing 11 modifies the previous example slightly. This version adds a where clause that limits the results to only those where the content of the `<source>` element is equal to the string `"Wikipedia"`.

Listing 11   Restricting results with the where clause

```
SELECT @x.query
(
  N'for $i in //concept
  let $j := ($i/name/text())[1], $k := ($i/source/text())[1]
  where $k eq "Wikipedia"
  order by $j ascending
  return <topic>{$j}</topic>'
);
```

The predicate in the where clause uses the same operators as predicates in path expressions. These operators are described in the next section.

XQuery comparison operators

XQuery supports several operators for comparing values, nodes, and sequences. A sequence is an ordered collection of zero or more items. The items can be nodes or atomic values, although SQL Server supports only homogenous sequences, or those that don't mix nodes and atomic values in a single XQuery sequence.

NOTE   The term *ordered*, as it applies to XQuery sequences, generally means document order as opposed to alphabetic or numeric order. In the XPath 1.0 recommendation, the concept of *node sets* is used instead of sequences. In node sets, the order is unimportant and duplicate nodes are disallowed. XQuery sequences stress the importance of order (as order is important in XML documents), and allow duplicate nodes.

Sequences are represented as follows in XQuery:

```
(10, 1, (2, 3), 5, 4, 6, 7, 8, 8, (), 9)
```

Sequences are a core concept within XQuery, and worth discussing further. Some of the important things to notice about the preceding sequence:

- Sequences in XQuery can be represented as comma-separated lists of values wrapped in parentheses.
- XQuery understands the concept of the empty sequence, represented by empty parentheses: ().

- XQuery sequences can contain subsequences, such as the (2, 3) sequence, which is a component of the larger sequence in the example.
- Sequences can contain numeric values, character strings, and values of other data types.

A sequence like the one shown is "flattened out" so that subsequences become part of the larger sequence, and empty sequences are removed. After this initial processing, the preceding sequence looks like the following to the XQuery processor:

```
(10, 1, 2, 3, 5, 4, 6, 7, 8, 8, 9)
```

An interesting and useful property of sequences is that any sequence containing only a single atomic scalar value is equivalent to that atomic scalar value. Because of this property, the sequence (3.141592) is equal to the atomic scalar value 3.141592, and the code sample in listing 12 returns a result of `true`.

Listing 12   Comparing a sequence with a single value to a scalar value

```
DECLARE @x xml;
SET @x = N'';
SELECT @x.query('(3.141592) eq 3.141592');
```

XQuery supports several operators that can be used in expressions and predicates. These operators are listed in table 2.

Table 2   XQuery comparison operators

Value comparison operators		General comparison operators	
eq	Equal to	=	Equal to
ne	Not equal to	!=	Not equal to
gt	Greater than	>	Greater than
ge	Greater than or equal to	>=	Greater than or equal to
lt	Less than	<	Less than
le	Less than or equal to	<=	Less than or equal to
Node comparison operators			
is	Node identity equality		
>>	Left node follows right node		
<<	Left node precedes right node		

XQuery comparison operators are classified in three groups, as shown in table 2. *Value comparison operators* are those operators that allow you to compare scalar atomic values to one another. Listing 13 demonstrates the `lt` value comparison operator. The result returned is `true`.

Listing 13   Comparing with the value comparison operators

```
DECLARE @x xml;
SET @x = N'';
SELECT @x.query('"ABC" lt "XYZ"');
```

The second group of operators, *general comparison operators*, contains those operators classified as *existential* operators. Existential operators compare all atomic values contained in sequences on both sides of the operator, and if any of the comparisons return true, the result of the entire comparison is true. Consider the two general comparisons in listing 14.

Listing 14   Comparing sequences with general comparison operators

```
DECLARE @x xml;
SET @x = N'';
SELECT @x.query('(1, 2, 3) > (3, 4, 5)');
SELECT @x.query('(1, 2, 3) = (3, 4, 5)');
```

The first comparison uses the general comparison > (greater-than) operator. Because none of the scalar atomic values in the sequence on the left are greater than any of the scalar atomic values in the sequence on the right, the result of the entire comparison is false. The second comparison uses the = general comparison operator. Because the "3" in the sequence on the left is equal to the "3" in the sequence on the right, the result of the comparison is true.

The final group of operators consists of the *node comparison operators*. These operators allow you to compare nodes. In listing 15, the first expression uses the node comparison << operator to determine whether the /family/mother node appears before the /family/father node, in document order. The second expression uses the is operator to determine whether the first node returned by the //child path is the same as the first node returned by the /family/child path expression. The result of both expressions in the example is true.

Listing 15   Comparing nodes with the node comparison operators

```
DECLARE @x xml;
SET @x = N'<?xml version = "1.0"?>
<family surname = "Adams">
  <mother>Morticia</mother>
  <father>Gomez</father>
  <child>Pugsley</child>
  <child>Wednesday</child>
  <uncle>Fester</uncle>
</family>';
SELECT @x.query('(/family/mother)[1] << (/family/father)[1]');
SELECT @x.query('(//child)[1] is (/family/child)[1]');
```

The is operator checks whether two nodes are actually the same node. Two nodes that might otherwise be considered equivalent (same node name, same character data content, and so on), but aren't the exact same node, aren't considered the same by the is operator.

XML indexes and XQuery performance

Whenever you query XML data on SQL Server, it is automatically converted to relational format behind the scenes. In this way, SQL Server can leverage the power of the relational query engine to fulfill XQuery queries. But on-the-fly shredding is an expensive process that can slow down overall processing. One answer to this problem is to use XML indexes. You can create a primary XML index on an xml data type column on a table to "pre-shred" your XML data. By pre-shredding the XML data, you avoid the overhead involved with on-the-fly shredding.

You can also create secondary XML indexes on your xml data type columns. These secondary XML indexes are relational indexes created on top of the primary XML index. You can choose from three types of secondary XML indexes, each designed to optimize access for different types of XQuery expressions. The creation and administration of XML indexes is beyond the scope of this chapter, but bear in mind that they're available to help increase XQuery performance efficiency. The downside to XML indexes is that they can substantially increase the storage requirements for xml data type columns.

NOTE   More information on XML indexes is available at http://msdn. microsoft.com/en-us/library/ms191497.aspx.

Summary

This concludes our introduction to the basics of XQuery. XQuery is a powerful XML querying language, with far more features than we can cover in this introductory chapter. With built-in support for XQuery path expressions, standard XQuery comparison operators, FLWOR expressions, XML DML, and a wide variety of additional functions and operators, SQL Server provides a powerful XQuery implementation that can be used to query and manipulate XML on SQL Server.

About the author

Michael Coles is a SQL Server MVP and consultant based in New York City. Michael has written several articles and books on a wide variety of SQL Server topics, including *Pro SQL Server 2008 XML* and the *Pro T-SQL 2008 Programmer's Guide*. He can be reached at http://www.sergeantsql.com.

11 SQL Server XML frequently asked questions

Michael Coles

With the SQL Server 2005 release, Microsoft implemented new and exciting XML integration into SQL Server. These features include the following:

- A new native xml data type
- XML content indexing
- Improvements to the FOR XML clause
- Improvements to the OPENROWSET function
- Integrated support for XML Schema
- Native XQuery (XML Query Language) support
- Access to additional XML-specific functionality via SQL CLR integration

All of this functionality, with some additional improvements, is included in SQL Server 2008. Many developers have questions about how to take advantage of this new functionality. This chapter is structured in a frequently-asked-questions (FAQ) format, and will answer many of the most common questions raised by developers who want to use SQL Server–based XML functionality in their applications. We will start with the basics.

XML basics

XML introduces a lot of terminology and concepts that can be new and confusing to SQL developers, or developers coming from other languages. In this section we will discuss some of these basic concepts.

What's XML?

XML is an acronym for *Extensible Markup Language*. XML is a specification for creating custom *markup languages*. A markup language is an artificial language that consists of textual annotations, or *markup tags*, that control the structure or display of textual data. XML allows you to create your own custom markup language, meaning you define the markup tags that give structure and additional context to your textual data. Listing 1 shows a simple XML document.

Listing 1   Sample XML document

```
<?xml version = "1.0"?>
<!-- This is a simple XML document -->
<country name = "United States of America">
  <states>
    <state>
      <abbreviation>NJ</abbreviation>
      <name>New Jersey</name>
    </state>
    <state>
      <abbreviation>NY</abbreviation>
      <name>New York</name>
    </state>
  </states>
</country>
```

This XML document consists of a root-level markup tag named `country`. Nested within this tag, in a hierarchical structure, is a `states` markup tag with additional `state` tags nested within it, and so on. XML is handy for representing hierarchical textual data, and is useful for manipulating and sharing text-based data over the internet.

The XML specification divides the different types of supported markup annotations into logical structures known as *nodes*. Nodes are a useful logical construct for working with XML content. A node can be one of the following types, as shown in the sample XML document:

- *Element nodes*—Element nodes consist of markup tags that wrap other nodes and textual data. The element `<abbreviation>NJ</abbreviation>` in the example is an element named `abbreviation` that contains the text data `NJ`.

- *Attribute nodes*—Attribute nodes are name/value pairs associated with element nodes. In the example, the `country` element has an associated attribute named `name`, which is assigned the value `"United States of America"`.

- *Text nodes*—Text nodes are the bottom-level nodes that contain character data within element nodes. The second `name` element contains a text node containing the character data `New York`.

- *Comment nodes*—Comment nodes are human-readable comments that can appear anywhere in XML documents outside of other markup. The `<!--` and `-->` delimiters are used to indicate a comment node, as in the example where the comment `<!-- This is a simple XML document -->` appears.

- *Processing instructions*—Processing instructions provide a means to pass additional information to the application parsing the XML data. Processing instructions are indicated by delimiting them with `<?` and `?>`. In the example, a special processing instruction known as the *prolog* is used to indicate the version of the XML recommendation that this document conforms to. The prolog in this example is `<?xml version = "1.0"?>`.

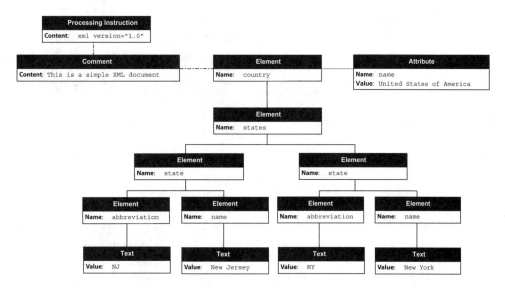

Figure 1   XML tree structure

XML data can be logically viewed as a set of nodes in a hierarchical tree structure. Figure 1 shows the sample XML document when viewed as a tree.

The XML node tree structure works well in support of other XML-based processing and manipulation recommendations that logically view XML data as hierarchical tree-like structures. These recommendations include XML Infoset, XML Schema, XML DOM, and XQuery/XPath Data Model, to name a few. Each of these recommendations can define extra node types in addition to these basic node types, such as *document nodes* and *namespace nodes*.

What's "well-formed" XML?

XML data must conform to certain syntactical requirements. XML that follows the syntactical requirements below is considered well-formed:

1 Well-formed XML data must contain one or more elements.

2 Well-formed XML data must contain one, and only one, *root element*. In the sample XML document presented in the previous section, the country element is the root element. It contains all other elements within its start and end tags.

3 Well-formed XML data must have all elements properly nested within one another. This means no overlapping start and end tags. The start and end tags of the states element don't overlap the other tags, such as the nested state, abbreviation, and name tags.

In addition to these requirements, XML character data must be properly *entitized*, which we will talk about in the next section. XML data that conforms to all of these rules is considered well-formed.

XML data that isn't well-formed must still follow these rules, with one exception: it can have more than one root node. Consider, for example, extracting only the `state` elements from the previous sample data and creating an XML result like listing 2.

Listing 2   Extracting `state` elements from XML document

```
<state>
  <abbreviation>NJ</abbreviation>
  <name>New Jersey</name>
</state>
<state>
  <abbreviation>NY</abbreviation>
  <name>New York</name>
</state>
```

This XML document isn't well-formed because it has multiple top-level elements. It still must conform to all other rules for well-formed documents, though. XML data that follows all of the rules for well-formedness, other than the requirement of a single root node, is sometimes referred to as an *XML fragment*.

What's the prolog?

The *prolog* of an XML document is an optional special processing instruction at the top of the XML document (see the answer to "What's XML?" for more information). When it is included, the prolog must be the first entry (no leading whitespace, data, or markup) of the XML document. The prolog generally includes a version number, and can also include an encoding specifier. The version number indicates the version of the W3C XML recommendation that your XML document conforms to. It is generally version 1.0 (or 1.1), as shown in the sample prolog in listing 3.

Listing 3   Sample prolog

```
<?xml version = "1.0"?>
```

The prolog can also include an encoding specifier. The encoding is generally ISO-8859-1, UTF-8, WINDOWS-1252, or UTF-16. If specified, the encoding must match the character encoding used in the source XML data. For instance, if your source XML is Unicode (nvarchar in SQL) data, you can't use an 8-bit character encoding such as ISO-8859-1. The sample prolog in listing 4 includes both a version and a 16-bit encoding specifier.

Listing 4   Sample prolog with encoding specifier

```
<?xml version = "1.0" encoding = "UTF-16"?>
```

Keep in mind that the prolog isn't required, but if it is included, it must match the source XML data's encoding.

What's an entity?

XML allows you to mark up textual data, but it assigns special meaning to certain characters, such as the greater-than and less-than symbols (< and >). *Entitizing* is the process of converting these characters that have special meaning in XML to special codes known as *entities*. The less-than symbol (<), for instance, must be converted to the entity <. XML defines five *predeclared XML entities*, which all programs that process XML must recognize. These predeclared XML entities are listed in table 1.

Table 1   Predeclared XML entities

Entity	Description
&	Ampersand (&)
'	Apostrophe (')
>	Greater-than symbol (>)
<	Less-than symbol (<)
"	Quotation marks (")

In addition to these predeclared XML entities, you can use numeric character references to represent any character in your XML data. Numeric character references resemble entities with a decimal or hexadecimal character code. The less-than character, for example, can be represented using any of the following forms in your XML data:

```
&lt;
&#60;
&#x3c;
```

SQL Server's XML parser automatically expands XML entities when you retrieve XML data.

What's a DTD?

The XML standard supports a special construct known as a *document type definition (DTD)*. In simple terms, the XML recommendation defines a DTD as a basic mechanism for constraining your XML structure and content. SQL Server supports a minimal subset of the DTD standard; specifically, you can use DTDs in your XML documents to declare your own user-defined entities. In order to process XML data that contains a DTD in SQL Server, you have to use the CONVERT function, as shown in listing 5. The result is shown in figure 2.

Listing 5   Converting XML with a DTD

```
DECLARE @x xml = CONVERT
(
  xml,
  N'
  <!DOCTYPE bookdoc [
    <!ENTITY manning "&#xa9;2008 Manning Publications Co.">
  ]>
  <book>
    <title>C# In Depth</title>
    <publisher>&manning;</publisher>
```

```
    </book>
    ',
    2
);
SELECT @x;
```

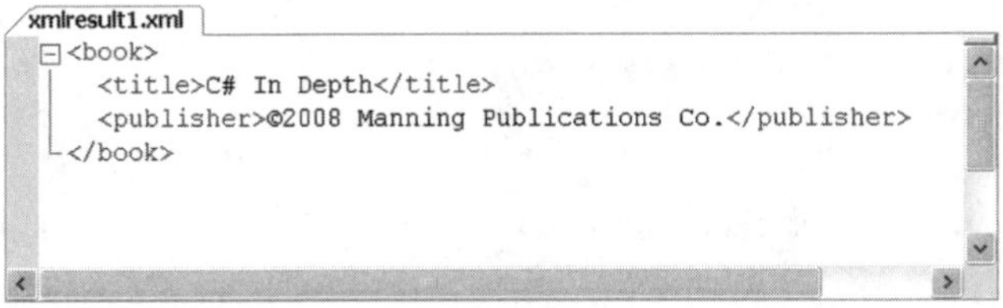

```
xmlresult1.xml
 <book>
    <title>C# In Depth</title>
    <publisher>©2008 Manning Publications Co.</publisher>
 </book>
```

Figure 2   XML document with a DTD processed by the SQL Server XML parser

The CONVERT function accepts three parameters: the target data type (in this case xml), the source data (an XML document with DTD), and a third style parameter. The third parameter must be set to the number 2 or 3 when you want SQL Server to parse an XML document containing a DTD.

You will notice three important things about the result shown in figure 2. First, the SQL Server XML parser replaces the XML entities in your document with the equivalent character data. Second, the SQL Server XML parser strips away the DTD when it has finished parsing the XML data. Finally, note that SQL Server doesn't natively support external DTDs, or DTDs that are stored outside of the current XML document.

The xml data type

The cornerstone of SQL Server 2005 and SQL Server 2008 XML functionality is the xml large object (LOB) data type. This data type provides a lot of native XML functionality through its various built-in methods, it can be validated via an XML schema, and its contents can be indexed with XML indexes. We will consider the xml data type in this section.

Why does SQL Server remove the DTD from my XML data?

When you store XML data using SQL Server's xml data type, SQL Server converts it to an internal binary representation based on the XQuery/XPath Data Model (XDM) recommendation. The XDM recommendation defines a hierarchical representation for XML data. When you retrieve XML data stored as the xml data type, SQL Server literally re-creates the XML text based on the XDM instance contents. The XDM allows for several changes to be made to the textual representation of the XML data, including the following:

- The DTD is used to expand entities in the XML data, and then the DTD is stripped from the XML data. The DTD isn't stored with the XML data. See the answer to "What's a DTD?"
- CDATA sections are expanded and the CDATA markers are stripped from the XML data.

- Insignificant whitespace (spaces, tabs, linefeeds, and carriage returns between markup tags) is removed. See the answer to "How do I preserve whitespace in my XML?"
- Entities are expanded to their textual representations.

In addition, typed data, such as integers, is stored in an internal binary format. An integer such as 00150 can be stored in a numeric representation, returning the textual representation 150 (creating a typed representation of your XML data requires storing the data in a typed xml instance).

NOTE The W3C XQuery/XPath Data Model recommendation is available at http://www.w3.org/TR/xpath-datamodel.

If you need to store exact copies of the text of your XML data with DTD, CDATA sections, insignificant whitespace, entities, and exact character-for-character representations of data, store your XML data using a character or binary data type such as varbinary(max), varchar(max), or nvarchar(max). The downside to this method of storing XML data in SQL Server is that you will not have access to the xml data type methods that allow you to query and manipulate your XML data.

How do I preserve whitespace in my XML?

As mentioned in the answer to "Why does SQL Server remove the DTD from my XML data?" SQL Server also strips away insignificant whitespace. Insignificant whitespace consists of tab characters, spaces, linefeeds, and carriage returns between XML markup tags. By default, when SQL Server converts your XML data to an internal XDM representation, it strips away insignificant whitespace. You can use the CONVERT function with 3 specified for the style option to convert your text-based XML data to an xml instance and preserve insignificant whitespace in the process. This conversion using CONVERT with style 3 isn't 100 percent exact, and some whitespace characters may not be preserved in the conversion process.

NOTE See the answer to "What's a DTD?" for an example of using the CONVERT function to convert text-based XML to the xml data type.

Why am I getting strange characters in my XML?

XML supports different character encodings, such as ISO-8859-1 or UTF-8 for single-byte character encodings and UTF-16 for Unicode character representations. The code in listing 6 contains Chinese characters, which can't be represented with single-byte character encodings. The problem in this example is that the text-based XML is being converted from a single-byte varchar encoding to the xml data type. The result of the code in listing 6 is shown in figure 3.

Figure 3   Result of single-byte encoding applied to Chinese characters

Listing 6   Applying single-byte encoding to Unicode characters

```
DECLARE @x xml = '<?xml version="1.0"?>
  <text> 繁體中文版 </text>';
SELECT @x;
```

As you can see in the example, there's a mismatch when trying to store or convert Chinese characters to single-byte encodings. SQL Server replaces the Chinese characters with question marks to indicate that it couldn't convert them to a single-byte encoding. The fix for this problem is simple: use nvarchar as the source when you need to represent character data that requires Unicode encoding. To do so, you can prefix string literals with the N prefix, as shown in listing 7. The result is shown in figure 4.

Figure 4   Result of properly encoding international characters in source XML

Listing 7   Eliminating single-byte-to-Unicode conversion problems

```
DECLARE @x xml = N'<?xml version="1.0"?>
  <text> 繁體中文版 </text>';
SELECT @x;
```

If you specify the wrong encoding in your XML, as shown in listing 8, you'll get an error.

Listing 8   Invalid single-byte-to-Unicode conversion

```
DECLARE @x xml = '<?xml version="1.0" encoding="UTF-16"?>
  <Music>
    <Band>Wu Tang Clan</Band>
  </Music>';
```

This statement returns an error like the following:

```
Msg 9402, Level 16, State 1, Line 1
XML parsing: line 1, character 39, unable to switch the encoding
```

The problem is that the character data you are converting to XML is single-byte varchar data, whereas the prolog specifies a Unicode UTF-16 encoding. SQL Server's XML parser can't reconcile this conflict. You can fix this by changing your source XML data to nvarchar Unicode data. In the case of a string literal, as in the example, prefix your string with the N character, as shown in listing 9.

Listing 9   Avoiding single-byte-to-Unicode conversion problems

```
DECLARE @x xml = N'<?xml version="1.0" encoding="UTF-16"?>
  <Music>
    <Band>Wu Tang Clan</Band>
  </Music>';
```

I recommend always using Unicode, or binary format with the proper encoding specified in the prolog, to accurately represent your XML data and prevent conversion problems like these. See the answer to "What's the prolog?" for more information about the XML prolog.

How do I query XML data?

You can query XML data using the `.query()` method of the `xml` data type. This method allows you to query XML data using XQuery path expressions. The code sample in listing 10 creates a simple XML document and uses the `.query()` method to return the book with ISBN 1430215941. Results are shown in figure 5.

Listing 10 Querying XML data

```
DECLARE @x xml = N'
<books>
  <book isbn = "1590599837">
    <title>Pro SQL Server 2008 XML</title>
  </book>
  <book isbn = "143021001X">
    <title>Pro T-SQL 2008 Programmer&apos;s Guide</title>
  </book>
  <book isbn = "1430215941">
    <title>Pro Full-Text Search in SQL Server 2008</title>
  </book>
</books>
';
SELECT @x.query
(
  N'/books/book[@isbn = "1430215941"]'
);
```

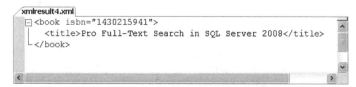

Figure 5   Result of executing an XQuery query against XML data

The results of the `.query()` method return entire XML nodes as `xml` data type instances.

How do I query a single value from my XML data?

Sometimes you might want to grab a single scalar value from your XML data instead of entire XML nodes. The `xml` data type `.value()` method provides this functionality. As with the `.query()` method, you pass an XQuery query to the `.value()` method. You also need to pass a T-SQL data type to the method. After SQL Server retrieves the scalar value from your XML data, it converts it to a T-SQL data type. The example in listing 11 retrieves the name of the book with ISBN 143021001X. The scalar value returned is converted to an `nvarchar` result. Results are shown in figure 6.

Listing 11   Retrieving a single scalar value from XML

```
DECLARE @x xml = N'
<books>
  <book isbn = "1590599837">
    <title>Pro SQL Server 2008 XML</title>
  </book>
  <book isbn = "143021001X">
    <title>Pro T-SQL 2008 Programmer&apos;s Guide</title>
  </book>
  <book isbn = "1430215941">
    <title>Pro Full-Text Search in SQL Server 2008</title>
  </book>
</books>
';
SELECT @x.value
(
  N'(/books/book[@isbn = "143021001X"]/title)[1]',
  N'nvarchar(100)'
);
```

Figure 6   Result of retrieving a scalar value
from XML data

How do I shred XML data?

Shredding is the process of converting XML documents to relational format—viewing
your XML data as if it were a relational table. SQL Server provides two options for
shredding XML data. The first, simplest option takes advantage of the `xml` data type
`.nodes()` method. This method accepts an XPath-style path expression and returns
a rowset consisting of `xml` data type values. The example in listing 12 shows how to
use the `.nodes()` method to shred your XML data. The results are shown in
figure 7.

Listing 12   Shredding XML data

```
DECLARE @x xml = N'<inventory store-num = "1983">
  <product ean = "0051500241776">
    <name>Jif Creamy Peanut Butter</name>
    <size>28 oz</size>
  </product>
  <product ean = "0024600010030">
    <name>Morton Iodized Sale</name>
    <size>26 oz</size>
  </product>
  <product ean = "0086600000138">
    <name>Bumble Bee Chunked White Albacore in Water</name>
    <size>6 oz</size>
```

```
    </product>
</inventory>';

SELECT Col.value(N'./@ean[1]', N'nvarchar(15)') AS EAN,
  Col.value(N'./name[1]', N'nvarchar(100)') AS Name,
  Col.value(N'./size[1]', 'nvarchar(100)') AS Size
FROM @x.nodes(N'//product') Tab(Col);
```

	EAN	Name	Size
1	0051500241776	Jif Creamy Peanut Butter	28 oz
2	0024600010030	Morton Iodized Sale	26 oz
3	0086600000138	Bumble Bee Chunked White Albacore in Water	6 oz

Figure 7   Result of shredding XML data

NOTE   The values returned by the .nodes() method are a functionally limited version of the xml data type. You can't access or retrieve these values directly; instead you have to use the xml data type methods, such as .query() and .value(), to access the content of the xml data type values returned by .nodes().

As you can see, the .nodes() method has to be aliased with both a table name and a column name. In this case, we used the alias Tab(Col) for simplicity. We used the xml data type .value() method to retrieve scalar values from the Col column of the result set.

The xml data type .nodes() method is a fairly simple way to shred your XML data, but there's a second option. The OPENXML rowset provider function is backward-compatible with SQL Server 2000. Like the .nodes() method, the OPENXML rowset provider OPENXML can be used to shred any binary or character data type, or (beginning with SQL Server 2005) the xml data type. OPENXML is a little more complicated than the .nodes() method. To use it, you first have to call the sp_xml_preparedocument stored procedure, which returns a handle to the XML document. This procedure invokes the COM-based Microsoft XML Core Services Library (MSXML) to convert your textual XML data to an internal XML Document Object Model (XML DOM) representation. sp_xml_preparedocument allocates memory for the XML DOM representation of your XML and returns an integer identifier, known as a *document handle*.

Once you've created the XML DOM representation of your XML data, you can call the OPENXML function to shred it. OPENXML takes three parameters: the document handle you generated previously with the call to sp_xml_preparedocument, an XPath-style path expression to indicate the nodes to shred, and an optional integer flag value that determines whether the input XML is element-centric or attribute-centric. The OPENXML function WITH clause allows you to specify the structure of the output rowset. Each column of the rowset can be defined with a column name, T-SQL data type, and a path expression indicating where the data should be pulled from relative to the current context node.

Finally, OPENXML requires you to clean up after yourself by calling sp_xml_ removedocument with the previously generated document handle. This procedure removes the XML DOM representation of your XML data and frees up the memory MSXML was using.

The example in listing 13 shows how to shred the same XML document we shredded previously, with the exact same result, but this time we will use OPENXML instead of the .nodes() method.

Listing 13   Shredding XML with OPENXML

```
DECLARE @x xml = N'<inventory store-num = "1983">
  <product ean = "0051500241776">
    <name>Jif Creamy Peanut Butter</name>
    <size>28 oz</size>
  </product>
  <product ean = "0024600010030">
    <name>Morton Iodized Sale</name>
    <size>26 oz</size>
  </product>
  <product ean = "0086600000138">
    <name>Bumble Bee Chunked White Albacore in Water</name>
    <size>6 oz</size>
  </product>
</inventory>';

DECLARE @handle int;

EXEC sys.sp_xml_preparedocument @handle OUTPUT, @x;

SELECT *
FROM OPENXML
(
  @handle,
  N'//product',
  3
)
WITH
(
  EAN nvarchar(15) N'./@ean[1]',
  Name nvarchar(100) N'./name[1]',
  Size nvarchar(100) N'./size[1]'
);

EXEC sys.sp_xml_removedocument @handle;
```

Advanced query topics

Many frequently asked questions about SQL Server XML concern advanced topics such as using XML namespaces and retrieving all element names and values from an XML document. In this section, we will cover some of these advanced query topics.

How do I specify an XML namespace in my XQuery queries?

Different XML-based standards may have element names in common. It is not uncommon to see different XML-based standards that specify elements named `Name` and `Price`, for instance. Each of these element names can have a completely different meaning, depending on the standard. In one standard, the `Name` element might be a customer name; in another standard, it might be a product name.

To differentiate between the different uses for the same name in different standards, XML provides the concept of *XML namespace*. An XML namespace is a qualifier for XML elements and attributes that allows you to associate them with XML documents. Using an XML namespace, you can differentiate between the `Name` elements used in different standards, as shown in listing 14.

```
Listing 14  Sample XML with namespaces
```

```
<customers:Name>John Jacob Jingleheimer-Smith</customers:Name>
<products:Name>Little Red Wagon</products:Name>
```

The XML namespace associates a namespace prefix (`customers` and `products` in listing 14) with a URI for a document. If you are using XQuery to query data that contains one or more explicit namespaces, you can use the XQuery `declare` element's `namespace` option to define the namespace in your query, as shown in listing 15. The results are shown in figure 8.

```
Listing 15  Querying XML with namespaces
```

```
DECLARE @x xml = N'
<sale xmlns:products = "urn:store:products"
      xmlns:customers = "http://www.tempuri.org/customerdata">
  <customers:Name>Jerry Lee Lewis</customers:Name>
  <products:Name>Baby Grand Piano</products:Name>
</sale>';

SELECT @x.query(N'declare namespace products = "urn:store:products";
  /sale/products:Name/text()') AS ProductName;

SELECT @x.query(N'declare namespace customers = "http://www.tempuri.org/
    ➥customerdata";
  /sale/customers:Name/text()') AS CustomerName;
```

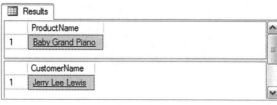

Figure 8   Querying XML with namespaces defined

In this example, we've defined two namespaces in the XML document: one to denote customer-specific elements and another for product-specific elements. When we query the data we use the XQuery declare namespace statement to assign a namespace prefix to a URI before we define the path expression. Once we've declared the namespace, we can use the namespace prefix to differentiate between elements in the path expression—even elements with the same local name (like the Name element in our example).

SQL Server also provides a WITH XMLNAMESPACES clause that can be used with queries, common table expressions (CTEs), and data manipulation language (DML) statements to declare your XML namespaces. The example in listing 16 modifies the previous example to use the WITH XMLNAMESPACES clause to generate the same result.

Listing 16   Using WITH XMLNAMESPACES clause

```
DECLARE @x xml = N'
<sale xmlns:products = "urn:store:products"
      xmlns:customers = "http://www.tempuri.org/customerdata">
  <customers:Name>Jerry Lee Lewis</customers:Name>
  <products:Name>Baby Grand Piano</products:Name>
</sale>';

WITH XMLNAMESPACES('urn:store:products' AS products)
SELECT @x.query(N'/sale/products:Name/text()') AS ProductName;

WITH XMLNAMESPACES('http://www.tempuri.org/customerdata' AS customers)
SELECT @x.query(N'/sale/customers:Name/text()') AS CustomerName;
```

How do I get all element names and values from my XML document?

XQuery is a handy query language when you know the structure of your XML document in advance, because you can specify the hierarchical path structure to get to the elements you are interested in. But what happens when you don't know the XML document structure in advance? In some cases you might want to grab the names and values of the elements in your XML document no matter where they occur. In those cases, you can take advantage of the xml data type's .nodes() method and XQuery wildcard querying. In XQuery, the asterisk (*) can stand in as a wildcard in your path expressions. The example in listing 17 grabs the XML namespace, name, and text content of every element in any XML document. The results are shown in figure 9.

Listing 17   Retrieving all element names and values from XML

```
DECLARE @x xml = N'
<Companies xmlns:info = "urn:corp:info"
           xmlns:address = "urn:corp:address">
  <info:Company>
    <info:Ticker>MSFT</info:Ticker>
    <info:Name>Microsoft Corporation</info:Name>
    <address:Address>One Microsoft Way, Redmond, WA</address:Address>
  </info:Company>
```

```
    <info:Company>
      <info:Ticker>IBM</info:Ticker>
      <info:Name>International Business Machines</info:Name>
      <address:Address>1 New Orchard Road, Armonk, NY</address:Address>
    </info:Company>
</Companies>';
SELECT CASE NodeUri WHEN N'' THEN N''
  ELSE N'{' + NodeUri + N'}' END + NodeName AS [Name],
  NodeUri,
  NodeName,
  NodeValue
FROM
(
  SELECT node.value(N'fn:namespace-uri(.[1])', N'nvarchar(1000)') AS
➥NodeUri,
    node.value(N'fn:local-name(.[1])', N'nvarchar(1000)') AS NodeName,
    node.query(N'./text()') AS NodeValue
  FROM @x.nodes(N'//*') T(node)
) sub;
```

	Name	NodeUri	NodeName	NodeValue
1	Companies		Companies	
2	{urn:corp:info}Company	urn:corp:info	Company	
3	{urn:corp:info}Ticker	urn:corp:info	Ticker	MSFT
4	{urn:corp:info}Name	urn:corp:info	Name	Microsoft Corporation
5	{urn:corp:address}Address	urn:corp:address	Address	One Microsoft Way, Redmond, WA
6	{urn:corp:info}Company	urn:corp:info	Company	
7	{urn:corp:info}Ticker	urn:corp:info	Ticker	IBM
8	{urn:corp:info}Name	urn:corp:info	Name	International Business Machines
9	{urn:corp:address}Address	urn:corp:address	Address	1 New Orchard Road, Armonk, NY

Figure 9   Retrieving all element names and nodes from an XML document

This sample query takes advantage of the XQuery wildcard character to match every node in the XML data, regardless of location or XML namespace. We also use the XQuery `fn:namespace-uri` and `fn:local-name` functions to retrieve the XML namespace URI and local name for every element found.

NOTE   XML automatically expands XML namespace prefixes (internally) to their matching namespace URIs whenever it encounters them in your XML data. To represent this, we've included a column that shows the fully expanded element names in the results. This column looks like this: `{urn:corp:info}Company`.

How do I load XML documents from the filesystem?

The `OPENROWSET` function has a `BULK` option that allows you to load data into SQL Server directly from the filesystem. Using this option, you can load a single file from the filesystem directly into a variable or column in a table. For our example, we will assume an XML file named state-list.xml exists in the root directory of your C: drive. This file looks something like listing 18.

Listing 18   Sample state-list.xml file

```
<?xml version="1.0"?>
<capitals>

    <state name="Alabama"
      abbreviation="AL"
      capital="Montgomery"
      flag="AL.gif"
      date="December 14, 1819"
      fact="Rosa Parks refused to give up her seat on a Montgomery bus in
      1955.  The Montgomery Bus Boycott kicked off the Civil Rights era a few
      days later."
      address="600 Dexter Ave"
      zip="36130"
      long="-86.301963"
      lat="32.377189" />

    <state name="Alaska"
      abbreviation="AK"
      capital="Juneau"
      flag="AK.gif"
      date="January 3, 1959"
      fact="In 1867 United States Secretary of State William H. Seward
      offered Russia $7,200,000, or two cents per acre, for Alaska."
      address="120 4th Street"
      zip="99801"
      long="-134.410699"
      lat="58.301072" />

    ...

</capitals>
```

You can use the OPENROWSET function with BULK option to load this XML file from the filesystem into an xml variable, as shown in listing 19. Partial results are shown in figure 10.

Listing 19   Loading XML data from the filesystem

```
DECLARE @xml XML;

-- Use OPENROWSET to read an XML file from the filesystem
SELECT @xml = BulkColumn
FROM OPENROWSET(BULK 'c:\state-list.xml', SINGLE_BLOB) TempXML

-- View the result
SELECT @xml;
```

```
xmlresult1.xml
<capitals>
   <state name="Alabama" abbreviation="AL" capital="Montgomery" flag="AL.gif" d
   <state name="Alaska" abbreviation="AK" capital="Juneau" flag="AK.gif" date="
   <state name="Arizona" abbreviation="AZ" capital="Phoenix" flag="AZ.gif" date
   <state name="Arkansas" abbreviation="AR" capital="Little Rock" flag="AR.gif"
   <state name="California" abbreviation="CA" capital="Sacramento" flag="CA.gif
   <state name="Colorado" abbreviation="CO" capital="Denver" flag="CO.gif" date
   <state name="Connecticut" abbreviation="CT" capital="Hartford" flag="CT.gif"
   <state name="Delaware" abbreviation="DE" capital="Dover" flag="DE.gif" date=
```

Figure 10   XML file loaded from filesystem into SQL Server

A few things you need to keep in mind with this method:

- The SQL Server service must have access to the drive, directory, and file you are trying to load.
- The source file name must be a string literal. You can't replace it with a variable name. If you want to use a variable name, you'll have to use this method with dynamic SQL.
- We used the SINGLE_BLOB option in this example—it is the preferred method, because SINGLE_BLOB supports all Windows encoding conversions. You can also use SINGLE_CLOB for character files or SINGLE_NCLOB for national character (Unicode) files.

Summary

This concludes my answers to some of the most frequently asked questions about SQL Server XML. SQL Server provides powerful XML functionality, especially with the introduction of the xml data type in SQL Server 2005. Now that SQL Server supports XQuery via the xml data type methods, improved FOR XML capabilities, and additional improved support for XML via SQL CLR and other functions, you can easily query, manipulate, modify, and process XML server-side.

About the author

Michael Coles is a SQL Server MVP and consultant based in New York City. Michael has written several articles and books on a wide variety of SQL Server topics, including *Pro SQL Server 2008 XML* and the *Pro T-SQL 2008 Programmer's Guide*. He can be reached at http://www.sergeantsql.com.

12 Using XML to transport relational data

Matija Lah

The principal subject of this chapter is the use of XML to transport data between locations. To make the demonstration more interesting, we'll use XML to transport *relational* data.

Before we start developing the database solution, we have to analyze and understand our business case. Only after identifying *every relevant fact* about the business case should you attempt any development work.

In the course of this chapter, through planning and developing activities, we'll learn the basics of how XML can be used in a Microsoft SQL Server 2005 (or later) database, but not before we touch on some basic truths about the XML standard itself.

Understanding before coding

To make the essence of this chapter as simple to understand as possible, our business case will cover a subject everyone should be fairly familiar with: discography.

What's a *discography*? In plain English, a discography is a collection of data about recorded music. It contains data about the composers, performers, compositions themselves, and so on.

For the purposes of analyzing this chapter's business case, we will interview a long-time employee of the music business—meet Joe "Mix-Remix" Quickfinger, our imaginary recording engineer/producer/former roadie, and a self-claimed recording industry expert. We should listen to Joe carefully, but at the same time not take everything for granted.

The concept

Before we unleash Joe, let's think for a second about our objectives. We need to design a data-centric solution capable of maintaining a discography, which also supports the exchange of business data between similar solutions using XML.

You might ask, why XML? XML is a well-known standard supporting both *data exchange* and *data storage*, although we'll focus on the former. XML is *humanly readable*. It can be read and written by people; its usability doesn't require any specific tools; it comes with a standard way of *enforcing the validity* of individual XML entities (namely the XML Schema); and—last but not least—the *querying language* used in the automation of XML retrieval as well as modification operations is also a standard (the XML Querying Language or XQuery). As we'll see later in this chapter, there's another benefit in using XML, but let this be enough theory for now.

> ### XML, XML Schema, XML Path Language, and XML Querying Language recommendations
>
> All these standards have been developed by the World Wide Web Consortium (or W3C), an international consortium of individuals and organizations that focuses on the development of protocols and guidelines aimed at ensuring long-term growth for the web.
>
> You can find more information on W3C at its web site: http://www.w3.org/.
>
> You can learn more about XML, XML Schema, XPath, and XQuery online:
>
> - XML (Extensible Markup Language): http://www.w3.org/XML/
> - XML Schema: http://www.w3.org/XML/Schema/
> - XML Path Language (XPath): http://www.w3.org/TR/xpath/
> - XML Query (XQuery): http://www.w3.org/XML/Query/

Joe has just had his fifth coffee and he's as ready to share his knowledge with us as he'll ever be. Because this isn't Joe Quickfinger's autobiography, I've taken the liberty of reducing the monologue to the bare essentials. Joe begins:

> The music industry isn't a business as much as it's a *big* mess, let me tell you. First of all, music is written by authors and performed by artists. Sometimes artists write their own music, and sometimes authors perform their own music themselves.
>
> Generally, artists are sociable people, and in the course of socializing they tend to form bands. A band would then consist of several artists. Some artists, on the other hand, are less sociable—they prefer to 'go solo,' but sometimes they too have to hire someone to help them perform their music.

So far we can safely say that a *Song* can be authored by one or more *Persons* and that a Person can author one or more Songs. Also, we can safely say that a *Band* is a collection of one or more Persons, and that a Person can be a member of one or more Bands. Joe continues to explain:

> In order to make a living and also be able to have some time off to socialize, the bands select one or more of their songs, record them, and publish them in the

form of an album. People in the recording business for some reason think the word song is inappropriate and the word composition is too long; therefore they call songs *tracks* instead.

Sometimes bands will invite other bands to help them put together an album. More often than that, the *producers* do a bit of "composing" on their own and end up with albums containing tracks performed by several bands and authored by several authors. Despite all this confusion, these albums aren't called *complications*.

We can safely say that a single Band can perform one or more *Tracks* and be present on one or more *Albums*, and that a single album may contain Tracks by one or more Bands.

When music was first created back in the Stone Age there weren't very many musicians, let alone bands! Nowadays, regardless of the number of musicians in it, each band is given a name. Usually the names are unique, but don't bet on it.

Each track is given a definite title, and as soon as it's ready to be put on an album it's also marked with a track number.

Albums also have titles. And we can tell when they were released, and—thanks to the devoted and sometimes psychotic fans—we can know this fact down to the very second the delivery truck reached the first store.

The information provided by Joe contains the essence of what you'd need to know about discographies in order to design a solution that could support Joe and his colleagues in their work.

We can identify individual business *entities*, the relationships that exist between them, and the attributes that describe them. And that's exactly what we need for the next step.

The logical model

To get a clear picture of all the elements that constitute the discography business case, see table 1, which shows individual business entities and facts about them.

Table 1   Entities, the facts about them, and the roles those facts play in the business case

Entity	Fact	Type of fact
Discography	Contains Albums	Relationship
Album	Consists of Tracks	Relationship
	Has a Title	Attribute
Track	Exists on Albums	Relationship
	Is authored by Persons	Relationship
	Is performed by Bands	Relationship
	Has a Title	Attribute
	Has a Track Number	Attribute

Table 1   Entities, the facts about them, and the roles those facts play in the business case *(continued)*

Entity	Fact	Type of fact
Person	Authors Tracks	Relationship
	Is in Bands	Relationship
	Has a First Name	Attribute
	Has a Middle Name	Attribute
	Has a Last Name	Attribute
Band	Performs Tracks	Relationship
	Contains Persons	Relationship
	Has a Name	Attribute
	Has an Established date/time	Attribute
	Has a Disbanded date/time	Attribute

A few words on logical modeling

Entities are intellectual concepts representing objects (things) and subjects (persons) present in a particular business; in fact, they exist at the center of the business. Everything in any business revolves around the entities. In our case, we've identified individual entities in Joe's statements.

The position of the entities in regard to the business is reflected in our summary of Joe's explanations through the *relationships* that exist between them and the *attributes* that describe them.

Put as simply as possible, a relationship can be represented by a *verb* designating an *action* or a *state* involving at least two entities. Verbs designating *ownership*, on the other hand, represent a different kind of relationship—a reference to an attribute. Relationships describe what *happens* and/or what *is* in regard to *several* entities, whereas attributes *describe* a *single* entity.

The entity-relationship schema is an essential part of the logical model, though not the only one, just like the data store in itself is not the only part of a data-centric solution. *Business logic* is the other essential part of the logical model. It defines all the data management operations needed for maintenance of the business entities. For the purposes of this chapter, we'll focus on the basic operations presented in table 2.

Table 2   Data management operations supported by our solution

Operation	Description
Create	Entity is created; the data is imported into the database.
Update	Entity is modified; the data in the database is changed.
Read	Entity is retrieved; the data is read from the database.

One particular operation isn't present in table 2: delete, the removal of entities from the database, won't be supported by our solution.

Before continuing, please take another good look at the tables.

The physical model

There may be other facts about the discography business, but for the sake of keeping this example simple, let's agree that they're not important right now.

In order to implement the logical model in our solution, we need to transform it into a physical model. This transformation is a science of its own, and is as such outside the scope of this chapter. Therefore we'll now move straight to the finished physical model, shown in figure 1.

The bold outlined boxes represent our entities along with their attributes. The arrows and the light outlined boxes represent the relationships: the *one-to-many* (for example, several Albums can have the same Title) and the *many-to-many* relationships (for example, several Persons can be members of several Bands), respectively. The callouts connected to each box list the attributes of each individual entity, and also contain other information—specifically the *constraints* that need to be implemented.

We can see that one new entity has been added to the physical model, named *Title*, and that it's referenced by both the Album as well as the Track entity. This new entity

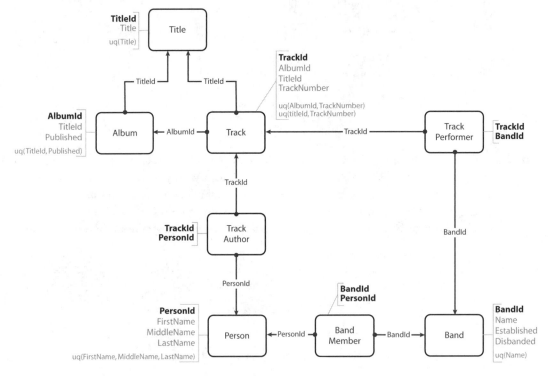

Figure 1   The physical model

is the result of a process called *normalization,* an explanation of which is also beyond the scope of this chapter. In brief, one of the objectives of *normalization* is the removal (or at least the reduction) of data redundancy. In plain English, each individual unit of information (such as an attribute or relationship) that's used in the business is only stored in a single place throughout the data model. To achieve this, we've also introduced *surrogate* keys representing each entity (the AlbumId, TrackId, PersonId, BandId, and TitleId columns or a combination thereof, shown in bold in figure 1) in addition to the *natural* keys present in the data itself—one or more columns containing values that uniquely identify each individual row in a table. (In our model, every Title is unique, and no more than one Album can be Published on the same day using the same Title.) The keys in our data model are enforced using *primary key constraints,* shown in bold, and *unique constraints,* shown in parentheses preceded by the abbreviation *uq* in figure 1. The question of surrogate keys versus natural keys is another issue that exceeds the scope of this chapter.

As you can observe from figure 1, one entity that we identified in the section "The logical model" seems to be missing from the physical model—the Discography. But is that really true? Based on the sole fact about this entity (that it "contains Albums") and the rest of the facts about the Album entity, we could define the Discography entity as the *container* of all other entities.

The database

The principal purpose of the physical model is to serve as a set of well-defined guidelines used in the development of our data store. As we can see from figure 1, no specific data store is implied, which means that we're free to decide on using any relational database management system (RDBMS). But because the RDBMS used throughout this book is Microsoft SQL Server, we'll use our data model to create a SQL Server database. Put more accurately: we'll implement the physical model of our business case in the form of a SQL Server database.

What shall we name this new database? First of all, it'll *contain* all the entities. By naming it *Discography* we could also implement the Discography entity as the container of every other entity.

One down, five to go. The data model has eight entities: five *primary* entities defined in the logical model (shown in table 1), and three *associative* entities (Track-Author, TrackPerformer, and BandMember) representing the many-to-many relationships between the primary entities.

You're welcome to design the database and the tables yourself, or use the scripts published at http://www.manning.com/SQLServerMVPDeepDives.

The XML Schema

At the beginning of this chapter, we decided on using XML as a means of transporting data to and from our database. We also mentioned the essential benefits of using XML, one of them being a standard method of enforcing the validity of our XML entities—the XML Schema. Again, the subject of XML and XML Schema exceeds the scope of this article; therefore let's emphasize one principal benefit of using the XML Schema.

In SQL Server, the XML standard is implemented as a *data type*, and because all data types typically represent (implement) a specific *(data) domain*, the purpose of the XML Schema in regards to the XML data type is to enforce its domain.

The XML Schema will provide us with a guarantee that the discography data coming in or going out of our database is valid—that it complies with the business rules.

Data domain

A data domain defines which values are allowed in a specific data element (such as a variable, a column, and so on).

For instance, a data element of a numerical type can only contain numerical data (numbers)—it can't, for instance, contain letters or punctuation marks (with the obvious exception of the decimal point). A data element of the `integer` numerical type can only contain numbers, and no other characters.

The XML data domain is similar to the two examples in the previous paragraph, but is governed by a much more complex set of rules defined by an XML Schema.

ENTITIES OF PRINCIPAL IMPORTANCE

Let's take another look at the physical model. We can see two entities that stand out as being more significant to the business compared to the rest.

The first such entity is the Album—even from Joe's narrative it should be quite clear that the Album represents a principal business entity. It contains all the information vital to the discography business: all the data about the Tracks and about the Album itself.

The other principal entity—also verifiable both in the logical and the physical models, as well as in Joe's statements—is the Band. Bands represent (at least in our particular model) the groups of Persons collectively responsible for the existence of the discography business.

This means that we'll require two XML Schemas: one to represent the Albums, and one to represent the Bands. By using two separate schemas, we'll also be able to isolate the two principal business entities (allowing independent exchange of information regarding each of them), and we'll be able to eliminate some redundancy. We'll illustrate that last statement in a minute.

Let's now implement our physical model in the form of XML Schemas. We'll be implementing the same data model as before, but this time using a different technology. See listing 1.

Listing 1   The Album XML Schema

```xml
<xs:schema
 xmlns:xs="http://www.w3.org/2001/XMLSchema"
 xmlns:ma="http://schemas.milambda.net/Music-Album"
 xmlns:m="http://schemas.milambda.net/Music"
 elementFormDefault="qualified"
 attributeFormDefault="qualified"
 targetNamespace="http://schemas.milambda.net/Music-Album">

<xs:import namespace="http://schemas.milambda.net/Music"
 ➥ schemaLocation="common.xsd"/>

<xs:element name="discography">
 <xs:complexType>
  <xs:sequence>
   <xs:element name="album" maxOccurs="unbounded">
    <xs:complexType>
     <xs:sequence>
      <xs:element name="track" maxOccurs="unbounded">
       <xs:complexType>
        <xs:sequence>
         <xs:element name="author" type="m:person" maxOccurs="unbounded"/>
         <xs:element name="band" maxOccurs="unbounded">
          <xs:complexType>
           <xs:attribute name="bandName" type="m:bandName"/>
          </xs:complexType>
         </xs:element>
        </xs:sequence>
        <xs:attribute name="title" type="m:entityTitle" use="required"/>
        <xs:attribute name="trackNumber" type="xs:integer"
            ➥ use="required"/>
       </xs:complexType>
      </xs:element>
     </xs:sequence>
     <xs:attribute name="title" type="m:entityTitle" use="required"/>
     <xs:attribute name="published" type="xs:dateTime" use="required"/>
    </xs:complexType>
   </xs:element>
  </xs:sequence>
 </xs:complexType>
</xs:element>

</xs:schema>
```

In listing 1, we can observe how our data model can be implemented as an XML Schema from the perspective of the Album entity: a Discography contains one or more Albums, which contain one or more Tracks written by one or more Authors and performed by one or more Bands.

Because we'll be using a separate XML Schema for the Band entity, we can leave out the Band Members from the Album definition, clearly eliminating unnecessary data redundancy, as shown in listing 2.

Listing 2   The Band XML Schema

```
<xs:schema
 xmlns:xs="http://www.w3.org/2001/XMLSchema"
 xmlns:mb="http://schemas.milambda.net/Music-Band"
 xmlns:m="http://schemas.milambda.net/Music"
 elementFormDefault="qualified"
 attributeFormDefault="qualified"
 targetNamespace="http://schemas.milambda.net/Music-Band">

 <xs:import namespace="http://schemas.milambda.net/Music"
    ➥ schemaLocation="common.xsd"/>

 <xs:element name="bands">
  <xs:complexType>
   <xs:sequence>
    <xs:element name="band" maxOccurs="unbounded">
     <xs:complexType>
      <xs:sequence>
       <xs:element name="member" type="m:person" maxOccurs="unbounded"/>
      </xs:sequence>
      <xs:attribute name="bandName" type="m:bandName" use="required"/>
      <xs:attribute name="established" type="xs:dateTime" use="required"/>
      <xs:attribute name="disbanded" type="xs:dateTime" use="optional"
         ➥ default="9999-12-31T00:00:00.000"/>
     </xs:complexType>
    </xs:element>
   </xs:sequence>
  </xs:complexType>
 </xs:element>

</xs:schema>
```

In listing 2 we can observe how the data model can be implemented from the perspective of the Band entity: a Discography is a collection of one or more Bands, containing one or more Members.

 This way, each individual Band entity can exist independently of any Album entity, but the consistency of the Discography as a whole remains intact as long as each Album entity references the appropriate Band entity (or entities).
In listings 1 and 2 we can observe that both XML Schemas *import* a third one. This is due to yet another simplification, based on the fact that both the Album and the Band

A few comments on the structure of the XML Schemas

The entities are implemented as *XML elements*. Their attributes are implemented as *XML attributes* of the XML element implementing the corresponding entity.

The relationships between the entities are implemented in the *structuring* of the XML, and the *nesting* of XML elements. For example, following the logical model rule, which states that the Discography entity *contains* Album entities, the Album element is placed inside the Discography element, and because an Album entity contains Track entities, the latter are represented by elements nested inside the Album element.

XML Schemas use a shared collection of *types*. These shared types are defined in the Common XML Schema, shown in listing 3.

For instance, the Person entity is present in the Album XML as well as the Band XML; therefore both can use the same type for the Person entity, rather than explicitly implementing two separate types with the same set of properties.

Listing 3   Common XML Schema

```
<xs:schema
 xmlns:xs="http://www.w3.org/2001/XMLSchema"
 xmlns:m="http://schemas.milambda.net/Music"
 elementFormDefault="qualified"
 attributeFormDefault="qualified"
 targetNamespace="http://schemas.milambda.net/Music">

<xs:simpleType name="personName">
 <xs:restriction base="xs:string">
  <xs:maxLength value="150"/>
 </xs:restriction>
</xs:simpleType>

<xs:simpleType name="bandName">
 <xs:restriction base="xs:string">
  <xs:minLength value="1"/>
  <xs:maxLength value="450"/>
 </xs:restriction>
</xs:simpleType>

<xs:simpleType name="entityTitle">
 <xs:restriction base="xs:string">
  <xs:minLength value="1"/>
  <xs:maxLength value="450"/>
 </xs:restriction>
</xs:simpleType>

<xs:complexType name="person">
 <xs:attribute name="firstName" use="required">
  <xs:simpleType>
   <xs:restriction base="m:personName">
    <xs:minLength value="1"/>
   </xs:restriction>
  </xs:simpleType>
 </xs:attribute>
 <xs:attribute name="middleName" type="m:personName" use="required"/>
 <xs:attribute name="lastName" type="m:personName" use="required"/>
</xs:complexType>

</xs:schema>
```

Now, if you want to see an example of the amount of redundancy eliminated because we chose to separate the two principal entities and implemented two XML Schemas instead of one, look at the XML examples containing partial discography data of two well-known rock bands published at http://www.manning.com/SQLServerMVPDeep Dives (both XML Schemas are also located there).

Enabling and maintaining the data flow

After implementing the data store part of the data model, we can now focus on the operational part of the logical model. We mentioned three data management operations that will be supported by our solution: entity creation, entity modification, and entity retrieval.

Regarding their relationship to the data flow, we can divide the supported data management operations into two groups:

- *Inbound operations*—Govern the flow of data into the database. *Create* and *Update* are both inbound operations;
- *Outbound operations*—Govern the flow of data out of the database. *Read* is the outbound operation.

With inbound operations, our objective should be clear. We'll have to

- Extract the data from the XML source.
- Insert the data into the data store that doesn't yet exist there.
- Update data that already exists in the data store to reflect the data extracted from the source.

With outbound operations, the objective is to

- Read the data from the database and return it in XML format.

Preparing the inbound data flow

Before we begin coding, we must consider all the relevant facts about the XML sources used in our solution.

Both XML Schemas allow the XML to contain more than one entity. The related entities are nested in the source, which reflects the relationships between them. Not only must we extract the entities from the XML source, but we also have to do this in the correct order.

How do we determine the correct order? By reviewing the physical model, shown in figure 1, the *dependency* of individual sets of data can be observed (follow the arrows and identify where they all point to). When importing the data into the database, we should start with the *independent* entities and finish with *dependent* ones.

This is a valid order of inbound operations for the Album XML Schema:

1. Title (doesn't depend on any other entity)
2. Album (depends on Title)
3. Track (depends on Title and Album)
4. Person (doesn't depend on any other entity)
5. Track Author (depends on Person and Track)
6. Band (doesn't depend on any other Entity)
7. Track Performer (depends on Band and Track)

This is a valid order of inbound operations for the Band XML Schema:

1 Band (doesn't depend on any other entity)

2 Person (doesn't depend on any other entity)

3 Band Member (depends on Person and Band)

EXTRACTING DATA FROM XML USING TRANSACT-SQL

You can choose from three data retrieval methods implemented in SQL Server 2005 and SQL Server 2008, and all the details regarding them are available in Books Online. In this chapter, we only need to know the bare essentials about these methods:

- The purpose of the `value()` method is to extract the value from a single XML data element (a *singleton*) and return it in the designated data type. We'll use this method to extract the values from the XML nodes.

- The purpose of the `query()` method is to read data from one or more XML *nodes* and return a sequence of XML data elements or a single XML data element. The `query()` method can also be used to *create* XML data, but in this chapter we'll only use it to retrieve data. The return type of the `query()` method is XML. We'll use this method to specify the target of the extraction operation and to transform the source data if needed.

- The purpose of the `nodes()` method is to read data from an XML entity and return a set of XML *nodes*. This method returns a row of XML data for each node in the XML entity that corresponds to the given criteria. We'll use this method to retrieve the data from the XML source in the form of a dataset representing a single entity or a single relationship between our entities.

The execution of all three methods is governed through an *XQuery statement* or an *XPath expression* passed to each of the methods as an argument. A detailed explanation of XQuery and XPath expressions is once again outside the scope of this chapter, but a brief version of the explanation is presented in the sidebar, "A few words on XPath expressions and XQuery statements."

A few words on XPath expressions and XQuery statements

The *XPath expression* is the principal expression used in retrieving data from XML entities. It guides the *XML processor* as it traverses the XML entity toward the targets containing the data that you want to extract.

For example, the `/orders/order/orderDate` XPath expression points to all elements named `orderDate` that exist inside elements named `order`, which in turn exist inside the element named `orders`, which exists at the root of the XML entity.

We could compare the XPath expression with the `FROM` clause of a Transact-SQL (T-SQL) query.

An XPath expression can be extended with an *XPath predicate*, the purpose of which is to restrict the traversal of the XML entity even further.

A few words on XPath expressions and XQuery statements *(continued)*

For example, the `/orders/order/orderDate[. > 20080101]` XPath expression contains an XPath predicate (enclosed in square brackets) restricting the XPath expression to point to only those elements named `orderDate` that contain values greater than 20080101.

We could compare the XPath predicate with the `WHERE` clause of a T-SQL query.

Compared to the XPath expression, the *XQuery statement* provides additional functionality needed in extracting the data from XML entities and transforming it. An XQuery statement can also be used to write XML data. One or more XPath expressions are used in every XQuery statement.

In this chapter, no data management operations against XML entities will require any knowledge of XQuery.

In table 3, we can see the XPath expressions pointing to individual entities of the Album XML Schema, and in table 4 we can see the XPath expressions pointing to individual entities of the Band XML Schema.

Table 3   XPath expressions used to extract the entities from the Album XML

Entity	XPath expression
Title	`/ma:discography/ma:album` `/ma:discography/ma:album/ma:track`
Album	`/ma:discography/ma:album`
Track	`/ma:discography/ma:album/ma:track`
Person	`/ma:discography/ma:album/ma:track/ma:author`
Band	`/ma:discography/ma:album/ma:track/ma:band`

Note that in tables 3 and 4, the names of the elements are prefixed with a reference to the respective XML namespace implemented by each XML Schema. You can observe all of the XML namespace declarations in listings 1 through 3. The namespaces are declared in the `xmlns` attributes of the root (`schema`) element of each XML Schema. Each XML Schema also targets a specific XML namespace, as declared in the `target-Namespace` attribute of the `schema` element. This specifies the namespace of the XML entity in which a particular XML Schema is used.

Table 4   XPath expressions used to extract the entities from the Band XML

Entity	XPath expression
Band	`/mb:bands/mb:band`
Person	`/mb:bands/mb:band/mb:member`

A few words about XML namespaces

First of all, the subject of XML namespaces exceeds the scope of this chapter. But what you should know about XML namespaces in order to understand their role in these examples is that they represent the business domain in which a particular XML entity exists.

In our examples, we've introduced three XML namespaces: one for Album data, another for Band data, and a third to represent a shared domain used both by the Album and the Band domains.

Think about it: does an Album represent the same business entity as a Band? No, absolutely not! Therefore, if we've decided on using XML to represent each of them, we need a way to distinguish between them, and this is where XML namespaces come in.

An XML entity that exists in the Album namespace can't be mistaken for an XML entity that exists in the Band namespace, although they're both represented as XML. In plain English: an Album can't be a Band and a Band can't be an Album.

Microsoft SQL Server 2005 and later versions support XML namespaces and introduces two methods used to declare them using T-SQL. Throughout this chapter we'll be using the `WITH XMLNAMESPACES` clause to declare XML namespaces that will be used in XPath expressions. All the details regarding XML namespaces in SQL Server and the `WITH XMLNAMESPACES` clause can be found in Books Online.

General information regarding XML namespaces can also be found online: http://www.w3.org/TR/xml-names/.

Importing the data

Using the XPath expressions listed in tables 3 and 4, we can prepare individual T-SQL SELECT statements used to extract the data from the XML source. In these SELECT statements, we'll use the XML retrieval methods mentioned earlier, and in the final definition of the query, we'll include them in INSERT statements that will be used to import the data extracted from the XML source into the corresponding tables of our Discography database.

Note that in the INSERT statements, we'll also have to prevent certain constraint violations—most of all, we'll need to prevent the import of data that already exists in the database.

EXTRACTING ALBUM DATA

The source of the Album data is an XML entity based on the Album XML Schema shown in listing 1 earlier in this chapter. This XML Schema provides the structure to hold the data for the Title, Album, and Person entities, including data for the Track Author and Track Performer associative entities.

All the details regarding XPath functions implemented in SQL Server are available in the Books Online article titled "XQuery Functions against the xml Data Type."

In the following examples, `@xml` designates a variable of the XML type holding the XML data in question. First off, listing 4 shows the code to extract the titles.

Listing 4   Extracting the titles

```
with    xmlnamespaces
        (
        'http://www.w3.org/2001/XMLSchema-instance' as xsi
        ,'http://schemas.milambda.net/Music' as m
        ,'http://schemas.milambda.net/Music-Album' as ma
        )
select  Discography.Album.query
                ('
                data(@ma:title)
                ').value
                    (
                    '.'
                    ,'nvarchar(450)'
                    ) as Title
        from    @xml.nodes
                    ('
                    /ma:discography/ma:album
                    ') Discography (Album)
union
select  Discography.Track.query
                ('
                data(@ma:title)
                ').value
                    (
                    '.'
                    ,'nvarchar(450)'
                    )
        from    @xml.nodes
                    ('
                    /ma:discography/ma:album/ma:track
                    ') Discography (Track)
```

The Title entity contains both the Album and the Track titles. Because in SQL Server 2005 it's not possible to specify a *union* XPath expression, the two sets must be merged into one using the T-SQL UNION clause.

Using the union XPath expression, the query could be simplified as shown in listing 5.

Listing 5   Simplified query with union XPath expression

```
with    xmlnamespaces
        (
        'http://www.w3.org/2001/XMLSchema-instance' as xsi
        ,'http://schemas.milambda.net/Music' as m
        ,'http://schemas.milambda.net/Music-Album' as ma
        )
select  Discography.Album.query
                ('
```

```
                    data(@ma:title)
                    ').value
                        (
                        '.'
                        ,'nvarchar(450)'
                        ) as Title
        from    @xml.nodes
                        ('
                        /ma:discography/ma:album
                        |
                        /ma:discography/ma:album/ma:track
                        ') Discography (Album)
```

Next up, listing 6 shows the code to extract the albums.

Listing 6   Extracting the albums

```
with    xmlnamespaces
        (
        'http://www.w3.org/2001/XMLSchema-instance' as xsi
        ,'http://schemas.milambda.net/Music' as m
        ,'http://schemas.milambda.net/Music-Album' as ma
        )
select  Discography.Album.query
                ('
                data(@ma:title)
                ').value
                        (
                        '.'
                        ,'nvarchar(450)'
                        ) as Title
        ,Discography.Album.query
                ('
                data(@ma:published)
                ').value
                        (
                        '.'
                        ,'datetime'
                        ) as Published
        from    @xml.nodes
                        ('
                        /ma:discography/ma:album
                        ') Discography (Album)
```

Listing 7 shows the code to extract the tracks.

Listing 7   Extracting the tracks

```
with    xmlnamespaces
        (
        'http://www.w3.org/2001/XMLSchema-instance' as xsi
        ,'http://schemas.milambda.net/Music' as m
        ,'http://schemas.milambda.net/Music-Album' as ma
        )
select  Discography.Track.query
```

```
                       ('
                       data(@ma:title)
                       ').value
                               (
                               '.'
                               ,'nvarchar(450)'
                               ) as TrackTitle
          ,Discography.Track.query
                       ('
                       data(@ma:trackNumber)
                       ').value
                               (
                               '.'
                               ,'int'
                               ) as TrackNumber
          ,Discography.Track.query
                       ('
                       data(parent::ma:album/@ma:title)
                       ').value
                               (
                               '.'
                               ,'nvarchar(450)'
                               ) as AlbumTitle
          ,Discography.Track.query
                       ('
                       data(parent::ma:album/@ma:published)
                       ').value
                               (
                               '.'
                               ,'datetime'
                               ) as Published
          from    @xml.nodes
                               ('
                               /ma:discography/ma:album/ma:track
                               ') Discography (Track)
```

Listing 8 shows the code to extract the persons.

Listing 8   Extracting the persons

```
with    xmlnamespaces
        (
        'http://www.w3.org/2001/XMLSchema-instance' as xsi
        ,'http://schemas.milambda.net/Music' as m
        ,'http://schemas.milambda.net/Music-Album' as ma
        )
select  distinct
        Discography.Person.query
                ('
                data(@m:firstName)
                ').value
                        (
                        '.'
                        ,'nvarchar(150)'
                        ) as FirstName
```

```
,Discography.Person.query
        ('
        data(@m:middleName)
        ').value
                (
                '.'
                ,'nvarchar(150)'
                ) as MiddleName
,Discography.Person.query
        ('
        data(@m:lastName)
        ').value
                (
                '.'
                ,'nvarchar(150)'
                ) as LastName
from    @xml.nodes
                ('
                /ma:discography/ma:album/ma:track/ma:author
                ') Discography (Person)
```

Listing 9 shows the code to extract the bands.

Listing 9   Extracting the bands

```
with    xmlnamespaces
        (
        'http://www.w3.org/2001/XMLSchema-instance' as xsi
        ,'http://schemas.milambda.net/Music' as m
        ,'http://schemas.milambda.net/Music-Album' as ma
        )
select  distinct
        Discography.Band.query
                ('
                data(@ma:bandName)
                ').value
                        (
                        '.'
                        ,'nvarchar(450)'
                        ) as [Name]
        from    @xml.nodes
                        ('
                        /ma:discography/ma:album/ma:track/ma:band
                        ') Discography (Band)
```

EXTRACTING BAND DATA

The source of the Band data is an XML entity based on the Band XML Schema shown in listing 2 earlier in this chapter. This XML Schema provides all the data for the Band and Person entities, including the data for the Band Member associative entity.

Compare the XML namespace declarations in listing 10 with the declaration in the code listings presented earlier. Is there something different? Why?

Listing 10   Extracting the bands

```
with    xmlnamespaces
        (
        'http://www.w3.org/2001/XMLSchema-instance' as xsi
        ,'http://schemas.milambda.net/Music' as m
        ,'http://schemas.milambda.net/Music-Band' as mb
        )
select  distinct
        Bands.Band.query
                ('
                data(@mb:bandName)
                ').value
                        (
                        '.'
                        ,'nvarchar(450)'
                        ) as [Name]
        ,nullif(Bands.Band.query
                ('
                data(@mb:established)
                ').value
                        (
                        '.'
                        ,'datetime'
                        ), N'') as Established
        ,nullif(Bands.Band.query
                ('
                data(@mb:disbanded)
                ').value
                        (
                        '.'
                        ,'datetime'
                        ), cast(N'99991231' as datetime)) as Disbanded
        from    @xml.nodes
                        ('
                        /mb:bands/mb:band
                        ') Bands (Band)
```

Listing 11 shows the code to extract the persons.

Listing 11   Extracting the persons

```
with    xmlnamespaces
        (
        'http://www.w3.org/2001/XMLSchema-instance' as xsi
        ,'http://schemas.milambda.net/Music' as m
        ,'http://schemas.milambda.net/Music-Band' as mb
        )
select  distinct
        Bands.Band.query
                ('
                data(@mb:bandName)
                ').value
                        (
                        '.'
```

```
                            ,'nvarchar(450)'
                            ) as [Name]
          ,nullif(Bands.Band.query
                    ('
                    data(@mb:established)
                    ').value
                            (
                            '.'
                            ,'datetime'
                            ), N'') as Established
          ,nullif(Bands.Band.query
                    ('
                    data(@mb:disbanded)
                    ').value
                            (
                            '.'
                            ,'datetime'
                            ), N'') as Disbanded
          from      @xml.nodes
                            ('
                            /mb:bands/mb:band
                            ') Bands (Band)
```

By combining the queries listed previously into a workflow of data management operations, we can design two SQL procedures, each with a specific purpose based on the
two principal business entities mentioned in the section "The XML Schema": one procedure to save the Album data and one procedure to save the Band data.

TIP   Here's a beginner's trick for memorizing XML retrieval methods: *Nodes*
provide the set, *query* retrieves the data element, and *value* extracts the
data.

We haven't discussed one important issue yet—the question of associative entities. As
you may have observed in our examples, only the primary entities are listed. Why is
that? The answer is simple: associative entities, representing the many-to-many relationships between the primary entities, can be retrieved from the XML source by combining the queries used in retrieving the data of the individual primary entities of a
particular relationship. The combinations are listed in table 5.

Table 5   Retrieving the associative entities

Associative entity	Provided by combining these primary entities
Track Author	Track joined with Person—based on the nesting of the Author XML ele-ment inside the Track XML element of the Album XML
Track Performer	Track joined with Band—based on the nesting of the Band XML ele-ment inside the Track XML element of the Album XML
Band Member	Band joined with Person—based on the nesting of the Person XML ele-ment inside the Band XML element of the Band XML

Similarly, the one-to-many relationships between primary entities can be retrieved:

- A Track is related to the corresponding Album based on the nesting of the Track XML element inside the Album XML element.
- A Track is related to a Title based on the value of the Title XML attribute of the Track XML element.
- An Album is related to a Title based on the value of the Title XML attribute of the Album XML element.

The scripts containing the definitions of the two procedures can be downloaded from http://www.manning.com/SQLServerMVPDeepDives.

You should study both definitions thoroughly before creating and/or attempting to use the procedures.

Note that in both procedures, table variables are used as temporary storage, which provides the primary keys (based on IDENTITY columns) needed for preserving referential integrity in the Discography database. The dependency of individual business entities was mentioned in the section "Preparing the inbound data flow."

In both procedures, in the INSERT statements used to import the data into the tables of the Discography database, observe the methods used to prevent the unique and primary key constraint violations.

In brief, this is the operational flow used in both procedures:

1 From the XML source, extract the data that represents each primary entity (in the order mentioned in the section "Preparing the inbound data flow").
2 Insert the data into the database table, but exclude rows that already exist at the destination (using the EXCEPT clause or the NOT EXISTS predicate).
3 Save the data of each primary entity in a table variable, including the surrogate key values that the rows received when they were inserted into the database table.
4 After both primary entities of a particular one-to-many relationship have been inserted and temporarily saved in the corresponding table variables, insert the data representing these relationships to the associative database tables.
5 After all the data has been extracted and all primary and associative entities have been inserted, the process finishes.

After you've carefully studied both stored procedures and have identified all the concepts presented in this chapter, prepare a T-SQL script to import the XML samples. Execute the script in steps: one XML file at a time, observe the progress, and inspect the tables of the Discography database after each step of the script has finished.

A sample script can also be downloaded from http://www.manning.com/SQLServerMVPDeepDives.

Exporting the data

To provide the outbound data flow, we pretty much have to do the opposite of what we achieved in the previous section: extract the data from the database and return it as XML.

In the data export, we'll also implement both XML Schemas designed earlier; therefore we'll need two retrieval procedures—one for the Album data and another for the Band data.

You should study the following two queries carefully in order to understand how the FOR XML clauses using the PATH declaration instruct the database engine to construct the XML entity. You can find all the details regarding the FOR XML clause in Books Online.

Let's start with the simpler of the two queries. As we defined earlier in this chapter, a Discography contains one or more Bands containing one or more Members. In the Band XML Schema, the relationship between the Band and the Person entities is implemented in form of XML elements representing the Band Members nested inside the XML element representing each individual Band.

In listing 12, you can observe how the FOR XML query used to retrieve the Person entity data is nested inside the FOR XML query used to retrieve the Band entity data. The result from the nested query is exposed as a column in the outer query, and the name of this column is specified in the PATH declaration of the inner query's FOR XML clause (in our example, mb:member).

Listing 12　To export the Band data from the database

```
with    xmlnamespaces
        (
        'http://www.w3.org/2001/XMLSchema-instance' as xsi
        ,'http://schemas.milambda.net/Music' as m
        ,'http://schemas.milambda.net/Music-Band' as mb
        )
select  Music.Band.Name as [@mb:bandName]
        ,Music.Band.Established as [@mb:established]
        ,Music.Band.Disbanded as [@mb:disbanded]
        ,(
        select  Music.Person.FirstName as [@m:firstName]
                ,Music.Person.MiddleName as [@m:middleName]
                ,Music.Person.LastName as [@m:lastName]
                from    Music.Person
                        inner join      Music.BandMember
                                on      Music.BandMember.PersonId =
                                ➡ Music.Person.PersonId
                where   (Music.BandMember.BandId = Music.Band.BandId)
                order by        Music.Person.LastName
                                ,Music.Person.FirstName
                                ,Music.Person.MiddleName
                for xml path('mb:member'), type
        )
        from    Music.Band
        order by        Music.Band.Name
        for xml path('mb:band'), root('mb:bands'), type
```

The proper nesting of the data (namely, that the Band contains the correct Members) is achieved by correctly referencing the Band Member associative entity, where the many-to-many relationships between the Bands and the Persons are stored.

The outer query also uses a PATH declaration specifying the XML node (mb:band) together with the ROOT declaration specifying the name of the XML root node.

The TYPE declaration is used to instruct the database engine to return the resultset as XML data rather than character data, which is the default (if the TYPE declaration is omitted).

Once again, we began the T-SQL query with the XML namespaces declaration, providing us with all the necessary namespaces implemented by the corresponding Band XML Schema.

The first thing that should be apparent from listing 13 is the added complexity resulting from the deeper nesting of the Album XML entity. Remember how we defined the Album XML Schema: a Discography contains one or more Albums containing one or more Tracks written by one or more Authors and performed by one or more Bands.

Listing 13   To export the Album data from the database

```
with     xmlnamespaces
         (
         'http://www.w3.org/2001/XMLSchema-instance' as xsi
         ,'http://schemas.milambda.net/Music' as m
         ,'http://schemas.milambda.net/Music-Album' as ma
         )
select   Music.Title.Title as [@ma:title]
         ,Music.Album.Published as [@ma:published]
         ,(
         select  Music.Title.Title as [@ma:title]
                 ,Music.Track.TrackNumber as [@ma:trackNumber]
                 ,(
                 select  Music.Person.FirstName as [@m:firstName]
                         ,Music.Person.MiddleName as [@m:middleName]
                         ,Music.Person.LastName as [@m:lastName]
                         from     Music.Person
                                  inner join      Music.TrackAuthor
                                                  on
                         ➥ Music.TrackAuthor.PersonId = Music.Person.PersonId
                         where    (Music.TrackAuthor.TrackId =
                         ➥ Music.Track.TrackId)
                         order by         Music.Person.LastName
                                          ,Music.Person.FirstName
                                          ,Music.Person.MiddleName
                         for xml path('ma:author'), type
                 )
                 ,(
                 select  Music.Band.Name as [@ma:bandName]
                         from     Music.Band
                                  inner join      Music.TrackPerformer
                                                  on
                         ➥ Music.TrackPerformer.BandId = Music.Band.BandId
```

```
                    where    (Music.TrackPerformer.TrackId =
                    ⇒ Music.Track.TrackId)
                    order by        Music.Band.Name
                    for xml path('ma:band'), type
            )
            from     Music.Title
                     inner join      Music.Track
                                on       Music.Track.TitleId =
                                ⇒ Music.Title.TitleId
            where    (Music.Track.AlbumId = Music.Album.AlbumId)
            order by        Music.Track.TrackNumber
            for xml path('ma:track'), type
    )
    from     Music.Title
             inner join      Music.Album
                        on       Music.Album.TitleId =
                        ⇒ Music.Title.TitleId
    order by        Music.Album.Published
    for xml path('ma:album'), root('ma:discography'), type
```

The queries to retrieve Person and Band data are nested inside the outer query used to retrieve Track data, which is nested inside the outermost query used to retrieve Album data. The result of each inner query is exposed to the outer query as a column of the outer query's resultset, and its name is specified by the inner query's PATH declaration of the FOR XML clause.

The outermost query also uses the PATH declaration specifying the destination XML node and the ROOT declaration specifying the root node of the destination XML entity.

The XML namespaces declaration at the beginning of the query provides all the necessary namespaces implemented by the corresponding Album XML Schema.

The queries presented in listings 11 and 12 are used in two SQL procedures, the definitions of which can be downloaded from http://www.manning.com/SQLServer-MVPDeepDives.

Review both procedures carefully before creating them in the Discography database. Pay attention to the optional input parameters used by the procedures, and how they're used in the queries to restrict the resultset.

Can you predict what would happen if the parameters weren't specified when using the procedures to retrieve data?

Preparing the sample data

As the development of a client application to create and edit XML data is outside the scope of this chapter, you could resort to a generic solution such as Microsoft Info-Path, or design a custom application implementing the functionalities provided in this chapter, or even use a text editor to create XML data.

InfoPath, for instance, provides a fairly simple way of designing forms based on sample XML data or on an XML Schema, such as the two schemas used in this chapter.

In fact, the samples published to http://www.manning.com/SQLServerMVPDeep Dives have been created using two InfoPath forms based on the Album and the Band XML Schemas. These forms can also be downloaded from http://www.manning.com/ SQLServerMVPDeepDives.

Homework

Even though this chapter spans several diverse subjects, it's not as diverse as the reality it tries to imitate. We left a few gaps; for one, we haven't considered all the facts about the discography business that can be observed in reality.

Here are some things you could do to improve this solution:

1 Create additional sample data:
   - Use the editor of your choice to add data to the sample XML entities.
   - Design InfoPath forms based on the XML Schemas designed in this chapter.
   - Design a custom client application implementing the XML Schemas and SQL procedures designed in this chapter.
2 Extend the entities with additional attributes:
   - Track Duration.
   - Album Description.
   - Lyrics.
3 Think about other facts about discographies:
   - Tracks aren't performed by Bands; they're performed by Musicians. Sometimes, Bands hire additional Musicians who aren't Band Members to help them record.
   - Musicians play (different) Instruments and perform in different Roles as Band Members.
   - Persons *join* the Band at some time, and they can also *leave* the Band at some time. They can even join and leave a Band more than once.
   - More people are involved in making an Album than Authors and Artists.
   - Bands can share a Name, yet Bands with the same name rarely share their Origin.
4 Think about data management as presented in this chapter and data management in general:
   - Could the existing processes be optimized?
   - Could the error handling in the procedures be improved in any way?
   - What would be needed to support all data management operations (such as including Delete)?
   - What other possibilities in terms of data analysis does the data model provide?
5 Think about other possibilities of retrieving Album and/or Band data as XML corresponding to the appropriate XML Schema.

Summary

We took a real-life business and analyzed it, and interviewed an (imaginary) expert in the business and summarized his responses. We then collected all the facts and used them to design the logical model of the forthcoming software solution.

After applying a bit of good old normalization "magic," we transformed the logical model into a physical model that we could then implement in the form of a SQL Server database, and also in the form of two XML Schemas.

The Discography database will serve as *permanent storage* for our discography data, and the schema-governed XML will serve as *temporary storage* and provide a way of transporting the data in and out of the permanent data store.

We've seen examples of the XML retrieval functionalities provided in Microsoft SQL Server's T-SQL language. Essential information was provided regarding the XML standard, the XML Schema, the XML Query (or XQuery), the XPath expression and XPath predicates, and last but not least, the XML namespaces. This essential information provides a first step into the world of XML, and shows ways of bridging the gap between the world of XML and the world of SQL, using SQL Server 2005 or later.

About the author

Matija Lah graduated at the Faculty of Law at the University of Maribor, Slovenia, in 1999. As a lawyer with extensive experience in IT, in 2001 he joined IUS SOFTWARE d.o.o., the leading provider of legal information in Slovenia, where he first came into contact with Microsoft SQL Server. In 2005, he decided to pursue a career as a freelance consultant in the domain of general, business, and legal information. In 2006 this led him to join AI-in-Law Future Technologies, Inc., a company that applies artificial intelligence to the legal information domain. Based on his continuous contributions to the SQL community, Microsoft gave him the Most Valuable Professional award for SQL Server in 2007.

13 Full-text searching

Robert C. Cain

Search is everywhere. In addition to the powerful search engines available to us, it seems like every website we visit has a search box for searching within that site. Wouldn't it be great to incorporate search within your applications? Fortunately, SQL Server provides a powerful text search engine that's as easy to use as one-two-three!

Foundations of full-text searching

Before we begin the step-by-step process of creating and using full-text indexes, there are a few fundamentals that you'll need to understand. Full-text search isn't a fancy way of doing a `LIKE` search with SQL. Instead, every word is placed into a special type of index called a *full-text index*. These indexes are organized and stored in full-text catalogs, which act as containers to organize our indexes.

Each word in a full-text index also includes a unique key for that record. You should note that in order to full-text index a table, SQL Server requires the table to have a unique, single-column key. This single-column key is used as part of the ranking functions we'll cover later in this chapter.

All of the text-based data types are eligible for full-text searching. The complete list is `char`, `nchar`, `varchar`, `nvarchar`, `text`, `ntext`, `xml`, `image`, and `varbinary(max)`. According to online documentation from Microsoft, `text`, `ntext`, and `image` data types will be deprecated in future versions of SQL Server, so I suggest avoiding these if you can.

`Char`, `nchar`, `varchar`, and `nvarchar` all make sense as candidates for full-text indexing. XML also makes sense, because it's text based, but adds the advantage that markup tags are ignored—only the data is full-text indexed. The data type that might have you scratching your head is `varbinary(max)`. To understand this, we have to briefly delve into the history of the full-text engine.

The code base for the full-text search engine included with SQL Server descended from a product called *Microsoft Index Server*. With it, you could index various document types stored on your server, be it a Windows NT 4.0 server or IIS

(Internet Information Server). The ability to look inside documents and index their content was retained and lives on in SQL Server's full-text search engine.

SQL Server allows you to store various types of unstructured documents, such as Microsoft Word, Excel, and many others inside a `varbinary(max)` field. If the full-text engine recognizes the type of document stored in a `varbinary(max)` field, it'll open the document and index all words contained in the document.

We're almost ready to dig into some code, but before we do, you should note that all of the examples in this chapter use the AdventureWorks2008 database. This is freely available from Microsoft's CodePlex site. As of this writing, you can find AdventureWorks at http://www.codeplex.com/MSFTDBProdSamples/Release/ ProjectReleases.aspx.

Creating and maintaining catalogs

The "one" in our one-two-three concerns the catalog. The catalog is a logical container to hold a group of one or more full-text indexes. Creating a catalog is fairly straightforward. Let's look at the basic statement to create one (for a complete syntax diagram, refer to the SQL Server Books On Line):

```
CREATE FULLTEXT CATALOG AdventureWorksFTC
AS DEFAULT;
```

First, note that you'll want to supply the name of your catalog in place of `Adventure-WorksFTC`. If you only have one full-text catalog for your database, I suggest using the same name as the database followed by *FTC* (for *full-text catalog*), as in the example.

The optional `AS DEFAULT` tells SQL Server to use this particular catalog as the default for all full-text commands if no catalog is specified. It's a good idea to specify at least one catalog as the default, and if you only have one, you definitely want to add this to the statement.

That's all there is to it; you now have an empty catalog waiting for your indexes. Before we start loading it with full-text indexes, though, let's take a moment to look at a few commands available for maintaining the catalog.

The first two are similar to each other, in that they update all of the indexes in the catalog, but they do it in quite different ways. The first is the `REBUILD` command.

```
ALTER FULLTEXT CATALOG AdventureWorksFTC REBUILD;
```

This will go through each index and rebuild it from the source tables. It's the fastest, most efficient way to rebuild an entire catalog, but it has the side effect of taking the catalog offline—your catalog won't be available for your users to do any full-text searching. If your operation is a 9-to-5 shop and you're doing a rebuild during off hours, then `REBUILD` is the way to go. But what if your operation runs 24 hours a day?

For those situations, we have the `REORGANIZE` command:

```
ALTER FULLTEXT CATALOG AdventureWorksFTC REORGANIZE;
```

The `REORGANIZE` command will rebuild all indexes, without taking the catalog offline. Your users will still be able to use and query the catalog normally. The downside is that this is a lot slower than doing a rebuild.

Fortunately, doing either a rebuild or a reorganize to your catalog is fairly rare. The most likely call for this is during database updates that span the majority of tables in the database. When making mass updates, you may find a significant speed increase by turning off full-text indexing (using techniques later in this chapter), doing the updates, turning indexing back on, and then rebuilding/reorganizing the entire catalog.

The final command is quite simple: it sets a catalog to be the new default catalog.

```
ALTER FULLTEXT CATALOG AdventureWorksFTC AS DEFAULT;
```

Like the previous commands, this isn't something you'll use often. Perhaps in a long script, you may want to change the default catalog temporarily to make your coding easier.

Creating and maintaining full-text indexes

Now that the catalog exists, we're ready to create indexes to put in it. In this section, we'll see not only how to create a full-text index, but how to maintain it.

Creating the full-text index

The second step in our one-two-three process is to create a full-text index. In the AdventureWorks database is a table called Production.ProductDescription. Full-text searching through product descriptions seems like a logical thing users would want to do, so we'll use this table. The next piece of information we need to know is what columns to search on. If you examine the table in SQL Server Management Studio, you'll see it only has one column that's eligible for full-text searching: Description. The final thing we need to know is the name of the unique index. Expanding the Keys branch in Management Studio shows us one key, named PK_ProductDescription_Product-DescriptionID. Armed with this information, we can now issue the command to create our full-text index on this table:

```
CREATE FULLTEXT INDEX ON Production.ProductDescription
([Description])
KEY INDEX PK_ProductDescription_ProductDescriptionID
ON AdventureWorksFTC
WITH CHANGE_TRACKING AUTO;
```

We start by issuing CREATE FULLTEXT INDEX ON XXX (replacing XXX with the name of the table we want to index). Note something interesting, though: at no point do we give the full-text index a name. With full-text indexing, each table is allowed to have one and only one full-text index. Because of this, SQL Server takes care of creating a unique index name for us, allowing us to refer to it by the table name.

The single full-text index per table isn't the limitation it might seem at first, because you can have as many columns as you want in the index, as line two of the preceding code shows. List each column in parentheses, separated by commas. You can also add and remove columns later, as we'll see momentarily.

The next line, KEY INDEX, asks you to specify the unique index for your table. This will typically be your primary key index. The important thing is that it be a single-column, non-nullable unique index. SQL Server requires this in order to perform its ranking functions, discussed later in this chapter.

The fourth line, `ON AdventureWorksFTC`, is optional if you have AdventureWorks as your default catalog. If you omit it, the full-text index will be placed into the default catalog. If you have multiple catalogs for your system, you can add the catalog name in order to place your new full-text index in a catalog other than the default.

The next line, `WITH CHANGE_TRACKING`, is probably the most important line in the statement. It defines how SQL Server will manage your full-text index; therefore, understanding the options is key to understanding how your index will get updated. The `AUTO` option is the most straightforward, so we'll tackle it first.

With `AUTO`, every time a row in your table is updated, SQL Server will update the full-text index associated with that table. This is by far the easiest way to manage your full-text indexes, but it can cause performance penalties if your table has a large number of updates in a short time span. I'd like to give you a more definitive statement than "large," but it depends on a variety of variables. How beefy is your server? How much RAM is installed? What's the speed of the disks? And is the catalog on the same drive as the database or a different one? All of these come into play; my best advice is to set up your index in a test environment with the change tracking set to `AUTO`, and then test with a load that simulates your production environment. If you can measure an unacceptable decrease in performance, you can instead set change tracking to `MANUAL`.

With `MANUAL` change tracking, each time a row is updated in your table, SQL Server sets an internal flag that marks that row as having been updated—but no action is taken to update your full-text index. To update the full-text index, you must issue an `ALTER` command, which we'll cover in detail shortly. This method is much more efficient and faster than using `AUTO`. It does have a downside, though, in that there's a time delay. You have to set up a job using SQL Server's job agent to issue the `ALTER` command at a frequency acceptable to your users. Thus, there will be some time delay between when a user updates a record in a table and when that data is available to be full-text searched on. For tables with large numbers of updates, `MANUAL` is definitely the preferred method.

The last option, `OFF`, will create the full-text index and populate it, but then cause no further updates to the index to be exercised. It won't track changes to the table, as with manual mode, nor will it set up the index to be automatically updated. `OFF` mode would be useful with static tables—tables where you don't plan on doing updates. Perhaps these are lookup tables, or they're tables from a legacy system you want to be able to report on for historical purposes, but that will never be updated.

With all three options, when you create the index, SQL Server immediately populates the full-text index from the source table. There may be times when this is undesirable. With `AUTO` or `MANUAL`, you don't have much choice, but with `OFF` mode, there's an additional option: `OFF, NO POPULATION`. When you tack on `NO POPULATION`, SQL Server will create the full-text index but not populate it. This would be useful when you want to break your scripts into two parts—one to create the full-text indexes, and a second you'd use later to populate them, perhaps during off hours, using the ALTER statement as shown later in this chapter.

Now that the full-text index has been created, we're ready for step three, querying data from our full-text index. Before we proceed, let's take a few moments to examine how to maintain our full-text indexes.

Maintaining full-text indexes

Anyone with five minutes of experience in the computer industry knows that the one thing that's constant is change. SQL Server provides many ways to change our full-text indexes, most of which are variations of the ALTER command. Let's look at some ways to maintain the index we just created in the previous section. The first statement is

```
ALTER FULLTEXT INDEX ON Production.ProductDescription
START UPDATE POPULATION;
```

This is the command to update the full-text index when CHANGE_TRACKING is set to MANUAL, and probably the command you'll use the most. When issued, SQL Server will roll through all of the rows in the table, and will update the corresponding full-text index for rows that have been marked as updated. To make life easier, you could issue this command from a scheduled SQL Server job on a timed basis.

A corresponding command is the full population command:

```
ALTER FULLTEXT INDEX ON Production.ProductDescription
START FULL POPULATION;
```

This command will rebuild the entire full-text index for this table from the ground up. You'd likely want to use this if you had turned off full-text indexing in order to update the source table and were now ready to get it back in sync with the full-text index.

The next two commands will allow us to add and remove columns from our full-text index:

```
ALTER FULLTEXT INDEX ON Production.ProductDescription
ADD ([Description]);
```

```
ALTER FULLTEXT INDEX ON Production.ProductDescription
DROP ([Description]);
```

All you need to do is indicate the column you want to add or drop, and SQL Server will take care of the rest.

It's also possible to alter the change-tracking mode after you create the full-text index. The change-tracking mode works like it does when creating the index. For example, if we wanted to change the tracking mode on the product description table, we'd issue this:

```
ALTER FULLTEXT INDEX ON Production.ProductDescription
SET CHANGE_TRACKING MANUAL;
```

To set it back to AUTO:

```
ALTER FULLTEXT INDEX ON Production.ProductDescription
SET CHANGE_TRACKING AUTO;
```

Or to turn it off:

```
ALTER FULLTEXT INDEX ON Production.ProductDescription
SET CHANGE_TRACKING OFF;
```

If you need to, you can also disable or enable a full-text index:

```
ALTER FULLTEXT INDEX ON Production.ProductDescription DISABLE;
```

```
ALTER FULLTEXT INDEX ON Production.ProductDescription ENABLE;
```

The DISABLE command will turn off all change tracking, but will leave the data in the index intact. You may want to disable an index if you'll no longer be using a table for updates, or if you're about to make a huge number of updates to the table and have change tracking set to AUTO. Be aware, though, that while disabled, no change tracking is performed. Thus, immediately after issuing the ENABLE command, you'll want to issue the ALTER command with START FULL POPULATION to rebuild the index.

Finally, you may want to remove the full-text index altogether. To do so, issue the DROP command:

```
DROP FULLTEXT INDEX ON Production.ProductDescription;
```

Querying full-text indexes

So far we've created a catalog, and then created a full-text index to put in the catalog. But users are strange creatures; not only do they expect us to keep their data safe, but they expect to get it back! So let's proceed to step three in our one-two-three—querying our full-text index.

Basic searches

SQL Server provides an assortment of ways to query our full-text index. The first we'll look at is the CONTAINS keyword, which is added to the WHERE clause of a query. The form is CONTAINS(column, 'word'), where column is the name of the column you want to look for the text in and 'word' is the word or phrase you want to look for. If you want to look at all of the columns in the table you've indexed, you can use an asterisk (*) in place of the column name. Let's do a simple search of our product description table:

```
SELECT ProductDescriptionID as PDID, [Description]
FROM [Production].[ProductDescription] pd
WHERE CONTAINS(pd.[Description], 'ride');
```

Running this query returns 10 rows back to us. Note that we could also have used CONTAINS(*, 'ride') and received the same results, because we only have one column in the full-text index. CONTAINS looks for an exact match of the word you pass in. Most of the time, searching for an exact match is what you'll want to do. Sometimes, though, you'll want something less exact, which returns a broader scope of results. For those times, SQL Server provides the FREETEXT keyword. The format is identical to CONTAINS: FREETEXT(column, 'text').

```
SELECT ProductDescriptionID AS PDID, [Description]
FROM [Production].[ProductDescription] pd
WHERE FREETEXT(pd.[Description], 'ride');
```

When you run this, you get 22 rows back. If you run this and look through the results, in addition to the word *ride*, you'll also see descriptions that contain the word *riding*. This is because of the way FREETEXT functions. FREETEXT works in a two-step process:

1 *Stemming*—The full-text search engine takes the word, in this case *ride*, and adds the variants of the word to its search. Thus it would have *ride, rides, rode, ridden,* and *riding* in the list.

2 *Thesaurus*—After doing the stemming, FREETEXT then goes to the thesaurus and retrieves the list of words that go with *ride*. For example, it might add words such as *drive, commute,* and *transportation* to the list. The process is repeated for each word found in the stemming process.

FREETEXT then performs a search on all of the words and returns the results to you.

Whereas CONTAINS looks for an exact match, FREETEXT looks to match the meaning of the word you're searching for. Which will be better for your application depends on your users and their needs.

So far, we've looked at some fairly simple queries, but we don't have to limit ourselves. Here's a slightly more complex example that uses FREETEXT and joins data from three different tables in the AdventureWorks database. This example is closer to what you might do in a production application:

```
SELECT [Name], ProductNumber, [Description]
FROM [Production].[Product] p
, [Production].[ProductDescription] pd
, [Production].[ProductModelProductDescriptionCulture] pmpdc
WHERE p.ProductModelID = pmpdc.ProductModelID
AND pmpdc.ProductDescriptionID = pd.ProductDescriptionID
AND FREETEXT(pd.[Description], 'shift');
```

FORMSOF

CONTAINS and FREETEXT are both powerful, but there are times when you want something a little looser than CONTAINS, but perhaps not quite as free as FREETEXT. SQL Server provides a way to get to this middle ground by using FORMSOF inside the text string we're searching for. The syntax is admittedly arcane, so let's look at an example:

```
SELECT [Name], ProductNumber, [Description]
FROM [Production].[Product] p
, [Production].[ProductDescription] pd
, [Production].[ProductModelProductDescriptionCulture] pmpdc
WHERE p.ProductModelID = pmpdc.ProductModelID
AND pmpdc.ProductDescriptionID = pd.ProductDescriptionID
AND CONTAINS(pd.[Description], 'FORMSOF(INFLECTIONAL, light)' );
```

As you can see, to use this, place FORMSOF inside the text string you're passing into the CONTAINS keyword. This strange syntax throws a lot of people, so I'm going to say it again to emphasize the point. *You must enclose FORMSOF inside the string you're passing to the CONTAINS keyword.*

After FORMSOF, use either the word INFLECTIONAL or THESAURUS, then a comma, and then the word we're looking for—in this example, *light*. When using FORMSOF INFLECTIONAL, the full-text engine will go through the stemming process, generating the words *light, lightest, lit,* and so on. But unlike FULLTEXT, it'll stop and not go to the thesaurus to add any more words. Conversely, you can also use the thesaurus without the stemming by using FORMSOF THESAURUS:

```
SELECT [Name], ProductNumber, [Description]
FROM [Production].[Product] p
, [Production].[ProductDescription] pd
, [Production].[ProductModelProductDescriptionCulture] pmpdc
WHERE p.ProductModelID = pmpdc.ProductModelID
AND pmpdc.ProductDescriptionID = pd.ProductDescriptionID
AND CONTAINS(pd.[Description], 'FORMSOF(THESAURUS, light)' );
```

In this second case, the full-text engine will look for all the words in its thesaurus that match the word *light*, but will not look for any stemmers of *light*.

Phrases, NEAR, OR, and prefixed terms

We can pull a few other tricks out of our hat when performing searches. It's possible to search for exact phrases by enclosing them inside double quotes. If we wanted to search for the phrase *stiff ride*, all we'd have to do is pass it into the CONTAINS predicate like this: CONTAINS(pd.[Description], '"stiff ride"'). In this case, the full-text engine will only return results when it finds that exact phrase.

Let's say your marketing folks are typical of those in most companies: they throw great parties, but aren't very consistent when it comes to data entry. Sometimes they use *stiff ride*, but other times *stiff, ride* and perhaps even *stiff stable ride*. Yet we still want to find results when *stiff* and *ride* are in the same description, in close proximity. For those searches, the NEAR keyword was created. Phrase your CONTAINS clause like CONTAINS(pd.[Description], 'stiff NEAR ride') and it will return all of the results you're looking for.

In order to use NEAR most effectively, it should be combined with the ranking features provided by CONTAINSTABLE and FREETEXTTABLE, discussed later in this chapter. Behind the scenes, NEAR returns all results where both words are found. It then assigns a rank to them, based on how far apart in the text the two words occur. The closer together, the higher the rank; the more distant, the lower. A rank of zero is given when the two words are more than 50 words apart. Therefore, you'll need to combine NEAR with the ranking feature so that results can be sorted in a way most useful to your users.

You may also see times where a tilde (~) is substituted for the word *near*, as in CONTAINS(pd.[Description], 'stiff ~ ride'). Although this syntax is acceptable, it's not nearly as readable and thus not widely used. I highly encourage you to stick to the word NEAR for readability.

It's also possible to pass an OR clause into the full-text engine: CONTAINS (pd.[Description], 'stiff OR ride'). This will return all matches where either word—*stiff* or *ride*—is in the results.

The final way to search is using prefixed terms. This is the closest to a form of the traditional SQL LIKE syntax, but with some important differences. LIKE performs pattern matching, and will search for the characters. If you were to enter and pd.[Description] like '%light%' as part of a SQL statement, it would return a hit on *semilightweight*. Assuming you only wanted search results that began with the word *light*, this would be an undesirable result.

Prefixed term search, on the other hand, only looks for full words (not patterns) that begin with the word you're searching for. To use a prefixed term, append an asterisk (*) to the end of the word, like so: CONTAINS(pd.[Description], '"light*"'). If you look at the results of a query with *light**, you'll see the word *lightweight* returned. This word hasn't been in any of our previous results because it was neither a stemmer nor a thesaurus match. Instead, the full-text engine went to the index and found all words that began with *light* and bypassed any stemming or thesaurus activity. It's necessary to enclose the prefixed term inside double quotes; otherwise the search engine will only look for *light* and ignore the *. Additionally, even though they're called *prefixed terms*, you can place the * at the front of the search word as well as the end.

Note that you may have seen *light-weight* in some results. This is because the hyphen (-) acted as a word breaker and the full-text engine considered *light-weight* to be two words—*light* and *weight*.

Ranking

When searching, especially with FREETEXT, it can be desirable to order your search results in terms of relevance—returning results that most closely match your search term or phrase first, then those that match the least last. To achieve this, SQL Server provides two more functions: CONTAINSTABLE and FREETEXTTABLE. These directly correspond to the way CONTAINS and FREETEXT searching work, but instead of being used in the WHERE clause, they return a table. Because they both act the same in terms of how to use them, we'll use FREETEXTTABLE for our example:

```
SELECT [KEY], RANK
FROM FREETEXTTABLE([Production].[ProductDescription]
, [Description]
, 'light' );
```

The first thing to notice is that FREETEXTTABLE is used in the FROM clause. As stated, both of these return a table for you to work with. Into the function we pass three parameters. The first is the name of the table we're free-text searching, in this case Production.ProductDescription. The second item is the column we're searching, here Description. We could've also passed in an * to search through all full-text-indexed columns in our table. The final item is the word we're looking for; here I used *light*.

Note our SELECT statement. Both FREETEXTTABLE and CONTAINSTABLE return two columns: KEY and RANK. KEY is the unique key for the row in the source table. RANK is an indicator of relevance.

RANK will be a number from 0 to 1000. Remember some important things when dealing with this number. First of all, it's not sequential. There will be gaps in the numbers returned. Second, the numbers aren't unique. You may have multiple rows returned that all have the same rank. Table 1 shows the results of the preceding query run against our AdventureWorks database.

As you can see, we have multiple rows with a rank of 113, as well as 310. I think you'd agree that this simple query isn't overly useful. Let's look at a slightly more complex query:

Table 1   Simple ranking query results

KEY	RANK
249	113
409	310
457	113
704	310
1090	113
1183	437
1185	310
1199	310
1206	310

```
SELECT fts.[KEY], fts.[RANK], [Description]
FROM [Production].[ProductDescription] AS pd
INNER JOIN FREETEXTTABLE([Production].[ProductDescription]
, [Description]
, 'light' ) AS fts
ON fts.[KEY] = pd.ProductDescriptionID
ORDER BY fts.[RANK];
```

Table 2 shows the results from the query.

Table 2   Results for medium-complexity ranking query

KEY	RANK	Description
249	113	Value-priced bike with many features of our top-of-the-line models. Has the same light, stiff frame, and the quick acceleration we're famous for.
457	113	This bike is ridden by race winners. Developed with the AdventureWorks Cycles professional race team, it has an extremely light heat-treated aluminum frame, and steering that allows precision control.
1090	113	Our lightest and best quality aluminum frame made from the newest alloy; it is welded and heat-treated for strength. Our innovative design results in maximum comfort and performance.
1185	310	Aluminum cage is lighter than our mountain version; perfect for long-distance trips.
1199	310	Light-weight, wind-resistant, packs to fit into a pocket.
1206	310	Simple and light-weight. Emergency patches stored in handle.
704	310	A light yet stiff aluminum bar for long-distance riding.
409	310	Alluminum-alloy frame provides a light, stiff ride, whether you are racing in the velodrome or on a demanding club ride on country roads.
1183	437	Affordable light for safe night riding—uses three AAA batteries.

This gives us more information than the previous query, but, as per listing 1, let's take it further and create a query you might use in a real-world production application.

Listing 1   Real-world example using `FREETEXTTABLE`

```
SELECT fts.[KEY], fts.[RANK], [Name]
, ProductNumber, [Description]
FROM [Production].[ProductDescription] pd
INNER JOIN FREETEXTTABLE([Production].[ProductDescription]
  , [Description], 'light' ) as fts
ON fts.[KEY] = pd.ProductDescriptionID
INNER JOIN [Production].[ProductModelProductDescriptionCulture] AS pmpdc
ON pmpdc.ProductDescriptionID = pd.ProductDescriptionID
INNER JOIN [Production].[Product] AS p
ON p.ProductModelID = pmpdc.ProductModelID;
```

Here we combine data from multiple tables and order them in a manner most relevant to the user. Because this query returns 43 rows, I'll leave it to your inquiring mind to key it in and see the results.

Whereas querying completes step three of our one-two-three, you'll often want to customize the behavior of your searches, especially when using `FREETEXT`. To do that we'll need to looking at customizing the thesaurus and stopwords.

Custom thesaurus and stopwords

Using `FREETEXT` or `FormsOf-Thesaurus`, it's possible to search for words using the thesaurus to augment your search. A natural question is, can we add our own words to the thesaurus?

The answer is a definite yes. In this section, we'll look at how to customize your thesaurus, and then cover the concept of stopwords.

Custom thesaurus

The first step is tracking down the name of your thesaurus. SQL Server stores the location in the registry. Open regedit or your favorite registry tool and navigate to HKEY_LOCAL_MACHINE > SOFTWARE > Microsoft > Microsoft SQL Server > [insert your instance name here] > MSSearch > Language > [insert your language abbreviation here].

WARNING Be careful not to accidentally change your registry entry. We only want to examine values here.

My instance name is MSSQL10MSSQLSERVER. For residents of the United States, the language abbreviation is ENU (short for English, US). (If you don't know your abbreviation, don't worry; shortly we'll look at a simple query that will let you discover it.) Regardless of where you live, navigate to the branch with your appropriate language abbreviation. Looking at the name TsaurusFile, you'll discover the name is tsenu.xml.

Now we need to go to the appropriate place on your hard drive. Assuming your instance is typical, this will be in C:\Program Files\Microsoft SQL Server\[your instance name]\MSSQL\FTData\. For me, this was

```
C:\Program Files\Microsoft SQL Server\MSSQL10.MSSQLSERVER\MSSQL\FTData\
```

Now that we've located it, let's navigate to the folder and open it up in your favorite text editor. (Be sure your text editor can handle Unicode files. Notepad works fine for this.)

TIP   If you're running on Vista, Windows 7, or Windows Server, make sure you run the text editor in Administrator mode so you can save changes!

Take a look at listing 2.

Listing 2   Default thesaurus XML file

```
<XML ID="Microsoft Search Thesaurus">
<!--  Commented out
    <thesaurus xmlns="x-schema:tsSchema.xml">
      <diacritics_sensitive>0</diacritics_sensitive>
        <expansion>
            <sub>Internet Explorer</sub>
            <sub>IE</sub>
            <sub>IE5</sub>
        </expansion>
        <replacement>
            <pat>NT5</pat>
            <pat>W2K</pat>
            <sub>Windows 2000</sub>
        </replacement>
        <expansion>
            <sub>run</sub>
            <sub>jog</sub>
        </expansion>
    </thesaurus>
-->
</XML>
```

The first thing to notice is the file is commented out. We'll want to uncomment it as the first step. Next you'll see the <thesaurus...> section. We won't need to change it, nor the diacritics tag, which specifies accent sensitivity.

The next three sections are examples. Ultimately you'll delete them and replace them with your own, but let's take a moment to look at what's there. The first section is an <expansion>...</expansion> tag. With an expansion set, all terms are equivalent. With the expansion tags, if the user enters any of those terms, it's the same as if they'd entered all of the terms. Thus in the first example, if a user were to type in Internet Explorer, a full-text search would return all records that contained *Internet Explorer*, *IE*, or *IE5*.

Replacement sets, the next section, are something you'll use less often. With replacements, SQL Server doesn't look for the word in the <pat> (pattern) tag;

instead it looks for the word in the <sub> tag. In this case, if a user types in W2K, the full-text search engine will instead look for *Windows 2000*. One true-life situation I can think of where this would be useful is addresses. If you know your system converts all street or state abbreviations to their full expanded name, then you could use this as a trap with full-text searching. For example:

```
<replacement>
  <pat>St</pat>
  <pat>Str</pat>
  <sub>Street</sub>
</replacement>
```

Thus a user typing in Elm St would be able to find Elm Street in your system. You could also expand this with states. Let me reiterate: this example assumes your source system automatically replaces all abbreviations with their full words. Using a replacement prevents the full-text search engine from looking for words that won't be there.

Replacements can also be useful in situations of error correction. For example, your database of addresses is used by your company's offshore support center, where they frequently misspell *Street* as *Stret*. You could add <pat>Stret</pat> to the thesaurus and help the users.

Of the two, you'll probably use expansions most of the time, but know that replacement sets exist and what they can be useful for. Finally, please note there are a handful of restrictions around the thesaurus file:

- You must have system administrator rights to be able to edit the file.
- You should make sure the editor understands Unicode format.
- Entries can't be empty.
- Phrases placed in the thesaurus have a maximum of 512 characters.
- You may not have any duplicate entries among the <sub> tags of expansion sets or the <pat> tags of replacement sets.

So let's create a simple example to test out our custom thesaurus. Open up your tsenu.xml file, and change it to this:

```
<XML ID="Microsoft Search Thesaurus">
    <thesaurus xmlns="x-schema:tsSchema.xml">
      <diacritics_sensitive>0</diacritics_sensitive>
        <expansion>
           <sub>light</sub>
           <sub>doodleysquat</sub>
        </expansion>
    </thesaurus>
</XML>
```

Here I'm going to make the word *light* and the word *doodleysquat* substitutable for each other. In case you're wondering, we're picking a nonsense word that we're sure we won't find in the AdventureWorks database. Save the changes.

Unfortunately, saving the changes isn't enough to make the full-text search engine pick up the updates to our thesaurus file. We have to tell SQL Server the file has been updated. In SQL Server 2008, this is fairly simple. Make sure you're in the right database for your catalog (in this case, AdventureWorks2008) and execute the stored procedure:

```
exec sys.sp_fulltext_load_thesaurus_file 1033;
go
```

The *1033* on the end refers to the local identifier (LCID) for the language of your thesaurus file. 1033 is for English, US. To discover your LCID, use this simple query:

```
select [name], lcid from sys.fulltext_languages order by [name];
```

Okay, we're at the finish line. Assuming your full-text engine has restarted, it should've picked up your new, customized thesaurus file. Let's go back to a query we used earlier, slightly altered:

```
SELECT [Name], ProductNumber, [Description]
FROM [Production].[Product] p
, [Production].[ProductDescription] pd
, [Production].[ProductModelProductDescriptionCulture] pmpdc
WHERE p.ProductModelID = pmpdc.ProductModelID
AND pmpdc.ProductDescriptionID = pd.ProductDescriptionID
AND CONTAINS(pd.[Description], 'FORMSOF(Thesaurus, doodleysquat)' );
```

We should get the same results as if we'd used the word *light* instead of *doodleysquat.*

As you can see, adding custom entries to the SQL Server Full Text Search Thesaurus isn't difficult; there are a few steps you need to follow in order to make it happen. Once you know how, you can use the functionality to make searches for your users more productive.

Stopwords and stoplists

Every language has some words that are used so often that indexing them for full-text searching would be useless—words such as *a, an, and, the, or,* and so forth. These words are known as *noise words* and will be ignored when you're doing any full-text indexing. In some companies, certain words become noise words. For example, your company may have a rule that its company name must appear in all comment records in the form of a copyright notice. In that case, your company name would become a noise word because it appears so often as to be meaningless to search for.

SQL Server 2005 had support for custom noise words for its full-text search, but it was in the form of a simple text file that applied to the entire server. SQL Server 2008 has moved to a new concept, *stopwords.* This change is much deeper than just a rebranding. With the change comes a lot more flexibility and functionality.

SQL Server 2008 introduces two new tools: stopwords and stoplists. A stoplist acts as a named container for a group of stopwords. You can then associate a stoplist with one or more tables. This is a great enhancement over noise words, which applied to the entire server. Now you can associate a group of stopwords, in a stoplist, with specific tables without affecting the rest of the tables in the database or server.

Let's run a query to demonstrate. We'll use the same query we've used elsewhere in this chapter:

```
SELECT [Name], ProductNumber, [Description]
FROM [Production].[Product] p
, [Production].[ProductDescription] pd
, [Production].[ProductModelProductDescriptionCulture] pmpdc
WHERE p.ProductModelID = pmpdc.ProductModelID
AND pmpdc.ProductDescriptionID = pd.ProductDescriptionID
AND CONTAINS(pd.[Description], 'shifting');
```

To create a stoplist, you can use the first of the new SQL Server 2008 commands, CRE-ATE FULLTEXT STOPLIST:

```
CREATE FULLTEXT STOPLIST ArcanesStoplist;
```

The stoplist will act as a holder for a specific set of words that we want to ignore. We refer to that group of words by the name we gave it, ArcanesStoplist. Now we need to add some words to the list. Here are two ways to do so; both use the ALTER FULLTEXT STOPLIST statement:

```
ALTER FULLTEXT STOPLIST ArcanesStoplist
  ADD 'shifting' LANGUAGE 1033;
```

```
ALTER FULLTEXT STOPLIST ArcanesStoplist
  ADD 'light' LANGUAGE 'English';
```

The command is straightforward; use the ALTER FULLTEXT STOPLIST statement and provide the name of the list you want to add a word to. Then comes the command ADD, followed by the word you want to add. Next you have to specify the language. You can specify the language in two ways, either by using the language ID (in this example, 1033) or the name for the language.

If you were to jump the gun and rerun our query, you'd think it would now ignore the word *shifting* because we just added it as a stopword to our stoplist. But there's still one more step.

You need to attach your stoplist to a table that has a full-text index on it. This is a major improvement over 2005, where stopwords were implemented as noise words, one simple text file that applied to the entire server. SQL Server 2008 now allows you to get granular with the application of custom groups of words. You're limited to one stoplist per table, though. On the plus side, one stoplist can be applied to multiple tables. Here's the code to associate our stoplist with a table:

```
ALTER FULLTEXT INDEX ON [Production].[ProductDescription]
SET STOPLIST ArcanesStoplist;
```

All we need to do is specify the table name and the stoplist to associate with that table. Now go run our test query. You should get back zero rows.

Congratulations! You've now associated your stoplist with the full-text index.

I'm sure you don't want to leave it this way, so let's look at what it will take to clean up the mess. First, you can decide you no longer want the stoplist associated with the full-text index. Time to use the ALTER command again:

```
ALTER FULLTEXT INDEX ON [Production].[ProductDescription]
SET STOPLIST system;
```

Setting the stoplist to the keyword system will change from your custom stoplist to the system stoplist. You can also use the word OFF instead of SYSTEM to turn off stopwords altogether for the specified table. If you want to use the standard system set of stopwords instead of using a custom set, use the SYSTEM keyword, as in the previous example. You can also use an INSERT INTO statement to copy the system stopwords into your custom stoplist, and then add or remove words as needed.

There may be times when you want to remove only a word or two from a stoplist, but not disassociate the entire list. It's possible to easily remove individual words from the list:

```
ALTER FULLTEXT STOPLIST ArcanesStoplist
  DROP 'shifting' LANGUAGE 1033;
ALTER FULLTEXT STOPLIST ArcanesStoplist
  DROP 'light' LANGUAGE 'English';
```

The syntax for the DROP is identical to ADD, except for using the word DROP instead of ADD.

Finally, you may want to drop the stoplist altogether. There's a DROP statement for that as well:

```
DROP FULLTEXT STOPLIST ArcanesStoplist;
```

This covers the basic use of stopwords and stoplists in 2008. Let's take a moment now to look at some advanced queries that will help you manage your stopwords and stoplists.

USEFUL QUERIES PERTAINING TO STOPWORDS AND STOPLISTS

Our first query returns a list of all the user-defined stoplists in our database:

```
SELECT stoplist_id, name
FROM sys.fulltext_stoplists;
```

Our next query returns a list of stopwords for our user-defined stoplists in the database. Note the linking to get the associated stoplist name and language:

```
SELECT sl.name as StoplistName
, sw.stopword as StopWord, lg.alias as LanguageAlias
, lg.name as LanguageName, lg.lcid as LanguageLCID
FROM sys.fulltext_stopwords sw
JOIN sys.fulltext_stoplists sl
ON sl.stoplist_id = sw.stoplist_id
JOIN master.sys.syslanguages lg
ON lg.lcid = sw.language_id;
```

This next query gets a list of all of the stopwords that ship with SQL Server 2008:

```
SELECT ssw.stopword, slg.name
FROM sys.fulltext_system_stopwords ssw
JOIN sys.fulltext_languages slg
ON slg.lcid = ssw.language_id;
```

Used together, these queries can help you discover the state of your stopwords and stoplists.

Useful system queries

So far we've learned how to create catalogs and full-text indexes, along with a variety of ways to get information back out of our indexes. All are great tools for the database developer. If you're a database administrator, though, there are few more tricks you can use to administer and take care of your full-text indexes.

Basic queries to discover what catalogs, indexes, and columns exist

Let's start with a few basic queries. First, let's retrieve a list of the catalogs that are associated with the current database.

```
SELECT fulltext_catalog_id, name, is_default
FROM sys.fulltext_catalogs;
```

This may return one or more rows, depending on how many catalogs you have. If you created the AdventureWorksFTC catalog, it'll appear in the name column. The fulltext_catalog_id is a numbered auto incrementing primary key without any meaning. The is_default column will contain a 1 if this catalog is the default; otherwise the value will be 0.

This is useful, so let's dig further. Let's get a list of all of the indexes in our database. To do so, we'll delve into the sys.fulltext_indexes view, adding it to the information provided by the sys.fulltext_catalogs view we used in the previous example:

```
-- List names of all FTS indexes
SELECT cat.[name] as CatalogName
, object_name(object_id) as table_name
, is_enabled
, change_tracking_state_desc
FROM sys.fulltext_indexes, sys.fulltext_catalogs cat
ORDER BY cat.[name], table_name;
```

The results of this query are shown in table 3.

Our query returns four rows, including the row for the Document table we created earlier in the chapter. Note that the query shows that all of these indexes are enabled, and it also displays the change-tracking mode being used.

Table 3   Query results to list all full-text indexes

CatalogName	table_name	is_enabled	change_tracking_state_desc
AdventureWorksFTC	Document	1	AUTO
AdventureWorksFTC	JobCandidate	1	AUTO
AdventureWorksFTC	ProductDescription	1	AUTO
AdventureWorksFTC	ProductReview	1	AUTO

We can extend the prior query one step further, adding in information about the unique index used for full-text searching and the associated stoplist for a given table, as shown in listing 3.

Listing 3 Full information about tables and full-text searching

```
SELECT c.name as CatalogName
, t.name as TableName
, idx.name as UniqueIndexName
, case i.is_enabled
  when 1 then 'Enabled'
  else 'Not Enabled'
  end as IsEnabled
, i.change_tracking_state_desc
, sl.name as StoplistName
FROM sys.fulltext_indexes i
JOIN sys.fulltext_catalogs c
ON i.fulltext_catalog_id = c.fulltext_catalog_id
JOIN sys.tables t
ON i.object_id = t.object_id
JOIN sys.indexes idx
ON i.unique_index_id = idx.index_id
AND i.object_id = idx.object_id
LEFT JOIN sys.fulltext_stoplists sl
ON sl.stoplist_id = i.stoplist_id;
```

So far we've looked at catalogs and tables. The next logical question most would ask is "Which columns are full-text indexed?" I'm glad you asked! The query shown in listing 4 will tell us. The results of the query are shown in table 4.

Listing 4 List all columns that are full-text indexed

```
SELECT t.[Name] as TableName
, c.[Name] as ColumnName
, (case ColumnProperty ( (t.[object_id], c.[Name], 'IsFulltextIndexed')
  when 1 then 'True'
  when 0 then 'False'
  else 'Invalid Input'
  end) as IsFullTextIndexed
FROM sys.tables t
JOIN sys.all_columns c ON t.[object_id] = c.[object_id]
WHERE ColumnProperty(t.[object_id], c.[Name], 'IsFulltextIndexed') = 1
ORDER BY t.[Name], c.column_id;
```

Table 4 Query results to list all columns that are full-text indexed

TableName	ColumnName	IsFullTextIndexed
Document	DocumentSummary	True
Document	Document	True
JobCandidate	Resume	True
ProductDescription	Description	True
ProductReview	Comments	True

Note that our ProductDescription.Description column appears in the list. If you want to check the status of all columns, and not only the ones that are full-text indexed, omit the WHERE clause from the query.

Advanced queries

It would be nice to return more information about our catalogs, such as their size, how many items are in them, and so forth. SQL Server provides a useful function called `FullTextCatalogProperty`. You provide it two parameters: the name of the catalog and the name of the property you wish to examine. A handful of the properties you can check this way turn out to be useful, so let's look at a query that returns these as a single result set. Listing 5 shows the query, and table 5 shows the results.

Listing 5   Using `FullTextCatalogProperty` to get information

```
SELECT [name] as CatalogName
, FullTextCatalogProperty('AdventureWorksFTC', 'IndexSize')
  AS IndexSizeMB
, FullTextCatalogProperty('AdventureWorksFTC', 'ItemCount')
  AS ItemCount
, FullTextCatalogProperty('AdventureWorksFTC', 'UniqueKeyCount')
  AS UniqueKeyCount
, CASE FullTextCatalogProperty('AdventureWorksFTC', 'PopulateStatus')
  WHEN 0 THEN 'Idle'
  WHEN 1 THEN 'Full population in progress'
  WHEN 2 THEN 'Paused'
  WHEN 3 THEN 'Throttled'
  WHEN 4 THEN 'Recovering'
  WHEN 5 THEN 'Shutdown'
  WHEN 6 THEN 'Incremental population in progress'
  WHEN 7 THEN 'Building index'
  WHEN 8 THEN 'Disk is full. Paused.'
  WHEN 9 THEN 'Change tracking'
  ELSE 'Error reading FullTextCatalogProperty PopulateStatus'
  END AS PopulateStatus
, CASE is_default
  WHEN 1 then 'Yes'
  ELSE 'No'
  END AS IsDefaultCatalog
FROM sys.fulltext_catalogs
ORDER BY [name];
```

Table 5   Query results for catalog information query

Catalog name	Index size (MB)	Item count	Unique key count	Populate status	Is default catalog
AdventureWorksFTC	0	762	3194	Idle	Yes
AW2008FullTextCatalog	0	762	3194	Idle	No

After the catalog name, you'll see the size of the index, in megabytes. Don't be alarmed that what you see in the table is 0; this means the catalog is less than 1 megabyte in size. This is due to the fact that we're running our query against the small sample database. The next column is the Item Count. This indicates the number of rows from the source system that were indexed.

Unique Key Count, on the other hand, is an indication of the number of entries in the catalog—in other words, how many unique word/primary key combinations are in the catalog.

Populate Status returns a number from 0 to 9, indicating what activity the full-text catalog is performing. Because we don't want to have to remember what each number means, the query uses a simple case statement to let us know in language we can understand.

Finally, the Is Default Catalog column tells us whether the catalog is the default for this database. Normally it returns 1 (for default) or 0 (for not the default), but because the case statement was useful for populate status, we might as well use it here as well.

At the beginning of the chapter, we talked about the varbinary(max) data type. As you'll recall, varbinary(max) is used to store a document whose type SQL Server understands; the full-text engine will open the document and index the contents. It's possible to retrieve a list of all document types understood by SQL Server, using the following query:

```
SELECT document_type, path, [version], manufacturer
FROM sys.fulltext_document_types;
```

This returns four columns. Because SQL Server 2008 understands 50 types right out of the box, I won't list them all here. The main column is the document_type; in it you'll see extensions such as .txt, .doc, .xls, .aspx, .cmd, .cpp, and many more. If the document saved in a varbinary(max) column has one of the extensions from the document_type column, SQL Server will understand it.

SQL Server uses the library located in the path column to do the work of opening and reading the document. The last two columns, version and manufacturer, are informational and let us know who made the library and what version it is.

If your full-text performance begins to suffer over time, you might want to check and see how many fragments exist. Internally, SQL Server stores index data in special tables it calls *full-text index fragments*. A table can have one or more fragments associated with it, but if that number gets too high, it can degrade performance.

The query shown in listing 6 will tell you how many fragments exist for your full-text index.

Listing 6 Determining the number of fragments for your full-text indexes

```
-- See how many fragments exist for each full text index.
-- If multiple closed fragments exist for a table do a REORGANIZE to help
➥ performance
SELECT t.name as TableName
, f.data_size
, f.row_count
, case f.status
```

```
   WHEN 0 THEN 'Newly created and not yet used'
   WHEN 1 THEN 'Being used for insert'
   WHEN 4 THEN 'Closed ready for query'
   WHEN 6 THEN 'Being used for merge input and ready for query'
   WHEN 8 THEN 'Marked for deletion. Will not be used for query and merge
➥source'
   ELSE 'Unknown status code'
   END
FROM sys.fulltext_index_fragments f
JOIN sys.tables t on f.table_id = t.object_id;
```

When this query returns, look for rows whose type is 4, or `Closed ready for query`. A table will be listed once for each fragment it has. If it turns out that you have a high number of closed fragments, you should consider doing a `REORGANIZE` on the index (using the `ALTER FULLTEXT INDEX` statement). Note two things: first you must do a reorganize, as opposed to a rebuild. Second, the exact number of fragments that will cause you issues is somewhat dependant on your hardware. But as a rule of thumb, if it exceeds 50, start planning a reorganize, and if it's over 100, start planning in a hurry.

The keywords

We'll close this chapter out by answering one of the most-often-asked questions: how can I find out what words are contained in my full-text index? New with SQL Server 2008 are a pair of dynamic management functions (DMFs) that can help us answer that very question.

The first is `sys.dm_fts_index_keywords`. To use this function, pass in the database ID and object ID for the table you want to discover the keywords for. It returns a table with many columns; this query shows you the more useful ones. Note that it also references the `sys.columns` view in order to get the column name:

```
SELECT keyword, display_term, c.name, document_count
FROM sys.dm_fts_index_keywords(db_id()
, object_id ('Production.ProductDescription')) fik
JOIN sys.columns c on
c.object_id = object_id('Production.ProductDescription')
AND c.column_id = fik.column_id;
```

The `db_id()` function allows us to easily retrieve the database ID. We then use the `object_id` function to get the ID for the table name, passing in the text-based table name. Table 6 shows a sampling of the results.

Table 6   Sample of results for query to find keywords

Keyword	Display term	Column	Document count
0x006C0069006700680074	light	Description	7
0x006C006900670068007400650072	lighter	Description	1
0x006C0069006700680074006500730074	lightest	Description	1
0x006C006900670068007400770065006900670068.0074	lightweight	Description	11

Table 6   Sample of results for query to find keywords *(continued)*

Keyword	Display term	Column	Document count
0x006C00690067006E0065	ligne	Description	3
0x006C0069006E0065	line	Description	5
0x006C0069006E006B	link	Description	2

The Keyword column contains the Unicode version of the keyword in hexadecimal format, and is used as a way to link the Display Term—the real indexed word—to other views. The Column column is obvious; the Document Count indicates how many times this keyword appears in the table.

One oddity about this particular DMF is that it doesn't appear in the Object Explorer—at least, the version used in the writing of this chapter doesn't. But not to worry: the view still works, and it's found in the Books Online documentation.

To add to the oddities, there's a second dynamic management function, one that doesn't display in the Object Explorer. It's sys.dm_fts_index_keywords_by_document, and can also return valuable information about your keywords. Here's a query that will tell us not only what the keywords are, but what rows they are located on in the source table:

```
SELECT keyword, display_term, c.name
, document_id , occurrence_count
FROM sys.dm_fts_index_keywords_by_document(db_id()
, object_id('Production.ProductDescription'))
JOIN sys.columns c on c.object_id =
    object_id('Production.ProductDescription')
ORDER BY display_term;
```

Like its sister DMF, you pass in the database ID and the object ID for the table. Table 7 shows a sampling of the data returned.

Table 7   Sample of results for query to find keywords and their source row

Keyword	Display term	Column name	Document ID	Occurrence count
0x006C0069006700680074	light	Description	249	1
0x006C0069006700680074	light	Description	409	1
0x006C0069006700680074	light	Description	457	1
0x006C0069006700680074	light	Description	704	1
0x006C0069006700680074	light	Description	1183	1
0x006C0069006700680074	light	Description	1199	1
0x006C0069006700680074	light	Description	1206	1

Keyword and Display Term are the same as the previous view, as is the Column Name. The Document ID is the unique key from the source table, and the Occurrence Count is how many times the word appears in the row referenced by the document ID.

Using this information, we can construct a query that combines data from the source table with this view. This will create a valuable tool for debugging indexes as we try to determine why a particular word appears in a result set:

```
SELECT  d.keyword, d.display_term
, d.document_id --primary key
, d.occurrence_count, p.Description
FROM sys.dm_fts_index_keywords_by_document(db_id()
, object_id('Production.ProductDescription')) d
JOIN Production.ProductDescription p
ON p.ProductDescriptionID = d.document_id
ORDER BY d.display_term;
```

As you can see from the results shown in table 8, we can pull the description for the row with the keyword we want.

Table 8   **Partial results of expanded query combining keywords with source data**

Keyword	Display term	Document ID	Occurrence count	Description
0x006C0069006700680074	light	249	1	Value-priced bike with many features of our top-of-the-line models. Has the same light, stiff frame, and the quick acceleration we're famous for.
0x006C0069006700680074	light	409	1	Alluminum-alloy frame provides a light, stiff ride, whether you are racing in the velodrome or on a demanding club ride on country roads.
0x006C0069006700680074	light	457	1	This bike is ridden by race winners. Developed with the AdventureWorks Cycles professional race team, it has a extremely light heat-treated aluminum frame, and steering that allows precision control.
0x006C0069006700680074	light	704	1	A light yet stiff aluminum bar for long-distance riding.
0x006C0069006700680074	light	1183	1	Affordable light for safe night riding; uses 3 AAA batteries.
0x006C0069006700680074	light	1199	1	Light-weight, wind-resistant, packs to fit into a pocket.
0x006C0069006700680074	light	1206	1	Simple and light-weight. Emergency patches stored in handle.

Summary

This concludes our look at full-text searching with SQL Server 2008. We began by creating a catalog to hold our indexes, then proceeded to step two, creating the indexes themselves. Our third step was querying the full-text indexes in a variety of ways. Finally, we looked at some queries that will help us maintain and discover the state of our full-text indexes.

Hopefully you'll find that using full-text searching can be as easy as one-two-three!

About the author

Robert C. Cain is a Microsoft MVP in SQL development, and is a consultant with COMFRAME as a senior business intelligence architect. Prior to his current position, Robert worked for a regional power company, managing, designing, and implementing the SQL Server data warehouse for the nuclear division. He also spent 10 years as a senior consultant, working for a variety of customers in the Birmingham, Alabama, area using Visual Basic and C#. He maintains the popular blog http://arcane-code.com.

In his spare time, Robert enjoys spending time with his wife and two daughters, digital photography, and amateur radio, holding the highest amateur license available and operating under the call sign N4IXT.

14 Simil: an algorithm to look for similar strings

Tom van Stiphout

Are you a perfect speller? Is everyone in your company? How about your business partners? Misspellings are a fact of life. There are also legitimate differences in spelling: what Americans call *rumors*, the British call *rumours*. *Steven A. Ballmer* and *Steve Ballmer* are two different but accurate forms of that man's name. Your database may contain a lot of legacy values from the days before better validation at the point of data entry.

Overall, chances are your database already contains imperfect textual data, which makes it hard to search. Additionally, the user may not know exactly what to look for. When looking for a number or a date, we could search for a range, but text is more unstructured, so database engines such as SQL Server include a range of tools to find text, including the following:

- EQUALS (=) and LIKE
- SOUNDEX and DIFFERENCE
- CONTAINS and FREETEXT
- Simil

Equals and LIKE search for equality with or without wildcards. SOUNDEX uses a phonetic algorithm based on the sound of the consonants in a string. CONTAINS is optimized for finding inflectional forms and synonyms of strings.

Simil is an algorithm that compares two strings, and based on the longest common substrings, computes a similarity between 0 (completely different) and 1 (identical). This is sometimes called *fuzzy string matching*. Simil isn't available by default. Later in this chapter we'll discuss how to install it.

In this chapter, we take a closer look at these various methods, beginning with the simplest one.

Equals (=) and LIKE

In this section we'll discuss two simple options for looking up text.

Equals (=) is appropriate if you know exactly what you're looking for, and you know you have perfect data. For example, this statement finds all contacts with a last name of *Adams*. If you have an index on the column(s) used in the WHERE clause, this lookup is very fast and can't be beat by any of the other techniques discussed later in this chapter:

```
SELECT FirstName, LastName
  FROM Person.Person
  WHERE (LastName = 'Adams')
```

NOTE Throughout this chapter, I'm using SQL Server 2008 and the sample database AdventureWorks2008, available at http://www.codeplex.com/ SqlServerSamples.

LIKE allows wildcards and patterns. This allows you to find data even if there's only a partial match. For example, this statement finds all contacts with a last name starting with *A*:

```
SELECT FirstName, LastName
  FROM Person.Person
  WHERE (LastName LIKE 'A%')
```

The wildcards % and _ are used as a placeholder for *any text* and *any character*. If you omit wildcards altogether, the statement returns the same records as if = were used. If, as in the preceding example, you use LIKE with a wildcard at the end, you have the benefit of a fast indexed lookup if there's an index on the column you're searching on. Wildcard searches such as WHERE (LastName LIKE '%A') can't use an index and will as a result be slower.

LIKE also supports patterns indicating which range of characters are allowed. For example, this statement finds last names starting with *Aa* through *Af*:

```
SELECT FirstName, LastName
  FROM Person.Person
  WHERE (LastName LIKE 'A[a-f]%')
```

Whether the lookup is case sensitive depends on the collation selected when the server was installed. A more detailed discussion of case sensitivity isn't in scope of this chapter.

But what if you don't know the exact string you're looking for? Perhaps you heard a company name on the radio and only know what it sounds like.

SOUNDEX and DIFFERENCE

If you're looking for words that sound alike, SOUNDEX and DIFFERENCE are the built-in functions to use. They only work for English pronunciation.

To get the SOUNDEX value, call the function:

```
SELECT FirstName, LastName, SOUNDEX(LastName)
  FROM Person.Person
  WHERE (LastName LIKE 'A%')
```

SOUNDEX returns a four-character string representing the sound of a given string. The first character is the first letter of the string, and the remaining three are numbers representing the sound of the first consonants of the string. Similar-sounding consonants get the same value; for example the *d* in Adams gets a value of 3, just like a *t* would. After all substitutions, *Adams* and *Atoms* have the same SOUNDEX value of A352. One typical use for SOUNDEX is to store the values in a table, so that you can later run fast-indexed lookups using =.

The DIFFERENCE function is used to compare SOUNDEX values in expressions. It converts its two arguments to SOUNDEX equivalents and computes the difference, expressed in a value between 0 (weak or no similarity) and 4 (strong similarity or identical). For example, this statement finds contacts with last names somewhat similar to Adams:

```
SELECT FirstName, LastName
  FROM Person.Person
  WHERE (DIFFERENCE(LastName, 'Adams') = 3)
```

Resulting names from the sample database include Achong, Adina, Ajenstat, and Akers. As you can see, not all of them would we immediately associate with Adams. That's one of the limitations of this simple algorithm. Keep reading for more sophisticated options.

CONTAINS and FREETEXT

So far we've covered a few fairly simple ways of finding text: by literal value, using literal values and wildcards, and by comparing the sounds of strings. Now we're going to check out the most powerful text-matching features built into SQL Server.

The keywords CONTAINS and FREETEXT are used in the context of full-text indexes, which are special indexes (one per table) to quickly search words in text. They require the use of a special set of predicates. Let's look at a few of these powerful statements.

The first one looks for all records with the word *bike* in them:

```
SELECT ProductDescriptionID, Description
  FROM Production.ProductDescription
  WHERE CONTAINS(Description, 'bike')
```

You might think that's equivalent to the following:

```
SELECT ProductDescriptionID, Description
  FROM Production.ProductDescription
  WHERE (Description LIKE '%bike%')
```

But the two statements aren't equivalent. The former statement finds records with the word *bike*, skipping those with *bikes*, *biker*, and other forms. Changing the latter statement to LIKE '% bike %' doesn't work either, if the word is next to punctuation.

The CONTAINS and FREETEXT keywords can also handle certain forms of fuzzy matches, for example:

```
SELECT Description
  FROM Production.ProductDescription
  WHERE CONTAINS(Description, 'FORMSOF (INFLECTIONAL, ride) ')
```

This statement finds words that are inflectionally similar, such as verb conjugations and singular/plural forms of nouns. So words such as *rode* and *riding-whip* are found, but *rodeo* isn't.

FREETEXT is similar to CONTAINS, but is much more liberal in finding variations. For example, a CONTAINS INFLECTIONAL search for *two words* would find that term and its inflections, whereas FREETEXT would find the inflections of *two* and *words* separately.

Another aspect of fuzzy matches is using the thesaurus to find similar words. Curiously, the SQL Server thesaurus is empty when first installed. I populated the tsglobal.xml file (there are similar files for specific languages) with the following:

```
<expansion>
    <sub>bicycle</sub>
    <sub>bike</sub>
</expansion>
```

Then I was able to query for any records containing *bike* or *bicycle*.

```
SELECT Description
  FROM Production.ProductDescription
  WHERE CONTAINS(Description, 'FORMSOF (THESAURUS, bike) ')
```

The thesaurus can also hold misspellings of words along with the proper spelling:

```
<replacement>
    <pat>visualbasic</pat>
    <pat>vb</pat>
    <pat>visaul basic</pat>
    <sub>visual basic</sub>
</replacement>
```

If I were writing a resume-searching application, this could come in handy.

The last option I want to cover here is the NEAR keyword, which looks for two words in close proximity to each other:

```
SELECT Description
  FROM Production.ProductDescription
  WHERE CONTAINS(Description, 'bike NEAR woman')
```

CONTAINS and FREETEXT have two cousins—CONTAINSTABLE and FREETEXTTABLE. They return KEY and RANK information, which can be used for ranking your results:

```
SELECT [key], [rank]
  FROM CONTAINSTABLE(Production.ProductDescription, Description, 'bike')
  ORDER BY [rank] DESC
```

So far we've covered the full range of text-searching features available in T-SQL, and we've been able to perform many text-oriented queries. If it's impractical to build a thesaurus of misspellings and proper spellings, we have to use a more generic routine. Let's get to the core of this chapter and take a closer look at one answer to this problem.

Simil

As shown earlier, T-SQL allows us to perform a wide range of text searches. Still, a lot remains to be desired, especially with regard to misspellings. If you want to find a set of records even if they have misspellings, or want to prevent misspellings, you need to perform fuzzy string comparisons, and Simil is one algorithm suited for that task.

One use for Simil is in data cleanup. In one example, a company had a table with organic chemistry compounds, and their names were sometimes spelled differently. The application presents the user with the current record and similar records. The user can decide which records are duplicates, and choose the best one. One button click later, all child records are pointed to the chosen record, and the bad records are deleted. Then the user moves to the next record.

Another typical use for Simil is in preventing bad data from entering the database in the first place. Our company has a Sales application with a Companies table. When a salesperson is creating or importing a new company, the application uses Simil to scan for similar company names. If it finds any records, it'll show a dialog box asking the user if the new company is one of those, or indeed a new company, as shown in figure 1.

Other uses include educational software with open-ended questions. One tantalizing option the original authors mention is to combine Simil with a compiler, which could then auto-correct common mistakes.

Let's look at Simil in more detail, and learn how we can take advantage of it.

In 1988, *Dr. Dobb's Journal* published the Ratcliff/Obershelp algorithm for pattern recognition (Ratcliff and Metzener, "Pattern Matching: The Gestalt Approach," http://www.ddj.com/184407970?pgno=5). This algorithm compares two strings and returns a similarity between 0 (completely different) and 1 (identical). Ratcliff and Obershelp wrote the original version in assembly language for the 8086 processor. In 1999, Steve Grubb published his interpretation in the C language (http://web.archive.org/web/

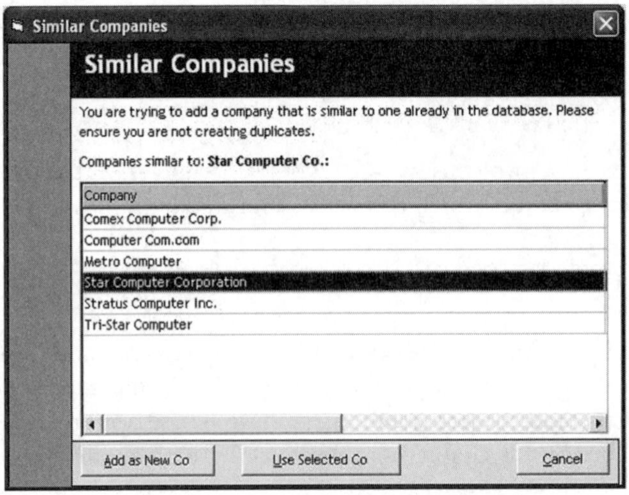

Figure 1   A form showing similar database records

20050213075957/www.gate.net/~ddata/utilities/simil.c). This is the version I used as a starting point for the .NET implementation I'm presenting here.

The purpose of Simil is to calculate a similarity between two strings.

Algorithm

The Simil algorithm looks for the longest common substring, and then looks at the right and left remainders for the longest common substrings, and so on recursively until no more are found. It then returns the similarity as a value between 0 and 1, by dividing the sum of the lengths of the substrings by the lengths of the strings themselves.

Table 1 shows an example for two spellings of the word *Pennsylvania*. The algorithm finds the largest common substrings *lvan*, and then repeats with the remaining strings until there are no further common substrings.

Table 1   Simil results for Pennsylvania

Word 1	Word 2	Common substring	Length
Pennsylvania	Pencilvaneya	lvan	8
Pennsy ia	Penci eya	Pen	6
nsy ia	ci eya	a	2
nsy i	ci ey	(none)	0
Subtotal			*16*
Length of original strings			*24*
Simil = 16/24			*0.67*

Simil is case sensitive. If you want to ignore case, convert both strings to uppercase or lowercase before calling Simil.

At its core, Simil is a *longest common substring* or *LCS* algorithm, and its performance can be expected to be on par with that class of algorithms. Anecdotally, we know that using Simil to test a candidate company name against 20,000 company names takes less than a second.

Simil has good performance and is easy to understand. It also has several weaknesses, including the following:

- The result value is abstract. Therefore it'll take some trial and error to find a good threshold value above which you'd consider two strings similar enough to take action. For data such as company names, I recommend a starting Simil value of about 0.75. For the organic chemistry names, we found that 0.9 gave us better results.

- It's insensitive for very small strings. For example, *Adams* and *Ramos* have three out of five characters in common, so the Simil value is 0.6. Most people wouldn't call those names similar.
- It treats every letter the same, without regard for vowels or consonants, or for letters that often occur together, or for the location in the string, or any other criteria. Some other algorithms do; for example, in the English language the letters Q and U nearly always occur together and in that order, so much so that they could almost be considered a single letter. In a more comprehensive algorithm, such occurrences could be given special consideration. SOUNDEX is another algorithm that does take into account that some consonants are almost the same (for example, *d* and *t*).
- Simil can't be precalculated, always requires a table scan, and can't take advantage of indexes. This may be a problem for large datasets.

Implementation in .NET

Several years ago I used the C version from Steve Grubb to create a classic Windows DLL that was called from the business layer of an application, and it has served me well. This DLL is available in the download package.

In a search for higher levels of performance, I rewrote the code for .NET in two ways. The first is a straight port from C to VB.NET; the second is a pure .NET interpretation. Why two ways? When a new development platform comes out, some developers stay with what they know and mold the platform to their way of programming, while others go with the flow and change their way of programming to what the platform has to offer. I was curious to find out which approach would yield the best performance.

The straight port is available in the `Simil` method of the `clsSimil` class in Simil-CLR.dll.

The pure .NET version is available in the `Simil` method of the `RatcliffObershelp` class in SimilCLR.dll. This version is the one we're using in the next section.

To me, it was gratifying to find out that the pure .NET version performed 30 percent better than the straight port.

Installation

SimilCLR.dll is a .NET assembly. An *assembly* is a unit of execution of a .NET application. SQL Server 2005 introduced the ability to run .NET assemblies in the SQL Server process space. Running inside of the SQL Server process offers performance benefits over the previous method of calling an extended stored procedure. If you're using an older version of SQL Server, I suggest using the classic DLL from your client or middle-tier code. All code modules discussed here can be downloaded from the book's download site at http://www.manning.com/SQLServerMVPDeepDives.

Because they can pack tremendous power, by default SQL Server doesn't allow .NET assemblies to run. To enable this capability, use the following:

```
EXEC sp_configure 'clr enabled', 1
GO
RECONFIGURE
GO
```

Please note that this is a server-wide setting.

Next copy SimilCLR.dll to a folder of your choice on the database server machine. To register an assembly with SQL Server, use the following:

```
CREATE ASSEMBLY asmSimil
    AUTHORIZATION dbo
    FROM N'C:\Windows\SimilCLR.dll'   --Enter your path.
    WITH PERMISSION_SET = SAFE;
GO
```

Once the assembly is registered, we need to make its methods accessible to T-SQL. This code creates a scalar function that takes the two strings to be compared, calls the `Simil` method in the assembly, and returns the Simil value for them:

```
CREATE FUNCTION dbo.fnSimil(@s1 nvarchar(max), @s2 nvarchar(max))
RETURNS float WITH EXECUTE AS CALLER
AS
EXTERNAL NAME asmSimil.[SimilCLR.RatcliffObershelp].Simil
```

In the next section, we'll use this function to run the Simil algorithm.

Usage

The simplest use of this function, as shown in listing 1, is a procedure that takes a pair of strings and returns the result through the output parameter.

> **Listing 1   Calling the `fnSimil()` function from a stored procedure**

```
CREATE PROCEDURE dbo.spSimil
    @str1 nvarchar(max),
    @str2 nvarchar(max),
    @dblSimil float output
AS
SET NOCOUNT ON
SELECT @dblSimil = dbo.fnSimil(@str1, @str2)
RETURN
```

You can call this procedure like this:

```
DECLARE @dblSimil float
EXEC dbo.spSimil 'some string', 'some other string', @dblSimil OUTPUT
SELECT @dblSimil     --0.786
```

A more powerful use of the function, shown in listing 2, is where you search an entire table for similar strings, only returning those more similar than some threshold value. This procedure returns all Person records where the Person's name is more similar to the given name than a certain threshold.

Listing 2   Using the `fnSimil()` function to search an entire table

```
CREATE PROCEDURE dbo.spSimil_FirstNameLastName
    @str1 nvarchar(max),
    @threshold float
AS
SET NOCOUNT ON
SELECT *
    FROM (SELECT dbo.fnSimil(@str1, Person.Person.FirstName + N' ' +
➥Person.Person.LastName) AS Simil, * FROM Person.Person) AS T
    WHERE T.Simil >= @threshold
    ORDER BY T.Simil DESC;
```

This procedure can be called like this:

```
EXEC dbo.spSimil_FirstNameLastName N'John Adams', 0.75
```

A query like this can be used to ensure that only genuinely new persons are added to the database, and not simple misspellings.

Testing

In order to test the new .NET code, I used NUnit (http://www.nunit.com) to write test scenarios and execute them. I highly recommend this tool, especially for code modules such as Simil that don't have a user interface. The test scripts are available in the download package, and include tests for null strings, similar strings, case sensitive strings, and more. One test worth mentioning here is one where the new code is compared with the results from the previous classic DLL based on Steve Grubb's work, for all CompanyNames in the Northwind database.

This test shown in listing 3 opens an ADO.NET data table and loops over each record. It compares the Simil value from our .NET assembly with the previous classic DLL version (the "expected" value). The two values are compared in the Expect method and, if not equal, an exception is thrown and the test fails.

Listing 3   Comparing Simil values between a .NET assembly and a classic DLL

```
<Test()> _
Public Sub TestCompanyNames()
Dim dt As dsNorthwind.dtCustomersDataTable = m_Customers.GetData()
For Each r1 As dsNorthwind.dtCustomersRow In dt.Rows
    For Each r2 As dsNorthwind.dtCustomersRow In dt.Rows
        Dim similNew As Double =
        ➥SqlServerCLR.RatcliffObershelp.Simil(r1.CompanyName, r2.CompanyName)
        Dim similClassic As Double =
        ➥similClassic(r1.CompanyName, r2.CompanyName)
        Dim strMsg As String = "s1=" & r1.CompanyName & ", s2=" &
➥r2.CompanyName & ": simil new=" & similNew & ", expected=" & similClassic
        Expect(similNew, EqualTo(similClassic), strMsg)
    Next
Next
End Sub
```

NUnit allows the developer to run the tests repeatedly until all tests get a passing grade. This test even helped me find a bug. In the .NET version, I was using a `Byte` array to store the characters of the two strings to be compared, and for characters with accents such as in *Antonio Moreno Taquería*, the classic DLL and the .NET version aren't the same. I quickly switched to using a `Char` array and the values agreed again. Without NUnit, this bug would likely have been found by one of you, the users, rather than by the developer/tester.

Summary

In this chapter, we presented several ways to look up text in a database table. We presented a modern implementation of Simil as a .NET assembly. With a free download and a few simple T-SQL scripts you can start using it today in your applications.

About the author

Tom van Stiphout is the software development manager of Kinetik I.T. (http://www.kinetik-it.com). Tom has a degree from Amsterdam University and came to the United States in 1991. After a few years with C++ and Windows SDK programming, he gradually focused more on database programming. He worked with Microsoft Access from version 1.0, and Microsoft SQL Server from version 4.5. During the last several years, Tom added .NET programming to his repertoire.

Tom has been a frequent contributor to the online newsgroups for many years. He's a former Microsoft Regional Director and a current Microsoft Access MVP.

15 LINQ to SQL and ADO.NET Entity Framework

Bob Beauchemin

In ADO.NET 3.5 and 3.5 SP1, Microsoft introduced two models designed to abstract SQL statements into a high-level language and to operate on database data as objects. The first, LINQ to SQL, is a lightweight mapping of LINQ (Language Integrated Query) calls to the SQL Server database. The other model, ADO.NET Entity Framework (EF), consists of an object-relational mapping (ORM) framework as well as query and view services built over the ADO.NET provider model. The Entity Framework has its own dialect of SQL (Entity SQL or ESQL) and can use ESQL statements or LINQ queries to access data. Although neither framework uses vanilla T-SQL as its query language, both frameworks can generate SQL statements or use existing stored procedures to access the database. This chapter is not an introduction to these frameworks as I assume that you already know their basics, but I will discuss how these frameworks interact with SQL Server, especially with respect to performance.

One way to look at the performance of an abstraction layer is to examine and profile the ADO.NET code, but both EF and LINQ to SQL are T-SQL code generators (EF is not database-specific, but I'm only talking about SQL Server here); therefore, another way to address performance is to examine the generated T-SQL code. I will look at performance from the generated T-SQL code perspective.

Many programmers who specialize in query tuning salivate over the prospect of tuning the bad queries that will assuredly result from these two data access stacks. In addition, many DBAs would like to ban LINQ or EF use when coding against their companies' databases. Most people who profess a dislike for the generated code have never seen (or have seen very little of) the generated code. For someone who writes and tunes T-SQL code, code generating programs and frameworks that rely on code generation can be worrisome if the code generation compromises database performance. Both Entity Framework and LINQ to SQL have API calls that can expose their generated T-SQL; you can also use SQL Profiler to look at the generated T-SQL. This chapter outlines some of the performance and manageability concerns that arise through the use of these models, beginning with the dynamic generation of SQL inside applications.

LINQ to SQL and performance

CONCERN

LINQ to SQL and EF will proliferate the use of SQL code in applications, and will almost surely produce suboptimal dynamic SQL, causing database performance problems and plan cache pollution.

It's almost dogma among database programmers that *static SQL* in stored procedures is better for security than dynamic SQL constructed using string concatenation. Besides the obvious association between dynamic SQL and SQL injection, using dynamic SQL means that all users must be given access to the underlying tables, unless you use LINQ to SQL/EF strictly with views and stored procedures. Using stored procedures, the DBA doesn't need to give access to underlying tables to each user, only to EXECUTE permission. Using views, the DBA gives permission to the view, not the underlying tables.

Plan cache pollution refers to the fact that using many different variations of the same SQL statement produces multiple plans in the cache for what is the same query. For example,

```
SELECT au_fname, au_lname FROM dbo.authors WHERE au_lname = 'Smith'
```

would produce a different query plan from this query:

```
SELECT au_fname, au_lname FROM dbo.authors WHERE au_lname = 'Jones'
```

In simple cases like this, the SQL Server query optimizer can perform what's known as auto-parameterization, in which case either of the queries above becomes

```
(@1 varchar(8000))SELECT [au_fname],[au_lname] FROM [dbo].[authors] WHERE
    [au_lname]=@1
```

LINQ to SQL and EF make every attempt to use parameterized SQL, rather than dynamic SQL, in their code generation. Microsoft claims that LINQ to SQL minimizes if not eradicates the potential for SQL injection.

In the context of Plan cache pollution, given their code generation nature, LINQ to SQL and EF are more likely to generate more homogenous SQL than programmers who write parameterized queries themselves. And programmers who use dynamic SQL, especially those most likely to use only LINQ to SQL/EF in future projects, are likely causing plan cache pollution right now. For an extensive discussion of how the SQL Server plan caches work, I'd recommend Sangeetha Shekar's blog series on the plan cache in the SQL Programmability and API Development Team Blog.[1] In these

---

[1] Sangeetha Shekar's blog series "Plan Cache Concepts Explained," on the SQL Programmability & API Development Team Blog, begins with this entry: http://blogs.msdn.com/sqlprogrammability/archive/2007/01/08/plan-cache-concepts-explained.aspx.

articles Sangeetha (who works on the plan cache team) states that there's no cacheability difference between dynamic parameterized SQL and a stored procedure. Nonparameterized SQL suffers a slight cacheability difference unless it's reused, which is highly unlikely.

So far, it's been my experience that LINQ to SQL, being more table-centric in mapping, will in general generate code that's closer to the code a T-SQL programmer would generate. EF is more *object-centric* and sometimes generates SQL that's meant to construct object graphs and therefore more expensive plans result. But, as an example of the fact that code generation can carry us only so far, neither framework can generate a full outer join when using LINQ without extension methods. Entity Frameworks can use full outer joins when using the Entity SQL language directly.

One current plan cache pollution issue occurs when string literals are used in queries. The LINQ to SQL query

```
var query = from a in ctx.authors where a.city = "Oakland" select a;
```

generates the following parameterized query:

```
(@p0 varchar(7))SELECT [t0].[au_id], [t0].[au_lname], [t0].[au_fname],
     [t0].[phone], [t0].[address], [t0].[city], [t0].[state], [t0].[zip],
     [t0].[contract]  FROM [dbo].[authors] AS [t0]  WHERE [t0].[city] = @p0
```

The same Entity Framework query generates a T-SQL query with a string literal, to get the parameterized query you'll need to use the LINQ to Entities query:

```
string city = "Oakland";
var query = from a in ctx.Authors where a.city == city select a;
```

Note that the parameter length is seven characters exactly (the size of the string). If I replaced this with `"where a.city = "Portland" "` the result would be a parameterized query with a different string length (`nvarchar(8)`) for @p0. This pollutes the plan cache with one query for each different string size, when it's only necessary to use the field size of the city field (20 in this case). SQL Server's built-in auto-parameterization always uses the string length of 8000 characters or 4000 Unicode characters, and using one string size in the query parameter is preferable to one different query per string size. Both LINQ to SQL and the EF have addressed the parameter length issue in the upcoming .NET 4.0 release by choosing a default length when none is specified, but in the meantime, using these frameworks means making query plan reuse compromises.

Generating SQL that uses projection

CONCERN

Using LINQ to SQL and EF will encourage SELECT * FROM. . .—style coding because you get back a nice, clean object instead of the less-useful anonymous type you receive by doing projection. This will also make covering indexes useless.

LINQ to SQL and EF can return something other than a whole object instance. Here's an example:

```
// This returns a collection of author instances
var query =  from a in ctx.authors
 select a;
```

```
// this returns a collection of anonymous type instances
var query =  from a in ctx.authors
             join ta in ctx.titleauthors on a.au_id equals ta.au_id
             join t in ctx.titles on ta.title_id equals t.title_id
             select new { a.au_id, t.title_id };
```

The collection of authors returned by the first query is updatable, and a reference to it can be used outside the function in which it's created. The anonymous type is not updatable and cannot be used outside the function in which it's created without using reflection or `CastByExample<T>`. I can see a use for anonymous types in data binding: the good old dropdown list.

You don't necessarily need to return an anonymous type. You can define (by hand) a class that represents the projection of `authorid` and `titleid`. Or query a view that returns an instance of an object. But, in order to do this on a large-scale project, you'd need to define a class for each projection in the entire project. As a database programmer, ask yourself, "Can I list every different projection (rowset) that every query in my project returns?" Very few programmers can answer "yes" to that question, even though it may be a great tuning aid to be able to enumerate every projection your project returns. Therefore, writing a class for every anonymous type is a good idea, but it's a lot of extra work. Perhaps there will be a tool that automatically does this in the future. If you don't write your own objects for each projection, you're using *whole objects*. That is `SELECT * FROM` in SQL.

This is similar to the issue you'd run into using stored procedures that return rowsets with LINQ to SQL; the designer generates a named type for the first rowset based on the shape of the first result set that a stored procedure returns, and doesn't generate anything for the additional result sets in a multiple result set procedure. It's a good practice to handcode named types for the multiple result set procedure yourself. Using rowset-returning procedures with EF forces you to define a class to contain the rowset produced, and aside from the extra work involved because the EF designer doesn't do this automatically, that's a good idea. But EF can't use procedures that return more than one rowset (`SqlDataReader.NextResult` in ADO.NET).

How does this style relate to covering indexes? An overly-simplistic definition of a covering index would be "nonclustered index defined over the set of columns used by one table in a projection." These indexes make for nicely optimized query plans, and sometimes even help with concurrency issues in `SELECT`s. But if we're always doing `SELECT * FROM`, forget those covering indexes. The index used most commonly is the clustered index on the base table.

You shouldn't define a covering index for every projection just because you can. Every index consumes space and affects the performance of inserts, updates, and deletes; therefore, there's a tradeoff. In fact, I've also heard it said that if you need many, many covering indexes, perhaps your database isn't as well normalized as it could be, but I'm not really sure I buy this argument.

I'd say that the ease with which every projection can become a `SELECT * FROM` query when using objects is, for the most point, a valid worry. If you're concerned about database performance, you need to do coding beyond what the APIs provide.

Updating in the middle tier

> **CONCERN**
>
> Using LINQ to SQL and EF will encourage *SELECT to middle-tier, then UPDATE or DELETE* rather than issuing SQL `UPDATE` or `DELETE` statements that are set-based.

Neither LINQ to SQL nor Entity Framework currently contains analogs to SQL's `INSERT`, `UPDATE`, or `DELETE` statements. Entity SQL could be expanded to include DML in the future, but LINQ to SQL doesn't have a language that extends SQL. Both APIs can cause insert, update, and delete operations on the database. You create or manipulate object instances, then call `SaveChanges` (EF) or `SubmitChanges` (LINQ to SQL).

The manipulate-objects-and-save pattern works well in LINQ to SQL and reasonably well in EF. The distinction is that in EF, if there are related entities (for example, a `title` row contains an integrity constraint that mandates that the title's publisher must exist in the `publisher`'s table), you must fetch the related entities first, causing an extra round trip to the database. One way to avoid the extra round trip is to synthesize a reference using `EntityKey`. I described this in a set of blog posts about deleting a single row without fetching related entities.[2]

What about performing an update? The `SaveChanges` (EF) and `SubmitChanges` (LINQ to SQL) methods can perform multiple insert, update, and delete operations in a single round trip. But let's consider the number of database round trips involved to change a single customer row. This requires one round trip to select the row and another to update the row. And what about a searched update in SQL (`UPDATE...WHERE`) that updates multiple rows, or an update based on a SQL join condition, or using `MERGE` in SQL Server 2008? My favorite example, using update over a recursive common table expression, gathers all employees reporting to a certain manager and gives them all a raise. The number of fetches required just to do the update increases if you don't code the fetch statements in batches. Even if this doesn't increase the number of round trips required to get the rows, the sheer number of required fetches (database-generated network traffic) increases.

Let's address the general get-then-update pattern first. I worried about this one until I realized that in most applications I've worked on, you don't usually do a blind update or delete. A customer web application fetches a row (and related rows); a pair of eyes inspects the row to ensure this is indeed the right row, and then presses the user-interface button that causes an update or delete. Therefore, get-then-update is an

---

[2] See "Entity Framework Beta3—Deleting without fetching" on my blog: http://www.sqlskills.com/BLOGS/ BOBB/post/Entity-Framework-Beta3-Deleting-without-fetching.aspx.

integral part of most applications anyway. If the update or delete of a row affects related rows, this can be accomplished with cascading update or delete in the database.

But how about multiple, searched updates without inspecting and fetching all the rows involved? Neither LINQ to SQL nor EF has a straightforward way to deal with this. Alex James wrote an excellent four-part blog series about rolling your own searched update in EF with an underlying SQL Server using .NET extension methods getting the SQL query text and string handling to turn it into an update,[3] but this method is neither compact nor straightforward. It also looks SQL Server–dependent; therefore, Microsoft would need to replicate this for each provider to make it part of the Entity Framework in a future release.

LINQ to SQL contains the ultimate fallback method for this case. The `Data-Context.ExecuteCommand` method lets you execute any SQL command, including parameters. An example would look like this:

```
// Initialize the DataContext using constructor of your choice
DataContext db = new DataContext(fileOrServerOrConnection);
// Use SQL statement directly
db.ExecuteCommand("UPDATE Products SET UnitPrice = UnitPrice + 1.00");
```

EF doesn't have the equivalent because your data store is an object model over a conceptual data source, not the data source itself, but EF does expose the underlying `DbConnection` instance; therefore, you can issue your own commands against the database tables.

I'd suggest (or even mandate) using stored procedures in searched `update` or `delete`. The blind searched operation or multiple-statement update is accomplished in a single database round trip, and you can even use the `OUTPUT` clause in SQL Server's DML to obtain information in rowset form showing exactly what was changed or deleted. Because this is a database-specific operation, using a stored procedure sounds like a good workaround for this problem. With the use of stored procedures as needed and the realization that most apps use the get-then-update pattern anyway, I think I'll dismiss this worry.

Optimizing the number of database round trips

CONCERN

Queries generated by LINQ to SQL and EF get too much or too little data at a time. Too much data in one query is a waste. Too little data is also bad because it means extra database round trips.

Both LINQ to SQL and EF have good mechanisms to optimize data retrieval. In addition, the problem at hand does not necessarily apply only to an ORM (object-relational

---

[3] See "Rolling Your Own SQL Update On Top Of the Entity Framework," by Alex James: http://blogs.msdn.com/alexj/archive/2007/12/07/rolling-your-own-sql-update-on-top-of-the-entity-framework-part-1.aspx.

mapping) or even only to databases. In a filesystem graphical user interface, you don't normally pre-fetch all of the files' information throughout the entire filesystem when someone wants to look at the content of the C drive? On the other hand, if you know you're going to eventually display all of the related entities' information you likely do want to get them. If not, perhaps you want to get related entities all at once, when the first child entity is selected, or get the children one at a time when each child entity is selected.

LINQ to SQL addresses this by implementing a property on the DataContext, the DeferredLoadingEnabled property. It is set to True by default, which means it will retrieve only the Customer object when the customer has orders, for example. The related Orders objects are retrieved with extra round trips to the database, one row at a time, when the Customer instance's Orders property is accessed in code. The related property, LoadOptions, also on the DataContext, takes a DataLoadOptions instance that allows you to control exactly how much related data is retrieved. That is, do you want only related orders or would you rather have the framework fetch orders, order details, and associated products in a single round trip? The DataLoadOptions also allows you to filter the amount of data you get from related tables; that is, you can specify that you want each customer's associated orders, but only OrderID and OrderDate.

ADO.NET Entity Framework does this a bit differently. It doesn't have a property that allows you to control whether deferred loading is enabled; rather, deferred loading is done by default. In order to load associated entities, there is a separate Load method, and an IsLoaded property that you can check before loading. EF also has an Include property of the query which lets you to specify which related entities can be loaded, if eager loading is desired. With EF you can also use Entity-Splitting in your design if you know you always want to retrieve OrderID and OrderDate, but no other properties, from the Orders table. Object purists may frown on composing objects based only on commonly used queries.

You can also retrieve only certain columns from a table (i.e., all the columns in Customers table except the column that contains the customer's picture) with either a related type (Entity-Splitting) or an anonymous type. And you can always specify a join that returns an anonymous type, if desired, to get only the properties you need from related tables.

So I'd say that this worry is not only completely unwarranted, but that LINQ to SQL and EF make programmers think more about lazy loading versus eager loading. Using eager loading may be clearer and more maintainable than a join, which always returns an anonymous rowset with columns from all tables interspersed. That is, you know exactly what related data (at an object level) is being requested and retrieved. But be careful with eager loading and a join with more than two tables. The generated SQL code will produce an anonymous rowset for the first two tables, and separate queries for the remaining tables.

LINQ to SQL and stored procedures

CONCERN

Adoption of LINQ to SQL and EF will discourage the use of stored procedures to return rowsets. In addition, the code generators will use a subset of T-SQL query constructs, that is, only the constructs that the LINQ or ESQL language supports, rather than the full power of the T-SQL query language.

Aficionados always think that a stored procedure represents a contract between consumer and provider. Although the database metadata indicates number and type of parameters, and comprises a contract, this is absolutely not true for rowsets returned by stored procedures. There is no database metadata that records anything about the returned rowsets, or even how many rowsets a stored procedure will return. In addition, errors that occur in the middle of a stored procedure might result in rowsets not being returned. Finally, there's always the possibility of returning multiple and/or different rowsets by using a stored procedure with conditional code. That's not much of a rowset contract at all.

One way to ameliorate this problem in SQL Server is to use multi-statement table-valued functions to return one rowset with known metadata. The main problem with this is performance; a multi-statement table-valued function (TVF) is the equivalent of filling a table variable in code and then returning it. Almost always there is extra disk I/O involved: the I/O of reading the base tables, plus the I/O of filling the table variable, plus the I/O of reading the table variable at the consumer. There are also performance considerations as SQL Server table variables have no statistics. Therefore if the table-valued function is used as a row source in a larger query, there is no way to estimate the number of rows returned by the TVF. SQL Server 2008's strongly typed table-valued parameters would be an analogous concept, but currently these are limited to being input-only in procedures. No strongly typed rowset result is currently supported.

Now that we've determined that there is no more of a rowset contract for stored procedures than for ad hoc SQL (the difference is in SQL encapsulation), what about T-SQL extensions that Entity SQL doesn't support? There are database-specific extensions like SQL Server's PIVOT operator, or ANSI SQL standards, like ranking and windowing functions.

LINQ aficionados are quick to talk about implementation through extension methods but the long and short of this is that these are a LINQ-ism, unrelated to LINQ to SQL. That is, the LINQ construct to SQL dialect statement mapping is fixed and embedded in the LINQ to SQL product. Using extensions to the SQL statement mapping can't change which T-SQL statement is produced. To control what is produced, you'd need to implement equivalent concepts on the client side and leave the generated database code alone.

EF may have a better story with this because each provider/writer implements the ESQL to query mapping. Conceivably you could write a custom provider to encapsulate the supplied provider including the T-SQL–specific extensions. The ESQL language itself does not have the capability of ODBC-like escape clauses; therefore, there'd be no way to express this extended SQL-based functionality in ESQL.

I'd classify the "subset of SQL" and "stored procedure rowset is an anonymous type" problems as issues that might be worked out in future releases of databases and frameworks. Until LINQ to SQL or EF provides escape clauses in the framework, the easiest way out is the ultimate escape clause, using the stored procedure that returns (anonymous) rowsets. And the more stored procedures are used (not insert, update, and delete procedures, which enhance the model, but rowset-returning procedures), the farther away from the model you get. This interferes with the usefulness of the model in general.

Tuning and LINQ to SQL queries

CONCERN
LINQ to SQL and EF generated queries will be *untunable* because, even if you discover a performance problem, you can't change the underlying API code to produce the exact SQL query that you want. There are too many layers of abstraction to change it.

T-SQL is a declarative language; a query is simply a description of what you want, not a description of how to physically retrieve it. Sometimes, however, the programmer has the ability to rephrase queries, resulting in better performance. Part of query tuning can consist of changing the SQL to get the plan you want, based on your intimate knowledge of the current data and the current use cases. As a simple example, you can switch between joins, correlated subqueries, and nested subqueries to see which one gives the best performance, or use EXISTS rather than a JOIN, or UNION ALL rather than an IN clause. The limitation is that, in the future, the query processor can get smarter, as a result making your past work unnecessary. Usually though, you've benefited from rewriting SQL for those extra years until the query processor changes.

Because the LINQ to SQL or ESQL queries are programmatically transformed into SQL queries, it is time consuming, but not impossible, to rephrase LINQ or ESQL queries to produce subtly different SQL queries and thus better performance. Because this optimization technique (rephrasing LINQ queries to change the generated SQL) is in its infancy, and is also one layer removed from simply tuning the SQL, we'll have to see how it progresses as the frameworks become more popular. The Entity Framework team is thinking of introducing hints and providing direct control over query composition in future releases.

Besides query rewrites, you can also hint queries, and T-SQL allows a variety of query hints. This helps when the query processor chooses a suboptimal plan (uncommon, but not unheard of) or you have intimate knowledge or data and use cases. Another reason for hints is to service different use cases with the same query. SQL queries have only one plan at a time (modulo parallelized plans) and you might have to satisfy different use cases by hinting the same query differently. Because the translation to SQL is deeply embedded in the LINQ and EF source code, I can't hint in the LINQ or ESQL code if I find a performance problem that can be helped with a hint. This means going back to using stored procedures (they work with hints) rather than using model-generated queries.

Hinting is usually not preferred over rewriting the SQL because hints tie the query processor's hands. For example, if the statistics change so that a different plan would work better, the query processor can't use this information because you've told it how to accomplish the query. You've changed SQL from a declarative language to an imperative language. It's best not to put query hints in code, but separate them to a separate layer. SQL Server 2005 calls this separate layer *plan guides*. The plan guide is a named database object that relates a hint to a query without changing the underlying code. You can add and drop plan guides, turn them on and off at will, or re-evaluate them when things (the statistics or use cases) change.

Can you use plan guides with LINQ to SQL or EF queries? There are two things to keep in mind. First, a plan guide for a SQL statement requires an exact match on a batch-by-batch basis. Machine-generated SQL will likely make an exact match easier, but you will have to check that the guides are being used each time LINQ/EF libraries change. Second, plan guides work best if you have a limited number in your database. They're meant to be special-case, not to add another level of complexity to a situation that is complex and becomes more complex as the layers of abstraction increase. Therefore, although you can use plan guides, use them with care.

Is this issue worth worrying about? I think we'll need to wait and see. Will you fix a few bad SQL or bad query problems in LINQ/EF before giving up entirely, or fix performance problems in the generated SQL by going to stored procedures?

Summary

New database APIs that promise to abstract the programming model away from the underlying database model and its declarative SQL language are always exciting to programmers who want to concentrate on presentation, use cases, and business logic, and spend less time with database optimization. LINQ to SQL and EF (as well as other object-relational mappers) show promise in this area but the proof is in the efficiency of the generated code and the size and reuse potential of the plan cache that results. Should folks be waiting in anticipation of LINQ to SQL/EF related performance problems? I'm not the only one who thinks optimizing declarative languages will always have its place; we've seen much written already in books and blogs about the right and wrong way to use LINQ to SQL and the ADO.NET Entity Framework. This chapter should provide you with hints and concerns from a database performance perspective.

About the author

Bob Beauchemin is a database-centric application practitioner and architect, instructor, course author, writer, and Developer Skills Partner for SQLskills. Over the past few years he's been writing and teaching his SQL Server 2005 and 2008 courses to students worldwide through Microsoft-sponsored programs, as well as private client-centric classes. He is the lead author of the books *A Developer's Guide to SQL Server 2005* and *A First Look at SQL Server 2005 For Developers*, author of *Essential ADO.NET*, and writes a database development column for MSDN magazine.

16 Table-valued parameters

Don Kiely

A major goal of the new Transact-SQL (T-SQL) features in SQL Server 2008 is to reduce the amount of code you need to write for common scenarios. Many new language features simplify code, and *table-valued parameters* probably do so most dramatically.

Such an innocuous name for a radical new feature! It's the sort of thing that only a geek could love: the ability to pass a table to a procedure. It's a simple enhancement but will change the way you think about programming SQL Server forever. If you've ever passed a comma or other delimited list of data values to a stored procedure, then split them up, and processed them, or bumped up against stored procedure parameter limits, you know the pain that is now forever gone. In this chapter I'll explore the syntax and use of this new T-SQL feature, both in SQL Server code as well as client code. By the end of the chapter, you'll wonder how you ever programmed without it!

What's the problem?

Before SQL Server 2008, there was no easy way to pass data containers—arrays, DataSets, DataTables, and so on—to stored procedures and functions. You could pass single scalar values with no problem, although if you had to pass many parameters you might run into the limit on parameters, which is 2,100. Objects like arrays, in-memory tables, and other constructs are not the kind of set-based objects that T-SQL deals with. Yet sometimes it is necessary to pass data containers to a code module.

Over the years, the ever-resourceful SQL Server community has devised plenty of ways to get around this problem. Some of the more common workarounds have included the following:

- Pass in a delimited string, and parse it using T-SQL's less-than-robust string-handling features.
- Pass data to the procedure as XML and shred it into a relational form.

- Create long parameter lists with plenty of optional parameters to accommodate varying needs.
- Create a global temporary table or even a permanent Parameters table to store lists of parameter data, which is often linked to a particular user connection.

The problem has plenty of other creative solutions. Unfortunately, making these solutions work requires either convoluted code or a shared resource or both, thereby creating maintenance nightmares.

Another kind of problem with T-SQL's inability to pass a data container as a parameter occurs when you pass data from a client application to be stored or processed in SQL Server. The canonical problem of this type is creating a new customer order along with one or more order line items. The overall workflow between client application and database server goes something like this: Pass the order header information, including customer ID, order date, and other order details. Get the new order ID back (normally the primary key of the Order table), then make multiple calls to an Insert-OrderDetail stored procedure to insert each order detail line item's data. Because there has been no easy way to encapsulate all this in a single call to the database server, the application has a chatty relationship with the server, causing many round trips and creating a fragile situation. You had to be careful with transactions, because whenever so much data was flowing back and forth between the application server and the database server, too many things could go wrong. In addition, it's never a good idea to leave data fragments lying around a database.

Table-valued parameters to the rescue!

Microsoft has felt our pain, and their solution is *table-valued parameters* (TVPs). This is not a new data type, but rather an object variable of type TABLE, an in-memory collection of rows. TABLE variable types are not new in SQL Server 2008. What's new is that you can now pass a variable of this type as a parameter to a stored procedure or other code module.

What? That's all that's new? Yes, indeed! This seemingly simple change has enormous implications for the code you write, vastly simplifying code whenever you need to pass rows of data to a code module. The parameter is a strongly typed database object with a table schema that you define, with all of the normal benefits of such variables. TVPs are great for passing tabular data around the code modules that make up an application, meeting a need that is surprisingly common in relational databases.

Let's take a look at a simple example of creating and using a TVP. You create and use TVPs in five steps:

1 Create a table type and define its structure.
2 Declare a code module that accepts a parameter of the table type.
3 Declare a variable of the table type and reference it.
4 Fill the table variable with data.
5 Call the code module, passing the variable to it.

The code for this example is in the Simple.sql file. The first step is to create the table type and define its structure. This is a persistent database object that you can reuse all you want within the database. Here, `MyTbl` has an integer ID field—presumably a primary key—and a string field.

```
CREATE TYPE MyTbl AS TABLE
    (ID INT, String NVARCHAR(100))
GO
```

You can treat the type almost like any kind of persisted table, such as by defining a primary key, `CHECK` constraints, default values for fields, and computed columns, and you can even set permissions. One of the few limitations is that you can't call user-defined functions from types.

The next step is to create a stored procedure that uses a parameter of the `MyTbl` type. The `dkSelectFromTVP` procedure takes the TVP as its only parameter and returns the contents of the table using a `SELECT` statement. As I said, this is a simple example.

```
CREATE PROCEDURE dkSelectFromTVP(@TVParam MyTbl READONLY)
AS
    SET NOCOUNT ON;
    SELECT * FROM @TVParam;
GO
```

Next, create an instance of the `TABLE` type and populate it from data. The code that follows creates the `@TVP` variable and inserts some data with the names of some cities and locations in Alaska. Notice that you can populate `TABLE` types using the same T-SQL statements used to insert data in regular, persisted tables.

```
DECLARE @TVP AS MyTbl;

INSERT INTO @TVP(ID, String) VALUES (1, 'Fairbanks');
INSERT INTO @TVP(ID, String) VALUES (2, 'Juneau');
INSERT INTO @TVP(ID, String) VALUES (3, 'Anchorage');
INSERT INTO @TVP(ID, String) VALUES (4, 'Denali');
```

`@TVP` behaves like any other kind of local variable, with a well-defined scope—the code module in which you declare it—that is cleaned up when it goes out of scope. One benefit is that using a table-valued parameter with a stored procedure generally causes fewer recompilations than using temporary tables.

The final step is to run the stored procedure, passing the `@TVP` table-valued parameter. Here's the code:

```
EXEC dkSelectFromTVP @TVP;
```

This produces the result shown in figure 1. Amazing! We have a stored procedure that returns the result of a `SELECT` statement!

Let's take the example a few steps further. Say that you want to change the data within the stored procedure before returning it. Here is a revised stored procedure that shows

Figure 1   Results of passing a TVP to a stored procedure with list of Alaska place names

some civic pride by adding "Rocks!" to every city name other than Anchorage (which is just a big city that is more like Seattle than anything else in Alaska).[1]

```
ALTER PROCEDURE dkSelectFromTVP(@TVParam MyTbl READONLY)
AS
    SET NOCOUNT ON
    UPDATE @TVParam SET String=String + ' Rocks!' WHERE String <>
➡ 'Anchorage'
    SELECT * FROM @TVParam
GO
```

But when you run this ALTER code, it produces an error message:

```
Msg 10700, Level 16, State 1, Procedure dkSelectFromTVP, Line 5
The table-valued parameter "@TVParam" is READONLY and cannot be modified.
```

Oops! We forgot to remove the READONLY keyword in the definition. After making that change, here is the new code:

```
ALTER PROCEDURE dkSelectFromTVP(@TVParam MyTbl)
AS
    SET NOCOUNT ON
    UPDATE @TVParam SET String=String + ' Rocks!'
        WHERE String <> 'Anchorage'
    SELECT * FROM @TVParam
GO
```

But when you run this code, you still get an error message:

```
Msg 352, Level 15, State 1, Procedure dkSelectFromTVP, Line 1
The table-valued parameter @TVParam must be declared with the READONLY
    option.
```

This shows that a TVP must be declared as READONLY within the code module where you use it as a parameter. This means that you can't change the contents of the table from within the code module. This is a disappointing limitation of TVPs in SQL Server 2008, but Microsoft is receiving pressure to ease this restriction in an update or future version. For now, you can work around the problem by making changes to the content of the table variable before passing it to a code module. The following code shows an example of how you could do that:

```
DECLARE @TVP AS MyTbl

INSERT INTO @TVP(ID, String) VALUES (1, 'Fairbanks')
INSERT INTO @TVP(ID, String) VALUES (2, 'Juneau')
INSERT INTO @TVP(ID, String) VALUES (3, 'Anchorage')
INSERT INTO @TVP(ID, String) VALUES (4, 'Denali')

UPDATE @TVP SET String=String + ' Rocks!' WHERE String <> 'Anchorage'

EXEC dkSelectFromTVP @TVP
```

---

[1] Editor's note: The author of this chapter is from Fairbanks, Alaska, which is several times smaller than Anchorage. He assures me that there is, in fact, no rivalry between the two cities at all.

An interesting characteristic of a TVP is that it has a non-null default value: an empty recordset. That means that this statement,

```
EXEC dkSelectFromTVP
```

does not cause an error, even though the stored procedure definition does not define a default value for the parameter, nor does it allow nulls. The default value for a TVP is an empty recordset, even if you never initialize the variable. Keep that behavior in mind as you work with TVPs, because it is quite different for other variable types.

Another TVP example

Okay, that wasn't the most extraordinary use of a TVP. But it shows the steps and syntax that you'll use with TVPs. Let's look at another example of how to use TVPs. This example, in the Products.sql file, uses a TABLE type to read product data from the AdventureWorksLT2008 database and insert new rows into another products table along with inventory data and the current date through a stored procedure. The first step is to create the TABLE type, which contains two fields for product information:

```
CREATE TYPE ProductsType AS TABLE
    (ProductName NVARCHAR(50), ProductNumber NVARCHAR(25));
GO
```

NOTE Microsoft no longer ships sample databases with SQL Server, but they do make them available on CodePlex. You can download the full set of sample SQL Server 2005 and 2008 databases from http://www.codeplex.com/ MSFTDBProdSamples.

The Products table will contain the new information. The Name and ProductNumber fields will contain the data from the AdventureWorksLT2008 database, while the ItemsInStock and CreatedDate fields will be populated when the data is inserted into the table.

```
CREATE TABLE Products
    (Name NVARCHAR(50),
    ProductNumber NVARCHAR(25),
    ItemsInStock INT,
    CreatedDate DATETIME);
GO
```

The next bit of code creates the stored procedure that receives the TVP with the product name and number data. It uses an INSERT statement to add data to the new Products table, setting ItemsInStock to zero and using the GETDATE() function to insert the current date and time.

```
CREATE PROCEDURE dkInsertProducts
    @ProductsTVP ProductsType READONLY
AS
    SET NOCOUNT ON
    INSERT INTO dbo.Products (Name, ProductNumber, ItemsInStock,
        CreatedDate)
        SELECT Name, ProductNumber, 0, GETDATE() FROM @ProductsTVP;
GO
```

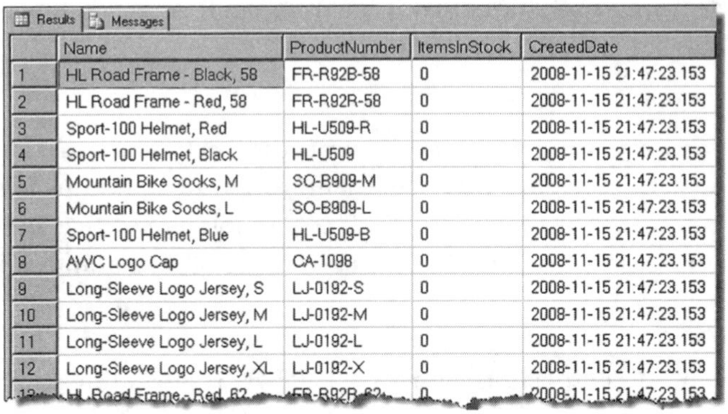

	Name	ProductNumber	ItemsInStock	CreatedDate
1	HL Road Frame - Black, 58	FR-R92B-58	0	2008-11-15 21:47:23.153
2	HL Road Frame - Red, 58	FR-R92R-58	0	2008-11-15 21:47:23.153
3	Sport-100 Helmet, Red	HL-U509-R	0	2008-11-15 21:47:23.153
4	Sport-100 Helmet, Black	HL-U509	0	2008-11-15 21:47:23.153
5	Mountain Bike Socks, M	SO-B909-M	0	2008-11-15 21:47:23.153
6	Mountain Bike Socks, L	SO-B909-L	0	2008-11-15 21:47:23.153
7	Sport-100 Helmet, Blue	HL-U509-B	0	2008-11-15 21:47:23.153
8	AWC Logo Cap	CA-1098	0	2008-11-15 21:47:23.153
9	Long-Sleeve Logo Jersey, S	LJ-0192-S	0	2008-11-15 21:47:23.153
10	Long-Sleeve Logo Jersey, M	LJ-0192-M	0	2008-11-15 21:47:23.153
11	Long-Sleeve Logo Jersey, L	LJ-0192-L	0	2008-11-15 21:47:23.153
12	Long-Sleeve Logo Jersey, XL	LJ-0192-X	0	2008-11-15 21:47:23.153
13	HL Road Frame - Red, 62	FR-R92R-62	0	2008-11-15 21:47:23.153

Figure 2 Results of running TVP-stored procedure

The final set of server-side code creates the variable of the `TABLE` type `ProductsType`, reads data from the AdventureWorksLT2008.SalesLT.Product table, and passes the TVP to the stored procedure.

```
DECLARE @Prods AS ProductsType;
INSERT INTO @Prods (ProductName, ProductNumber)
    SELECT [Name], ProductNumber FROM AdventureWorksLT2008.SalesLT.Product;

EXEC dkInsertProducts @Prods;
GO
SELECT * FROM Products;
```

Figure 2 shows the results of running the code.

The usefulness of TVPs becomes apparent only with more real-world examples that are called from ADO.NET client applications, so we'll explore that next.

Using TVPs from client applications

Microsoft has a huge job keeping its various database and development platforms in sync so that developers can take advantage of new SQL Server 2008 features. To make full use of TVPs, you'll need to use both Visual Studio 2008 and ADO.NET 3.5. Neither has full support yet for all new SQL Server 2008 features, but fortunately the initial releases of both products support TVPs.

From client applications, you can use TVPs to pass multiple rows of data in a single round trip to the server, without any special server-side processing logic or temporary tables to hold data for set operations. The data you pass must have the correct number of fields to match the TVP definition on the server, but the column names don't have to match. The data types must correspond to the types defined in the code module in SQL Server, or be implicitly convertible. If you violate these requirements, you'll get an error message from SQL Server.

You can pass a TVP from ADO.NET code to SQL Server using any of three ADO.NET objects:

- `System.Data.DataTable`
- `System.Data.DbDataReader`
- `System.Collections.Generic.IList<SqlDataRecord>`

ADO.NET and SQL Server collaborate to perform the conversions necessary to create a new TABLE type that is usable by T-SQL. The DataTable object is probably the easiest to use and familiar to most .NET database application developers. The DbDataReader object is part of ADO.NET's alternative factory-method-based objects. SqlDataRecord is used within SQL CLR code, which is the .NET code that executes within the SQL Server process.

Most often, you'll need to identify the parameter as a TVP by using the TypeName property of a SqlParameter object, setting the property to SqlDbType.Structured. The type you use must match the name of a compatible TABLE type in the database on SQL Server. Otherwise you'll get an error.

Using a DataTable

The sample client is an ASP.NET website application contained in the Client directory in this chapter's sample files. The Simple.aspx page shows two methods of using TVPs from ADO.NET with the DataTable and DbDataReader objects. The first of two buttons on the form uses the dkSelectFromTVP stored procedure created earlier in the chapter to return the list of rows in the TVP passed to it. Listing 1 shows the two methods. The BuildDataTable method creates a new DataTable and populates it with data, this time with some cities and villages in the Alaska Interior. The real meat of the code is in the DataTableButton Click event procedure.

Listing 1   Code to use a `DataTable` to pass a TVP to a stored procedure

```
private DataTable BuildDataTable()
{
    DataTable dt = new DataTable("AlaskaCities");
    dt.Columns.Add("ID", typeof(System.Int32));
    dt.Columns.Add("String", typeof(System.String));

    dt.Rows.Add(1, "Ester");
    dt.Rows.Add(2, "Chena");
    dt.Rows.Add(3, "North Pole");
    dt.Rows.Add(4, "Chatanika");
    dt.Rows.Add(5, "Fox");
    return dt;
}

protected void DataTableButton_Click(object sender, EventArgs e)
{
    DataTable dt = BuildDataTable();

    using (SqlConnection cnn = new SqlConnection(ConfigurationManager
        .ConnectionStrings["TVPs"].ConnectionString))
    {
        SqlCommand cmd = new SqlCommand("dkSelectFromTVP", cnn);
        cmd.CommandType = CommandType.StoredProcedure;
        cmd.Parameters.AddWithValue("@TVParam", dt);
        cnn.Open();

        SqlDataReader dr = cmd.ExecuteReader();
        GridView1.DataSource = dr;
```

```
        GridView1.DataBind();
    }
}
```

The event procedure starts by creating the Data-
Table object to be passed to the stored procedure.
The rest of the code is fairly typical ADO.NET code
that creates a command object, adds the DataTable
as a parameter, and calls the ExecuteReader
method to return the resultset, which is bound to a
GridView control on the web form. Figure 3 shows
the results.

TVP Simple Client Example

**Figure 3   Results of passing a
DataTable as a TVP**

The notable thing about this example is that
there isn't anything notable about it, compared to
how you've been writing ADO.NET code for years.
And because the structure of the DataTable is such
a close match for the TABLE type defined earlier, the code doesn't even have to specify
the SqlDbType of the table-valued parameter. Usually specifying the type is not
optional, so you should get into the habit of always providing that information. You'll
see how in the next example.

Using a DbDataReader

The second button on the Simple.aspx page uses a DbDataReader object, one of the
factory-based objects provided by ADO.NET. This example reads the ProductID and
Name fields from the Product table in the AdventureWorksLT2008 database and populates a DbDataReader object with that data. It then passes the object to the dkSelect-
FromTVP stored procedure and again binds the results to the GridView control on the
web page.

This time the code that defines the parameter is a bit different than our last example, because you have to specify the TypeName and SqlDbType properties of the Sql-
Parameter object. Set the TypeName property to the name of the TABLE type you
defined in the database and set the SqlDbType property to the SqlDbType.Structured
enumeration value.

```
SqlParameter param = cmd.Parameters.AddWithValue("@TVParam", ddr);
param.TypeName = "dbo.MyTbl";
param.SqlDbType = SqlDbType.Structured;
```

Listing 2 shows the full code for the button's Click event procedure, and figure 4
shows a partial list of the results.

Listing 2   Using a DbDataReader object as a TVP

```
protected void DbDataReaderButton_Click(object sender, EventArgs e)
{
    DbProviderFactory factory =
        DbProviderFactories.GetFactory("System.Data.SqlClient");
```

```
DbConnection cnnAW = factory.CreateConnection();
cnnAW.ConnectionString = ConfigurationManager
    .ConnectionStrings["AWLT"].ConnectionString;

DbCommand dbCmd = cnnAW.CreateCommand();
dbCmd.CommandText = "SELECT Productid, [Name] FROM SalesLT.Product";
dbCmd.CommandType = CommandType.Text;
cnnAW.Open();

DbDataReader ddr = dbCmd.ExecuteReader();

using (SqlConnection cnn = new SqlConnection(ConfigurationManager
    .ConnectionStrings["TVPs"].ConnectionString))
{
    SqlCommand cmd = new SqlCommand("dkSelectFromTVP", cnn);
    cmd.CommandType = CommandType.StoredProcedure;
    SqlParameter param = cmd.Parameters.AddWithValue("@TVParam", ddr);
    param.TypeName = "dbo.MyTbl";
    param.SqlDbType = SqlDbType.Structured;
    cnn.Open();

    SqlDataReader dr = cmd.ExecuteReader();
    GridView1.DataSource = dr;
    GridView1.DataBind();
}
}
```

Figure 4　Results of passing a DbDataReader as a TVP

Using TVPs to enter orders

The next example shows a more realistic use for TVPs. The code is part of an order entry system, and one of the application requirements is to reduce the number of round trips between the client application and the database server. The code in Orders.sql takes the order header information and line items and inserts them into the appropriate tables in the database in a single round trip. The code in listing 3 shows the T-SQL used to create the database objects. The OrderDetailsType is a TABLE type that the client application will pass to the stored procedure with the list of products selected by the user. Pricing and other information will be gathered from other tables in the AdventureWorksLT2008 database. Then the code creates the Orders and OrderDetails tables to hold the data. Finally, the code creates the dkPlaceOrder stored procedure that receives the CustomerID and OrderDetailsType TVP. It gets the next order ID from the Orders table, then inserts the data into the Orders and OrderDetails tables. Note that all the data is either passed to the procedure or gathered from related tables in the AdventureWorksLT2008 database.

NOTE   To keep things simple and to focus on TVPs, I didn't make this code robust enough to handle concurrency issues. For example, the method of getting the next OrderID number will likely result in duplicate IDs in a multiuser environment. So don't use this code in a production environment without beefing it up to handle your environment!

Listing 3   Code to create database objects to insert orders

```
-- Create type to hold user product selections
CREATE TYPE OrderDetailsType AS TABLE
    (ProductID INT NOT NULL, Quantity INT NOT NULL)
GO

CREATE TABLE Orders (
    OrderID INT NOT NULL,
    CustomerID INT NOT NULL,
    OrderDate Datetime NOT NULL)
GO

CREATE TABLE OrderDetails (
    OrderID INT NOT NULL,
    ProductID INT NOT NULL,
    Cost MONEY NOT NULL,
    Quantity INT NOT NULL)
GO

CREATE PROCEDURE dkPlaceOrder (
    @CustomerID INT,
    @Items OrderDetailsType READONLY)
AS
    -- Get the next OrderID
    -- CAUTION! Simple, but not robust for concurrent apps
    DECLARE @OrderID INT
    SET @OrderID = (SELECT ISNULL(MAX(OrderID)+1, 1) FROM Orders)

    -- Create the order
    INSERT INTO dbo.Orders VALUES(@OrderID, @CustomerID, GETDATE())

    -- Insert the products
    INSERT dbo.OrderDetails(OrderID, ProductID, Cost, Quantity)
        SELECT @OrderID, tvp.ProductID, prd.StandardCost, tvp.Quantity
            FROM @Items AS tvp
            INNER JOIN AdventureWorksLT2008.SalesLT.Product AS prd
                ON tvp.ProductID = prd.ProductID
GO
```

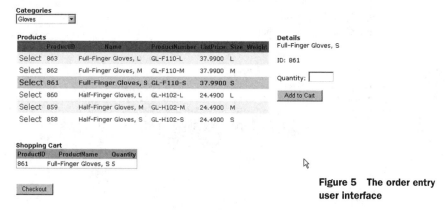

Figure 5   The order entry
user interface

Orders.sql also has some code you can use to test the stored procedure by entering an order.

Figure 5 shows that the Orders.aspx page in the Client sample website application has the user interface. The user selects a product category, then selects one of the available products. To order the item, the user enters the quantity and clicks the Add to Cart button. The Shopping Cart section keeps track of the selected items. When the user is done, she clicks the Checkout button to place the order, which inserts the data into the Orders and OrderDetails tables. To maximize profits, there is no way to remove an item from the shopping cart after it is placed there.

Most of the code behind the Orders.aspx page manages the user interface and is not included here; you can explore that code on your own. The shopping cart is managed with a `DataTable` that is saved as a session variable as the user interacts with the page and selects products. This makes it easy to pass to the stored procedure when the user is ready to place the order.

But there is a twist in the code: to make displaying the contents of the shopping cart convenient, the `DataTable` includes a `ProductName` field in addition to the two fields that the stored procedure expects. So before passing the `DataTable` to the procedure, the code removes that extra field. It does this by creating a copy of the `DataTable` object and removing the column from the copy instead of the original object. If you tried to pass the `DataTable` with the extra field, SQL Server would refuse it and raise an error.

Listing 4 contains the code for the `Click` event of the Checkout button. The code uses a hardcoded `CustomerID` of 1, and sets up to pass the `dt DataTable` object as a TVP.

Listing 4   Checkout code that creates the order in the database

```
protected void CheckoutButton_Click(object sender, EventArgs e)
{
    // Need to get rid of extra column
```

```
DataTable dt = dtCart.Copy();
dt.Columns.Remove("ProductName");

using (SqlConnection cnn = new SqlConnection(ConfigurationManager
    .ConnectionStrings["TVPs"].ConnectionString))
{
    SqlCommand cmd = new SqlCommand("dkPlaceOrder", cnn);
    cmd.CommandType = CommandType.StoredProcedure;
    cmd.Parameters.AddWithValue("@CustomerID", 1);
    SqlParameter param = cmd.Parameters.AddWithValue("@Items", dt);
    param.TypeName = "dbo.OrderDetailstype";
    param.SqlDbType = SqlDbType.Structured;

    cnn.Open();

    cmd.ExecuteNonQuery();

    dtCart.Rows.Clear();
    gridCart.DataSource = dtCart;
    gridCart.DataBind();
}
}
```

Summary

The primary benefit of using TVPs is that you can write simpler code than in older versions of SQL Server because you don't have to deal with the lack of container objects supported in T-SQL. As a result you have more flexibility in working with sets of data as well as better performance because you can take advantage of T-SQL's set-based operations.

The variable that contains the TVPs is scoped to the procedure to which they are passed, just as with other types of parameters. They abide by all of the security features in SQL Server, which means that you can assign permissions on the TABLE type object and limit how they are used and by whom. And like other database objects, various catalog views can provide information about the table objects.

TVPs do have limitations:

- TVPs are passed by reference (BY REF) for the sake of performance. (This is not the same way that objects are passed by reference in .NET programming languages; see the explanation that follows.)

- The parameter must be marked as READONLY, which means that you can't modify in any way the data in the TVP from within the procedure you pass it to. This is probably the most significant limitation of TVPs, one that hopefully Microsoft will ease in the future.

- No statistics are created on the TABLE object variable, which means that you may end up with expensive table scans more often than you would with a regular persisted table.

It is important to remember that the default value for a TABLE variable is an empty recordset, *not* a null. This makes it different from any other data type, so you have to remember this and not expect that a TABLE variable will ever be null.

As mentioned above, one of the limitations of TVPs is that they are passed by reference. The TVP is materialized as a temporary table in the tempdb database, and when you pass it to a code module, you are actually passing a reference to that table. SQL Server manages it all for you, so unless you dig (or read the documentation!) you'll never know this. The code samples for this chapter include a `TempDB.sql` script that lets you explore this behavior, by displaying `tempdb`'s `sys.tables` and `sys.columns` catalog views to list the structure of the TVP from within a stored procedure.

Nevertheless, despite these limitations, TVPs do a remarkable job in reducing the amount of code that you need to write when you need to pass a set of data to a code module. They are probably among the best of the productivity features that Microsoft introduced in SQL Server 2008.

About the author

Don Kiely, MVP, MCSD, is a technology consultant who develops secure desktop and web applications using tools including SQL Server, VB, C#, AJAX, and ASP.NET. He writes regularly for many industry journals, including *Visual Studio Magazine*, MSDN *Magazine*, *CoDe Magazine*, and *asp.netPRO*. Don trains developers and speaks regularly at industry conferences, including TechEd, SQL PASS, DevConnections, DevTeach, and others, and is a member of the INETA and MSDN Canada speaker bureaus. He writes courseware and records videos for AppDev. In his other life he roams the Alaska wilderness by foot, dog sled, skis, and kayak. Contact him at donkiely@computer.org.

17 Build your own index

Erland Sommarskog

Consider this SQL query:

```
SELECT person_id, first_name, last_name, birth_date, email
FROM    persons WHERE email LIKE '%' + @word + '%'
```

You can immediately tell that the only way the SQL Server can evaluate this query is to look through every single email address, be that by scanning the table or by scanning an index on the email column. If the table is large, say, ten million rows, you can expect an execution time of at least a minute.

Imagine now that there is a requirement that in most cases the response time for a search should be only a few seconds. How could you solve this? Regular indexes do not help, nor do full-text indexes; to be efficient both require that there is no leading wildcard in the search string.

There is one way out: you have to build your own index. In this chapter I will look at three ways to do this. The first two methods more or less require SQL 2005 or later, whereas the last method is easily implementable on SQL 2000.

The database and the table

In this chapter we will work with the persons table shown in listing 1.

Listing 1 Creating the persons table and index on email

```
CREATE TABLE persons (
    person_id   int           NOT NULL,
    first_name  nvarchar(50)  NULL,
    last_name   nvarchar(50)  NOT NULL,
    birth_date  datetime      NULL,
    email       varchar(80)   NOT NULL,
    other_data  char(73)      NOT NULL DEFAULT ' '
    CONSTRAINT pk_persons PRIMARY KEY (person_id))

CREATE INDEX email_ix ON persons (email)
```

The aim is to implement queries that permit users to look up persons by searching on parts of an email address. The column other_data is a filler to make the table wider; in a real-life table you would instead find other columns, such as address, city and so on.

If you want to work with the examples in this chapter, you should get the file Ch.17.zip from the download area for this book. This file includes a number of scripts that we will work with. The scripts assume that you have Microsoft SQL Server 2005 or later installed. Note also that some of the scripts require that you have enabled the Common Language Runtime (CLR) on you server; by default the execution of user-written CLR code is disabled.

Different file names denote different versions of the scripts for SQL 2005 and SQL 2008. The zip file also includes a BCP file from which the persons table is loaded.

The script 01_build_database.sql creates a database called yourownindex, which is 1.7 GB, whereof 700 MB are the log files. Before you run the script, run a find-and-replace to match the path to which you extracted the files. The database collation is Latin1_General_CI_AS.

The script loads one million rows into the persons table from the BCP file. Because including real email addresses in a download file could be sensitive, I have generated the addresses from a list of Slovenian words that I happened to have lying around. Slovenian is a language which is very rich in inflections, and this list has over a million entries.

The user section of the addresses is completely random. There are some 20,000 different domains, with a skewed distribution to make some domains more common than others to mimic a real-world situation. The top domains are the normal ones, with the distribution taken from a real-world source. About 58 percent of the addresses end in .com or .net. The email addresses are lowercase only, and I have replaced all accented characters so that only international A through Z characters appear. There are no digits in the data.

The data in the columns first_name, last_name, and birth_date are taken from the AdventureWorksDW database.

The build script also creates a few more items that I will present as we encounter them. Expect the script to run for 2–3 minutes; it's a good idea to run the script at this point.

Plain search and introducing tester_sp

One should never go on a performance quest without a baseline. In our case this is the SELECT statement in the beginning of the article. This also gives me the opportunity to introduce the stored procedure tester_sp, created by 01_build_database.sql. Tester_sp expects a single parameter: the name of the procedure to be tested. Tester_sp assumes that the tested procedure takes a single parameter containing a search string, and that the procedure returns the columns person_id, first_name, last_name, birth date, and email for all persons whose email address contains the search string.

Tester_sp calls the tested procedure with four different search strings, and records the number of rows returned and the execution time in milliseconds. The procedure makes two calls for each search string, and before the first call for each string, tester_sp also executes the command DBCC DROPCLEANBUFFERS to flush the buffer cache. Thus, we measure the execution time both when reading from disk and when reading from memory.

Of the four search strings, two are three-letter strings that appear in 10 and 25 email addresses respectively. One is a five-letter string that appears in 1978 email addresses, and the last string is a complete email address with a single occurrence.

Here is how we test the plain_search procedure. (You can also find this script in the file 02_plain_search.sql.)

```
CREATE PROCEDURE plain_search @word varchar(50) AS
SELECT person_id, first_name, last_name, birth_date, email
FROM   persons WHERE email LIKE '%' + @word + '%'
go

EXEC tester_sp 'plain_search'
go
```

The output when I ran it on my machine was as follows:

```
6660 ms, 10 rows. Word = "joy".
6320 ms, 10 rows. Word = "joy". Data in cache.
7300 ms, 25 rows. Word = "aam".
6763 ms, 25 rows. Word = "aam". Data in cache.
17650 ms, 1978 rows. Word = "niska".
6453 ms, 1978 rows. Word = "niska". Data in cache.
6920 ms, 1 rows. Word = "omamo@petinosemdesetletnicah.com".
6423 ms, 1 rows. Word = "omamo@petinosemdesetletnicah.com". Data in cache.
```

These are the execution times we should try to beat.

Using the LIKE operator—an important observation

Consider this procedure:

```
CREATE PROCEDURE substring_search @word varchar(50) AS
SELECT person_id, first_name, last_name, birth_date, email
FROM   persons WHERE substring(email, 2, len(email)) = @word
```

This procedure does not meet the user requirements for our search. Nevertheless, the performance data shows something interesting:

	joy	aam	niska	omamo@
Disk	5006	4726	4896	4673
Cache	296	296	296	296

The execution times for this procedure are better than those for plain_search, and when the data is in cache, the difference is dramatic. Yet, this procedure, too, must scan, either the table or the index on the email column. So why is it so much faster?

The answer is that the LIKE operator is expensive. In the case of the substring function, SQL Server can examine whether the second character in the column matches the first letter of the search string, and move on if it doesn't. But for LIKE, SQL Server must examine every character at least once. On top of that, the collation in the test database is a Windows collation, so SQL Server applies the complex rules of Unicode. (The fact that the data type of the column is varchar does not matter.)

This has an important ramification when designing our search routines: we should try to minimize the use of the LIKE operator.

Using a binary collation

One of the alternatives for improving the performance of the LIKE operator is to force a binary collation as follows:

```
COLLATE Latin1_General_BIN2 LIKE '%' + @word + '%'
```

With a binary collation, the complex Unicode rules are replaced by a simple byte comparison. In the file 02_plain_search.sql, there is the procedure plain_search_binary. When I ran this procedure through tester_sp, I got these results:

```
         joy    aam   niska   omamo@
Disk    4530   4633    4590     4693
Cache    656    636     733      656
```

Obviously, it's not always feasible to use a binary collation, because many users expect searches to be case insensitive. However, I think it's workable for email addresses. They are largely restricted to ASCII characters, and you can convert them to lowercase when you store them. The solutions I present in this chapter aim at even better performance, but there are situations in which using a binary collation can be *good enough*.

NOTE In English-speaking countries, particularly in the US, it's common to use a SQL collation. For varchar data, the rules of a SQL collation encompass only 255 characters. Using a binary collation gives only a marginal gain over a regular case-insensitive SQL collation.

Fragments and persons

We will now look at the first solution in which we build our own index to get good performance with searches using LIKE, even on tens of millions of rows.

To achieve this, we first need to introduce a restriction for the user. We require his search string to contain at least three contiguous characters. Next we extract all three-letter sequences from the email addresses and store these fragments in a table together with the person_id they belong to. When the user enters a search string, we split up the search string into three-letter fragments as well, and look up which persons they map to. This way, we should be able to find the matching email addresses quickly.

This is the strategy in a nutshell. We will now go on to implement it.

The fragments_persons table

The first thing we need is to create the table itself:

```
CREATE TABLE fragments_persons (
      fragment  char(3) NOT NULL,
      person_id int     NOT NULL,
```

```
        CONSTRAINT pk_fragments_persons PRIMARY KEY (fragment, person_id)
)
```

You find the script for this table in the file 03_fragments_persons.sql. This script also creates a second table that I will return to later. Ignore it for now.

Next, we need a way to get all three-letter fragments from a string and return them in a table. To this end, we employ a *table of numbers*. A table of numbers is a one-column table with all numbers from 1 to some limit. A table of numbers is good to have lying around as you can solve more than one database problem with such a table. The script to build the database for this chapter, 01_build_database.sql, created the table *numbers* with numbers up to one million.

When we have this table, writing the function is easy:

```
CREATE FUNCTION wordfragments(@word varchar(50)) RETURNS TABLE AS
RETURN
    (SELECT DISTINCT frag = substring(@word, n, 3)
     FROM   numbers
     WHERE  n BETWEEN 1 AND len(@word) - 2
)
```

Note the use of DISTINCT. If the same sequence appears multiple times in the same email address, we should store the mapping only once. You find the wordfragments function in the file 03_fragments_persons.sql.

Next, we need to load the table. The CROSS APPLY operator that was introduced in SQL 2005 makes it possible to pass a column from a table as a parameter to a table-valued function. This permits us to load the entire table using a single SQL statement:

```
INSERT fragments_persons(fragment, person_id)
    SELECT w.frag, p.person_id
    FROM   persons p
    CROSS  APPLY wordfragments(p.email) AS w
```

This may not be optimal, though, as loading all rows in one go could cause the transaction log to grow excessively. The script 03_fragments_persons.sql includes the stored procedure load_fragments_persons, which runs a loop to load the fragments for 20,000 persons at a time. The demo database for this chapter is set to simple recovery, so no further precautions are needed. For a production database in full recovery, you would also have to arrange for log backups being taken while the procedure is running to avoid the log growth.

If you have created the database, you may want to run the procedure now. On my computer the procedure completes in 7–10 minutes.

Writing the search procedure

Although the principle for the table should be fairly easy to grasp, writing a search procedure that uses it is not as trivial as it may seem. I went through some trial and error, until I arrived at a good solution.

Before I go on, I should say that to keep things simple I ignore the possibility that the search string may include wildcards like % or _, as well as range patterns like [a-d] or [^a-d]. The best place to deal with these would probably be in the wordfragments function. To handle range patterns correctly would probably call for an implementation in the CLR.

THE QUEST

The first issue I ran into was that the optimizer tried to use the index on the email column as the starting point, which entirely nullified the purpose of the new table. Thankfully, I found a simple solution. I replaced the LIKE expression with the logical equivalent as follows:

```
WHERE  patindex('%' + @wild + '%', email) > 0
```

By wrapping the column in an expression, I prevented SQL Server from considering the index on the column.

My next mistake was that I used the patindex expression as soon as an email address matched any fragment from the search string. This was not good at all, when the search string was a .com address.

When I gave it new thought, it seemed logical to find the persons for which the email address included all the fragments of the search string. But this too proved to be expensive with a .com address. The query I wrote had to read all rows in fragments_persons for the fragments *.co* and *com.*

ENTER STATISTICS

I then said to myself: what if I look for the least common fragment of the search string? To be able to determine which fragment this is, I introduced a second table as follows:

```
CREATE TABLE fragments_statistics
     (fragment char(3) NOT NULL,
      cnt      int     NOT NULL,
      CONSTRAINT pk_fragments_statistics PRIMARY KEY (fragment)
)
```

The script 03_fragments_persons.sql creates this table, and the stored procedure load_fragments_persons loads the table in a straightforward way:

```
INSERT fragments_statistics(fragment, cnt)
   SELECT fragment, COUNT(*)
   FROM   fragments_persons
   GROUP  BY fragment
```

Not only do we have our own index, we now also have our own statistics!

Equipped with this table, I finally made progress, but I was still not satisfied with the performance for the test string omamo@petinosemdesetletnicah.com. When data was on disk, this search took over 4 seconds, which can be explained by the fact that the least common fragment in this string maps to 2851 persons.

THE FINAL ANSWER

I did one final adjustment: look for persons that match both of the *two* least common fragments in the search string. Listing 2 shows the procedure I finally arrived at.

Listing 2   The procedure `map_search_five`

```
CREATE PROCEDURE map_search_five @wild varchar(80) AS
DECLARE @frag1 char(3),
        @frag2 char(3)

; WITH numbered_frags AS (
   SELECT fragment, rowno = row_number() OVER(ORDER BY cnt)
   FROM   fragments_statistics
   WHERE  fragment IN (SELECT frag FROM wordfragments(@wild))
)
SELECT @frag1 = MIN(fragment), @frag2 = MAX(fragment)
FROM   numbered_frags
WHERE  rowno <= 2

SELECT person_id, first_name, last_name, birth_date, email
FROM   persons p
WHERE  patindex('%' + @wild + '%', email) > 0
  AND  EXISTS (SELECT *
              FROM   fragments_persons fp
              WHERE  fp.person_id = p.person_id
                AND  fp.fragment = @frag1)
  AND  EXISTS (SELECT *
              FROM   fragments_persons fp
              WHERE  fp.person_id = p.person_id
                AND  fp.fragment = @frag2)
```

The common table expression (CTE) `numbered_frags` ranks the fragments by their frequency. The condition `rowno <= 2` extracts the two least common fragments, and with the help of `MIN` and `MAX`, we get them into variables. When we have the variables, we run the actual search query.

You may think that a single `EXISTS` clause with a condition of `IN (@frag1, @frag2)` would suffice. I tried this, but I got a table scan in the fragments_persons table, where there are two separate `EXISTS` clauses.

When I ran `map_search_five` through `tester_sp`, I got this result:

	joy	aam	niska	omamo@
Disk	373	260	4936	306
Cache	16	16	203	140

The performance is good. It still takes 5 seconds to search *niska* from disk, but for 2,000 hits, this should be acceptable. Nevertheless, there are still some problematic strings. For instance the string *coma* matches only 17 persons, but it takes over 10 seconds to return these, as both the strings *com* and *oma* are common in the material.

You find the script for `map_search_five` in the file 04_map_search.sql. This file also includes my first four less successful attempts. If you decide to look at, say, the three least common fragments, you can use a procedure that is more extensible called `map_search_six`, which uses a different technique to find the least two common fragments.

Keeping the index and the statistics updated

Our story with the fragments_persons table is not yet complete. Users may add persons, delete them, or update their email addresses. In this case we must update our index, just as SQL Server maintains its indexes. You do this by using a trigger.

In the download archive, you find the files 05_fragments_persons_trigger-2005.sql and 05_fragments_persons_trigger-2008.sql with triggers for SQL 2005 and SQL 2008. There are two versions because in the SQL 2008 trigger I use the new MERGE statement.

The triggers are fairly straightforward, but there are a few things worth pointing out. In listing 3, I show the version for SQL 2008, as it is considerably shorter.

Listing 3   The trigger keeps `fragment_persons` updated.

```
CREATE TRIGGER fragments_persons_tri ON persons
   FOR INSERT, UPDATE, DELETE AS

SET XACT_ABORT ON
SET NOCOUNT ON

-- Exit directly if now row were affected.
IF NOT EXISTS (SELECT * FROM inserted) AND          ❶
   NOT EXISTS (SELECT * FROM deleted)
   RETURN

-- If this is an UPDATE, get out of email is not touched.
IF NOT UPDATE(email) AND EXISTS (SELECT * FROM inserted)  ❷
   RETURN

DECLARE @changes TABLE
    (fragment char(3) NOT NULL,
     person_id int    NOT NULL,
     sign       smallint NOT NULL CHECK (sign IN (-1, 1)),
     PRIMARY KEY (fragment, person_id))

INSERT @changes (fragment, person_id, sign)         ❸
   SELECT frag, person_id, SUM(sign)
   FROM   (SELECT w.frag, i.person_id, sign = 1
           FROM    inserted i
           CROSS  APPLY wordfragments(i.email) w
           UNION ALL
           SELECT w.frag, d.person_id, -1
           FROM    deleted d
           CROSS  APPLY wordfragments(d.email) w) AS u
   GROUP  BY frag, person_id
   HAVING SUM(sign) <> 0

MERGE fragments_persons AS fp                        ❹
USING @changes c ON fp.fragment  = c.fragment
                AND fp.person_id = c.person_id
WHEN NOT MATCHED BY TARGET AND c.sign = 1 THEN
   INSERT (fragment, person_id)
      VALUES (c.fragment, c.person_id)
WHEN MATCHED AND c.sign = -1 THEN
   DELETE;

MERGE fragments_statistics AS fs                     ❺
```

```
USING (SELECT fragment, SUM(sign) AS cnt
       FROM   @changes
       GROUP  BY fragment
       HAVING SUM(sign) <> 0) AS d ON fs.fragment = d.fragment
WHEN MATCHED AND fs.cnt + d.cnt > 0 THEN
  UPDATE SET cnt = fs.cnt + d.cnt
WHEN MATCHED THEN
  DELETE
WHEN NOT MATCHED BY TARGET THEN
  INSERT (fragment, cnt) VALUES(d.fragment, d.cnt);
go
```

The trigger starts with two quick exits. At ❶ we handle the case that the statement did not affect any rows at all. In the case of an UPDATE operation, we don't want the trigger to run if the user updates some other column, and this is taken care of at ❷. Observe that we cannot use a plain IF UPDATE, as the trigger then would exit directly on any DELETE statement. Thus, the condition on IF UPDATE is only valid if there are also rows in the virtual table *inserted*.

At ❸ we get the changes caused by the action that fired the trigger. Inserted fragments get a weight of 1 and deleted fragments get a weight of -1. If a fragment appears both in the new and old email addresses, the sum will be 0, and we can ignore it. Otherwise we insert a row into the table variable @changes. Next at ❹ we use this table variable to insert and delete rows in the fragments_persons table. In SQL 2008, we can conveniently use a MERGE statement, whereas in the SQL 2005 version, there is one INSERT statement and one DELETE statement.

Finally, at ❺ we also update the fragments_statistics table. Because this is only a statistics table, this is not essential, but it's a simple task—especially with MERGE in SQL 2008. In SQL 2005, this is one INSERT, UPDATE, and DELETE each.

To test the trigger you can use the script in the file 06_map_trigger.sql. The script performs a few INSERT, UPDATE, and DELETE statements, mixed with some SELECT statements and invocations of map_search_five to check for correctness.

What is the overhead?

There is no such thing as free lunch. As you may expect, the fragments_persons table incurs overhead. To start with, run these commands:

```
EXEC sp_spaceused persons
EXEC sp_spaceused fragments_persons
```

The reserved space for the persons table is 187 MB, whereas the fragments_persons table takes up 375 MB—twice the size of the base table.

What about the overhead for updates? The file 07_trigger_volume_test.sql includes a stored procedure called volume_update_sp that measures the time to insert, update, and delete 20,000 rows in the persons table. You can run the procedure with the trigger enabled or disabled. I ran it this way:

```
EXEC volume_update_sp NULL   -- No trigger enabled.
EXEC volume_update_sp 'map'  -- Trigger for fragments_persons enabled.
```

I got this output:

```
SQL 2005                    SQL 2008
INSERT took 1773 ms.        INSERT took 700 ms.
UPDATE took 1356 ms.        UPDATE took 1393 ms.
DELETE took 826 ms.         DELETE took 610 ms.
INSERT took 40860 ms.       INSERT took 22873 ms.
UPDATE took 32073 ms.       UPDATE took 35180 ms.
DELETE took 30123 ms.       DELETE took 28690 ms.
```

The overhead for the fragments_persons table is considerable, both in terms of space and update resources, far more than for a regular SQL Server index. For a table that holds persons, products, and similar base data, this overhead can still be acceptable, as such tables are typically moderate in size and not updated frequently. But you should think twice before you implement something like this on a busy transactional table.

Fragments and lists

The fragments_persons table takes up so much space because we store the same fragment many times. Could we avoid this by storing a fragment only once? Yes. Consider what we have in the following snippet:

```
fragment     person_id
--------     ---------
aam              19673
aam              19707
aam              43131
aan              83500
aan             192379
```

If we only wanted to save space, we could just as well store this as follows:

```
fragment     person_ids
--------     -----------------
aam          19673,19707,43131
aan          83500,192379
```

Most likely, the reader at this point gets a certain feeling of unease, and starts to ask all sorts of questions in disbelief, such as

- Doesn't this violate first normal form?
- How do we build these lists in the first place?
- And how would we use them efficiently?
- How do we maintain these lists? Aren't deletions going to be very painful?
- Aren't comma-separated lists going to take up space as well?

These questions are all valid, and I will cover them in the following sections. In the end you will find that this outline leads to a solution in which you can implement efficient wildcard searches with considerably less space than the fragments_persons table requires.

There is no denial that this violates first normal form and an even more fundamental principle in relational databases: *no repeating groups*. But keep in mind that, although we store these lists in something SQL Server calls a table, logically this is an index helping us to make things go faster. There is no data integrity at stake here.

Building the lists

Comma-separated lists would take up space, as we would have to convert the id:s to strings. This was only a conceptual illustration. It is better to store a list of integer values by putting them in a `varbinary(MAX)` column. Each integer value then takes up four bytes, just as in the fragments_persons table.

To build such a list you need a user-defined aggregate (UDA), a capability that was added in SQL 2005. You cannot write a UDA in T-SQL, but you must implement it in a CLR language such as C#. In SQL 2005, a UDA cannot return more than 8,000 bytes, a restriction that was removed in SQL 2008. Thankfully, in practice this restriction is insignificant, as we can work with the data in batches.

In the download archive you can find the files integerlist-2005.cs and integerlist-2008.cs with the code for the UDA, as well as the compiled assemblies. The assemblies were loaded by 01_build_database.sql, so all you need to do at this point is to define the UDA as follows:

```
CREATE AGGREGATE integerlist(@int int) RETURNS varbinary(MAX)
EXTERNAL NAME integerlist.binconcat
```

This is the SQL 2008 version; for SQL 2005 replace `MAX` with `8000`.

Note that to be able to use the UDA, you need to make sure that the CLR is enabled on your server as follows:

```
EXEC sp_configure 'clr enabled', 1
RECONFIGURE
```

You may have to restart SQL Server for the change to take effect.

Unwrapping the lists

The efficient way to use data in a relational database is in tables. Thus, to use these lists we need to unpack them into tabular format. This can be done efficiently with the help of the numbers table we encountered earlier in this chapter:

```
CREATE FUNCTION binlist_to_table(@str varbinary(MAX))
RETURNS TABLE AS
RETURN (SELECT DISTINCT n = convert(int,
                         substring(@str, 4 * (n - 1) + 1, 4))
        FROM    numbers
        WHERE   n <= datalength(@str) / 4)
```

`DISTINCT` is needed because there is no way to guarantee that these lists have unique entries. As we shall see later, this is more than a theoretical possibility.

This is an inline table-valued function (TVF), and normally that is preferred over a multi-statement function, because an inline TVF is expanded into the query, and the optimizer can work with the expanded query. This is not the case with a multi-statement TVF which also requires intermediate storage. I found when testing various queries that the optimizer often went astray, and using a multi-statement function gave me better performance. A multi-statement function also permitted me to improve performance by using the IGNORE_DUP_KEY option in the definition of the table variable's primary key and thereby remove the need for DISTINCT:

```
CREATE FUNCTION binlist_to_table_m2(@str varbinary(MAX))
RETURNS @t TABLE
     (n int NOT NULL PRIMARY KEY WITH (IGNORE_DUP_KEY = ON)) AS
```

I have to admit that I am not a big fan of IGNORE_DUP_KEY, but when the duplicates are only occasional, it tends to perform better than using DISTINCT.

The code for these functions is available in the file 09_list_search.sql, which also includes the search procedures that we will look at later.

The fragments_personlists table

I have given an outline of how to construct and unpack these lists. To put it all together and write queries, we first need a table. When designing the table, there is one more thing to consider: it is probable that new persons will be added one by one. If the varbinary(MAX) column grows at the rate of one id at a time, this could lead to fragmentation. Therefore it seems like a good idea to use a pre-allocation scheme, and permit the actual list to be longer than required by the number of entries. This leads to this table definition:

```
CREATE TABLE fragments_personlists(
    fragment            char(3)         NOT NULL,
    stored_person_list  varbinary(MAX)  NOT NULL,
    no_of_entries       int             NOT NULL,
    person_list AS substring(stored_person_list, 1, 4 * no_of_entries),
    listlen    AS datalength(stored_person_list) PERSISTED,
    CONSTRAINT pk_fragments_personlists PRIMARY KEY (fragment)
)
```

The column stored_person_list is the allocated area, but the one we should use in queries is person_list which holds the actual person_id:s for the email addresses containing the fragment. The column listlen is used when maintaining the table. There may not be much point to have it persisted, but nor is the cost likely to be high.

You find the definition of this table in the files 08_fragments_personlists-2008.sql and 08_fragments_personlists-2005.sql. These files also include the preceding CREATE AGGREGATE statement, and the load procedure for the table, which is what we will look at next.

Loading the table

The conceptual query to load this table is simple:

```
INSERT fragments_personlists
    (fragment, stored_person_list, no_of_entries)
    SELECT w.frag, dbo.integerlist(w.person_id), COUNT(*)
    FROM   persons p
```

```
    CROSS  APPLY wordfragments(p.email) w
    GROUP  BY w.frag
```

Because of the size limitations imposed on UDA:s in SQL 2005, this query will not run
on this version of SQL Server, but we must employ batching just as we did when we
loaded the fragments_persons table. With SQL 2008 batching is a good idea as it keeps
the size of the transaction log in check. Listing 4 shows the version of the load procedure for SQL 2008.

Listing 4   Loading the fragments_personlists table

```
CREATE PROCEDURE load_fragments_personlists AS

SET NOCOUNT ON
SET XACT_ABORT ON

DECLARE @batchstart int,
        @batchsize  int,
        @totalrows  int

SELECT @batchstart = 1, @batchsize = 20000          ❶
SELECT @totalrows = COUNT(*) FROM persons

TRUNCATE TABLE fragments_personlists

WHILE @batchstart <= @totalrows
BEGIN
   ; WITH numbered_persons(person_id, email, rowno) AS (    ❷
       SELECT person_id, email, row_number()
                OVER(ORDER BY email, person_id)
       FROM   persons
   ),

       personlists(fragment, person_list, cnt) AS (         ❸
       SELECT w.frag, dbo.integerlist(p.person_id), COUNT(*)
       FROM   numbered_persons AS p
       CROSS  APPLY wordfragments (p.email) AS w
       WHERE  p.rowno >= @batchstart
         AND  p.rowno < @batchstart + @batchsize
       GROUP  BY w.frag
   )

   MERGE fragments_personlists AS fp
   USING personlists AS p ON fp.fragment = p.fragment
   WHEN  MATCHED THEN UPDATE
   SET no_of_entries = fp.no_of_entries + p.cnt,
       stored_person_list.write(p.person_list +
           CASE WHEN fp.listlen < 7000 AND           ❹
                     fp.listlen < 4 *
                         (fp.no_of_entries + p.cnt)
                THEN convert(varbinary(2000),
                     replicate(0x0, 4 *
                         (fp.no_of_entries + p.cnt)))
                ELSE 0x
           END,
       4 * fp.no_of_entries, 4 * p.cnt)
   WHEN NOT MATCHED BY TARGET THEN
```

```
    INSERT(fragment, no_of_entries, stored_person_list)
       VALUES (p.fragment, p.cnt, p.person_list +
              CASE WHEN p.cnt < 7000
                   THEN convert(varbinary(2000),
                              replicate(0x0, 4 * p.cnt))
                   ELSE 0x
              END);

    SELECT @batchstart = @batchstart + @batchsize
END

ALTER INDEX pk_fragments_personlists ON
    fragments_personlists REORGANIZE
```

❺

❻

At ❶ we set up variables to control the batch. Because this is SQL 2008, we can freely select the batch size. On SQL 2005, the batch size must not exceed 1999, as the `inte-gerlist` aggregate cannot return more than 7996 bytes of data on this version of SQL Server (7996 and not 8000, because of the internal implementation of the `integer-list` aggregate).

The CTE at ❷ numbers the persons, so that we can batch them. The reason we number by email first is purely for performance. There is a nonclustered index on email, and like any other nonclustered index, this index also includes the key of the clustered index, which in the case of the persons table is the primary key, and thus the index covers the query.

The next CTE, `personlists` at ❸, performs the aggregation from the batch. The `MERGE` statement then inserts new rows or updates existing ones in a fairly straightforward fashion, save for the business that goes on at ❹ and ❺. This is the pre-allocation scheme that I mentioned earlier. You can perform pre-allocation in many ways, and choosing a scheme involves trade-offs for speed, fragmentation, and wasted space. The scheme I've chosen is to allocate double the length I need now, but never allocate more than 2000 bytes at a time. Note that when the length exceeds 7000 bytes I don't pre-allocate at all. This is because the fragmentation problem exists only as long as the column is stored within the row. When the column is big enough to end up in large object (LOB) storage space, SQL Server caters for pre-allocation itself.

Finally, at ❻ the procedure reorganizes the table, to remove any initial fragmentation. The reason I use `REORGANIZE` rather than `REBUILD` is that `REORGANIZE` by default also compacts LOB storage.

The SQL 2005 version of `load_fragments_personlists` is longer because the `MERGE` statement is not available. We need separate `UPDATE` and `INSERT` statements, and in turn this calls for materializing the `personslists` common table expression (CTE) into a temporary table.

On my machine, the procedure runs for 7–9 minutes on SQL 2008 and for 15–17 minutes on SQL 2005.

The system procedure `sp_spaceused` tells us that the table takes up 106 MB, or 27 percent of the space of the fragments_persons table.

A search procedure

In the preceding section, we've been able to save space, but will we also be able to write a stored procedure with the same performance we got using the fragments_persons table?

The answer is yes, but it's not entirely straightforward. I started with the pattern in map_search_five, but I found that in the query that determines the two least common fragments, SQL Server was scanning the fragments_personlists table. To work around this, I saved the output from the wordfragments function into a table variable.

Next I realized that rather than getting the fragments from this query, I could just as well pick the lists directly, and after some experimentation I arrived at the procedure shown in listing 5.

Listing 5   Search procedure using fragments_personlists

```
CREATE PROCEDURE list_search_four @wild varchar(80) AS
DECLARE @list1 varbinary(MAX),
        @list2 varbinary(MAX)

DECLARE @wildfrags TABLE (frag char(3) NOT NULL PRIMARY KEY)
INSERT @wildfrags(frag)
   SELECT frag FROM wordfragments(@wild)

; WITH numbered_frags AS (
   SELECT person_list,
          rowno = row_number() OVER(ORDER BY no_of_entries)
   FROM   fragments_personlists
   WHERE  fragment IN (SELECT frag FROM @wildfrags)
)
SELECT @list1 = MIN(person_list), @list2 = MAX(person_list)
FROM   numbered_frags
WHERE  rowno <= 2

SELECT person_id, first_name, last_name, birth_date, email
FROM   persons p
WHERE  patindex('%' + @wild + '%', email) > 0
  AND  EXISTS (SELECT *
               FROM   binlist_to_table_m2(@list1) b
               WHERE  b.n = p.person_id)
  AND  EXISTS (SELECT *
               FROM   binlist_to_table_m2(@list2) b
               WHERE  b.n = p.person_id)
```

I'd like to emphasize here that I used a multi-statement version of the binlist_to_table function. When I used the inline version, it took a minute to run the procedure for the string *niska*!

The results for list_search_four with our test words follow:

	joy	aam	niska	omamo@
Disk	203	266	6403	473
Cache	16	0	500	46

Compared to the results for map_search_five, the performance is better in some cases, but worse in others.

The file 09_list_search.sql contains the code for list_search_four, as well as five other list_search procedures. The first three illustrate my initial attempts, and they do not perform well. The last two are variations with more or less the same performance as list_search_four.

Keeping the lists updated

As in the case with fragments_persons, we need a trigger on the persons table to keep fragments_personlists up to date. Handling new persons is no problem; this is similar to the load procedure, and this is also true for new data in UPDATE statements. But how do we handle deletions, and the old data in UPDATE? If a person is deleted, to keep the lists accurate, we should delete the person_id from all lists it appears in. As you can imagine, deleting a person with a .com address would be costly.

Thankfully, there is a simple solution: don't do it. This table is only an index, and we use it only to locate rows that may match the user's search condition. The real search condition with LIKE or patindex must always be there. So although we will get some false positives, they will not affect the result of our queries. As the number of outdated mappings grows, performance will suffer. Thus, you will need to re-run the load procedure from time to time to get rid of obsolete references. But that is not really much different from defragmenting a regular SQL Server index.

As a consequence the person_list column for a fragment could include duplicate entries of the same person_id. A simple example is when a user mistakenly changes the email address of a person, and then restores the original address—hence, the need for DISTINCT in the binlist_to_table function.

You can find the code for the trigger in the files 10_fragments_personlists_trigger-2005.sql and 10_fragment_personlists_trigger-2008.sql. In the file 11_list_trigger_test.sql there is a script for testing the trigger. I'm not including the trigger code here in full, as it's similar to the load procedure. The trigger for SQL 2008 does not resort to batching, but in the trigger for SQL 2005 batching is unavoidable, due to the size restriction with the UDA. One thing is a little different from the load procedure, though: in case of UPDATEs we should not store fragment-person_id mappings that do not change. Listing 6 shows how this looks in the trigger for SQL 2005.

Listing 6   Filtering out unchanged `fragment-person_id` mappings

```
; WITH fragmentpersons(fragment, person_id) AS (
   SELECT w.frag, p.person_id
   FROM   (SELECT person_id, email,
                  rowno = row_number() OVER(ORDER BY person_id)
           FROM   inserted) AS p
   CROSS  APPLY wordfragments (p.email) AS w
   WHERE  rowno >= @batchstart
     AND  rowno < @batchstart + @batchsize
   EXCEPT
   SELECT w.frag, p.person_id
   FROM   (SELECT person_id, email,
                  rowno = row_number() OVER(ORDER BY person_id)
           FROM   deleted) AS p
```

```
CROSS   APPLY wordfragments (p.email) AS w
WHERE   rowno >= @batchstart
  AND   rowno < @batchstart + @batchsize
)
```

The EXCEPT operator, introduced in SQL 2005, comes in handy when dealing with this issue. Also, observe that here the batching is done differently from the load procedure. In the load procedure we numbered the rows by email for better performance, but if we were to try this in our trigger, things could go wrong. Say that the email address for person 123 is changed from a@example.com to z@example.com in a mass update of more than 2,000 rows. If we number rows by email, the rows for person 123 in *inserted* and *deleted* would be in different batches, and so would the rows for at least one more person. By batching on the primary key, we avoid this.

You can use the procedure volume_update_sp from 07_trigger_volume_test.sql to measure the overhead of the trigger. I got these numbers:

```
SQL 2005                 SQL 2008
INSERT took 23570 ms.    INSERT took 11463 ms.
UPDATE took 21490 ms.    UPDATE took 9093 ms.
DELETE took 610 ms.      DELETE took 670 ms.
```

Thus on SQL 2008, there is a considerable reduction in the overhead compared to the trigger for the fragments_persons table. To be fair, that trigger handles deletions as well.

Using bitmasks

The last technique we will look at uses an entirely different approach. This is not my own invention; Sylvain Bouche developed it and was kind to share his idea with me.

In contrast to the other two techniques that rely heavily on features added in SQL 2005, this technique can easily be applied on SQL 2000. This method also has the advantage that it doesn't put any restriction on the user's search strings.

The initial setup

Sylvain assigns each character a weight that is a power of 2, using this function:

```
CREATE FUNCTION char_bitmask (@s varchar(255))
RETURNS bigint WITH SCHEMABINDING AS
BEGIN
   RETURN CASE WHEN charindex('e',@s) > 0 THEN 1 ELSE 0 END
        + CASE WHEN charindex('i',@s) > 0 THEN 2 ELSE 0 END
        + ...
        + CASE WHEN charindex('z',@s) > 0 THEN 33554432 ELSE 0 END
END
```

The idea here is that the less common the character is, the higher the weight. Then he adds a computed column to the table and indexes it:

```
ALTER TABLE persons ADD email_bitmask AS dbo.char_bitmask(email)
CREATE INDEX email_bitmask_ix ON persons(email_bitmask) INCLUDE (email)
```

I'd like to emphasize that it's essential to include the email column in the index. I tried to skip that, and I was duly punished with poor performance.

Searching with the bitmask

When you conduct a search, you compute the bitmask for the search string. With help of the bitmask you can find the rows which have all the characters in the search string and apply only the expensive LIKE operator on this restricted set. That is, this condition must be true:

```
email_bitmask & char_bitmask(@wild) = char_bitmask(@wild)
```

This condition cannot result in a seek of the index on email_bitmask, but is only good for a scan. From the preceding equation, this condition follows:

```
email_bitmask >= char_bitmask(@wild)
```

The bitmask value for the column must be at least equal to the bitmask for the search string. Thus, we can constrain the search to the upper part of the index. This leads to the procedure shown in listing 7.

Listing 7   Search function using the bitmask

```
CREATE PROCEDURE bit_search_two @wild varchar(50) AS
SET NOCOUNT ON
DECLARE @bitmask bigint

SELECT @bitmask = dbo.char_bitmask(@wild)

SELECT person_id, first_name, last_name, birth_date, email
FROM   persons
WHERE  email_bitmask >= @bitmask
  AND  CASE WHEN email_bitmask & @bitmask = @bitmask
            THEN patindex('%' + @wild + '%', email)
            ELSE 0
       END > 0
```

The sole purpose of the CASE statement is to make absolutely sure that SQL Server evaluates only the patindex function for rows with matching bitmasks.

Adapting the bitmask to the data

When I tested Sylvain's code on my data, the performance was not good. But he had selected the weights in his function to fit English, and my data was based on Slovenian. To address this, I created this table:

```
CREATE TABLE char_frequency (
    ch    varchar(2) NOT NULL,
    cnt   int        NULL,
    rowno int        NOT NULL,
    CONSTRAINT pk_char_frequency PRIMARY KEY (ch),
    CONSTRAINT u_char_frequency UNIQUE (rowno)
)
```

Then I wrote a stored procedure, load_char_frequency, that loads this table, and inserted the frequency for all characters. In the column rowno, I put the ranking, and I excluded the at (@) and period (.) characters, because they appear in all email addresses.

Next I wrote a stored procedure, build_bitmask_sp, that reads the char_frequency table, and from this table builds the char_bitmask function. Depending on the number of entries in the char_frequency table, the return type is either int or bigint. Because scalar user-defined functions (UDFs) come with some overhead, I opted to inline the bitmask computation in the column definition. The procedure also creates the index on the bitmask column.

Build_bitmask_sp is perfectly rerunnable. If the column already exists, the procedure drops the index and the column and then re-adds them with the new definition. Because it is only a computed column, it does not affect how data pages for the table are stored on disk. This makes it possible for you to change the bitmask weights as you get more data in your table.

I don't include any of that code here, but you can find these procedures, as well as Sylvain's original function and the procedure bit_search_two, in the file 12_bitmask.sql.

Performance and overhead

When you have set up the data you can execute tester_sp for bit_search_two to test the performance. You will find that it does not perform as well as the fragment searches:

```
       joy    aam   niska   omamo@
Disk   293   5630   13953      470
Cache   16   4760    2756      123
```

There is a considerable difference between *joy* and *aam*. The reason for this is that *y* is a rare character in Slovenian, and therefore has a high bitmask value. On the other hand both *a* and *m* are common, so the bitmask value for *aam* is low, and SQL Server has to go through the better part of the index on email_bitmask.

Because this is a regular SQL Server index, we don't need to write a trigger to maintain it. It can still be interesting to look at the overhead. When I ran

```
EXEC volume_update_sp NULL
```

with the index on email_bitmask in place, I got this result:

```
INSERT took 4633 ms.
UPDATE took 6226 ms.
DELETE took 2730 ms.
```

On my machine, it takes about 3 minutes to create the index, and it takes up 45 MB in space. Thus, the bitmask index is considerably leaner than the fragment tables.

The big bitmask

You could add characters directly to the char_frequency table, and because the table has a char(2) column, you could add two-character sequences as well. But because the bitmask is at best a bigint value, you cannot have more than 63 different weights.

Mainly to see the effect, I filled char_frequency with all the two-letter sequences in the data (save those with the at (@) and period (.) characters). In total, there are 561. I then wrote the procedure build_big_bitmask_sp, which generates a version of char_bitmask that returns a binary(80) column. Finally, I wrote the procedure bit_search_three which uses this big bitmask. Strangely enough, the & operator does not support binary types, so I had to chop up the big bitmask into 10 bigint values using substring, resulting in unwieldy code.

On my machine it took 1 hour to create the index on SQL 2005, and on SQL 2008 it was even worse: 90 minutes. The total size of the index is 114 MB, a little more than the fragments_personlists table.

The good news is that bit_search_three performs better for the string *aam* although it's slower for the full email address:

```
        joy    aam   niska   omamo@
Disk    156    516   13693     1793
Cache     0     93    2290      813
```

But the result from the volume test is certainly discouraging:

```
INSERT took 77203 ms.
UPDATE took 151096 ms.
DELETE took 76846 ms.
```

It's clear that using the big bitmask in my implementation is not a viable solution. One problem is that 561 charindex calls are far too many. The char_bitmask function could be implemented more efficiently, and I would at least expect the CLR to offer a few possibilities. The other problem is that as the mask grows, so does the index. Because the method works by scanning part of the index, this has a direct effect on the performance. You would need to find a more efficient storage format for the bitmask to overcome this.

Summary

You've now seen two ways to use fragments, and you've seen that both approaches can help you considerably in speeding up searches with the LIKE operator. You have also seen how bitmasks can be used to create a less intrusive, but lower performance, solution.

My use case was searching on email addresses which by nature are fairly short. Fragments may be less appropriate if your corpus is a column with free text that can be several hundred characters long. The fragments table would grow excessively large, even if you used the list technique.

You can take a few precautions, however. You could filter out spaces and punctuation characters when you extract the fragments. For instance, in the email example, we could change the `wordfragments` function so that it does not return fragments with the period (.) and at (@) characters.

You could achieve a more drastic space reduction by setting an upper limit to how many matches you save for a fragment. When you have reached this limit, you don't save any more mappings. You could even take the brutal step to throw those matches away, and if a user enters a search string with only such fragments, you tell him that he must refine his search criteria.

In contrast, the space overhead of the bitmask solution is independent of the size of the column you track. Thus, it could serve better for longer columns. I see a potential problem, though: as strings get longer, more and more characters appear in the string and most bitmask values will be in the high end. Then again, Sylvain originally developed this for a `varchar(255)` column, and was satisfied with the outcome.

In any case, if you opt to implement any of these techniques in your application, you will probably be able think of more tricks and tweaks. What you have seen here is only the beginning.

About the author

Erland Sommarskog is an independent consultant based in Stockholm, Sweden. He started to work with relational databases in 1987. He first came in contact with SQL Server in 1991, even if it said Sybase on the boxes in those days. When he changed jobs in 1996 he moved over to the Microsoft side of things and has stayed there. He was first awarded MVP in 2001. You can frequently see him answer SQL Server questions on the newsgroups. He also has a web site, www.sommarskog.se, where he has published a couple of longer articles and some SQL Server–related utilities.

18 Getting and staying connected—or not

William Vaughn

It seems that I spend quite a bit of my time answering questions—from family, friends and neighbors—who want to know how to resurrect their computers, or from developers who need to figure out how to get around some seemingly impossibly complex problem. Thankfully, not all of their problems are that complex. I expect that many of you are confronted by many of the same queries from those that look up to you as a technical resource—like the doctor who lives up the street who listens patiently while you describe that pain in your right knee.

A couple of the most common questions I get on the public Network News Transfer Protocol (NNTP) newsgroups (such as Microsoft.public.dotnetframe-work.adonet and ..sqlserver.connect[1]), are "How do I get connected?" and "Should I stay connected?" This chapter attempts to explain how the SQL Server connection mechanism works and how to create an application that not only can connect to SQL Server in its various manifestations but stays connected when it needs to. I don't have room here to provide all of the nuances, but I hope I can give you enough information to solve some of the most common connection problems and, more importantly, help you design your applications with best-practice connection management built in.

What is SQL Server?

Before I get started, let's define a few terms to make sure we're all on the same page. When I refer to *SQL Server*, I mean all versions of Microsoft SQL Server except SQL Server Compact edition. The connection techniques I discuss here apply to virtually all versions of SQL Server, starting with SQL Server 2000 and extending beyond SQL Server 2008. If I need to discuss a version-specific issue, I'll indicate the

---

[1] No, I don't hang out on the MSDN forums—they're just too slow.

specific version to which the issue applies. Getting connected to SQL Compact is done differently—you provide a path to the .SDF file and a few arguments in the connection string to configure the connection. SQL Server Compact Edition is discussed in two other chapters so I suggest looking there for details.

Instances of SQL Server run as a service, either on the same system as the *client* (the program that's asking for the connection) or on another system (often referred to as a *server*). The service communicates with the outside world via the interactive Tabular Data Stream (TDS) protocol that's documented online (http://msdn.microsoft.com/en-us/library/cc448435.aspx). But it's unwise to code directly to TDS, as it's subject to change without notice, and, frankly, that's what the `SqlClient` .NET and DB-Library data access interfaces are for.

SQL Server has several entry points:

- A specifically enabled TCP/IP port
- A named pipe
- The VIA protocol
- The shared memory provider

Depending on the SQL Server version, some or all of these protocols (except shared memory) are disabled by default. This hides any installed SQL Server instances from the network and prevents clients from connecting. To enable or disable one or more of these protocols, I recommend the SQL Server Configuration Manager (SSCM) as shown in figure 1. The SQL Server Surface Area Configuration Utility has been dropped from SQL Server 2008 but you can also use `sp_configure` to make protocol changes.

If you expect to share SQL Server databases over a network, the client data access interfaces must address them through VIA, an IP port, or a named pipe. If the client is running on the same system as the SQL Server instance, your code should connect through the (far faster) shared memory provider. I'll show you how to do that a bit later (see "Establishing a connection" later in this chapter).

Understanding the SQL Server Browser service

In SQL Server 2005 and later, Microsoft uses the SQL Server Browser service to decouple IP assignment and port broadcasting functionality from the SQL Server instance,

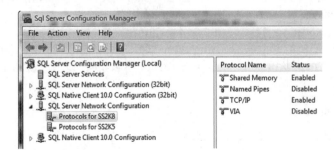

Figure 1   The SQL Server Configuration Manager

in order to improve functionality and security. By default, the SQL Server Browser service is disabled on some stock-keeping units (SKUs), so it needs to be enabled if you need to expose SQL Server instances to network clients. The SQL Server Configuration Manager can also set the startup state of this or any SQL Server–related service.

On startup, the SQL Server Browser service claims UDP port 1434, reads the registry to identify all SQL Server instances on the computer, and notes the ports and named pipes that they use. When a server has two or more network cards, SQL Server Browser will return all ports enabled for SQL Server.

When SQL Server clients request SQL Server resources, the client network library sends a UDP message to the server using port 1434, requesting access to a specific named or default instance. SQL Server Browser responds with the TCP/IP port or named pipe of the requested instance. The network library on the client application then completes the connection by sending a request to the server using the information returned by the service.

When your application accesses SQL Server across a network and you stop or disable the SQL Server Browser service, you must hard-set a specific port number to each SQL Server instance and code your client application to always use that port number. Typically, you use the SQL Server Configuration Manager to do this. Keep in mind that another service or application on the server might use the port you choose for each instance, causing the SQL Server instance to be unavailable. If you plan to expose your instance via TCP/IP address and penetrate a firewall, this is the only approach you can choose.

Diagnosing a connectivity problem

Getting connected to SQL Server can be troublesome as there are so many layers of security and physical infrastructure to navigate. The following sections walk you through the layers and explain how to test to see if each layer is working, disabled, or protected, thus making the connection attempt fail. These steps include the following:

- Testing the network (if necessary). Can you see the network? Is the host server visible and responding?
- Testing the SQL Server instance service state. Is the instance running?
- Connecting to the instance and initial catalog (default database) given the appropriate credentials.

Testing for network availability

When troubleshooting a connection issue, it's best for your application to use your own diagnostics to test for network and service availability, as the human running the application is often unable to return reliable information about the state of the network, SQL Server services, or the weather. For this reason, I encourage developers to add a few lines of code to test for the presence of the network and test the state of the selected SQL Server instance. As shown in listing 1, in Visual Basic.NET (or C#) it's easy to use the .NET Framework `Devices.Network` class.

NOTE   All of the code examples in this chapter are in Visual Basic.NET.

> **Listing 1   Testing for network availability in Visual Basic.NET**

```
Dim WithEvents myNet As New Devices.Network
    Function TestServerAvailability( _
      ByVal uriServiceName As System.Uri) As Boolean
        If myNet.IsAvailable Then
            ' Continue
        End If
    End Function

    Private Sub myNet_NetworkAvailabilityChanged( _
        ByVal sender As Object, _
        ByVal e As
    ➥ Microsoft.VisualBasic.Devices.NetworkAvailableEventArgs) _
        Handles myNet.NetworkAvailabilityChanged
        ' Report network has changed state.
        If e.IsNetworkAvailable = False Then
            ' Report network is down...
        End If
    End Sub
```

After you determine that the network is available, and you can ping a known server within the domain hosting the SQL Server, you know that the connection problem is likely on the server hosting the SQL Server instance. If the network is down, there might well be other issues such as an improperly configured Network Interface Card (NIC) or Wi-Fi interface, a disconnected cable, a bad router, or improperly configured firewall that make testing the SQL Server instance irrelevant and unnecessary.

Managing the SQL Server instance state

Because SQL Server is a service, it must be running before it can accept connections. Although this might seem obvious, for some implementations—as when using SQL Server Express Edition—the server instance might not be needed by other applications and might be consuming resources between uses. In this case the service might be shut down after the application quits. There are any number of architectural, administrative, and performance considerations to resolve when taking this approach, but given the expanding number of SQL Server Express implementations it's wise to understand how to configure the server so the instance is running when needed and not in the way when SQL Server is not required. I usually suggest another approach: install the SQL Server Express instance on a spare system and leave it running at all times. This makes connection, administration, and countless other issues less complex.

Again, the SSCM can be used to set the startup state of any of the SQL Server–related services, including SQL Server Reporting Services and BS Analysis Services. You can also use Services.msc or command-line scripts to start or stop selected services as shown in listing 2—assuming you have admin rights (run the script as Administrator). I do this on my demo laptop to bring up SQL Server, Reporting Services, and other services on demand before a session. Note that the service name (for example, `mssql`) is followed by the instance name (ss2k8) separated by a $ even for SQL Server 2008. You can also use NET START in a similar way but it does not return as much detailed information about the status of the service as it starts (or doesn't). In any case, you can include a script like this in a batch file that you execute before (or after) you run a job that requires SQL Server.

Listing 2 Starting SQL Server and supporting services in a command batch

```
cls
echo on
rem sc start w3svc
sc start  mssql$ss2k8
sc start  reportserver$ss2k8
sc start sqlagent$ss2k8
sc start sqlbrowser
sc start mssql$sqlexpress
start msdtsServer
start sqlwriter
pause
```

It's also possible to start SQL Server (or any service) using .NET factory classes, and I'll show you how to do that a bit later (in listing 4).

Finding visible SQL Server instances

Okay, so the network is available (at least as far as your application can tell) and the server hosting your SQL Server instance is visible on the network. Next, you can query the .NET Framework to see what SQL Server instances are visible. This is a two-step process that's simplified somewhat because we're interested only in *SQL Server* instances (and not other services like Reporting Services or Exchange). In summary, the code shown in listing 3 performs the following steps:

1 First, use the ADO.NET (2.0) `System.Data.Common.DbProviderFactories` object's `GetFactoryClasses` method to harvest the .NET data providers installed on the system. This method returns a `DataTable`.

2 Pick out the `SqlClient` data provider row and pass it to the `DbProviderFactories.GetFactory` method. In this case you get a `DbDataSourceEnumerator` object that can be inspected via the `GetDataSources` method to find the visible SQL Server instances.

This is the same technique used by the Data Connection dialog box in Visual Studio and SSMS (you know, the dialog box that takes 10 seconds or so to enumerate the visible servers). This means you need to expect a similar delay before the `GetFactory` method completes. A code segment to perform these operations is shown in listing 3.

Listing 3 Capturing the list of visible SQL Server instances

```
Private Sub ShowInstance(ByVal drProvider As DataRow)
       Try
           Me.Cursor = Cursors.WaitCursor
```

```
    Dim factory As DbProviderFactory = _
        DbProviderFactories.GetFactory(drProvider)
    Dim dsE As DbDataSourceEnumerator = _
        factory.CreateDataSourceEnumerator()
    If dsE Is Nothing Then
        DataGridView1.DataSource = Nothing
        MsgBox("No instances visible for this provider(" _
            & drProvider(0).ToString & ")")
    Else
        DataGridView1.DataSource = dsE.GetDataSources()
    End If
Catch exNS As NotSupportedException
    MsgBox("This provider does not support data source
➥ enumeration...")
Catch exCE As System.Configuration.ConfigurationException
    MsgBox("The " & drProvider(0).ToString & " could not be
➥ loaded.")
Finally
    Me.Cursor = Cursors.Default
End Try

End Sub
```

NOTE This method exposes only those instances that can be referenced by the `SqlClient` .NET data provider. This means that only SQL Server instances are shown; Reporting Services, Analysis Services, and other related services are not included.

If everything has gone well, you can *see* the target SQL Server instance—so you know the service is being exposed by the SQL Browser. Remember that the code shown previously searches the registry for installed instances, but you still don't know if the SQL Server instance has been started or if, perhaps, a DBA has paused the instance. The code to determine the instance state is quicker and simpler than searching for visible server instances. In this case, your code calls the `System.ServiceProcess.Services-Controller` class to test the current service status. This same class can also be used to set the service status. This means you'll be able to start, stop, or pause a specific SQL Server instance (if you have sufficient rights).

The trick here is to pass the correct arguments to the `ServicesController` class to properly identify the SQL Server instance. When the industry transitioned from SQL Server 2000 (version 8.0) to SQL Server 2005 (version 9.0), the method of referencing instances changed. SQL Server 2000 uses the service name of `MSSQLSERVER`. From SQL Server 2005 on, the service name changed to `MSSQL` followed by the instance name (separated with a $). For example, on my web site I have an instance of SQL Server 2005 named SS2K8, which shows up in services.msc as *SQL Server (SS2K8)* with a service name of `MSSQL$SS2K8`. Unfortunately, the .NET factory classes require you to pass in the same string that appears in services.msc when asked for the *service name*. It can be a bit confusing. Perhaps the example in listing 4 will make this easier.

For purposes of this exercise, let's assume we're working with SQL Server 2005 or later. Listing 4 illustrates a routine that starts a selected SQL Server instance on a specified network server. In the example, we pass in the server's name (in this case *BetaV1*, which is the name of the server hosting the desired SQL Server instance) and the Service Name which is composed of *SQL Server* concatenated with the instance name in parenthesis. For example, when I choose BetaV1 and the SS2K8 SQL Server instance on that server, the arguments passed to the ServiceController class would be *SQL Server (SS2K8)* and BETAV1. After you have instantiated a ServiceController object for the given SQL Server instance (or any service for that matter), you can determine its running state by examining the Status property. Likewise, you can use a controller method to do the following (and much more):

- Start, stop, or pause the service.
- Determine if the service can be paused and continued.
- Determine if the service can be stopped or shut down.
- Determine if the service has dependent services.

This assumes that the service can be started—and you can use the ServiceController class to test for this state as well. I tuned this code up a bit to leverage the WaitFor-Status method as it seemed a bit more elegant than polling the state. Note that the Controller.Start method is asynchronous, so it returns immediately—usually before the service has had a chance to start.

Listing 4   Starting a selected service

```
Private Sub btnStart_Click(ByVal sender As System.Object, _
    ByVal e As System.EventArgs) Handles btnStart.Click
    Dim Controller As New System.ServiceProcess.ServiceController( _
        txtServiceName.Text, txtServerName.Text)
    lblControllerStatus.Text = Controller.Status.ToString
    If Controller.Status = ServiceControllerStatus.Running Then
    Else
        Timer1.Enabled = True
        Controller.Start()
        Do Until intTimeout > 20 _
        Or Controller.Status = ServiceControllerStatus.Running
            Controller.Refresh()
            lblControllerStatus.Text = Controller.Status.ToString
            lblControllerStatus.Refresh()
        Loop
    End If
    Timer1.Enabled = False
End Sub
```

What is a connection?

Now that you know the network is up and the SQL Server instance being targeted is visible and running, you're ready to try to open a connection. Too many applications assume these facts and expect the exception messages returned from the various layers between the application and the server are useful—unfortunately, they aren't (at least in most cases).

NOTE Make sure your code includes complete and robust connection exception handling. Consider that the user trying to connect with your application is the person least likely to be able to diagnose what's wrong.

A *connection* to a SQL Server instance is a logical link between an application and a specific SQL Server instance. Once established, it's the only means of communicating with the instance. When you execute the `SqlClient` `Open` method on a `SqlConnection` object, the .NET data access interface establishes a bi-directional link to accept SQL commands and return the result sets containing the rows or other information back from the server—including exceptions and messages.

When it comes time to establish a connection to SQL Server, developers have faced a dizzying array of data access interfaces that are designed to make, use, and break connections, as well as manage pools of connections as the need arises. Data access interfaces, including ODBC, OLE DB, RDO, COM-based ADO, and ADO.NET, all use TDS behind the scenes to establish a link between the client application and a specific instance of SQL Server, so they all share a common purpose—to expose TDS to one programming interface or another that can be easier to use. Connections can be established over a network (WAN or LAN), or established directly by using a shared memory data access provider if the client and SQL Server service are running on the same system. As you add logical or physical layers between the client and SQL Server, more issues are exposed—issues that make connecting more and more difficult. This means you should try to use the Shared Memory provider whenever possible. No, this does not mean you should avoid multi-tiered systems or service-oriented architectures which centralize access to the SQL Server instance, but it does mean that when building an object layer or service that's hosted on a system that's *also* hosting the SQL Server instance, it makes abundant sense to bypass the network layer and use the shared memory provider.

A SQL Server 2008 instance can support up to 32,767 connections, which is an order of magnitude more than you'll ever need. In reality, the upper limit of connections is limited by available resources like RAM, available CPU cycles, the version of SQL Server installed, and how the DBA has configured the system. Even SQL Server Express edition can support hundreds (or even thousands) of connections, but because of further version-specific constraints applied to RAM and processor utilization, it's not likely that you'll be able to maintain more than a few hundred viable connections.

Contrary to popular myth, connections are not expensive. Unlike other DBMS systems that create full-duplex heavyweight connections or perform burdensome DDL queries when connecting, a SQL Server connection has a fairly small impact on the server (and client). SQL Server's connections are *half-duplex*. This means that a connection can handle only one operation at a time—a connection is either in *talk* mode or *listen mode*.

TIP Think of a connection like a CB radio conversation in which only one person can talk at a time. This is why radio operators use established protocols to end a *packet* of conversation by saying "Over" when they've finished talking. 10–4?

To connect or not to connect...

Although establishing a connection is fairly cheap, it's not free, so when designing highly scalable applications it makes sense to minimize the total number of times an application opens and closes connections, thereby getting the most out of each open/close cycle. This is especially true for ASP or Web Service applications that have to service dozens to thousands of connections a minute.

Because an ASP/ASP.NET/Web Service application cannot (or should not) attempt to maintain a globally referenced Connection object, applications are designed around a just-in-time connection strategy. This usually means acquiring a connection just before it's needed and releasing the connection back to the connection pool right after the results are captured by the client. I discuss the connection pool a little later (see "Connection management" later in this chapter). I think this makes sense to an extent. If you know that your application plans to make several queries in quick succession, some might suggest a broader-scope connection paradigm that holds the connection until all of these operations are complete. This approach comes with an element of risk. One of the more common failure modes for ASP-type applications is *leaking connections*—that is, when connections are acquired (by the Connection.Open method) but not released (with the Connection.Close method). Because the .NET Framework's garbage collector (GC) does not run that often,[2] orphaned connection objects (that have not been released) might languish in the object garbage heap for minutes to hours. Because of this, any connection strategy must ensure that any connection that's acquired (opened) is release (closed).

To facilitate ASP-type application connection churn, the data access providers have implemented a mechanism to cache connections—it's called the *connection pool*. I'll devote some time to this mechanism a bit later when I discuss properties, methods, and events that the data access interfaces expose to help manage connections.

NOTE ADO.NET 2.0 and later supports the option to use Multiple Active Resultsets (MARS) connections. Although these permit developers to reuse connections that have pending results, there are so many restrictions and evil side effects, that there are few real scenarios in which this approach provides any benefit over opening another connection.

Another myth that I hope to bust is that all applications should always use a *connect-query-disconnect* connection strategy. I can see how this myth got started, as this is a best practice for ASP, ASP.NET, and Web Service applications. If you're building a Microsoft Windows Presentation Foundation (WPF), Windows Forms, or other client-side executable, it does not always (or even usually) make sense. Instead, I often recommend connecting to the server when connectivity is first required and maintaining the connection for the life of the application. The benefits to this approach are compelling. First, your application need not spend resources opening (and closing) connections.

---

[2] The garbage collector runs when memory resources demand it—so perhaps not for some time.

But the most significant benefit is the ability to manage connection-scoped server state. For example, you can create

- Temporary tables (in tempdb) that can be indexed to hold intermediate query results based on the current client. These can be used to dramatically improve query performance.
- Connection-specific connection settings that need be applied only once and *stick with* the connection scope.
- Server-side cursors against live data, although this is not often done.

Consider that when you open a connection, SQL Server has to launch an agent to manage your requests, allocate memory, and prepare for your work. When you close a connection, the server has to clean up the mess you left behind like the maid who comes into your hotel room after that all-nighter. Any connection-owned resources, such as temporary tables or server-side cursors, have to be freed, and the agent has to be shut down. These operations can be postponed by using connection pooling, as I'll discuss later (see "Managing the connection pool" later in this chapter).

Connection management

So, when you discover that you cannot perform another operation on the existing connection, what should you do? Simply open another connection? I suggest you rethink your application strategy. Consider the following scenario. Your application has opened a connection and executed a query, which returns a rowset as a DataReader. In an attempt to save time and resources, you've decided *not* to create and populate a memory-resident `DataTable` (or `DataSet`). To implement your decision, you execute a query and ADO.NET supplies a `SqlDataReader`, which is a pipe to the rowset. While processing the DataReader row by row, you determine that some changes are needed in the database based on a row's data values. At this point you discover that you can't reuse the DataReader object's connection to make the change, so you're tempted to open another connection or somehow figure out how MARS works.

Can you see the problem here? Because you're using SQL Server (and not some toy database), it makes a lot more sense to perform this type of operation *on the server*. After all, SQL Server is a service designed to manage database operations. In this case, I would recommend that you write a stored procedure to make these changes in place. And no, I'm not suggesting that you build a cursor in a stored procedure to walk through and edit the rows. In many cases row-by-row operations can be performed by a simple (and sometimes not-so-simple) UPDATE statement with far better performance. Why don't developers do this in the first place? Well, some are uncomfortable with more than basic T-SQL operations. My suggestion in this case is to get familiar with T-SQL and stored procedures and learn how to leverage the server-side power of SQL Server.

Consider that any number of scenarios resemble the one I described previously. That said, some situations require multiple connections, but before your application charges off to open a second connection (or even consider MARS) I suggest you reconsider what the application is trying to accomplish. It usually makes a lot of sense to complete rowset population as quickly as possible to free up server-side resources being consumed by your connection. This means leveraging the `TableAdapter Fill` or `DataTable Load` methods to construct or load a memory-resident DataTable with the selected rowset(s).

NOTE Rowset population is the process of bringing the entire selected rowset to the client. Doing so frees any pending locks on the data rows, pages, and extents on the server. It can also free your connection for additional operations by your application (or others) needing SQL Server resources your application might be holding.

Connection strategies

Although you have little control over some parts of SQL Server query processing, there are other aspects of application implementation where you *can* manage to improve performance. These include limiting the number of demands your application makes on the server as well as the *quality* or intelligence of these requests. Most data access developers agree that it's not only the number of server requests, but the intelligence of them that makes a difference between an application that can support 100 users and one that can support thousands.

Each time you execute a query or perform a data definition language (DDL) operation, the client-side data access provider (typically implemented by ADO.NET's `Sql-Client` namespace) must build a set of TDS packets, hook up the connection, pass the query to the server, and process the result sets as they are made available by SQL Server. This process is called a *round trip*. Generally, anything you can do in your application to make each round trip more efficient can help improve performance—it's like avoiding a trip down the mountain for an egg when you know you'll need another tomorrow or in an hour. This means if you can bundle several queries or other operations together in a batch instead of sending the commands individually, you can improve performance by reducing round trips. It also means executing queries that return enough rows to satisfy the user's *immediate* requirements and perhaps a few more to permit the user to browse or filter the returned rowsets.

But consider this scenario: you want your application to start quickly but your design requires execution of a number of time-consuming queries against one or more SQL Server (or other DBMS) databases to populate pick lists and fetch current status. Does it make sense to open more than one connection to perform parallel (possibly asynchronous) operations to improve performance? Sure, in some cases I can see this as a viable approach—especially if the extra connections are closed after use. But another approach that I've been recommending lately uses the new Visual Studio 2008 Local Data Cache classes that leverage SQL Server Compact edition to persist lookup table data on the client system. Although this does not make sense for ASP.NET applications, for applications that are permitted to use the client systems' resources, I think letting the replication *connection* (that works independently of your own SQL Server connection) handle these independent operations has appeal.

Another solution to application initialization, where you need to summarize server data for the user, is to not perform the summary on the client and not open a connection at all. I've found that it's often far more efficient and easier to code when I use the `MicrosoftReportViewer` control to launch and render a SQL Server Reporting Services server-generated report to summarize (even complex) data. This eliminates the need to open and manage a `SqlClient` connection or worry about unwanted server load caused by clients performing duplicate operations. Consider that reports generated from the same data can be cached (as a report Snapshot) on the Reporting Services server and regenerated only when the data changes. This way, your application does not need to include the code to generate the summary, process the summary data, manage the presentation UI, or tie up a connection to do so.

Establishing a connection

You've determined that you need a connection. If you haven't skipped down to this section, you're aware that it's not always necessary to open a connection (or another connection). Let's step through the process of configuring a `SqlClient.SqlConnection` object.

NOTE   You can connect to SQL Server in other ways, including using one of the older one-size-fits-all data access interfaces (DAI) like ODBC or OLE DB, or one of the more recent DAIs like COM-based ADO that uses ODBC or OLE DB behind the scenes. You can also use the `OleDb` namespace to connect to SQL Server, but because of its COM legacy and inefficiency, you'll be hobbled by a lack of features that are supported only in the managed `SqlClient` namespace. If you're still working with OLE DB and non-.NET applications, I suggest using the SQL Server Native Client (SNAC) provider as it's the most efficient and includes support for SQL Server 2008.

Many of these steps are performed automatically when you create a Visual Studio Data Connection in the Server Explorer, after you provide the essential ingredients and perhaps a few values.

You can specify a host of options when defining a `SqlConnection` object—all of which are configured in the `ConnectionString` property or passed in the `SqlConnection`. All of these options are specified by key and value pairs. Note that if you don't spell the key correctly or pass a value that's not within the acceptable range of values, ADO.NET throws an exception. This is different than the behavior you might have seen with OLE DB or ODBC connection strings. Note also that the keys are not case sensitive and whitespace is ignored. If you repeat a key, only the last value is used. Some might suggest using the `ConnectionStringBuilder` to construct the `ConnectionString` but unless you're charging by the line, this seems like going to the emergency room to take out a splinter. Consider that Visual Studio exposes application settings that can also be used to construct the `ConnectionString` and persist it in your project, so it can be easily referenced in code. This paradigm provides an interactive dialog box to create and test a connection string at design time.

The essential keys and values in the `ConnectionString` include the following:

- `Server` or `Data Source`—The *name* of the server and instance name of the targeted SQL Server.
- `Integrated Security`—The security mode to use. This setting determines whether ADO.NET uses *trusted* (SSPI) Windows authentication or *untrusted* SQL Server authentication. In the latter case, this includes a specific Login Name and matching password. The default is `False`. See the section "Trusted or untrusted security?" later in this chapter.
- `User ID` and `Password` (or `PWD`)—Only specified when not including the Integrated Security key or when integrated security is not set to `True` or SSPI. Specifies the SQL Server Login account name and matching password that has rights to access the `Initial Catalog`. These keys are ignored if you've requested `Integrated Security`.
- `Initial Catalog`—Specifies the SQL Server database to use for all operations (if not specifically overridden in the query or after opening the connection). Although `Initial Catalog` is not *required*, it's essential that your connection avoid depending on the default database set by the DBA for the login account. If the DBA-set default database is changed, your application will break. Leave it off at your own peril.

NOTE Some of these keys have (several) alternate names. I'm showing the most common.

Some of the more interesting (and commonly used) options include the following:

- `Application Name`—This key identifies the connection so it can be identified when you're using SQL Profiler filters.
- `Async`—Used to determine if the connection should permit asynchronous operations.
- `AttachDBFilename`—Used with detached SQL Server database files. This approach has a number of side effects that I discuss later.
- `ConnectTimeout` or `Connection Timeout`—How long should the client application wait for the connection to be established? The default is 15 seconds—an eon in SQL Server terms. A typical Windows Forms connection should open in about a second; in an ASP.NET application using connection pooling, even less time—unless the pool is full or the server is too busy. See the section "Connection pooling" later in this chapter for more information.
- `Enlist`—When set to `True`, the connection pooler automatically enlists the connection in the current transaction context.
- `Encrypt`—When `True`, SSL encryption is used for all data sent between the client and SQL Server—but only if the server has an SSL certificate installed.
- `TrustServerCertificate`—When set to `True`, SSL is used to encrypt the channel when walking the certificate chain to validate trust. If `TrustServerCertificate`

is set to `True`, and `Encrypt` is set to `False`, the channel is not encrypted. A setting of `True` has no effect if the server is not configured to accept SSL connections.

- `User Instance`—Used with SQL Server Express to create a user-specific instance of SQL Server in the user's process space. Microsoft plans to deprecate this approach in a future version of SQL Server. (See "Accessing user instances" later in this chapter for more information.)

NOTE   Key values that accept true/false settings also accept *yes* or *no* and in some parts of Minnesota, *you betcha* is also acceptable—well, it should be.

Notice anything missing here? Well, the Connection Reset key has been removed in ADO.NET 3.5. This key gave developers the option to leave the connection state in place between uses. Each application sharing the pool could leverage work done by other instances of the application (even if it was the same application). For some reason, Microsoft has seen fit to remove this feature.

Before we move on, let's revisit the essential connection string keys to pick up a few more details. I discuss the keys associated with the connection pool a bit later (see "Connection pooling" later in this chapter).

The server key

The server key in the connection string names the server (system) and instance of the target server. If you plan to address the SQL Server *default* (unnamed) instance, leave off the `\<instance name>` portion of the key value. Remember, specifying a server by name requires the Windows Directory Name Service (DNS) to locate the named server, so if there is something wrong with the DNS service or it can't be reached, attempts to connect by name can fail.

TIP   Using "." or "`(local)`" indicates that the SQL Server service instance specified is on the same system as the client application and enables the shared memory data provider.

I rarely hard-code a server name in my applications. Instead, I either reference a connection string kept in a separate file (`appconfig` or `webconfig`) or better yet, I use an alias. Using the SSCM you can create a named alias to dereference the server/instance to a specific name used in the connection string. This way, when you're ready to move the application into production, you change the alias and run the application.

If you want to simplify your connection strategy, bypassing needless overhead can usually help. If your client application is connecting to a SQL Server instance that's running on the client's system—as when using SQL Server Express, or a SQL Server Workgroup instance running on the same system as your ASP.NET application—it makes a lot of sense to use the shared memory provider (SMP). That's because this provider does not need to navigate through ports, protocols, or the network stack to get to SQL Server and SQL Server does not need to wade through these layers to return your result sets.

To activate the SMP, all you need to do is specify "`.`" or "`(local)`" for the Server or Data Source key. You still need to specify the SQL Server instance being addressed unless you're connecting to the default instance. That's done by tacking on the instance name to the "`.`" or "`(local)`" in the connection string. Although it makes a lot of sense to use the local connection whenever possible, there might be drawbacks to this approach if the SQL Server has to compete with other resource-hungry applications on the same system, such as Reporting Services, Office, or Age of Empires. In a production environment, even when using SQL Express, I prefer to build a dedicated system whose sole purpose is to host an instance of SQL Server.

Table 1 shows a number of example server key settings.

Table 1 Typical server key settings

The server key syntax SERVER=	SMP?	Addresses
`<server name>;` as in `MyServer`	No	Default instance on `<server name>` server
`.;` or `(local);`	Yes	Default instance on the local server
`.\<MyInstance>;` as in `.\SS2K8;`	Yes	`<MyInstance>` named instance on the local server
`<domain>\<server>\<instance>;`	No	Named instance on named server on named domain
`<IP>,<Port>;` as in `209.20.233.22,1433;`	No	The specified server by IP address and port

I don't recommend addressing any SQL Server instance via IP address and port. Why? Well, it's tough to do, given the number of firewalls most (serious) organizations put up to prevent direct-port operations. It also assumes you've gone to the trouble of disabling the dynamic IP port assignment scheme used by SQL Server 2005 and later. Accessing a SQL Server instance over the Internet? IMHO: madness.

Trusted or untrusted security?

One of the critical components you need to include in your connection string is your application's or your user's credentials. You have two choices:

- Request a *trusted* connection. This approach captures the Windows user or IIS credentials and passes them to SQL Server for authentication.
- Supply a user ID and password that are passed to SQL Server for authentication.

In either case you must create a login for the specified user or for the domain group that includes the user's Windows login ID—unless you're connecting as the SQL Server system administrator or a member of the administrator's group.

WARNING Connecting any production application that's accessible to users using the SA Login ID and password is a fundamental mistake. Although there are rare exceptions, developers should never build or test applications using SA credentials.

Let's visit each of these approaches in a bit more detail.

Using trusted or integrated security

Microsoft seems to support the trusted approach for most production applications. I also endorse it, but with a few caveats. You enable the trusted security option by including `Integrated Security=SSPI;` or `Trusted_Connection=True;` in the connection string. After you do, keep in mind that the connection inherits the rights granted to the user. The *user* might be a human with domain or system login rights or a service (like the ASP.NET service running under IIS). In the case of IIS services you need to determine the version of IIS you're using to host the application making the connection and the username IIS is using to log into SQL Server. I discuss this in the next section.

If the user has limited rights in the database, the application might not be able to access all of the data objects (like stored procedures, tables, views, or functions) that it needs to function properly. In addition, if the user has *super rights*, the application might have access to more data objects than necessary. The reason I mention this is that trusted security may open your database to Trojan attacks, where a block of SQL is embedded surreptitiously that can be executed only when a user with sufficient rights runs the program.

When you use this approach, consider that each time your code opens a connection, the user credentials are verified. This also applies to pooled connections (as discussed in "Connection pooling" later in this chapter). Trusted connections are enabled by default when you install SQL Server, and cannot be disabled.

ASP.NET considerations

When connecting from an ASP.NET application hosted by Internet Information Services (IIS), it's IIS that usually acts as a proxy user. The real *users* (the humans) accessing your web page are usually not members of your domain, so Active Domain authentication credentials won't help get them connected. Over the years the default user account name used by IIS has changed. Today's defaults are as follows:

- In IIS 6.0, the system uses *<machinename>*\ASPNET.
- In IIS 7.0, the system uses *<NT Authority>**<network service>*.

It's also possible, and probably a good idea in some cases, to have your ASP.NET applications log on with application-specific SQL Server authentication credentials instead of these defaults, which are used when you specify `Integrated Security = SSPI`. This gives you more control over the rights this particular application is granted.

As these accounts may not have been assigned rights to your database or to the objects they contain, you'll have to make some changes using SQL Server Management Studio to grant these rights. If you don't, you won't be able to connect, or you'll get a rights exception as the connection attempts to access the initial catalog.

A considerable number of articles discuss techniques to protect the credentials used by applications that choose to use SQL Server authentication (untrusted) connections. Some advise creating an entry in the Web.Config file, although others say this is a mistake. In my opinion, if you create a login account on SQL Server and grant rights to only those specific objects that the application needs and no other, the surface area of exposure is reduced dramatically. So what if the credentials are leaked? All the hacker can do is run the permitted stored procedures or extract data using the read-only views.

WARNING Trusted security can make your application vulnerable to Trojan attacks. Remember that 80 percent of all hacking comes from *within* the corporate firewall.

I don't have the space here to discuss much more on security. Suffice it to say, that you need to make sure to deny access to all objects in the database and carefully consider which server logins, database users, schemas, or roles should have rights.

Using SQL Server authentication

I'm of the opinion that SQL Server authentication eliminates the opportunity for a high-privilege user to access more data than the application is intended to expose. With this approach I recommend setting up a SQL Server Login ID for the specific application or for the group of related applications that need identical rights. Not everyone agrees with this approach, but in my experience many customers find it far easier to let the DBA, not the developer, control access to the database and its contents.

To use SQL Server *untrusted* authentication, you must first enable that option during SQL Server installation (setup) or via SQL Server Management Studio by setting the Security Server Authentication option to permit SQL Server and Windows Authentication Mode, as shown in figure 2.

Next, you need to include the `UID=<Login ID>;` and `Password=<password>;` keys and values. I don't build a SQL Server account for each individual in the company; this avoids the problem of creating a login account for the payroll clerk *Betty* who is replaced by *Bob* while she's on maternity leave (giving Bob a complex). Instead, I created a *PayRollClerk15* login account or role that's used by the application (or Betty and Bob). Note that this strategy (of individual or even role-based) accounts is not a good idea for ASP.NET applications.

Figure 2   Setting SQL Server and Windows Authentication mode in SSMS

WARNING   As a general rule of thumb, you should never expose the SA password nor create applications that use it. Do not permit developers to build applications using the SA account. Doing so masks any number of complex issues that will have to be addressed at some time in the future—hopefully before your data is compromised.

Accepting user login credentials—or not

I often drone on and on about why it's important to avoid login dialog box strategies that capture a user ID and password. I don't use them to capture SQL Server authentication credentials but I sometimes use them to determine the user rights level. The application (protected by HTTPS or Windows ACL rights protections) logs on with its own unique credentials. If I expose a user login, it's to restrict user access to only those portions of the data to which they have permission to see and (perhaps) change.

If you must expose a user login dialog box, make sure that you don't permit the user to guess indefinitely until they get the right combination of username and password. Make sure you insist on strong passwords and introduce a delay that hobbles hackers with keystroke generators. I also cripple the login dialog box for some long period of time after *N* number of login attempts.

Accessing user instances

About the time that SQL Server Express was born, Microsoft felt a need to replace the Access/JET database with a suitably equivalent engine. Because of this, the developers at Microsoft decided to implement the (expletive deleted) user instance option. As a result, the Visual Studio data access code generators were adapted to use this feature, so it's likely that there are any number of applications that implement it. I don't want to spend a lot of time on this approach as I don't endorse it—and neither does Microsoft at this point in time. It's on the chopping block for deprecation in a later version. Although I would advise avoiding it and moving on, I'll give you an idea of what it does to your user's system.

When you include the key User Instance = True; in the connection string, the first time the database connection opens, the following series of operations is started (or at least attempted):

1   ADO.NET's SqlClient data provider looks for an installed instance of SQL Express. This option works only against SQL Server Express.
2   If found, the SQL Server Express master and msdb databases are copied to the user's directory.
3   The database file (.mdb) as specified in the AttachDBFilename key is also copied to the user directory.
4   A user-owned instance of SQL Server is started as a process owned by the user—not as a service, so it does not appear in Services.msc.
5   At this point, tempdb, model, trace, and the transaction log files are created.

6 The instance name is generated and appears as a number; for example: 69651E0A-5550-46.

7 A named pipe connection is established to the user instance and passed back to ADO.NET.

As you can see, the first time a user instance connection is made, it can take a considerable amount of work to get the connection established. For this reason, it makes sense to bump up the ConnectTimeout key value. The next time the User Instance key is used, the process is far simpler. Because the master and other system databases are already in place, the SQL Server instance belonging to the user is restarted. The AttachDBFilename key-specified database is not reinstalled.

WARNING When accessing a user instance, the connection is given full SA rights when using the Trusted Connection option. You can see how this might impact the security of the database—especially when the database's contents do not belong to the user but are the value-added provided by a vendor.

After the database connection is closed, the SQL Server instance owned by the user remains running for 60 minutes, by default. This can be reduced by executing sp_configure 'user instance timeout', <minutes>. An acceptable value is anything between 5 and 65,535, so even after the user application ends, SQL Server hangs around waiting for another connection for at least 5 minutes.

Typically, it takes less than a second to get connected to SQL Server from a Windows Forms application, but the connection operation can be delayed by a clogged network, a busy server, or a yellow cable dangling from the router. In an ASP.NET application, consider that the website might be under considerable load (due to the success of your Super Bowl ad or the inefficiency of your code). If your code does not complete its data operation quickly enough, the server might be unable to keep up. If the provider cannot get connected immediately, it continues to wait (and retry) for the number of seconds specified by the ConnectTimeout key. After the time expires, it throws an exception.

TIP When ADO.NET attempts to connect to SQL Server, the ConnectTimeout counter begins. After SqlClient finds the server, the counter stops—even though you might not yet be able to use the connection.

Connection pooling

Again, quite a bit has been written about connection pooling. This is one of the most common areas of concern, especially for ASP.NET applications, and I've written my share of articles and blog entries. When you understand how the mechanism works, you'll understand how to keep it working. These are the basic functions:

- When the SqlConnection.Open method passes a connection string to SqlClient, the provider looks for a matching connection pool. Each pool is uniquely identified by its connection string.

- Each `AppDomain` or `Process` gets its own pool. This means other ASP.NET applications get their own pool(s).
- Each transaction scope gets its own pool.
- An application can have as many pools as necessary—just change the connection string.
- Since ADO.NET 2.0, developers have been able to clear a specific pool or all pools owned by the `AppDomain` or Process.
- When the `SqlConnection.Open` method is called, either a new pool is created, or an existing pool is reused.
- If the pool exists, the provider attempts to find and use a dormant (unused) connection in the pool. Otherwise, a new connection to SQL Server is established and its handle is placed in the pool.
- If a dormant connection is found, the connection state is cleared (by default) so the new owner inherits a *clean* connection state—identical to the state when it was first opened.
- As more requests for connections are passed to the provider, the process is repeated until the number of pooled connections reaches an upper limit. The default is 100 connections.
- When the `Connection.Close` method is called, the connection is marked as *dormant* and reusable. The connection is then placed in the pool, ready for reuse. No attempt is made to clean out the connection state until the connection is reused.
- If a connected application fails in a way that forces the connection to be closed, the pooled connection is dropped. In some cases, all connections in the pool are dropped when an error occurs.
- If the server cannot be accessed for whatever reason or the `AppDomain` or Process ends, the pool is flushed and dropped.
- If a pooled connection is not reused after 4 to 8 minutes, it is closed and dropped from the pool until there are `Min Pool Size` connections left.

NOTE   Connection pools are created on the *client*, not on the server.

TIP   When debugging applications with Visual Studio, you'll notice that Visual Studio owns the connection pools. This means connections might be held for some time if the application under development does not properly close the connection (as often happens). Eventually, you'll overflow the pool or exhaust the number of connections permitted by the SQL Server configuration.

As you can see, managing the connection pool can be somewhat complex—at least behind the scenes. Typically an active ASP.NET site uses about a dozen connections per pool—even those sites that support thousands of users. If you need to adjust the connection pooling mechanism, you can do so using the specific connection string keys, as shown in table 2.

Table 2   Connection pooling connection string keywords

Key name	Default	Purpose
Connection Lifetime	0	Has no effect on lifetime of dormant pools except for clustered servers.
Load Balance Timeout	0	Has no effect on lifetime of dormant pools except for clustered servers.
Max Pool Size	100	Specifies the maximum number of connections to be pooled. (If you have to increase this, you're doing something wrong.)
Min Pool Size	0	Sets the number of connections kept in the pool regardless of age.
Pooling	True	Enables or disables connection pooling.

Despite what the documentation says, you can't change the length of time a connection is left in the pool after it's closed. The Connection Lifetime and Load Balance Timeout keys are used only in clustered servers. After a connection is closed by the Connection.Close method, the dormant connection remains aging in the pool (holding its server-side state) for 4 to 8 minutes (the time is chosen randomly). The only way to force the connections to close is to flush the pool or stop the process or AppDomain that owns it.

Closing the connection

Before closing out this chapter, I'd like to include a few tips about closing a connection. As discussed earlier, when connection pooling is enabled and the Connection.Close method is executed, the Connection is released back to the pool but the server-side state is not touched—not for 4 to 8 minutes. When the connection is reused, the first TDS packet sent to the server instructs the agent to reset the connection. You can't alter this behavior now that the Connection Reset key has been removed. This means that if the server is holding resources for the connection, they remain held until the connection is reused or the application ends. Microsoft suggests that developers disable connection pooling to immediately release these resources. I suggested to Microsoft that it give developers the option of resetting the connection on Close.

Summary

Based on the feedback I get at conferences and from my customers, readers, and the developers I support online, connecting to SQL Server continues to be one of the most trouble-prone areas for both novice and expert developers. Sadly, it seems that there are as many opinions about how, when, and if to connect as there are health-card lobbyists in Washington. For instance, Microsoft wants developers to use SSPI authentication. I do too, but I also urge caution. Some suggest that accessing SQL

Server directly via ports is OK but I beg to disagree as I'm concerned with hard-coding ports and network snooping.

Building any connection strategy is all about what works for your application architecture and security infrastructure. In some cases the just-in-time connection strategy makes sense, but in others it incurs needless overhead. Sometimes the connection pool helps improve performance, but at other times it just gets in the way.

Sometimes we as writers, consultants, and pundits make things a lot more complicated than they have to be by overloading our readers and clients with a lot of unnecessary detail. Considering that most SQL Server implementations are SQL Server Express, those that mold opinions need to remember to keep things simple whenever possible without compromising security or performance. For the most part, the developers I work with want solutions, not options. I hope this chapter has provided some of these solutions.

About the author

William (Bill) Vaughn is an industry-recognized author, mentor, and subject-matter expert on Visual Studio, SQL Server, Reporting Services, and data access technologies. He's worked in the computer industry for over 37 years. In 2000, after 14 years at Microsoft, Bill stepped away to work on his books, consulting, mentoring, and independent training seminars. He's written over a dozen books, including *Hitchhiker's Guide to Visual Studio and SQL Server (7th Edition)* and *Hitchhiker's Guide to SQL Server Compact Edition*. He and Peter Blackburn also wrote the critically acclaimed *Hitchhiker's Guide to SQL Server 2000 Reporting Services*.

19 Extending your productivity in SSMS and Query Analyzer

Pawel Potasinski

Many SQL Server developers and administrators prefer to use T-SQL code instead of a graphical interface to perform their common duties. I'm definitely one of those T-SQL maniacs. That's why the ability to define custom keyboard shortcuts in SQL Server Management Studio (SSMS) in Microsoft SQL Server 2005 and 2008, and SQL Server Query Analyzer in Microsoft SQL Server 2000, is one of my favorite features of those applications. I love the idea that during the development of my database, which contains more than 100,000 objects at the moment, I can use my utils to easily perform everyday tasks such as searching for a specific object, showing the object definition, or finding dependencies between database objects. If you spend some time on writing your own utils to fit your needs, I can promise you won't regret it.

Custom keyboard shortcuts

Both Query Analyzer and SSMS provide the ability to call T-SQL code with custom keyboard shortcuts. You can define the shortcuts using the main menus of those applications (note that the way you define the shortcuts in both applications is slightly different).

To define custom shortcuts in Query Analyzer:

1 On the Tools menu, click Customize... (see figure 1).

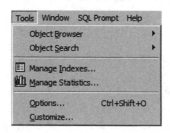

Figure 1   To define custom keyboard shortcuts in Query Analyzer, in the Tools menu, click Customize...

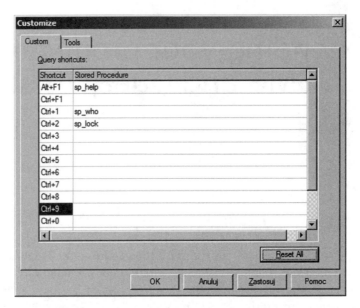

Figure 2   Keyboard shortcuts defined in the Customize window in Query Analyzer

- In the Customize window (shown in figure 2), add your T-SQL code next to the chosen keyboard shortcut and click OK.

To define custom shortcuts in SSMS:

1   On the Tools menu, click Options... (see figure 3).

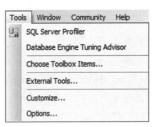

Figure 3   To define custom keyboard shortcuts in SSMS, in the Tools menu, click Options...

2   In the Options window, in the Environment node, click Keyboard (see figure 4).

3   Add your T-SQL code next to the chosen keyboard shortcut and click OK.

In both applications, some shortcuts are reserved by default for system stored procedures—for example, sp_who and sp_help.

What makes this feature powerful is that you can use these shortcuts with the text selected in the query editor window. You select the text, press the appropriate shortcut, and then the code assigned to the shortcut is concatenated with the text you've selected and the result of concatenation is executed. Let's see some examples. By default, the Alt-F1 shortcut is reserved for the sp_help system stored procedure. Open

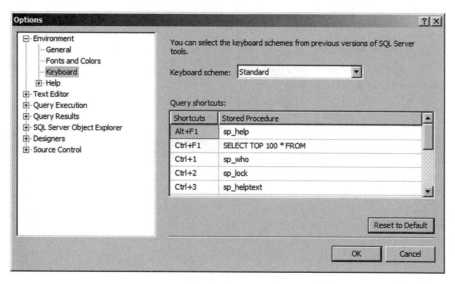

Figure 4   Keyboard shortcuts defined in the Options window in SSMS

a new query window in SSMS (or Query Analyzer), connect to any SQL Server 2005 or 2008 instance, and type the following:

```
'sys.objects'
```

Then select the text you've just written and press Alt-F1. This should display the result of the sp_help procedure executed with `'sys.objects'` as a parameter (the result should consist of the metadata of the sys.objects catalog view).

NOTE   In Query Analyzer, custom keyboard shortcuts also work with text selected in the Results or the Messages tabs. In SSMS, you can't use custom shortcuts with text selected in any of the mentioned tabs.

Creating your custom utility to use with keyboard shortcuts

When you know how to define your own keyboard shortcuts, you can create some custom stored procedures to use with the feature. I call those procedures *utilities* or—shorter—*utils*, probably because of their frequent use in my everyday work. Most of my utils are procedures to query the metadata and return some information needed for writing some new T-SQL code. Let's create a sample util to demonstrate the idea.

How often do you need to get the list of a table's columns or procedure's parameters? In my experience, this needs to be done on a regular basis. Let's write a utility named sp_getcolumns, which will return a list of columns or parameters of a database object of our choice.

NOTE   The sample stored procedure sp_getcolumns demonstrated in this chapter will work in SQL Server 2005 and 2008.

The prefix sp_ isn't accidental here. If you want the procedure to work with database objects in every single database in your SQL Server instance, the best way is to create it in the master database and name it with an sp_ prefix so that you can easily call it no matter what the current database of your session is (SQL Server will search the master database for objects prefixed with *sp_*).

Listing 1 shows an example of what the procedure's code can look like. You can add some improvements. I'll provide some suggestions later in this chapter.

Listing 1   Creating sample utility `sp_getcolumns`

```
USE  master
GO

IF OBJECT_ID('dbo.sp_getcolumns','P') IS NOT NULL
  DROP PROC dbo.sp_getcolumns
GO

CREATE PROC [dbo].[sp_getcolumns]
@object sysname,
@horizontal tinyint = 0
AS
SET NOCOUNT ON

DECLARE @lines TABLE (
  line_id int identity(1,1) primary key,
  line nvarchar(4000)
)

IF EXISTS (SELECT 1 FROM sys.all_columns WHERE [object_id] =
➥OBJECT_ID(@object))
BEGIN
  IF @horizontal = 1 BEGIN
    DECLARE @line nvarchar(4000)
    SET @line = N''
    SELECT @line = @line + [name] + N', '
    FROM sys.all_columns
    WHERE [object_id] = OBJECT_ID(@object)
    ORDER BY column_id
    INSERT @lines (line)
    SELECT LEFT(@line,LEN(@line)-1)
  END
  ELSE BEGIN
    INSERT @lines (line)
    SELECT [name] + N','
    FROM sys.all_columns
    WHERE [object_id] = OBJECT_ID(@object)
    ORDER BY column_id
    UPDATE @lines
    SET line = LEFT(line,LEN(line)-1)
    WHERE line_id = @@IDENTITY
  END
END
SELECT line AS ' ' FROM @lines ORDER BY line_id
GO
```

First of all, note that I use the `sys.all_columns` catalog view to retrieve the column list (to retrieve the column list in SQL Server 2000, you should use the dbo.syscolumn system table).

NOTE Normally you should avoid the *sp_* prefix for your stored procedures. Use it only in development or for testing, and not in your production databases. Also, it may be required to mark your newly created procedure as a system object with an undocumented stored procedure—`sp_MS_MarkSystemObject`. Otherwise your procedure may not work properly with all databases within the SQL Server instance. Remember that the `sp_MS_MarkSystemObject` system procedure is for internal use only and isn't supported by Microsoft; therefore, never use it against objects in your production databases.

The procedure has two parameters: `@object` (the name of the database object for which the column list should be returned) and `@horizontal`—this parameter decides whether the columns are returned as a single line (`@horizontal = 1`) or each column is returned as a single line in a result set (`@horizontal <> 1`).

The `SET NOCOUNT ON` line should be used as a best practice in every stored procedure you write to limit the information messages (such as the number of rows affected by the query) sent by SQL Server to the applications.

My procedure uses a table variable called `@lines`. A simple `IF` condition controls the way the column/parameter list is inserted into the `@lines` variable. I wanted the result list to be comma separated; therefore, the comma is concatenated to every column/parameter name. The last comma is unnecessary, so I remove it, either by using `LEFT` function (for column/parameter list returned horizontally) or by simple `UPDATE` statement (for the list returned vertically).

Finally, all rows from the `@lines` table variable are returned in the appropriate order. Simple, isn't it?

All you have to do after you create the procedure is to assign a custom keyboard shortcut to it. Then you can test the util. Go to one of your databases, write the name of one of your database objects (if you use the fully qualified name of the object, put it in single quotes), and press the appropriate keys on your keyboard. The example is shown in figure 5. A parameter list of the `sp_getcolumns` stored procedure is returned (current database: master).

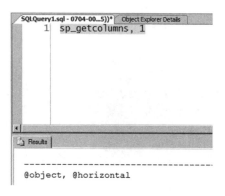

Figure 1 Sample use of the `sp_getcolumns` utility

Some thoughts on how you can improve the procedure presented in this chapter:

- Add an option to return the data types of the columns/parameters.

- Use nvarchar(max) data type for line column in the @lines table variable and for the @line variable (in SQL Server 2005/2008 only).
- Perform concatenation with FOR XML PATH clause (in SQL Server 2005/2008 only) or CLR aggregate function (this will let you avoid the nasty string concatenation performed on the @line variable).
- Use the NOLOCK hint to avoid unnecessary locking on the system objects.

Some ideas for utilities to implement

Here are some ideas of other utilities that might be useful for you:

- Searching for database objects by name
- Searching for database objects depending on the given object
- Scripting database objects
- Selecting sample rows from a table

This is a call to action! Create your own utilities, assign them to the custom shortcuts, and make your everyday work more efficient than ever before.

Summary

With custom keyboard shortcuts and your own stored procedures, you can immensely improve your productivity. A skilled developer can avoid using the mouse in a graphical interface and just use a keyboard to execute T-SQL code. As a result, some SQL Server developers are considered magicians because they can do everything just by quickly tapping the keyboard.

About the author

Pawel Potasinski is a database developer and consultant working for Asseco Business Solutions S.A. corporation. He's been working with SQL Server since 2000. His focuses are data transfer processes, performance troubleshooting, and dynamic code generation. Pawel holds MCT certification since 2004 and is a SQL Server MVP since 2008. In 2007, he founded the Polish SQL Server User Group.

20 Why every SQL developer needs a tools database

Denis Gobo

SQL isn't an object-oriented language. There's no notion of inheritance. The closest thing that SQL has to objects are views, user-defined functions, and stored procedures. Picture a developer at a software shop; this developer has written a distance calculation algorithm in SQL. Other developers copied this same code for use in their projects. After some time, the original developer finds a small defect in the code he wrote. He updates his code and contacts the other developers so that they can make the modification in their code.

This approach has a few problems; here are three of them:

- The original developer could forget to contact another developer to make the code change.
- A lot more people have to make changes now; this will increase the chance of mistakes.
- All the other developers have to update and test their code to make sure it works as expected.

As you can imagine, it's much easier to change and test the code in one place. This is the primary reason you need a tools database. Ideally, the tools database should have loosely coupled code and data; it shouldn't have data and code that depend on another user-created database. To give you an example, the tools database shouldn't format dates based on a calendar table from the human resources database; the calendar table should be stored in the tools database itself.

What belongs in the tools database?

The following are examples of what should go in a tools database:

- ZIP code and address tables
- Auxiliary table of numbers
- Maintenance procedures for the database server

283

- Reporting procedures showing connected users, free space, or file sizes
- ISO country and currency code tables
- Region- and country-specific calendar tables

Creating the tools database

Begin by creating the following database on your server:

```
CREATE DATABASE Tools
GO

USE Tools
GO
```

Using an auxiliary table of numbers

A numbers table can be useful for a variety of reasons. You can create result sets on the fly without having to store the data itself. Using a numbers table, you can also do set-based operations; this will speed up some operations dramatically because you aren't looping anymore. To find gaps in identity values, all you need to do is left-join your table with a numbers table and select the rows that have no value. Splitting off strings can also be accomplished fairly easy with a numbers table, as you'll see later on.

How big should a numbers table be? To store a million numbers in a numbers table, you'll need about 13 megabytes. If you're just doing date ranges and splitting off strings, then 10,000 rows might be enough; if you need to find identity gaps, then you need more rows than the maximum value in your identity column.

Let's start by creating our numbers table. We do this by creating an empty table, into which we insert 251 rows with values between 0 and 250 with the SQL script in listing 1.

Listing 1   Script to create a numbers table

```
CREATE TABLE Numbers(number int primary key not null)
GO

DECLARE @Loop int
SET @Loop = 0

SET NOCOUNT ON
WHILE @Loop <=250
BEGIN
    INSERT Numbers(number) VALUES (@Loop)
    SET @Loop = @Loop + 1
END
GO
```

Generating a calendar on the fly

Let's look at how you can use a numbers table to create a result set of dates. When working with dates and number tables, you'll use the DATEADD function. The syntax for DATEADD function looks like this: DATEADD (datepart , number, date).

The first argument is `datepart`; if we use `mm` for `datepart`, we're telling the function to use months. The second argument is `number`; this tells the function what to add to the date. You can also pass in negative values for subtraction.

The third argument is `date`; this is a valid date or something that can be converted to a date. To see how this works, run the following piece of code:

```
SELECT DATEADD(mm,1,'20090501')

(Result set)
2009-06-01 00:00:00.000
```

As you can see after passing a value of 1 for the `number` argument, the date was incremented by a month. If we pass in a negative number, we'll get a date that's a month earlier than we passed in, as the following code demonstrates:

```
SELECT DATEADD(mm,-1,'20090501')

(Result set)
2009-04-01 00:00:00.000
```

Now it's time to use our numbers table to create some dates. The query in listing 2 will add one month multiplied by the number in the numbers table to today's date and return the next 100 months, beginning with today's date.

Listing 2 Query to create dates from the numbers table

```
SELECT DATEADD(mm,number,CONVERT(varchar(8),GETDATE(),112))
FROM dbo.Numbers
WHERE number < 100
ORDER BY number
```

The query creates the dates in the result set in listing 3.

Listing 3 Abridged result set of dates created from the numbers table

```
2008-10-29 00:00:00.000
2008-11-29 00:00:00.000
2008-12-29 00:00:00.000
2009-01-29 00:00:00.000
....
....
2017-01-29 00:00:00.000
```

If you add a minus sign in front of number, it'll go back in time. As shown in listing 4, we can use the minus sign before a number to go back in time.

Listing 4 Query to create dates in the past from the numbers table

```
SELECT DATEADD(mm,-number,CONVERT(varchar(8),GETDATE(),112))
FROM dbo.Numbers
WHERE number < 100
ORDER BY number
```

The query creates the dates in the result set in listing 5.

Listing 5   Abridged result set of dates created in the past from the numbers table

```
2008-10-29 00:00:00.000
2008-09-29 00:00:00.000
2008-08-29 00:00:00.000
....
....
2000-07-29 00:00:00.000
```

The query in listing 6 will return the first and last day of every quarter from January, 2000, until December, 2024.

Listing 6   Query to return the first and last day of every quarter from 2000 to 2024

```
DECLARE @Date datetime
SELECT @Date = '2000-01-01 00:00:00.000'
SELECT DATEADD(qq,number,@Date),DATEADD(qq,number+1,@Date)-1
FROM dbo.Numbers
WHERE number < 100
```

The result set of the query is listed in listing 7.

Listing 7   Abridged result set of query in listing 6

```
2000-01-01 00:00:00.000    2000-03-31 00:00:00.000
2000-04-01 00:00:00.000    2000-06-30 00:00:00.000
2000-07-01 00:00:00.000    2000-09-30 00:00:00.000
....
....
2024-10-01 00:00:00.000    2024-12-31 00:00:00.000
```

Splitting strings with a numbers table

Numbers tables are also handy if you need to split delimited strings. Take, for example, the following string: 'Z,X,A,B,D,F,Z,Z,Z,Z,A,V,S,Q,L,B,B,B,B,B'. You want to get all the characters in that string without duplicates. This is easily accomplished with a numbers table. First, create the stored procedure in listing 8.

Listing 8   Stored procedure to split delimited strings with the numbers table

```
CREATE PROCEDURE SplitString
@StringToSplit varchar(1000),
@Delimiter varchar(10)
AS

SELECT DISTINCT SUBSTRING(@Delimiter + @StringToSplit + @Delimiter, number
➥+ 1,
CHARINDEX(@Delimiter, @Delimiter + @StringToSplit + @Delimiter, number + 1)
➥- number -1) As StringItem
FROM Numbers
WHERE number <= LEN(@Delimiter + @StringToSplit + @Delimiter) - 1
AND SUBSTRING(@Delimiter + @StringToSplit + @Delimiter, number, 1) =
➥@Delimiter
ORDER BY StringItem
GO
```

Here's how you'd call that stored procedure with a string delimited with commas:

```
EXEC SplitString 'Z,X,A,B,D,F,Z,Z,Z,Z,A,V,S,Q,L,B,B,B,B,B',','
```

The result set of unique characters in a string is shown in listing 9.

Listing 9   Result set of unique characters in a string

```
A
B
D
F
L
Q
S
V
X
Z
```

Here's an example with a pipe symbol as delimiter:

```
EXEC SplitString 'Z|X|A', '|'

(Result set)
A
X
Z
```

The same code from the stored procedure, but with comments explaining how it works, is shown in listing 10.

Listing 10   Stored procedure with comments

```
-- This will hold the delimited string
DECLARE @StringToSplit varchar(1000)
SELECT @StringToSplit ='Z|X|A'

-- This is the delimiter
DECLARE @Delimiter varchar(10)
SELECT @Delimiter= '|'

-- Return unique values
SELECT DISTINCT
-- Add the delimiters to the string and add 1 to the start position
SUBSTRING(@Delimiter + @StringToSplit + @Delimiter, number + 1,
-- Until you find the next delimiter
CHARINDEX(@Delimiter, @Delimiter + @StringToSplit + @Delimiter, number + 1)
➡- number -1) As StringItem
-- Use the numbers table to loop
FROM Numbers
-- Keep going until you arrive at the end of the string
WHERE number <= LEN(@Delimiter + @StringToSplit + @Delimiter) - 1
-- Return only positions between delimiters
AND SUBSTRING(@Delimiter + @StringToSplit + @Delimiter, number, 1) =
➡@Delimiter
ORDER BY StringItem
```

As you can see, I created a stored procedure and made it accept different delimiters; this provides flexibility and also one codebase. I don't need to have a stored procedure for every delimiter that can possible be used.

Placing common code in the tools database

Common code is code that typically can be written and consumed only one way. Converting from Celsius to Fahrenheit, converting from miles to kilometers, and calculating sales tax are some examples.

Let's look at a sales tax calculation example; each state will have a current tax rate and a previous tax rate in a table. The row where the EndDate is NULL is the current tax rate; the row where the EndDate isn't NULL is a previous tax rate. When we add a new tax rate, we simply update the row where the EndDate column has a NULL value with the current date and insert a new row with a NULL value for the EndDate.

Create the StateTaxRates table in listing 11 and insert four rows for state tax rates.

Listing 11 Table for state tax rates

```
CREATE TABLE StateTaxRates(StateCode char(2) NOT NULL,
StartDate datetime NOT NULL,
EndDate datetime,
TaxRate decimal(4,4) NOT NULL)
GO

INSERT StateTaxRates VALUES('NJ','20010101','20070101',.07)
INSERT StateTaxRates VALUES('NJ','20070102',NULL,.08)
INSERT StateTaxRates VALUES('CA','20010101','20080101',.0825)
INSERT StateTaxRates VALUES('CA','20080102',NULL,0.09)
```

The user-defined function that calculates the tax is shown in listing 12.

Listing 12 User-defined function to calculate tax

```
CREATE FUNCTION CalculateStateTax(@Value decimal(20,8),@StateCode
➥char(2),@Date datetime)
RETURNS decimal(20,4)
AS
BEGIN
    DECLARE @TaxRate decimal(4,4)

    --Grab latest tax rate
    IF @Date IS NULL
    BEGIN
        SELECT @TaxRate = TaxRate
        FROM StateTaxRates
        WHERE StateCode = @StateCode
        AND EndDate IS NULL
    END
    ELSE
       --Grab tax rate for a specific day
    BEGIN
        SELECT @TaxRate = TaxRate
        FROM StateTaxRates
```

```
        WHERE StateCode = @StateCode
        AND @Date >= StartDate
        AND @Date < EndDate
    END

    --Do the calculation by multiplying the tax with the amount
    RETURN @Value * @TaxRate
END
GO
```

Four example calls and their results are shown in listing 13.

Listing 13   Four example calls and their results

```
SELECT dbo.CalculateStateTax(100,'NJ',null)
(Result set)
8.0000

SELECT dbo.CalculateStateTax(100,'NJ','20020101')
(Result set)
7.0000

SELECT dbo.CalculateStateTax(10000,'CA',null)
(Result set)
900.0000

SELECT dbo.CalculateStateTax(100000,'CA','20020101')
(Result set)
8250.0000
```

Formatting

In general, formatting should be done in the presentation layer, but sometimes you need to generate a file and the recipient needs certain values to be in a specific format. Take a date for example; what if you want a date in the format YYYY-MM-DD? SQL Server has a bunch of formats built in, but it doesn't have that one. Create the function in listing 14.

Listing 14   Function to format a date

```
CREATE FUNCTION FormatDateDash(@Date datetime)
RETURNS varchar(10)
AS
BEGIN
RETURN CONVERT(varchar(10),@Date,120)
END
GO
```

Now call it like this:

```
SELECT dbo.FormatDateDash(getdate()),dbo.FormatDateDash('20010101')
(Result set)
2008-10-29    2001-01-01
```

Calling code from a different database

In order to call code that resides in a different database, you'll need to use three-part notation. Three-part notation looks like this:

```
DatabaseName.Schema.Object
```

A stored procedure named `SplitString` exists in the tools database within the dbo schema. In order to execute this stored procedure from the temp database, your code would look like this:

```
USE tempdb
GO
EXEC Tools.dbo.SplitString 'Z|X|A', '|'
GO
```

You need to have appropriate permissions in order to call objects in a database from another database!

Summary

Hopefully this chapter has given you an idea of how a tools database can help you save time and headaches. Next time when you have to make code changes in several places to fix a bug or make a change request, consider a tools database: it'll make your life easier.

About the author

Denis Gobo resides in Princeton, New Jersey, with his wife and three kids. For the last four years, Denis has been working for Dow Jones, where his task is to optimize the storage and retrieval of a good amount of data; most of this data is stored in SQL Server. Denis is a cofounder of http://lessthandot.com, a community site for tech professionals, where he also blogs and answers questions in the forums. In his free time, Denis likes to read, watch horror movies, and spend time with his family.

21 Deprecation feature

Cristian Lefter

With every release of SQL Server, new features are added. Also, some features are discontinued or marked as *deprecated*, which means that they'll be removed in a future version of SQL Server. Starting with SQL Server 2008, the deprecation policy is taken very seriously. How seriously? Seriously enough to mention that the first public CTP of the product came with a feature that allows you to monitor usage of deprecated functionality. You may ask yourself: why would I need to track the usage of deprecated features?

Among the possible reasons are the following two:

- You can obtain greater longevity for an application if you're an application developer.
- You can identify possible upgrade problems for your existing applications before the next release of SQL Server hits the shops.

The deprecation feature consists of two components:

- The `SQLServer:Deprecated Features` object performance counter.
- The `Deprecation` category of trace events, including the `Deprecation Announcement` event class (indicates that a feature will be removed in a future version of SQL Server) and the `Deprecation Final Support` event class (indicates that a feature will be removed in the next major release of SQL Server).

The complete list of deprecated features can be found in Books Online and has more than nine printed pages. Table 1 displays a few of them.

Table 1 Deprecated features

Deprecated feature	Replacement
DATABASEPROPERTY	DATABASEPROPERTYEX
The 80 compatibility level and upgrade from version 80	Only compatibility levels for the last two versions of the product available

Table 1 Deprecated features *(continued)*

Deprecated feature	Replacement
sp_dboption	ALTER DATABASE
text, ntext, image data types	varchar(max), nvarchar(max), varbinary(max) data types
sp_attach_db	CREATE DATABASE statement with the FOR ATTACH option

A simple usage example

To get a feel for how the deprecation feature works, listing 1 shows how to read the performance counter SQLServer:Deprecated Features before and after using the DATABASEPROPERTY function (which will be replaced by the DATABASEPROPERTYEX function). Note that if you run the sample on a named instance, you have to change the counter name.

Listing 1 Reading the SQLServer:Deprecated Features counters

```
-- Declare a variable to hold the current value of the counter
DECLARE @CurrentCount bigint;
SELECT
    @CurrentCount = cntr_value
FROM sys.dm_os_performance_counters
WHERE
    object_name='SQLServer:Deprecated Features'
    AND instance_name='DATABASEPROPERTY';

-- Increase the value of the counter by 1
-- using the deprecated feature the function DATABASEPROPERTY
SELECT DATABASEPROPERTY('master','IsTruncLog') AS IsTruncLog;

-- Retrieve the difference between the current counter value
-- and the original value
-- The value returned is 1 (or greater if another session used the
-- DATABASEPROPERTY function after saving the counter value
SELECT
    (cntr_value - @CurrentCount) AS SessionUsage
FROM sys.dm_os_performance_counters
WHERE
    object_name='SQLServer:Deprecated Features'
    AND instance_name='DATABASEPROPERTY';
```

The example in the listing reads the performance counters from T-SQL by using the sys.dm_os_performance_counters dynamic management view. A more attractive image can be obtained using the Performance Monitor. From the SQLServer:Deprecated Features performance object, select and add the DATABASEPROPERTY counter. Then back in the SQL Server Management Studio, run again the next statement:

```
SELECT DATABASEPROPERTY('master','IsTruncLog') AS IsTruncLog;
```

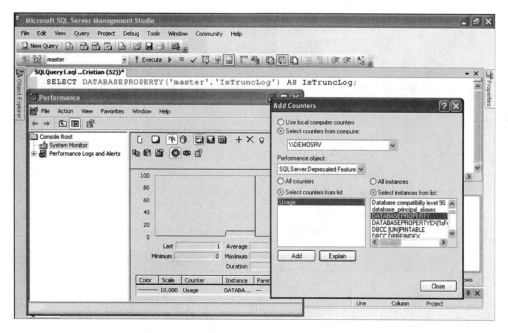

Figure 1   Tracking deprecated features using Performance Monitor

Figure 1 shows the SQLServer:Deprecated Features performance object in Performance Monitor.

Methods of tracking deprecated features

Probably the most useful scenario based on tracking deprecated features is to collect data and save it on a data store, and then build a report over the data store and optionally include the report in SQL Server Management Studio. The frequency of collection, the synchronous or asynchronous mode of collection, and the data store used are a matter of choice (personally I prefer using Extended Events). Some of the possible tracking methods follow:

- *Performance Monitor*—Can be used to display graphically the values of counters for the SQLServer:Deprecated Features performance object.
- *The sys.dm_os_performance_counters Dynamic Management View*—Based on the same SQLServer:Deprecated Features performance object, it allows taking snapshots for the current values of the counters.
- *The performance logs and alerts*—Use the same object as for Performance Monitor; the difference is that the values can be tracked over time.
- *SQL Profiler and SQL Trace*—This method is based on the Deprecation Announcement and the Deprecation Final Support event classes.

- *Event notifications*—This method consists of creating an event notification for the DEPRECATION_ANNOUNCEMENT and DEPRECATION_FINAL_SUPPORT events. A stored procedure can be used to log the events.
- *Extended Events*—The sqlserver.deprecation_announcement and the sqlserver.deprecation_final_support events support this method. An example is provided later on.
- *SQL Trace Collector*—If you need automation for collecting deprecation events, the SQL Trace Collector part of the Data Collector architecture can be helpful.
- *WMI*—This method consists of creating SQL Agent alerts based on WMI queries. It's mentioned only as a possible option, not as a suggestion, because it doesn't bring any advantages over the other methods.

The next section highlights two of the mentioned methods. First, a simple skeleton for the event notifications method is displayed in listing 2.

Listing 2 Event notification method

```
-- Create a queue
CREATE QUEUE DeprecationFeatures_Queue;
GO

-- Create a service
CREATE SERVICE DeprecationFeatures_Service
ON QUEUE DeprecationFeatures_Queue([http://schemas.microsoft.com/SQL/
    Notifications/P
ostEventNotification]);
GO

-- Create a route
CREATE ROUTE DeprecationFeatures_Route
WITH SERVICE_NAME = N'DeprecationFeatures_Service',
ADDRESS = N'LOCAL';
GO

-- Create the actual event notification
CREATE EVENT NOTIFICATION DeprecationFeatures_Notification
ON SERVER
FOR DEPRECATION_ANNOUNCEMENT, DEPRECATION_FINAL_SUPPORT
TO SERVICE 'DeprecationFeatures_Service', 'current database';
GO
```

For using Extended Events, listing 3 creates a session and then adds the two deprecation events. For storage, a ring buffer with maximum 1000 entries is used.

Listing 3 Extended Events method

```
-- Create an event session and add the two deprecation events
CREATE EVENT SESSION TrackDF
ON SERVER
ADD EVENT sqlserver.deprecation_announcement,
ADD EVENT sqlserver.deprecation_final_support;
GO
```

```
-- Add a the ring buffer target and configure it
-- to retain 1000 events
ALTER EVENT SESSION TrackDF
ON SERVER
ADD TARGET package0.ring_buffer
(
     SET occurrence_number = 1000
);
GO

-- Start the session and begin event collection
ALTER EVENT SESSION TrackDF
ON SERVER
STATE = start
GO

-- Use a deprecated feature
SELECT DATABASEPROPERTY('master','IsTruncLog') AS IsTruncLog;

-- View the collected events
SELECT CAST(xet.target_data as xml)
FROM sys.dm_xe_session_targets xet
JOIN sys.dm_xe_sessions xe
ON (xe.address = xet.event_session_address)
WHERE xe.name = 'TrackDF'
GO

-- Stop the event session and remove it from the server
ALTER EVENT SESSION TrackDF
ON SERVER
STATE = STOP;
GO

DROP EVENT SESSION TrackDF
ON SERVER
GO
```

The result of the previous SELECT query is displayed in listing 4.

Listing 4   XML result

```
<RingBufferTarget eventsPerSec="0" processingTime="0"
➡totalEventsProcessed="1" eventCount="1" droppedCount="0"
➡memoryUsed="424">
  <event name="deprecation_final_support" package="sqlserver" id="207"
➡version="1" timestamp="2008-10-30T08:54:31.689Z">
    <data name="feature">
      <type name="unicode_string" package="package0" />
      <value>DATABASEPROPERTY</value>
      <text />
    </data>
    <data name="message">
      <type name="unicode_string" package="package0" />
      <value>DATABASEPROPERTY will be removed in the next version of SQL
    ➡Server. Avoid using this feature in new development work, and plan to
    ➡modify applications that currently use it.</value>
      <text />
```

```
    </data>
  </event>
</RingBufferTarget>
```

Summary

SQL Server 2008 makes it easy to track the features that will be removed in future releases of the product. Pick any of the methods mentioned in this chapter and make sure that your applications will have a greater longevity.

About the author

Cristian Lefter is a SQL Server MVP and a former SQL Server developer, currently working as a consultant at Micro Training, a consulting and training company. Cristian is a writer, blogger, SQL expert, and frequent reviewer for Manning, Apress, Wiley, and other publishers, as well as for ASPToday, Simple-Talk, Microsoft E-Learning, Asentus, Content Master, GrandMasters, and more. He's based in Bucharest, Romania.

You can reach him at his blog at http://sqlserver.ro/blogs/cristians_blog/default.aspx, or his email address at Cristian-Lefter@hotmail.com.

22 Placing SQL Server in your pocket

Christopher Fairbairn

SQL Server is a database engine that can scale to cope with the largest data centers and astronomically sized datasets, but it can also scale down to support incredibly small and resource-constrained scenarios.

Many workforces are increasingly becoming mobile and working outside the fixed confines of an office environment. This presents a challenge to system architects, as they need to consider how to make their company data accessible to field workers while coping with issues such as the high costs and slow speeds (and potential unavailability) of network connectivity.

In building a traditional three-tier distributed application, you may have used SQL Server 2008 to store your data on a large centralized server and had clients retrieve data over the network on an as-needed basis.

When building mobile applications for devices such as laptops, Tablet PCs, and PDAs, you're more likely to place a local data store on each client. This is required to store data so that the application can continue to function while offline. It may also be desirable to locally cache large fairly static datasets (such as customer or product lists) to avoid repeatedly transferring data over expensive or slow networks.

SQL Server Compact Edition is the smallest member of the SQL Server family and is optimized to be an embedded database for single-user applications running on the Tablet PC, Windows Mobile PDA, and desktop platforms. It's designed to fit in your pocket with a disk footprint of less than 4 MB.

Design goals

Providing a complete relational database engine that also supports replication and synchronization in less than 4 MB of disk space does lead to some trade-offs. For starters, SQL Server Compact Edition has a completely separate implementation that doesn't share a common code base with any other edition of SQL Server.

SQL Server Compact 3.5 has been designed with the following concepts and goals in mind:

- *Cross-platform*—SQL Server Compact Edition runtimes are available for a wide range of devices running the Windows CE and Windows Mobile operating systems on ARM, MIPS, and SH4 platforms. This is in addition to the traditional Windows operating system running on x86 CPUs found in your desktop or Tablet PC machine.

- *Small*—The typical runtime size is 2 to 3 MB of disk space with less than 5 MB of RAM required—although the exact requirements depend upon OS and processor type.

- *Secure*—The contents of database files can be encrypted with 128-bit encryption that complies with industry standards such as RSA and AES.

- *Data synchronization*—Mobility gives the freedom to work anywhere at the expense of making it harder to provide a consistent view across the enterprise. Although a local data store is useful, it typically needs to be synchronized back to a centralized server at some stage to ensure that all users share a common set of data. SQL Server Compact Edition supports merge replication and remote data access (RDA) synchronization technologies.

- *Multi-user support*—Although there's no concept of database users or access roles, SQL Server Compact Edition supports multiple applications accessing one database file at the same time. The storage engine provides row- and page-level data locking, along with various isolation levels to help guarantee data integrity during concurrency.

- *Familiar tools*—The database engine is integrated into familiar development tools such as SQL Server Management Studio (SSMS) and Visual Studio to give developers an experience as close to the full version of SQL Server as possible while promoting the reuse of existing techniques and knowledge.

- *Simplified deployment*—As well as traditional CAB- and MSI-based installations that require administrative privileges, SQL Server Compact Edition supports XCOPY-style deployment. You can include the database engine as part of your own setup and deploy it within your application folder.

The underlying design goal is to provide a complete SQL relational database management system that allows the reuse of existing developer experience and training while being mindful of the resource constraints and runtime environment typical of smaller mobile and embedded systems.

Architecture

SQL Server Compact Edition doesn't run as a Windows service that clients connect to via inter-process communication mechanisms. Instead, when an application wants to access a SQL CE database, it creates an instance of the database engine directly within the application process. Internally the database engine is a set of dynamic link libraries as demonstrated in figure 1.

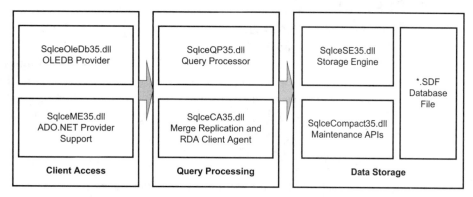

Figure 1   An overview of the architecture of SQL Server Compact Edition showing the various DLLs that make up the database engine. These DLLs are loaded directly into the process space of the client application wanting access to the database.

Because the database engine is hosted within the client application, traditional data access penalties such as the number of server round trips and network latency don't have the same impact on performance. Microsoft has used this fact to their advantage in an effort to further reduce the size of the core database engine. Traditional RDBMS features such as views, triggers, and stored procedures aren't implemented. Instead the developer is encouraged to implement these features within the client application via procedural code in languages such as C++, C#, or VB.NET while accessing the database via standard ADO.NET functionality. Unique database engine features such as low-level row and index access mechanisms further reduce the penalty of implementing these features outside of the core database engine.

A SQL Server Compact Edition database is physically implemented as a single file with a 4 GB size limit. The traditional file extension is *.SDF. Database files are portable, allowing a database file to be generated on a server and then copied for use by one or more PDA devices.

Deployment

You can use a number of mechanisms to deploy SQL Server Compact Edition onto client machines and devices. If you intend to distribute the database engine as part of your own product, the first step is to sign up for a redistribution license by filling in a form available at http://www.microsoft.com/Sqlserver/2005/en/us/compact-redistribute.aspx. This enables Microsoft to keep track of the number of ISVs distributing SQL Server Compact Edition and potentially allows them to notify you of issues such as critical security updates.

Deploying on a desktop

The SQL Server Compact 3.5 runtime components support both 32-bit (x86) and 64-bit (x64) environments, and are required to run SQL Server Compact 3.5–based applications on the desktop. The runtime components can be downloaded from the web in the form of an MSI-based installation[1] named SSCERuntime-ENU-x86.msi or SSCE-Runtime-ENU-x64.msi for 32-bit and 64-bit systems, respectively. Service Pack 1 or above will be required for true 64-bit support.

The MSI installation requires administrative privileges, as it installs a single copy of the database engine in a system-wide location. Having a sole installation of the database engine reduces disk usage when it's used by multiple applications and enables administrators and mechanisms such as Windows Update to easily perform system-wide updates.

Deploying on a device

Deployment to devices that run the Windows Embedded CE or Windows Mobile operating systems is slightly more complicated, due to the wider range of platforms and processors available. The SQL Server Compact 3.5 for Devices installation (SSCEDeviceRuntime-ENU.msi)[2] installs a series of CAB files within the %PROGRAMFILES%\Microsoft SQL Server Compact Edition\v3.5\Devices folder that can then be used to install the database engine on each supported combination of platform and processor type.

XCOPY deployment

If database functionality isn't a central part of your application, or will be installed by consumers rather than IT administrators, it may be more convenient to install SQL Server Compact Edition behind the scenes as part of your own installation procedure rather than having a separate installer. The downloads outlined previously also provide a series of loosely bundled .DLL files such as sqlceoledb35.dll. These files implement the database engine and can be packaged and deployed within your own application folder. No COM-style registration is required. The disadvantage of this deployment model is that system updates won't be able to update your instance of the database engine. In some cases, the advantage of a streamlined application installation is worth the complexity of handling security patches yourself.

Tool support

The SQL Server Compact database engine is supported by the same set of development tools used by desktop editions of SQL Server. This enables you to use the tools you're already familiar with to create, maintain, and manipulate SQL Server Compact databases. As an example of this tight integration, figure 2 shows the Connect to Server dialog box within SQL Server Management Studio.

All you need to modify in order to connect to a SQL Server Compact Edition database is to set the Server Type to SQL Server Compact Edition. This enables you to

---

[1] Runtime components in the form of an MSI-based installation available at http://www.microsoft.com/downloads/details.aspx?FamilyID=dc614aee-7e1c-4881-9c32-3a6ce53384d9&displaylang=en.

[2] SQL Server Compact 3.5 for Devices installation available at http://www.microsoft.com/downloads/details.aspx?FamilyId=FCE9ABBF-F807-45D6-A457-AB5615001C8F&displaylang=en.

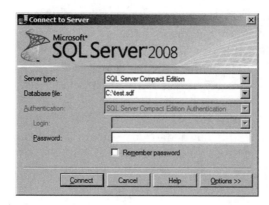

Figure 2   The Connect to Server dialog box within SQL Server Management Studio allows a developer to connect to a SQL Server Compact Edition database by selecting SQL Server Compact Edition as the server type.

connect to a Compact Edition database file located on your current machine or any ActiveSync-connected device.

Once connected to a database file, you can use most SQL Server Management Studio features. For example, figure 3 demonstrates the Object Explorer pane, and executing SQL queries via a query window. Even more advanced features, such as the display of estimated and actual query plans, are supported. But many of these features have simplified or reduced feature sets reflecting the limited capabilities of the underlying database engine. As an example, most dialog boxes don't support scripting their changes to a query window.

Most programmers will be more familiar with working within the Visual Studio IDE, and SQL Server Compact Edition has the same richness of support within this tool. For example, a new SQL Server Compact Edition database file can be added to a project by selecting the Local Database option within the Add New Project Item dialog box.

Once a database file has been added, double-clicking on it within Solution Explorer will open up the Server Explorer pane. This pane provides some of the same

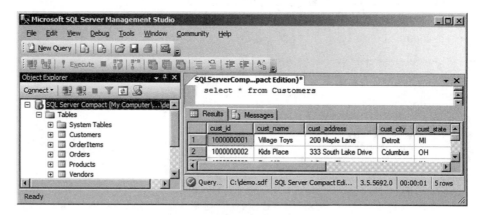

Figure 3   An example session with SQL Server Management Studio demonstrating the Object Explorer and Query panes accessing a SQL Server Compact Edition database.

functionality available within SQL Server Management Studio and enables the user to modify the database schema and perform queries against it.

The seamless integration with SQL Server Management Studio and Visual Studio also makes it easier to migrate a solution between the full SQL Server database engine and the Compact Edition. In many cases, it's enough to switch ADO.NET data providers in code and verify that your SQL statements don't rely on features or optional T-SQL syntax unique to one RDBMS implementation.

Developer tool integration is unfortunately tied to a particular combination of tool and database engine versions. In order to use SQL Server Compact 3.5 and get full support of the IDE features, you'll need Visual Studio 2008 and SQL Server Management Studio 2008. If you try to open a database file from an older version of the database engine (such as SQL Server 2005 Mobile Edition), you may be prompted to upgrade the file to the latest file format. This is an irreversible process that'll render the database file unreadable by the GUI tools within earlier versions of the IDE.

Programming support

SQL Server Compact Edition provides both a native OLE DB provider and a managed ADO.NET data provider in order to support a wide range of development tools and environments.

To use the managed ADO.NET data provider, you need to add a reference to the `System.Data.SqlServerCe.dll` assembly and make use of the classes within the `System.Data.SqlServerCe` namespace. The developer experience is similar to using the standard `System.Data.SqlClient` namespace for SQL Server 2008. The main difference is that instead of a `Sql` prefix, the ADO.NET data provider classes use a `SqlCe` prefix.

As well as standard ADO.NET data provider functionality, the SQL Server Compact Edition provider includes a number of extensions that can potentially provide more efficient access to data. These features tend to make up for the lack of views, triggers, and stored procedures. For example, listing 1 demonstrates how the query processor can be bypassed completely to more efficiently implement a `select * from customers where cust_name like 'F%'` style query.

Listing 1   Bypassing the query processor

```
using (SqlCeCommand cmd = new SqlCeCommand("Customers",    ❶
  cnn))
{
  cmd.CommandType = CommandType.TableDirect;    ❷
  cmd.IndexName = "IDX_CustName";                              ❸
  cmd.SetRange(DbRangeOptions.Prefix, new object[]
      { "F" }, null);

  using (SqlCeResultSet rs =
        cmd.ExecuteResultSet(ResultSetOptions.Sensitive))    ❹
  {
    while (rs.Read())
```

```
    {
      Console.WriteLine("Customer: Id={0}, Name={1}",        ❺
        rs["cust_id"], rs["cust_name"]);
    }
  }
}
```

The code sample starts off by creating a `SqlCeCommand` instance ❶. This uses a previously established (and opened) database connection called cnn. The command string is the name of the Customers table. This is further reinforced by setting the `Command-Type` property ❷ to `TableDirect`. `TableDirect` mode allows you to access all rows within the specified table, and in effect behaves similar to a traditional database cursor.

When using `TableDirect` mode, you can also optionally provide an index range to filter the rows that will be returned. In this example, we restrict the result set ❸ to only include rows where the `IDX_CustName` index has a value beginning with the letter *F.*

Once we've specified which rows from the table we want to access, we're ready to send the command to the database engine via a call to the `ExecuteResultSet` method ❹. Because we've explicitly provided the database engine with the required table and index names, the database engine will have a lot less difficulty processing this query than if we passed it an opaque string containing T-SQL.

The call to `ExecuteResultSet` will return quickly, as it has in effect opened the equivalent of a database cursor. It's only when we start stepping over each row with successive calls to the `Read` method that data is fetched. While processing each row, you can access the columns within the result set by using the indexer operator ❺. Because the result set was created with the `ResultSetOptions.Sensitive` flag, it's even possible to assign columns new values, and these changes will make their way back to the database engine.

Although ADO.NET provider features such as `TableDirect` mode can provide immense speed and performance benefits, the disadvantage of such techniques is that they tie the application logic closer to database implementation details such as the chosen indexing strategy. Depending upon how stable your database schema is, this could lead to brittle and hard-to-maintain code.

Summary

SQL Server Compact Edition has grown into a mature and comprehensive database platform for mobile and disconnected environments. It can be used for a wide range of scenarios, including local online and offline data caches, client-side data stores, or even as a structured document format for data transfer between devices.

A major advantage of SQL Server Compact Edition over other mobile database products is the ability to leverage many of the same tools and development practices familiar to desktop SQL Server developers. Not only does this shorten the time required to come up to speed with the new database engine, but it also provides a reasonable transition path between SQL Server Express Edition and SQL Server Compact

Edition, should an application grow to exceed the capabilities of SQL Server Compact Edition, or conversely need to be migrated to a PDA-based application.

I encourage you to give SQL Server Compact Edition a try the next time you need an easy-to-deploy-and-maintain database engine for a mobile or offline based application.

About the author

Christopher Fairbairn is a Device Application Development MVP from Christchurch, New Zealand, with more than eight years experience in mobile application development on a range of platforms including Palm OS, J2ME, Windows Mobile, and the iPhone. Christopher actively blogs at http://www.christec. co.nz/blog/ and loves to get feedback from the community.

23 Mobile data strategies

John Baird

In recent months, there have been many headlines decrying the loss of thousands and millions of sensitive data records on disks, laptops, and portable media. This is a concern to many users of Windows Mobile and handheld devices. If my phone is lost or stolen, how safe is the data contained within it? If I lose network connectivity, what happens to my data? In this chapter, we'll discuss how to solve the data issues that arise from carrying a device that must store its data locally and operate independently of any network connectivity.

Microsoft has recognized this need and has provided a number of strategies for the mobile developer to use in solving the disconnected data problem: two older techniques and one recent addition are available to the mobile developer. This chapter will focus mainly on the recent release of the Microsoft Sync Framework (MSF) and how it applies to mobile development and synchronization of data between the .NET Compact Framework (.NET CF) and SQL Server.

Much information exists on older technologies, such as remote data access (RDA) and merge replication (MR), and is readily available via an internet search. The following books provide excellent coverage of these topics:

- Rob Tiffany's *Windows Mobile Data Synchronization with SQL Server 2005 and SQL Server Compact 3.1*, Hood Canal Press, 2007.
- Andy Wigley, Daniel Moth, and Peter Foot's *Mobile Development Handbook*, Microsoft Press, 2007.

By utilizing SQL Server Compact Edition (SQL CE) as the local data store, we can take advantage of both RDA and MR to maintain the integrity of our data, whether connected or not. With SQL CE, the mobile application can read from the database using typical SQL data access techniques. Subsequently, when and if we are connected, the chosen data management strategy kicks in to synchronize our data with the remote server.

NOTE Tables 1 through 5 are reproduced from MSDN, courtesy of Microsoft, Inc.

Microsoft Sync Framework (MSF)

MSF is Microsoft's newest entry into the information replication and synchronization arena. It combines the ease and usefulness of RDA with the power and scalability of MR. It is highly developer centric and requires little setup. RDA will soon be deprecated in favor of MSF because of its ease of use and scalability.

MSF uses the provider model as shown in figure 1, and is transport agnostic. The provider model allows developers to create synchronization technology for any client and for any server. A number of providers are already available as listed here:

- File Systems
- Sync Services for Feed Sync
- Sync Services for ADO.NET

Most major software vendors are developing providers for their technology to interface with MSF.

The main pieces of this architecture are the client and server synchronization providers, the synchronization adapter, and the synchronization agent.

Client synchronization provider

The client synchronization provider's main responsibilities are the following:

- Store information in client tables that are enabled for synchronization.
- Retrieve changes from client database since the last synchronization.
- Apply incremental changes to the client database.
- Detect conflicting changes.

Server synchronization provider

The server synchronization provider's main responsibilities are the following:

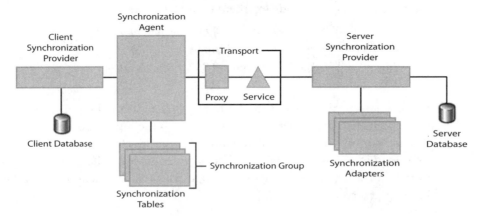

Figure 1   Synchronization architecture

- Store information in server tables that are enabled for synchronization.
- Retrieve changes from server database since the last synchronization.
- Apply incremental changes to the server database.
- Detect conflicting changes.

Synchronization adapter

The synchronization adapter is the communication gateway between the server synchronization provider and the server database. It is analogous to the data adapter in ADO.NET. Each table added to the syncTables collection will have an adapter defined for it. The adapter stores and serves the commands necessary for it to interact with the provider. These commands include the basic create, read, update, and delete (CRUD) operations. The commands can use any command type supported by ADO.NET, such as T-SQL, stored procedures, views, and functions. The properties and public methods available are shown in tables 1 and 2.

Table 1 `SyncAdapter` **properties**

Name	Description
ColumnMappings	Gets a collection of `SyncColumnMapping` objects for the table. These objects map columns in a server table to the corresponding columns in a client table.
DeleteCommand	Gets or sets the query or stored procedure that is used to delete data from the server database.
Description	Gets or sets a description for the synchronization adapter.
InsertCommand	Gets or sets the query or stored procedure that is used to insert data into the server database.
SelectConflictDeletedRowsCommand	Gets or sets the query or stored procedure that is used to identify deleted rows that conflict with other changes.
SelectConflictUpdatedRowsCommand	Gets or sets the query or stored procedure that is used to identify updated rows that conflict with other changes.
SelectIncrementalDeletesCommand	Gets or sets the query or stored procedure that is used to retrieve deletes made in the server database since the last synchronization.
SelectIncrementalInsertsCommand	Gets or sets the query or stored procedure that is used to retrieve inserts made in the server database since the last synchronization.
SelectIncrementalUpdatesCommand	Gets or sets the query or stored procedure that is used to retrieve updates made in the server database since the last synchronization.

Table 1 `SyncAdapter` properties *(continued)*

Name	Description
TableName	Gets or sets the name of the table at the server for which to create the `SyncAdapter`.
UpdateCommand	Gets or sets the query or stored procedure that is used to update data in the server database.

Table 2 `SyncAdapter` methods

Name	Description
FillSchema	Populates the schema information for the table that is specified in `TableName`.
GetClientColumnFromServerColumn	Gets the client column name that corresponds to the specified server column name.
ToString	Overridden. Returns a string that represents the `SyncAdapter` object.

Synchronization agent

The synchronization agent's responsibilities include the following:

- Track tables involved in the synchronization through a synchronization group.
- Instantiate the client and server synchronization providers.
- Retrieve changes from the client synchronization provider and apply them to the client database.
- Retrieve changes from the server synchronization provider and apply them to the server database.

The synchronization agent class has one major method: `synchronize`. This method makes sure the data in both databases is the same. A number of properties and events are available (table 3). For more information on these items, go to MSDN and the MSF online information. When adding tables to a synchronization group, a couple of enumerations are used to specify how to create the database (table 4) and for which direction the updates are allowed (table 5).

Table 3 Synchronization agent properties

Property	Description
Configuration	Gets a `SyncConfiguration` object that contains information about tables and synchronization parameters.
LocalProvider	Gets or sets an object derived from `ClientSyncProvider` that is used to communicate with the local data store.
RemoteProvider	Gets or sets an object derived from `ServerSyncProvider` that is used to communicate with the remote data store.

Table 3   **Synchronization agent properties** *(continued)*

Property	Description
SessionState	Gets or sets a `SyncSessionState` object that is used to define whether the session is currently synchronizing. This property is not compliant with Common Language Specification (CLS).
SyncStatistics	Gets a `SyncStatistics` object that represents statistics for a synchronization session.

Table 4   `TableCreationOption` **enumerations**

Enumeration	Description
CreateNewTableOrFail	Create the table in the client database. If an existing table has the same name, throw an exception.
DropExistingOrCreateNewTable	Create the table in the client database. If an existing table has the same name, drop the existing table first.
TruncateExistingOrCreateNewTable	Create the table in the client database if the table does not exist. If an existing table has the same name, delete all rows from this table.
UploadExistingOrCreateNewTable	Create the table in the client database if the table does not exist. If an existing table has the same name, upload all rows from this table on the first synchronization. This option is only valid with a `SyncDirection` of `Bidirectional` or `UploadOnly`.
UseExistingTableOrFail	Use an existing table in the client database that has the same name. If the table does not exist, throw an exception.

Table 5   `SyncDirection` **enumerations**

Enumeration	Description
Bidirectional	During the first synchronization, the client typically downloads schema and an initial data set from the server. On subsequent synchronizations, the client uploads changes to the server and then downloads changes from the server.
DownloadOnly	During the first synchronization, the client typically downloads schema and an initial data set from the server. On subsequent synchronizations, the client downloads changes from the server.
Snapshot	The client downloads a set of data from the server. The data is completely refreshed during each synchronization.
UploadOnly	During the first synchronization, the client typically downloads schema from the server. On subsequent synchronizations, the client uploads changes to the server.

Using MSF

I will explain how to create a Windows Communication Foundation (WCF) service, which will be used as the transport mechanism between the client synchronization agent (which lives on the mobile device) and the server synchronization provider (which is part of the WCF service). To use the MSF, you must supply the client and server synchronization providers and the sync agent.

To do this, you need code that creates a proxy service to connect to the WCF service, which will request synchronization of the SQL CE database on the mobile device with the SQL Server on the network. The code discussed in this section is referred to in an excellent post on the MSF blog; links to both the blog and the code can be found on this book's web page: http://www.manning.com/SQLServerMVPDeepDives.

THE WCF SERVICE

Listings 1, 2, and 3 show the code necessary to create the service. After you have created the project, added the files, added the references indicated in the USING statements, and compiled the service project, you need to deploy the service to Internet Information Services (IIS). You will add the code in listing 3 to your project's app.config.

Listing 1   WCF service IService.cs

```
using System.Runtime.Serialization;
using System.ServiceModel;
using System.Data;
using Microsoft.Synchronization.Data;
namespace WcfSyncService
{
  [XmlSerializerFormat]
  [ServiceContract]
  public interface IService
  {
    [OperationContract]
    string GetData(int value);

    [OperationContract]
    CompositeType GetDataUsingDataContract(CompositeType composite);
    [OperationContract]
    SyncServerInfo GetServerInfo(SyncSession syncSession);

    [OperationContract]
    SyncContext ApplyChanges(
                      SyncGroupMetadata groupMetadata,
                      DataSet dataSet,
                      SyncSession syncSession);

    [OperationContract]
    SyncContext GetChanges(
                      SyncGroupMetadata groupMetadata,
                      SyncSession syncSession);

    [OperationContract]
    SyncSchema GetSchema(
                  string[] tableNames,
```

```
                              SyncSession syncSession);
  }

  [DataContract]
  public class CompositeType
  {
    bool boolValue = true;
    string stringValue = "Hello ";

    [DataMember]
    public bool BoolValue
    {
      get { return boolValue; }
      set { boolValue = value; }
    }

    [DataMember]
    public string StringValue
    {
      get { return stringValue; }
      set { stringValue = value; }
    }
  }
}
```

Listing 2   WCF service.cs

```
using System;
using System.Data;
using System.Data.SqlClient;
using Microsoft.Synchronization.Data;
using Microsoft.Synchronization.Data.Server;
using System.Collections.ObjectModel;
using System.IO;
namespace WcfSyncService {
  public class Service : IService {
    static DbServerSyncProvider _serverSyncProvider;
    public Service(){
      if (_serverSyncProvider == null) {
        CreateServerProvider();
      }
    }
    private void CreateServerProvider() {
      SqlConnection conn = new SqlConnection(
            @"server=Thinkpad;database=AdventureWorks2008;
              integrated security = true");
      conn.Open();
      _serverSyncProvider = new DbServerSyncProvider { Connection = conn };

      SqlSyncAdapterBuilder builder = new SqlSyncAdapterBuilder {
                      Connection = conn,
                      SyncDirection = SyncDirection.Bidirectional,
                      TableName = "SyncTable",
                      CreationTrackingColumn = "CreationDate",
                      UpdateTrackingColumn = "LastEditDate",
                      DeletionTrackingColumn = "DeletionDate",
                      TombstoneTableName= ("SyncTable_Tombstone")};
```

```
    _serverSyncProvider.SyncAdapters.Add(builder.ToSyncAdapter());
    SqlCommand selectNewAnchorCmd = new SqlCommand {
                    CommandText = ("SELECT @" +
                        SyncSession.SyncNewReceivedAnchor +
                        " = GETUTCDATE()")};

    SqlParameter newRecAnchor = new SqlParameter {
                    ParameterName = ("@" +
                        SyncSession.SyncNewReceivedAnchor),
                        DbType = DbType.DateTime,
                        Direction = ParameterDirection.Output};
    selectNewAnchorCmd.Parameters.Add(newRecAnchor);
    _serverSyncProvider.SelectNewAnchorCommand =
                        selectNewAnchorCmd;
}

public string GetData(int value)
{
    return string.Format("You entered: {0}", value);
}

public CompositeType GetDataUsingDataContract(
                        CompositeType composite) {
    if (composite.BoolValue)
    {
        composite.StringValue += "Suffix";
    }
    return composite;
}

public SyncServerInfo GetServerInfo(SyncSession syncSession) {
    try {
        Logger.Log("In GetServerInfo()");
        return _serverSyncProvider.GetServerInfo(syncSession);
    }
    catch (Exception e) {
        Logger.Log(e.ToString());
        throw;
    }
}


public SyncContext ApplyChanges(SyncGroupMetadata groupMetadata,
                        DataSet dataSet,
                        SyncSession syncSession)  {
    try {
        Logger.Log("In ApplyChanges()");
        return _serverSyncProvider.ApplyChanges(groupMetadata,
                                dataSet,
                                syncSession);
    }
    catch (Exception e) {
        Logger.Log(e.ToString());
        throw;
    }
}

public SyncContext GetChanges(SyncGroupMetadata groupMetadata,
```

```
                                    SyncSession syncSession) {
      SyncContext context;
      Try {
        Logger.Log("In EnumerateChanges()");
        context = _serverSyncProvider.GetChanges(groupMetadata,
                                          syncSession);
      }
      catch (Exception e) {
        Logger.Log(e.ToString());
        throw;
      }
      return context;
    }

  public SyncSchema GetSchema(string[] tableNames,
                            SyncSession syncSession)  {
      try {
        Logger.Log("In GetSchema()");
        Collection<string> tables = new Collection<string>();
        foreach (string s in tableNames) {
          tables.Add(s);
        }
        return _serverSyncProvider.GetSchema(tables, syncSession);
      }
      catch (Exception e) {
        Logger.Log(e.ToString());
        ApplicationException newex = new ApplicationException(
                                "failed in GetSchema()", e);
        throw newex;
      }
    }
  }

  public class Logger
  {
    static readonly Object thisLock = new Object();
    private const string logfile = @"\wcftestlog.log";

    public static void Log(string msg)
    {
      using (StreamWriter sw = File.AppendText(logfile))
      {
        sw.WriteLine(DateTime.Now + " : " + msg);
        sw.Flush();
      }
    }
  }
}
```

Listing 3 WCF service App.config

```
<system.serviceModel>
  <services>
   <service name="Service" behaviorConfiguration="ServiceBehavior">
    <endpoint address="" binding="basicHttpBinding"
        contract="IService">
     <identity>
```

```
      <dns value="localhost" />
     </identity>
   </endpoint>
   <endpoint address="mex"
             binding="mexHttpBinding"
             contract="IMetadataExchange" />
   <host>
    <baseAddresses>
     <add baseAddress="http://localhost/WcfSyncService/Service/" />
    </baseAddresses>
   </host>
  </service>
 </services>
 <behaviors>
  <serviceBehaviors>
   <behavior name="WcfSyncService.Service1Behavior">
    <serviceMetadata httpGetEnabled="True"/>
    <serviceDebug includeExceptionDetailInFaults="True" />
   </behavior>
  </serviceBehaviors>
 </behaviors>
</system.serviceModel>
```

THE MOBILE APPLICATION

This example involves setting up the client to test the MSF via the WCF service. You need to create a console application and add the two classes in listings 4 and 5. After you have compiled and built the project, add a service reference to the WCF service you created and hosted in IIS.

Listing 4   Mobile console app TestSync.cs

```
using System;
using System.Linq;
using System.Collections.Generic;
using System.Text;
namespace SyncSample {
  public class TestSync {
    static void Main(string[] args) {
      ServiceClient svc = new ServiceClient();
      string testString = svc.GetData(3);
      SyncClient client = new SyncClient();
      client.SetupAgent();
      client.Sync();
    }
  }
}
```

Listing 5   Mobile class SyncClient

```
using System;
using Microsoft.Synchronization;
using Microsoft.Synchronization.Data;
using Microsoft.Synchronization.Data.SqlServerCe;
namespace SyncSample {
```

```
public class SyncClient {
  SyncAgent sa;
  public void SetupAgent(){
    SqlCeClientSyncProvider clientProvider = new
          SqlCeClientSyncProvider(
                    @"data source=testsync.sdf", true);
    ServiceClient svc = new ServiceClient();

    ServerSyncProvider serverProvider = new
                      ServerSyncProviderProxy(svc);
  cagent
    sa = new SyncAgent {
                      LocalProvider = clientProvider,
                      RemoteProvider = serverProvider};
    if (sa != null) {
      sa.Configuration.SyncTables.Add(
              "MyTableToSync",
              TableCreationOption.CreateNewTableOrFail,
              SyncDirection.DownloadOnly);
    }
  }
  public void Sync() {
    try {
      sa.Synchronize();
    }
    catch (Exception e) {
      Console.WriteLine(e.ToString());
    }
  }
}
}
```

The Microsoft .NET Compact Framework (.NET CF) 3.5 includes a subset of WCF for smart devices, enabling them to communicate with remote WCF components. The .NET CF version of WCF ships with support only for message-level communications; a code generation tool is available which allows you to consume other WCF services.

On the desktop, this utility is called `svcutil.exe` and generates a proxy client in code, which can consume the WCF service; however, its output does not compile against the .NET CF. Microsoft has provided the `NETCFSvcUtil.exe` tool contained in the Power Toys for .NET Compact Framework 3.5. You can find this download at http://www.microsoft.com/downloads/details.aspx.

This tool is analogous to the `svcutil.exe` and supports many of the same command-line switches but performs a few additional and modified steps, including the following:

- Verifies that the service being consumed offers endpoints compatible with the feature subset included in .NET CF 3.5.
- Generates the client proxy class in C# or VB that compiles against .NET CF or desktop WCF.
- Generates code for a `.NETCFClientBase` class that fills in where .NET CF doesn't support calling WCF services.

Unlike `svcutil.exe`, this process will not generate a .config file to store the endpoint information. This information is stored in the client proxy code.

To use this tool:

1   Open a Visual Studio command window.
2   Change the directory to your mobile application directory.
3   Enter this command:

    `NETCFsvcutil.exe http://<machinename>/yourservice/service.svc`

    The preceding command should generate two source files. The one named after your service will contain the proxy class you will use to consume the WCF service you created. Add these classes to your project and compile the code. The code can be found at this book's website, http://www.manning.com/ SQLServerMVPDeepDives.

Comparison

Much thought has been given to creating solutions to ensure that data remains in sync during periods of connectivity. All of the techniques—RDA, MR, and MSF—allow data synchronization and replication; however, each has its own strengths and disadvantages, as shown in table 6.

Table 6   Key feature comparison of the three synchronization methodologies

Key feature	RDA	MR	MSF
Synchronize by using services	No	No	Yes
Supports heterogeneous databases	No	No	Yes
Incremental change tracking	No	Yes	Yes
Conflict detection and resolution	No	Yes	Yes
Easily create data views on the client	No	No	Yes
Automatically initialize schema and data	Yes	Yes	Yes
Supports large data sets	Yes	Yes	Yes
Query processor is locally available	Yes	Yes	Yes
Automatically propagate schema changes	No	Yes	No
Automatically repartition data	No	Yes	No
Use on devices	Yes	Yes	Yes

Summary

Which replication strategy you use is up to you, but if you are looking for a robust, developer-centric, scalable solution, the MSF should be your choice. Notice the comparison in table 6. MSF replaces the functionality in RDA with an enhanced plan and copies the functionality of MR. If you require a DBA-centric approach with little code to set up the process, then MR is your choice. Both MSF and MR will keep your data in sync. With the techniques and code samples we have shown in this chapter, you will be able to take advantage of these methodologies to transfer, create, modify, and replicate your data from your mobile device to your desktop server.

About the author

John Baird began his computer programming career while in the US Navy. In 1982, he helped form and direct the first PC-based computer processing department for training and manpower in the Department of Defense. After leaving the military in 1988, John began a varied career as a consultant developing business applications ranging from computer-based training to vertical market software for resellers.

Today, John is working for the industry leader in financial software for fund administration. John was awarded his MVP status for device application development beginning in 2008.

Database Administration

Edited by Paul S. Randal
and Kimberly L. Tripp

A database administrator (DBA) has a tiresome and sometimes thankless job—until things go wrong. It's then that a DBA's skills are most apparent. But the less frequently anyone has to visit their DBA, the better that DBA is doing! So how does a good DBA do it?

A good DBA works with actions rather than words: automating, monitoring, tuning, but above all learning and constantly realizing what they don't know. No one can know everything, and a good DBA recognizes that—even embraces it. A good DBA is always looking to improve their systems, learn tips and tricks, and prototype new configurations. A good DBA sets up alerts to be notified of errors and problems as soon as they begin to happen, possibly solving them before they turn into disasters. Just as in life, the sooner you know there's a problem, the easier it may be to fix! (Did you know that you can set up SQL Server Alerts based on error severity levels—not just specific error numbers? For severity levels 19 and higher, a generic alert should notify you that an error has occurred.)

So, how does a DBA make this happen? Not only does a good DBA proactively look for faults before they become catastrophic but, when something does go wrong, a good DBA takes the time to do a root-cause analysis to make sure the risk is avoided in the future. Leveraging the SQL Server toolkit is imperative in making this happen. Auditing, leveraging the Dynamic Management Views (DMVs), using PowerShell, knowing the ins and outs of backup and restore, understanding security, understanding availability; there are a lot of areas to understand, and a good DBA must be a jack of all trades *and* a master of at least some! It's not easy, and it's more than just a job for a good DBA. SQL Server is a passion for these DBAs—a hobby in addition to their job—and they're constantly learning and expanding on what they know to improve their uptime, minimize data loss, and even allow them to take a vacation once in a while...

This book won't teach you everything you need to know to be a good DBA, but it's one important part in the lifelong quest to get you there. Specifically, this section consists of tips and tricks from some of the many MVPs who are either full-time DBAs (or used to be) or who consult with DBAs who are constantly improving their systems and skills. Many of these topics are the particular passions of the authors, and they've donated their time and experiences to help us all become better DBAs. We truly want to thank them for their time and especially their passion.

SQL Server is a passion for both of us and we've enjoyed reading and learning from these chapters and experiences. Whether you're a seasoned DBA or a newcomer to SQL Server, we know you'll find material in this section that will help you learn, grow, and become a better DBA.

About the editors

Paul S. Randal and Kimberly L. Tripp are a husband-and-wife team who own and run SQLskills.com, a world-renowned SQL Server consulting and training company. They are both SQL Server MVPs and Microsoft Regional Directors, with over 30 years of combined experience on SQL Server.

Paul worked on the SQL Server team for nine years in development and management roles, writing many of the DBCC commands, with responsibility for core Storage Engine for SQL Server 2008. Paul writes extensively on his blog (SQLskills.com/blogs/Paul) and for *TechNet Magazine*, where he is a Contributing Editor.

Kimberly worked on the SQL Server team in the early 1990s as a tester and writer before leaving to found SQLskills and embrace her passion for teaching and consulting. Kimberly has been a regular at worldwide conferences since she first presented at TechEd in 1996, and she blogs at SQLskills.com/blogs/Kimberly.

Paul and Kimberly have written Microsoft white papers and books for SQL Server 2000, 2005, and 2008, and are regular, top-rated presenters worldwide on database maintenance, high availability, disaster recovery, performance tuning, and SQL Server internals. Together they teach the SQL MCM certification throughout Microsoft.

In their spare time they like to find frogfish in remote corners of the world.

24 What does it mean to be a DBA?

Brad M. McGehee

If you ask ten database administrators (DBAs) what their job roles are, you'll get ten different answers. For example, one organization may need a DBA to manage the day-to-day administration of SQL Server instances, whereas another organization may want a DBA to write both Transact-SQL (T-SQL) and C# code. Another organization might want a DBA who specializes in SQL Server Integration Services (SSIS) packages, whereas another organization may want a DBA who specializes in database design.

The job of DBA encompasses many different roles (and often job titles), and these vary widely from one organization to the next. In short, there is no standard job description for a DBA. This is partly because the job title doesn't have a long history (relational databases were first used in the 1970s, and Microsoft SQL Server Version 4.21 was released in 1993) and partly because the DBA role is quickly evolving as new technologies are released.

Because there is no commonly-accepted definition of a DBA, the goal of this chapter is to describe the types of tasks and roles that DBAs commonly perform, with the aim of explaining to those new to the profession what DBAs do day-in and day-out.

The first section of this chapter describes many of the tasks DBAs commonly perform. The second section classifies these tasks into specialty roles, as you will rarely find a DBA who performs all of these tasks all the time. Throughout this chapter, I try to answer the question: "What does it mean to be a DBA?"

Typical DBA tasks: A to Z

DBAs perform so many different tasks that it is hard to categorize them all. The alphabetized list that follows outlines the common DBA tasks. This list is by no means comprehensive, and some of the tasks overlap.

APPLICATION INTEGRATION

Most organizations use some combination of in-house and third-party applications; and few of these applications work in isolation. Therefore, DBAs often have to make disparate applications talk to one another, using a database as the means of sharing data. DBAs commonly get involved in figuring out the best way to integrate applications, and often perform the integration themselves.

ARCHIVING DATA

Data grows over time and can become costly to store and difficult to manage. In addition, increased data tends to exacerbate performance problems. DBAs are often responsible for monitoring data size and growth, and determining the best way to store it. In some cases, this may include archiving seldom-used data in another database, or it might mean purging data that is no longer needed. Often, choices are limited, as company policy and government regulations can restrict how and where data is stored.

ATTENDING MEETINGS

Most DBAs hate attending meetings because it detracts from work time. Meetings are a fact of working life and, if used wisely, aren't necessarily a waste of time. With correct planning and preparation, meetings are great opportunities for improving communications. The responsibilities of the DBA are often unknown or misunderstood by co-workers, so DBAs should always take advantage of opportunities, such as meetings, to share with others what they do.

AUDITING

An emerging task of the DBA is to identify which users are accessing, inserting, updating, or deleting data, and when. Auditing might only be necessary for limited time periods, for specific data, or it might be required 24/7 for all data. DBAs often work with people outside their organization, such as external auditors, to perform this task. And to further complicate the lives of DBAs, many industries are subject to specific regulations on how data is accessed and protected, which means that DBAs have to comply with some specific rules, with the potential for significant penalties, should they not fully comply.

BACKUP AND RECOVERY

One of the most fundamental aspects of the DBA's job is to protect the organization's data. This includes making periodic backups of data and keeping it safe from accidental or intentional destruction. In addition, a well-developed recovery plan needs to be implemented and tested so that when problems arise, data and access to critical systems can be restored quickly.

BUSINESS INTELLIGENCE AND DATA WAREHOUSING

Another emerging trend is for DBAs to be tasked with the creation and maintenance of data warehouses and business intelligence applications, so organizations can better use their data to make more effective business decisions. Increasingly, DBAs are specializing in this fast-growing area.

CAPACITY PLANNING

In most organizations, the number and size of databases grow rapidly. It is the responsibility of the DBA to monitor data growth, and plan how best to deal with it. This may include archiving it, compressing it, increasing the size of current hardware, or adding new hardware.

CHANGE MANAGEMENT

SQL Server configurations, database schema, T-SQL code, and many other facets of the application ecosystem change over time. It is often the responsibility of the DBA to perform impact analysis before changes are made, implement changes, test changes, and document them.

DATA MODELING AND DATABASE DESIGN

The foundation of all efficient and scalable databases is good design. DBAs often create database designs by performing needs and requirements analysis, creating a logical model, and then implementing the physical model. Larger organizations may have DBAs who specialize in database design.

DATABASE APPLICATION DEVELOPMENT

Many DBAs are application developers who specialize in writing code to access data stored in SQL Server databases. Although this is most commonly done using T-SQL, it can include writing code that is used to access SQL Server data. Many DBAs decide to make this their area of specialty, because of the depth of knowledge required to be a good database applications developer.

DEVELOPING AND MAINTAINING BEST PRACTICES

Successful DBAs are proactive in their work, and one of the best ways to be proactive is to develop sound database best practices, and to implement them in a consistent manner. The better organized and managed the database operations, the more efficient they will be. One of the many ways that DBAs can perform this task is to create a runbook that describes the organization's best practices and internal procedures. This document is the DBA's bible for performing all DBA-related functions.

DISASTER RECOVERY

At some point in their careers, DBAs will have to recover lost data. This may be as simple as restoring a database and its log files, or it may be as complex as moving a weather-damaged data center from one city to another. To make dealing with disasters easier (small or big), it's the DBA's responsibility to plan, implement, and regularly test disaster recovery scenarios.

HARDWARE SETUP AND CONFIGURATION

In some organizations, hardware is handled by dedicated hardware technicians. In others, the DBA is responsible for building, installing, and configuring their own hardware, including servers and storage area networks (SANs). In addition, DBAs may also perform regular hardware troubleshooting and maintenance.

HIGH AVAILABILITY

A DBA needs to ensure that the databases are available to users when they need access to data. You can help ensure high availability in many different ways, including use of log shipping, clustering, database mirroring, and other technologies. Because of the specialized knowledge required for high availability techniques, many DBAs choose this as their main area of focus.

INSTALLING, CONFIGURING, AND UPGRADING SQL SERVER SOFTWARE

One of the most time-consuming of all database tasks is installing, configuring, patching, and upgrading SQL Server instances. Although it might sound like an easy task, it usually isn't. One of the difficulties is finding a good time to perform such work, especially in 24/7 shops. In addition, each time SQL Server is patched or upgraded, there is the risk that after the patch or upgrade the applications that access the database, or the databases themselves, might not work properly. On top of this, DBAs often have to battle third-party vendors who are unwilling to certify that their application will work after you have made the changes. This requires the completion of planning, testing, and backout preparation before implementing major changes.

LOAD BALANCING

Over time, the load put on individual databases changes. DBAs are responsible for monitoring workloads and figuring out how to maximize hardware resources to get the best SQL Server performance. This may involve moving a database from a heavily loaded server to a server with a lighter load. SQL Server virtualization, and how it can benefit load balancing, is becoming a hot topic for many DBAs. For more information on SQL Server virtualization, see chapter 39, "Running SQL Server on Hyper-V," by John Paul Cook.

MAINTAINING DOCUMENTATION

Writing and maintaining documentation is probably the most boring and loathed task that a DBA will encounter. However boring, it is a critical part of the DBA's job. If you don't document, then there is no easy way to rebuild the current infrastructure should major problems arise.

MANAGING PEOPLE

Many DBAs find themselves in management positions, such as a senior DBA in charge of junior DBAs. Some DBAs at large organizations do this full time, whereas others combine people management with other DBA duties. On the other hand, when some DBAs get a taste of management, they give it up to get back to more technical work. Managing people is not for everyone.

MANAGING SQL SERVER–BASED APPLICATIONS

A surprise for many new DBAs is the realization that they are responsible not only for managing SQL Server and its databases, but in many organizations, they are also responsible for managing any applications that access the database. In some organizations, the DBA spends more time managing applications than SQL Server itself.

MANAGING TEST ENVIRONMENTS

In many organizations, DBAs manage test environments that not only include test SQL Servers and test databases, but also test applications. The purpose of this is to allow applications (both in-house and third-party) to be tested before new versions of either the application or SQL Server are rolled out into production.

MENTORING

Oftentimes, DBAs have to share their knowledge with other DBAs, developers, or end users. This might be informal one-on-one tutoring, or it might include classroom training.

MONITORING

This is a wide-ranging task that includes multiple subtasks, such as performance monitoring, monitoring server disk space, viewing logs, ensuring jobs have run successfully, and scrutinizing for errors. Although a variety of third-party tools are available to perform these tasks, DBAs commonly spend a lot of time performing monitoring manually because they don't have a budget for such tools, or they are not familiar with them.

NEEDS AND REQUIREMENTS ANALYSIS

Whether DBAs are involved in development, or just supporting third-party applications, they often get involved in needs and requirements analysis. This can include talking to users, finding out their needs and requirements, and determining the best way to meet them. This often includes researching available third-party solutions and determining if it's best to develop the application in-house, or to invest in a third-party application.

NEGOTIATING SERVICE LEVEL AGREEMENTS

In many organizations, DBAs become involved in negotiating service level agreements (SLAs). An SLA is an agreement between parties in which one is the customer and the other is the service provider. The customer (the owner of the business application accessing SQL Server databases) and the DBA (the service provider), must agree on acceptable levels of service, such as defining what is an acceptable response time for a specific type of transaction. Part of the negotiating process often requires the DBA to set expectations and educate the customer on what is feasible given the resource constraints of the organization.

OPERATING SYSTEM SETUP, CONFIGURATION, AND ADMINISTRATION

Just as many DBAs manage their own hardware, many DBAs also manage the operating system on their SQL Server instances. Not only must SQL Server be configured optimally, the operating system it is running on must also be configured optimally, and be properly maintained.

PERFORMANCE TUNING

Everyone wants their data right now. It is the job of the DBA to monitor performance and to determine ways to optimize database performance. This can be complex, and many DBAs specialize in this area.

PROJECT MANAGEMENT

Oftentimes, DBAs find themselves in charge of a large project involving many other people. This could entail writing a new in-house application, or managing the migration of a data center from one location to another. DBAs with good project management skills are in high demand.

REPLICATION

Data is often moved from one server to another, and one of the most popular ways to perform this task is to use SQL Server replication. DBAs often research various ways data can be replicated from server to server, decide on the most appropriate method, implement replication, and then manage it after it is up and running.

REPORT WRITING

With the advent of SQL Server Reporting Services, many DBAs find themselves writing reports against databases. This might include writing the T-SQL code to extract the data, or it could include the creation and formatting of physical reports. This is a new and growing area, and some DBAs are specializing in it.

RUNNING JOBS

Virtually every SQL Server has jobs that run periodically. They might include backups, data imports or exports, index rebuild jobs, and data integrity checks. DBAs are responsible for determining what jobs are needed, creating the jobs, and scheduling them.

SCRIPTING

DBAs often write their own T-SQL scripts to perform a wide range of tasks, including monitoring and maintenance. With the advent of PowerShell, many DBAs are writing PowerShell scripts to enhance their productivity.

SECURITY

DBAs control who can access data and what they can do with it. This has many aspects, including creating SQL Server logins and users, assigning permissions, moving security between servers, and implementing data encryption.

SSIS AND ETL

DBAs often move data in and out of databases, and at the same time, perform transformations on the data as it is moved. This is often done for data warehouses and application integration. This process is often referred to as extract, transform, and load (ETL), and in SQL Server this is commonly performed using SQL Server Integration Services (SSIS).

TESTING

DBAs frequently perform all sorts of testing. This can include testing of the following: databases, applications, management tools, and disaster recovery plans. DBAs test because they want to ensure the high availability and integrity of their data.

TROUBLESHOOTING

Virtually every day, DBAs troubleshoot one problem or another. Often when a problem occurs, the DBA is expected to drop everything and focus on resolving the problem at hand. This can result in long hours and high levels of stress. As with many technical positions, effective DBAs are good problem solvers.

WORKING WITH TEAMMATES

DBAs rarely work alone. In most cases, DBAs interact with many people, including other DBAs, developers, end users, product-knowledge specialists, vendors, accountants, hardware experts, and networking experts. Because of this, DBAs need good people skills.

DBA specialties

As you can see, DBAs perform many different tasks and take on a wide variety of roles. Usually, DBAs are generalists because they need to know a little about many different areas. On the other hand, you seldom find a DBA who is a master of all the previously described tasks. This is for two reasons. First, most people don't have the time to master every DBA-related subject. Second, there is the added burden of having to keep up with rapidly changing technology. For most people, it's impossible to carry out all aspects of the DBA role. To become a successful DBA, you don't have to know everything there is to know about SQL Server. In fact, you have a much better chance of becoming a successful DBA if you narrow your focus and specialize in a handful of SQL Server subjects.

In this section, we take a look at some of the common areas in which DBAs specialize.

DBA SYSTEM ADMINISTRATOR

The DBA system administrator is a generalist who knows a little about many different subjects. Also known as a production DBA, the DBA system administrator is generally in charge of setting up, configuring, and maintaining test and production SQL Server instances. This can include such routine tasks as monitoring, performance tuning, backups and restores, security, creating jobs, and so on. In medical terms, think of the DBA system administrator as the general practitioner. All of the other DBA specialists are more like medical specialists.

DBA DATABASE ARCHITECT

Think of a DBA database architect as the employee who sees the big picture of data storage and access in an organization, and whose job it is to research the organization's data needs, research the available options, and then recommend policies the organization should implement. In many organizations, the title of database architect is another name for the lead DBA, DBA manager, or DBA project manager.

DBA DATABASE DESIGNER

DBA database designers focus on creating new database schemas. They define user needs and requirements, develop logical database designs, create physical databases, and so on. In most cases, the DBA database designer works with DBA developers, or other developers, to develop and maintain applications.

DBA DEVELOPER

The DBA developer writes code, be it T-SQL scripts, stored procedures, functions, Common Language Runtime (CLR) objects, or any other kind of code that is used to access SQL Server data. Often, the DBA developer works with DBA system administrators, DBA database designers, project managers, and other developers to develop and maintain applications.

DBA HIGH AVAILABILITY AND DISASTER RECOVERY SPECIALIST

For many of today's online businesses, it is more critical than ever that SQL Server is available around the clock. Therefore, DBAs often need to specialize in high availability. Their job is to determine what high availability methods are best for their environment, and then to implement and maintain them, helping to prevent the loss of data in the first place. Other DBAs specialize in disaster recovery, after the fact. In other words, they are brought in to try to recover data from corrupted databases because existing high availability and disaster recovery procedures failed.

DBA BUSINESS INTELLIGENCE SPECIALIST

DBA BI (business intelligence) specialists design, create, and maintain data warehouses and online analytical processing (OLAP) cubes, so that data can more easily be retrieved and analyzed by organizations. This often involves developing BI-based applications written using Multidimensional Expressions (MDX) queries. In most cases, they are also heavily involved in extract, transform, and load (ETL) and designing and implementing SSIS packages.

DBA REPORT WRITER

In the past, the DBA report writer has often been lumped in with the business intelligence specialist. SQL Server Reporting Services has evolved to a point that many DBAs are now specializing in designing and creating reports to extract data from databases in meaningful ways.

Summary

Given that the DBA job description is so varied and constantly changing, it is hard to list all the possible DBA specialties on which you might want to focus, so don't consider the list in this chapter to be anything more than an informal guide.

You may find that you want to develop your own specialty, one that is even more focused than the broad specializations I've listed. For example, you might want to focus on performance tuning, clustering, SSIS, or replication only. Nothing prevents you from specializing as much as you like, other than the fact that the more narrow your specialty, the fewer jobs available.

As we have seen, being a DBA means many different things. It is not a single job title with a single skill set. Instead, the job title of DBA encompasses a wide range of job tasks and roles that are tied together with a single common denominator—DBAs are the guardians of the organization's data. As DBAs, it is our job not only to protect an organization's data, but also to make it available to everyone in the organization who needs it to perform their jobs effectively. How well we fulfill this responsibility determines how successful we are as DBAs.

About the author

Brad M. McGehee is an MCSE+I, MCSD, and MCT (former) with a bachelor's degree in Economics and a master's in Business Administration. Involved in the industry since 1982, Brad is currently the Director of DBA Education for Red Gate Software, and is an accomplished Microsoft SQL Server MVP with over 14 years of experience with SQL Server and over 6 years of training experience. Brad is a frequent speaker at SQL PASS, European PASS, SQL Connections, SQLTeach, SQLBits, SQL Saturdays, TechFests, Code Camps, SQL Server user groups, and other industry seminars. He blogs at www.bradmcgehee.com.

25 Working with maintenance plans

Tibor Karaszi

Just like a car or a house, you want to maintain your databases so that they run smoothly and safely over time. You probably have actions you want to perform that are specific to your application and data, but some actions are common to most databases, like backups and defragmentation. This is why Microsoft created maintenance plans that make the implementation of standard actions easy. We specify which of these standard actions we want to perform, for which databases, and at what intervals—no T-SQL coding required. Of course, some DBAs want more control over the actions than the maintenance plans allow for, but for those who are not full-time DBAs, maintenance plans are a good solution.

What is a maintenance plan, and how do I create one?

The implementation of maintenance plans (MPs) has changed over time. From SQL Server 6.5 to 2000, an MP was executed by sqlmaint.exe through a SQL Server Agent (Agent) job. As of SQL Server 2005, an MP is a SQL Server Integration Service (SSIS) package, executed by an Agent job.

You create a plan using SQL Server Management Studio (SSMS) and right-clicking the Maintenance Plans folder under the Management folder. You can use either a wizard or a trimmed-down version of the SSIS package Designer, available inside SSMS. For beginners, I recommend using the wizard, and, as you get more comfortable using MPs, you can dive into the Designer.

The SSIS package is saved directly to the msdb database (not out in the filesystem as a .dtsx file) along with some metadata in the msdb database, indicating that the plan exists. This metadata allows SSMS to list your plans in the Maintenance Plans folder, where you can right-click and edit them. If you choose to schedule the plan, which you typically will want to do, then one or more Agent jobs will be created.

Versions and service packs

If you are using SQL Server 2005, I strongly encourage you to be at least on Service Pack 2 (SP2) on both the server and the client (SSMS). SP2 added some functionality, like a separate schedule per task, and it also added the Maintenance Cleanup Task to the wizard. In fact, if you are using SQL Server 2005, you want to be at least slightly higher than the original SP2 release because of some bugs in that original release.

TIP What build number you want to be using, and how to check it, is slightly complicated and depends on whether you have applied a hotfix or not. I suggest you check out http://blogs.msdn.com/psssql/archive/2007/04/ 06/post-sql-server-2005-service-pack-2-sp2-fixes-explained.aspx and verify that you aren't using the original SP2.

I will assume SQL Server 2008 in this section. An MP in SQL Server 2005 with SP2 looks the same and has the same functionality as in 2008 (with the addition that for SQL Server 2008 you can compress a backup if you are using Enterprise Edition).

One or several schedules per plan?

You might not be familiar with some of the terms I use here; therefore, it's time for some explanations. A *maintenance plan* (plan) is what is created by the Designer or wizard. It's implemented as an SSIS *package*, which is saved directly to the msdb database. An SSIS package consists of several SSIS *tasks*, where each task is of a certain type (backup database, check integrity, and so on). You decide whether to *schedule* the plan (typically you will want to do this), which will create one or several Agent *jobs*, where each job has one Agent *schedule*.

As of SP2, you can decide whether you want to have one schedule per task or one schedule for the entire plan (the latter was the only option prior to SQL Server 2005 SP2). Having several schedules will result in *several* Agent jobs—one per schedule. There are advantages with both alternatives; therefore, think a few minutes about how you want to do this. As an example, say you want to perform these tasks:

- Weekly defragmentation and removal of backup history
- Daily database backup, removal of old backup files, and checking of database integrity
- Transaction log backup every 15 minutes

If you have one schedule per task, you can have only one plan, but you will end up with six Agent jobs (called *subplans*), each scheduled separately. This means you have to decide for each job when it is to be executed. If you don't want the jobs to overlap each other, you'll have to plan out the timing.

On the other hand, if you want only one schedule for the plan, you will end up with several plans—three plans in the preceding example. You would have one plan for the weekly tasks, another for the daily tasks, and yet another for the log backup task. For each plan, you can decide in what order the tasks are to be performed.

Regardless of how you do the scheduling, you need to specify what databases to operate on *for each task* (for the task types that operate at the database level). This differs from MPs in SQL Server 2000 and earlier, where you specified the databases at the plan level.

The dialog boxes will look slightly different depending on whether you are using the wizard or the Designer, on how you want to schedule the plan, and on what version and service pack you are using, but, in the end, the tasks you perform inside the plan are the same. The screenshots that follow in this chapter are from SQL Server 2008, and have one schedule for the whole plan, using the wizard. You will find that your dialog boxes will look very similar even if some of these attributes differ.

Wizard dialogs

If you create your plan using the wizard, you will be presented with a number of dialog boxes that are specific to the wizard. It is pretty obvious what they do, so I will only mention them briefly here:

- *Select Plan Properties page*—Here you specify the name of the plan, an optional description, and whether you want to have one schedule for the entire plan or one schedule per task. If you want one schedule for the entire plan, you can enter the scheduling page from here.
- *Select Maintenance Tasks page*—Here you select what tasks you want to include in the plan.
- *Select Maintenance Task Order page*—This page allows you to specify in what order each task is to be performed.

Task types

In the following sections, I will describe the task types that are available in an MP. You will see that I also mention which T-SQL command or stored procedure is executed for each task. Whenever you feel you want to dive deeper and learn about the options for each command, don't hesitate to read about the command in the SQL Server Books Online. Each command is documented with all its options, and you will also learn about options that are not exposed in an MP, which can be valuable and help you decide whether or not to replace that task with your own T-SQL command.

Sometimes the most difficult thing is to decide what tasks to include, and in what order, so let's start with some advice on that. I typically include the following tasks in my MPs:

- Database check integrity
- Reorganize index or rebuild index (not both)
- Update statistics
- History cleanup
- Backup database (often both full and transaction log and sometimes also differential)
- Maintenance cleanup task

The one thing I strongly discourage you from including is the shrink database task. See the following section, "Shrink database task," for details.

As for the order in which tasks are performed, it doesn't matter much as long as you follow best practices (for example, don't shrink and don't update index statistics if you also rebuild your indexes). One could argue that you want to check integrity before a backup (and don't do a backup if the integrity check doesn't pass), and you could argue that the other way around is better (check integrity after the backup so that you know the backup was clean). I don't recommend spending too much time on this; the important thing is choosing which tasks to perform and following best practices.

Check database integrity task

The check database integrity task executes the `DBCC CHECKDB` command, which searches for various types of corruption in the database. I prefer to execute this as often as I can (once a day if possible), because I want to know as soon as possible if I have a corruption problem in a database.

The `DBCC CHECKDB` command has a lot of options, but only Include Indexes (which toggles the `NOINDEX` option) is available through maintenance plans, as shown in figure 1.

Shrink database task

Don't ever be tempted to run the shrink database task, shown in figure 2. Regularly shrinking database files can have a huge negative performance impact, among other things.

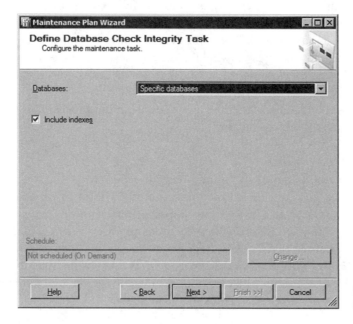

Figure 1 Defining the check database integrity task

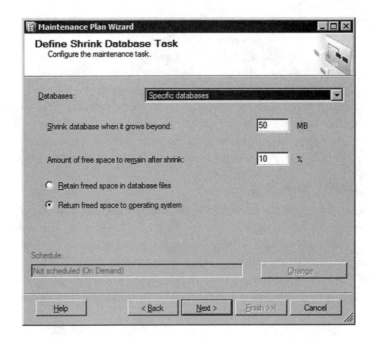

Figure 2   Defining the shrink database task

For instance, shrinking fragments your indexes; therefore, it is useless to first defragment your indexes and then shrink your database. People often think that they can get around this by shrinking the files first, and then rebuilding the indexes, but the rebuild operation uses temporary space that then becomes "free" at the completion of the index rebuild. This often leads to confusion as to why there is free space, and to an incorrect assertion that the shrink operation failed to reclaim this space. In any case, it's best practice to have a fair amount of free space in your database files.

Still, I frequently see shrinking being scheduled, and I have an article on my website describing why you want to avoid doing it. Check it out at http://www.karaszi.com/ SQLServer/info_dont_shrink.asp if you need more convincing.

I recommend shrinking database files only in special circumstances. This task executes the DBCC SHRINKDATABASE command.

Reorganize index task

The reorganize index task, shown in figure 3, executes the ALTER INDEX command using the REORGANIZE option. This is something you might want to do in order to defragment your indexes, which in turn can improve performance. Note, though, that the task is pretty stupid—it will execute the command for every index in the database, regardless of whether the index is fragmented in the first place. You can be smarter than that, and you will even find T-SQL code in Books Online that checks the fragmentation level for each index and only defragments the fragmented indexes (see the Books Online topic for sys.dm_db_index_physical_stats).

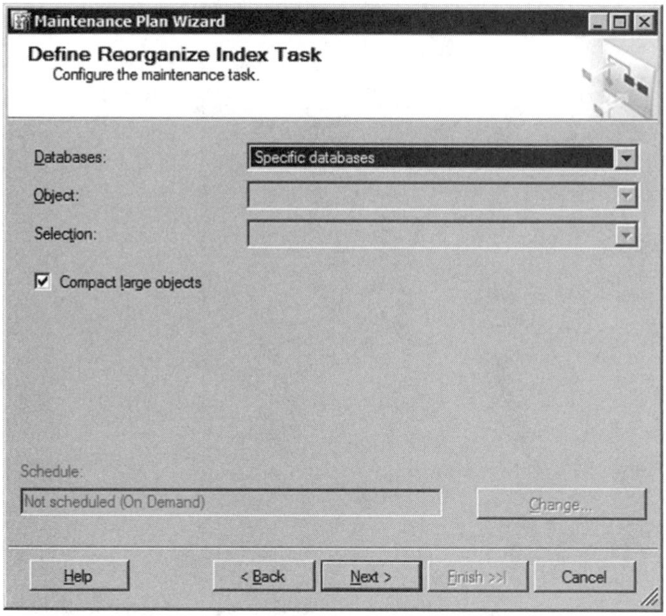

Figure 3 Defining the reorganize index task

Rebuild index task

The rebuild index task, shown in figure 4, is pretty much the same as the reorganize index task, but it uses the REBUILD option of the ALTER INDEX command and can generate more problems (in terms of data and log file growth) if misused. This also operates on every index in the database, regardless of the fragmentation level.

Let me again point out that you shouldn't both rebuild and reorganize—that is a waste of time and resources. There's a lot to say about index fragmentation and defragmenting indexes, such as why you might want to do it, whether you should reorganize or rebuild, how each operation is implemented, and so on. Such elaborations are outside the scope of this chapter, but Paul S. Randal has a section about index fragmentation in his great TechNet article about database maintenance, titled "Top Tips for Effective Database Maintenance." I encourage you to read the article, which you'll find at http://technet.microsoft.com/en-us/magazine/cc671165.aspx.

Update statistics task

The update statistics task uses the UPDATE STATISTICS command, which can improve performance for your queries by providing the optimizer with more accurate statistics for the data in your tables. A database option is available that will cause this to be performed automatically, but that does not kick in until you have modified about 20 percent of the data for a column. The more data you sample, the more accurate the statistics will be, but the longer the statistics collection will take. A full scan, which samples 100 percent of the rows, delivers the most accurate statistics, but it obviously takes the most time.

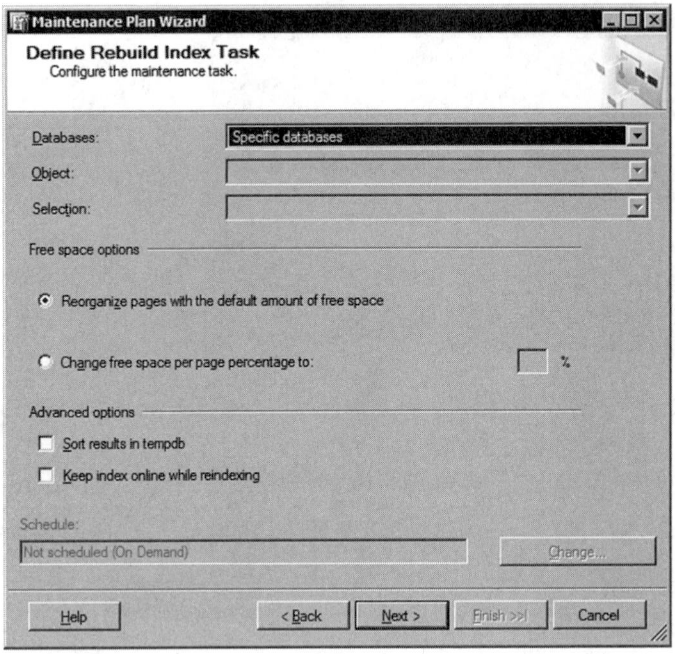

Figure 4   Defining the rebuild index task

Note that if you rebuild your indexes, you will get updated statistics (based on a full scan) for free, but only for the index statistics of the indexes that are rebuilt, not for column statistics. What you don't want to do is first rebuild indexes (which updates statistics for all indexes, based on all data) and then use this task to update index statistics. At best, this will waste time and resources to update the statistics twice. At worst, it will run this task after index rebuild, with less than a 100 percent sample rate, resulting in less precise statistics than after the index rebuild.

I recommend that you include this task in your plans. If you also rebuild indexes (in contrast to reorganizing, which does nothing for statistics), configure it to update Column Statistics Only. If you don't rebuild indexes, configure it to update All Existing Statistics, as shown in figure 5. Use as high a Scan Type as you have time for—ideally a full scan.

History cleanup task

If you don't delete old history information from your various history tables, you will find your msdb database growing over time. I've seen some pretty extreme cases with large msdb databases because of frequent transaction log backups or many databases in the SQL Server instance. This task, shown in figure 6, makes it a no-brainer to remove old history information.

The following procedures are used by this task:

- sp_delete_backuphistory
- sp_purge_jobhistory
- sp_maintplan_delete_log

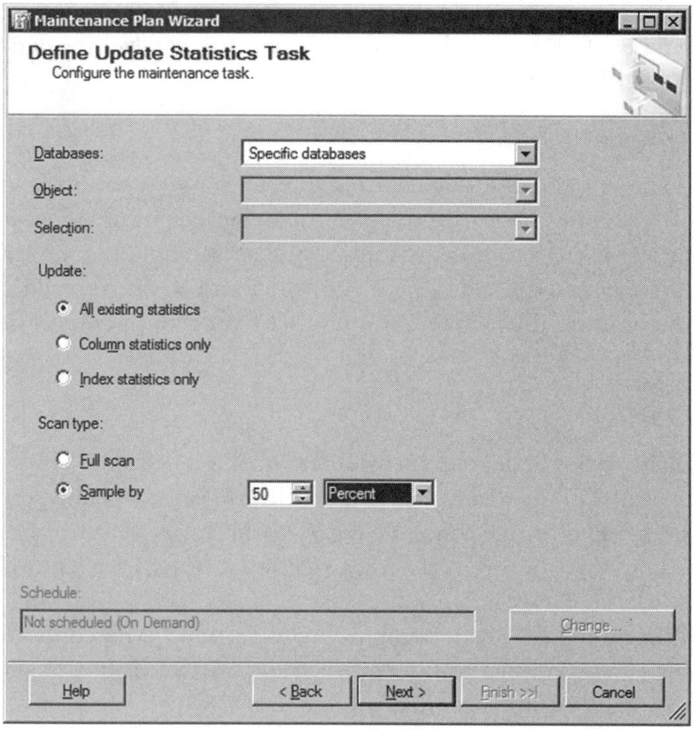

Figure 5 Defining the update statistics task

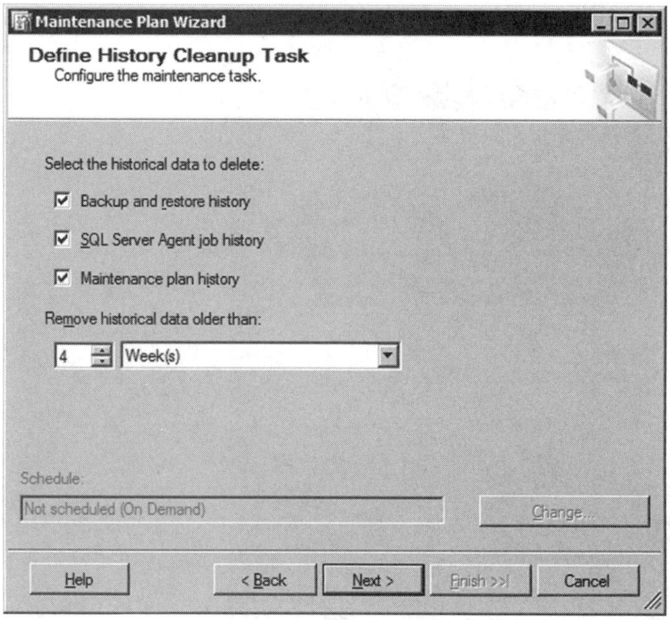

Figure 6 Defining the history cleanup task

I typically keep three to six months of history. It can be useful to look at the history a few weeks back in time or even a couple of months, but I haven't ever needed to check history for several months back in time.

Execute SQL Server Agent job task

There isn't much to say about the execute SQL Server Agent job task, shown in figure 7. You can expand on the functionality of an MP by executing Agent jobs from within an MP. You might want to execute a batch file, executable file, or script from within the plan to create folders, move files, copy files, and so on. You can create an Agent job to do this and call the job from this task. The procedure used by this task is msdb.dbo.sp_start_job.

Back up database task

The look of this dialog box will depend on whether you see it from the wizard or from the Designer. When used in the wizard (as in figure 8), you cannot change the backup type because it was selected in the initial dialog box where you selected what operations to perform. The topmost three choices specify what type of backup will be performed and for which databases.

The expiration section is, in my opinion, pretty useless and even confusing. Many users believe that this will automatically remove or overwrite backups; for instance, those older than 14 days. That is not what these options (which set RETAINDAYS and EXPIREDATE behind the scenes) are for. All they do is cause an error if you try to overwrite that backup file earlier than the specified days or date. If it were up to me, these options would not be present in the MP backup task.

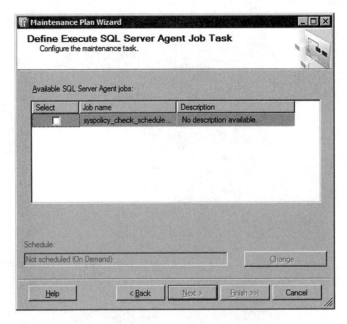

Figure 7   Defining the execute SQL Server Agent job task

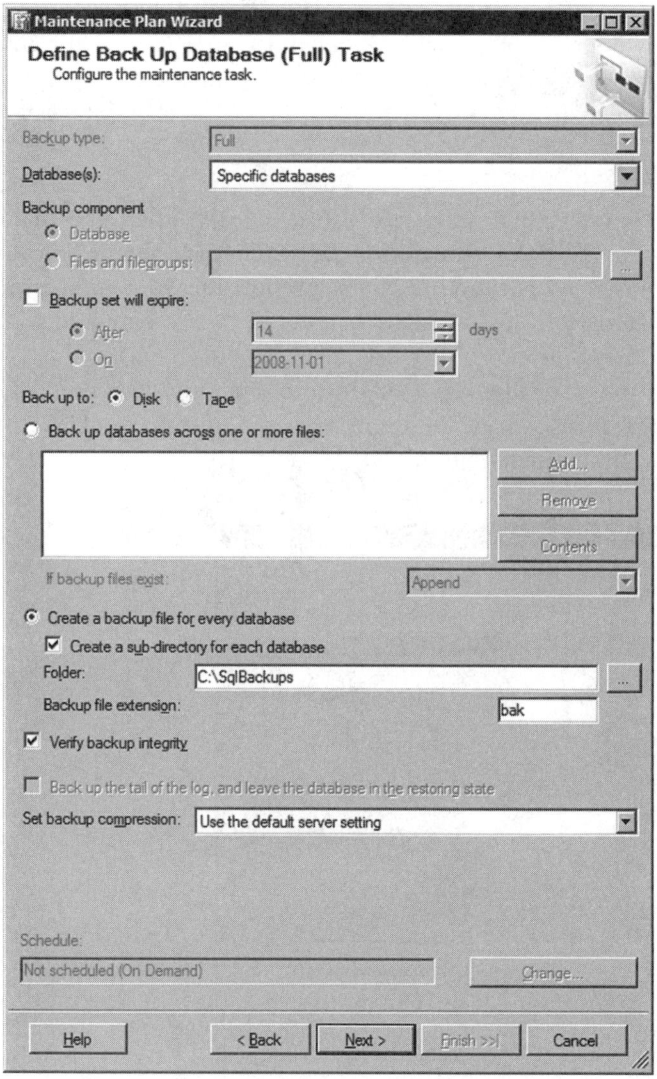

Figure 8 Defining the back up database task

You can also specify whether to back up to a specific backup device or create a new backup device (file) for each backup. Most often, you want the latter, because this will allow for the removal of old backup files. Note, though, that the removal of old backup files is performed in a separate task, not in this task. I've been to several installations where the disks were approaching full because there was no function to remove old backup files.

You can also decide to verify the backup after it is produced, which uses the RESTORE VERIFYONLY command. An option to include the CHECKSUM option for the backup command in the MP backup task is not available, so the information the verification has to work with is somewhat limited. Performing backup using the CHECKSUM option is a best practice, but unfortunately MPs do not allow us to do that.

Finally, if you are on SQL Server 2008 and have Enterprise Edition, you can decide whether to compress the backup (which coincidently causes the backup to be done using CHECKSUM, regardless of whether CHECKSUM, NO_CHECKSUM, or none of those options are specified).

Maintenance cleanup task

If you are on SQL Server 2005 and haven't installed SP2, then the maintenance cleanup task, shown in figure 9, is not in the wizard. That is a shame, because this is the task that will remove old backup files (or MP report files, depending on the setting). You can, of course, add it from the Designer, but I was happy to see that SP2 included this task in the wizard.

The options are pretty straightforward. Unfortunately the task uses an undocumented command, xp_delete_file; therefore, we are in unsupported land if we want to use this procedure from our own jobs.

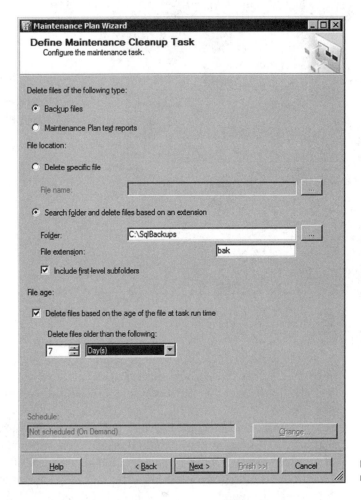

Figure 9   Defining the maintenance cleanup task

Select reporting options

You should think about the reporting options. The dialog box shown in figure 10 is not from the wizard, it is from the Designer. The Designer dialog box is a superset of the wizard dialog box, so you'll find all options in the wizard discussed here. The reason I decided to show this dialog box from the Designer is that it has some options that the wizard does not have.

If something goes wrong (like a backup fails or DBCC CHECKDB detects database corruption), you definitely want to know about it as soon as possible and with as much information as possible so that you can take appropriate action without any unnecessary delay. I find a report file good to have, even if there is history for each execution of the plan available (right-click an existing plan and select View History). For most cases, I like to enable email support within SQL Server and configure the jobs to email the operator. The exception is for jobs that execute frequently. In most cases, you will hopefully also have some monitoring solution for errors in the Windows Event Log, various error log files, high-severity errors (such as 823, 824), and the like.

Execute T-SQL statement task

For some reason, this task, shown in figure 11, is not available from the wizard. If you want to add this task, finish the wizard and let it save the plan, and then right-click the

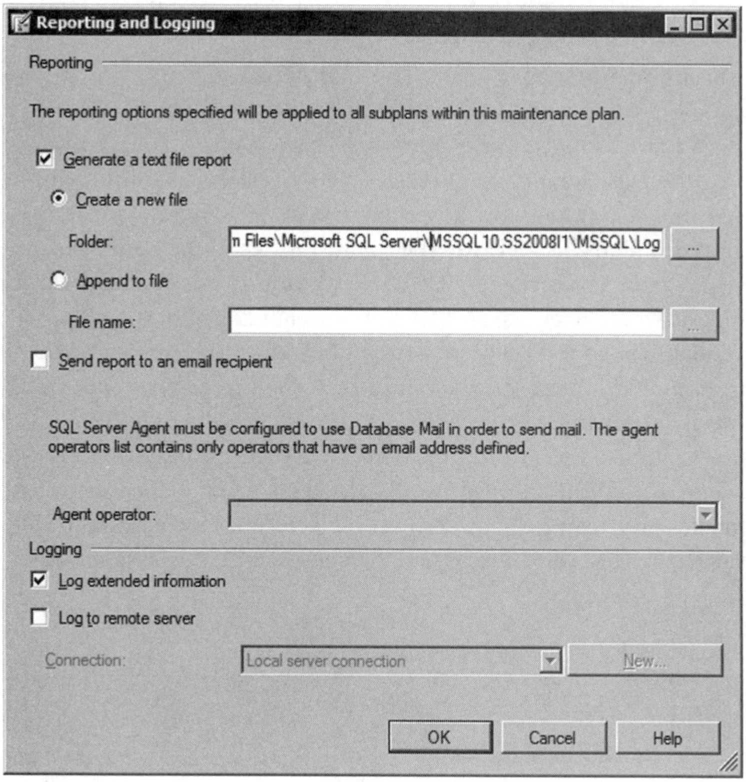

Figure 10
Selecting the
reporting options

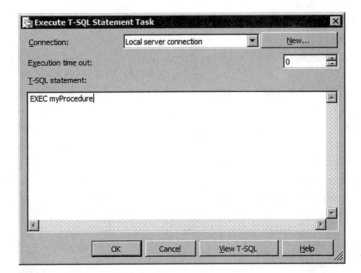

Figure 11   Executing the
T-SQL statement task

plan and select Modify, which will open the Designer. I find this task useful, because it allows us to add whatever T-SQL commands we wish to an MP. Not only can we set the order in which tasks run in the plan, we can execute other Agent jobs as well as T-SQL commands from within our MPs.

Executing and monitoring the plan

So now you have a maintenance plan. The Maintenance Plan Wizard or Designer, whichever you used, has created one or several Agent jobs for you. Make sure that the Agent is running and using an appropriate service account (the Windows account that is used for the SQL Server Agent service). The service account should exist as a Windows login in SQL Server, having `sysadmin` privileges. If you can start the Agent, you know you've fulfilled this, because the Agent refuses to start unless it can log in to SQL Server with `sysadmin` privileges. Also, the account needs access to the right folders and shares and other resources for whatever you perform in the MP.

When the plan has been executed, you might want to be notified. You can either set up notification of an Agent operator in the MP's Select Report Options dialog box, or you can specify notification at the job level. I prefer the former, because this allows me to include the information from the MP report file in the email, which means I can immediately start troubleshooting possible problems when I receive the email. You can also right-click an existing MP in SSMS and select View History, which will show the history information from MP history tables in msdb, such as sysmaintplan_log and `sysmaintplan_logdetail`.

Summary

MPs are powerful tools. They allow you to easily and quickly define various types of maintenance operations for your SQL Server instance without needing any T-SQL programming. As you become more experienced and see a need for more tailored plans, you can refine your existing MPs. You can pick and choose between the options in the predefined tasks, and replace some of those with your own T-SQL or SQL Server Agent job tasks.

Some DBAs prefer to skip the MPs altogether, and do everything using some combination of T-SQL code, scripting language, and a job scheduler (like SQL Server Agent). I've done my share of that. What you should remember if you do this is that although it is extremely powerful and allows for ultimate flexibility (you write your own code, after all), the code you write needs to be written, debugged, tested, and maintained over time. I hesitate to leave home-grown maintenance jobs with customers who do not have the competency to maintain this code over time.

In many cases, MPs provide a good middle ground, and with the added flexibility introduced in SQL Server 2005, they become even more powerful and versatile.

About the author

Tibor Karaszi has been a SQL Server MVP since 1997, and he is an independent consultant and trainer, focusing on the relational database engine. His experience with SQL Server goes all the way back to the late 1980s and the first version of Microsoft SQL Server. Tibor lives in Stockholm, Sweden. His web site is at http://www.karaszi.com.

26 PowerShell in SQL Server

Richard Siddaway

PowerShell is the automation engine that Microsoft is now building into all of its major products. It started with Exchange Server 2007, Windows Server 2008, and various members of the System Center family, and is now available in SQL Server 2008. You can expect to see it appearing in even more products in the future, as PowerShell is part of Microsoft's Common Engineering Criteria. Other vendors such as Quest, Special Operations Software, Citrix, and IBM are building Power-Shell support into their products. Version 1 became available in November 2006. PowerShell Version 2 is in CTP as of the time of writing. It's expected to ship with the release of Windows 7 and Windows Server 2008 R2, in which it'll be installed by default.

So what's PowerShell and what can we do with it?

PowerShell overview

PowerShell is usually exposed as a command shell and scripting language. It's .NET based and can access the .NET framework.

NOTE You do NOT have to be a .NET programmer to learn or use PowerShell!

PowerShell is designed to be used interactively and as a scripting language. Anything that can be performed at the command prompt can be performed interactively and vice versa. One of the design goals of PowerShell is that it should be easily extensible. The PowerShell team provides the core PowerShell engine and other product teams build PowerShell snap-ins with the functionality that they require.

PowerShell features

The most striking PowerShell features are *cmdlets*, *providers*, and the *pipeline*. The scripting language has the looping, branching, and control features that you'd expect. Its syntax is similar to that of C#.

CMDLETS

Cmdlets are self-contained commands that perform a single task; for instance `Get-Service` returns a list of the services installed on the machine and includes information such as the status. Cmdlets can be thought of as being analogous to command-line utilities such as `ping` and `ipconfig` which we've used for years.

Cmdlets have a *verb-noun* naming convention. The verb part should adhere to the standard verb set,[1] and the noun is descriptive of the returned data. They may have an alias defined—for instance `get-childitem` is aliased to `dir` and `ls`. Cmdlets return .NET objects that may be altered to a greater or lesser extent by the cmdlet. It's possible to access the base object if required. When typing at the command line, it's possible to partially type the name of a cmdlet or parameter and press the Tab key to cycle through the available options that would complete the name.

PROVIDERS

In PowerShell terms, a *provider* is a way to expose a data store as if it were the filesystem. A command such as `dir c:\scripts` is common on Windows systems. Being able to type `dir hklm:\software\microsoft` and see registry keys opens a lot of functionality. The standard cmdlets for working with files and the standard navigation techniques used in the filesystem will work (with exceptions) in the other providers.

PowerShell ships with providers for the filesystem, registry, certificate store, and internal PowerShell features. Providers are available for other data stores, including Active Directory and IIS 7. SQL Server 2008 also exposes PowerShell functionality as a provider.

PIPELINE

We've been using pipelines since the days of DOS—for example `dir | more`. The PowerShell pipeline passes .NET objects rather than text, so that the functionality of the object is exposed:

```
Get-Service *sql* | Foreach {if($_.Status -eq "Stopped"){start-service
$_.Name -whatif}}
```

In this example, we get services that include *sql* in their name. You can use wildcards throughout PowerShell. We then loop through each object and check its status. The `$_` symbol represents the object moving along the pipeline. If the service is stopped, we start it. The `-whatif` parameter means that we'll show what would've happened if we'd performed the action. For any cmdlet that will alter the state of something, consider using the `-whatif` parameter first. It can save a lot of grief!

PowerShell issues and solutions

PowerShell has a number of issues that can trip up new users. Table 1 lists a few of them.

---

[1] See http://msdn.microsoft.com/en-us/library/ms714428(VS.85).aspx for more information about the Microsoft standard verb set.

Table 1   PowerShell issues

Issue	Solution
Can't run scripts when first installed	Open PowerShell as administrator and run the following: `Set-ExecutionPolicy -executionPolicy RemoteSigned` SQL Server PowerShell (SQLPS) has its own execution policy independent of PowerShell itself.
Can't run scripts in the current folder	Use this syntax: `./script_name.ps1`
Can't double-click to run script	By design. Don't change—this is a security feature to help prevent the automatic execution of malware, as has been seen with VBScript.
PowerShell only works on local machine	Remoting is in Version 2. WMI and .NET can be used for remote administration. Some providers do give remoting capability.
Not all .NET assemblies are loaded in PowerShell	Load ss required.

Having briefly looked at PowerShell itself, how can we use it with SQL Server?

PowerShell with SQL Server 2000 and 2005

PowerShell can work with SQL Server 2000 and 2005 in two ways. We can use ADO.NET within PowerShell to read, create, and modify data. Alternatively we can use Server Management Objects (SMO) to administer our servers. These two techniques can also be used with SQL Server 2008.

Data access

PowerShell is built using .NET, so we use ADO.NET to access data in SQL Server. If you've programmed ADO.NET in C# then listing 1 should appear familiar.

Listing 1   Accessing SQL Server data with PowerShell

```
$connString = "server=SQL1;Integrated
➥Security=SSPI;database=adventureworks"              ❶

$cn = new-object "System.Data.SqlClient.SqlConnection"
$connString                                          ❷

$cmd = new-object "System.Data.SqlClient.SqlCommand"
$cmd.CommandType = [System.Data.CommandType]"Text"
$cmd.CommandText = "SELECT * FROM Production.Product Where Color =   ❸
➥'Silver'"
$cmd.Connection = $cn

$dt = new-object "System.Data.DataTable"      ❹

$cn.Open()              ❺
$rdr = $cmd.ExecuteReader()         ❻

$dt.Load($rdr)       ❼
$cn.Close()        ❽

$dt | Format-Table       ❾
```

The starting point of any code to access a SQL Server database is to create a connection string ❶. This supplies the information to identify the server and database, as well as authenticate the user (in this case using an integrated logon). Once we have that information, we can create a connection ❷ to the database server.

NOTE As with many things in the .NET world, there are a number of ways to achieve a given goal and everyone has their own favorite code syntax. I use this syntax and I know it works. The other variations will work equally as well.

Next on the agenda is to create the command we'll execute ❸. In this case we're performing a select, though it could be any valid T-SQL command, including inserts, updates, and deletes. Stored procedures can also be used, though with slightly different syntax. When we retrieve our data, we need somewhere to put it, so we create a data table ❹. This is a .NET object that represents the data. After opening the connection ❺ we can select our data ❻ and load our data table ❼. We'd better close the connection as well, so the DBAs don't get upset with us ❽. Now the data can finally be displayed ❾. PowerShell v2 has an `Out-Gridview` cmdlet that'll display the data in a nice filterable GUI.

In addition to accessing user data, we can also use these techniques to read system information and Dynamic Management Views. The results could be piped into Power-Gadgets, which enables you to produce real-time updatable charts that can be used as Vista sidebar gadgets if required.

Administration

Being able to access the data is only part of the picture. We need to be able to administer SQL Server as well. PowerShell is an automation engine that lends itself to working across multiple servers. We need to be able to use SMO to perform the administrative tasks. SMO is covered in chapter 27, "Automating SQL Server management using SMO," but for the purposes of our discussion it's a hierarchical set of .NET objects, introduced with SQL Server 2005, that exposes the functionality we see in the SQL Server Management Suite.

PowerShell doesn't know anything about SMO, though the assemblies are automatically loaded by SQLPS, so we need to explicitly need to load the .NET assemblies into PowerShell when we want to use this functionality. We can perform the load in the PowerShell profile if we're going to be using SMO a lot, as shown in listing 2.

Listing 2 Accessing SMO with PowerShell

```
$null = [reflection.assembly]::LoadWithPartialName
➥("Microsoft.SqlServer.ConnectionInfo")
$null = [reflection.assembly]::LoadWithPartialName
➥("Microsoft.SqlServer.SmoEnum")
$null = [reflection.assembly]::LoadWithPartialName
➥("Microsoft.SqlServer.Smo")
```

 ❶ Load SMO

```
$Smo = "Microsoft.SqlServer.Management.Smo."
$server = new-object ($Smo + 'server') "SQL1"     ◁────❷ Create server object
$server.databases | Select Name | Format-Table    ◁────❸ Display data
```

The first three lines load the SMO assemblies ❶ into PowerShell. The SMO object hierarchy starts with a server object ❷. It's always created first, and other objects such as databases, logins, and jobs are accessed from the server object. In this case, I've defined a string to hold the first part of the class name and then use PowerShell's New-Object cmdlet to create the object. The only required parameter is a server name. If you use integrated security, the authentication is handled automatically.

The server object can then be used to access the databases collection. In this case, we're only accessing the name ❸, but all of the database properties available in the GUI management console are accessible through these objects.

NOTE   The SMO documentation doesn't include examples for PowerShell. The C# examples can usually be translated. Be prepared to work through SQL Server Books Online and MSDN documentation for the full details.

PowerShell gives you the ability to access and manipulate data from the command line and to administer your servers using SMO. In SQL Server 2008, PowerShell is built into the product and provides even more functionality.

PowerShell with SQL Server 2008

PowerShell is a prerequisite for installing SQL Server 2008, as with many of the latest versions of Microsoft products. The PowerShell functionality is exposed through sqlps.exe, a provider for SMO, and some cmdlets.

SQLPS

Sqlps.exe is a PowerShell mini-shell. It's a version of PowerShell that has been specially compiled to incorporate SQL Server functionality and remove some standard PowerShell functionality, such as the following:

- *The ability to add snap-ins*—The *-pssnapin cmdlets aren't available
- *The ability to create a console file*—The SQLPS configuration can't be exported for importing into another PowerShell session. This is different from the Exchange PowerShell configuration, for instance.

Use get-command | select noun -Unique | sort noun both in SQLPS and the standard PowerShell to see the differences. That still leaves the majority of PowerShell functionality available. This means we can administer services, processes, and event logs on our SQL Server machines, as shown in figure 1.

One slight oddity is that SQLPS doesn't appear on the Start menu when SQL Server 2008 is installed. I recommend creating an icon on the desktop or the Start menu. SQLPS can be found at C:\Program Files\Microsoft SQL Server\100\Tools\Binn\ SQLPS.exe.

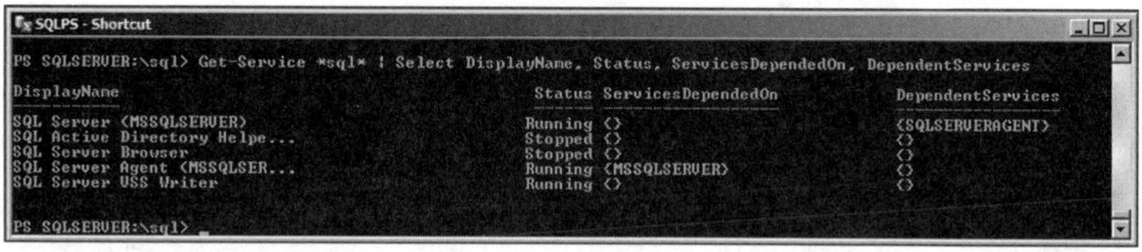

Figure 1   Service dependencies in SQL Server

During startup, SQLPS will attempt to run any PowerShell profiles that it finds. If the profile contains any commands that SQLPS can't process, an error will occur and the profile processing may halt. If an error doesn't occur, SQLPS will be pointing at the root of the SQL Server drive. SQLPS can also be started by right-clicking an object in SQL Server Management Studio (SSMS) and selecting Start PowerShell from the context menu.

Provider

As mentioned earlier, a provider exposes a data store as if it were the filesystem. In this case, it exposes the SMO hierarchy for SQL Server. The provider only gives access to databases and tables for administrative purposes. It's not possible to do a `dir` and scroll through the data in your table.

The provider is accessed as if it were another drive on your system—in this case, the sqlserver: drive. The normal navigation commands such as `cd` are used within the provider. When you open up the SQL Server mini-shell and perform `dir sqlserver:` the results are the following:

```
Name               Root                          Description
----               ----                          -----------
SQL                SQLSERVER:\SQL                SQL Server Database Engine
SQLPolicy          SQLSERVER:\SQLPolicy          SQL Server Policy Management
SQLRegistration    SQLSERVER:\SQLRegistration    SQL Server Registrations
DataCollection     SQLSERVER:\DataCollection     SQL Server Data Collection
```

If you use the following to step into the database engine and display the contents

```
cd sqlserver:\sql
dir
```

all you'll see is the current machine. You can access remote machines by typing `cd server_name` and you'll be connected to them. This also works in SSMS, where you can right-click on a remote registered server and point the provider to that particular server, including SQL Server 2005 instances. In effect, SQLPS has its own remoting system.

You can use the `dir` command, as in the next example, to list the features available in the database engine:

```
(cf)dir sqlserver:\sql\sql08\default
```

Here are the results for my server:

```
Audits
BackupDevices
Credentials
CryptographicProviders
Databases
Endpoints
JobServer
Languages
LinkedServers
Logins
Mail
ResourceGovernor
Roles
ServerAuditSpecifications
SystemDataTypes
SystemMessages
Triggers
UserDefinedMessages
```

We can use the `Get-Item` cmdlet to access the information:

```
cd sqlserver:\sql\sql08
$server = get-item default
$Server.Information.Properties | Select-Object Name, Value |
Format-Table -auto
```

Databases on the system be found by running the following:

```
cd sqlserver:\sql\sql08\default\Databases
dir | Select Name | Format-Table
```

To work with the system databases we need to use `Get-Item`:

```
Get-Item .
cd master
Invoke-Sqlcmd -Query "SELECT * FROM syslogins" | Where{$_.Sysadmin -eq 1} |
➥Select Loginname
```

The `Invoke-Sqlcmd` cmdlet can be used to access data. The one thing we can't do in the provider is use `New-Item` to create a database, table, or any other object. We need to revert to using SMO in PowerShell for creating objects. The provider allows us to access the configuration information in SQL Server easily.

Cmdlets

In SQL Server 2008, there are five cmdlets shipped with the provider:

- `Convert-UrnToPath`
- `Decode-SqlName`
- `Encode-SqlName`
- `Invoke-PolicyEvaluation`
- `Invoke-Sqlcmd`

`Convert-UrnToPath` converts an SMO URN to a PowerShell provider path. The URN indicates where we are in the object hierarchy. The next two in the list are concerned with translating names between PowerShell and SMO. `Invoke-PolicyEvaluation` evaluates one or more SQL Server Policy-Based Management policies against a target set, either reporting the compliance level of the set or bringing the set into compliance.

The final cmdlet, `Invoke-Sqlcmd`, enables us to send a T-SQL command to the server and access or manipulate data, for example:

```
Invoke-Sqlcmd -Database AdventureWorks2008
-Query "Insert INTO dbo.test1 values (1,2,3), (4,5,6)"

Invoke-Sqlcmd -Database AdventureWorks2008
-Query "Select * from dbo.test1"
```

We can now replace listing 1 with the code from listing 3.

Listing 3 Accessing data with PowerShell cmdlet

```
 Invoke-Sqlcmd -ServerInstance "SQL08" -Database "AdventureWorks2008"
-Query "SELECT * FROM Production.Product Where Color = 'Silver'" |
Format-Table
```

The `-ServerInstance` gives us the server to which we'll connect. It's assumed that integrated security is used. The query is exactly the same as used in listing 1. The listing ends by piping the results into a `Format-Table` that'll display the output as a neatly formatted table. The results could be read into a variable to enable further analysis if required.

Using this cmdlet is a lot easier than using ADO.NET, especially for nonprogrammers. It gives us easy-to-use command-line access to the data in our database.

Summary

PowerShell is an automation engine Microsoft is now building into all of its major products. The data in SQL Server can be accessed using scripts or cmdlets shipping with SQL Server 2008. SMO-based scripts can be used to administer all versions since SQL Server 2000. PowerShell providers enable us to administer and configure SQL Server. The new policy management features can also be accessed from PowerShell.

About the author

Richard Siddaway is a technical infrastructure architect with SCH plc. With more than 20 years of experience in various aspects of IT, Richard is currently concentrating on the Microsoft environment at an architectural level, especially around Active Directory, Exchange, and SQL Server. His initial programming background is still useful, as Richard is an experienced scripter always looking for the opportunity to automate a process. Richard is a PowerShell MVP who founded and currently leads the UK PowerShell User Group. Richard frequently presents on PowerShell at conferences and user groups. He can be contacted via his blog at http://richardsiddaway.spaces.live.com/.

27 Automating SQL Server Management using SMO

Allen White

When managing Microsoft SQL Server, there is rarely just one best way to accomplish any given task. Server Management Objects (SMO) and its sisters, Replication Management Objects (RMO) and Analysis Management Objects (AMO), are object libraries that enable you to manage SQL Server to best fit your needs.

Microsoft provides excellent tools to manage SQL Server, but they may not always fit the skill set of your administrative team. For example, your operations team may be more inclined to script all management tasks (not a bad idea and the graphical tools provided don't necessarily lend themselves to automation). SMO, introduced with SQL Server 2005, was built using the .NET Framework, so the objects it exposes are available in your language of choice. In this chapter, I'll give examples using Visual Basic .NET, but you can build your own application using any .NET language.

SMO was designed to be easier to use and more efficient than its predecessor, Distributed Management Objects (DMO). For example, when returning the collection of databases for a server, SMO returns only the name and the schema for the databases on the server. DMO returns the fully instantiated collections of every database on that server, taking additional time to both populate that collection and send it. In addition, DMO increases the network bandwidth required to pass that entire collection to the client. The point is that when you need additional detail from the server, SMO returns that detail, but not by default. SMO also supports a wealth of features new to SQL Server 2005 and SQL Server 2008.

In SQL Server 2008, Microsoft added the ability to launch a PowerShell window from the Object Explorer window of SQL Server Management Studio (SSMS). What loads is a special executable of PowerShell with two *snap-in* modules and the SMO assemblies already loaded. This executable is in the SQL Server binaries and is called `sqlps.exe`. In the PowerShell window, you can browse SMO objects just as you'd browse a file structure tree on a disk file system. As people are exposed to this feature, they'll create new and different ways to manage SQL Server through scripts, and understanding the SMO object library will help reduce the time required to write these scripts.

Another powerful use of SMO will be through the Policy-Based Management feature of SQL Server 2008. Although SSMS makes it easy to create conditions and policies, doing so across an enterprise can be tedious. By scripting these objects using PowerShell and SMO, you can maximize the consistency of your enterprise servers.

PowerShell is the new scripting environment for the Windows platform. For administrators who don't have access to the Visual Studio environment, or for the IT professional who prefers scripting to compiled code, PowerShell provides full access to the .Net Framework and all the objects available within. PowerShell is available as a free download from Microsoft at http://www.microsoft.com/powershell/.

Other chapters in this book provide a great amount of detail on PowerShell, so here we'll focus on the administrative tasks you can accomplish with PowerShell using SMO.

Loading required libraries

Before you can use SMO within PowerShell, you must load the SMO assembly into the environment. To load the basic SMO environment interactively, you must execute the following command:

```
[System.Reflection.Assembly]::LoadWithPartialName('Microsoft.SqlServer.SMO')
    | out-null
```

The results of the command are piped to the `out-null` device because we generally don't need to see the version number of the library when it's loaded.

When Microsoft introduced SQL Server 2008, they moved a number of objects from the SMO library into new dynamic-link libraries (DLLs) called SMOExtended.dll and SQLWMIManagement.dll. To allow the scripts to run in either environment, the example scripts will extract the `FullName` property from the `Assembly` object from the load of the SMO DLL, and then filter the string to determine the release number of the SMO DLL. If the release number indicates the DLL is from SQL Server 2005 (Version 9.0) no more work is required; otherwise the two new DLLs must be loaded, as shown in listing 1.

Listing 1   Code to load SMOExtended.dll and SQLWMIManagement.dll

```
# Load SMO assembly, and if we're running SQL 2008 DLLs load the
➥SMOExtended and SQLWMIManagement libraries
$v = [System.Reflection.Assembly]::LoadWithPartialName
    ➥('Microsoft.SqlServer.SMO')
$p = $v.FullName.Split(',')
$p1 = $p[1].Split('=')
$p2 = $p1[1].Split('.')
if ($p2[0] -ne '9') {
```

```
   [System.Reflection.Assembly]::LoadWithPartialName('Microsoft.SqlServer.
➡SMOExtended')  | out-null
   [System.Reflection.Assembly]::LoadWithPartialName('Microsoft.SqlServer.
➡SQLWMIManagement')  | out-null
   }
```

All the example scripts will contain these commands near the beginning just to be certain the library is loaded, but it's easier to edit your PowerShell profile file to include it, so the libraries are always loaded when you start the environment. You can learn how to do this on the MSDN site at http://msdn.microsoft.com/en-us/library/bb613488(VS.85).aspx.

Backup

The most important task of a database administrator is to maintain a reliable set of backups for the databases being managed. System and disk failures occur in the best hardware environments, so maintaining consistent backups is critical to the prevention of data loss.

SMO provides objects that provide the administrator a variety of ways to back up and restore databases, as we will see. First, let's take a look at the objects.

We need to find out where SQL Server stores the backup files by default; that location is specified in a property in the `Settings` collection of the `Server` object, as shown in figure 1.

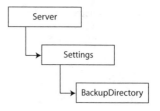

After creating a `Server` object and setting it to connect to our target server, we need to copy the `Server` object's `Settings.BackupDirectory` (figure 1) property to a variable. We'll use the variable to build the path to the file we create as the backup device.

Figure 1 The `BackupDirectory` property is in the server's `Settings` collection.

We also need to create a `Backup` object and set its properties. We need to add a backup device to the `Backup` object's `Devices` collection to have a place for the backup to go, and then we need to execute the `SqlBackup` method to perform the backup.

The `Action` property (figure 2) can be set to one of three values—`Database`, `Log`, or `File`—to define the type of backup to be performed. The `BackupSetDescription`, `BackupSetName`, and `MediaDescription` properties aren't required, but are useful when looking at a backup file later to determine what's contained in the file. The `Database` property contains the name of the database to be backed up. The `AddDevice` method of the `Devices` collection takes two arguments, the full path and filename of the file to contain the backup, and the device type of the backup, in our case `File`.

After the properties are set, the `SqlBackup` method is called, and we pass as its sole argument the `Server` object variable name.

The design of the code samples shown here is to perform a full database backup of all of the non-system databases on the target server, then, if the database is not in the SIMPLE recovery mode, to also perform a transaction log backup of the database. This code can then be executed every time your backup strategy calls for a full database backup of all databases on the target server. If you remove the full database backup logic from the code sample the code can be run every time transaction log backups are to be run for all databases on the server, improving your recovery interval to minimize the potential data loss in the event of a system failure.

In the following script, shown in listing 2, we'll connect to our target server, and then get the default backup directory from the Settings collection. We'll next grab the database collection and iterate through that to do the backups. For each database we'll get the current date and time and put it into a string to use in the backup filename. We'll do the full backup for the database, then we'll check to see if the database recovery model is Simple. If not, we'll perform a transaction log backup on the database as well.

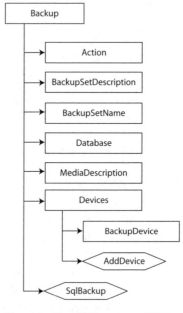

Figure 2   The SMO Backup object

Listing 2   Backing up user databases

```
#backup.ps1
#Performs a Full backup followed by a transaction log backup on all user
➥databases
param (
    [string]$srvname='MyServer\MyInstance'
    )

# Load SMO assembly, and if we're running SQL 2008 DLLs load the
➥SMOExtended and SQLWMIManagement libraries
$v = [System.Reflection.Assembly]::LoadWithPartialName
    ➥('Microsoft.SqlServer.SMO')
$p = $v.FullName.Split(',')
$p1 = $p[1].Split('=')
$p2 = $p1[1].Split('.')
if ($p2[0] -ne '9') {
    [System.Reflection.Assembly]::LoadWithPartialName('Microsoft.SqlServer.
  ➥SMOExtended')    | out-null
    [System.Reflection.Assembly]::LoadWithPartialName('Microsoft.SqlServer.
  ➥SQLWMIManagement')    | out-null
    }

$s = new-object ('Microsoft.SqlServer.Management.Smo.Server') $srvname
$bkdir = $s.Settings.BackupDirectory
$dbs = $s.Databases
foreach ($db in $dbs) {

  if ($db.IsSystemObject -eq $False -and $db.IsMirroringEnabled -eq $False)
➥{
```

```
$dbname = $db.Name
$dt = get-date -format yyyyMMddHHmmss
$bk = new-object ('Microsoft.SqlServer.Management.Smo.Backup')
$bk.Action = 'Database'
$bk.BackupSetDescription = "Full backup of " + $dbname
$bk.BackupSetName = $dbname + " Backup"
$bk.Database = $dbname
$bk.MediaDescription = "Disk"
$bk.Devices.AddDevice($bkdir + "\" + $dbname + "_db_" + $dt + ".bak",
➡ 'File')
$bk.SqlBackup($s)

# Simple Recovery Model has a Value Property of 3
# SQL Server 2008 doesn't recognize the enumerated value so the code is
➡slightly different
# Set a variable to run the transaction log backup, and if Simple, turn
➡it off
$trnbck = 1
if ($p2[0] -eq '9')
    {
    if ($db.DatabaseOptions.RecoveryModel -eq 'Simple') { $trnbck =
    ➡0 }
    }
else
    {
    if ($db.RecoveryModel.value__ -eq 3) { $trnbck = 0 }
    }
if ($trnbck -eq 1) {
    $dt = get-date -format yyyyMMddHHmmss
    $trn = new-object ('Microsoft.SqlServer.Management.Smo.Backup')
    $trn.Action = 'Log'
    $trn.BackupSetDescription = "Trans Log backup of " + $dbname
    $trn.BackupSetName = $dbname + " Backup"
    $trn.Database = $dbname
    $trn.MediaDescription = "Disk"
    $trn.Devices.AddDevice($bkdir + "\" + $dbname + "_tlog_" + $dt
    ➡+ ".trn", 'File')
    $trn.SqlBackup($s)
    }
    }
}
```

Restore

All the backups in the world don't do a bit of good if they can't be restored, and there are scenarios that require restores to be done. One is where a server or disk drive fails and the data needs to be recovered for business to continue. This is the primary reason we perform regular backups. For this case, the backup is restored (generally) to the same location where the original database files existed.

In addition to this there may be the case where data is inadvertently modified or deleted, and some alternate recovery method is required, usually restoring the database backup to a new database name, so that the original data can be copied to the production database without disturbing other transactional activity occurring.

Another use is for development and Quality Assurance (QA) testing, where a copy of the production database is restored in the development or QA environment to examine the effect of some application update. Finally, and this is often overlooked, database backups should be regularly tested in disaster recovery testing, to be certain that, should a problem occur, the backups are in fact usable.

A valuable piece of information is available to us via SMO for the restore process that isn't available through Management Studio or through straight T-SQL, and that is the location of the default data and log file paths (figure 3). We can use this in our restore scenario, using the following objects.

When we have this information, we can set the properties of the SMO Restore object (figure 4). We first connect to the server, then we create a BackupDeviceItem, specifying the name and path of the backup file we're going to use, and add that to the Devices collection of the Restore object. We need to create at least two RelocateFile objects (more if there are more logical files in the backup file) and add them to the RelocateFiles collection. These RelocateFile objects will allow us to specify both the LogicalFileName and the Physical-FileName properties of the new database. In the PhysicalFileName properties, we'll use the MasterDBPath and MasterDBLogPath properties from the server information shown previously. Figure 4 shows the object hierarchy for the Restore object.

As shown in listing 3, after we've set the properties, we can invoke the SqlRestore method to perform the restore; then the restored database is available for use.

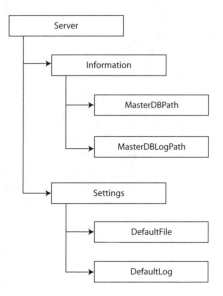

Figure 3   Database file path properties

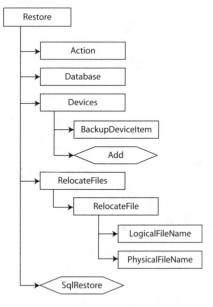

Figure 4   The SMO Restore object

Listing 3   Restoring a copy of an existing database from backup

```
#restore.ps1
#Restores a database with a new name from an existing backup
param (
```

```
        [string]$srvname='MyServer\MyInstance',
        [string]$dbname='AdWorks',
        [string]$bckfile='C:\MSSQL.2\MSSQL\Backup\AdventureWorks_db_20071227175
   ➥004.bak'
        )

# Load SMO assembly, and if we're running SQL 2008 DLLs load the
➥SMOExtended and SQLWMIManagement libraries
$v = [System.Reflection.Assembly]::LoadWithPartialName
    ➥('Microsoft.SqlServer.SMO')
$p = $v.FullName.Split(',')
$p1 = $p[1].Split('=')
$p2 = $p1[1].Split('.')
if ($p2[0] -ne '9') {
    [System.Reflection.Assembly]::LoadWithPartialName('Microsoft.SqlServer.
   ➥SMOExtended')   | out-null
    [System.Reflection.Assembly]::LoadWithPartialName('Microsoft.SqlServer.
   ➥SQLWMIManagement')   | out-null
    }

$srv = new-object ('Microsoft.SqlServer.Management.Smo.Server') $srvname

$bdi = new-object ('Microsoft.SqlServer.Management.Smo.BackupDeviceItem')
➥ ($bckfile, 'File')
$restr = new-object('Microsoft.SqlServer.Management.Smo.Restore')
$restr.Database = $dbname
$restr.Devices.Add($bdi)
$restrfile = new-object('Microsoft.SqlServer.Management.Smo.RelocateFile')
$restrlog = new-object('Microsoft.SqlServer.Management.Smo.RelocateFile')
$restrfile.LogicalFileName = "AdventureWorks_Data"
$restrfile.PhysicalFileName = $s.Information.MasterDBPath + '\'+ $dbname +
➥'_Data.mdf'
$restrlog.LogicalFileName = "AdventureWorks_Log"
$restrlog.PhysicalFileName = $s.Information.MasterDBLogPath + '\'+ $dbname
➥+ '_Log.ldf'
$restr.RelocateFiles.Add($rsfile)
$restr.RelocateFiles.Add($rslog)
$restr.SqlRestore($srv)
```

Creating a database

Using SMO to create databases and database objects may seem counterintuitive, because these objects are usually created using T-SQL scripts, but automating the processes that create the objects can provide consistency in an area that is usually quite inconsistent. Let's start with the database itself.

SQL Server requires that a database have a PRIMARY filegroup and that the system tables (the database metadata) reside in that filegroup (in fact their location cannot be changed). Best practices recommendations include keeping your application data out of the PRIMARY filegroup, to help in managing the disk files for the database. When using SSMS, it can be tedious to create a database with the desired size, file location, and with a separate, default, filegroup to hold the application data. This is a relatively simple process with SMO.

For the example database, we'll create a database called MyAppDB, which will have a 5 MB file in the PRIMARY filegroup to hold the database metadata. This file should never grow beyond 5 MB because it contains only database metadata. We'll use the logical name MyAppDB_SysData for this file and house it in the default data path for the server.

The application data will be located in a second filegroup called AppFG, which we'll set as the default filegroup for the database. We'll create one file with a logical name MyAppDB_AppData and house it in the default data path for the server as well. We'll set an initial size of 25 MB and allow it to grow by 25 MB each time it is required, but set a maximum size of 100 MB.

Log files in SQL Server do not use filegroups, so we'll add a log file to the LogFiles collection of the database with a logical name MyAppDB_Log and house it in the default log file path for the server. We'll set its initial size to 10 MB and allow it to grow by 10 MB each time it needs to do so, but we won't set a maximum size for the log file.

After we've created the structural objects for the database, we execute the Create method, but SQL Server automatically sets the default filegroup to PRIMARY when a database is created, so we have to go back in and set the default filegroup to AppFG using the Alter method at both the filegroup and database levels.

Figure 5 is a hierarchical diagram of the objects we'll use to create the database. Now let's look at the example code in listing 4.

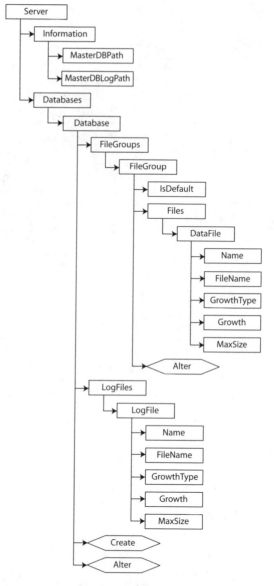

Figure 5   The SMO Databases collection and Database object

Listing 4   Creating a user database

```
#createdatabase.ps1
#Creates a new database using our specifications
param (
    [string]$srvname='MyServer\MyInstance',
    [string]$dbname='MyAppDB',
    [int]$datsize=25,
    [int]$maxsize=100,
    [int]$logsize=10
    )

# Load SMO assembly, and if we're running SQL 2008 DLLs load the
➥SMOExtended and SQLWMIManagement libraries
$v = [System.Reflection.Assembly]::LoadWithPartialName
    ➥('Microsoft.SqlServer.SMO')
$p = $v.FullName.Split(',')
$p1 = $p[1].Split('=')
$p2 = $p1[1].Split('.')
if ($p2[0] -ne '9') {
    [System.Reflection.Assembly]::LoadWithPartialName('Microsoft.SqlServer.
  ➥SMOExtended')  | out-null
    [System.Reflection.Assembly]::LoadWithPartialName('Microsoft.SqlServer.
  ➥SQLWMIManagement')  | out-null
    }

$srv = new-object ('Microsoft.SqlServer.Management.Smo.Server') $srvname

# Instantiate the database object and add the filegroups
$db = new-object ('Microsoft.SqlServer.Management.Smo.Database') ($srv,
➥$dbname)
$sysfg = new-object ('Microsoft.SqlServer.Management.Smo.FileGroup') ($db,
➥'PRIMARY')
$db.FileGroups.Add($sysfg)
$appfg = new-object ('Microsoft.SqlServer.Management.Smo.FileGroup') ($db,
➥'AppFG')
$db.FileGroups.Add($appfg)

# Create the file for the system tables
$dbdsysfile = new-object ('Microsoft.SqlServer.Management.Smo.DataFile')
➥ ($sysfg, 'MyAppDB_SysData')
$sysfg.Files.Add($dbdsysfile)
$dbdsysfile.FileName = $srv.Information.MasterDBPath +
➥'\MyAppDB_SysData.mdf'
$dbdsysfile.Size = [double](5.0 * 1024.0)
$dbdsysfile.GrowthType = 'KB'
$dbdsysfile.Growth = [double](5.0 * 1024.0)
$dbdsysfile.IsPrimaryFile = 'True'

# Create the file for the Application tables
$dbdappfile = new-object ('Microsoft.SqlServer.Management.Smo.DataFile')
➥ ($appfg, 'MyAppDB_AppData')
$appfg.Files.Add($dbdappfile)
$dbdappfile.FileName = $srv.Information.MasterDBPath +
➥'\MyAppDB_AppData.ndf'
$dbdappfile.Size = [double](25.0 * 1024.0)
$dbdappfile.GrowthType = 'KB'
```

```
$dbappfile.Growth = [double]($datsize * 1024.0)
$dbappfile.MaxSize = [double]($maxsize * 1024.0)

# Create the file for the log
$dblfile = new-object ('Microsoft.SqlServer.Management.Smo.LogFile') ($db,
➥ 'MyAppDB_Log')
$db.LogFiles.Add($dblfile)
$dblfile.FileName = $srv.Information.MasterDBLogPath + '\MyAppDB_Log.ldf'
$dblfile.Size = [double]($logsize * 1024.0)
$dblfile.GrowthType = 'KB'
$dblfile.Growth = [double]($logsize * 1024.0)

# Create the database
$db.Create()

# Set the default filegroup to AppFG
$appfg = $db.FileGroups['AppFG']
$appfg.IsDefault = $true
$appfg.Alter()
$db.Alter()
```

After this script is completed, the MyAppDB database will exist and user objects will be placed in the AppFG filegroup instead of PRIMARY, which will improve the long-term management of the database.

Scripting

The scripting of SMO is a vast improvement over the scripting of its predecessor, DMO. With SMO you can create T-SQL scripts from objects even if they don't yet exist. When you open almost any maintenance dialog box in SQL Server Management Studio, you'll see a button that allows you to generate a script from the changes you've made in that dialog box. You can then save that script for archival purposes, cancel out of the dialog box, and execute the script as written, or make changes to it before you execute it.

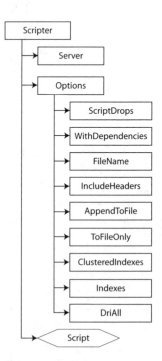

Another useful feature of scripting existing objects is to generate scripts of all database objects for documentation or source code control. This allows the administrators to then rebuild a database in the form it existed at the time the script was created.

At any time while creating or working with objects in SMO, you can script those objects for archival or later use. Figure 6 shows the `Scripter` object and the properties we need to set.

The `Server` property allows the `Scripter` object to connect to the server. The remaining properties that need to be set are in the `Scripter` `Options` collection.

Figure 6   The SMO `Scripter` object

The ScriptDrops property specifies whether the script will consist of drops for the objects or create for the objects. If you specify c to this property, the script will contain a DROP statement for the object (within an IF condition to ensure that it exists), but a False value will cause the scripter to generate the CREATE statement for the object. The WithDependencies property, if True, will cause the objects to be scripted in an order that respects the dependency of one scripted object on another. The FileName property contains the full path of the resultant script file. The IncludeHeaders property, when True, will include a comment indicating the name of the object and when the script was created in the script. The AppendToFile will append the script to the end of an existing file if True, and overwrite the file if False. By default the scripting process will send the results to the console, so setting the ToFileOnly to True will cause the scripter to send the script only to the file specified. Setting Clustered-Indexes to True will cause the clustered index for a table to be included in the script, and setting Indexes to True will cause the nonclustered indexes to be included in the script. The DriAll property, when set to True, will cause all objects with enforced declarative referential integrity to be included in the script.

The objects to be scripted need to be added to an array of type SqlSmoObject. This allows you to decide at what point you want the object included in the script. After the array has been populated with all the objects to be scripted you can invoke the Script method and the script will be created.

Now let's look at the example code in listing 5.

Listing 5 Scripting all objects in the AdventureWorks database

```
#scripting.ps1
#Script all the table objects in the AdventureWorks database
param (
    [string]$srvname='MyServer\MyInstance',
    [string]$dbname='AdventureWorks',
    [string]$scrname='c:\dbscript.sql'
    )

# Load SMO assembly, and if we're running SQL 2008 DLLs load the
➥SMOExtended and SQLWMIManagement libraries
$v = [System.Reflection.Assembly]::LoadWithPartialName
    ➥('Microsoft.SqlServer.SMO')
$p = $v.FullName.Split(',')
$p1 = $p[1].Split('=')
$p2 = $p1[1].Split('.')
if ($p2[0] -ne '9') {
    [System.Reflection.Assembly]::LoadWithPartialName('Microsoft.SqlServer.
➥SMOExtended')   | out-null
    [System.Reflection.Assembly]::LoadWithPartialName('Microsoft.SqlServer.
➥SQLWMIManagement')   | out-null
    }

$srv = new-object ('Microsoft.SqlServer.Management.Smo.Server') $srvname
$db = $srv.Databases[$dbname]

$scrp = new-object ('Microsoft.SqlServer.Management.Smo.Scripter') ($srv)
```

```
$scrp.Options.ScriptDrops = $False
$scrp.Options.WithDependencies = $True
$scrp.Options.FileName = $scrname
$scrp.Options.IncludeHeaders = $True
$scrp.Options.AppendToFile = $True
$scrp.Options.ToFileOnly = $True
$scrp.Options.ClusteredIndexes = $True
$scrp.Options.DriAll = $True
$scrp.Options.Indexes = $True

$scrp.Script($db.Tables)
```

Summary

This chapter presents just a few examples of methods for automating your management of SQL Server using SMO and PowerShell. You can find many additional examples on the web and on the Codeplex site to help you solve your SQL Server management problems. You'll also find additional examples in my blog at http://sql-blog.com/blogs/allen_white/default.aspx.

About the author

Allen White is a SQL Server trainer and consultant who's been using SQL Server since 1992. He has been awarded Microsoft's MVP Award for his work in the SQL Server community for three years.

28 Practical auditing in SQL Server 2008

Jasper Smith

In SQL Server 2008 Enterprise Edition, instance- and database-level audit is now built into the Database Engine with its own set of instance- and database-level objects—Server Audit and Server Audit Specification at the instance level, and Database Audit Specification at the database level.

SQL Server 2005 introduced event notifications and data definition language (DDL) triggers as mechanisms for auditing DDL statements, but coverage of events wasn't complete. There was no support for auditing access to data, and there was no tool support available in SQL Server Management Studio (SSMS).

Generating audit event s in SQL 2008 is extremely lightweight compared to previously available mechanisms, and is based on the new extended events infrastructure, which is designed to have an extremely low overhead even for large numbers of events. It also allows much finer-grained event filtering.

NOTE All of the new audit features described in this chapter require SQL Server 2008 Enterprise or Developer Edition, and aren't available in lower editions.

Overview of audit infrastructure

In SQL Server 2008, all events are now auditable using the new audit objects, including those not available via event notifications in previous versions of SQL Server. Configuration is greatly simplified with built-in tool support in SSMS. Figure 1 gives an overview of the various audit objects.

Server audit objects

You can define the properties of an audit, such as Queue Delay or Action on Audit Failure, as well as the output target, such as File, Windows Application Log, or Windows Security Log. You can create multiple server audits, each of which defines its own target.

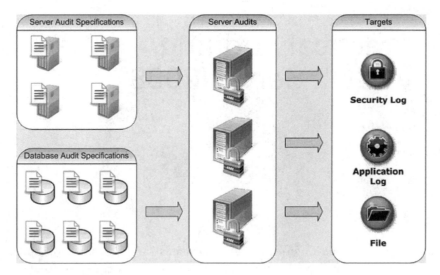

Figure 1   Overview of audit object relationships

Server audit specification objects

You can define the audit action groups that you want to audit at the instance level, along with the server audit they belong to. There can be a maximum of one server audit specification per server audit. You can create multiple server audit specifications, as long as each one uses a separate server audit.

Database audit specification objects

You can define the individual audit actions or action groups that you want to audit at the database level, including any filters and the server audit they belong to. There can be a maximum of one database audit specification per database per server audit. You can create multiple database audit specifications for the same database, but they need to belong to separate server audits.

Server audits

The Server Audit object is the first object you create when enabling auditing for an instance of SQL Server 2008. It defines the output target for audit events generated by audit specifications. You can choose from three possible audit output types for a Server Audit object:

- Windows Application Event Log
- Windows Security Event Log
- File (local or remote)

When you specify the Application or Security Log target, the settings listed in table 1 are available for configuration.

NOTE   Writing events to the Windows Security Log isn't allowed on Windows XP.

Table 1   Server Audit configuration settings for Application and Security Log targets

Setting	Description
Queue Delay	Amount of time in milliseconds that events are buffered before being forced to be processed. To enable synchronous event delivery, you'd set this to 0. Synchronous delivery may have a performance impact. The default value is 1000.
Shutdown on Failure	Whether the SQL instance will shut down if audit events can't be written to the target. The default value is CONTINUE.
Audit GUID	To support scenarios such as database mirroring, an audit needs a specific GUID that matches the GUID found in the mirrored database. The GUID can't be modified after the audit has been created.

Configuring the Windows Security Log target

In order to allow SQL Server to write events to the Windows Security Log, a number of additional configuration steps are required. The following walkthrough demonstrates how to enable the Windows Security Log target for Windows Server 2003. For details of how to configure this target for Windows Server 2008, see the SQL Server Documentation (http://msdn.microsoft.com/en-gb/library/cc645889.aspx).

1   Launch the Local Security Policy MMC snap-in by clicking Start > Run > secpol.msc.

2   Select the Audit Policy folder under the Local Policies folder and double-click Audit Object Access in the right pane.

3   Check both the Success and Failure check boxes in the resultant dialog, as shown in figure 2.

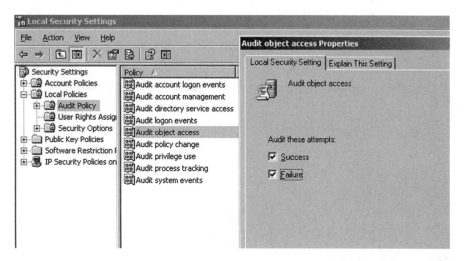

Figure 2   Enabling Audit Object Access

4 Click OK to apply the changes.

5 In the same snap-in, select the User Rights Assignment folder under Local Policies and double-click on Generate Security Audits in the right pane.

6 Add the SQL Service account as shown in figure 3 and click OK.

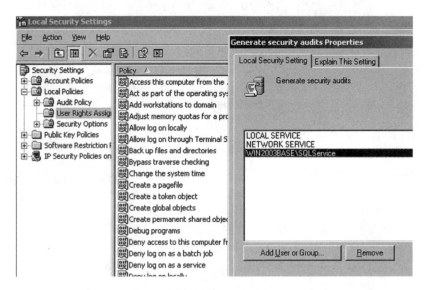

Figure 3   Enabling Generate Security Audit for SQL Service account

7 Restart the SQL Server service in order for the changes to take effect.

NOTE   The required options can be set by Group Policy in a domain environment, in which case local settings will be overwritten. You should discuss these settings with the team that manages Group Policy to ensure the required settings remain in effect for SQL Servers where you need to be able to write events to the Security Log.

Creating a server audit using the Windows Security Log target

To create a server audit, you can either use SSMS or T-SQL. The following example demonstrates how to create a server audit that uses the Windows Security Log using SSMS:

1 In SSMS Object Explorer, expand the Security node, right-click on the Audits node, and select New Audit from the context menu, as shown in figure 4.

Figure 4   Creating a new audit using SSMS

2 In the Create Audit dialog box shown in figure 5, specify the audit name as `SecurityLogAudit`, choose Security Log from the Audit drop-down list, and click OK.

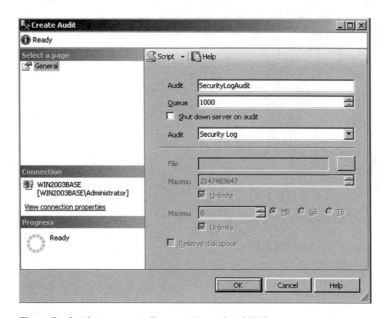

Figure 5   Setting server audit properties using SSMS

3 Note that the server audit has been created in a disabled state, as indicated graphically by the small downward-pointing red arrow on the server audit icon. In order to use this server audit, it must first be enabled. To enable the server audit, right-click on it and select Enable Audit from the context menu, as shown in figure 6.

Figure 6   **Enabling a server audit using SSMS**

The code in listing 1 is the equivalent of what we've just done via SSMS, but using T-SQL.

Listing 1   Creating a server audit using the Security Log target

```
CREATE SERVER AUDIT [SecurityLog]
TO SECURITY_LOG
WITH
(  QUEUE_DELAY = 1000,
   ON_FAILURE = CONTINUE
)
GO

ALTER SERVER AUDIT [SecurityLog]
WITH(STATE=ON)
GO
```

NOTE   Windows Security Log is the most secure destination for auditing events from system administrator activity. It can also be used to integrate with the ACS (Audit Collection Service) functionality in SCOM 2007 (System Center Operations Manager).

Creating a security audit using the Windows Application Log target

To create a server audit using the Windows Application Log target, use the code shown in listing 2. As with the previous example, the server audit can be created using SSMS or T-SQL. The same options are available as for the Security Log target described in table 1. The server audit will be created in a disabled state and must be enabled before a server or database audit specification can write audit events to it.

Listing 2 Creating a server audit using the Application Log target

```
CREATE SERVER AUDIT [ApplicationLog]
TO APPLICATION_LOG
WITH
( QUEUE_DELAY = 2000,
  ON_FAILURE = CONTINUE
)
GO

ALTER SERVER AUDIT [ApplicationLog]
WITH(STATE=ON)
GO
```

Configuring a server audit using the File target

When you specify the File target, the settings in table 2 are available for configuration.

Table 2 Server audit configuration settings for File targets

Setting	Description
Queue Delay	Amount of time in milliseconds that events are buffered before being forced to be processed. To enable synchronous event delivery, you'd set this to 0. Synchronous delivery may have a performance impact. The default value is 1000.
Shutdown on Failure	Whether the SQL instance will shut down if audit events can't be written to the target. The default value is CONTINUE.
Audit GUID	To support scenarios such as database mirroring, an audit needs a specific GUID that matches the GUID found in the mirrored database. The GUID can't be modified after the audit has been created.
Filepath	The folder used to store the audit files. The filenames are automatically generated based on the audit name and GUID.
Maxsize	The maximum size of an audit file. The default value is UNLIMITED.
Max Rollover Files	The maximum number of rollover audit files. The default value is 0 (unlimited).
Reserve Disk Space	Whether to preallocate disk space to the Maxsize value. The default value is OFF.

The code in listing 3 demonstrates creating a server audit that uses the File target. In this example, the audit folder is C:\Audit\Server, the maximum size on any individual file is 100 MB, the number of rollover files is unlimited, and we aren't preallocating disk space for the audit files. The queue delay is set to 2 seconds; therefore, this is an asynchronous audit and it won't cause the instance to shut down if audit events can't be written to the target.

Listing 3 Creating a server audit using the File target

```
CREATE SERVER AUDIT [ServerAuditFile]
TO FILE
( FILEPATH = N'C:\Audit\Server\'
```

```
    ,MAXSIZE = 100 MB
    ,MAX_ROLLOVER_FILES = 0
    ,RESERVE_DISK_SPACE = OFF
)
WITH
(   QUEUE_DELAY = 2000
    ,ON_FAILURE = CONTINUE
)
GO

ALTER SERVER AUDIT [ServerAuditFile]
WITH(STATE=ON)
GO
```

Server audit specifications

Server audit specifications define the audit action groups that you want to audit at the instance level, along with the server audit they belong to. There can be a maximum of one server audit specification per server audit. You can create multiple server audit specifications as long as each one uses a separate server audit.

At the instance level, you can specify one or more audit action groups (for database audit specifications, you can specify individual audit actions and filters as well). Note that actions that modify the audit itself (such as disabling or altering audit objects) are automatically audited. A large number of audit action groups are available; to find details on all of them, check Books Online (http://msdn.microsoft.com/en-gb/library/cc280663.aspx).

Creating server audit specifications

For the first example (demonstrated in listing 4), we'll create a server audit specification to audit changes to logins using the SERVER_PRINCIPAL_CHANGE_GROUP and use the ApplicationLog server audit we created earlier. If you don't specify the WITH clause, the server audit specification will be created in a disabled state. We'll also generate some events for the audit to capture.

> **Listing 4   Creating a server audit specification using the Application Log target**

```
CREATE SERVER AUDIT SPECIFICATION [AuditLoginChanges]
FOR SERVER AUDIT [ApplicationLog]
ADD (SERVER_PRINCIPAL_CHANGE_GROUP)
WITH (STATE = ON)
GO

-- create some events
CREATE LOGIN AuditLoginDemo
WITH PASSWORD = 'sdkfds*)&(9kdsafk',
CHECK_POLICY=OFF
GO
ALTER LOGIN AuditLoginDemo WITH
DEFAULT_DATABASE = model,
DEFAULT_LANGUAGE = British
```

```
GO
DROP LOGIN AuditLoginDemo
GO
```

In the next example, we'll create a server audit specification using SSMS that audits the SERVER_OPERATION_GROUP and SERVER_STATE_CHANGE_GROUP audit action groups and uses the ServerAuditFile server audit. To create a new server audit specification, follow these steps:

1 Expand the Security top-level node.
2 Right-click the Server Audit Specifications node and choose New Server Audit Specification. This will open the Create Server Audit Specification dialog box, as shown in figure 7.

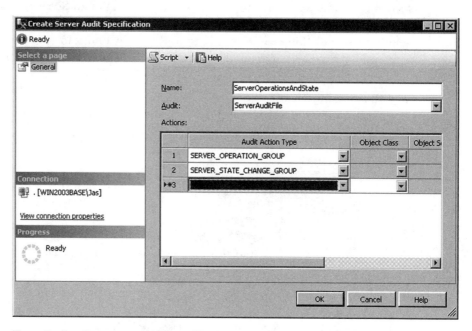

Figure 7 Creating a server audit specification using SSMS

3 Supply a name and select the server audit you want to use. Choose ServerAudit-File from the drop-down list.
4 You can then add one or more audit action groups. Select SERVER_OPERA-TION_GROUP and SERVER_STATE_CHANGE_GROUP.
5 Click OK to create the server audit specification.

The server audit specification will be created in a disabled state. To enable it:

1 Expand the Server Audit Specifications node in Object Explorer.
2 Right-click the ServerOperationsAndState audit specification and choose Enable Server Audit Specification.

The T-SQL code in listing 5 generates some events that will be captured by our audit in order for us to have some activity to view.

Listing 5   Creating events for the server audit specification

```
EXEC sp_configure 'show advanced options',1
RECONFIGURE
GO
EXEC sp_configure 'clr enabled',1
RECONFIGURE
GO
```

Viewing audit events

To view the audit events that are written to the Application or Security Log, we can use either Windows Event Viewer or SSMS. When viewing events using Event Viewer, it's helpful to create a filter for only Success and Failure audits, to cut down the number of records. When viewing the audit in SSMS, this is automatically done for you. Follow these steps to view the events in SSMS:

1 Expand the Security top-level node in SSMS.
2 Expand the Audits node and right-click the ApplicationLog Server Audit.
3 Select View Audit Logs, as shown in figure 8.

Figure 8   Viewing audit logs using SSMS

This launches the SSMS LogFile Viewer, which enables you to easily review audit events written to any of the available server audit targets, as shown in figure 9.

To view events from server audits that use the File target, we can use a new built-in system function called `sys.fn_get_audit_file`. This function allows you to extract the audit events from one or more audit files in a tabular format that can be queried with standard T-SQL or loaded into a table for further analysis. Listing 6 demonstrates how to query the `sys.server_file_audits` catalog view to obtain the audit folder and pass that to the `sys.fn_get_audit_file` function in order to view the audit events in SSMS.

Listing 6   Viewing audit events from T-SQL

```
DECLARE @folder VARCHAR(255)
SELECT @folder = log_file_path + '*'
FROM sys.server_file_audits WHERE name = 'ServerAuditFile'

SELECT * FROM sys.fn_get_audit_file(@folder,DEFAULT,DEFAULT)
ORDER BY event_time DESC
```

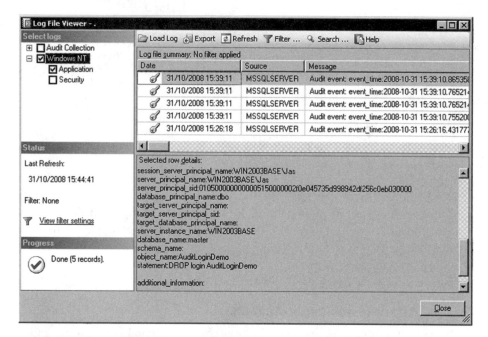

Figure 9   Viewing audit logs in the Log File Viewer

A number of new catalog views expose metadata about server audit specifications. The query in listing 7 demonstrates some of them and lists all server audit specifications, along with their properties.

Listing 7   Viewing details of all server audit specifications

```
SELECT sp.name AS ServerAuditSpecification,
     CASE WHEN sp.is_state_enabled =1
          THEN 'Y' ELSE 'N' END AS SpecificationEnabled,
     d.AuditActions,
     a.name AS ServerAudit,
     a.type_desc AS ServerAuditType,
     CASE WHEN a.is_state_enabled =1
          THEN 'Y' ELSE 'N' END AS AuditEnabled,
     st.status_desc AS AuditStatus,
     a.queue_delay AS QueueDelay,
     a.on_failure_desc AS OnFailure,
     st.audit_file_path AS CurrentFile,
     f.max_file_size AS MaxFileSize,
     f.max_rollover_files AS MaxRolloverFiles,
     CASE WHEN f.reserve_disk_space = 0 THEN 'N'
          WHEN f.reserve_disk_space = 1 THEN 'Y' END AS ReserveSpace
FROM sys.server_audit_specifications AS sp
JOIN sys.server_audits a
   ON sp.audit_guid = a.audit_guid
JOIN sys.dm_server_audit_status st
   ON a.audit_id = st.audit_id
LEFT JOIN sys.server_file_audits f
```

```
      ON a.audit_id = f.audit_id
LEFT JOIN (SELECT server_specification_id,
              STUFF((SELECT ',' + audit_action_name AS [text()]
                    FROM sys.server_audit_specification_details AS d2
                    WHERE d2.server_specification_id =
➥d1.server_specification_id
                    ORDER BY audit_action_name
                    FOR xml path('')), 1, 1, '') AS AuditActions
              FROM sys.server_audit_specification_details AS d1
              GROUP BY server_specification_id) AS d
   ON sp.server_specification_id = d.server_specification_id
ORDER BY ServerAuditSpecification
```

Database audit specifications

Database audit specifications define the audit action groups, individual audit actions, and filters that you use to audit events at the database level, as well as the server audit they belong to. There can be a maximum of one database audit specification per database per server audit. You can create multiple database audit specifications for a database as long as each one uses a separate server audit.

Creating database audit specifications

In the following examples, we'll create a number of database audit specifications for the AdventureWorks2008 sample database using a new file-based server audit.

NOTE   You can download the latest version of the AdventureWorks 2008 database from Codeplex: http://www.codeplex.com/MSFTDBProdSamples/Release/ProjectReleases.aspx.

We'll create a new file-based server audit that we'll use for our database audit specification. The T-SQL code is shown in listing 8.

Listing 8   Creating a server audit for a database audit specification

```
CREATE SERVER AUDIT [AWDMLAudit]
TO FILE
(  FILEPATH = 'C:\Audit\DB\AdventureWorks\AWDMLAudit'
   ,MAXSIZE = 100 MB
   ,MAX_ROLLOVER_FILES = 0
   ,RESERVE_DISK_SPACE = OFF
)
WITH
(  QUEUE_DELAY = 2000
   ,ON_FAILURE = CONTINUE
)
ALTER SERVER AUDIT [AWDMLAudit]
WITH(STATE=ON)
GO
```

We'll now create a new database audit specification to audit the DML (Select, Insert, Update, and Delete) events for the HumanResources.EmployeePayHistory and Sales.CreditCard tables. As for the audit action groups available in server audit specifications, we can also specify individual audit actions and filter them based on individual objects and the user or role accessing them. In this example, we'll specify the public database role so that DML for all users is captured. The T-SQL code is shown in listing 9.

Listing 9   Creating a database audit specification to audit DML activity

```
USE AdventureWorks2008
GO
CREATE DATABASE AUDIT SPECIFICATION AWSensitiveDMLAudit
FOR SERVER AUDIT AWDMLAudit
ADD (SELECT , INSERT , UPDATE, DELETE
     ON HumanResources.EmployeePayHistory
     BY PUBLIC),
ADD (SELECT , INSERT , UPDATE, DELETE
     ON Sales.CreditCard
     BY PUBLIC)
WITH (STATE = ON)
GO
```

Now generate some DML activity against the audited tables using the code in listing 10.

Listing 10   Creating DML activity

```
USE AdventureWorks2008
GO
SELECT TOP 10 * FROM Sales.CreditCard
GO
BEGIN TRAN
   UPDATE Sales.CreditCard
   SET ExpYear = 2009,ModifiedDate = GETDATE()
   WHERE CreditCardID = 6
ROLLBACK TRAN
GO
SELECT * FROM HumanResources.EmployeePayHistory
GO
```

To view the results of the DML activities, we'll use the `fn_get_audit_file` function. We can join the results of this function with the `sys.dm_audit_class_type_map` and `sys.dm_audit_actions` management views to translate the action and object types to help make the results easier to understand. The T-SQL code is shown in listing 11, followed by the results in figure 10.

Listing 11   Viewing DML activity audit events in File target

```
USE master
GO
-- get the audit file
DECLARE @filepattern VARCHAR(300)
DECLARE @folder VARCHAR(255)
DECLARE @auditguid VARCHAR(36)
SELECT @auditguid = audit_guid,@folder = log_file_path
FROM sys.server_file_audits WHERE name = 'AWDMLAudit'

SELECT @filepattern = @folder + '*_' + @auditguid + '*'
```

```
-- view the results
SELECT a.name AS Action,c.class_type_desc AS ObjectType,
f.server_principal_name,f.schema_name,f.OBJECT_NAME,f.statement
FROM fn_get_audit_file(@filepattern,NULL,NULL) AS f
JOIN sys.dm_audit_class_type_map c ON f.class_type = c.class_type
JOIN sys.dm_audit_actions a ON f.action_id = a.action_id
AND c.securable_class_desc = a.class_desc
WHERE f.action_id <> 'AUSC'
ORDER BY event_time DESC,sequence_number
```

	Action	ObjectType	server_principal_name	schema_name	OBJECT_NAME	statement
1	SELECT	TABLE	WIN2003BASE\Jas	Sales	CreditCard	SELECT TOP 10 * FROM Sales.CreditCard
2	SELECT	TABLE	WIN2003BASE\Jas	Sales	CreditCard	UPDATE [Sales].[CreditCard] set [ExpYear] = @1,[Mo(
3	UPDATE	TABLE	WIN2003BASE\Jas	Sales	CreditCard	UPDATE [Sales].[CreditCard] set [ExpYear] = @1,[Mo(
4	SELECT	TABLE	WIN2003BASE\Jas	HumanResources	EmployeePayHistory	SELECT * FROM HumanResources.EmployeePayHist

Figure 10   Results of listing 11

A couple of interesting points are raised by the results. As you can see, the update statement is present twice (because the table needs to be read to qualify rows for the update, which is why both SELECT and UPDATE actions appear for the UPDATE statement), even though the transaction it was in was rolled back. Also note that the statement for the update is the autoparameterized version, rather than the statement text. Database audits don't capture any before or after data images for DML actions.

NOTE   To capture the data that has changed, you could combine auditing with the new Change Data Capture functionality in SQL 2008 Enterprise Edition. See Books Online for details (http://msdn.microsoft.com/en-gb/library/bb522489.aspx).

Listing 12 shows more examples demonstrating the additional filtering available for database audit specifications. If you try to create these without deleting the previous database audit specification, they'll fail because of the limit of one database audit specification per database per server audit. In order to DROP or ALTER a database audit specification, it must first be disabled.

Listing 12   Additional examples of database audit specifications

```
USE AdventureWorks2008
GO

-- audit all execution of stored procedures
CREATE DATABASE AUDIT SPECIFICATION Example1
FOR SERVER AUDIT AWDMLAudit
ADD (EXECUTE
    ON DATABASE::AdventureWorks2008
    BY PUBLIC)
WITH (STATE = ON)
GO
```

```
-- audit all updates in the Sales schema
CREATE DATABASE AUDIT SPECIFICATION Example2
FOR SERVER AUDIT AWDMLAudit
ADD (UPDATE
     ON SCHEMA::Sales
     BY PUBLIC)
WITH (STATE = ON)
GO

-- audit all schema changes in the database
CREATE DATABASE AUDIT SPECIFICATION Example3
FOR SERVER AUDIT AWDMLAudit
ADD (SCHEMA_OBJECT_CHANGE_GROUP)
WITH (STATE = ON)
GO
```

SSMS has built-in tool support for database audit specifications. If you expand the Security node in a Database node in Object Explorer in SSMS, you'll see the new database audit specifications node. To create a new database audit specification, follow these steps:

1 Right-click on the Database Audit Specifications node and choose New Database Audit Specification, as shown in figure 11.

Figure 11 Creating a database audit specification in SSMS

2 This will bring up the Create Database Audit Specification dialog box, which allows you to select the audit actions and groups, along with any applicable filtering.

3 Select some audit action groups and click OK to create the database audit specification, as shown in figure 12.

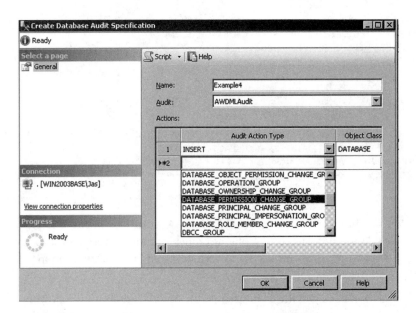

Figure 12   Configuring a database audit specification in SSMS

4 New database audit specifications are created in a disabled state. To enable the database audit specification, right-click on it and select Enable Database Audit Specification.

Summary

That brings us to the end of this introduction to the new built-in auditing features in SQL Server 2008. As you've seen, it's extremely easy to configure and administer via T-SQL or SSMS. It's also designed to be extremely lightweight and have less overhead than the existing mechanisms (SQL trace, DDL triggers, and event notifications).

About the author

Jasper Smith is an independent SQL Server consultant based in the UK, specializing in performance tuning and high availability solutions. He's been working with SQL Server for more than eight years and has been a Microsoft MVP for SQL Server for the past six years. He also runs http://www.sqldbatips.com, home of popular free SQL tools and utilities such as Reporting Services Scripter, Expressmaint, and SQL 2005 Service Manager.

29 My favorite DMVs, and why

Aaron Bertrand

This chapter covers some of my favorite Dynamic Management Views and Dynamic Management Functions in SQL Server 2005 and SQL Server 2008. I will start out by giving some background about DMVs. Then I will list some details about the individual views and functions that I use most frequently. Finally, I will show you some interesting queries you can use to take full advantage of the information that these objects expose.

What is so great about DMVs, anyway?

As an architect first and foremost, I have always been interested in the performance and usage information I can extract out of my SQL Server instances. In versions prior to SQL Server 2005, there was a wide range of ways to get this information, such as cryptic DBCC commands, bit flags in system tables (mostly undocumented), and system stored procedures (some unsupported). SQL Server 2005 introduced us to a new way to derive this data: Dynamic Management Views (DMVs) and Dynamic Management Functions (DMFs), collectively known as DMVs.

DMVs brought about a more consistent way to obtain the existing information we were used to retrieving. They also introduced new data that we had never had access to before, or could only access via auditing, extensive tracing, or memory dumps. Consistency is important, as we finally have a relatively stable set of conventions for how the DMVs and DMFs are named, present common data types and column names, and exist in the sys schema.

Another aspect about DMVs that I appreciate significantly over system stored procedures and DBCC commands is that I can query against them directly, making it easy to pull only the columns and rows that I want. As an example, in the past, if I only wanted to see sessions that were blocking or being blocked, I would have to create a temporary table up front, insert the results of sp_who2, and run filtered queries against the temporary table (or squint at the whole result set, scrolling up and down).

You should note a couple of important things about DMVs. First, they only contain data since the last time the instance was started. All metrics are literally thrown away when the SQL Server service is shut down. You can make this data persist between restarts, but that is out of scope for this topic (Paul Randal discusses the idea of persisting DMV data across SQL Server restarts at http://www.sqlskills.com/BLOGS/PAUL/ post/Indexes-From-Every-Angle-How-can-you-tell-if-an-index-is-being-used.aspx, and there is also the DMVStats CodePlex project from Tom Davidson and Sanjay Mishra, available at http://www.codeplex.com/sqldmvstats/). Because they also require VIEW SERVER STATE or VIEW DATABASE STATE permissions, depending on the DMV, it is not always possible to have access to the complete set of information that is available.

I feel that a couple of things are missing. For example, there is no DMV coverage whatsoever of SQL Server Agent, which has a crude API. This makes it tedious to cull information about jobs and schedules. And there is no way to extend the DMVs by creating my own custom views—this was one of my initial questions when the first beta version of SQL Server 2005 arrived in my mailbox. It is also impossible to distinguish, by name alone, between DMVs and DMFs. When using SQL Server Management Studio in SQL Server 2008, and against a SQL Server 2008 instance, IntelliSense will help out a little bit here. The AutoComplete list uses an icon to indicate whether it is a view or a function. Without this hint, I have often queried a DMF without any parameters:

```
SELECT * FROM sys.dm_exec_sql_text;
```

That results in this error:

```
Msg 216, Level 16, State 1, Line 1
Parameters were not supplied for the function 'sys.dm_exec_sql_text'.
```

This ambiguous naming convention is not helpful to me; similar to the way the same column can have a different name from one system table to the next. This is not the most efficient aspect of my own personal work. It has become a pattern of trial and error for me. The AutoComplete list has accelerated my learning curve when working against SQL Server 2008. I could look at the catalog views to determine the type, but this is a hard habit to get into when writing code and stumbling upon new views and functions in SQL Server 2008.

In a few isolated cases, information that we used to see in system tables has not been carried over to the new DMV structure. I will mention one of these cases briefly when I talk about sys.dm_exec_sessions further on. Thankfully, there is a decent workaround, but I am surprised at this well-publicized omission. It was reported early in the SQL Server 2005 development cycle, and has not been corrected in SQL Server 2008.

I don't want to write an entire chapter about the background and underlying concepts behind DMVs. I urge you to peruse the Books Online documentation to learn more about them. The starting point in the documentation, which has both SQL Server 2005 and SQL Server 2008 branches, is at the following URL: http:// msdn.microsoft.com/en-us/library/ms188754.aspx.

What I want to do is to share with you my most-often used DMVs, and some of the neat things you can do with them. First I will list and explain the objects I will use, and then I will show you some sample code that I currently use in my own production environments. I will also indicate which objects are new in SQL Server 2008.

A brief list of my favorite DMVs and DMFs

Here is some background information on the views and functions that I will be using in sample code later in the chapter.

sys.dm_os_sys_info

The first DMV I want to mention is `sys.dm_os_sys_info`, because I use it in many places further on. This view makes it easy to gather data about the underlying system, such as the amount of physical memory installed, the number of CPUs, and the number of buffers in the buffer pool.

One of the important columns added in SQL Server 2008 is `sqlserver_start_time`, which is useful in determining how much information is there when querying DMVs (because, as previously discussed, all of the data is discarded when the instance is restarted). When I am using SQL Server 2005, an easy workaround is to grab the created date/time of the `tempdb` database, or the `login_time` of spid 1 from `sys.sysprocesses`, both of which are reliable and usually close enough.

sys.dm_exec_sessions, sys.dm_exec_requests, and sys.dm_exec_connections

`sys.dm_exec_sessions`, `sys.dm_exec_requests`, and `sys.dm_exec_connections` are a complex replacement for the old system table sysprocesses, the system procedure `sp_who`, and the famously undocumented and unsupported system procedure `sp_who2`.

`sys.dm_exec_sessions` returns "one row per authenticated session on SQL Server." Long-time DBAs can translate this to mean "one row per SPID." Note that what we used to call a SPID is now referred to throughout all of the DMVs as `session_id`. The information provided here includes login information, host name, program name, status, environment settings, and metrics such as CPU, memory, and I/O used by the session. An important column that has been left out of this view is `database_id`. We used to be able to get this information for all SPIDs in sysprocesses, but now it is not accessible if the `session_id` does not have an active request (in which case you can get the information from other DMVs). Because of this, I continue to have to rely on `sys.sysprocesses`, which is provided for backward compatibility but in my opinion is still an essential view.

`sys.dm_exec_requests` returns data for all of the requests currently active against the server. An important note here is that it is possible to have multiple rows for any given `session_id` (for example, when executing a query where the degree of parallelism (DOP) > 1). The data includes start time, status, type of command (for example,

SELECT), and database information, and provides hooks that make it possible to determine the query being executed (or object being called). The data also includes blocking information, environment settings in place when the request started, and the CPU, memory, and I/O required by the request. Finally, in some scenarios (for example, BACKUP DATABASE) the view exposes how far along the process is, and the estimated completion time. In SQL Server 2008, there is also a group_id column for Resource Governor information, and the same query_plan and query_plan_hash columns that were added to sys.dm_exec_query_text.

sys.dm_exec_connections provides details about each connection attached to SQL Server. This includes connection time, protocol information, authentication method, and IP address.

Note that sys.sysprocesses is still provided for backward compatibility purposes. As I mentioned before, this is a good thing—in certain scenarios, this is the only place where database context is provided.

I use these DMVs almost exclusively as a package deal to create stored procedures that allow me to provide relational data about specific things that are going on in my instances that would otherwise require a lot of digging. Later I will show my own version of sp_who, which is much richer than what is provided out of the box.

sys.dm_exec_sql_text

sys.dm_exec_sql_text returns a table containing the database ID, object ID, and text of the SQL query. It also returns the number for deprecated numbered procedures, and a BIT indicating whether the SQL text is encrypted. I use this to correlate information in the sessions, requests, and connections DMVs so I can see exactly what queries these requests are running. This function can be applied inline when pulling data from DMVs like sys.dm_exec_requests, unlike the old ways to get query text (DBCC INPUTBUFFER or ::fn_get_sql()).

sys.dm_exec_query_stats

sys.dm_exec_query_stats returns a row for every query plan in the cache. I use this to find the queries that are being recompiled the most, and also to find inefficient query plans. The DMV returns information including the last compile time, number of times the query has been compiled, and various metrics about each plan including execution counts, physical and logical I/O, and minimum, maximum, and total elapsed times. In SQL Server 2008, two new columns were added. These are query_hash and query_plan_hash, which make it easier to aggregate queries with similar (but not identical) execution plans.

sys.dm_exec_procedure_stats

sys.dm_exec_procedure_stats contains a large number of metrics about all stored procedures that currently have plans in the cache. Like sys.dm_exec_query_stats, there are details about execution counts, I/O, and elapsed time. I use it to determine which of my stored procedures are running long, or to capture trends about stored procedures that are being executed more frequently. Prior to SQL Server 2008, this information wasn't readily available except via a SQL trace, or through custom logging inside each stored procedure or in the applications that call them. There is another companion DMV called `sys.dm_exec_trigger_stats`, but because I am not a big trigger user, it is less useful to me. I am hoping that in a future version they add another DMV, `sys.dm_exec_function_stats`. Then we will be able to better monitor the usage and efficiency of those objects.

sys.dm_db_index_usage_stats

This view returns the count and last occurrence of user (and system) seeks, scans, lookups, and updates. I use this to find indexes which are not very useful, for example where writes far outweigh reads. By comparing the number of reads to the number of writes, I can easily see where some indexes are being overtaxed or underutilized.

sys.dm_db_missing_index_details, sys.dm_db_missing_index_groups, and sys.dm_db_missing_index_group_stats

`sys.dm_db_missing_index_details`, `sys.dm_db_missing_index_groups`, and `sys.dm_db_missing_index_group_stats` allow to me find out which indexes might have been useful if they existed. By doing the work of the Database Engine Tuning Advisor (DETA) behind the scenes, the views let me quickly see where and how seeks or index scans could have improved queries that previously had to perform table scans due to the lack of an index. The recommendations here are not always stellar (for example, they are overly fond of using included columns), but they can provide a good starting point.

Honorable mentions

I didn't want to ignore a few objects that I use often. Due to limited space, I couldn't demonstrate queries for all of them. I urge you to investigate these and other objects on your own to get a better understanding of how they can make your database work easier.

sys.dm_os_performance_counters

Indispensable when troubleshooting, `sys.dm_os_performance_counters` allows me to gather various SQL-related performance counters in a relational format (note that you cannot query this DMV for counters that are not SQL-related). From Page Life Expectancy, to Logins per Second, to Lock Timeouts, to Cache Hit Ratios, it's all there, and much easier to consume and correlate than with a separate Performance Monitor session or log file.

sys.dm_db_partition_stats

Before SQL Server 2005, I had to rely on the system table `sysindexes` to determine the size and number of rows of a table, and had to be sure to run `DBCC UPDATEUSAGE` with `COUNT_ROWS` first; otherwise, acknowledge that the information may not be 100 percent accurate. Now `sys.dm_db_partition_stats` can tell me—accurately, and across all databases in my instance—which tables have the most rows, what is the number of pages, and how much LOB and other data is being stored off-row. This sure beats using the undocumented and unsupported `sp_msForEachDatabase` and `sp_msForEachTable` procedures to execute `sp_spaceused` for each database and table, and trying to collate the results myself.

sys.dm_db_index_physical_stats

This table-valued DMF provides physical information about each index and partition in a table. For each b-tree level, `IN_ROW_DATA` allocation unit, `LOB_DATA` allocation unit and `ROW_OVERFLOW_DATA` allocation unit in each partition, a row is returned that includes the index and allocation unit type, fragment counts and sizes, average fragmentation percentage, page count, and row count. I use this view to obtain a picture of indexes that are candidates for rebuilding or reorganizing. This is slightly better than an educated guess, less work than running `DBCC SHOWCONTIG` over and over again, and much better than blindly running maintenance against all indexes on a fixed schedule. I have used various adaptations of Ola Hallengren's index optimization scripts. They are located here, and are definitely worth some investigation: http://ola.hallengren.com/.

When composing this topic, I was asked the question, why is this DMF better than using `DBCC SHOWCONTIG`, given that they produce the same results? Well, for one, it is easier to apply a `WHERE` clause to the DMV, to limit the output to a set of tables without having to make multiple calls (or parse the verbose output to find the tables of interest). I can also use the DMV in a query that includes other tables or views. I can easily join against, say, `sys.dm_db_partition_stats` to get the row counts, and `sys.indexes` to get the index name and other details. The query in listing 1 demonstrates this.

> **Listing 1 Sample query against `sys.dm_db_index_physical_stats`**

```
SELECT TOP 10
    [object_name] = OBJECT_NAME(s.[object_id]),
    index_name = i.name,
    i.is_primary_key,
    i.is_unique_constraint,
    s.partition_number,
    s.index_type_desc,
    s.alloc_unit_type_desc,
    s.avg_fragmentation_in_percent,
    s.page_count,
    p.reserved_page_count,
    p.row_count
```

```
FROM
    sys.dm_db_index_physical_stats
    (
        DB_ID(), NULL, NULL, NULL, NULL
    ) AS s
INNER JOIN
    sys.dm_db_partition_stats AS p
ON
    s.[object_id] = p.[object_id]
    AND s.partition_number = p.partition_number
    AND s.index_id = p.index_id
INNER JOIN
    sys.indexes i
ON
    s.[object_id] = i.[object_id]
    AND s.index_id = i.index_id
WHERE
  OBJECT_NAME(s.[object_id]) LIKE 'pattern%'
ORDER BY
    OBJECT_NAME(s.[object_id]),
    s.index_id;
```

Try doing all of that with DBCC SHOWCONTIG.

sys.dm_sql_referenced_entities

sys.dm_sql_referenced_entities (and its companion, sys.dm_sql_referencing_ entities) should make dependency tracking in SQL Server 2008 much better, by maintaining information about references between objects in a more reliable way than sysdepends did. A few MVPs have found some bugs in these views, but I wrote a lengthy article about helping to automate dependency tracking slightly more accurately than the engine currently does on its own, using the new catalog view sys.sql_expression_dependencies. This was also introduced in SQL Server 2008: http://sqlblog.com/blogs/aaron_bertrand/archive/2008/09/09/keeping-sysdepends -up-to-date-in-sql-server-2008.aspx.

Setting up a utility database

Before I get started with some code, I'd like to get a few maintenance tasks out of the way. I usually create a utility database for generic stored procedures and functions. Many of the stored procedures I use on my own systems are system-wide and do not need to run in the context of any specific database. (There are exceptions. Other procedures I create further on do need to be created within each database.)

One of the things I do a *lot* for reporting purposes is to construct a two- or three-part name (schema.object or database.schema.object). Typically I would do this as follows (at least in SQL Server 2005 SP2 and above), given an @object_id in the current database:

```
SELECT ThreePartName = QUOTENAME(DB_NAME(DB_ID())) + '.'
    + QUOTENAME(OBJECT_SCHEMA_NAME(@object_id, DB_ID()))
    + QUOTENAME(OBJECT_NAME(@object_id, DB_ID()));
```

Because this can become quite tedious, I create two user-defined functions in my utility database, dbo.AB_GetTwoPartName() and dbo.AB_GetThreePartName(), to perform this work for me.

Another function I create in my utility databases is dbo.AB_Uptime(), which returns the start time of the SQL Server service and number of minutes the instance has been running. Note that I have not tried this on a server that has been running for 4,000 years, which would overflow the INT return value of the DATEDIFF() function. In SQL Server 2008 I use sys.dm_os_sys_info, but in SQL Server 2005, I must use other workarounds. You can use the SQL Server 2005 version of the function I include below if you are happy enough with using tempdb as your start time indicator. You could also parse the error logs or keep your own log using a startup procedure.

And finally, because I am looking at the results of sys.dm_exec_sql_text() often, and because extracting the relevant statement in the output is complex when the object is a stored procedure or function (because it includes the text for the entire object), I bury this logic in the utility database, in a function called dbo.AB_ParseSQLText(). Believe me, the logic looks much more complex in an already complicated query, when using columns like statement_start_offset instead of simple INT parameters. You can see this code in listing 2.

Listing 2 Creating a utility database

```
IF DB_ID(N'AB_Utility') IS NULL
    CREATE DATABASE AB_Utility;
GO
USE AB_Utility;
GO
IF OBJECT_ID(N'dbo.AB_GetThreePartName', N'FN') IS NOT NULL
    DROP FUNCTION dbo.AB_GetThreePartName;
GO
CREATE FUNCTION dbo.AB_GetThreePartName
(
    @object_id INT,
    @database_id INT
)
RETURNS NVARCHAR(1000)
AS
BEGIN
    RETURN (QUOTENAME(DB_NAME(@database_id)) + '.'
        + QUOTENAME(OBJECT_SCHEMA_NAME(@object_id, @database_id))
        + '.' + QUOTENAME(OBJECT_NAME(@object_id, @database_id)));
END
GO
IF OBJECT_ID(N'dbo.AB_GetTwoPartName', N'FN') IS NOT NULL
    DROP FUNCTION dbo.AB_GetTwoPartName;
GO
CREATE FUNCTION dbo.AB_GetTwoPartName
(
    @object_id INT,
    @database_id INT
)
```

```
RETURNS NVARCHAR(1000)
AS
BEGIN
  RETURN (QUOTENAME(OBJECT_SCHEMA_NAME(@object_id, @database_id))
    + '.' + QUOTENAME(OBJECT_NAME(@object_id, @database_id)));
END
GO
IF OBJECT_ID(N'dbo.AB_Uptime', N'IF') IS NOT NULL
    DROP FUNCTION dbo.AB_Uptime;
GO

/* -- you should uncomment one of these functions
    -- depending on the version of your instance:

-- SQL Server 2008 :

CREATE FUNCTION dbo.AB_Uptime()
RETURNS TABLE
AS
RETURN
(
  SELECT
    sqlserver_start_time,
    uptime = DATEDIFF(MINUTE, sqlserver_start_time, CURRENT_TIMESTAMP)
  FROM
    sys.dm_os_sys_info
);

-- SQL Server 2005:

CREATE FUNCTION dbo.AB_Uptime()
RETURNS TABLE
AS
RETURN
(
  SELECT
    sqlserver_start_time = create_date,
    uptime = DATEDIFF(MINUTE, create_date, CURRENT_TIMESTAMP)
  FROM
    sys.databases
  WHERE
    name = 'tempdb'
);

*/

IF OBJECT_ID(N'dbo.AB_ParseSQLText', N'FN') IS NOT NULL
    DROP FUNCTION dbo.AB_ParseSQLText;
GO
CREATE FUNCTION dbo.AB_ParseSQLText
(
    @text  NVARCHAR(MAX),
    @start INT,
    @end   INT
)
RETURNS NVARCHAR(MAX)
AS
BEGIN
```

```
    RETURN
    (
      SELECT COALESCE
      (
        SUBSTRING
        (
          @text,
          @start / 2 + 1,
          (CASE WHEN @end = -1
                THEN (DATALENGTH(@text))
                ELSE @end
           END - @start)/2 + 1
        ),
        N''
      )
    );
END
GO
```

Now that I have my underlying utility functions set up, I can get on with generating some interesting code for you to use on your own systems.

Some interesting applications of my favorite DMVs

In this section, I'll show you a number of ways you can use the DMVs I've covered above, beginning with a more refined version of sp_who.

A more refined sp_who or sp_who2

We've all used sp_who or sp_who2 at some point; however, I often find myself digging deeper and handcrafting queries myself, either to obtain more information than the procedures provide, or to whittle down the rows. This way, I can focus on the most important activity at the time. Both sp_who and sp_who2 provide a parameter @loginame, which enables you to pull activity for a specific session_id, or for a specific login, or for all active queries (those that are not sleeping, awaiting command, lazy writer, or checkpoint sleep). But I often want to search on other parameters (such as database name or a pattern match on the command) or limit the result set to only those sessions that are blocking or being blocked. The following procedure is a bit lengthy, and tries for the most part to mimic sp_who and sp_who2, but hopefully the code (and the sample calls that follow) will give you some ideas about how to write your own enhanced routines that allow you to dig into an issue without having to try too hard. An example of this is shown in listing 3.

Listing 3   An sp_who2 replacement

```
USE AB_Utility;
GO
IF OBJECT_ID(N'dbo.AB_who', 'P') IS NOT NULL
    DROP PROCEDURE dbo.AB_who;
GO
CREATE PROCEDURE [dbo].[AB_who]
```

```
      @loginame              SYSNAME = NULL,
      @ShowBlockersOnly         BIT = 0,
      @ShowSystemSpids          BIT = 0,
      @SearchDBName          NVARCHAR(255) = N'%',
      @SearchHostName         VARCHAR(255)  = N'%',
      @SearchCommand         NVARCHAR(255) = N'%'
AS
BEGIN
  SET NOCOUNT ON;

  WITH list AS
  (
    SELECT
      SPID = s.session_id,
      BlockedBy = NULLIF(r.blocking_session_id, 0),
      [database] = DB_NAME(COALESCE(r.database_id, sp.[dbid])),
      [host_name] = COALESCE(s.[host_name], ''),
      ip_address = COALESCE(c.client_net_address, ''),
      [program_name] = COALESCE(s.[program_name], ''),
      login_name = COALESCE(UPPER(s.login_name), ''),
      [status] = UPPER(COALESCE(r.[status], s.[status])),
      command = UPPER(COALESCE(r.command, '')),
      logical_reads = COALESCE(r.logical_reads, s.logical_reads),
      num_reads = COALESCE(r.reads, c.num_reads),
      num_writes = COALESCE(r.writes, c.num_writes),
      cpu_time = COALESCE(r.cpu_time, s.total_scheduled_time),
      row_count = COALESCE(r.row_count, s.row_count),
      memory_in_pages = COALESCE(r.granted_query_memory,
        s.memory_usage),
      s.login_time,
      last_request_start_time = COALESCE(
        r.start_time, s.last_request_start_time),
      request_active = CASE
        WHEN UPPER(s.[status]) IN
            ('SLEEPING', 'BACKGROUND')
        THEN 0
        ELSE 1
        END,
      wait_type = COALESCE(r.wait_type, r.last_wait_type, ''),
      exec_sql = CASE
        WHEN qs.[sql_handle] IS NULL
        THEN COALESCE(est.[text], '')
        ELSE ''
        END,
      exec_object = COALESCE(AB_Utility.dbo.AB_GetThreePartName(
        est.objectid, est.[dbid]), ''),
       exec_statement = AB_Utility.dbo.AB_ParseSQLText(est.[text],
            qs.statement_start_offset, qs.statement_end_offset)
    FROM
      sys.dm_exec_sessions AS s
    LEFT OUTER JOIN
      sys.sysprocesses AS sp
      ON s.session_id = sp.spid
    LEFT OUTER JOIN
      sys.dm_exec_requests AS r
```

```
    ON s.session_id = r.session_id
LEFT OUTER JOIN
  sys.dm_exec_connections AS c
  ON s.session_id = c.session_id
LEFT OUTER JOIN
  sys.dm_exec_query_stats AS qs
  ON qs.[sql_handle] = COALESCE(
    r.[sql_handle], c.most_recent_sql_handle)
OUTER APPLY
  sys.dm_exec_sql_text(COALESCE(
    r.[sql_handle], c.most_recent_sql_handle,
    qs.[sql_handle])) AS est
)
SELECT
  *
FROM
  list
WHERE
  SPID = CASE
    WHEN @loginame LIKE '[0-9]%'
    THEN CONVERT(INT, @loginame)
    ELSE SPID
  END
  AND SPID > CASE
    WHEN @ShowSystemSpids = 1
    THEN 0
    ELSE 50
  END
  AND login_name = CASE
    WHEN @loginame LIKE '[^0-9]%'
    AND UPPER(@loginame) <> 'ACTIVE'
    THEN UPPER(@loginame)
    ELSE login_name
  END
  AND request_active = CASE
    WHEN UPPER(@loginame) = 'ACTIVE'
    THEN 1
    ELSE request_active
  END
  AND UPPER([database])    LIKE UPPER(@SearchDBName)
  AND UPPER([host_name])    LIKE UPPER(@SearchHostName)
      AND
      (
        UPPER(exec_statement)    LIKE UPPER(@SearchCommand)
    OR UPPER(exec_object)    LIKE UPPER(@SearchCommand)
    OR UPPER(exec_sql)    LIKE UPPER(@SearchCommand)
  )
  AND
  (
    EXISTS
    (
      SELECT 1
        FROM list b1
              WHERE b1.BlockedBy = CASE
          WHEN @ShowBlockersOnly = 1
```

```
                  THEN list.SPID
                  ELSE b1.BlockedBy
                END
            )
          OR ISNUMERIC(CASE
            WHEN @ShowBlockersOnly = 1
            THEN BlockedBy
            ELSE '1'
          END) = 1
          )
      ORDER BY
        SPID;
END
GO
-- capture only those sessions that are actively running queries
EXEC AB_Utility.dbo.AB_who active;
-- capture only those sessions logged in as sa
EXEC AB_Utility.dbo.AB_who N'sa';
-- capture only spid 55
EXEC AB_Utility.dbo.AB_who 55;
-- capture only those blocking or being blocked
EXEC AB_Utility.dbo.AB_who @ShowBlockersOnly = 1;
-- include system spids
EXEC AB_Utility.dbo.AB_who @ShowSystemSpids = 1;
-- capture only those in the database AB_Utility
EXEC AB_Utility.dbo.AB_who @SearchDBName = 'AB_Utility';
-- capture only those running from the host machine "GREENLANTERN"
EXEC AB_Utility.dbo.AB_who @SearchHostName = 'GREENLANTERN';
-- capture only those running this procedure
EXEC AB_Utility.dbo.AB_who @SearchCommand = '%ab_who%';
```

Getting statistics for stored procedures (SQL Server 2008 only)

You can use the table-valued function in listing 4 to find all of the stored procedures that are being called frequently, or are taking a long time, or both.

Listing 4   Table-valued function for procedure statistics

```
USE AB_Utility;
GO
IF OBJECT_ID(N'dbo.AB_GetProcedureStats', N'IF') IS NOT NULL
    DROP FUNCTION dbo.AB_GetProcedureStats;
GO
CREATE FUNCTION dbo.AB_GetProcedureStats
(
    @database_name SYSNAME
)
RETURNS TABLE
AS
RETURN
(
    SELECT
        [name] = AB_Utility.dbo.AB_GetThreePartName
         (p.[object_id], p.[database_id]),
        u.sqlserver_start_time,
```

```
        uptime_minutes = u.uptime,
        p.execution_count,
            executions_per_minute = CONVERT(DECIMAL(15,2),
              (p.execution_count * 1.0 / u.uptime)),
        max_time_milliseconds = p.max_elapsed_time / 1000,
        avg_time_milliseconds = CONVERT(DECIMAL(15,2),
            ((1.0 * p.total_elapsed_time / 1000) / p.execution_count))
    FROM
        sys.dm_exec_procedure_stats AS p
    CROSS JOIN
        AB_Utility.dbo.AB_Uptime() AS u
    WHERE
        p.[database_id] = (COALESCE(DB_ID(@database_name),
        p.[database_id]))
        AND p.[database_id] <> 32767 -- resource database
);
GO
```

If you want to only return procedures that have executed at least 50 times, or only want to include those that take an average of 75 milliseconds or more, you can easily add those filters to the WHERE clause:

```
SELECT *
FROM dbo.AB_GetProcedureStats('msdb')
WHERE execution_count >= 50
-- WHERE avg_time_milliseconds >= 75
ORDER BY avg_time_milliseconds DESC;
```

Finding unused stored procedures (SQL Server 2008 only)

I often see the question, "How do I tell which stored procedures are not being used?" You can determine which procedures in a database have not been used recently by checking those that are not represented in sys.dm_exec_procedure_stats. Take note that there are no guarantees here. If you want to be certain, you should use auditing or your own logging methods to determine stored procedure usage. One common problem is that there are stored procedures that are run for monthly or annual reports, and sometimes these haven't been run since the last time SQL Server was started. Try to make sure that your uptime covers a full business cycle. This can still give you a decent starting list of under-utilized procedures, especially if SQL Server has been running for a long time.

Because this procedure needs to pull data directly from database-specific catalog view sys.procedures, you will need to create it in each database where you want to use it. This is a common scenario, and when I am setting up a new SQL Server instance, I typically create copies of all such utility-related objects in the model database. This way, I know they will be available in all user databases created from that point on. The procedure is shown in listing 5.

Listing 5   Finding unused stored procedures

```
USE [your_database];
GO
IF OBJECT_ID('dbo.AB_GetUnusedProcedures', N'P') IS NOT NULL
    DROP PROCEDURE dbo.AB_GetUnusedProcedures;
GO
CREATE PROCEDURE dbo.AB_GetUnusedProcedures
AS
BEGIN
    SET NOCOUNT ON;

    SELECT
        'These procedures have not been executed in the past '
        + RTRIM(uptime) + ' minutes (the last time SQL started)',
        sqlserver_start_time
    FROM
        AB_Utility.dbo.AB_Uptime();

    SELECT
        [name] = AB_Utility.dbo.AB_GetTwoPartName
         (p.[object_id], DB_ID()),
        p.create_date,
        p.modify_date
    FROM
        sys.procedures AS p
    LEFT OUTER JOIN
        sys.dm_exec_procedure_stats AS ps
    ON
        p.[object_id] = ps.[object_id]
    WHERE
        ps.[object_id] IS NULL
    ORDER BY
        p.[Name];
END
GO
```

If you want to avoid creating this object in each user database, you can create it in the master database so that it can be called from any user database with the original database context. Note that you must change the prefix to sp_ in order to use this method. For example, you would change the code from listing 5 to the code in listing 6. Note that I also changed the [name] function to return a three-part name; therefore, you can be sure it is being called from the right place.

Listing 6   Making a system stored procedure

```
USE [master];
GO
IF OBJECT_ID('dbo.sp_AB_GetUnusedProcedures', N'P') IS NOT NULL
    DROP PROCEDURE dbo.sp_AB_GetUnusedProcedures;
GO
CREATE PROCEDURE dbo.sp_AB_GetUnusedProcedures
AS
BEGIN
    SET NOCOUNT ON;
```

```
SELECT
    'These procedures have not been executed in the past '
    + RTRIM(uptime) + ' minutes (the last time SQL started)',
    sqlserver_start_time
FROM
    AB_Utility.dbo.AB_Uptime();

SELECT
    [name] = AB_Utility.dbo.AB_GetThreePartName
     (p.[object_id], DB_ID()),
    p.create_date,
    p.modify_date
FROM
    sys.procedures AS p
LEFT OUTER JOIN
    sys.dm_exec_procedure_stats AS ps
ON
    p.[object_id] = ps.[object_id]
WHERE
    ps.[object_id] IS NULL
ORDER BY
    p.[Name];
END
GO
EXEC dbo.sp_MS_marksystemobject N'dbo.sp_AB_GetUnusedProcedures';
GO
USE [your_database];
GO
EXEC dbo.sp_AB_GetUnusedProcedures;
GO
```

WARNING Although creating objects in the master database has been a relatively safe and well-known method for years, please proceed with the understanding that you may need to change it later. It is not documented, not supported, and likely to cease working in some future version of SQL Server. The main problem with using undocumented methods is that Microsoft does not need to warn you before they change or remove the functionality; therefore, your next upgrade might end up being a lot more work than you thought.

Finding inefficient and unused indexes

The following query will help you identify indexes in your database that are not used at all, or are used more during maintenance operations than for improving query performance. As with the query to find unused procedures, what you do with this information will rely heavily on how long SQL Server has been up and running. If you restarted SQL Server this morning, then these statistics may not yet represent an adequate sample of your workload. And as with the unused procedure code, you will need to create this object in each relevant database, because it returns metadata from the local catalog view `sys.indexes`. (If you want to use the system object technique, the changes to the code are similarly simple.) This code is shown in listing 7.

Listing 7 Measuring the usefulness of indexes

```
USE [your_database];
GO
IF OBJECT_ID('dbo.AB_MeasureIndexUsefulness', N'P') IS NOT NULL
    DROP PROCEDURE dbo.AB_MeasureIndexUsefulness;
GO
CREATE PROCEDURE dbo.AB_MeasureIndexUsefulness
AS
BEGIN
    SET NOCOUNT ON;

    SELECT 'These indexes have collected statistics for the past '
        + RTRIM(uptime) + ' minutes (the last time SQL started)',
        sqlserver_start_time
    FROM
        AB_Utility.dbo.AB_Uptime();

    WITH calced AS
    (
        SELECT
            [object_id],
            index_id,
            reads = user_seeks + user_scans + user_lookups,
            writes = user_updates,
            perc = CONVERT(DECIMAL(10,2), user_updates * 100.0 /
                    (user_seeks + user_scans + user_lookups + user_updates))
        FROM
            sys.dm_db_index_usage_stats
        WHERE
            database_id = DB_ID()
    )
    SELECT
        [status] = CASE
            WHEN reads = 0 AND writes = 0 THEN
                'Consider dropping : not used at all'
            WHEN reads = 0 AND writes > 0 THEN
                'Consider dropping : only writes'
            WHEN writes > reads THEN
                'Consider dropping : more writes (' +
                    RTRIM(perc) + '% of activity)'
            WHEN reads = writes THEN
                'Reads and writes equal'
        END,
        [table] = AB_Utility.dbo.AB_GetTwoPartName(
                c.[object_id], DB_ID()),
        [index] = i.Name,
        c.reads,
        c.writes
    FROM
        calced AS c
    INNER JOIN
        sys.indexes AS i
    ON
        c.[object_id] = i.[object_id]
```

```
            AND c.index_id = i.index_id
        WHERE
            c.writes >= c.reads;
END
GO
```

Note that because the read and write metrics are per operation, not per row, a DML operation that affects 100 rows will only count as one user update in this view.

Finding inefficient queries

The table-valued function in listing 8 will return the top *n* queries, ordered in descending order by longest average CPU time, longest average elapsed time, highest average reads, highest logical reads, highest writes, or highest number of executions. Because this one query does not rely on database-specific catalog views, it can be created in the utility database and called from anywhere (passing database name, number of rows, and ordering preference). You can also add a WHERE clause to restrict the result set to objects matching a certain naming pattern or queries that executed at least *n* times.

Listing 8   Finding inefficient queries

```
USE AB_Utility;
GO
IF OBJECT_ID(N'dbo.AB_GetInefficientQueries', N'IF') IS NOT NULL
    DROP FUNCTION dbo.AB_GetInefficientQueries;
GO
CREATE FUNCTION dbo.AB_GetInefficientQueries
(
    @database_name      SYSNAME,
    @number_of_rows    INT,
    @order_by          VARCHAR(15)
)
RETURNS TABLE
AS
RETURN
(
  SELECT TOP (@number_of_rows) * FROM
  (
    SELECT
      exec_object = AB_Utility.dbo.AB_GetTwoPartName(
        est.objectid, est.[dbid]),
      exec_statement = AB_Utility.dbo.AB_ParseSQLText(est.[text],
        qs.statement_start_offset, qs.statement_end_offset ),
      u.sqlserver_start_time,
      uptime_minutes = u.uptime,
      execution_count,
      first_execution_time = qs.creation_time,
      qs.last_execution_time,
      avg_cpu_time_milliseconds
        = qs.total_worker_time / (1000 * qs.execution_count),
      avg_logical_reads
        = qs.total_logical_reads / qs.execution_count,
```

```
      avg_physical_reads
        = qs.total_physical_reads / qs.execution_count,
      avg_writes
        = qs.total_logical_writes / qs.execution_count,
      avg_elapsed_time_milliseconds
        = qs.total_elapsed_time / (1000 * qs.execution_count)
    FROM
      sys.dm_exec_query_stats AS qs
    CROSS APPLY
      sys.dm_exec_sql_text(qs.[sql_handle]) AS est
    CROSS JOIN
      AB_Utility.dbo.AB_Uptime() AS u
    WHERE
      est.[dbid] = DB_ID(@database_name)
  ) x
  ORDER BY CASE @order_by
    WHEN 'cpu time'      THEN avg_cpu_time_milliseconds
    WHEN 'logical reads'    THEN avg_logical_reads
    WHEN 'physical reads'     THEN avg_physical_reads
    WHEN 'writes'         THEN avg_writes
    WHEN 'elapsed time'     THEN avg_elapsed_time_milliseconds
    WHEN 'executions'    THEN execution_count
    END DESC,
    exec_object
);
GO
USE [tempdb];
GO
SELECT *
FROM AB_Utility.dbo.AB_GetInefficientQueries
(
    'msdb',
    50,
    'cpu time'
)
-- WHERE exec_object NOT LIKE '%sp_get_composite_job_info%'
-- WHERE execution_count >= 50;
```

Finding missing indexes

Starting with SQL Server 2005, the database engine started keeping track of indexes that the optimizer would have taken advantage of, if they existed. The missing index DMVs should be used only as a guide, and not as the final authority on how you should change your index structures. (As with other DMVs, the data does not persist between restarts. Also, be careful about relying on data for tables with indexes that have changed recently, as this can also clear out missing index information.) The function in listing 9 will return a slightly more useful output structure to help you determine which tables and indexes you should further investigate for fine tuning. This includes information about how long SQL Server has been up, when the last user seek or scan was for that specific query (because it may represent an ad hoc query outside of your normal workload), and the CREATE INDEX DDL if you wanted to follow through with the suggestion. To use the function, you pass in the database name and the number of rows you want to return.

Listing 9 Finding missing indexes

```
USE AB_Utility;
GO
IF OBJECT_ID(N'dbo.AB_GetMissingIndexes', N'IF') IS NOT NULL
    DROP FUNCTION dbo.AB_GetMissingIndexes
GO
CREATE FUNCTION dbo.AB_GetMissingIndexes
(
    @database_name  SYSNAME,
    @number_of_rows INT
)
RETURNS TABLE
AS
RETURN
(
    SELECT TOP (@number_of_rows)
       *,
       -- must give credit to Tibor Karazsi here:
       [statement] = 'CREATE INDEX [<<index name>>]'
         + ' ON ' + [table] + ' ('
         + COALESCE(eq + COALESCE(', ' + iq, ''), iq)
         + ')' + COALESCE(' INCLUDE(' + ic + ');', ';')
    FROM
    (
      SELECT
        [table] = AB_Utility.dbo.AB_GetTwoPartName(
          d.[object_id], d.database_id),
        eq = d.equality_columns,
        iq = d.inequality_columns,
        ic = d.included_columns,
        relative_benefit = (s.user_seeks + s.user_scans)
          * (s.avg_total_user_cost * s.avg_user_impact),
        s.user_seeks,
        s.user_scans,
        s.last_user_seek,
        s.last_user_scan
      FROM
        sys.dm_db_missing_index_details AS d
      INNER JOIN
        sys.dm_db_missing_index_groups AS g
        ON d.index_handle = g.index_handle
      INNER JOIN
        sys.dm_db_missing_index_group_stats AS s
        ON g.index_group_handle = s.group_handle
      WHERE
        d.database_id = DB_ID(@database_name)
    ) x
    CROSS JOIN AB_Utility.dbo.AB_Uptime()
    ORDER BY relative_benefit DESC
);
```

```
GO
SELECT *
FROM AB_Utility.dbo.AB_GetMissingIndexes
(
    'Org00010001',
    50
);
```

DMV categories in SQL Server

Table 1 lists the DMV categories in both SQL Server 2005 and SQL Server 2008. Table 2 lists the new DMV categories in SQL Server 2008.

Table 1   DMV categories in SQL Server 2005 and 2008

DMV category	DMVs	URL for more information
Common Language Runtime (CLR)	`sys.dm_clr_*`	http://msdn.microsoft.com/en-us/library/ms179982.aspx
Database	`sys.dm_db_*`	http://msdn.microsoft.com/en-us/library/ms181626.aspx
Database mirroring	`sys.dm_db_mirroring_*`	http://msdn.microsoft.com/en-us/library/ms173571.aspx
Execution	`sys.dm_exec_*`	http://msdn.microsoft.com/en-us/library/ms188068.aspx
Full-text search	`sys.dm_fts_*`	http://msdn.microsoft.com/en-us/library/ms174971.aspx
Indexes	`sys.dm_db[_missing|_index_*`	http://msdn.microsoft.com/en-us/library/ms187974.aspx
Input/output (I/O)	`sys.dm_io_*`	http://msdn.microsoft.com/en-us/library/ms190314.aspx
Query notifications	`sys.dm_qn_*`	http://msdn.microsoft.com/en-us/library/ms187407.aspx
Replication	`sys.dm_repl_*`	http://msdn.microsoft.com/en-us/library/ms176053.aspx
Service broker	`sys.dm_broker_*`	http://msdn.microsoft.com/en-us/library/ms176110.aspx
SQL Server operating system	`sys.dm_os_*`	http://msdn.microsoft.com/en-us/library/ms176083.aspx
Transactions	`sys.dm_tran_*`	http://msdn.microsoft.com/en-us/library/ms178621.aspx

Table 2   New DMV categories in SQL Server 2008

	DMV	URL
Change data capture	`sys.dm_cdc_*`	http://msdn.microsoft.com/ en-us/library/bb522478.aspx
Extended events	`sys.dm_xe_*`	http://msdn.microsoft.com/ en-us/library/bb677293.aspx
Object (dependency)	`sys.dm_sql_*`	http://msdn.microsoft.com/ en-us/library/bb630390.aspx
Resource governor	`sys.dm_resource_governor_*`	http://msdn.microsoft.com/ en-us/library/bb934218.aspx
Security	`sys.dm_[audit|cryptographic|etc]_*`	http://msdn.microsoft.com/ en-us/library/bb677257.aspx

Summary

Gone are the days of running DBCC commands and system stored procedures over and over again, and keeping links to Profiler and Performance Monitor on every machine's desktop, when trying to peek into the usage characteristics of our SQL Server instances. I hope I have provided a glimpse of how much power we have been given through DMVs and DMFs, and that I have inspired you to use them more often when observing usage or troubleshooting performance issues.

About the author

Aaron Bertrand is the Senior Data Architect at One to One Interactive, a global marketing agency headquartered in Boston, Massachusetts. At One to One, Aaron is responsible for database design and application architecture. Due to his commitment to the community, shown through blogging at http://www.sql-blog.com, peer-to-peer support on forums and newsgroups, and speaking at user group meetings and code camps, he has been awarded as a Microsoft MVP since 1998. Aaron recently published a technical white paper for Microsoft, detailing how to use the new Resource Governor feature in SQL Server 2008.

30 Reusing space in a table

Joe Webb

People who have switched to Microsoft SQL Server from Microsoft Access sometimes ask, "If I delete a bunch of rows, do I need to compact my SQL Server database?"

It's been many years since I've used Access, but I still remember the reason for their concern. Access would continually add rows to the end of the table. If some, or even all, of the rows were deleted from the table, Access wouldn't reuse the space. It kept adding rows to the end of the table and never backfilled the *holes*. Compacting the Access database file would get rid of the holes.

Understanding how SQL Server automatically reuses table space

I'm not an expert in Access, and I'm certainly not knocking it. I haven't even used Access since v2.0 back in the 1990s. This behavior may have changed since then, or perhaps I misremember, but suffice it to say that with SQL Server this is not an issue. But don't take my word for it. Let's consider an example to prove the point.

To set up the example, let's create a table with three columns and then populate it with test data. The T-SQL code for doing this is shown in listing 1.

Listing 1   Creating and populating the dbo.Test table

```
USE tempdb ;
GO

--create a test table
CREATE TABLE dbo.Test
        (
         col1 INT
        ,col2 CHAR(25)
        ,col3 VARCHAR(4000)
        ) ;

--create some test data
DECLARE @cnt INT ;
SET @cnt = 0 ;
```

```
WHILE @cnt < 1000
        BEGIN
            SELECT
                @cnt = @cnt + 1 ;
            INSERT
                dbo.Test ( col1,col2,col3 )
            VALUES
                (
                 @cnt
                ,'test row # ' + CAST(@cnt AS VARCHAR(10)) + 'A'
                ,REPLICATE('ABCD', ROUND(RAND() * @cnt, 0))
                ) ;
        END
```

The CREATE TABLE statement creates a table called Test as part of the dbo schema in the tempdb database. The table is composed of three columns. The first is an integer, the second is a fixed length character string that contains 25 characters, and the third and final column is a variable length character string that can contain up to 1900 characters.

To add test data, we will use a simple INSERT statement. The INSERT statement has been placed inside a WHILE loop and is executed 1,000 times. Note that the last column in the table will vary in length from zero to a maximum of 4,000. Statistically, it should average around 1,000 characters.

Let's view the contents of the table to make sure we have what we think we have. We can do this by running a SELECT statement to retrieve the data, as shown in listing 2. The results of the query are shown in figure 1.

Listing 2   Querying the dbo.Test table

```
--view the table
SELECT
        *
FROM
        dbo.Test ;
```

To examine the amount of space the table consumes, we'll use a Dynamic Management View (DMV) called sys.dm_db_index_physical_stats. DMVs were first introduced in SQL Server 2005 and have been continued in SQL Server 2008. (For more on DMVs, see chapter 29, "My favorite DMVs, and why," by Aaron Bertrand.)

NOTE   The scripts that make use of DMVs will not work in SQL Server 2000.

The query in listing 3 returns a single row of data with four columns—the allocation unit type, the page count, the average page space used as a percentage, and the total

	col1	col2	col3
1	1	test row # 1A	ABCD
2	2	test row # 2A	ABCDABCD
3	3	test row # 3A	ABCDABCDABCD
4	4	test row # 4A	ABCDABCD
5	5	test row # 5A	ABCDABCD
6	6	test row # 6A	ABCDABCDABCDABCDABCDABCD
7	7	test row # 7A	ABCDABCDABCDABCD

Figure 1   Results from dbo.Test table

number of rows in the dbo.Test table. The alloc_unit_type_desc column describes the allocation unit type: valid values are IN_ROW_DATA, LOB_DATA, or ROW_OVERFLOW_DATA (see Books Online for a detailed explanation of these terms). The page_count column indicates the total number of data pages used by the table for IN_ROW_DATA (that is, the allocation unit that stores the table rows in our example). The avg_page_space_used_in_percent column reports the average percentage of space used in all data pages in the IN_ROW_DATA allocation type. The record_count intuitively contains the number of rows contained in the table.

Listing 3   Examining the space used by the dbo.Test table

```
--check the size of the table
SELECT
        alloc_unit_type_desc
       ,page_count
       ,avg_page_space_used_in_percent
       ,record_count
FROM
        sys.dm_db_index_physical_stats(
            DB_ID()
           ,OBJECT_ID(N'dbo.Test')
           ,NULL
           ,NULL
           ,'Detailed') ;
```

Figure 2 displays the results of the DMV query. As you can see on my test system, 158 data pages are used to store the 1,000 rows and each data page is, on average, 82.1 percent full.

Figure 2   Using a DMV to review space used

To continue with the example, let's delete half of the rows in our dbo.Test table and see what happens to the space used by the table. The T-SQL script in listing 4 uses the modulo operator, represented by the percent sign in T-SQL, to delete each row where the value in the first column, col1, is an odd number. So we are deleting every other row in the table.

Listing 4   Deleting the odd-numbered rows

```
--delete the odd rows
DELETE FROM
        Test
WHERE
        col1 % 2 = 1

--view the table
SELECT
        *
```

```
FROM
        dbo.Test ;
```

Figure 3 shows the results of the SELECT query. You can see that the table is left with test row #2, test row #4, and so on, for a total of 500 rows.

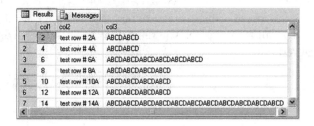

Figure 3   Deleting half the rows in the dbo.Test table

Now that half of the rows in the table have been deleted, let's look at the space the table consumes by running the DMV query from listing 3 again.

Figure 4 shows that the number of pages used to store the table's data remains constant but the percentage used of each page changes. It is cut in half, from 82.1 percent to 42.1 percent. Also notice that the number of rows reported in the record_count column has been cut in half, as expected.

Figure 4   Examining the space consumed by the dbo.Test table

So let's add some new rows to the table to prove that SQL Server will automatically reuse the newly freed space, thus filling in the *holes*, to go back to our Access comparison. Using the T-SQL script found in listing 5, we can quickly add 500 rows of data to the dbo.Test table. This script is similar to the one first used to populate the table with sample data. It inserts one row at a time in a WHILE loop. To help differentiate the new rows from the existing rows, I change the insert statement so that the third column is filled with WXYZ's rather than ABCD's as before, though it doesn't matter for our proof.

Listing 5   Adding new rows to the dbo.Test table

```
--add some more test data
DECLARE @cnt INT ;
SET @cnt = 0  ;
WHILE @cnt < 500
        BEGIN
                SELECT
                        @cnt = @cnt + 1 ;
                INSERT
                        dbo.Test ( col1,col2,col3 )
                VALUES  (
                        @cnt
                        ,'test row # ' + CAST(@cnt AS VARCHAR(10))
```

```
                ,REPLICATE('WXYZ', ROUND(RAND() * @cnt, 0))
                ) ;

       END
```

Now let's once again use the `sys.dm_db_index_physical_stats` DMV to see the space used by the table. Figure 5 displays the result of the query.

Figure 5 Reviewing the space used by the dbo.Test table after inserting new rows

Notice that the table is still using 158 data pages, but the average percent used for each page has increased to 62.9 percent from the prior value of 42.1 percent. The results confirm our expectations—the *holes* were indeed reused by SQL Server. No additional pages were allocated; the free space available was used.

At this point it is important to understand that, although SQL Server can and will automatically reuse space that was previously used by one or more rows, it will do so only under very specific circumstances. This behavior is most readily demonstrated through the use of a heap (a table without a clustered index) in which there is no pre-defined order of the rows. The behavior can also be observed in clustered tables when the newly inserted rows have key values that allow them to be inserted into the holes left by prior deletions. You shouldn't expect all newly inserted rows to fit nicely in the holes of a clustered table. The point is that SQL Server will reuse space as appropriate.

To clean up after this example, let's execute one final statement to drop the dbo.Test table. Listing 6 displays the `DROP` statement.

Listing 6   Dropping the dbo.Test table

```
--clean up
DROP TABLE dbo.Test ;
```

Recognizing when SQL Server does not reclaim space

Under certain circumstances SQL Server does not automatically reclaim space that is no longer being used. If a table definition is altered to drop one or more variable length columns, the space consumed by those columns is not immediately made available for reuse by SQL Server.

To illustrate this behavior, let's consider an example. Let's create another test table using the script in listing 7. The script creates the table and populates it with 1,000 rows of data.

Listing 7   Creating the dbo.Test2 table

```
USE tempdb ;
GO

--create the dbo.Test2 table
```

```
CREATE TABLE dbo.Test2
        (
         col1 INT
        ,col2 CHAR(25)
        ,col3 VARCHAR(4000)
        ) ;

--create some test data
DECLARE @cnt INT ;
SET @cnt = 0  ;
WHILE @cnt < 1000
        BEGIN
                SELECT
                        @cnt = @cnt + 1 ;
                INSERT
                        dbo.Test2 ( col1,col2,col3)
                VALUES  (
                         @cnt
                        ,'test row # ' + CAST(@cnt AS VARCHAR(10))
        ,REPLICATE('A', 4000)
        ) ;
          END
```

Figure 6 shows the results from the SELECT statement. This table has three columns of data, an integer in the first column, a character string in the second column that can contain up to 25 characters, and a variable length character string in the final column that contains 4,000 characters.

Figure 6   Viewing data in the dbo.Test2 table

Using the query shown in listing 3, we can see how much space our newly created dbo.Test2 table is consuming. Figure 7 shows the results. The newly created table takes up 500 data pages to store the 1,000 rows of data. Each data page is, on average, 99.9 percent full.

Figure 7   Space used by the dbo.Test2 table

Now to set up our test scenario, let's drop the third column, the one that consumes the most space. Listing 8 contains the ALTER TABLE script to drop col3; it then executes the DMV query to reveal the space used by the table.

Listing 8   Dropping a `varchar` column in the dbo.Test table

```
--drop the last column
ALTER TABLE dbo.Test2 DROP COLUMN col3 ;

--check the space used again
SELECT
        alloc_unit_type_desc
        ,page_count
        ,avg_page_space_used_in_percent
        ,record_count
FROM
        sys.dm_db_index_physical_stats(
            DB_ID()
            ,OBJECT_ID(N'dbo.Test2')
            ,NULL
            ,NULL
            ,'Detailed') ;
```

Looking at the results in figure 8, we can see that we get the same results as before—500 data pages, storing 1,000 rows, each 99.9 percent full, and this after dropping the column that consumed the most space.

Figure 8   Reviewing the space used after dropping a column

Why is this? When a table is altered to drop a column, SQL Server does not remove the column data from the data pages. Instead it updates the metadata in the system tables so that when queried, it appears as if the column no longer exists. The data is still present in the data pages, but it's not returned as a part of a result set. Thus, the space cannot be reused initially.

So let's add some additional rows to the table and see what happens. The script shown in listing 9 inserts 500 additional rows into the dbo.Test2 table. Notice that this script inserts only two columns of data because we've dropped the third column, col3.

Listing 9   Adding more rows to the dbo.Test2 table

```
--insert additional rows
DECLARE @cnt INT ;
SET @cnt = 0 ;
WHILE @cnt < 500
    BEGIN
            SELECT
                    @cnt = @cnt + 1 ;
            INSERT
                    dbo.Test2 ( col1,col2 )
            VALUES (
                     @cnt
                    ,'test row # ' + CAST(@cnt AS VARCHAR(10))
                    ) ;
    END
```

When we use the `sys.dm_db_index_physical_stats` DMV to examine the space used by the dbo.Test2 table, we find that the number of data pages increases slightly, indicating that the space once consumed by the dropped column was not automatically reused. Figure 9 shows the results.

Figure 9   Inserting rows after dropping a column

If the space had been automatically reused, there should have been more than enough space to contain the additional 500 rows without having to add more space. But because the columns were only marked as no longer being part of the table in the metadata, there is no space to reuse. So SQL Server added additional pages to make space for the new rows.

Using DBCC CLEANTABLE to reclaim unused table space

Although it is comforting to know that in certain cases SQL Server will automatically reuse space once consumed by deleted rows, we've just seen that it will not automatically reuse space once consumed by dropped columns.

Fortunately, this space is not lost forever; we can reclaim this space by issuing a DBCC command. The DBCC CLEANTABLE command allows us to specify a database and table, and it will free up any space once consumed by dropped variable length character columns.

To reclaim the space in our dbo.Test2 table, run the T-SQL command found in listing 10.

Listing 10   Reclaiming space using DBCC CLEANTABLE

```
--reclaim the space from the table
DBCC CLEANTABLE('tempdb', 'dbo.Test2') ;
```

If it succeeds, you should receive a message similar to the following as an output message in the query window.

```
DBCC execution completed. If DBCC printed error messages, contact your system
    administrator.
```

DBCC CLEANTABLE reclaims space from variable length columns that no longer exist as part of the table definition. In this context a variable length column can be one of the following data types: varchar, nvarchar, varchar(max), nvarchar(max), varbinary, varbinary(max), text, ntext, image, sql_variant, and xml.

Now that we've used the DBCC command to reclaim the space, let's return to our DMV query and examine the space used by the table by running listing 3.

Figure 10 shows the results. Notice that the number of data pages consumed by the table did not decrease; however, the average space used as a percentage decreased dramatically to 1.4 percent from 99.7 percent.

Figure 10   The space consumed by dbo.Test2 after running DBCC CLEANTABLE

To prove that the space is truly available for reuse, let's add another 3,000 rows to the table by altering and running listing 9.

Now checking the used space by again running the DMV query in listing 3, we see that the number of pages used to make the table did not increase. Notice, though, that the average page space used as a percentage did increase to 4.2 percent from 1.4 percent. Figure 11 shows the results.

Figure 11   Inserting rows into reclaimed space

Summary

When rows are deleted from a table without a clustered index (an object known as a heap), SQL Server can readily reuse the space that was once consumed by deleted rows. The same may hold true for clustered tables, as long as the newly inserted rows have the required key values that would allow them be placed in a *hole* created by a deleted row.

There are certain circumstances, in which *deleted* space is not immediately released for reuse; in particular when variable length character columns are dropped from a table. By employing the DBCC CLEANTABLE command we can reclaim the space once consumed by the dropped columns and make better use of the disk resources at hand.

About the author

Joe Webb, a Microsoft SQL Server MVP, serves as Chief Operating Manager for WebbTech Solutions, a Nashville-based IT consulting company. He has over 15 years of industry experience and has consulted extensively with companies in the areas of business process analysis and improvements, database design and architecture, software development, and technical training.

In addition to helping his consulting clients, Joe enjoys writing and speaking at technical conferences. He has delivered over 50 sessions at conferences in Europe and North America and has authored two other books.

Joe served for six years on the Board of Directors for the Professional Association for SQL Server (PASS), an international user group with 30,000 members worldwide. He culminated his tenure on the board by serving as the Executive Vice President of Finance for the organization. Joe also volunteers his time by serving on the MBA Advisory Board for Auburn University and the Computer Science Advisory Committee for Nashville State Community College.

When he's not consulting, Joe enjoys spending time with his family and tending to the animals and garden on his small farm in middle Tennessee. He can be reached at joew@webbtechsolutions.com.

31 Some practical issues in table partitioning

Ron Talmage

This chapter covers two practical topics in SQL Server table partitioning:

- Strategies for creating partition functions
- Minimizing data movement

Large SQL Server databases can become difficult to manage due to their size. Usually such large databases have only a couple of large tables that account for most of the databases' size. Table partitioning is a method for making those large tables easier to manage, and in some cases improving query performance against those large tables.

Table partitioning is an involved topic and can quickly become complex; therefore, this chapter is going to have a limited scope. Let's look at table partitioning from a general point of view, and then zero in on the two topics mentioned previously.

Table partitioning dependencies

Let's begin with a basic overview that'll introduce the terminology surrounding table partitioning. Our focus will be on SQL Server 2008 and SQL Server 2005. Table partitioning was introduced with SQL Server 2005 and enhanced a bit in SQL Server 2008, but the overall architecture of table partitioning remains the same between both versions.

NOTE Table partitioning is an Enterprise Edition–only feature in SQL Server 2008 and 2005. That means you can use the Developer and Evaluation Editions to learn about table partitioning, but you can put it into production only with the Enterprise Edition.

In a nutshell, a SQL Server–partitioned table is a table that's referred to as one table but is subdivided into multiple segments or partitions. In fact, technically all database tables in SQL Server 2005 and later are partitioned with one implicit partition.

Such tables aren't normally referred to as explicitly partitioned. They can't have more than one partition without also having been created on a partition scheme with a valid partition function. Only when a table has this additional property does it become a truly partitioned table.

The extra properties that a partitioned table needs concern two aspects:

- *Storage (partition scheme)*—Every partitioned table requires a definition for its storage, called a *partition scheme.* The partition scheme defines on which filegroups the table's multiple partitions will be stored.
- *Partition boundaries (partition function)*—Every partition scheme must be bound to a *partition function* that defines the partition boundaries, and therefore the partition ranges.

Before we examine these features in greater detail, look at the summary of the relationship of a partitioned table, the partition scheme, and the partition function in figure 1.

A partitioned table (a table that can have more than the single default partition) must be bound to a partition scheme. A given partition scheme could be used by more than one

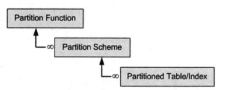

Figure 1   Dependency relations of the major table partitioning components

table. In turn, a partition scheme must be defined using exactly one partition function, though a given function might be used by more than one partition scheme.

Manipulating partitioned data

Once a partitioned table is defined using a partition scheme and function, data can be added and removed from the partitioned table, one partition at a time.

A single table can be loaded with external data and then swapped with an empty table partition, using what's called a SWITCH operation, something done by ALTERing the table. Next, by manipulating the table's partition function, two partitions in a table can be combined (using the MERGE option) to form one single new partition, and a single partition can be SPLIT into two partitions.

The end result is that you can use the SWITCH, MERGE, and SPLIT operations to modify a partitioned table so as to load new data and remove old data.

For example, to load new data into a partitioned table, follow these steps:

1 Load the new data into a staging table in the same database.

2 Use SPLIT to create an empty new partition at the "front" end of the table (where you want to load the data).

3 Swap the staging table with the empty partition, using the SWITCH operation.

Figure 2 shows the loading operation.

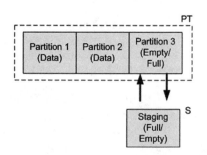

Figure 2   An initially empty partition is swapped with a full staging table.

In figure 2, partition 3 is initially empty and a staging table S is created and loaded with data. Then S is swapped with partition 3 using the SWITCH operation. The result is that partition 3 has the data and the staging table is now empty. This operation involves metadata only, and only takes milliseconds to complete, no matter what the size of the new table. Because there's no data transfer, no activity other than the metadata operation is logged in the transaction log. This is how table partitioning can load data quickly.

Although the metadata operations (SWTICH, MERGE, and SPLIT) occur almost instantaneously, to accomplish them SQL Server requires a schema modification lock on the partitioned table. If other transactions are running that prevent the schema modification lock, the metadata operations will be blocked until the required lock is granted.

To remove old data from a partitioned table, follow these steps:

1 Create an empty staging table in the same database.
2 Swap the staging table with the oldest full partition, using the SWITCH operation.
3 MERGE the old empty partition with an empty neighbor to remove it.

Figure 3 illustrates how data can be removed.

In figure 3, partition 1 has data and an empty staging table S is created. Then S is swapped with partition 1 using the SWITCH operation, resulting in an empty partition 1 but a full staging table S. As before, this operation involves metadata only, and only takes milliseconds to complete. Once the data has been swapped out to staging table S, partition 1 can be merged with partition 2 or another empty partition, and effectively disappear. Then the staging table data can optionally be copied out of the database for archiving, and the table truncated and reused later. This is how table partitioning can remove data quickly from a partitioned table.

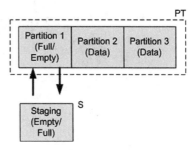

Figure 3   A full partition can be swapped with an empty staging table to remove data.

How the partition function works

So how does this all work? As figure 1 showed, it all starts with the partition function. This is a special type of function used in table partitioning, and is unlike other T-SQL functions in several ways. Like other functions, each partition function is scoped to the database it's created in. Although the partition function is a user-created database object, it's not visible by ordinary means in Management Studio; you can find partition functions, along with partition schemes, in the Storage node for each database. The reason is because the partition function is a special database object, not found in the sys.sysobjects table like other user-created and system functions.

What a partition function does is define the boundaries of a partitioned table based on the data type of the partitioning key of the table. The partition function splits up the range of all possible values that might be in the partitioning key of a table, and assigns each to a possible partition.

It's important to see that the partition function operates in a flexible way *that can change over time.* This is critical: you use the SPLIT and MERGE operations to add and remove partitions in a table by adding and removing partitions in the table's partition function.

For example, you can create a partition function using the following syntax:

```
CREATE PARTITION FUNCTION PFNExample1_Left (int)
AS RANGE LEFT FOR VALUES (10, 20, 30);
```

This code creates a partition function that

- Has a boundary range with data type integer
- Sets the range type to LEFT
- Sets the integer values 10, 20, and 30 as the initial boundary values
- Creates a total of four possible partitions

It's important to see that three boundary values results in four partitions. The boundary values are the points in the range of possible values where the "cuts" into partitions are. There's always one more partition than there are boundary values.

NOTE   The maximum number of boundary values allowed in a partition function is 999. Therefore, the maximum number of partitions in a partitioned table is—you guessed it—1,000.

The boundary values themselves can fall into the partition to the left or the right of the cut. In this example, placing values to the left produces the following partitions for this function:

```
{NULL, MinInt ... 10},
{11 ... 20},
{21 ... 30},
{31 ... MaxInt}
```

Here MinInt stands for the minimum integer value (–2,147,483,648) and MaxInt stands for the maximum integer value (2,147,483,647). The NULL value, if allowed in a table, always is the minimum value of the first partition.

You can verify these partition boundaries by using the $PARTITION operator. Using $PARTITION with a partition function shows you exactly how the partitions will be distributed based on possible values. To see this, execute the following queries:

```
SELECT $PARTITION.PFNExample1_Left(NULL);
SELECT $PARTITION.PFNExample1_Left(9);
SELECT $PARTITION.PFNExample1_Left(10);
SELECT $PARTITION.PFNExample1_Left(11);
SELECT $PARTITION.PFNExample1_Left(20);
SELECT $PARTITION.PFNExample1_Left(21);
```

The code shows that the integer value 10 falls into partition 1, whereas 11 will be in partition 2. The value 10 is the upper bound of partition 1, and a little exploration will show you that 20 is the upper bound of partition 2, and so forth.

Next, let's shift our example a bit and create the same partition function using the RIGHT range:

```
CREATE PARTITION FUNCTION PFNExample1_Right (int)
AS RANGE RIGHT FOR VALUES (10, 20, 30);
```

In this case, we end up placing the boundary value in the partition to the right of the cut:

```
{NULL, MinInt ... 9},
{10 ... 19},
{20 .. 29},
{30 ... MaxInt}
```

Again we end up with four partitions, but this time the boundary values fall into the partitions to the right: each boundary value becomes the lower bound of the right-most set of partitions. Execute the following queries:

```
SELECT $PARTITION.PFNExample1_Right(NULL);
SELECT $PARTITION.PFNExample1_Right(9);
SELECT $PARTITION.PFNExample1_Right(10);
SELECT $PARTITION.PFNExample1_Right(11);
SELECT $PARTITION.PFNExample1_Right(20);
SELECT $PARTITION.PFNExample1_Right(21);
```

Now we see that 10 is in partition 2 as the lower bound, 20 is the lower bound of partition 3, and so on. The lower bound of partition 1 is NULL.

So which is better, setting the range RIGHT or LEFT? Almost always, RANGE RIGHT will be superior, because it's easier to specify lower-bound values than upper-bound values. In fact, specifying lower-bound values is much more natural; we find it easier to think in terms of 10, 20, and 30 than in terms of 9, 19, and 29. Similarly, it's much easier to specify the first day of each month than it is to specify the last day of the month.

Drilling down: using SPLIT and MERGE

Now you can see how a partition can be split and merged. What you do is ALTER the partition function and use the SPLIT or MERGE options to perform the corresponding action. Remember that our PFNExample1_Right() function from the previous section has three boundary values (10, 20, 30), and we therefore have four partitions:

```
{NULL, MinInt ... 9},
{10 ... 19},
{20 ... 29},
{30 ... MaxInt}
```

Let's add a new partition with a boundary value 40. We do that by ALTERing the partition function and using the SPLIT function:

```
ALTER PARTITION FUNCTION PFNExample1_Right()
    SPLIT RANGE (40);
```

What the `ALTER PARTITION FUNCTION` command with the `SPLIT` option has done is add a new boundary value of 40, and therefore with four boundary values we now have five partitions:

```
{NULL, MinInt ... 9},
{10 ... 19},
{20 ... 29},
{30 ... 39},
{40 ... MaxInt}
```

You can verify this by running the following queries:

```
SELECT $PARTITION.PFNExample1_Right(39)
SELECT $PARTITION.PFNExample1_Right(40)
SELECT $PARTITION.PFNExample1_Right(41)
```

Next, you can `ALTER` the function to remove a boundary value, which effectively removes a partition by merging two neighboring partitions into one. The following code will remove boundary value 10 from our example function:

```
ALTER PARTITION FUNCTION PFNExample1_Right()
   MERGE RANGE (10);
```

Now we have the result of only three boundary values (20, 30, 40) because we removed 10 as a boundary value. Therefore, we're now back to only four partitions, but we've moved the range forward a bit:

```
{NULL, MinInt ... 19},
{20 ... 29},
{30 ... 39},
{40 ... MaxInt}
```

It's important to realize the dynamic nature of the partition function, because it allows partitions to be added and removed from a partition function and also from any partitioned table that uses that function.

Drilling down: using SWITCH

Using the `SWITCH` operation is conceptually much simpler than `SPLIT` and `MERGE`. All you do is `ALTER` the table and tell it what to swap. For example, in figure 2 we want to swap data into partitioned table P, partition 3, from staging table S. All that's required is this statement:

```
ALTER TABLE dbo.P SWITCH PARTITION 3 TO dbo.S;
```

In this case, staging table S was preloaded with data and an empty partition 3 was created using the `SPLIT` option. Then the `ALTER TABLE` with `SWITCH` command swaps the two, and in a matter of milliseconds the data from table S is in partition 3.

Conversely, figure 3 shows data being swapped out of the tail of a partitioned table. Partition 1 has data we want to put into the staging table S. This is the command:

```
ALTER TABLE dbo.S SWITCH TO dbo.P PARTITION 1;
```

Once the data is out of partition 1, you can remove the boundary value for it using the MERGE option of the ALTER PARTITION FUNCTION command, and it'll merge into its neighboring partition.

The key: avoiding data movement

The key to loading and removing data quickly from partitioned tables is to use the metadata operations of SWITCH, SPLIT, and MERGE without incurring any data movement. Data movement occurs when an operation requires that SQL Server move data from one partition to another.

The SWITCH operation always requires one side of the swap to be empty; therefore, it's always a metadata operation. On the other hand, it's possible that the SPLIT and MERGE operations, if you don't use them carefully, may cause data movement.

If you SPLIT a loaded partition in such a way that some of the partition's data must be moved to a new partition, data movement will occur as SQL Server moves that data to a new partition of the table. You can avoid this data movement by always using SPLIT to create new partitions that will be empty.

Similarly, if you MERGE two partitions of a table and each has data, then SQL Server must move data from one of the partitions into the final partition. If this is a lot of data, a lot of inserts will occur, resulting in a lot of I/O and potentially a lot of transaction log growth during the move operation. You can avoid data movement by always using MERGE with at least one empty partition.

Sources for more information

Here are a few places you can look for more information about table partitioning:

- For further information about all table partitioning topics, see SQL Server Books Online, for both SQL Server 2008 and 2005. Find the Partitioned Tables category in the Books Online Index tab.
- For a full discussion of SQL Server 2005 table partitioning, see the white paper, "Partitioned Tables and Indexes in SQL Server 2005" at http://msdn.microsoft.com/en-us/library/ms345146.aspx.
- For using table partitioning in data warehouses, see "Strategies for Partitioning Relational Data Warehouses in Microsoft SQL Server" at http://www.microsoft.com/technet/prodtechnol/sql/2005/spdw.mspx.
- Finally, for a summary of best practices for table partitioning, see "Top 10 Best Practices for Building a Large Scale Relational Data Warehouse" at http://sqlcat.com/top10lists/archive/2008/02/06/top-10-best-practices-for-building-a-large-scale-relational-data-warehouse.aspx.

Summary

Table partitioning is quite an involved topic, and in this chapter we only scratched the surface, but I hope we highlighted a couple of the most important bumps! These are the key takeaways:

- `RANGE RIGHT` is generally more useful than `RANGE LEFT` for partition functions.
- The key to making partition table data loading and removal fast is minimizing data movement, making sure `SPLIT` and `MERGE` are metadata operations only.

In order to cover these issues, there are many important topics that had to be left out. Here are a few of them, which you can use as directions for research:

- Placing filegroups for partition schemes
- The `NEXT USED` property of filegroups in a partition scheme
- Creating a table on a partition scheme
- Partitioned indexes and index alignment
- The sliding-window scenario

About the author

Ron Talmage is a mentor and cofounder of Solid Quality Mentors. He's a SQL Server MVP, a PASS Regional Mentor, and current president of the Pacific Northwest SQL Server Users Group. He has been writing white papers and articles on SQL Server since way back when.

32 Partitioning for manageability (and maybe performance)

Dan Guzman

Large tables are a bane to database administrators (DBAs). It takes seemingly forever to rebuild indexes on tables with many millions or billions of rows, not to mention the exorbitant space required to do so. For example, you must maintain more than 1 terabyte (TB) of database free space just to rebuild the clustered index on a 1 TB table, because both the old and new index must coexist until the rebuild is done. Developers are challenged to design applications that can load, purge, or archive vast amounts of data efficiently while providing high data availability.

SQL Server's table and index partitioning feature is a great way to address these manageability and load/purge/archive issues. But you must be aware that partitioning is a fundamental structural change that influences execution plans and query performance. Care is needed to implement partitioning wisely to maximize performance and manageability benefits while avoiding potential problems. Before I discuss important partitioned table design considerations and common pitfalls, let's first review core partitioning concepts.

Overview

The table partitioning feature is available in Enterprise and Developer editions of SQL Server 2005 and later versions. Partitioning a table or index divides it into partitions (subsets) based on the partitioning column value. Each partition has well-defined boundaries to ensure that a given partitioning column value is mapped to exactly one partition and a partition exists for all possible values. A table or index can be partitioned based on any persisted column value, with the exception of columns of data type `text`, `ntext`, `image`, `xml`, `timestamp`, `varchar(max)`, `nvarchar(max)`, `varbinary(max)`, and `FILESTREAM`. The `timestamp` data type is disallowed because it is a synonym for the `rowversion` data type and not related to date or time. Each partition is a complete heap or b-tree structure, as illustrated in figures 1 and 2. This allows a partition to be managed individually in data definition language (DDL) operations when it is advantageous to do so. For example, a

Figure 1   Partitioned heap with two partitions

fragmented index partition can be rebuilt or reorganized while avoiding other non-fragmented partitions of the same index. Furthermore, when an individual index partition is rebuilt, the available filegroup free space needed is determined by the partition size rather than the size of entire index. Yet SQL queries use a partitioned table like any other table, so partitioning is entirely transparent to application queries. The query optimizer strives to generate an execution plan with operators and filters to access only the partitions needed by a given query based on the partitioning column value. SQL 2008 includes improvements to better optimize partitioned table queries.

Partitioning is flexible so that a table and its indexes can be partitioned similarly, differently, or not at all. In practice, it is often advantageous to partition a table and its indexes similarly, a technique known as *alignment*. When aligned, corresponding data and index partitions have the same partitioning column and boundaries, and therefore include the same subset of data. Aligning tables and indexes makes it possible to switch an entire partition between objects with identical schema in a single DDL operation, as long as the source and target partitions reside on the same filegroups. Switching data in this manner allows massive amounts of data to be loaded or archived/purged nearly instantaneously, and provides a tremendous performance benefit compared to traditional data manipulation language (DML) methods. No physical data movement is required for the switch operation, and logging is minimal regardless of the database recovery model, again, as long as everything involved resides on the same filegroups.

Partitioning allows granular control of data placement within a single table. A database administrator (DBA) can place partitions on separate physical disks/arrays via filegroups in order to place infrequently accessed historical data on less-expensive, slower storage. Controlling intra-table data placement is difficult to accomplish without partitioning.

Queries that scan vast amounts of data may experience a performance benefit from partitioning. Depending on the particulars of a query, SQL Server can scan only those partitions needed, scan partitions in parallel using multiple threads, or join similarly partitioned tables more efficiently. Together with thoughtful file placement and multiple processors, performance of these concurrent scan operations can be maximized with partitioning.

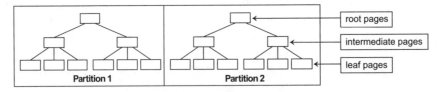

Figure 2   Partitioned table or b-tree index with two partitions

How to partition

Creating a partitioned table or index is fairly straightforward: create a partition function, create a partition scheme, and finally create the partitioned object by specifying the partition scheme and partitioning column. SQL Server uses the partition function internally during storage and retrieval operations to determine the appropriate partition number based on the partitioning column value. The partition scheme maps partitions defined by the partition function to filegroups for storage. Note that *no partitions are physically created until a partitioned table or index is created using the partition scheme.*

A *partition function* is a specialized scalar function that returns the partition number that corresponds to the specified value. The partition function lists the boundary values between partitions along with the partitioning column data type. The actual number of partitions is always one greater than the number of specified boundary values. Picture an infinite length of rope cut into pieces, with the cuts representing the partition boundaries as defined by the partition function, and the rope segments representing the resultant partitions. As figure 3 shows, the first and last pieces have no end on one side, so the number of segments (partitions) is equal to the number of cuts made (partition boundaries) plus one. A partition function with no boundaries listed results in a single unbounded partition.

Figure 3 Rope cuts representing two partition boundaries, resulting in three partitions

All rows within the range of adjacent boundaries are placed in the corresponding partition. The partition for an exact match on a boundary value is determined by the partition function RANGE LEFT or RIGHT. LEFT, the default, indicates that the lower partition number be used for an exact match, and RIGHT indicates that the higher number should be used. Figure 4 shows partitions resulting from RANGE LEFT and RIGHT partition functions.

```
CREATE PARTITION FUNCTION PF_SalesTransactions_Left(datetime)
    AS RANGE LEFT FOR VALUES(
        '2008-12-31T23:59:59.997','2009-01-31T23:59:59.997'
        );
```

<='2008-12-31T23:59:59.997'	>'2008-12-31T23:59:59.997' AND <='2009-01-31T23:59:59.997'	>'2009-01-31T23:59:59.997'
Partition 1	Partition 2	Partition 3

```
CREATE PARTITION FUNCTION PF_SalesTransactions_Right(datetime)
    AS RANGE RIGHT FOR VALUES(
        '2009-01-01T00:00:00','2009-02-01T00:00:00'
        );
```

<'2009-01-01T00:00:00'	>='2009-01-01T00:00:00' AND <'2009-02-01T00:00:00'	>='2009-02-01T00:00:00'
Partition 1	Partition 2	Partition 3

Figure 4 Partitions resulting from RANGE LEFT and RANGE RIGHT functions

```
CREATE PARTITION SCHEME PS_SalesTransactions_Data
    AS PARTITION PF_SalesTransactions_Right
    TO (N'FileGroup_Pre_20090101',N'FileGroup_20090101',N'FileGroup_20090201'
    );
```

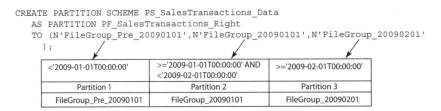

<'2009-01-01T00:00:00'	>='2009-01-01T00:00:00' AND <'2009-02-01T00:00:00'	>='2009-02-01T00:00:00'
Partition 1	Partition 2	Partition 3
FileGroup_Pre_20090101	FileGroup_20090101	FileGroup_20090201

Figure 5   Partition scheme filegroup mapping for RANGE RIGHT function

A *partition scheme* references a partition function and lists the filegroups corresponding to the partition numbers for mapping. Figure 5 shows a partition scheme and the partition/filegroup mappings using the RANGE RIGHT partition function from figure 4. A partitioned table/index is created much like any other. The only difference is that the CREATE statement specifies a partition scheme and column name instead of a filegroup name. When an index is created on a partitioned table, by default it is partitioned using the same partition scheme as the base table (aligned), unless a different partition scheme or a filegroup is specified. The script in listing 1 shows the DDL to create a partitioned sales transaction table with data and indexes explicitly aligned.

Listing 1   Creating a partitioned sales transaction table

```
CREATE TABLE dbo.SalesTransactions_Partitioned(
    SalesTransactionID uniqueidentifier NOT NULL,
    SalesTransactionTime datetime NOT NULL,
    StoreID int NOT NULL,
    ProductID int NOT NULL,
    Quantity int NOT NULL
    ) ON PS_SalesTransactions_Data(SalesTransactionTime);

CREATE CLUSTERED INDEX cdx_SalesTransactions_SalesTransactionTime
    ON dbo.SalesTransactions_Partitioned(SalesTransactionTime)
    ON PS_SalesTransactions_Data (SalesTransactionTime);

CREATE INDEX idx_SalesTransactions_StoreID_ProductID
    ON dbo.SalesTransactions_Partitioned(StoreID, ProductID)
    ON PS_SalesTransactions_Index1(SalesTransactionTime);

CREATE INDEX idx_SalesTransactions_ CustomerID
    ON dbo.SalesTransactions_Partitioned(CustomerID)
    ON PS_SalesTransactions_Index2(SalesTransactionTime);
```

This table and index DDL will create the partitioned table that we will use in the execution plan examples later in this chapter.

Planning and design considerations

Although partitioning a big table nearly always provides manageability benefits, performance is another matter. Some workloads and schema designs are well suited to partitioning, whereas others involve trade-offs between manageability and performance. Partitioning introduces schema and index design requirements that have major ramifications on query execution plans, and also influences how queries should be formulated to maximize performance. It is important to consider these factors as well as your partitioning objectives when partitioning an existing table or designing a new one.

A major design consideration is that partitioned indexes must contain the partitioning column, either as part of the key or as an included column. The partitioning column is required to be part of the clustered index key as well as part of unique index keys, including those that support primary key and unique constraints. With nonunique nonclustered indexes, the partitioning column can be an included column if not already part of the index key. If you don't want the partitioning column in a unique index key, the index must be partitioned differently, or not at all, and you must forgo the benefits of alignment for efficiently switching data in and out of tables. (Chapter 31, "Some practical issues in table partitioning," discusses partition switching in detail.)

Partitioning adds another dimension to query and index tuning. As I mentioned earlier, query execution plans that use a partitioned table or index include operators and/or filters to access only those partitions needed. Each partition needed during query execution will require a separate scan or seek. If the partitioning column value is specified as a constant in the query, SQL Server can invoke the partition function at query compile time. The resultant execution plan will include partition number constants for the needed partitions, and unneeded partitions will not be accessed. This is *static partition elimination.* When a query specifies the partitioning column value as a parameter or variable, the execution plan will use the partition function at run time to determine the required partition(s) and avoid those not needed. This is *dynamic partition elimination.*

The worst performance case is when the partitioning column value isn't specified in the query and all partitions must be accessed. Performance of a partitioned table/index scan without partition elimination is usually the same or better than the same query against a nonpartitioned version. A massive data skew between partitions can worsen scan performance, especially in SQL Server 2005.

On the other hand, performance of index seeks without partition elimination will likely be worse than that of a nonpartitioned index, because a nonpartitioned index requires only a single seek, whereas a partitioned index without partition elimination requires one seek per partition. Keep in mind that each seek operation must traverse all levels of the b-tree; therefore seek overhead is increased proportionally by the number of partitions touched. Note that the comparative seek performance of a partitioned versus nonpartitioned table query is pronounced when few rows match the seek predicate and many partitions are touched.

To illustrate comparative seek performance and execution plans, I created a partitioned SalesTransaction table and indexes using DDL from the earlier example, but with 36 monthly partitions plus empty first and last partitions. I also created a nonpartitioned version of the table and loaded several million rows of sales transactions spanning three years into both tables. The complete DDL and test data generation scripts

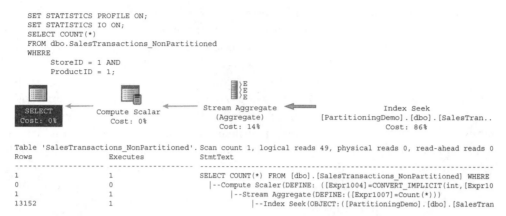

```
SET STATISTICS PROFILE ON;
SET STATISTICS IO ON;
SELECT COUNT(*)
FROM dbo.SalesTransactions_NonPartitioned
WHERE
        StoreID = 1 AND
        ProductID = 1;
```

Table 'SalesTransactions_NonPartitioned'. Scan count 1, logical reads 49, physical reads 0, read-ahead reads 0

Rows	Executes	StmtText
1	1	SELECT COUNT(*) FROM [dbo].[SalesTransactions_NonPartitioned] WHERE
0	0	|--Compute Scaler(DEFINE: ([Expr1004]=CONVERT_IMPLICIT(int, [Expr10
1	1	|--Stream Aggregate(DEFINE:([Expr1007]=Count(*)))
13152	1	|--Index Seek(OBJECT:([PartitioningDemo].[dbo].[SalesTran

Figure 6   SQL Server 2005 aggregate query nonpartitioned plan and statistics

are available for download from http://www.manning.com/SQLServerMVPDeep Dives. Figures 6 and 7 show the SQL Server 2005 execution plans and statistics output of an aggregate query against both tables.

Both execution plans include the expected nonclustered index seek operator using the covering index. The partitioned table plan adds a Constant Scan and Nested Loop operator to invoke a separate seek for each of the 38 partitions. The scan counts (1 versus 38) show the number of partitions accessed, and the logical reads (48 versus 144) reflect the cost of doing so. With the data distributed evenly over 36

```
SET STATISTICS PROFILE ON;
SET STATISTICS IO ON;
SELECT COUNT(*)
FROM dbo.SalesTransactions_Partitioned
WHERE
        StoreID = 1 AND
        ProductID = 1;
```

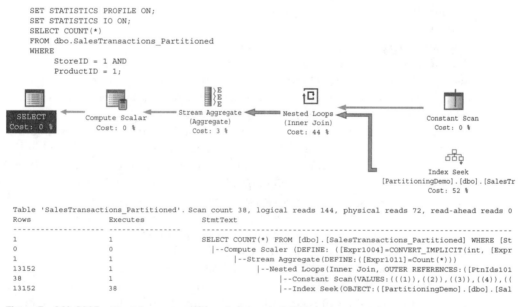

Table 'SalesTransactions_Partitioned'. Scan count 38, logical reads 144, physical reads 72, read-ahead reads 0

Rows	Executes	StmtText
1	1	SELECT COUNT(*) FROM [dbo].[SalesTransactions_Partitioned] WHERE [St
0	0	|--Compute Scaler (DEFINE: ([Expr1004]=CONVERT_IMPLICIT(int, [Expr
1	1	|--Stream Aggregate(DEFINE:([Expr1011]=Count(*)))
13152	1	|--Nested Loops(Inner Join, OUTER REFERENCES:([PtnIds101
38	1	|--Constant Scan(VALUES:(((1)),((2)),((3)),((4)),((
13152	38	|--Index Seek(OBJECT:([PartitioningDemo].[dbo].[Sal

Figure 7   SQL 2005 aggregate query partitioned plan and statistics

monthly partitions in this example, nearly three times as many logical reads were needed to process the same number of rows from the partitioned index.

The performance differential is exacerbated when few rows are actually retrieved because most of the index seeks are unproductive. Figure 8 shows a detail query of the nonpartitioned table by CustomerID, which returns only one row. In this case, the partitioned table query in figure 9 is 20 times more costly in terms of I/O than the nonpartitioned version. In my experience, simple queries like these that don't include the partitioning column are a common cause of poor performance of partitioned objects. If the partitioning column can't be included in queries, adding a nonpartitioned index can address the performance issue. Unfortunately, this will prevent alignment and negate partitioning manageability benefits for that index.

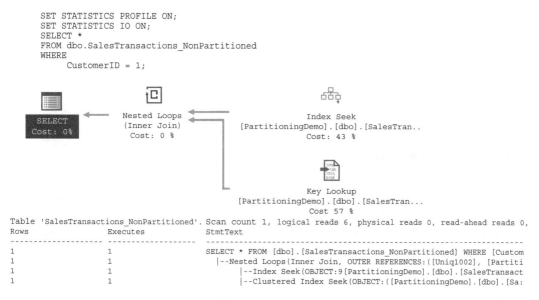

```
SET STATISTICS PROFILE ON;
SET STATISTICS IO ON;
SELECT *
FROM dbo.SalesTransactions_NonPartitioned
WHERE
      CustomerID = 1;
```

Figure 8   SQL Server 2005 detail query nonpartitioned plan and statistics

```
SET STATISTICS PROFILE ON;
SET STATISTICS IO ON;
SELECT *
FROM dbo.SalesTransactions_NonPartitioned
WHERE
      CustomerID = 1;
```

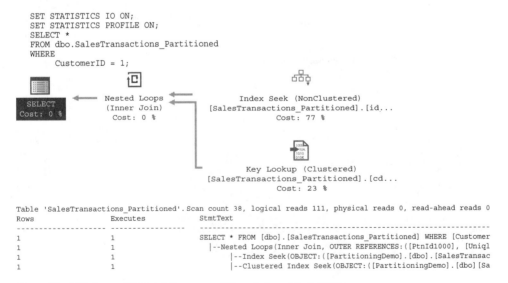

```
Table 'SalesTransactions_Partitioned'. Scan count 28, logical reads 111, physical reads 0, read-ahead reads 0
Rows                Executes           StmtText
------------------- ------------------ --------------------------------------------------------------------------
1                   1                  SELECT * FROM [dbo].[SalesTransactions_Partitioned] WHERE [Customer
1                   1                  |--Nested Loops(Inner Join, OUTER REFERENCES:([PtnIds1006], [Uniq
0                   0                  |--Compute Scaler(DEFINE:([PtnIds1006]=RangePartitionNew([Pa
1                   1                  |   |--Nested Loops(Inner Join, OUTER REFERENCES:([PtnIds10
38                  1                  |   |   |--Constant Scan(VALUES:((1)),((2)),((3)),((4)),(
1                   38                 |   |   |--Index Seek(OBJECT:([PartitioningDemo].[dbo].[Sa
1                   1                  |--Clustered Index Seek(OBJECT:([PartitioningDemo].[dbo].[Sa
```

Figure 9   SQL Server 2005 detail query partitioned plan and statistics

The difference in query plans between SQL Server 2005 and SQL Server 2008 with regard to partitioned index seeks is noteworthy. At first glance, the SQL Server 2008 plan listed in figure 10 looks nearly identical to the nonpartitioned plan in figure 8,

```
SET STATISTICS IO ON;
SET STATISTICS PROFILE ON;
SELECT *
FROM dbo.SalesTransactions_Partitioned
WHERE
      CustomerID = 1;
```

SELECT
Cost: 0 %   ◄─── Nested Loops
                (Inner Join)   ◄───   Index Seek (NonClustered)
                Cost: 0 %   [SalesTransactions_Partitioned].[id...
                                       Cost: 77 %

                                       Key Lookup (Clustered)
                                       [SalesTransactions_Partitioned].[cd...
                                       Cost: 23 %

```
Table 'SalesTransactions_Partitioned'. Scan count 38, logical reads 111, physical reads 0, read-ahead reads 0
Rows                Executes           StmtText
------------------- ------------------ --------------------------------------------------------------------------
1                   1                  SELECT * FROM [dbo].[SalesTransactions_Partitioned] WHERE [Customer
1                   1                  |--Nested Loops(Inner Join, OUTER REFERENCES:([PtnId1000], [Uniql
1                   1                  |--Index Seek(OBJECT:([PartitioningDemo].[dbo].[SalesTransac
1                   1                  |--Clustered Index Seek(OBJECT:([PartitioningDemo].[dbo].[Sa
```

Figure 10   SQL Server 2008 detail query partitioned plan and statistics

```
Seek Keys[1]:
    Start: PtnId1000 >= Scalar Operator((1)),
    End: PtnId1000 <= Scalar Operator((38)),
Seek Keys[2]:
    Prefix: [PartitionTest].[dbo].[SalesTransactions_Partitioned].CustomerID=Scalar
    Operator((5))
```

Figure 11　SQL Server 2008 partitioned index seek predicate including partition range expression

but a closer examination of the seek operator listed in figure 11 reveals that the seek predicate includes a range expression that touches all 38 partitions. Even though the SQL Server 2008 plan is less complex than the SQL Server 2005 partitioned plan due to the omission of the Constant Scan and Nested Loop operators, every partition must still be accessed, because the partitioning column wasn't included in the query.

As you can see from the seek predicate in figure 11, the partition number appears to the SQL Server 2008 query processor as if it were the high-order column of the index key. This optimization allows partition elimination to be pushed down into the seek operator instead of done through query plan operators as in the SQL Server 2005 plan. See the "Query Processing Enhancements on Partitioned Tables and Indexes" topic (http://msdn.microsoft.com/en-us/library/ms345599.aspx) in the SQL Server 2008 Books Online for a thorough discussion of enhancements related to partitioned index seeks.

Gotchas and tips

Partitioning is often used with large tables that are unforgiving by nature. Let me share some common pitfalls and tips that might help you achieve a successful partitioning implementation.

Boundary time values

Pay particular attention to boundary values of RANGE LEFT partition functions when the partitioning data type includes both date and time of day (smalldatetime, datetime, datetime2, and datetimeoffset). To ensure that all data for a given date ends up in the same partition, specify the maximum possible time value allowable for the partitioning data type, and be careful of boundary value rounding. For example, a datetime data type boundary value of 2009-12-31T23:59:59.999 will be rounded up to 2010-01-01T00:00:00.000, and rows that exactly match the date will then end up in the lower partition instead of the higher one. I find it more intuitive to use RANGE RIGHT for date/time data types so that I can specify exact date boundaries.

If the time value isn't needed by the application, you can avoid date/time partitioning ugliness with a column of the DATE data type. Not only does DATE simplify partition boundaries, but queries for specific dates or date ranges don't need to consider the time portion and are therefore easier to write and more intuitive. If the time portion is needed but not included in range searches, alternatives include creating separate DATE and TIME columns or creating a DATE column that's computed and persisted based on the existing date/time value.

SPLIT and MERGE performance

Plan your partition maintenance to avoid costly movement of large amounts of data. The easiest way to accomplish this is to plan so that only empty partitions are split and merged. Nonempty partitions can still be split or merged efficiently, but only if you are careful to avoid unnecessary data movement. With SPLIT, the newly created partition is the one that includes the specified boundary value (LEFT or RIGHT); data will be moved into the new partition as appropriate for the new boundaries. SQL Server can leverage existing indexes to determine what, if any, data needs to be relocated. Consequently, splitting a nonempty partition can be nearly instantaneous, as long as no data needs to be moved and a useful index on the partitioning column exists.

MERGE performance is also proportional to the amount of data moved. The partition that includes the merged boundary is the one removed, and all data will be moved from the removed partition into the adjacent retained one.

Update statistics after SWITCH

Always update statistics after a partition switch. SQL Server maintains statistics at the table level rather than the partition level; therefore index statistics are immediately stale after a switch and can result in suboptimal plans.

Shared partition functions and schemes

Partition functions can be shared by multiple partition schemes, and schemes can be used by many tables and indexes. Be aware that splitting or merging a shared partition function can therefore affect many tables and indexes.

It is often desirable to partition a staging table identically to the main table to guarantee alignment for switch operations. Ensure that the staging table is empty during partition function maintenance in order to avoid unnecessary movement of transient staging table data.

Summary

Mistakes made with large tables can lead to anguish for all involved. Perform due diligence in designing a new partitioned table or converting an existing one, especially when performance is critical or the workload demanding. Inventory queries that use the table, examine execution plans to ensure all are optimal, and take the time to test performance against representative data. Not only will this help you avoid unwanted surprises during your partitioning implementation, you'll be confident that the application is performing to its maximum potential while you enjoy the manageability benefits of partitioning.

About the author

Dan Guzman began using Microsoft SQL Server with version 4.21a on Windows NT 3.1 after several years as a mainframe DBA. He's been a SQL Server MVP since 2000, helping out in online SQL Server communities as well as in the local St. Louis SQL Server User Group and .NET events. Dan enjoys watching movies and playing Xbox games with his wife and teenage daughter.

33 Efficient backups
without indexes

Greg Linwood

As databases grow in size, the challenges associated with managing correspondingly larger backups also increase, as they require proportionally more storage space and processing time to complete.

The practice of compressing database backups has emerged over recent years to address these problems, but another opportunity still remains that can further reduce backup time, space, and energy consumption—simply by eliminating index data from backups! Because the proportion of data consumed by nonclustered indexes is significant in many databases (often 50 percent or greater), the savings to be made from eliminating these indexes from backups is also significant in many cases.

In this chapter, we'll investigate a practical method to reduce backup sizes and timing—by separating tables and indexes into different filegroups, and then using filegroup backups instead of full database backups to eliminate index data from routine backups.

The example scripts shown in this chapter have been tested on SQL Server 2005 and SQL Server 2008, but simple customizations could be applied to allow this technique to also be used with older versions.

It's OK to not back up nonclustered indexes!

Before describing *how* to eliminate index data from backups, it's first important to point out that a nonclustered index contains merely a copy of the rows from its associated table, sorted differently (by the index's keys) to allow efficient searching during processing of queries. Eliminating this redundant index data from routine database backups does not limit the recoverability of the database data from its backup; indexes can always be re-created by scanning and re-sorting their underlying table rows if necessary.

Re-creating indexes certainly adds additional time to the restore process, and some may argue that this overhead is unacceptable. But in real practice, high availability is usually implemented with techniques other than relying on restoration of database backups (for example, database mirroring, or log shipping), so the timing of restore operations is rarely significantly important.

In many cases, restoration of a database is only performed to recover specific data rather than for high availability purposes. In this common scenario, the elimination of indexes from the restore process increases restore speed—and therefore availability of data (as restoring a *tables-only* filegroup is obviously faster than restoring a full database backup that contains both tables *and* indexes).

A simple example

Let's walk through an example that demonstrates the steps involved in separating tables and indexes into different filegroups, then backup the tables-only filegroup, and finish with restoration of the backup.

We'll begin by reviewing SQL Server's default table and index filegroup placements to describe default behaviors (by which most databases operate), then move through the steps required to separate indexes from tables before looking at backup and restore.

We'll use an extremely simple example—a database with only a single table and a single nonclustered index to demonstrate the essential steps before moving into a deeper discussion on practical issues associated with more complex real-world databases.

Default table and index storage behavior

By default, SQL Server stores all table and index objects within a filegroup named PRIMARY (assuming a default installation of SQL Server, without any modifications to the model database). In the vast majority of cases, most SQL Server databases contain only a PRIMARY filegroup, with all tables and indexes contained within it.

Before we can create any tables or indexes, we first need a database so let's begin there—by creating an empty database. This will contain one filegroup named PRIMARY:

```
CREATE DATABASE BackupTest;
USE BackupTest;
```

NOTE   The CREATE DATABASE command does allow fine-grained control over many attributes and configurations of the new database, including which filegroups and associated files are created (including addition of multiple filegroups)—but we are only concerned with inspecting default behavior at this point.

To verify existence of the PRIMARY filegroup, you can right-click the database in SQL Server Management Studio (SSMS) and view the Files tab in the Properties dialog box, or run the following query against the sys.filegroups system catalog view within the newly created BackupTest database.

```
SELECT name, data_space_id, is_default FROM sys.filegroups;
```

The results should be similar to those displayed in figure 1, confirming the database has one default filegroup named PRIMARY.

name	data_space_id	is_default
PRIMARY	1	1

Figure 1   List of filegroups from sys.filegroups

By default, unless further filegroups are explicitly created, all tables created within the database are stored within this PRIMARY filegroup. Any indexes created on those tables are also stored within the same filegroup as their tables, and therefore will be stored within the PRIMARY filegroup.

Let's continue by creating a simple two-column table:

```
CREATE TABLE dbo.Table1 (
    Col1 INT NOT NULL primary key
  , Col2 INT NOT NULL
);
```

To verify that the preceding table is created within the PRIMARY filegroup, execute the following command:

```
SELECT d.*
FROM sys.data_spaces d, sys.indexes i
WHERE i.object_id = OBJECT_ID('dbo.Table1')
  AND d.data_space_id = i.data_space_id
  AND i.index_id < 2;
```

Results should be returned similar to those displayed in figure 2, confirming that Table1 was created on the default PRIMARY filegroup.

If we now create a nonclustered index on Table1 named ncix_Table1, it will also be created in the PRIMARY filegroup:

```
CREATE NONCLUSTERED INDEX ncix_Table1 ON dbo.Table1 (Col1);
```

To verify that our new index has also been created within the PRIMARY filegroup, run the following command:

```
SELECT i.name, i.index_id, i.type_desc, i.data_space_id
FROM sys.data_spaces d, sys.indexes i
WHERE i.object_id = OBJECT_ID('dbo.Table1')
  AND d.data_space_id = i.data_space_id
  AND i.index_id > 1;
```

Results should be returned similar to those displayed in figure 3, confirming that the index ncix_Table1 was created within data_space_id 1 (PRIMARY).

name	data_space_id	type	type_desc	is_default
PRIMARY	1	FG	ROWS_FILEGROUP	1

Figure 2   Confirm that Table1 was created on the default PRIMARY filegroup.

name	index_id	type_desc	data_space_id
ncix_table1	2	NONCLUSTERED	1

Figure 3   Confirm that index ncix_Table1 was created within data_space_id 1 (PRIMARY).

Our example so far represents the most common behavior for storing table and index objects in SQL Server databases—they're stored within the PRIMARY filegroup by default.

NOTE   Few database administrators (DBAs) bother to reconfigure the physical layout of their databases until growth in data or transaction processing volumes force them to fine-tune physical database layout across disk systems using filegroups.

When using the default filegroup configuration, there's no option other than to back up both tables and indexes together. Full database backups always back up all tables and indexes, regardless of filegroup configuration and a filegroup backup of only the PRIMARY filegroup would produce a similar result in this case, as the database's only table and index are both contained within the PRIMARY filegroup.

Adding a dedicated filegroup for nonclustered indexes

To enable us to eliminate nonclustered indexes from our backups via filegroup backups, we must first move our nonclustered index ncix_Table1 from the PRIMARY filegroup to another filegroup, allowing the PRIMARY filegroup to be backed up in isolation from any index filegroups. We must first create another filegroup, which we'll dedicate to the storage of nonclustered indexes.

To create a *nonclustered index only* filegroup, run the following command:

```
ALTER DATABASE BackupTest
ADD FILEGROUP NCIX_FG;
```

This creates another filegroup within the database named NCIX_FG (short for *nonclustered index filegroup*). But we must also add at least one physical operating system file to the filegroup before database objects can be stored within it (alter the FILENAME path as appropriate for your filesystem):

```
ALTER DATABASE BackupTest
ADD FILE (
   NAME = N'NCIX_FG_F1'
 , FILENAME = N'C:\ NCIX_FG_F1.ndf')
TO FILEGROUP NCIX_FG;
```

Moving nonclustered indexes into the new filegroup

Now that we have created a nonclustered index only filegroup to store our nonclustered index, we can relocate the nonclustered index into it. To accomplish this, we re-issue the CREATE INDEX statement, with two additional options, DROP_EXISTING and ON NCIX_FG:

```
CREATE NONCLUSTERED INDEX ncix_Table1 ON dbo.Table1 (Col1)
WITH DROP_EXISTING --, ONLINE = ON
ON NCIX_FG;
```

The DROP_EXISTING option causes the newly created index to be created as the replacement of the existing index, without needing to explicitly drop the existing index (which could damage query performance for queries that might be in flight, while the index is dropped). The ONLINE option can be used to further reduce concurrency impact with SQL Server 2005 or 2008 Enterprise Edition.

The ON NCIX_FG clause is the main focus of our attention in this statement, which defines the new location for the nonclustered index.

Backing up only the PRIMARY filegroup

Now that we've successfully separated our nonclustered indexes (one only) from the PRIMARY filegroup into a separate filegroup, it's now possible to perform a tables-only filegroup backup. Instead of issuing a standard BACKUP DATABASE command, add a filegroup specification to back up only the PRIMARY filegroup. For example:

```
BACKUP DATABASE BackupTest
FILEGROUP = 'PRIMARY'
TO DISK = 'E:\BackupTest_Primary.bak'
```

SQL Server will then perform a filegroup backup of the PRIMARY filegroup only, without copying any contents from the newly created NCIX_FG to the backup set.

NOTE   Although no data is backed up from NCIX_FG, the backup still contains *definitions* of nonclustered indexes because index metadata information is stored in system tables, which are located in the PRIMARY filegroup (sys.indexes, sys.index_columns and so on). This means that we can re-create the nonclustered indexes in the restore process from their definitions, even though we don't have their allocated data structures in our backup file.

Restoring the PRIMARY filegroup backup

The process required to restore the database from the PRIMARY filegroup backup differs depending on whether you're restoring only to perform data extraction purposes (re-creation of indexes *not* required), or whether you intend to bring the database fully online (re-creation of indexes *is* required).

Restoring from the PRIMARY filegroup backup to perform data extraction is simple and faster than restoring a full backup. On the other hand, restoring the database back to its full state to bring it back into a production role—including a rebuild of all nonclustered indexes—requires more steps than from a simple full database backup.

Let's quickly review both of the steps required in each scenario.

Restoring for extraction only

When restoring a database from the PRIMARY (tables-only) filegroup for data extraction/examination only, you include FILEGROUP and RECOVERY (or NORECOVERY if you also wish to restore a chain of log backups) clauses in your RESTORE command, as follows:

```
RESTORE DATABASE BackupTest
FILEGROUP = 'PRIMARY'
FROM DISK = 'E:\BackupTest_Primary.bak'
WITH RECOVERY
```

SQL Server will then restore the PRIMARY filegroup and recover the database, bringing it online and available for querying. This allows extraction of data by executing SELECT commands, but INSERT, UPDATE, or DELETE commands will fail with error 8607:

```
Msg 8607, Level 16, State 1, Line 1: The table '[Tablename]' cannot be modified
    because one or more nonclustered indexes reside in a filegroup which is not
    online.
```

It's also possible that SELECT statements might fail if a nonclustered index is used to process the query, either via selection by SQL Server's query optimizer or explicit index hint. In this case, error 315 will be returned:

```
Msg 315, Level 16, State 1, Line 2: Index "[IndexName]" on table "[TableName]"
    (specified in the FROM clause) is disabled or resides in a filegroup which
    is not online.
```

In this scenario, you might need to either remove index hints, or explicitly hint SQL Server to access the table via its heap or clustered index storage, instead of via the nonclustered index (which is offline).

Restoring for production use

Restoring a database from a PRIMARY filegroup backup for production use does require a few more steps than restoring from a regular full database backup. The most significant of these involves rebuilding nonclustered indexes from the underlying tables.

In summary, these are the steps required to bring a database fully online from a PRIMARY filegroup backup:

1　Restore the primary filegroup backup and recover the database.
2　Script out index definitions from the PRIMARY filegroup, using a new filegroup name.
3　Restart SQL Server in single-user mode (with -m startup parameter).
4　Connect to SQL Server using the Dedicated Administrator Connection.
5　Delete nonclustered index definitions from the sys.sysindexes system view.
6　Remove -m startup parameter and restart SQL Server in multi-user mode.
7　Create a new, renamed filegroup to re-create the nonclustered indexes in.
8　Rebuild nonclustered indexes in the new filegroup.

NOTE   Scripting nonclustered index definitions from the PRIMARY filegroup is still possible even though the nonclustered index filegroup hasn't been restored, because index definitions exist within the system meta tables in the PRIMARY filegroup, regardless of where the physical index storage allocations are located. This is a crucial fact that enables this technique to work.

Before walking through each of these steps, two issues associated with this technique should be discussed:

- An update to system views is required to re-create nonclustered indexes (step 5).
- The nonclustered index filegroup's name must be changed (step 7).

ISSUE 1: INDEX DEFINITIONS MUST BE REMOVED BY UPDATING A SYSTEM VIEW

The process of re-creating indexes following restoration of the PRIMARY filegroup requires deleting existing index metadata from the sys.sysindexes system view prior to re-creating indexes (step 3 in the previous list). This fact might discourage some from using this technique, but it should be pointed out that updating this system view does not, in and of itself, compromise the integrity of the database, as the database tables that contain the real data in our database are stored within the PRIMARY filegroup and are not affected by the update of this system view.

WARNING   Updating a system catalog is an operation that's not supported by Microsoft. An alternative supported solution is to reconstruct the database by scripting its definition, re-creating the database, exporting all table data from the backup, and re-importing to the new re-created database.

This system update is required because neither DROP INDEX nor CREATE INDEX WITH DROP_EXISTING work when only the PRIMARY filegroup has been restored. Each fails with an error stating that the index's filegroup is offline as SQL Server attempts to remove the index's allocations, which aren't available during execution of the command.

To avoid this system catalog update, an alternative is to re-create an entirely new database by scripting all database objects from the PRIMARY filegroup (tables, indexes, and all other objects) and exporting all data from the restored PRIMARY filegroup into that new database. This is obviously more time-consuming than only re-creating nonclustered indexes (as tables are also re-created in the new database), but it's a workable alternative that allows you to bring a database back online from PRIMARY filegroup backup without using any system catalog updates.

ISSUE 2: NEW NONCLUSTERED INDEX FILEGROUP MUST BE RENAMED

Another issue is that the filegroup that contained the nonclustered indexes in the source database (NCIX_FG in our example) cannot be fully removed from the restored database without further system catalog updates.

This is less of a problem though, as another filegroup can be added to the restored database and nonclustered indexes be built into it. The name of a filegroup is rarely important to an application, so this doesn't pose a serious problem—simply create another filegroup (for example NCIX_FG2) and rebuild nonclustered indexes into it instead. This is what we'll do in our example.

Restoring for production use—step by step

Let's walk through the individual steps required to restore our database for production use from a PRIMARY filegroup backup.

STEP 1—RESTORE THE PRIMARY FILEGROUP BACKUP AND RECOVER THE DATABASE
The first step is identical to the restore process for extraction only. Assuming our PRIMARY filegroup backup remains located in the root of E:\ drive, execute the following command:

```
RESTORE DATABASE BackupTest
FILEGROUP = 'PRIMARY'
FROM DISK = 'E:\BackupTest_Primary.bak'
WITH RECOVERY
```

This restores the database's PRIMARY filegroup, meaning that all tables, views, stored procedures, user-defined functions, and other database objects stored in the PRIMARY filegroup have been restored to the database. Index definitions have also been restored to the system catalogs (which reside in the PRIMARY filegroup), but their data structure allocations have not, as they are located within the dedicated nonclustered index filegroup (NCIX_FG in our example)—which was neither backed up nor restored.

STEP 2—SCRIPT OUT INDEX DEFINITIONS FROM PRIMARY FILEGROUP
In the current state of our database, it's not possible to rebuild our nonclustered indexes using more convenient options such as DBCC DBREINDEX, ALTER INDEX REBUILD, or CREATE INDEX WITH DROP_EXISTING. Each of these generates an error whether executed from a normal connection or dedicated administrator connection (DAC), because each requires existing index allocations to be available during execution of the command.

Instead, we'll script index definitions out to a file and use the script later (step 8), to rebuild the indexes, after we have dropped index definitions from the sys.sysindexes system catalog and created a new nonclustered index filegroup to contain the new indexes.

To generate the index scripts, use the utility stored procedure (SP) described later in this chapter, named usp_Manage_NCIX_FileGroup. This SP accepts two parameters—@ScriptOnlyOrExecute (nvarchar(6)) and @NCIXFGName (nvarchar(255)).

The @ScriptOnlyOrExecute parameter should be set to N'Script', which instructs the SP to generate scripts only, without executing them.

The @NCIXFGName parameter should be provided with the name of a new filegroup to rebuild nonclustered indexes into. At this stage, this filegroup does not exist, but we'll create it in step 7. The name provided for this new filegroup must be different from the existing nonclustered index filegroup for this database (which is NCIX_FG in our example) because that filegroup's descriptive metadata still exists in the system catalogs. For our example, we'll create another filegroup named N'NCIX_FG2'.

```
EXEC usp_Manage_NCIX_FileGroup N'Script', N'NCIX_FG2'
```

Output from the execution of this procedure should contain a list of CREATE INDEX statements, one per nonclustered index in the database. Save this output to a script file (for example NCIXScripts.sql) for later use in step 7. Note that each CREATE INDEX statement will include the filegroup name NCIX_FG2. When we run this script later, nonclustered indexes will be re-created within this filegroup, so we'll need to add it to the database (which we do in step 7).

STEP 3—RESTART SQL SERVER IN SINGLE-USER MODE

Before we can re-create our nonclustered indexes, we need to remove existing index definitions from the database by deleting them from the sys.sysindexes system catalog. This requires us to connect to SQL Server in single-user mode, using the DAC before we can perform the DELETE.

Starting SQL Server in single-user mode requires adding the -m startup parameter via the SQL Server 2005 or 2008 Configuration Manager utility, as displayed in figure 4.

1 Navigate to the SQL Server Program Files menu.

2 Open the SQL Server Configuration Manager utility.

3 Right-click on the relevant instance of SQL Server from the right-hand window.

4 Select the Properties menu.

5 Click on the Advanced tab.

6 Select the Startup Parameters configuration.

7 Add ; -m to the end of the existing list of Startup Parameters (or the beginning of Startup Parameters with SQL Server 2008).

8 Click Apply, and click OK in the warning dialog box that appears.

9 When the Properties dialog box closes, right-click on the SQL Server instance and select Restart.

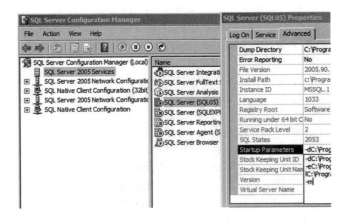

Figure 4   Adding the –m startup parameter in SQL Server Configuration Manager

STEP 4—CONNECT TO SQL SERVER USING DEDICATED ADMINISTRATOR CONNECTION

Once the SQL Server instance has been restarted, connect through the DAC to allow updates to the system catalogs. Connect or reconnect an SSMS connection by adding `ADMIN:` to the beginning of the server name in your connection dialog box, as displayed in figure 5.

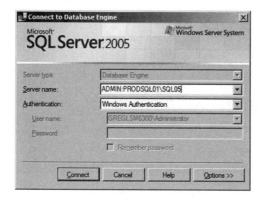

Figure 5   Specifying the Dedicated Administrator Connection using the SSMS connection dialog box

STEP 5—DELETE NONCLUSTERED INDEX DEFINITIONS

Once connected through the DAC, delete existing nonclustered index definitions from the system schema by running the following command:

```
DELETE
FROM  sys.sysindexes
WHERE OBJECTPROPERTY (id, 'IsUserTable') = 1
  AND indid > 1 AND indid < 255
```

Executing this command allows us to run the script generated in step 2 to re-create all nonclustered indexes—but first we need to remove the -m startup parameter, restart the SQL Server, and add a new nonclustered index using the filegroup name specified for the @NCIXFGName parameter in step 2.

STEP 6—REMOVE -M STARTUP PARAMETER AND RESTART SQL SERVER

To remove the -m startup parameter, follow the steps outlined in step 3 but remove ; -m from the Startup Parameters configuration before restarting the SQL Server instance.

STEP 7—CREATE A NEW, RENAMED FILEGROUP

Once the SQL Server instance has been restarted in multi-user (normal) mode, a new filegroup must be added prior to re-creating the database's nonclustered indexes. This is a two-step process; first we create the filegroup by executing the following command:

```
ALTER DATABASE BackupTest
ADD FILEGROUP NCIX_FG2;
```

Then, we add at least one file to the filegroup by executing the following command:

```
ALTER DATABASE BackupTest
ADD FILE (
```

```
    NAME = N'NCIX_FG2_F1'
  , FILENAME = N'C:\ NCIX_FG2_F1.ndf')
TO FILEGROUP NCIX_FG2;
```

NOTE   The name used for this new filegroup must match the name provided to the parameter @NCIXFGName in step 2 because the script generated in step 2 will attempt to build nonclustered indexes into this filegroup when it is run in step 8.

STEP 8—REBUILD NONCLUSTERED INDEXES IN THE NEW FILEGROUP

To re-create the nonclustered indexes in the new filegroup, connect to the database using SSMS and execute the script created in step 2.

usp_Manage_NCIX_Filegroup

This utility stored procedure has been designed to simplify two tasks described in this technique:

- Move a large number of nonclustered indexes into a dedicated filegroup, as part of reorganizing your database in preparation to perform PRIMARY (tables-only) filegroup-based backups.
- Generate a script to re-create nonclustered indexes during the restore process if necessary.

The workflow of this stored procedure iterates over a database's indexes, generating a CREATE INDEX statement for each index, and either executes the statement (when reorganizing the database in preparation for performing PRIMARY filegroup backups) or prints the statement (to generate scripts for re-creating nonclustered indexes during restore). The value supplied for the @ScriptOnlyOrExecute parameter defines which behavior will occur. Supply N'Execute' to execute the scripts (moving the indexes into the filegroup named in the other parameter @NCIXFGName) or N'Script' to script out the CREATE INDEX statements when restoring the database.

Note that slightly different CREATE INDEX statements are generated when N'Execute' is supplied to the @ScriptOnlyOrExecute parameter. When N'Execute' is supplied, WITH DROP_EXISTING is appended to the CREATE INDEX statement so that each existing index remains in place while a new copy is being created in the new, dedicated nonclustered index filegroup. In addition, the script identifies whether the edition of the SQL Server instance is Enterprise or Standard Edition and includes WITH ONLINE=ON if Enterprise Edition is detected. The idea here is to cause minimal interruption to queries during reorganization of the database, with close to zero interruption if the Enterprise Edition of SQL Server is in use.

Here's a sample usage. Move all nonclustered indexes into a newly created filegroup named 'NCIX_FG':

```
EXEC usp_Manage_NCIX_FileGroup N'Exec', N'NCIX_FG'
```

As in listing 1, script out CREATE INDEX statements into a newly created filegroup named 'NCIX_FG2'.

Listing 1   Scripting CREATE INDEX commands to a new filegroup

```
EXEC usp_Manage_NCIX_FileGroup N'Script', N'NCIX_FG2'

CREATE PROCEDURE [dbo].[usp_Manage_NCIX_FileGroup]
   @ScriptOnlyOrExecute NVARCHAR(6) /* N'Script' or N'Exec' */
 , @NCIXFGName NVARCHAR(255) /* the name new filegroup to move NCIXs into*/
AS
SET NOCOUNT ON

/*cursor variables*/
DECLARE @tnm NVARCHAR(128), @ixnm NVARCHAR(128), @cnm NVARCHAR(128)
      , @schnm NVARCHAR(128), @isPK BIT, @isUn BIT, @isIncCol BIT
      , @cixnm NVARCHAR(128), @ctbschnm NVARCHAR(256)
      , @ixcr NVARCHAR(4000), @ixcnt INT, @indid INT, @order NVARCHAR(5)
      , @inccols NVARCHAR(4000)
SELECT @ixcnt = 0, @cixnm = N'', @ctbschnm = N''

/*open cursor over schema / table / index / columns*/
DECLARE cr CURSOR FOR
SELECT ss.name, so.name, si.name, N'[' + sc.name + N']', is_primary_key
      , CASE WHEN is_descending_key = 0 THEN N'' ELSE N' DESC' END
      , is_included_column, si.index_id, is_unique
FROM sys.schemas ss
JOIN sys.objects so on ss.schema_id = so.schema_id
JOIN sys.indexes si on so.object_id = si.object_id
JOIN sys.index_columns ic ON si.object_id = ic.object_id
                        AND si.index_id = ic.index_id
JOIN sys.columns sc ON ic.object_id = sc.object_id
                  AND ic.column_id = sc.column_id
WHERE OBJECTPROPERTY (so.object_id, 'IsUserTable') = 1
  AND si.index_id > 1 AND si.index_id < 255 /*only interested in NCIXs*/
ORDER BY ss.name, so.name, si.name, ic.index_column_id
/*order crucial for cursor logic*/

OPEN cr

FETCH NEXT FROM cr INTO @schnm, @tnm, @ixnm, @cnm, @isPK, @order, @isIncCol,
      @indid, @isUn

/*move over cursor, constructing & executing a
  drop / create index statement per index*/
WHILE @@FETCH_STATUS = 0
 BEGIN

  IF @ixnm != @cixnm or (@schnm+@tnm != @ctbschnm) /*new index or table*/
    BEGIN
    /*if index, table or schema name changes, reinitialise*/
    IF @schnm+@tnm != @ctbschnm SET @ctbschnm = @schnm+@tnm

    SELECT @ixcnt = @ixcnt + 1
    IF @ixcnt > 1
     BEGIN
       SELECT @ixcr = LEFT(@ixcr, LEN(@ixcr) - 2) + N')'
         + CASE WHEN LEN(@inccols) > 1 THEN N' INCLUDE ('
         + LEFT(@inccols, LEN(@inccols) - 2) + N')' ELSE N'' END
         + N' WITH (DROP_EXISTING = ON'
         + CASE WHEN SERVERPROPERTY('EngineEdition') = 3
```

```
              THEN N', ONLINE = ON)' ELSE N')' END
          + N' ON [' + @NCIXFGName + ']'
        /*execution of create NCIX in other FG occurs
          on first row of NEXT index*/
        PRINT @ixcr; IF @ScriptOnlyOrExecute = N'Exec' EXEC(@ixcr)
      END
      SELECT @cixnm = @ixnm, @inccols = ''
      SET @ixcr = N'create ' + CASE WHEN @isUn = 1
                               THEN N'unique ' ELSE N'' END
            + N'nonclustered index [' + @ixnm + N'] on ['
            + @schnm + N'].[' + @tnm + N'] (' + @cnm + @order
            + N', '
    END
  ELSE
    BEGIN
      /*if same index, build key of included cols csv list*/
      IF @isIncCol != 0 SET @inccols = @inccols + @cnm + N', '
      ELSE SET @ixcr = @ixcr + @cnm + @order + N', '
    END

  FETCH NEXT FROM cr INTO @schnm, @tnm, @ixnm, @cnm, @isPK, @order,
    @isIncCol, @indid, @isUn
END

/*should usually be one last index (assuming there were any)*/
IF @ixcnt > 1
  BEGIN
    SELECT @ixcr = LEFT(@ixcr, LEN(@ixcr) - 2) + N')'
      + CASE WHEN LEN(@inccols) > 1 THEN N' INCLUDE ('
      + LEFT(@inccols, LEN(@inccols) - 2) + N')' ELSE N'' END
      + N' WITH (DROP_EXISTING = ON'
      + CASE WHEN SERVERPROPERTY('EngineEdition') = 3
             THEN N', ONLINE = ON)' ELSE N')' END
      + N' ON [' + @NCIXFGName + ']'
    PRINT @ixcr; IF @ScriptOnlyOrExecute = N'Exec' EXEC(@ixcr)
  END

CLOSE cr ; DEALLOCATE cr
```

Note the following points about the preceding script:

- The script iterates over all schemas and their user tables within the current database, identifying all nonclustered indexes and generating a CREATE INDEX .. WITH DROP_EXISTING ON [NCIX_FG] script for each index, which is then executed dynamically to move each nonclustered index.
- The script will not attempt to move tables. Heaps or clustered indexes are eliminated by the cursor query's WHERE filter:

  ```
  and si.index_id > 1 and si.index_id < 255"
  ```
- Unique definitions, key order, and included columns are all also preserved, so nonclustered indexes should be moved identically with their current definitions.
- Each individual CREATE INDEX statement is also printed, allowing easy review of the commands that have been dynamically executed by the script.

Planning before moving NCIXs into a dedicated filegroup

Using the usp_Manage_NCIX_FileGroup utility stored procedure makes moving all of your database's nonclustered indexes into a new, dedicated nonclustered index filegroup an easy process, but there are some important considerations that need to be addressed before doing this.

Moving NCIXs temporarily requires additional disk space

As nonclustered indexes are moved into the new, dedicated nonclustered index filegroup, extra space needs to be consumed in the filesystem by the filegroup to allocate new page extents to contain the moved nonclustered indexes.

At the same time, space is being freed within the PRIMARY filegroup (as each nonclustered index is moved out to the new filegroup) but this space is not freed back to the filesystem. Filegroup space is only returned to the filesystem if the filegroup's files are explicitly shrunk, using DBCC SHRINKFILE. This doesn't happen automatically, so moving nonclustered indexes out of the PRIMARY filegroup to a new dedicated nonclustered index filegroup will require consumption of more filesystem space.

How much more space is required depends on how much nonclustered index data your database contains. The more nonclustered index data you have, the more filesystem space you need for the new filegroup but the more space you will save in your tables-only filegroup backups.

The amount of space consumed by nonclustered indexes can be roughly estimated in SQL Server 2005 and SQL Server 2008 by running the following query:

```
SELECT SUM(page_count) * 8192.0 / 1048576 as NCIXs_Mb
FROM sys.dm_db_index_physical_stats(db_id(), NULL, NULL, NULL , 'LIMITED')
WHERE OBJECTPROPERTY (object_id, 'IsUserTable') = 1
  AND index_id > 1 AND index_id < 255
```

Here is a similar query for SQL Server 2000:

```
SELECT SUM(dpages) * 8192.0 / 1048576 as NCIXs_Mb
FROM sysindexes
WHERE OBJECTPROPERTY (id, 'IsUserTable') = 1
  AND indid > 1 AND indid < 255
```

Moving NCIXs creates empty space in PRIMARY filegroup

Once nonclustered indexes have been moved out of the PRIMARY filegroup to a new dedicated nonclustered index filegroup, a significant amount of space will have been freed within the PRIMARY filegroup.

This space can be returned to the filesystem by shrinking the filegroup's files via DBCC SHRINKFILE, but using this command will significantly fragment any clustered indexes within the filegroup.

Another option is to add another dedicated filegroup for table storage (heaps and clustered indexes), leaving the PRIMARY filegroup for system tables only. The process of building this additional filegroup requires even more filesystem space, but allows you to re-create the table storage structures within it without fragmenting those structures. After completion of this step, you can shrink the PRIMARY filegroup without significant impact.

Alternatively, you can leave the free space in the PRIMARY filegroup. A problem with this approach is that restoring backups of the database in this state requires equivalent filesystem space on the server the backup is being restored to. Given that the PRIMARY filegroup contains a significant amount of empty space, this might create difficulties in restoring backups on standby or development servers.

Log shipping

So what about combining this technique with log shipping and piecemeal restore? Log shipping standby databases are typically initialized by restoring a full backup of the primary database, and then continuously synchronized by performing regular transaction log backups on the primary database, and restoring those transaction log backups on the standby with NORECOVERY until the standby database needs to be brought online.

It's also possible to initialize a standby database by restoring a tables-only filegroup, then continuously synchronizing via a similar process—except that restoration of log files on the standby utilizes SQL Server 2005's new piecemeal restore feature to include a FILEGROUP clause to the RESTORE LOG commands. Consider this example:

```
RESTORE LOG StandbyDatabase
FILEGROUP = 'PRIMARY'
FROM DISK = 'E:\PrimaryDatabase_LogBackup_20090301090005.lbak'
WITH NORECOVERY
```

Using the FILEGROUP clause directs the RESTORE command to ignore entries in the transaction log that belong to the dedicated nonclustered index filegroup, only restoring log entries that relate to tables (ignoring log entries that relate to nonclustered indexes).

An advantage from combining this technique with log shipping and piecemeal restore is that initialization of the log shipping standby database is faster because a smaller tables-only filegroup backup only needs to be copied from the log shipping primary server to the standby server and restored to the standby database. Unfortunately, there's no way to eliminate index-related transaction log entries from the log backup files, so this technique does not solve the widespread problem of routine index maintenance breaking log shipping systems.

On the other hand, it might be considered a disadvantage that this technique complicates the process of bringing the standby database online in the event of a failover requirement, as indexes also need to be rebuilt.

It's important to point out that it's also possible to continue using regular log shipping (without piecemeal filegroup level restore) while still taking advantage of the disk space, time, and energy savings from switching regular daily full database backups to tables-only filegroup backups. Initializing log shipping in this scenario still requires a full backup of the primary database, but this is still possible because full database backups can still be taken—irrespective of whether tables and indexes have been separated into separate filegroups or not.

In this mode of regular backups and log shipping, you can continue to take regular tables-only filegroup backups of the primary database while still fully restoring transaction log backups against a standby database that has been initialized from a full backup. If log shipping ever breaks, take an ad hoc full backup to re-initialize the log shipping standby database.

Summary

You have much to gain from eliminating index data from backups by the method described in this chapter. Reductions in disk space required to store backups, time taken to process routine backups, and also energy consumed in the process, are all real, tangible benefits.

As with many other technology choices, these advantages need to be weighed against the inconvenience of a slightly more complex and time-consuming restore process in the event that a database needs to be fully reconstructed from backup. In many cases, though, restoration of backups is only performed for ad hoc extraction of historical data, in which case using this technique makes the restoration process faster, allowing quicker recovery of data.

Another benefit is that the reduction in size of backup files from this technique also allows for more copies of historical backups to be maintained. Although this might not be of significant value with smaller databases, with larger databases it could make the difference between being able to store a second backup file rather than only a single full database backup.

Perhaps Microsoft might consider including a feature that allows backups to be taken of table data only, without requiring updates to the system schema, in a future release of SQL Server. Such a feature might even extend to filtering log backups to contain only table-related entries so that log shipping standby servers can be kept in a tables-only state without needing to copy all transaction log entries (including unnecessary index entries) during log shipping.

Although some might consider the updates to system catalogs or increased time required to restore a database as unacceptable, the benefits gained every day in disk space, backup processing time, and energy saved should outweigh these issues in many cases.

About the author

Greg Linwood is the Managing Director of MyDBA—a dedicated SQL Server support business—and also Australian Director of SQLskills, a specialist provider of SQL Server training. Greg has worked in a range of developer and DBA capacities with SQL Server since 1993, and was the first Australian to receive Microsoft's SQL Server MVP award in 2003. He has gained significant expertise in SQL Server tuning, and most of his professional time is currently spent tuning customer SQL Server systems. Greg is passionate about building high-quality SQL Server community events in Australia, and is one of the founders of the Australian SQL Server User Group, leading the Melbourne SQL Server User Group.

34 Using database mirroring to become a superhero!

Glenn Berry

This chapter covers how to use database mirroring not only to increase availability in the traditional sense, but also for less common situations that are not typically mentioned in the SQL Server documentation or literature. One example is using database mirroring to seamlessly upgrade from SQL Server 2005 to SQL Server 2008 with a 10–15-second outage. Another example is using database mirroring to move multiple terabytes of data from one storage system to another with a 10–15-second outage. This chapter reveals these *secret* techniques.

Why should I use database mirroring?

SQL Server 2005 introduced database mirroring, and SQL Server 2008 enhanced it. Back in the pre-SQL Server 2005 days, you had several choices for high availability solutions with SQL Server, including failover clustering, log shipping, and replication. In many situations, database mirroring offers key advantages over all older technologies. It is simple to set up and administer, it offers fast automatic failover, it works at the database level (rather than at the instance or table level), and it can be used with commodity-level hardware.

Database mirroring offers fast failover (usually much faster than failover clustering), and automatic failover (unlike log shipping or replication). It also avoids the single point of failure that you have with the shared storage in failover clustering. In addition, it is much easier to administer than failover clustering (where adding and removing drives can be pretty painful, for example).

How does database mirroring work?

If you are unfamiliar with how database mirroring works, here is a quick primer.

You have one user database, which must be running with the FULL recovery model, which is called the *principal*. The principal is available for client connections, and does most of the work. You also have a complete, synchronized copy of that database (which must be running on another SQL Server instance, preferably on another server). The copy, known as the *mirror*, is *not* available for client connections. Optionally, if you want automatic failover, you have a third instance of SQL Server, hopefully on its own server, which is the *witness*. The witness can run on older hardware, and it can be SQL Server Express Edition. Its job is to help determine when a failover is required, by communicating with the principal and mirror. One witness instance can be used for multiple principal/mirror pairs if needed, because the witness is not doing intense work, and it can also be used as a Central Management Server with SQL Server 2008.

All of the write activity on the principal (including DDL and DML) is sent over your network to the mirror, where it is replayed on the mirror. Depending on how your database mirroring is configured, this may be happening synchronously or asynchronously. You must be running in high-safety mode (synchronous) with a witness, to allow automatic failover. If you are running Enterprise Edition of SQL Server, you can run in high-performance mode (asynchronous), which does not allow automatic failover, but can still be useful for many situations.

With database mirroring, you have two complete copies of your data, which can be a good thing. Failover clustering uses shared, external storage, usually a storage area network (SAN), where drives are *owned* by a particular node in the cluster. Shared storage is a common single point of failure. If unavailable, the cluster service will not start, and SQL Server will not start on the cluster.

From a storage perspective, having a second copy of the data with the mirror can be expensive, but it protects you from the single point of failure you have with a failover cluster (assuming the mirror database is on a different storage system than the principal database). This second copy of your data is ready to go after recovery has completed. The mirror database can be available much faster than a database restored from backups or SAN snapshots. As a DBA responsible for multiple, mission-critical databases, having the databases mirrored gives me additional peace of mind, because the mirrors represent additional copies of the data, over and above my normal backups and SAN snapshots.

How do you set up database mirroring?

You have several ways to do this, depending on your objectives, available infrastructure, and budget. You should invest sufficient time and resources in testing your infrastructure (including server and network hardware) to make sure it can handle your anticipated workload reliably. Make sure you have enough disk space available to accommodate possible log file growth if you encounter temporary issues with the mirroring session.

If you need or want a robust, high availability solution with automatic failover and the ability to run comfortably on the *mirror* server for an extended period, consider using these best practices.

Make sure that both the principal and mirror have identical hardware:

- Server model
- Number and types of CPUs
- Amount of RAM
- Amount of I/O capacity, space, and RAID level on separate storage devices

Using best practices is important to ensure that the mirror can keep up during normal operation and especially when you do log-intensive operations like index rebuilds or reorganizations. This will also ensure that you can comfortably run your workload on the mirror hardware for an extended period.

Make sure that both the principal and mirror are running a 64-bit version of Windows Server 2008 or better. Windows Server 2008 R2 will be 64-bit only; and it is likely that the next version after SQL Server 2008 will be 64-bit only; therefore, time is running out on the 32-bit era. Improved memory management alone is a great reason to switch to a 64-bit version.

You should choose a 64-bit version of the Enterprise Edition of SQL Server 2008, because Enterprise Edition has several valuable enhancements (such as parallel log restore and log stream compression) that are important for database mirroring. SQL Server 2008 native backup compression is helpful when you are initially setting up a mirror, because your backups and restores will be smaller and will usually complete more quickly. The compressed backup files will be easier to move from the principal to the mirror (because they are smaller). SQL Server 2008 also offers automatic page repair for database mirroring. SQL Server 2005 database mirroring also works well, although it lacks the enhancements that were added in SQL Server 2008.

Both sides of the partnership should be running the same build of SQL Server, that is, the same Service Pack and Cumulative Update level. If you want automatic failover, you must have a witness instance, which should be on the same build of SQL Server as the principal and mirror.

You also should standardize on common drive sizes, drive letters, and paths for certain SQL Server uses, such as data files, transaction logs, tempdb, backups, and so on. For example, you might decide to use P:, Q:, R:, and S: for data files; L: for your transaction log; T: for tempdb; and G: and H: for database backups, for both the principal and mirror sides of the mirroring partnership. This is important, because if you decide to add a new data file to your principal, the G: drive, for example, but there is no identical drive letter and path on the mirror, your database mirroring state will be suspended (and the transaction log will not be truncated) until you correct the situation. Backup drives should also have the same drive letters, because if you end up running on the mirror hardware for an extended period, you would want to be running your normal full and transaction log backup routine on the mirror side (which is now the principal). Having identical drive letters and paths makes this much easier. Even though tempdb cannot be mirrored, you still should include it in your drive letter standardization efforts, for consistency's sake, because that will help you make sure that both instances are configured identically.

One valid objection that you may hear regarding database mirroring is that it is only available at the user database level; therefore, it does not include things like logins and SQL Agent jobs. This is easy enough to correct with a little preparation. You should try hard to use Windows Authentication instead of SQL Server Authentication for your logins, and then create the same Windows logins on the mirror instance. This will avoid the possibility of *orphaned users* that you can get with SQL Server Authentication. If you must use SQL Server Authentication, you can create the SQL Server logins on the mirror instance with the same SID as on the principal instance, which will also avoid the orphaned users issue. The queries in listing 1 show how to create a SQL Server login with an identical SID on the mirror instance.

Listing 1   Script to create a login with identical `SID` on the mirror instance

```
-- Get the SID for an existing login
SELECT [name], sid
FROM sys.server_principals
      WHERE type_desc = 'SQL_LOGIN'
-- Create SQL Server login with a specific SID
--(to avoid orphaned user problem)
CREATE LOGIN yourloginname WITH PASSWORD =
  'yourpassword',
sid = 0xA306A5DFBF321A4D98D71520DAE1C1D3, CHECK_POLICY
  = OFF
```

You can script SQL Agent jobs out on the principal, and then create them on the mirror ahead of time, keeping them disabled on the mirror until you need them. However, ensuring that the SQL Agent jobs are maintained on the mirror will require some discipline. Job changes are migrated over time.

You should make sure that both sides of the mirroring partnership are properly configured for SQL Server 2008, depending on your type of workload. For both online transaction processing (OLTP) and decision support system (DSS) types of workloads, I would grant the Lock Pages in Memory and Perform Volume Maintenance Tasks rights to the SQL Server Service Account. Prior to SQL Server 2008 SP1 CU2 (Build 2714), the Lock Pages in Memory right worked only with the Enterprise Edition of SQL Server 2005/2008. The Perform Volume Maintenance Tasks right is necessary for the Windows Instant File Initialization feature to work. This allows SQL Server to allocate file space for data files (during database creation, file grows, and database restores), without zeroing out the file first. This can pose a small security risk, but I think the benefit far outweighs the risk. Database restores are much quicker with Windows Instant File Initialization enabled. This is important when you are trying to establish a mirror on a busy production database.

You should also set instance level options with `sp_configure` for things like max server memory (MB), max degree of parallelism, optimize for ad hoc workloads, clr enabled, and backup compression default to appropriate values depending on your workload type. Max degree of parallelism is usually set to "1" for OLTP workloads and half the number of processor cores for DSS workloads. Optimize for ad hoc workloads and backup compression default should both be enabled in most cases. If you have any .NET CLR assemblies in the database that you want to mirror, you need to make sure that clr enabled is set to "1" on the SQL Server instance where the mirror database will live.

How do you prepare the mirror?

Finally, after all of the preliminary configuration work, you are ready to *prepare the mirror* for database mirroring. If possible, you should try to do this during non-peak hours, and you should also consider deferring normal index maintenance tasks while you are trying to establish the mirror, so that log-intensive operations are minimized as much as possible. This will make it much easier to establish the mirror.

To prepare the mirror, you need to take a full database backup of the user database that you want to mirror (which must be running in FULL recovery model). Using backup compression, whether it is SQL Server native backup compression or a solution from a third party, is highly recommended in this situation, because it will make the backup file(s) much smaller, and it will allow the full backup to complete much more quickly. When the full backup is complete, you will need to copy the database backup to the *mirror* instance. Speed is of the essence here, because your full backup is falling behind the live database each second during this process.

If you are using a modern SAN on your principal instance, you may be able to *snap* the backup drive(s) over to the *mirror* host nearly instantaneously. Otherwise, you will have to copy the backup file(s) over your network to the mirror host, which may take quite a bit of time. If both servers are running Windows Server 2008, network copy time can be reduced courtesy of the improvements in Server Message Block 2.0. If the backup file(s) are compressed, that will obviously reduce the copy and restore time even further.

After the backup file(s) are available on the mirror host, you should restore the database with the NORECOVERY option. This is important. If you restore with RECOVERY (which is the default for both the SQL Server Management Studio (SSMS) GUI and T-SQL), you will not be able to establish the mirror, and you will have to restore all over again. You should always script out the restore, to double-check it, and you should change the progress update setting to 1 percent, so that you can get a better estimate of how long the restore will take. Depending on the size and activity level of your database, and your hardware and network infrastructure, this full backup, copy, and restore sequence could take several hours. You can dramatically reduce this time frame by having a robust I/O subsystem, using backup compression, making sure the mirror instance SQL Server Service account has the Perform Volume Maintenance Tasks right, and using Windows Server 2008.

Again, depending on your level of write activity on the principal and the time elapsed for the full backup, copy, and restore sequence, you will probably have taken one or more transaction log backups on the principal during this period. You should also use backup compression here if possible. Each of these backup files should be copied over to the mirror instance, where they need to be restored with NORECOVERY, in sequence. Depending on how long the full backup took, some of the initial transaction log backup restores will be skipped when you try to restore them, because their log sequence numbers will be included in the full backup. With SQL Server 2008, you must back up and restore at least one log backup; otherwise you will not be able to establish the mirror.

For example, if your full backup, copy, and restore took six hours, your mirror will be about six hours behind the principal after the full restore is finished. You will usually find that the transaction log restores go relatively quickly, and you will start to rapidly catch up to the principal. If you are taking hourly transaction log backups on the principal, you will typically see the restore take a few minutes (depending on several factors, mainly I/O capacity on the mirror), which will allow you to eventually catch up to the principal. It is important to try to catch up as much as possible, because SQL Server will refuse to establish the mirror if it is too far behind the principal.

After you are caught up as closely as possible, you need to create the mirroring endpoints and issue the appropriate ALTER DATABASE commands to establish the mirror. The database mirroring wizard in SQL Server Management Studio (SSMS) works well enough for this, but beware that it will want to start the mirroring session in high-safety mode (synchronous) by default, which I do not recommend. You can also use T-SQL to do this. In most cases, you should start database mirroring in high-performance mode (asynchronous), to make sure that the performance of the principal is not negatively affected by the mirror trying to get fully synchronized. The SSMS tool called Database Mirroring Monitor, which was introduced with SQL Server 2005 SP1, makes it much easier to watch what is going on as the databases get synchronized. You can also watch some database mirroring specific counters in Performance Monitor (under SQL Server: Database Mirroring), and you can run some system catalog and Dynamic Management View (DMV) queries to monitor database mirroring. Some of these are shown in listing 2.

Listing 2   Queries to monitor database mirroring

```
-- Basic info about mirrored databases
SELECT DB_NAME(database_id) AS 'database_name', *
FROM sys.database_mirroring
WHERE database_id > 4 -- eliminate system databases
AND mirroring_state != NULL
-- Check mirroring endpoints
SELECT *
FROM sys.database_mirroring_endpoints
-- Check witness status
SELECT *
FROM sys.database_mirroring_witnesses
-- Check mirroring connections
SELECT *
FROM sys.dm_db_mirroring_connections
-- Check auto page repair history (SQL 2008 only)
SELECT DB_NAME(database_id) AS 'database_name', *
FROM sys.dm_db_mirroring_auto_page_repair
```

You should not rely on the status message in the Object Explorer tree in SSMS to tell you the status of your database mirror, because it does not auto refresh. If you do not manually refresh the database status in Object Explorer, you will never know the true status of the database mirroring session. This will give you a false sense of security and well-being, because the status might say Principal, Synchronized, even if the true status is something else like Principal, Suspended (unless you manually refresh it). Perhaps a future version of SQL Server will have a feature that would let you configure SSMS to let it automatically refresh this status periodically. In the meantime, you can use Database Mirroring Monitor to configure alerts that can automatically notify you about the status of your database mirror. You can also query sys.databases and check the log_reuse_wait_desc column to see if the description is DATABASE_MIRRORING (which tells you that mirroring has a problem), as you see below:

```
-- Get log reuse wait description
SELECT [name], log_reuse_wait_desc
FROM sys.databases
```

If a problem with your database mirroring session is preventing the transaction log from being truncated internally when you take a transaction log backup, the transaction log on the principal database will start to fill up and eventually grow (if auto-grow is enabled). This is usually caused by a communications problem or a REDO queue on the mirror.

One final tip about establishing your first database mirroring session on a production server is to try creating a small test database on the principal for a trial run on that server. Create an empty database running FULL recovery model, then take a full backup and log backup (even though it is empty, with no activity). Then restore the full backup and log backup, with no recovery. Finally, create the endpoints and alter the database to create the mirror. This should take you less than five minutes, and it will validate connectivity and security for all of the servers and instances involved. It will also validate that you are performing all of the tasks correctly, in the right sequence, before you try it on your production database. This tip is also useful for troubleshooting if you run into problems later on a production server.

One last thing you need to take care of is to talk to your developers about how and where they store their application-level connection strings, and what data access technologies they are using to connect to your database. With most data access technologies, you will be able to use *transparent client redirect*, by adding a failover partner to the connection string. This will allow clients to automatically connect to the server that is acting as the principal before and after a failover, whether it is automatic or manual. This modified connection string should be in place before you attempt a database failover. If the modified connection string is not available, implicit client redirection will usually work, but explicit client redirection is a better choice. If you ever need or want to remove mirroring from the database, you should remove the failover partner information from the connection strings for that database.

Now you have mirroring set up and running well, with no performance issues. What superhero functions can you perform with database mirroring?

Using database mirroring for routine maintenance

Routine maintenance on a database server is much more difficult than the equivalent maintenance on a middle-tier server (such as a web or application server). With a middle-tier server that is behind a load balancer, you can remove the server from the pool, allow it time to drain its pending requests, and then do whatever is required, whether it be applying Windows updates, updating the BIOS or firmware, or updating the application. It is easy to do *rolling maintenance* in the middle tier. Database mirroring makes rolling maintenance almost as easy for the data tier. Let's imagine that you need to apply a critical Windows update on your database servers in production. You have tested this update in a development/QA environment to make sure that it does not cause issues for SQL Server or your application(s), and you have confirmed that the update requires a reboot of the server.

If you had a standalone database server with no high availability solution in place, you would be looking at about five to ten minutes of downtime for all of the applications that use that server (because that is about the average time it takes most commodity level servers to completely reboot and then restart SQL Server). The downtime varies based on your hardware and environment, and could be much longer. That one standalone database server restart would use up all your downtime for the entire year if you are trying to achieve *five nines* availability, which is 99.999 percent.

With a SQL Server Failover Cluster, you would be looking at about 60–90 seconds of downtime for each node as you moved an instance from one node to another to perform a rolling upgrade. SQL Server Clustering takes much longer to fail over than database mirroring does, because it has to start SQL Server on the new node when you fail over. With database mirroring, you would be able to perform the same routine maintenance with either one or two 15–30-second failovers (if the mirroring state is SYNCHRONIZED and there is no REDO queue on the mirror), depending on whether you had equivalent hardware on both sides of the mirror. How would you do this?

Before you start, you should confirm that you have valid failover partner information in all of your application connection strings. You would also want to defer index maintenance that was scheduled during this time frame, because you don't want extra transaction log activity. Then you would apply the Windows update to the server where the mirror copy of the database was running, and reboot the server. After the server comes back up and the SQL Server is restarted, you can watch in Database Mirroring Monitor, until the database(s) are again fully synchronized. Depending on your hardware and workload, this might take awhile.

After the database(s) are synchronized, you would manually fail over from the principal to the mirror (thereby swapping their roles). This will usually take less than a minute depending on your workload and hardware. During this relatively short time, your applications will be unavailable, but after the mirroring roles are switched, your applications will automatically reconnect (with no user intervention), assuming the failover partner information is correct in the connection strings, and the application has been coded to reconnect after a failure. If you have multiple mirrored databases on that server, you would manually fail over each of those databases. Finally, you could apply the Windows update to the original principal server, which now has the mirror database(s), and then allow it to restart. If your hardware is equivalent on both sides, you could run on the normal mirror side until the next time you needed to do some maintenance (assuming you have a SQL license). If not, you can wait for the mirror to become synchronized, and then failover again to be back on the original server. Either way, database mirroring can give you *much less downtime* (seconds instead of minutes) than any other method.

If you *do not* have equivalent hardware and I/O capacity on both sides of the mirror, you can use a variation on this strategy. If your budget will not allow you to buy sufficient hardware and I/O capacity for the mirror, you can run database mirroring in high-performance mode (asynchronous) during normal operations. That way, your principal database is not slowed down waiting on your mirror hardware and I/O subsystem during times of peak workload. In high-safety mode (synchronous), transactions are not committed on the principal until they have been sent to the mirror, committed there, and then acknowledged back to the principal. When it comes time for routine maintenance, you follow nearly the same sequence of steps, with a few key changes.

You apply the Windows Update and reboot the mirror server, and you wait for the mirror to get synchronized again. On the principal side, you switch from high-performance to high-safety mode, which is a quick and easy change. You should once again confirm that the database is fully synchronized, which might take awhile, and then failover the database from the principal to the mirror. The failover usually takes less than a minute. After the roles are switched, go to the new principal, and quickly switch back to high-performance mode. Next, you apply the Windows update to the original principal server and allow it to reboot. Then you wait for the database to get fully synchronized and then switch back to high-safety mode and fail over that database back to the original server. Finally, you switch back to high-performance mode, and you are done, with two relatively quick failovers.

One drawback to running normally in high-performance mode is that you lose your automatic failover capability, which requires high-safety mode, with a witness. It also makes it more difficult to quickly recover from losing the principal database. If you ever permanently lost the principal database (due to a catastrophic hardware failure, for example), you could break the mirroring partnership and recover the orphaned mirror by running the commands below:

```
-- Remove the mirror
ALTER DATABASE yourdatabase SET PARTNER OFF

-- Restore the database on the mirror side
RESTORE DATABASE yourdatabase WITH RECOVERY
```

You could always restore from your regular SQL Server backup set. This could take quite awhile, during which time your application(s) will be down. If the database(s) had a mirroring state of SYNCHRONIZED when the failure occurred, you could be back up and running much more quickly on the *broken* mirror, with no data loss.

Using database mirroring to upgrade to SQL Server 2008

Let's say that you are ready to upgrade your production database servers from SQL Server 2005 running on Windows Server 2003 to SQL Server 2008 running on Windows Server 2008. This technique would also work with an upgrade to SQL Server 2008 running on Windows Server 2003, but you would lose the benefits of Windows Server 2008. You could do this several ways, each with varying degrees of risk and downtime.

One way would be to upgrade both the operating system and SQL Server in place, on the existing server. This would be risky (in my opinion), and would incur at least a couple of hours of downtime for both upgrades, assuming everything went smoothly. I would never upgrade in place like this, unless I had no other choice. Another method would be to install a fresh copy of Windows Server 2008 on a new server, get it fully patched and configured, then install SQL Server 2008, and get it fully patched and configured (including transferring logins, SQL Agent jobs, and so on). After the new server was completely ready and tested, you could use one of the following methods:

- Detach your SQL Server 2005 database(s), and copy (not move) them over to the new server and attach them.
- Go through a full backup, copy, and restore sequence from the old server to the new server.
- Use database mirroring to minimize the downtime.

The detach/attach route would be faster than the other methods, but you would still be offline for the time it took to copy the database files to the new server. This time could be minimized by using a third party compressed backup or using a SAN snapshot to copy the database files to the new server. Detach/attach is slightly riskier than the other two methods, because you will upgrade the copy (not the original, which is still back on the old server) of the database to 2008 format when you attach it in SQL Server 2008. If the attach does not succeed, you still have the original on the old server. Be sure you never detach your database and move the live copy to the new server to attach it there. This is a good way to lose your live copy if the attach does not succeed.

The full backup, copy to new server, and restore sequence would take much longer than the detach/attach route, but it is safer. Depending on the size of your database(s) and your infrastructure, you would probably be looking at several hours of downtime with a full backup/restore sequence.

You could also use log shipping to get your data from the old server to the new server. You would need to change the old database to read-only before you switched to the new server, and then back up the tail of the log and restore it on the new server. This would be more complicated to implement, but it would be low risk and have relatively short downtime (probably a few minutes).

A much better solution would be to use SQL Server Database Mirroring to migrate from SQL Server 2005 on the existing server to SQL Server 2008 on a new server with a single relatively short outage. This works well, is low risk, and is easy to implement.

One caveat is that your SQL Server 2005 instance must be on Build 3215 (SP2 Cumulative Update 5) or better. If you are on an older build of SQL Server 2005, you will not be able to establish a mirroring session with a SQL Server 2008 instance.

To use this method, you would install a fresh copy of Windows Server 2008 on a new server, get it fully patched and configured, then install SQL Server 2008, and get it fully patched and configured (including transferring logins and SQL Agent jobs). Then you would go though the normal steps to *prepare the mirror*—full database backup, copy and restore with NORECOVERY, then log backups, copy and restore with NORECOVERY, until you were ready to create the endpoints and establish the mirror.

After the mirror was established and synchronized, you could run that way as long as needed until you were ready to fail over each database to the mirror. You would also need to ensure that all of your applications had the failover partner information added to their connection strings. Failing over from SQL Server 2005 to SQL Server 2008 usually takes less than a minute, depending on your workload. Be aware that this is a one-way trip. After you have failed over from SQL Server 2005 to SQL Server 2008, you cannot go back (and, in fact, your 2005 copy of the database will be corrupted).

After you failed over each database from SQL Server 2005 to 2008, you would remove the mirroring session for that database. You would change the compatibility level to SQL Server 2008 (100) because it will still be SQL Server 2005 (90)—you originally restored it from a SQL Server 2005 backup. This assumes that your application has been tested and is fully compatible with SQL Server 2008 (100) compatibility mode. I would also consider running sp_updatestats on the upgraded database(s) during a non-peak period. Then you would enable all of your transferred SQL Server Agent jobs on the new server. Finally, you are ready to take advantage of the great new features in SQL Server 2008, and you were able to upgrade with a small outage and no loss of data.

Using database mirroring to move data seamlessly

Another common problem that can be easily solved with database mirroring is moving large volumes of live SQL Server data from one location to another, with little downtime. This could be from one server to another server, from one storage device to another storage device, or from one geographic location to another.

Case study of moving data with database mirroring

A couple of years ago, I was faced with moving about 3 TB of data that was in several busy SQL Server 2005 OLTP databases from an older server host and SAN to a new server host and SAN about 50 yards away. Let's examine a case study in which I employed database mirroring for exactly this purpose. The system ran 24/7/365, with a five nines availability requirement. These business constraints eliminated any possibility of using a conventional full backup and restore sequence, because I estimated that it would take about 18 hours for a full backup, file copy, and full restore to complete, which was unacceptable to the business.

Another possibility was using a database detach, file copy, and attach operation. We had 2Gbps host bus adapters (HBAs) in each server, and copying the detached database files would be much faster over fiber links than with Gigabit Ethernet. Even so, we would be looking at several hours to copy the database files from the old server to the new server, plus a significant risk of something going awry during the file copy. None of these conditions was acceptable. Once again, the superhero solution is database mirroring.

In this case, I was able to deploy a new server attached to the new SAN in the new location. We installed a fresh copy of the x64 version of Windows Server 2003 R2 and got it fully configured and updated, including provisioning all the required SAN drives. Then we installed the x64 version of SQL Server 2005 Enterprise Edition and got it fully configured and updated to the same SQL Server build as on the original instance. Then we started the mirror preparation process.

I ran a full database backup on the original server, and had our SAN engineer take a SAN snapshot of the backup drives, which he then presented to the mirror host machine. This allowed me to start the full restore with NORECOVERY process in a few minutes (because I did not have to wait hours to copy the backup files over the network). As the full restore was running, I periodically copied my transaction log backup files over the network from the old server to the new server, so that they would be ready to restore as soon as the full restore finished. This is important with a busy OLTP database, because you are racing to catch up as you are preparing the mirror. After the full restore finished, I started restoring the transaction log backups on the new server. Scripting multiple log restores out with a 1 percent progress update setting and some PRINT statements after each log restore gave me a much better idea of my progress and how far the timing of the mirror database was behind the principal database. After I was caught up to being less than an hour behind the principal database, I configured security, and established the mirror in high-performance mode. Because the new SAN had much more I/O capacity than the old SAN, it only took a few minutes to get each database synchronized.

We ran in high-performance mode for a few days while we were moving other hardware, and were making sure we were ready to fail over the mirrored databases. Finally, we switched to high-safety mode and failed over each database to the new server and SAN. After some application testing, we were ready to remove the mirroring session for each database, making the move permanent. Then we powered down the old server and SAN, and moved them to the new location, rebuilt the server with a fresh copy of the operating system and SQL Server, and reestablished all of our database mirrors.

Lessons learned from case study

Depending on your workload and I/O capacity, it may take some time for the principal and mirror databases to get fully synchronized after you initially establish a database mirror. If you have less I/O capacity on the mirror side, you will see the unrestored log size grow on the mirror side if you are watching in Database Mirroring Monitor. Eventually it should catch up, and allow the two databases to become fully synchronized. After the databases are synchronized, you are ready to fail over from the principal to the mirror.

In order to fail over seamlessly, you need to make sure that you have the correct failover partner information added to all of your application connection strings. When you are ready, you can switch to high-safety mode and fail over the database. After your expected 10–15-second outage, your applications will be running against the principal database on the new server and SAN, in the new location. Next, you can remove mirroring from the database, and you will have moved the data, with a brief outage. After you remove mirroring from the database, make sure to remove the failover partner information from all of your connection strings. Later, after you have repeated this sequence with all of your databases, you can power down the old server and SAN and move them if necessary. This general strategy can also be used to move data over longer geographic distances. As the geographic distance increases, you have to be careful about increasing network latency if you are running in high-safety mode, which will cause delays for the principal as it waits for the mirror to harden its transactions. This is much less of a problem with high-performance mode, and SQL Server 2008 also helps with log stream compression, which is helpful over high-latency WAN links.

Once again, using Windows Server 2008 in combination with SQL Server 2008 Enterprise Edition makes it much quicker and easier to prepare the mirror, because you get much better network file copy performance, you can use backup compression for your backups and restores, and you can run database mirroring in high-performance mode. In the end we were able to fail over from the old server and SAN to the new server and SAN with a single 15-second outage, which was a great success, made possible with database mirroring.

Summary

For some reason, few DBAs have tried out database mirroring. When I go to various SQL Server–related events, I often ask for a show of hands on how many people have tried or are using database mirroring with SQL Server, and usually the percentage is low, which always amazes me. Don't be afraid to start using SQL Server database mirroring.

As you've seen, database mirroring is easy to set up and administer, it offers the fastest possible automatic failover (under the right conditions), and it can be used with commodity hardware for a reliable high availability solution. It can replace or complement failover clustering or log shipping. For example, databases within a clustered instance can be mirrored to either a standalone instance of SQL Server or another SQL Server failover cluster. This provides both hardware redundancy through the Windows cluster and storage redundancy through database mirroring.This would give you additional hardware redundancy at the host level because of the Windows cluster, and storage redundancy because of the database mirroring.

With this configuration, you could also take advantage of the much faster failovers available with database mirroring to reduce your downtime for normal maintenance. Using a database mirror in combination with a cluster makes it much easier to do maintenance on the entire cluster (such as applying a Windows or SQL Server Service pack or cumulative update), because you can failover all of your databases to the mirror, and then do whatever you need to do to the cluster, without being in a rush.

If you are going to combine failover clustering with synchronous database mirroring (with automatic failover), you will want to change the default mirroring partner timeout to a higher value, so that a mirroring fail over is not initiated during the time that you are in the middle of a cluster failover (from one node to another). You can change this value with the following command:

```
ALTER DATABASE mydatabase SET PARTNER TIMEOUT 90;
```

Another possibility is to combine failover clustering with asynchronous database mirroring, which will avoid the potential for *dueling* failovers, at the cost of the loss of another layer of automatic redundancy. This is still a useful configuration, because you have a second copy of the database available (although it may not be synchronized) in the event of a catastrophic cluster or storage failure.

You can also take advantage of database mirroring for the non-traditional uses described in this chapter. Database mirroring can dramatically reduce your downtime for rolling maintenance tasks. It also makes it much easier to migrate to SQL Server 2008 in a production situation, with little risk or downtime. Hopefully this chapter has inspired you to try out database mirroring and given you ammunition to convince your company to upgrade to both Windows Server 2008 and SQL Server 2008, not because they are new and shiny, but because of tangible benefits that they provide together.

About the author

Glenn Berry works as a Database Architect at NewsGator Technologies in Denver, Colorado. He is a SQL Server MVP, and he has a whole collection of Microsoft certifications, including MCITP, MCDBA, MCSE, MCSD, MCAD, and MCTS, which proves that he likes to take tests.

He is also an Adjunct Faculty member at University College, University of Denver, where he has been teaching since 2000.

35 The poor man's SQL Server log shipping

Edwin Sarmiento

Let's imagine that you've got a new line of business application up and running smoothly. You're extending your disaster recovery plan to include this new application. For database, you're thinking along the lines of log shipping until you read the documentation provided by the vendor: *The installation program installs SQL Server 2005 Express Edition.*

Log shipping is a high availability solution of SQL Server, in which the SQL Server Agent automates the process of generating transaction log backups of the source database, copying them over to a remote SQL Server instance, and restoring them in either no-recovery or read-only, standby mode. It has gained popularity as a high availability solution because of the option to use different hardware for a standby server and the licensing options available for setting it up. This feature is available in the Enterprise Edition for SQL Server 2000, whereas even the Standard and Workgroup Editions of SQL Server 2005 and 2008 have it. But for those who are using editions other than those specified, there are no other options except to do it outside of the "supported" scenarios. Many third-party applications use editions such as Express and the old Microsoft SQL Server Desktop Engine (MSDE) including those from Microsoft, such as Office SharePoint Server 2007, with its default installation option. This chapter will discuss how to implement log shipping even when Microsoft says it cannot be done.

It is important to understand what log shipping does so that we can come up with a process that can implement a similar mechanism. *Process* is more important than the technology itself. Log shipping consists of three steps:

1 Back up the transaction log within a specified interval, say every 15 minutes.
2 Copy the log backup from the primary server to the standby server.
3 Restore the copied log backup while leaving the database in either no-recovery or read-only, standby mode.

Because we'll be dealing with SQL Server 2005 and 2008 Express Edition (or even SQL Server 2000 editions that do not support log shipping), defining a primary and a standby server could mean working with nonserver operating systems such as Windows 2000 Professional, Windows XP, or even Windows Vista or Windows 7. References to these terms throughout the chapter should not be confused with using Windows server operating systems.

Understanding these steps will help you create an automated job that involves all of these processes. First, you need to create a full backup of the database that you will be configuring for log shipping, and restore the backup on the standby SQL Server. Make sure that the restore options for the database should either be read-only and standby or with no recovery (the T-SQL script for this is defined in listing 5, which shows restoreLOG.vbs). This ensures that we can restore additional transaction logs later in the process. After we restore the database backup on the standby server, we are now ready to configure log shipping. The following items are needed:

- *ROBOCOPY (Robust File Copy Utility)*—This is a command-line file copy tool available in the Windows Resource Kit tools. This copies files from a source folder to a destination folder and resumes interrupted copies. It also preserves Windows NT File System (NTFS) permissions and access control lists (ACLs).
- *Shared folder*—You should share the folder, which will contain the log backup files, and make sure that you have at least read-only access.
- *Domain*—This will have the primary and standby servers as member servers.
- *Domain account*—This has dbo permissions on the database, which you will be configuring for log shipping. We'll use this account to copy and restore the log backups from the primary server to the standby server.

Now, we're ready to configure any database for log shipping. We'll start with the SQL Server instance that will act as the primary server. To be more structured, we'll create folders on both the primary and standby servers that will contain the log backups, the script files, the script execution results, and the UNDO files. The scripts are dependent on the file and folder structure you create, so make sure you update your scripts accordingly.

- *E:\LogShipFolder*—Location of the log backups, segregated by database name (for example, E:\LogShipFolder\Northwind for the Northwind database). This folder should be on both the primary and the standby servers.
- *E:\LogShipFolder\UNDO*—Location of UNDO files that will be specified as part of the RESTORE LOG command when the choice is to restore the log backup and leave the database in the read-only, standby mode. This folder should be created in the standby server. Each UNDO file is identified by the fact that it has the database name as its prefix.
- *E:\LogShipFolder\scripts*—Location of all the T-SQL scripts, VBScripts, batch files, and EXE files that will be used for this process. This folder should be on both the primary and the standby servers.

- *E:\LogShipFolder\scripts\SQL*—Location of the dynamically generated T-SQL script files, which will contain the RESTORE LOG command. This SQL script file will be run by a command-line call to sqlcmd.exe (or osql.exe for SQL Server 2000 or MSDE), the command-line utility for SQL Server. This folder should be created in the standby server and will also store the query execution results file, which will be generated using the sqlcmd.exe command-line utility. The results file is for records and troubleshooting.

Creating the T-SQL script

First, you need to create a T-SQL script that generates transaction log backups. Let's say, we'll back up the Northwind database in our SQL Server 2005 Express instance, as shown in listing 1. We'll name the file backupLog.sql.

Listing 1 T-SQL script (backupLog.sql) generates transaction log backups

```
DECLARE @strTimeStamp NVARCHAR(12) --variable for timestamp value
DECLARE @SQL VARCHAR(1000) --variable for dynamic SQL
SET @strTimeStamp=convert(char(8), getdate(), 112)
SET @strTimeStamp=@strTimeStamp + REPLACE(convert(char(8), getdate(),
    108),':','')

SELECT @SQL = 'BACKUP LOG [Northwind] TO DISK =
    ''E:\LogShipFolder\Northwind\Northwind_tlog_' + @strTimeStamp +'.trn''
    WITH INIT'
EXEC (@SQL)
```

When you run this backup script, make sure that you have no other log backups running, as this would break the log sequence that is necessary to restore the transaction logs.

Creating a cleanup script

We'll need to create a cleanup script that will delete the log backups older than a specified number of days or whatever retention period you have set as a corporate policy. The script will also log the delete activities in a file for reference. To accomplish this task, a VBScript will be used, as shown in listing 2.

Listing 2 VBScript (deleteTRN.vbs) cleans up the transaction log backups

```
On Error Resume Next
Dim fso, folder, files, sFolder, sFolderTarget, intDaysOld
Set fso = CreateObject("Scripting.FileSystemObject")

'The number of days would be the value passed to the script as a parameter
intDaysOld= Wscript.Arguments.Item(0)
strDatabaseName= Wscript.Arguments.Item(1)

'Location of the database backup files
sFolder = "E:\LogShipFolder\" & strDatabaseName & "\"

Set folder = fso.GetFolder(sFolder)
Set files = folder.Files
```

```
    'Variable used for writing to textfile-generate report on database backups
        deleted
Const ForAppending = 8

    'Create a folder named "scripts" for ease of file management &
    'a file inside it named "LOG.txt" for delete activity logging
Set objFile = fso.OpenTextFile(sFolder & "scripts\LOG.txt", ForAppending)

objFile.Write "=================================" & VBCRLF & VBCRLF
objFile.Write "DATABASE BACKUP FILE REPORT  " & VBCRLF
objFile.Write "DATE:   " & FormatDateTime(Now(),1)   & "" & VBCRLF
objFile.Write "TIME:   " & FormatDateTime(Now(),3)   & "" & VBCRLF & VBCRLF
objFile.Write "======================================" & VBCRLF

    'iterate thru each of the files in the database backup folder
For Each itemFiles In files
    'retrieve complete path of file for the DeleteFile method and to extract
    'file extension using the GetExtensionName method
    a=sFolder & itemFiles.Name

    'retrieve file extension
    b = fso.GetExtensionName(a)
        'check if the file extension is TRN
        If uCase(b)="TRN" Then
            'check if the database backups are older than intDaysOld days
            If DateDiff("d",itemFiles.DateCreated,Now()) >= intDaysOld Then
                'Delete any old BACKUP files to cleanup folder
                fso.DeleteFile a
                objFile.WriteLine "BACKUP FILE DELETED: " & a
            End If
        End If
Next

objFile.WriteLine "======================================"&VBCRLF & VBCRLF

objFile.Close

Set objFile = Nothing
Set fso = Nothing
Set folder = Nothing
Set files = Nothing
```

Creating a batch file

We need to create the batch file that will call both the T-SQL script and the VBScript file. The contents of the batch file will be a simple call to sqlcmd.exe and a call to the VBScript file using either wscript.exe or calling the file, as shown in listing 3. Save the file as E:\LogShipFolder\scripts\databaseBackup.cmd and save it in the scripts subfolder.

Listing 3   Batch file (databaseBackupLog.cmd) calls the backup and cleanup scripts

```
REM Run TSQL Script to backup database transaction logs
sqlcmd -S<PRIMARYINSTANCENAME> -E -i"E:\LogShipFolder\scripts\backupLog.sql"

REM Run database backup cleanup script, passing the number of days
REM old and the database name
E:\LogShipFolder\scripts\deleteTRN.vbs 2 Northwind
```

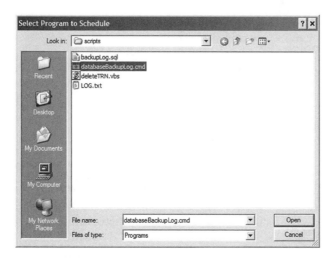

**Figure 1 Selecting a
program to schedule**

We'll now create a Scheduled Task to run this batch file every 15 minutes or so, depending on the frequency of your transaction log backups. This is the alternative to SQL Server Agent, as it is not available on the Express Editions. Scheduled Tasks can be found in the Control Panel > Scheduled Tasks or under Start > All Programs > Accessories > System Tools > Scheduled Tasks (this is the same as the Task Scheduler if you're running on Windows Vista).

Because we are using Windows authentication to run the T-SQL script, we should use a Windows account that is a member of the db_backupoperator role of all the databases, as outlined in the list and figures that follow:

1   Launch Scheduled Tasks.
2   Click on Add Scheduled Task.
3   Browse to the E:\LogShipFolder\scripts\ folder and select databaseBackup-Log.cmd (see figure 1).
4   Select the frequency and time for running the backups (see figures 2 and 3).

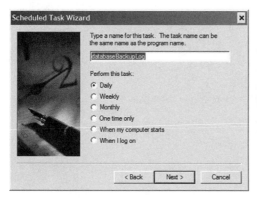

Figure 2   Naming a task

Figure 3   Entering a start time and day for the task

Figure 4   Entering the user's name and password

5   Enter a Windows account that has at least db_backupoperator role privileges for all of the databases (see figure 4).

After creating the scheduled task, open the properties of the job you just created. On the Schedule tab, click the Advanced button. On the Advanced Schedule Options window (figure 5), click the Repeat Task check box. Enter the values as defined by your log backup frequency, in this case 15 minutes, and specify a duration of 24 hours.

Now that we have created the automated job to generate the log backups, we need to share the folder that will contain the log backups. We'll share the E:\LogShipFolder in this scenario in case you plan to create log shipping jobs for more than one database on this instance. This should be accessible from the standby server, either via the IP address or the DNS name.

On the standby server, copy the robocopy.exe file into the E:\LogShipFolder\scripts folder. Then create a batch file that will call the robocopy.exe utility, passing the corresponding parameters. This batch file will copy the log backups from the primary server to the standby server and should be run in the standby server. Let's call the batch file logShipRobocopy.cmd and save it in the same folder. We add another line on the batch file to call a VBScript file that will be responsible for restoring the log backups on the standby server based on time stamps. The batch file will contain the commands shown in listing 4.

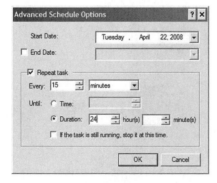

Figure 5   Using Advanced Schedule Options

```
REM ROBOCOPY job to copy the transaction log backups from the primary
REM server to the standby server
ROBOCOPY \\primary-server\LogShipFolder E:\LogShipfolder /COPY:DATSO /MIR

REM Call the VBScript file that will run a RESTORE LOG command
REM The VBScript file accepts 2 parameters—the folder containing the
REM transaction log backups and the database name
E:\LogShipFolder\scripts\restoreLOG.vbs E:\LogShipFolder\ Northwind
```

The /COPY option, in the ROBOCOPY command, with the corresponding flags copies the files together with the file information as specified by the following switches:

- D—File data
- A—File attributes
- T—File timestamps
- O—File ownership information
- U—File auditing information
- S—File security (NTFS ACLs)

Both source and destination volumes must be formatted using NTFS to allow copying of Security, Ownership, and Auditing information. If this switch is omitted, the default is /COPY:DAT, or /COPY:DATS if /SEC is specified. The /MIR (short for *mirror*) switch is used to maintain an exact mirror of the source directory tree. This ensures that whatever the users did on their machines is replicated on the server.

The restoreLOG.vbs file will contain the commands shown in listing 5.

```
'This script does a custom log shipping job using ROBOCOPY and VBScript
'with FileSystemObject querying the specified folder for files created
'within the past 15 minutes or less and generates a TSQL RESTORE LOG
'command which is executed after the ROBOCOPY script
'Syntax: restoreLOG.vbs folder databaseName

On Error Resume Next

Dim sFolder, sFolderTarget, strParentFolder, strDatabaseName
Dim fso, folder, files, strFileNameResults, objShell

Set fso = CreateObject("Scripting.FileSystemObject")
Set objFSO = CreateObject("Scripting.FileSystemObject")

strParentFolder=Wscript.Arguments.Item(0)
strDatabaseName=Wscript.Arguments.Item(1)

sFolder = strParentFolder & strDatabaseName

Set folder = fso.GetFolder(sFolder)
Set files = folder.Files

SET objShell = CreateObject("Wscript.Shell")

For each itemFiles In files
```

```
    a=sFolder & "\" & itemFiles.Name

    'retrieve file extension
    b = fso.GetExtensionName(a)

    'check if the file extension is TRN
    If uCase(b)="TRN" Then

        'check for DateCreated attribute of file and compare with current
        'date/time
          If (DateDiff("N", itemFiles.DateCreated, Now) <=15) Then
              'Create the file to contain the script
                If (objFSO.FileExists("E:\LogShipFolder\scripts\SQL\" &
            ➥strDatabaseName & ".sql")) Then
                    objFSO.DeleteFile ("E:\LogShipFolder\scripts\SQL\" &
                ➥strDatabaseName & ".sql")
                    End If

                Set objMyFile =
➥objFSO.CreateTextFile("E:\LogShipFolder\scripts\SQL\" & strDatabaseName
➥& ".sql", True)

                    str1="RESTORE LOG " & strDatabaseName
                    str2="FROM DISK='" & a & "'"
                    str3="WITH STANDBY='E:\LogShipFolder\UNDO\UNDO_" &
                ➥strDatabaseName & "_ARCHIVE.DAT',"
                    str4="DBO_ONLY"

                    objMyFile.WriteLine (str1)
                    objMyFile.WriteLine (str2)
                    objMyFile.WriteLine (str3)
                    objMyFile.WriteLine (str4)

                    objMyFile.Close
                    Set objFSO = Nothing
                    Set objMyFile = Nothing

                    'Run an OSQL command that uses a RESTORE LOG WITH MOVE,
                ➥STANDBY
                    objShell.Run("sqlcmd -S<STANDBYINSTANCENAME> -E -
➥iE:\LogShipFolder\scripts\SQL\" & strDatabaseName & ".sql -
➥oE:\LogShipFolder\scripts\SQL\" & strDatabaseName & "-results.txt")

                    'Call subroutine to read the results file for RESTORE
                ➥errors
                    strFileNameResults="E:\LogShipFolder\scripts\SQL\" &
                ➥strDatabaseName & "-results.txt"
                    Call CheckforErrors(strFileNameResults, strParentFolder,
                ➥strDatabaseName)
              End If
    End If
Next

objFile.Close
SET objFile = NOTHING
SET fso = NOTHING
SET folder = NOTHING
SET files = NOTHING
SET objShell = NOTHING
```

```
SET objFSO = NOTHING
SET objMyFile = NOTHING

'SUBROUTINE - used to read the results of the SQLCMD query to check for
'errors
Sub CheckforErrors(fileNameResults,parentFolder,databaseName)

strFileNameResults=fileNameResults
strParentFolder=parentFolder
strDatabaseName=databaseName

Const ForReading = 1

SET objShell = CreateObject("Wscript.Shell")
Set objFSO = CreateObject("Scripting.FileSystemObject")
Set objFile = objFSO.OpenTextFile(strFileNameResults, ForReading)
strContents = objFile.ReadAll

'The value=0 means that it cannot find the phrase RESTORE LOG successfully
'processed and thus means an error
If Instr(strContents,"RESTORE LOG successfully processed")=0 then
   objShell.Run(strParentFolder & "scripts\sendEmailSMTP.vbs " &
 ➥strDatabaseName & " RESTORE ")
End If

objFile.Close

Set objFSO=NOTHING
Set objFile=NOTHING
Set objShell=NOTHING

End Sub
```

The script accepts two parameters—the folder containing the copied log backups and the database name. It iterates through the contents of the folder and retrieves the file extension of all the files—in this case, TRN. It then checks for the DateCreated attribute of the file and compares it to the system date and time. If the value for the Date-Created attribute for the file differs in less than or equal to 15 minutes from the system date and time, it creates a SQL file containing the RESTORE LOG command for the database you've passed as a parameter to the script. Notice how the script is dynamically generated, passing the filename of the retrieved log backup. After the SQL file has been generated, a call to the sqlcmd.exe utility is made, passing the filename of the SQL file generated as an input and generating an output file, which we'll use to send email alerts should the RESTORE LOG command fail. Because the script will be executed using the Windows Task Scheduler, we need something to send us email alerts for notification, as SQLMail and Database Mail are not available in SQL Server Express. The script calls another VBScript file, sendEmailSMTP.vbs, which accepts two parameters—the database name and the job type, which in this case is a RESTORE job. Listing 6 shows the script for the sendEmailSMTP.vbs file. Make sure to change the SMTP server address and the recipient email address.

Listing 6   VBScript file (sendEmailSMTP.vbs) sends email notifications

```
'Accept input parameters
Dim databaseName
Dim jobType

'first parameter
databaseName= Wscript.Arguments.Item(0)
'second parameter
jobType= Wscript.Arguments.Item(1)

Set objMessage = CreateObject("CDO.Message")
objMessage.Subject = "Message Alert from STANDBY SQL Server: " & databaseName
     & " " & jobType & "  job failed"
objMessage.From = "admin@domain.local"
objMessage.To = "sqladmin@domain.local"
objMessage.TextBody = "The " & databaseName & " " & jobType & " job running
➡in the STANDBY SQL Server instance failed on " & Now() & vbCrLF &
➡vbCrLf & "Please look at this problem ASAP " & vbCrlf & vbCrlf & vbCrlf
➡& vbCrlf  & "- The SQL Server Administrator/DBA -"

'This section provides the configuration information for the remote SMTP
'server.Normally you will only change the server name or IP.
objMessage.Configuration.Fields.Item("http://schemas.microsoft.com/cdo/
➡configuration/sendusing") = 2

'Name or IP of Remote SMTP Server
objMessage.Configuration.Fields.Item("http://schemas.microsoft.com/cdo/
➡configuration/smtpserver") = "smtp.domain.local"

'Server port number(typically 25)
objMessage.Configuration.Fields.Item("http://schemas.microsoft.com/cdo/
➡configuration/smtpserverport") = 25

objMessage.Configuration.Fields.Update

objMessage.Send
Set objMessage = Nothing
```

After all the required scripts have been created, we'll use the same process we used in the primary server by creating a Scheduled Task that will call the logShipRobocopy.cmd batch file. This is the tricky part. You need to make sure that the batch file will execute after the log backup in the primary server is generated but before the new one starts. We must monitor this after implementation as the log backup time in the primary server may increase due to increased transactions, which means increased file size resulting in increased file transfer time.

To illustrate, if we enabled log backups on the primary server to run every 15 minutes starting from 12:00 a.m., the log backups will be generated in 15-minute sequences: 12:00 a.m., 12:15 a.m., 12:30 a.m., and so on. On the standby server, the scheduled task to call the logShipRobocopy.cmd batch file should be scheduled to run every 15 minutes but after 12:00 a.m. To be safe, it should run in sequences that are two-thirds of the time sequences of the primary server, say 12:10 a.m. This would provide ample time for a medium-sized database with an average-to-high number of transactions to generate the log backups. Using a trial-and-error process to find the appropriate timing, you could begin by setting 5 minutes for copying the log backups from the primary to the standby and to restoring them.

To reiterate, when the log backup job runs on the primary server at 12:00 a.m., your Scheduled Task on the standby server should be scheduled to execute at 12:10 a.m. When you create the Scheduled Task, make sure that the domain account that you use has the appropriate rights to copy from the shared folder and dbo or dbcreator privileges to restore the log backups. You also need to take into account password changes on the account, as changes will cause the jobs on the primary and standby servers to fail. Note that all the scripts used in the entire process are interdependent. Changing the frequency of the transaction log backups would mean changing the VBScript file that reads the DateCreated attribute of the log backup file to reflect that interval. It also means changing the frequency of the Scheduled Task created on the standby server. Overall, understanding the entire process will give you the flexibility to modify parameters used in all the scripts.

Improving the log shipping process

You can improve the process of log shipping in many ways such as by using Windows PowerShell instead of VBScript. Windows PowerShell is an extensible command-line shell and associated scripting language that runs on top of .NET Framework 2.0, and it makes writing scripts much easier. A few lines of VBScript can be translated in a single line of code in PowerShell.

For example, consider the deleteTRN.vbs file that is responsible for cleaning up the transaction log backup files. Listing 7 shows the script translated into PowerShell. This does not log the delete activity in a text file, but it does the job as expected.

Listing 7   PowerShell translation of deleteTRN.vbs

```
Get-ChildItem E:\LogShipFolder\Northwind | Where {$_.CreationTime -lt (get-
↪date).AddDays(-2) -and ($_.Extension -eq ".trn")} | Remove-Item
```

Notice how a couple of lines of VBScript codes can translate to a single line in PowerShell. It's a great alternative to administering servers and workstations with scripts.

Summary

The process in this chapter gives you an opportunity to implement a custom log shipping solution on SQL Server editions that do not support it—even older versions. You can improve the process in many ways including using Windows PowerShell instead of VBScript. Custom log shipping gives you an opportunity to implement a high availability solution for your SQL Server Express databases even though they may be running on a Windows XP Professional machine. Have fun!

About the author

Edwin Sarmiento works as a Senior SQL Server DBA/Systems Engineer for The Pythian Group in Ottawa, Canada. He is passionate about technology but has interests in music, professional and organizational development, leadership, and management, when not working with databases. He lives up to his primary mission statement, "To help people grow and develop their full potential as God has planned for them."

36 Understated changes in SQL Server 2005 replication

Paul Ibison

This chapter aims to cover the following areas:

- Useful undocumented or partially documented replication behavior
- Using the more efficient methodologies available in SQL Server 2005 to replace older replication techniques

That means we'll be covering some of the less obvious changes made to the replication engine between SQL Server 2000 and SQL Server 2005.

Our main source of replication information—Books Online (BOL)—has a dedicated section describing the new replication enhancements found in SQL Server 2005. This section mostly concentrates on the main areas of functionality, such as setting up merge-over-HTTPS, Oracle publishers, peer-to-peer transactional publishing, and so on. Over time, though, various other subtle changes have come to light as the DBA community has gained more experience using SQL Server 2005 replication. Some of these configuration changes are not described at all in BOL, and in certain cases they'll result in different (and preferred!) replication behavior. In other cases, the details are listed in BOL, but it is only with experience that others and I have realized that the new functionality is intended as a replacement for a previous way of administering replication.

This chapter presents a hodgepodge of such lesser-known methods, and hopefully, as a replication administrator, you can find some details that will improve the efficiency of your system and reduce or remove the administrative burden.

Undocumented or partially documented changes in behavior

In this section, we'll look at some useful replication functionality that isn't found in the help guide.

Reading the text of hidden replication stored procedures

Consider the case when you need to examine the text of a replication system stored procedure. You might want to see this text for several reasons. Perhaps you want to perform the same actions as the SQL Server Management Studio (SSMS) GUI, but hope to gain programmatic control of the process for yourself. Perhaps you want to get a better understanding of what happens under the hood in order to increase your replication expertise and troubleshooting ability. Whatever the reason, usually you will need to know the name of the system stored procedure and then use sp_helptext or the OBJECT_DEFINITION function to see the whole procedure definition. For some of the replication stored procedures, though, you will find that the text is hidden and these two methods will not work. For example, if you try the following code in a normal query window, you will have NULL returned:

```
SELECT OBJECT_DEFINITION (OBJECT_id('sys.sp_MSrepl_helparticlecolumns'))
```

On the other hand, if you use the dedicated administrator connection (DAC), you will be able to access the underlying text of the procedure. The process is pretty straightforward and is shown here:

1   Enable remote access to the DAC:

```
sp_configure 'remote admin connections', 1;
GO
RECONFIGURE;
GO
```

2   Connect to the server using the DAC.

Use a query window to connect to yourservername by using ADMIN:yourservername in the server name section (or use the sqlcmd command-prompt utility with the -A switch).

3   Execute the script:

```
SELECT OBJECT_DEFINITION (
    OBJECT_id('sys.sp_MSrepl_helparticlecolumns')
)
```

You should find the procedure text returned as expected, and if you are on a production system, don't forget to close the DAC connection when you are done with it!

Creating snapshots without any data—only the schema

When we look in BOL at the definition of a replication stored procedure or a replication agent, we find that the permitted values for the parameters are all clearly listed. But it occasionally becomes apparent that there are other acceptable values that have never been documented. The exact number of these hidden parameters is something we'll never know, and in all cases they will be unsupported for the general public. Even so, sometimes they start being used and recommended prior to documentation, usually in order to fix a bug. A case in point is the sp_addpublication procedure, in which there is now the acceptable value of database snapshot for the @sync_method.

This value was for some time known about, undocumented and yet used, but it now exists in fully documented (and supported) form in BOL. The usual caveats apply if you decide to use any such workaround; you must take full responsibility, and any such modifications are completely unsupported.

Another example that exists in the public domain but is not yet in BOL is also available. If your distributor is SQL Server 2005, the Snapshot Agent has an undocumented /NoBcpData switch that will allow you to generate a snapshot without any BCP data. This can be useful when you need to (quickly) debug schema problems generated on initialization.

You can access the command line for running the Snapshot Agent from SSMS as follows:

1 Expand the SQL Server Agent node.
2 Expand the Jobs node.
3 Double-click on the Snapshot Agent job, which typically has a name of the form <Publisher>_<PublisherDB>_<Publication>_<number> (for example, Paul-PC-TestPub-TestPublication-1). You'll know if this is the correct job because the category will be listed as REPL-Snapshot.
4 Select Steps from the left pane.
5 Select the second Run Agent step, and click the Edit button to open it. You should see the command line in the Command text box.

Once you have added the /NoBcpData parameter to the command line, as shown in figure 1, click OK in the Job Step dialog box and click OK again in the Job dialog box to make sure that the change is committed. The /NoBcpData switch tells the Snapshot Agent to create empty BCP files instead of bulk-copying data out from the published tables.

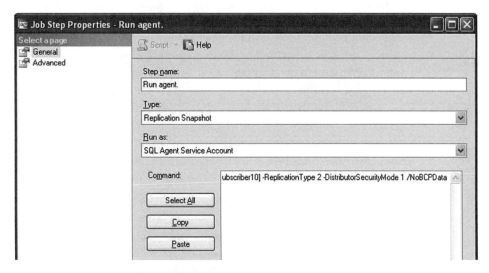

Figure 1   In the Snapshot Agent's job step, the unofficial (unsupported!) /NoBcpData is entered.

Some changed replication defaults

Many replication defaults changed between SQL Server 2000 and SQL Server 2005—far too many to cover in this section. Most of the new defaults are obvious and self-explanatory, but occasionally some of the following changes catch people out.

ROW-LEVEL CONFLICT DETECTION

In SQL Server 2000, column-level conflict detection was the default for merge replication, and this has changed to row-level conflict detection in SQL Server 2005. Which one is correct for your business is something only you can determine, but if you previously left this setting alone and intend to do the same now, you might find an unexpected set of records in the conflict viewer.

NEW MERGE IDENTITY RANGE MANAGEMENT

The following changes to identity range management for merge publications have been introduced in SQL Server 2005:

- Range allocation is automatic.   In SQL Server 2005 merge publications, the article identity range management is set to automatic by default. In SQL Server 2000, the default identity range management was manual. What is the difference?

  Automatic range management ensures that each subscriber is reseeded with its own identity ranges without any extra configuration, whereas manual means that you will need to change either the seed or the increment of the identity range on each subscriber to avoid conflicts with the publisher. If you previously relied on leaving this article property alone and chose to manually administer the identity range, beware because a range of 1,000 values will have already been allocated to each of your subscribers.

- Default range sizes have increased.   The publisher range has changed from 100 to 10,000, and the subscriber range size has increased from 100 to 1,000.

- Overflow range is allocated.   The merge trigger code on the published article implements an overflow range that is the same size as the normal range. This means that by default you will have two ranges of 1,000 values allocated to a subscriber. The clever part is that the overflow range is automatically allocated by the merge insert trigger and therefore doesn't require a connection to the publisher. However, the reseeding performed in the trigger is restricted to those cases where a member of the db_owner role does the insert.

- The threshold parameter is no longer used.   Although it appears in the article properties dialog box much the same as in SQL Server 2000, the threshold parameter only applies to subscribers running SQL Server Mobile or previous versions of SQL Server.

"NOT FOR REPLICATION" TREATMENT OF IDENTITY COLUMNS

Identity columns have a new default behavior. These columns are automatically marked as Not for Replication (NFR) on the publisher and are transferred with the identity NFR property intact at the subscriber. This retention of the NFR property applies to both transactional and merge replication.

Why might this be a useful change? First, it means that you don't need to wade through all the tables before creating the publication in order to manually set each identity column as NFR. This is a huge improvement because the method used in SQL Server 2000 by Enterprise Manager to set the NFR attribute involved making whole (time-consuming) copies of the table data. It also means that if you are using transactional replication as a disaster recovery solution, there is now one less hoop you will need to jump through on failover because you don't have to change this setting on each table at the subscriber. That particular part of your process can now be removed.

(If you are now thinking that it is not possible in T-SQL to directly add the NFR attribute to an existing identity column, please take a look inside the `sp_identitycolumnforreplication` system stored procedure, because this is the procedure that marks the identity column as NFR.)

DEFERRED UPDATE TRACE FLAGS

For transactional replication, you might be using deferred update trace flags unnecessarily. In SQL Server 2000, updates to columns that do not participate in a unique key constraint are replicated as updates to the subscriber unless trace flag 8202 is enabled, after which they are treated as deferred updates (paired insert/deletes). On the other hand, updates to columns that do participate in unique constraints are always treated as deferred updates (paired insert/deletes) unless trace flag 8207 is enabled. In SQL Server 2005, all such changes are replicated as updates on the subscriber regardless of whether the columns being updated participate in a unique constraint or not.

PARTITIONING OF SNAPSHOT FILES

The following change to a replication default is more complicated to explain, but it deals with a significant improvement that has been made to the initial snapshot process. In SQL Server 2000, when an article is BCP'd to the filesystem (the distribution working folder) during the snapshot generation, there is always one file created that contains the table's data. In SQL Server 2005, when you look in the distribution working folder after creating a snapshot, you might be surprised to find many such files for each article, each containing a separate part of the table data, as shown in figure 2.

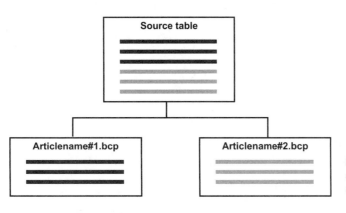

Figure 2   Snapshot data from a table is now partitioned across several text files.

Clearly there has been a big change in the processing rules. I'll refer to this overall process of splitting data files as *BCP partitioning*, borrowing the term from a Microsoft developer who once pointed this out in a posting in the Microsoft Replication Newsgroup (microsoft.public.sqlserver.replication). This section explains why BCP partitioning exists, what the expected behavior is, and how to troubleshoot if it all goes wrong.

BCP partitioning has several benefits. First, it helps in those cases where there has been a network outage when the snapshot is being applied to the subscriber. In SQL Server 2000, this would mean that the complete snapshot would have to be reapplied, and in the case of concurrent snapshots, this would all have to be done in one transaction. In contrast, if you have a SQL Server 2005 distributor and SQL Server 2005 subscribers, there is now much greater granularity in the process. The article rows are partitioned into the separate text files, and each partition is applied in a separate transaction, meaning that after an outage, the snapshot distribution is able to continue with the partition where it left off and complete the remaining partitions. For a table containing a lot of rows, this could lead to a huge saving in time.

Other useful side effects are that this can cause less expansion of the transaction log (assuming that the migration crosses a backup schedule or the subscriber uses the simple recovery model), and it can lead to paths of parallel execution of the BCP process for those machines having more than one processor. (It is true that parallel execution existed in SQL Server 2000, but this was only for the processing of several articles concurrently and not for a single table.)

Similarly, the same benefits apply when creating the initial snapshot using the Snapshot Agent. Note that the -BcpBatchSize parameter of the Snapshot and Distribution Agents governs how often progress messages are logged and has no bearing at all on the number of partitions.

To disable BCP partitioning, you can add the unofficial -EnableArticleBcp-Partitioning 0 switch to the Snapshot Agent and a single data file will be produced, just like in SQL Server 2000. Why would you want to turn off such a useful feature? Well, anecdotally, things may get worse for folks who don't start off with empty tables (archiving or roll-up scenarios) or if the CPU, disk I/O, or network bandwidth is the bottleneck in the attempt to extract more snapshot processing throughput when using BCP partitioning.

Finally, for those tables that expand the transaction log, some DBAs like to enable the bulk-logged recovery mode to try to minimize logging, but this will not always work when dealing with multiple partitions. To ensure that there is a maximum chance of going down the bulk-logged path, you should use -MaxBcpThreads X (where X > 1) for the Distribution Agent and ensure that the target table doesn't have any indexes on it before the Distribution Agent delivers the snapshot.

More efficient methodologies

In the previous section, we looked at several undocumented techniques that can be used to enhance the replication behavior. We'll now look at some capabilities that are fully documented, but that are not always understood to be replacements for less-efficient methodologies.

Remove redundant pre-snapshot and post-snapshot scripts

In SQL Server 2000 publications, we sometimes use pre-snapshot and post-snapshot scripts. The pre-snapshot scripts are T-SQL scripts that run before the snapshot files are applied, whereas the post-snapshot scripts apply once the snapshot has completed. Their use is often to overcome DRI (declarative referential integrity) issues on the subscriber.

Remember that the initialization process starts by dropping tables on the subscriber. If all the tables on the subscriber originate from one publication, this is not an issue, but if there is more than one publication involved, we might have a scenario where the dropping of tables at the subscriber during initialization would be invalid because of relationships between articles originating from different publications. There might also be other tables on the subscriber that are related to replicated articles and that are not themselves part of any publication. Either way, we find the same DRI problem when initialization tries to drop the subscriber's table. In such cases, the pre-snapshot and post-snapshot scripts are needed—a pre-snapshot script would drop the foreign keys to allow the tables to be dropped, and a post-snapshot script would then add the foreign keys back in. Such scripts are not difficult to write, but each needs to be manually created and maintained, causing (another!) maintenance headache for the DBA.

In SQL Server 2005 there is a new, automatic way of achieving this on initialization at the subscriber. Initially, there is a call to the `sys.sp_MSdropfkreferencingarticle` system stored procedure, which saves the relevant DRI information to the following three metadata tables:

- dbo.MSsavedforeignkeys
- dbo.MSsavedforeignkeycolumns
- dbo.MSsavedforeignkeyextendedproperties

Once the information is safely hived away, the foreign keys are dropped. To re-add the foreign keys, the Distribution Agent calls the new `sp_MSrestoresavedforeignkeys` system stored procedure once the snapshot has been applied. Note that all this happens automatically and requires no manual scripts to be created.

Take a look at your existing pre-snapshot and post-snapshot scripts. If they deal with the maintenance of foreign keys, there's a good chance they are doing work that is already done by default, in which case you'll be able to drop the scripts entirely and remove the maintenance issue.

Replace merge -*EXCHANGETYPE* parameters

In SQL Server 2005 merge replication, we can now mark articles as download-only, meaning that changes to the table are only allowed at the publisher and not at the subscriber. Previously, in SQL Server 2000, we would use the -EXCHANGETYPE value to set the direction of merge replication changes. This was implemented by manually editing the Merge Agent's job step and adding -EXCHANGETYPE 1|2|3 as text.

When using SQL Server 2000, entering a value of -EXCHANGETYPE 2 means that changes to a replicated article at the subscriber are not prohibited, are recorded in the merge metadata tables via merge triggers, and are subsequently filtered out when the Merge Agent synchronizes. This means there may be a huge amount of unnecessary metadata being recorded, which slows down both the data changes made to the table and the subsequent synchronization process.

This -EXCHANGETYPE setting is not reflected directly in the GUI and is hidden away in the text of the Merge Agent's job. Despite being a maintenance headache and causing an unnecessary slowing down of synchronization, it was the only way of achieving this end, and judging by the newsgroups, its use was commonplace.

In SQL Server 2005, when adding an article, there is an option to define the subscriber_upload_options either using the article properties screen in the GUI or in code, like this:

```
sp_addmergearticle @subscriber_upload_options = 1
```

This parameter defines restrictions on updates made at a subscriber. The parameter value of 1 is described as "download only, but allow subscriber changes" and seems equivalent to the -EXCHANGETYPE = 2 setting mentioned previously, but in the SQL Server 2005 case there are no triggers at all on the subscriber table. Another distinction is that this setting is made at the more granular article level rather than set for the entire publication. This means that although the -EXCHANGETYPE and sp_addmergearticle methods are logically equivalent, the implementation has become much more sophisticated in SQL Server 2005. Triggers that unnecessarily log metadata at the subscriber are no longer fired; therefore both subscriber data changes and the subsequent synchronization are significantly faster.

Put simply, you should replace the use of EXCHANGETYPE with download-only articles!

Incidentally, this setting is also implemented by a separate check box in SSMS, as shown in figure 3. This check box does a similar job but sets the value of @subscriber_upload_options to 2, which again makes the changes download-only, but in this case any subscriber settings are prohibited and rolled back.

Figure 3   Merge replication articles can be marked as download-only to prevent subscriber changes and reduce metadata.

Summary

We have looked at many of the lesser-known replication techniques useful in SQL Server 2005. Some of these involve using parameters or procedures that are partially documented but that might help solve a particular issue. Other methods are fully documented, but we have looked at how these methods can be used to replace replication techniques used in SQL Server 2000 and improve our replication implementation and reduce administration.

About the author

Paul Ibison is a contractor SQL Server DBA in London. He runs the website www.replicationanswers.com—the only site dedicated to SQL Server replication—and has answered over 6,000 questions on the Microsoft SQL Server Replication newsgroup. When not working, he likes spending time with his wife and son, Ewa and Thomas, going fell-walking in the Lake District, and learning Ba Gua, a Chinese martial art.

37 High-performance transactional replication

Hilary Cotter

The purpose of this chapter is to educate DBAs on how to get maximum performance from their high-performance transactional replication topology across all versions and editions. Most DBAs are concerned with latency—in other words, how old the transactions are when they are applied on the Subscriber.

To set expectations, you should know that the minimum latency of any transactional replication solution will be several seconds (lower limits are between 1 and 2 seconds). Should you need replication solutions which require lower latencies, you should look at products like Golden Gate, which is an IP application that piggybacks off the Log Reader Agent.

Focusing solely on latency will not give you a good indication of replication performance. The nature of your workload can itself contribute to larger latencies. For example, transactions consisting of single insert statements can be replicated with small latencies (that is, several seconds), but large batch operations can have large latencies (that is, many minutes or even hours). Large latencies in themselves are not necessarily indicative of poor replication performance, insufficient network bandwidth, or inadequate hardware to support your workload.

Consequently, in this study we'll be looking at the following:

- *Throughput*—The number of transactions and commands SQL Server can replicate per second. These can be measured by the performance monitor counters SQLServer:Replication Dist:Dist:Delivered Trans/sec and SQL-Server:Replication Dist:Dist:Delivered Cmds/sec.
- *Worker time*—How long it takes for SQL Server to replicate a fixed number of transactions and commands. This statistic is logged when the replication agents are run from the command line.
- *Latency*—How old the transactions are when they arrive at the Subscriber. Latency can be measured using the performance monitor counter SQLServer:Replication Dist:Dist:Delivery Latency.

Although these performance monitor counters are the best way to get a handle on your current throughput and latency in your production environments, in this study we'll be focusing primarily on throughput. We'll focus mainly on worker time, or how long the distribution agent has to work to replicate a given set of commands. We'll focus on the Distribution Agent metrics, as the Log Reader is rarely the bottleneck in a replication topology. Additionally the Log Reader Agent operates asynchronously from the Distribution Agent; therefore, the Log Reader Agent can keep current with reading the log, while the Distribution Agent can be experiencing high latencies. By studying the output of the replication agents themselves, when you replay your workloads through them (or measure your workloads as they are replicated by the agents), you can determine the optimal configuration of profile settings for your workloads, and determine how to group articles into different publications for the maximum throughput.

This chapter assumes that you have a good understanding of replication concepts. Should you be unfamiliar with replication concepts, I advise you to study the section *Replication Administrator InfoCenter* in Books Online, accessible online at http://msdn.microsoft.com/en-us/library/ms151314(SQL.90).aspx.

Before we begin it is important to look at factors that are the performance kiss of death to any replication solution. After we look at these factors and possible ways to mitigate them, we'll look at tuning the replication agents themselves for maximum performance.

Performance kiss of death factors in transactional replication

The following factors will adversely affect the throughput of any replication solution:

- Batch updates
- Replicating text
- Logging
- Network latency
- Subscriber hardware
- Subscriber indexes and triggers
- Distributor hardware
- Large numbers of push subscriptions

We'll look at each of these in turn.

Batch updates

Transactional replication replicates transactions within a transactional context—hence the name *transactional*. This means that if I do a batch update, insert, or delete, the batch is written in the log as singleton commands. Singletons are data manipulation language (DML) commands that affect at most one row. For example, the following are all singletons:

```
insert into tableName (Col1, Col2) values(1,2)
update tableName set Col1=1, Col2=2 where pk=1
delete from tableName where pk=1
```

Each singleton is wrapped in a transaction. Contrast this with the following batch updates (the term *update* refers to any DML—an insert, update, or delete:

```
insert into tableName

select * from tableName1

update tableName set col1=1 where pk<=20
delete from tableName where pk<=20
```

In the insert statement the insert batch update will insert as many rows as there are in tableName1 into tableName (as a transaction). Assuming there were 20 rows with a pk less than or equal to 20 in tableName, 20 rows would be affected by the batch update and batch deletes.

If you use any transaction log analysis tool, you'll see that the batch updates are decomposed into singleton commands. The following update command

```
update tableName set col1=1 where pk<=20
```

would be written in the log as 20 singleton commands, that is:

```
update tableName set col1=1 where pk=1
update tableName set col1=1 where pk=2
update tableName set col1=1 where pk=3
...
update tableName set col1=1 where pk=20
```

The Log Reader Agent reads committed transactions and their constituent singleton commands in the log and writes them to the distribution database as the constituent commands.

Details about the transaction are written to MSrepl_transactions along with details about the constituent commands.

The Distribution Agent wakes up (if scheduled) or polls (if running continuously) and reads the last applied transaction on the subscription database for that publication. It then reads MSrepl_transactions on the distribution database and applies the corresponding commands for that transaction it finds in MSrepl_commands one by one on the Subscriber.

Transactions are committed to the database depending on the settings of the BatchCommitSize and BatchCommitThreshold settings for the Distribution Agent. We'll talk about these settings later.

Key to understanding the performance impact of this architecture is realizing that replicating large transactions means that a transaction will be held on the Subscriber while all the singleton commands are being applied on the Subscriber. Then a commit is issued. This allows the Distribution Agent to roll back the entire transaction, should there be a primary key violation, foreign key violation, lack of transactional consistency (no rows affected), or some other event that causes the DML to fail (for example, the subscription database transaction log filling up). This can mean that a lengthy period of time is required to apply large batch updates. While these batch updates are being applied, the Distribution Agent will wrap them in a transaction so that it can roll them back on errors, and Subscriber resources are consumed to hold this transaction open. Latencies that were previously several seconds can quickly grow to many minutes, and occasionally to hours (for large numbers of modified rows). SQL Server will get bogged down when replicating transactions that affect large numbers of rows—typically in the tens or hundreds of thousands of rows. Strategies for improving performance in this regard are presented in the sections that follow.

REPLICATING THE EXECUTION OF STORED PROCEDURES

Replication involves doing your batch DML through a stored procedure and then replicating the execution of the stored procedure. If you choose to replicate the execution of a stored procedure, every time you execute that stored procedure its name and its parameters will be written to the log, and the Log Reader Agent will pick it up and write it to the distribution database, where the Distribution Agent will pick it up and apply it on the Subscriber. The performance improvements are due to two reasons:

- Instead of 100,000 commands (for example) being replicated, only one stored procedure statement would be replicated.
- The Log Reader Agent has to read only the stored procedure execution statement from the log, and not the 100,000 constituent singleton commands.

Naturally this will only work if you have a small number of parameters to pass. For example, if you're doing a batch insert to 100,000 rows, it will be difficult to pass the 100,000 rows to your stored procedure.

SP_SETSUBSCRIPTIONXACTSEQNO

Another trick is to stop your Distribution Agent before you begin your batch update. Use the sp_browsereplcmds stored procedure to extract commands that have not been applied to the Subscriber and issue them on the Subscriber to bring it up to date with the Publisher. Then perform the batch update on your Publisher and Subscriber. The Log Reader Agent will pull all the commands from the Publisher into the distribution database, but make sure that they are not replicated (and hence applied twice at the Subscriber). Use sp_browsereplcmds to determine the transaction identifier (xact_ seqno) for the last batch update command that the Log Reader Agent writes into the distribution database. Note that you can select where to stop and start sp_browsereplcmds as it will take a long time to issue unqualified calls to sp_browsereplcmds.

You may have to wait awhile before the Log Reader Agent reads all the commands from the Publisher's log and writes them to the distribution database.

When you detect the end of the batch update using sp_browsereplcmds, note the value of the last transaction identifier (xact_seqno) and then use sp_setsub scriptionxactseqno to tell the subscription database that all the batch updates have arrived on the Subscriber. Then restart your Distribution Agent, and the agent will write only transactions that occurred after the batch update.

Take care to note any transactions that may be in the distribution database and occurred after the batch update started and before it stopped. You'll need to ensure that these commands are also applied on the subscription database.

The problem with this approach is that the Log Reader Agent still has to process all of the batch update commands that are written to the log. This approach will eliminate the lengthy time required for the Distribution Agent to apply the commands to the Subscriber, but will not address the time that it takes for the Log Reader Agent to read the batch commands from the log and write them to the distribution database.

MAXCMDSINTRAN

MaxCmdsInTran is a Log Reader Agent parameter, which will break a large transaction into small batches. For example, if you set this to 1,000 and do a batch insert of 10,000 rows, as the Log Reader Agent reads 1,000 commands in the log it will write them to the distribution database, even before that batch insert has completed. This allows them to be replicated to the Subscriber. If this batch insert was wrapped in a transaction on the Publisher and the batch insert failed before the transaction was committed, the commands read by the Log Reader Agent and written in the distribution database would not be rolled back. For example, if the batch insert failed on the 9,999th row, the entire 10,000-row transaction would be rolled back on the Publisher. The log reader would already have read the 9,000 rows out of the transaction log and written them to the distribution database, and then they would be written in 1,000 row batches to the Subscriber.

The advantage of this method is reduced latency because the Log Reader Agent can start reading these commands out of the Publisher's log before the transaction is committed, which will mean faster replication of commands. The disadvantage is that consistency may be lacking between your Publisher and Subscriber. Appropriate use cases are situations in which being up to date is more important than having a complete historical record or transactional record. For example, a media giant used this method with the understanding that their peak usage would occur during a disaster. For example, during 9/11 everyone used the news media resources for the latest news, and if a story was lost, its rewrite swiftly came down the wire. A large book seller also used this method when they wrote off a few lost orders, knowing that the bulk of them would be delivered to the subscribers on time.

Replicating text

Text in this context refers to any of the large-value data types—text, ntext, image, nvarchar(max), varchar(max), varbinary(max) with filestream enabled, varbinary(max), and XML.

Like a batch update, when you replicate text, the constituent commands may be spread over multiple rows in MSrepl_commands.

For example, this statement,

```
Insert into tableName (col1) values(replicate('x',8000)
```

is spread over eight rows in MSrepl_commands. When the text is being replicated, there is overhead not only when the command is read out of the Publisher's log and broken into eight commands in MSrepl_commands, but there is also overhead for the Distribution Agent in assembling these eight commands into one insert statement to apply on the Subscriber.

Unfortunately there is no easy way of getting around the overhead, other than using vertical filtering to avoid replicating text columns. On the newsgroups I frequently encounter misconceptions about the `max text repl size (B)` option, the value of which can be set using sp_configure. The misconception is that this setting somehow helps when replicating text. Some people think that if you are replicating text values larger than the setting of `max text repl size`, then the value is not replicated; others think that special optimizations kick in. In actuality your `insert` or `update` statement will fail with this message: "Length of text, ntext, or image data (x) to be replicated exceeds configured maximum 65536."

Although you can use this option to avoid the expense of replicating large text values, ensure that your application can handle the error that is raised.

Logging

This is a catch-22. The agents need to log minimal replication activity so that the replication subsystem can detect hung agents. However, logging itself will degrade replication performance. Figure 1 illustrates the impact of various settings of the `HistoryVerboseLoggingLevel` when replicating 10,000 singleton insert statements.

The y axis is worker time (ms), and the x axis is `OutputVerboseLevel`. Notice how a setting for `HistoryVerboseLevel` of 0 and using the default for `OutputVerboseLevel` (1) will give you the best performance and replicate 20 percent faster than its nearest competitor; 20 percent faster meant a total of 18,356 transactions per second.

The characteristics are completely different for 100 transactions of 100 singleton inserts as displayed in figure 2.

The y axis is worker time, and the x axis is `OutputVerboseLevel`.

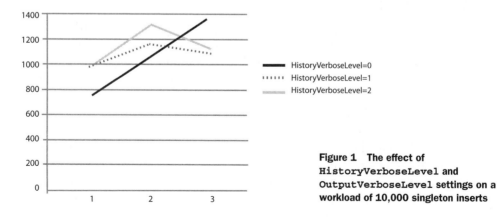

Figure 1   The effect of `HistoryVerboseLevel` and `OutputVerboseLevel` settings on a workload of 10,000 singleton inserts

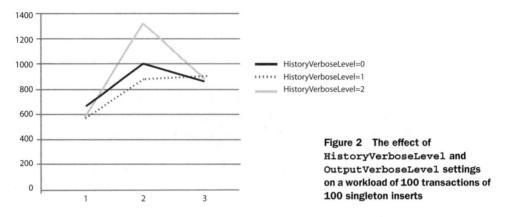

Figure 2   The effect of `HistoryVerboseLevel` and `OutputVerboseLevel` settings on a workload of 100 transactions of 100 singleton inserts

Notice how the default settings (`HistoryVerboseLevel` = 1, and `OutputVerboseLevel` = 1) are optimal for this workload. You'll need to create custom profiles and adjust them for your workload. A setting for `HistoryVerboseLevel` of 0 means no history, 1 means only the current history is retained, and 2 means that all history will be retained. An `OutputVerboseLevel` setting of 1 means minimal output, 2 means detailed output, and 3 means debugging information is included in the output.

The above examples occur when you run the Distribution Agent from the command line. For comparative purposes, when you run in SQL Server Management Studio using the defaults, the maximum number of commands per second on the same test system is 7,892. We get a performance boost of 25 percent when we run the agents from the command line; this is because of the overhead in running and monitoring the agents from within SQL Server. If you run your agents from the command line, you'll have to roll your own monitoring agent to ensure that the agents are not hung, and there are no errors.

As the performance improvements are significant, this is definitely an option to use in environments requiring minimal latency.

Network latency

If you are replicating from one server to another, the impact of network latency can cripple high performance replication solutions. You should examine two factors—network bandwidth and speed. Although network latency is typically not a factor when replicating between servers on the same network segment or switch, it can be painful when replicating over a WAN.

For example, a financial client of mine was replicating between their New York City office and offices in Europe. The ping response time between local servers was 0 ms, and between New York and the European offices was 7 ms. Replication latency was typically several seconds during the day; however while replicating batch commands at night the latency would shoot up to several hours. Contrast this with local subscribers which would apply the batches within minutes. Sniffer analysis revealed minimal network congestion at the time. The best response to minimizing the effect of network latency is to increase the network packet size. You can increase the network packet size to 32 KB by issuing the following command:

```
sp_configure 'Show Advanced Options', 1
reconfigure with override
go
sp_configure 'network packet size (B)', 14000
reconfigure with override
go
```

Note that the maximum network packet size is 32,767 bytes. Prior to SQL 2005 SP3 and SQL 2008 SP1 there is a bug that causes exceptions using the maximum value for network packet size. The threshold appears to be somewhere around 14,000 bytes. You can experiment with binary elimination to fine tune this limit further—unfortunately there isn't a knowledge base (KB) article that describes this.

Increasing the network packet size allows SQL Server to encapsulate more replication commands within a single packet. Should an error occur, the network stack will request this packet be retransmitted. Lossy or congested networks will benefit from lower packet sizes; otherwise you should be using a larger value.

Although this client found the effects of network latency particularly painful with batch updates, each time you replicate over WANs or distances you can benefit from increased packet sizes.

Anecdotally, I heard that to circumvent this problem one client batched all the update statements into a text file, copied them over manually to the subscribers, and then issued them on the subscribers. The client was able to live with the synchronization issues that the solution presented. The batch update was wrapped in a stored procedure on the Publisher, the execution of which was replicated, and the code for the stored procedure on the subscribers was replaced with a no-op.

Subscriber hardware

Subscriber hardware impacts replication performance. For most non-trivial workloads, the Subscriber's hardware does not have to be the same as the Publisher's. You should be running a multi-proc box, with ample memory. Preferably you should be running SQL Server 2005/2008 64-bit. Should your hardware be inadequate you'll run into a problem called hardware impedance mismatch, where the Subscriber will degrade the performance of your Publisher.

Subscriber indexes and triggers

Subscriber indexes and triggers will add to the latency of every replicated command being applied. Ensure that the indexes on the Subscriber are as lightweight as possible. Unfortunately, transactional replication is most frequently used to replicate to a reporting environment, which usually requires a different set of indexes on the Subscriber than on the Publisher, and consequently this is not an easy task. However, the effort spent in careful elimination of marginally effective indexes and triggers will pay dividends. If at all possible, trigger logic should be incorporated into the replication stored procedures, and sometimes can be incorporated into a different article with careful use of custom sync objects.

Distributor hardware

As replication impacts the performance of the Publisher, using a clustered remote Distributor is necessary when you have any appreciable throughput. Ensure that your Distributor is running RAID 10, and has ample memory—64 GB is recommended. Please refer to this blog post for an analysis of distributor hardware: http://blogs.technet.com/lzhang/archive/2006/05/12/428178.aspx.

Large numbers of push subscriptions

If you have a large number of push subscriptions, you should migrate to pull subscribers to transfer the processing requirements from the Distributor to the Subscriber. Also, using pull subscribers over WANs has performance advantages.

In the remainder of this chapter we'll look at optimal replication settings. Most of these settings can be configured using custom profiles.

Optimal settings for replication

Most of the tuning should be done on the Distribution Agents. Log Reader Agents are rarely bottlenecks. Naturally, you should separate log files on I/O paths different from the data drives to prevent I/O contention; this will help log reader performance.

Use the settings `ReadBatchSize` and `ReadBatchThreshold` to most significantly improve the Log Reader Agent settings.

`ReadBatchSize` determines when the log reader will distribute the transactions it has read from the log to the distribution database. The default is 500, which means that the log reader will batch up 500 transactions before writing them to the distribution database. `ReadBatchThreshold` determines when the log reader will distribute the commands it has read from the log to the distribution database. The default for `ReadBatchThreshold` is 0.

This concept is key to understanding how these parameters work: the parameters honor transactional boundaries. For example, if I had a `ReadBatchSize` and `ReadBatchThreshold` settings of 500 and 100 respectively, and I issued a batch update which affected 1000 rows, neither of these parameters would trigger a message telling the Log Reader Agent to write the buffered data to the distribution database. If I issued a singleton insert, both transactions would fly as the `ReadBatchThreshold` is reached (or exceeded). The `PollingInterval` determines how long transactions will remain in the buffer before being sent to the distribution database even if `ReadBatchSize` or `ReadBatchThreshold` have not been exceeded.

Figure 3 illustrates the impact of various settings for `ReadBatchSize` and `ReadBatchThreshold`.

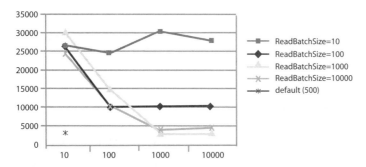

Figure 3   The effect of worker time with varying settings of `ReadBatchSize` and `ReadBatchThreshold` for a workload of 10,000 singleton inserts on the Log Reader Agent

The y axis is worker time in ms, and the x axis is `ReadBatchThreshold`. As you can see, the higher values produce the lowest worker times for this particular workload. In this case, the workload is 10,000 singleton inserts.

CommitBatchSize and CommitBatchThreshold

`CommitBatchSize` and `CommitBatchThreshold` settings are analogous to `ReadBatch-Size` and `ReadBatchTheshold`. `CommitBatchSize` refers to the number of transactions that will be sent in a batch to the Subscriber, and `CommitBatchThreshold` refers to the number of commands. Similar to `ReadBatchSize` and `ReadBatchThreshold`, higher numbers are better, but they will consume more resources on the Subscriber. In some cases the snapshot isolation model can be used to minimize the effect of higher `CommitBatchSize` and `CommitBatchThreshold` settings, keeping in mind the added pressure put on tempdb and possible performance problems associated with it. Figure 4 shows the results of 10,000 singleton inserts with varying values of `CommitBatchSize` and `CommitBatchThreshold` settings.

In figure 4 the y axis is worker time in ms, and the x axis is `CommitBatchThreshold`. The lower values of worker time are better. As you can see, the best values for `Commit-BatchSize` and `CommitBatchThreshold` are 1,000 and 1,000. The defaults are `Commit-BatchSize=100` and `CommitBatchThreshold=1,000`.

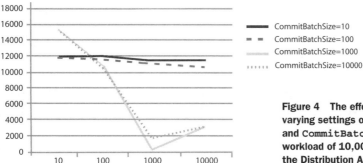

Figure 4   The effect of worker time with varying settings of `CommitBatchSize` and `CommitBatchThreshold` for a workload of 10,000 singleton inserts on the Distribution Agent

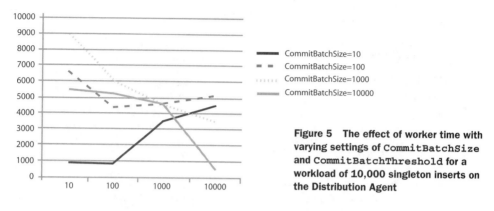

Figure 5 **The effect of worker time with varying settings of** `CommitBatchSize` **and** `CommitBatchThreshold` **for a workload of 10,000 singleton inserts on the Distribution Agent**

Characteristics for 100 batch inserts of 100 rows are illustrated in figure 5.

In figure 5 the y axis is worker time in ms, and the x axis is `CommitBatchThreshold`. The lower values of worker times are better. As you can see the best values for `CommitBatchSize` and `CommitBatchThreshold` are 10 and 10 or 100, or a second sweet spot at 10,000 and 10,000. The defaults are `CommitBatchSize=100` and `CommitBatchThreshold=1,000`.

Clearly if your workload is characterized by singleton inserts, or if you have transactions consisting of 100 row updates or inserts, one of the preceding settings will work best for you, but these are edge cases. By measuring the number of transactions and commands in your workloads using the performance monitor counters SQLServer:Replication Dist:Dist:Delivered Trans/sec and SQLServer:Replication Dist:Dist:Delivered Cmds/sec you can get an idea of the ratio of transactions to commands that characterizes your overall workload. You can then adjust the settings on your custom profile for the appropriate `CommitBatchSize` and `CommitBatchThreshold` settings.

You'll get maximum performance by grouping `msrepl_commands` by `article_id` and discovering which articles generate the most replication activity. Then you can publish these articles in different publications and use the independent agent option. Also use customer profile settings for `CommitBatchSize` and `CommitBatchThreshold` for these articles.

Update proc

Use the stored procedure `sp_scriptdynamicupdproc` to generate a custom update stored procedure and use it in place of the automatically generated one. This pays dividends when you update only a small portion of the total columns in the replicated table. You must use the MCALL format in your article in order to use this stored procedure. In my test performing 10,000 singleton updates where one column out of 10 was updated, the performance improvement was 32 percent.

SubscriptionStreams

The `SubscriptionStreams` Distribution Agent parameter also has a dramatic impact on mixed workloads. `SubscriptionStreams` allows replication of parallel streams of data to a Subscriber. Should an error occur, the Distribution Agent will throttle down to a single thread until the error is cleared and then spin up to the number of streams defined by the `SubscriptionStreams` parameter. In my tests I have found an improvement of 20 percent using a `SubscriptionStreams` parameter of 4.

Summary

This chapter presented methods for delivering high-performance replication solutions. In the first part of the chapter we looked at factors that limit your ability to deliver high performance—so called performance kiss of death factors. I have presented several solutions to these performance blockers.

In the second part of the chapter we looked at how to optimize the performance of the replication agents. If you have workloads that are uniform (unmixed workloads) you can easily select settings for `ReadBatchSize`, `ReadBatchThreshold`, `CommitBatchSize`, and `CommitBatchThreshold` for optimal performance. If you have mixed workloads (varying numbers of commands affected by each transaction) you'll need to use the replication performance monitor counters for your agent to determine the average values to use to set the parameters for these agents. Usage of `SubscriptionStreams` and the dynamic update proc can also result in significant performance improvements.

You can achieve maximum performance for your replication solution by using these methods: continually monitor your workloads for each Distribution Agent; adjust your Log Reader and Distribution Agents, placing them in their own publications; and use appropriate settings for these workloads.

About the author

Hilary Cotter is a New Jersey–based consultant specializing in replication and other high-availability technologies, full-text search, and performance tuning. He has over 20 years of experience in IT.

38 Successfully implementing Kerberos delegation

Scott Stauffer

Kerberos delegation is a method of securely transferring a user's credentials from the client's PC to the middle application tier such as a web server, then on to a back-end database tier. In this chapter, I'll explain some of the issues, talk about the prerequisites, and discuss the steps of implementing Kerberos delegation in your environment.

I first became interested in digging deeper into Kerberos delegation when I asked a group of approximately 50 database professionals the following question at a local PASS chapter meeting: "How many people have attempted to set up Kerberos delegation?" I was shocked to see so few hands, and then shocked again after hearing that not one of them was successful.

I've implemented Kerberos with a client for a scaled-out SharePoint and Reporting Services environment and ran into little difficulty doing so. It did take time to troubleshoot, but in the end there was victory. So why was I so successful? I think it was partially due to a fantastic relationship with the system administrator, who was patient, curious, and not operating a systems environment in fire-fighting mode. I also had an old colleague who'd traveled the Kerberos delegation path before and forwarded us some notes and resources. I'm indebted to Goran and Richard for their help in the past, in turn making this chapter possible.

Over the last few months, I've scoured many Microsoft Knowledge Base articles, white papers, webcasts, blogs, books, and magazines to see that there are truly a lot of factors that can affect whether a Kerberos delegation implementation is successful. Upon setting up a virtual fictitious environment with which to test my findings, I quickly felt the pain of others who'd traveled this path before me. I spent a number of hours troubleshooting some pretty mind-numbing errors. This chapter draws together what I've absorbed and distills it into a package to make your implementation of Kerberos delegation successful.

Understanding the issues that Kerberos delegation resolves

It isn't uncommon for a new technology solution to come along and for IT people to look around to see if they have a business problem that this new technology will resolve. This isn't always a bad thing, but sometimes businesses get skeptical and wonder if their IT staff are just looking for a reason to play with something new. Kerberos delegation is likely not one of those technologies. What Kerberos delegation gives us is fantastic for business, but there's no shiny exterior or crinkly wrapper. In fact I'd guess that a large percentage of IT people didn't know that Kerberos delegation was introduced in Windows Server 2000 to lay a foundation for single sign-on. I'd imagine Kerberos is often stumbled upon only after a scale-out project is embarked upon, and things don't go quite as planned, as is the case with the sidebar titled "Twelve Angry Techs."

> **Twelve Angry Techs—humorous *SQL Server Magazine* article**
>
> Hopefully this chapter will help prevent you from running into some of the issues this group encountered:
>
> http://www.sqlmag.com/Article/ArticleID/99207/Twelve_Angry_Techs.html.

The double hop

The difficulty with Kerberos delegation is that people often "don't know what they don't know." They're forced to take error messages (the symptoms of the problem) and do some research until they uncover the mystery of their problem. Frequently, this problem is the one referred to as the *double-hop issue*. Out of the box, the Windows Server platform isn't configured to have users' credentials passed from the client machine to a middle business tier, which in turn passes the users' credentials on to the back-end data tier. The environment can be set up to operate that way, but it requires effort and understanding before this scenario will be possible. This chapter will step you through the configurations needed to successfully accomplish a double hop (and multi hops) in the most common environments.

A generic infrastructure—our business challenge

In order to understand this double hop issue better, it might be helpful to provide a simple scenario to use as an example. Let's assume the following scenario as laid out in figure 1.

A business user, Joan, needs to access her corporate intranet server called vWebTier. This is shown in figure 1 as the *1st Hop*. When she runs her intranet applications, the intranet server passes her credentials on to the database server called vDataTier. This step is shown in the figure as the *2nd Hop*. The database recognizes Joan's credentials on the domain and gives her the appropriate information based on her

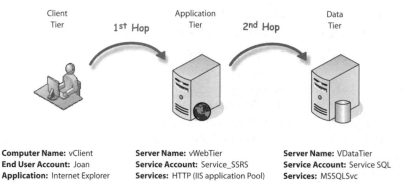

Client Tier   1st Hop   Application Tier   2nd Hop   Data Tier

Computer Name: vClient
End User Account: Joan
Application: Internet Explorer

Server Name: vWebTier
Service Account: Service_SSRS
Services: HTTP (IIS application Pool)

Server Name: VDataTier
Service Account: Service SQL
Services: MSSQLSvc

Figure 1   Our fictitious "SSTB.local" Active Directory domain

predefined access, mapped to a SQL Server login and associated database user. An audit application installed on the database server is able to recognize that it was Joan who requested customer information, and logs her user account in the audit log.

This scenario was made possible because Kerberos delegation was put in place. The next section explains some of the important aspects of delegation you need to understand before implementing it in your environment.

Understanding Kerberos delegation

Kerberos is an involved authentication protocol developed at MIT. Microsoft's implementation of Kerberos debuted with the advent of Active Directory (AD) in Windows Server 2000. There are many detailed Knowledge Base articles, white papers, blogs, and webcasts on the subject. Many of these resources are referenced at the end of the chapter if you need a more detailed explanation of Kerberos delegation. This section focuses on what you need to understand before you talk with your Windows admin, so that you can get her support and cooperation in implementing a Kerberos delegation solution.

Service principle names

Microsoft Product Support Services has indicated that when troubleshooting Kerberos delegation issues with customers, the bulk of problems commonly revolves around service principle names (SPNs). An SPN is a registration in Active Directory that enables the user to locate a service in an Active Directory domain. The SPN is made up of a few basic parts:

1 The service being provided
2 The computer hosting the service
3 The port number (if you aren't using the service's default port)
4 The user or computer account context that the service is running

Now that we have an idea what an SPN is, let's look at the ones we'll need to create. Someone with Domain Admin or Enterprise Admin privileges creates an SPN by using setspn.exe. Setspn ships with Windows Server 2008, but for Windows Server 2003 it's part of the Windows Server 2003 Service Pack 2 32-bit Support Tools package, which is available from http://www.microsoft.com/downloads.

NOTE I don't provide the direct link to the support tools mentioned in this section because they would be long hyperlinks, and when new service packs come out in the future, it's best you use the latest files. Use the search bar at the top of http://www.micosoft.com/Downloads to find the most up-to-date version for your edition of Windows Server 2003.

The setspn.exe command-line tool provides the three main functions of listing, adding, and deleting SPNs. When the support tools are installed, a new Programs group is added to your Start menu. Click on Command Prompt in the Windows Support Tools group so that you're in the path of the installed applications. Let's start off by listing the SPNs that are set in the functioning environment where delegation is in place, as shown in listing 1.

Listing 1   Finding out the SPNs that are currently in place

```
C:\Program Files\Support Tools>setspn -l vWebTier          Lists SPN for
Registered ServicePrincipalNames for                    ① machine vWebTier
    CN=VWEBTIER,CN=Computers,DC=SSTB,DC=local:
    HOST/VWEBTIER
    HOST/vWebTier.SSTB.local

C:\Program Files\Support Tools>setspn -l SSTB\Service_SSRS    Lists SPN
Registered ServicePrincipalNames for                         for user
    CN=Service_SSRS,CN=Users,DC=SSTB,DC=local:            ② Service_SSRS
    http/vwebtier
    http/vwebtier.sstb.local

C:\Program Files\Support Tools>setspn -l vDataTier          Lists SPN for
Registered ServicePrincipalNames for                    ③ machine vDataTier
    CN=VDATATIER,CN=Computers,DC=SSTB,DC=local:
    HOST/VDATATIER
    HOST/vDataTier.SSTB.local

C:\Program Files\Support Tools>setspn -l Service_SQL        Lists SPN for user
Registered ServicePrincipalNames for                    ④ Service_SQL
    CN=Service_SQL,CN=Users,DC=SSTB,DC=local:
    MSSQLSVC/vdatatier.sstb.local:1433
    MSSQLSVC/vdatatier:1433
```

In the first command ①, we're using setspn to list the service principle names in place for the machine named vWebTier. You can also see that the machine is part of the SSTB.local domain and there are two HOST registrations for vWebTier. One entry is for HOST/VWEBTIER, which registers the NetBIOS name of the machine, and a second entry HOST/vWebTier.SSTB.local registers the fully qualified domain name (FQDN) for the server. Windows automatically creates these two registrations as soon as the machine is added to the domain.

The second command ② lists the SPNs for the services associated with the user account Service_SSRS. Note that the HTTP service is running on the host vWebTier, but the service is registered to the user account, not to the machine. This causes confusion for many, and is the reason why duplicate SPNs are mistakenly created. We chose to register the service to the user account Service_SSRS as opposed to the computer account vWebTier, because we're going to run the IIS application pool under the context of Service_SSRS. Service_SSRS will be responsible for passing credentials on to the vDataTier database server. You'll also notice that the domain name SSTB was specified in this command, but all of the commands in listing 1 return DC=SSTB,DC=local, indicating that Active Directory already knows the domain context regardless of whether SSTB is indicated in the command.

The third command ❸ lists the SPNs for the computer vDataTier, and again, because this machine is a member of the domain, the HOST services were automatically registered with the NetBIOS name and the FQDN.

The last command ❹ lists the SPNs for the service account with which the SQL Server service is running on vDataTier. If the SQL Server was originally installed with LocalSystem as opposed to using a domain user for its service account, SQL Server would've automatically created an SPN on the vDataTier computer account.

DUPLICATE SPNS

When SQL is installed with a domain account, no automatic registration takes place. If you originally installed SQL with LocalSystem, ensure that you list the SPNs for the computer account to check that the SPNs are no longer there (or delete them if they are), as duplicate SPNs listed in both the user account and the computer account will prevent Kerberos Delegation from functioning.

NOTE   Some services do automatic registration under certain circumstances; therefore, always list SPNs for both user accounts (under which the service runs) and computer accounts to see that a service for a host doesn't show up in two accounts.

CREATING SPNS

Now that we've shown the results we're looking for, let's demonstrate how to create those registrations.

In figure 1, the SSTB.local Active Directory domain has an IIS web server called vWebTier with an application pool running under the context of a domain user account called Service_SSRS. The following command shows how to create an SPN for this service:

```
setspn.exe -A HTTP/vWebTier SSTB\Service_SSRS
```

The syntax for the command is

```
setspn.exe -A {service}/{server}[:port] [{domain}\{user account}]
```

As discussed earlier, you need to create a second SPN that's similar to the previous one, but the second must have the fully qualified domain name (FQDN) for the server:

```
setspn.exe -A HTTP/vWebTier.SSTD.local SSTB\Service_SSRS
```

That takes care of the web server; now let's look at the database server. The data tier needs to be in the same domain or a trusted domain within the Active Directory forest. For more information on domains and forests, see the sidebar titled "Forest, trees, and domains." The SQL Server vDataTier is in the same domain, and the SQL Server service runs under the context of a domain user account, Service_SQL. The two registrations that we'll need to enter are as follows:

```
setspn.exe –A MSSQLSVC/vDataTier SSTB\Service_SQL
setspn.exe –A MSSQLSVC/vDataTier.SSTD.local SSTB\Service_SQL
```

Forests, trees, and domains

Wikipedia explains the structure of the Active Directory in the following manner:

"The forest, tree, and domain are the logical parts in an AD network. The AD forest contains one or more transitive, trust-linked trees. A tree is a collection of one or more domains and domain trees, again linked in a transitive trust hierarchy."

For a more in-depth explanation, please see http://en.wikipedia.org/wiki/Active_Directory.

This SQL Server is installed as a default instance, and therefore listens on port 1433 for SQL traffic. If the instance of SQL Server were configured on port 2433, then the registrations would change to look like this:

```
setspn.exe –A MSSQLSVC/vDataTier:2433 SSTB\Service_SQL
setspn.exe –A MSSQLSVC/vDataTier.SSTD.local:2433 SSTB\Service_SQL
```

WARNING It's important to note the direction of the slashes that separate the service from the host and the domain from the account. The `setspn` tool won't tell you if you have them incorrect!

Adding yet another tier to our example

Let's say we have another server that an application from vWebTier attempts to access called vOLAPCube, and it houses SQL Server 2005 Analysis Services cubes for the sales department. The OLAP Services also runs under the domain user account Service_OLAP. The SPN necessary is

```
setspn.exe –A MSOLAPSvc.3/vOLAPCube SSTB\Service_OLAP
```

Constrained delegation

Kerberos delegation allows the authentication process to trust a computer or a user account to pass along credentials to another computer. This concept concerned some people, and rightly so, as it allows the account to pass credentials of the current user to *any* service on *any* server in the domain or forest. For that reason, constrained delegation was introduced with Windows Server 2003. This allows only specified services running on specified servers to impersonate a user, not carte blanche impersonation privileges for the account.

Figure 2 shows the dialog box with the Delegation tab of a user account participating in Kerberos constrained delegation. As configured, this account is only able to delegate credentials to the SQL Server Service on computer vDataTier over port 1433. Trust This User for Delegation to Specified Services Only is the option that enforces constrained delegation.

If a user clicks on the radio button next to Trust This User for Delegation to Any Service (Kerberos Only) then the account is unconstrained; this means that the account can impersonate the domain user when accessing any service on any machine. This scenario is shown in figure 2.

If the constrained delegation option isn't showing up on the Delegation tab in figure 2, this could mean that you need to raise the domain functional level to a minimum of Windows Server 2003, as is shown in figure 3. To see the domain function level, have your domain admin open the Active Directory Domains and Trusts management console found in the Administrative Tools group located in the Control Panel. Once in the Active Directory Domains and Trusts console, right-click the domain and click Raise Domain Functional Level as shown in figure 4.

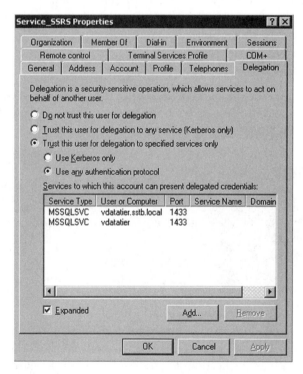

Figure 2   User account tab for Service_SSRS

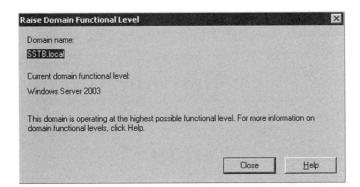

Figure 3 Dialog box showing that the current domain functional level is set to Windows Server 2003

NOTE If your machines aren't in the same Active Directory domain, but are within the same Active Directory forest and the domains trust one another, the forest functional level will need to be raised to Windows Server 2003 in addition to the domains. Raising the forest functional level can also be accomplished with the Active Directory Domains and Trust management console. Right-click Active Directory Domains and Trusts and click Raise Forest Functional Level, as shown in figure 5.

Implementing Kerberos delegation step by step

This section provides a checklist for each of the components needed to successfully implement Kerberos delegation. Get your domain admin or enterprise admin on board with this project early, as you'll need them to do many of the tasks for you, especially in the Active Directory subsection.

Configuring the Active Directory

Many of the Active Directory requirements will likely already be in place, but there are some things worth checking. I don't provide exhaustive explanations and solutions to

Figure 4 Checking the domain functional level within the Active Directory Domains and Trusts

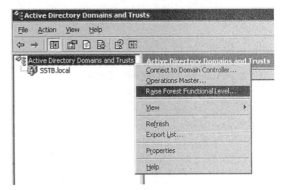

Figure 5 Checking the forest functional level within Active Directory Domains and Trusts

these requirements, as further details can be found on the internet with your favorite search engine.

TIME SYNC

If the system time on the computers is more than a few minutes out of sync, you might want to look further into this item. You can adjust the tolerance which Kerberos forgives for the spread of the clocks, but it's advisable to set up Time Services with a central time source with which to sync.

DNS

DNS is required for Kerberos, as it's used in querying Active Directory service principle names (SPNs).

SAME DOMAIN OR TRUSTED DOMAIN IN THE FOREST

The computers involved need to trust one another in order to encrypt and decrypt the Kerberos-delegated credentials passed from one tier to the next, as previously discussed and illustrated in figure 1.

DOMAIN USERS FOR SERVICE ACCOUNTS

In order for Kerberos delegation to function, it's necessary that the application tier have an IIS application pool configured with a domain user account. For the data tier, it's possible to use LOCAL SYSTEM to run the SQL Server service; but I strongly recommend you use a domain account, as it's generally considered a best practice to do so.

SPNS SET FOR SERVICES

As shown in the section "Constrained delegation," SPNs are added with setspn.exe. Ensure that SPNs are entered for all services participating in delegation. In our fictitious environment, we entered the following commands to register the SPNs:

```
setspn.exe -A HTTP/vWebTier SSTB\Service_SSRS
setspn.exe -A HTTP/vWebTier.SSTD.local SSTB\Service_SSRS
setspn.exe -A MSSQLSVC/vDataTier SSTB\Service_SQL
setspn.exe -A MSSQLSVC/vDataTier.SSTD.local SSTB\Service_SQL
```

NO USER ACCOUNTS ARE MARKED AS SENSITIVE

No accounts involved in Kerberos delegation can be marked as sensitive, or delegation won't succeed. Your domain admin can check this by opening the Active Directory User and Computers management console found in the Administrative Tools group, located in the Control Panel. Once in there, right-click the users, click Properties, and click the Account tab to reveal the Account options, as shown in figure 6.

RAISE FOREST FUNCTIONAL LEVEL

If you plan on using constrained delegation, you'll need to ensure your domain and forest functional levels are at a Windows Server 2003 level, as discussed earlier in the section "Constrained delegation."

SET ACCOUNTS FOR DELEGATION IN THE
ACTIVE DIRECTORY USERS AND COMPUTERS MANAGEMENT CONSOLE

You'll need to trust the user account for delegation under which the IIS Application pool runs. You accomplish this with the Active Directory User and Computers management console. Select either Trust This User for Delegation to Any Service (Kerbe-

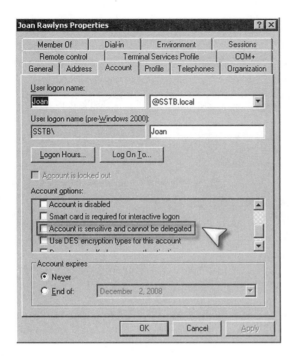

Figure 6   Properties of domain user account Joan Rawlyns showing that Account Is Sensitive and Cannot Be Delegated isn't selected

ros Only) for unconstrained, or Trust This User for Delegation to Specified Services Only for constrained Kerberos delegation. In our example, shown back in figure 2, you see the Account tab of the user Service_SSRS configured with constrained Kerberos delegation.

Configuring the client tier

If the client computer was purchased in the last five years, it's more than likely that the workstation meets the requirements for delegation. After meeting the AD requirements in the previous section, make sure the following points are addressed on the client side.

WINDOWS 2000 OR HIGHER FOR THE CLIENT OPERATING SYSTEM

Kerberos delegation isn't supported in any Windows operating system lower than Windows 2000.

INTERNET EXPLORER 5.X OR HIGHER FOR YOUR BROWSER

As Internet Explorer is free, and most versions of Windows now come preinstalled with a newer version of IE, having version 5.5 or higher isn't likely to be an issue.

LAN SETTINGS

Deselect the option Automatically Detect Settings, as shown in figure 7. To get to the LAN Settings dialog box, go into the Windows Control Panel and choose Internet Options, select the Connections tab, and click on the LAN Settings button.

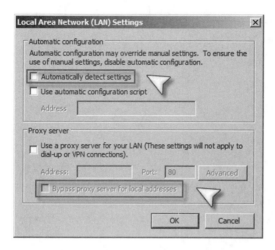

Figure 7   **Confirm that the Automatically Detect Settings option is *not* selected, and ensure that you Bypass Proxy Server for Local Addresses if you do have a proxy server configured.**

The Automatically Detect Settings option seems to be selected by default on many of the desktops that I've tested.

NOTE   If you don't deselect the Automatically Detect Settings option, you may be faced with some 502 Bad Gateway error messages, as shown in figure 8.

If you have a proxy server, ensure that you configure it in the Local Area Network (LAN) Settings dialog box discussed previously, but ensure that you've also selected Bypass Proxy Server for Local Addresses. Figure 7 doesn't show entries for a proxy, as no proxy is present in my environment, but you can see the options available to be enabled if required.

SET ENABLE INTEGRATED WINDOWS AUTHENTICATION

Within the Advanced tab of the Internet Options dialog box, ensure that Enable Integrated Windows Authentication* is set, as shown in figure 9. To get to the Internet Options dialog box, go into the Windows Control Panel and choose Internet Options.

Figure 8   **502 Bad Gateway error message appears if Automatically Detect Settings is enabled.**

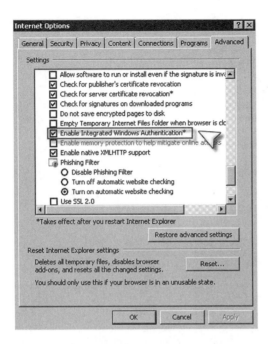

Figure 9 Ensuring that Enable Integrated Windows Authentication* is selected

SET AUTOMATIC LOGON ONLY IN INTRANET ZONE

Security settings for the local intranet zone should have this option set as shown in figure 10. This is the default setting for this option.

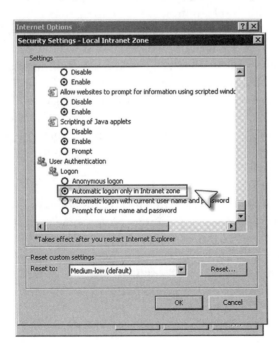

Figure 10 Ensuring that Automatic Logon Only in Intranet Zone is selected

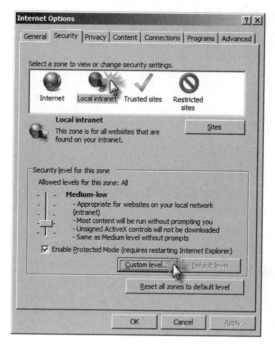

Figure 11   Accessing the local intranet zone's security settings

To get to the Security Settings - Local Intranet Zone dialog box from the Security tab of the Internet Options dialog box, first select the Local Intranet zone at the top of the box, and then click the Custom Level... button as shown in figure 11.

The client requirements can be loosened to allow for other browsers and other operating systems on the client side if constrained delegation is used in conjunction with the Use Any Authentication Protocol option shown in figure 2. If this is selected, Kerberos isn't required between the client and the server involved in the first hop. Kerberos is required, though, to make the second hop involving delegation. This configuration is also known as *protocol transition* and is discussed further in the resources provided in the section "Resources to assist in more complex infrastructures."

Configuring the web tier

Now that the SPNs have been set, and the Active Directory and client tier requirements have been met, we must now configure the web tier. At this point, you'll need to configure IIS to host the application. You might want to ask for some assistance from your system administrator or an IIS guru if this isn't your area of expertise.

This section steps you though making the necessary configuration changes in IIS to support Kerberos delegation. In this section, we'll configure the IIS web tier by calling the IIS Manager from the Administrative Tools group found in the Windows Control Panel.

CREATE AN IIS APPLICATION POOL

To create a new application pool, right-click Application Pool and choose New Pool from within the IIS Manager management console. Give the pool a name and choose to use the default settings for the new application pool.

CONFIGURE THE APPLICATION POOL TO USE A DOMAIN ACCOUNT

After creating the new application pool, right-click the entry and choose Properties. Click on the Identity tab, select the radio button next to Configurable, and enter the domain user account and password for which you earlier created an SPN. Figure 12 shows the new application pool Delegation, with the identity of SSTB\Service_SSRS.

CREATE A NEW VIRTUAL DIRECTORY FOR OUR APPLICATION

Now that we have an application pool, we need to set up a virtual directory within a website. To create a virtual directory, right-click the website in which you want the application to reside. Choose New > Virtual Directory to open the Virtual Directory Creation Wizard. Now enter the alias name for your virtual directory. In my example I've used the Default Web Site and used an alias of Delegation for the name of the virtual directory. Continue by specifying the path to the website's ASP.NET code. Next ensure that you choose the permission Run Scripts (such as ASP), then choose Next and Finish.

CONFIGURE VIRTUAL DIRECTORY TO USE APPLICATION POOL

Now that we've created the virtual directory, we'll need to make sure it uses the newly create application pool. Right-click the virtual directory, navigate to the Virtual Directory tab, and ensure that the drop-down selection box for Application Pool has the

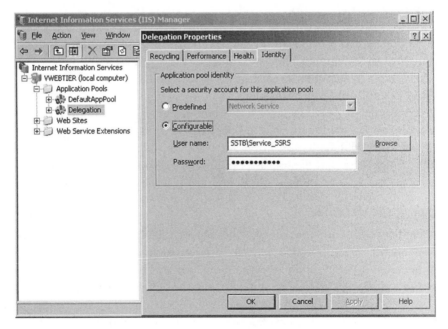

Figure 12 Setting the identity of the application pool

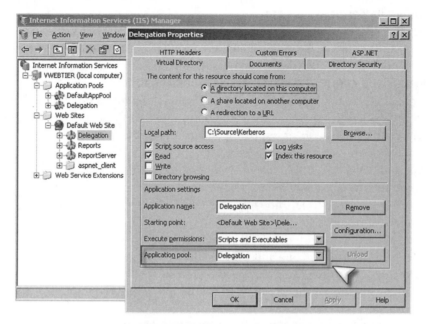

Figure 13   Selecting the application pool you just created for your new virtual directory

name of the pool that you recently created. This step is captured in the screenshot in figure 13.

MODIFY THE AUTHENTICATION METHOD FOR THE WEBSITE

While we're still in the virtual directory's Properties dialog box, click on the Directory Security tab and click the Edit button to modify the authentication methods. In this dialog box, set Integrated Windows authentication and clear the Enable Anonymous Access option, as shown in figure 14.

ENABLE THE DEFAULT CONTENT PAGE

As the last step, we must ensure that the default page is chosen for the site. Specify the ASPX file that's used for the landing page for this virtual directory. In our example, the page is called default.aspx. For easy navigation to the site content, ensure that you specify the page so that the user isn't required to do so. Figure 15 shows the Add and Move Up buttons used to place our default page at the top of the list.

Configuring the data tier

In our demonstration scenario, the SQL Server relational engine is the last stop for our Windows credentials to be passed. In order to achieve success, we must have the SQL Server service running under the same user account as we defined in the SPN, as discussed previously. To change this, we'd use the SQL Server Service Manager.

If this is the last machine and credentials don't need to be passed to another machine, then setting the service's user account to allow delegation isn't necessary. These settings are only necessary if you have any distributed queries that use data

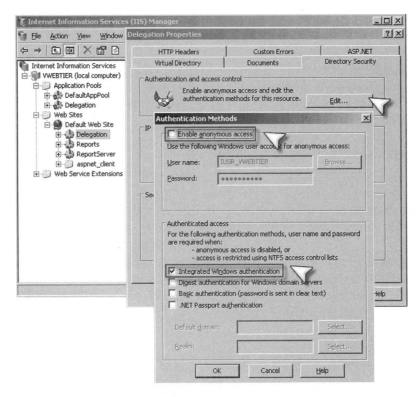

Figure 14   Enabling integrated Windows authentication and disabling anonymous access

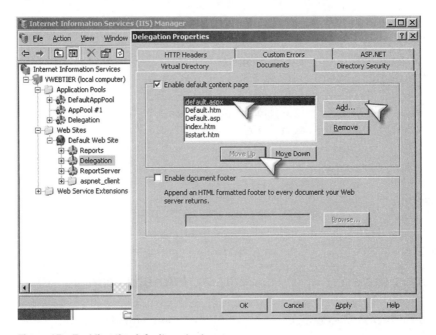

Figure 15   Enabling the default content page

sources located on another machine, requiring the credentials to hop to one more machine. Now that we've confirmed the last tier, it's time to test out our configuration.

Validating delegation from end to end

Now it's time to test whether we've successfully created an environment that will support Kerberos delegation. Luckily we have an application to let us know whether we were successful. This tool is called *DelegConfig*.

Downloading and installing DelegConfig

DelegConfig was developed by Brian Murphy-Booth from Microsoft, who has frequently had to work with clients to troubleshoot their Kerberos delegation issues. DelegConfig is an ASP.NET application that helps identify what's preventing you from successfully accomplishing Kerberos delegation. DelegConfig is available from http://www.iis.net/1434/ItemPermalink.ashx. Installing the application on your middle-tier web server will confirm that you can connect from your client application (in this case Internet Explorer) to the IIS Server and pass your credentials on to a back-end database server with Kerberos delegation. Detailed installation instructions can be found here: http://blogs.iis.net/bretb/archive/2008/03/27/How-to-Use-DelegConfig.aspx.

Running DelegConfig from the web tier

DelegConfig can help create the necessary SPNs to make things work, as it can perform the same duties as setspn.exe. I prefer to use DelegConfig after my SPNs are in place. First run DelegConfig from the web tier; then, once successful, call DelegConfig from the client tier.

Running DelegConfig from the client tier

After successfully following the instructions in the "Downloading and installing Deleg-Config" section, you should see results similar to figure 16, showing green check boxes. If not, don't despair, as there are plenty of places to go for further assistance.

First off, if DelegConfig doesn't show a green check, it'll likely point you in the right direction as to how to fix it. You'll notice that each section has an expandable Explanation section with insight and background explaining what settings and configurations will lead you toward success. Additionally, revisit the instructions once again located at http://blogs.iis.net/bretb/archive/2008/03/27/How-to-Use-DelegConfig.aspx.

If you're still stuck, the section "Resources to assist in more complex infrastructures" provides troubleshooting resources and tools to help expose what's preventing you from successfully implementing Kerberos delegation.

Resources to assist in more complex infrastructures

These resources have proven helpful at bettering my understanding of the complexities of Kerberos delegation, and I hope you find them equally helpful.

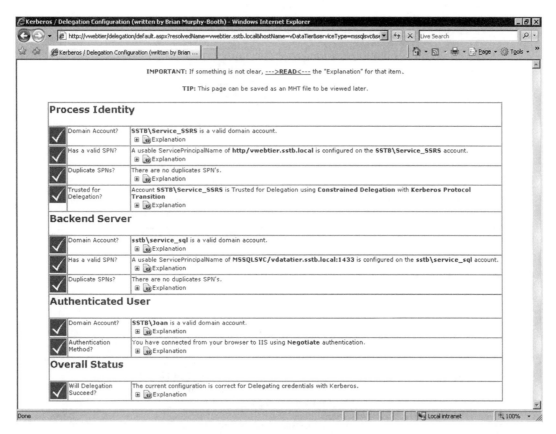

Figure 16   DelegConfig confirms a successful Kerberos implementation with big green check boxes.

Table 1 lists free tools that I've found useful. Table 2 lists various blog posts full of helpful information. Table 3 lists Microsoft TechNet articles related to Kerberos. Table 4 lists Microsoft Help and Support articles on the subject. Table 5 lists Microsoft white papers that may be of interest. Finally, table 6 lists some Microsoft webcasts that may be helpful.

Table 1   Free tools for testing and implementing

Title	URL
Windows Server 2003 Service Pack 2 32-bit Support Tools	http://www.microsoft.com/downloads/details.aspx?FamilyID= 96a35011-fd83-419d-939b-9a772ea2df90&DisplayLang=en
Windows Server 2003 Resource Kit Tools (contains KList.exe and KerbTray.exe for troubleshooting)	http://www.microsoft.com/downloads/details.aspx? FamilyID=9d467a69-57ff-4ae7-96ee-b18c4790cffd&DisplayLang=en
DelegConfig (Kerberos/delegation configuration reporting tool)	http://www.iis.net/1434/ItemPermalink.ashx

Table 1   Free tools for testing and implementing *(continued)*

Title	URL
gssMonger—tool for verifying Kerberos authentication interoperability between Windows and other platforms	http://www.microsoft.com/downloads/details.aspx?FamilyID=986a0a97-cfa9-4a45-b738-535791f02460&DisplayLang=en
Kerberos/delegation worksheet	http://blogs.inetium.com/blogs/jdevries/archive/2006/06/26/245.aspx

Table 2   Blog posts

Title and author	URL
Ask the Directory Services Team (all articles tagged with Kerberos)	http://blogs.technet.com/askds/archive/tags/Kerberos/default.aspx
Kerberos Delegation to SQL Server Darwin, Australian in UK—Delegation Guy	http://blogs.msdn.com/darwin/archive/2005/10/19/482593.aspx
The Problem with Kerberos Delegation Brad Turner, ILM MVP (Gilbert, AZ, US)	http://www.identitychaos.com/2008/03/problem-with-kerberos-delegation.html
Spat's Weblog: "Kerberos delegation .. end to end" Steve Patrick (Spat), Critical Problem Resolution, Microsoft Corporation	Part I: http://blogs.msdn.com/spatdsg/archive/2007/11/14/kerberos-delegation-end-to-end-part-i.aspx Part 2: http://blogs.msdn.com/spatdsg/archive/2007/11/20/kerberos-delegation-end-to-end-part-ii.aspx Part 3: http://blogs.msdn.com/spatdsg/archive/2007/11/26/kerb-part-3.aspx
DelegConfig (Kerberos/delegation configuration reporting tool) Brian Murphy-Booth, Support Escalation Engineer, Microsoft Corporation	http://blogs.iis.net/brian-murphy-booth/archive/2007/03/09/delegconfig-delegation-configuration-reporting-tool.aspx
Essential Tips on Kerberos for SharePoint Developers James World, Microsoft Developer Consultant, Microsoft UK	http://blogs.msdn.com/james_world/archive/2007/08/20/essential-guide-to-kerberos-in-sharepoint.aspx
Microsoft BI with Constrained Kerberos Delegation Rob Kerr, MCDBA, MCTS; Principal Consultant, BlueGranite	http://www.robkerr.com/post/2008/05/Microsoft-BI-with-Constrained-Kerberos-Delegation.aspx
Enterprise Portal Kerberos Delegation for connecting to Reporting/Analysis Services on a different box Microsoft's Enterprise Solutions blog	http://blogs.msdn.com/solutions/archive/2008/02/28/enterprise-portal-kerberos-delegation-for-connecting-to-reporting-analysis-services-on-a-different-box.aspx
Understanding Kerberos and NTLM authentication in SQL Server Connections Microsoft SQL Server Protocols team	http://blogs.msdn.com/sql_protocols/archive/2006/12/02/understanding-kerberos-and-ntlm-authentication-in-sql-server-connections.aspx

Table 2 Blog posts *(continued)*

Title and author	URL
SQL 2008, Kerberos and SPNs Tomek Onyszko, Warsaw, Poland	http://blogs.dirteam.com/blogs/tomek/archive/2008/04/09/ sql-2008-kerberos-and-spns.aspx

Table 3 Microsoft TechNet articles

Title	URL
Kerberos Authentication in Windows Server 2003: Technical Resources for IT Pros	http://technet2.microsoft.com/windowsserver/en/technologies/ featured/kerberos/default.mspx
Kerberos Explained	http://technet.microsoft.com/en-us/library/bb742516.aspx
How to: Configure Windows Authentication in Reporting Services	http://technet.microsoft.com/en-us/library/cc281253.aspx
Configure Kerberos authentication (Office SharePoint Server)	http://technet.microsoft.com/en-us/library/cc263449.aspx

Table 4 Microsoft Help and Support articles pertaining to Kerberos delegation

Title	URL
Unable to negotiate Kerberos authentication after upgrading to Internet Explorer 6	http://support.microsoft.com/default.aspx/kb/299838
How to enable Kerberos event logging	http://support.microsoft.com/default.aspx/kb/262177
How to configure IIS to support both the Kerberos protocol and the NTLM protocol for network authentication	http://support.microsoft.com/default.aspx/kb/215383
How to configure IIS Web site authentication in Windows Server 2003	http://support.microsoft.com/default.aspx/kb/324274
How to use Kerberos authentication in SQL Server	http://support.microsoft.com/default.aspx/kb/319723
How to make sure that you are using Kerberos authentication when you create a remote connection to an instance of SQL Server 2005	http://support.microsoft.com/default.aspx/kb/909801
How to configure a Windows SharePoint Services virtual server to use Kerberos authentication	http://support.microsoft.com/default.aspx/kb/832769
You receive an "HTTP Error 401.1 - Unauthorized: Access is denied due to invalid credentials" error message when you try to access a Web site that is part of an IIS 6.0 application pool	http://support.microsoft.com/default.aspx/kb/871179
Authentication may fail with "401.3" Error if Web site's "Host Header" differs from server's NetBIOS name	http://support.microsoft.com/default.aspx/kb/294382

Table 4   Microsoft Help and Support articles pertaining to Kerberos delegation *(continued)*

Title	URL
How to troubleshoot the "Cannot generate SSPI context" error message	http://support.microsoft.com/default.aspx/kb/811889

Table 5   Microsoft white papers

Title	URL
Troubleshooting Kerberos Delegation	http://www.microsoft.com/downloads/details.aspx?FamilyID=99B0F94F-E28A-4726-BFFE-2F64AE2F59A2&displaylang=en
Planning and Implementing Multitier Applications Using Windows Server 2003 Security Services	http://www.microsoft.com/downloads/details.aspx?FamilyID=edfb4607-fda9-4f9b-82e2-aea54197eb21&DisplayLang=en
Kerberos Protocol Transition and Constrained Delegation	Downloadable: http://www.microsoft.com/downloads/details.aspx?FamilyID=f856a492-ad87-4362-96d9-cbdf843e6634&DisplayLang=en Online: http://technet.microsoft.com/en-us/library/cc739587.aspx Samples: http://www.microsoft.com/downloads/details.aspx?FamilyID=0d066110-7c48-453a-a1af-d6a8b1944ce2&DisplayLang=en
Kerberos Authentication for Load Balanced Web Sites	http://www.microsoft.com/downloads/details.aspx?FamilyID=035465f0-5090-4f9c-ac44-fc0500769be9&DisplayLang=en
Troubleshooting Kerberos Errors	http://www.microsoft.com/downloads/details.aspx?FamilyID=7dfeb015-6043-47db-8238-dc7af89c93f1&DisplayLang=en
Windows 2000 Kerberos Authentication	http://technet.microsoft.com/en-us/library/bb742431.aspx

Table 6   Microsoft webcasts

Title	URL
Introduction to Kerberos	http://support.microsoft.com/kb/822248
Troubleshooting Kerberos authentication with secure web applications & SQL Server	http://support.microsoft.com/kb/842861
How to understand, implement, and troubleshoot Kerberos double-hop authentication	http://support.microsoft.com/kb/887682
Configuring Microsoft SQL Server 2005 Analysis Services for Kerberos authentication	http://support.microsoft.com/kb/916962
Understanding, implementing, and troubleshooting Kerberos double-hop authentication	http://support.microsoft.com/servicedesks/webcasts/seminar/shared/asp/view.asp?url=/servicedesks/webcasts/en/WC102704/manifest.xml

Summary

Kerberos delegation is a method of securely transferring a user's credentials from the client's PC to the middle application tier such as a web server, then on to a back-end database tier. In the chapter, I discussed what service principle names (SPNs) are and how to register them. I explained constrained and unconstrained Kerberos delegation and how to configure accounts to support these two methods. I stepped through requirements for Active Directory and the client, web, and data tiers. I then stepped through implementing and testing Kerberos delegation.

I hope you have a better understanding of Kerberos delegation, and why and when you need it. Most of all, I hope that you were able to successfully implement Kerberos in your environment after reading this chapter.

About the author

Scott Stauffer is an independent consultant working out of the metro Vancouver area, assisting clients with data systems solutions to their business challenges. He has worked in IT for more than 13 years, and although Scott has managed systems with early version SQL Server on OS/2, he really started digging deep into SQL Server with the release of SQL Server 6.5. With a keen interest in continuous learning, sharing knowledge, and building community, Scott founded the Vancouver PASS chapter (http://www.Vancouver.SQLPASS.org) back in September 2004. More recently, he started the Vancouver BI PASS chapter (http://www.VancouverBI.SQLPASS.org) in order to dive deep into the business intelligence features that SQL Server has to offer.

39 Running SQL Server on Hyper-V

John Paul Cook

Virtualization is a popular term covering several technologies. In the server space, virtualization is beneficial for several reasons:

- Disaster recovery is simple. You merely copy a small number of files from your normal production environment to your disaster recovery environment. Your disaster recovery hardware doesn't have to match your production hardware.

- Provisioning a virtual machine is simpler and faster than provisioning a physical machine. Virtualization tools make it simple to clone a production server and run it on different hardware. Development and test servers can be provisioned quickly, which can boost the efficiency of regression testing.

- With fewer physical servers needed, less rack space, cooling, and electricity are consumed, making for a greener and more affordable infrastructure.

- Microsoft offers savings on licenses. A single copy of Windows 2008 Server Standard Edition on a physical machine allows you to also run one virtual copy of Windows 2008 Server Standard Edition at no additional licensing cost. With Windows 2008 Server Enterprise Edition, up to four virtual copies of Windows 2008 Server can be run at no additional cost. One copy of Windows 2008 Server Datacenter Edition allows an unlimited number of Windows Server virtual machines to be run on the same physical machine, all covered by the one datacenter license. Licensing can be complicated by assignment and downgrade rights which are explained here: http:// blogs.technet.com/mattmcspirit/archive/2008/11/13/licensing-windows-server-in-a-virtual-environment.aspx.

In this chapter, we will begin with an overview of virtualization architecture before exploring a number of key issues such as configuration, clock drift, and backups.

Virtualization architecture

Virtualization technologies can be organized by technology type, as you can see in table 1.

Table 1   Types and examples of virtualization technologies

Server hardware virtualization (hypervisor)	Microsoft Hyper-V, VMware ESX, Xen Hypervisor
Server software virtualization	Microsoft Virtual Server 2005 R2, VMware Virtual Server (formerly GSX)
Presentation virtualization	Terminal Services, Citrix XenApp
Application virtualization	Microsoft App-V, VMware ThinApp, Citrix XenApp streaming
Desktop virtualization	Microsoft Virtual PC and MED-V, VMware Workstation, Parallels Desktop

A hypervisor is a small software layer installed directly on physical hardware. It allows multiple and disparate operating systems to be installed on the hypervisor layer. Hypervisors introduce little overhead, allowing the performance of the virtual machines to be close to the performance of a physical machine. They are currently the enterprise standard in virtualization because they offer better performance and higher capacity than server virtualization applications such as Microsoft Virtual Server 2005 R2 Service Pack 1 (SP1) and VMware Server.

When the Hyper-V role is enabled on Windows 2008 Server, the original Windows 2008 operating system is transformed into a virtual machine, which is called the parent partition. The virtual machines are called child partitions. Each partition is isolated from the other. Figure 1 highlights this relationship.

For supported operating systems, additional software may be installed into a virtual machine to facilitate interaction with the physical hardware devices. For Hyper-V, this software is called Integration Services. It provides special device drivers call synthetic drivers, which are optimized for the virtual world and which are necessary for achieving near native performance. With synthetic drivers, the overhead of hardware emulation is avoided.

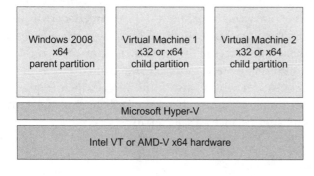

Figure 1   A virtual machine running on Hyper-V only passes through a thin hypervisor layer to access the physical hardware.

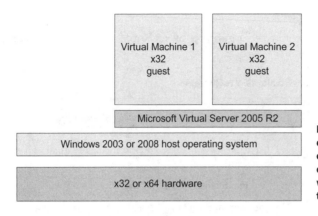

Figure 2   A virtual machine running on Virtual Server 2005 R2 passes its operating system calls to the host operating system for execution, which results in a longer, slower path to the hardware.

Server software virtualization products such as Microsoft Virtual Server 2005 R2 SP1, as shown in figure 2, incur more overhead than hypervisors and are slower. Virtual Server 2005 R2 SP1 is installed as an application running on the physical machine's operating system. Virtual operating systems are installed into Virtual Server 2005 R2 SP1. The virtual operating system must pass all of its hardware calls to the virtualization application, which in turns passes them to the host operating system. For example, if Windows 2003 Server is installed as a guest operating system in Virtual Server 2005 R2 SP1, which is installed on Windows Server 2008, operating system calls in 2003 Server are passed through Virtual Server 2005 SP1 to Windows Server 2008 to finally be executed. The path is less direct than that of a hypervisor and this adversely impacts performance.

Even with the inherent overhead of software virtualization, small volume SQL Servers with limited demands on the hardware can perform acceptably using server software virtualization such as Virtual Server 2005 R2. For more demanding database applications, hypervisor-based server hardware virtualization is needed. Hyper-V offers significantly improved disk I/O performance when compared to Microsoft Virtual Server 2005 R2.

Benefits of isolation

When a virtual machine crashes, it doesn't affect the other virtual machines or the physical machine because each virtual machine is isolated from the others and the physical machine. Processes in one virtual machine (VM) can't read, corrupt, or access processes running in other virtual machines. Because of this complete isolation, it is possible to have multiple default instances of SQL Server running on a single physical server by having each default instance in its own virtual machine. This is particularly important when trying to consolidate third-party applications which require default instances of SQL Server. Each application can run in its own virtual machine with each virtual machine running a default instance of SQL Server.

Configuring virtual machines

To obtain the best possible results from a virtual machine, it must be configured properly. Configuration of virtual disks, virtual processors, and virtual network adapters affect performance.

Configuring disks

Microsoft Hyper-V offers the following choices for its virtual disks:

- Passthrough disks
- Virtual hard disks (VHDs)
- Dynamically expanding
- Fixed size
- Differencing

Passthrough disks are physical disks directly accessed by the virtual machine. Because they offer the most direct path, they provide the best performance and are well suited for large data volumes. They lack flexibility and portability.

A virtual hard disk is a file that resides on the parent partition's file system or storage area network (SAN).

Dynamically expanding VHDs are best suited for development and test environments because they conserve disk space. Dynamically expanding VHDs grow as needed, which minimizes space usage but tends to cause fragmentation. Because the virtual machine's operating system is isolated from the physical machine, it has no knowledge of the amount of physical disk space available. The virtual machine only knows the maximum allowable size of the dynamic VHD. This can create a disparity between what the virtual machine sees as free space and the reality of free space on the physical machine.

In figure 3, the virtual machine running in the window on the right shows 117 GB of free space in its VHD. But because this dynamically expanding VHD resides on physical disk D, which has no free space left, the 117 GB of free space doesn't actually exist. Hyper-V places the virtual machine into a paused state because it has no physical space to continue operating. SQL Server can be configured to provide you with low free disk space alerts, but if you are using dynamically expanding VHDs, you may not get the alert. The virtual machine doesn't know when there isn't room for a dynamically expanding disk to grow.

Fixed-size VHDs perform better than dynamically expanding VHDs because all of their space is preallocated, although the performance difference has been lessened with the R2 release of Hyper-V. When a fixed VHD is created and its size specified, it takes all of its space from the physical machine. If there isn't enough space, an error occurs and it is not created.

Differencing VHDs also grow as needed, but they are linked to another VHD in a parent- child relationship. When a differencing VHD is used, all changes are written to the differencing VHD instead of the parent VHD. Although this causes an overall slight decrease in disk performance, it allows changes to be made without altering the

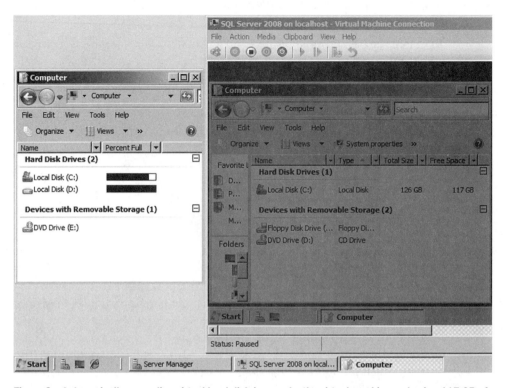

Figure 3   A dynamically expanding virtual hard disk is seen by the virtual machine as having 117 GB of free space when there is actually no disk space left on the physical file system. This forces the virtual machine into a paused state..

parent VHD. Differencing VHDs are useful in test environments because extensive changes to a virtual machine can be made without changing the original VHD. When differencing VHDs are used, any changes to the parent VHD breaks the parent-child relationship rendering the children differencing VHDs nonfunctional. To prevent this from happening accidentally, it is advisable to set a parent VHD to read only. You can create more than one differencing VHD from the same parent VHD. Doing this allows you to create different branches sharing a common ancestor. For example, you might have a parent VHD with a client application that accesses SQL Server. You could use two different differencing VHDs for testing two independent and different enhancements to the client application.

Hyper-V allows you to take a snapshot of a running virtual machine. After creating a snapshot, all changes to the virtual machine are written to a separate virtual disk file. This is similar to a differencing disk in that performance is reduced slightly because of the additional overhead of a file depending on another file. Snapshots are particularly useful in testing service packs. Before applying a service pack, create a snapshot. After testing the service pack you can create another snapshot, revert to your snapshot made before the service pack was applied, or merge the snapshot's changes to the initial VHD. Although snapshots allow recovery of a virtual machine to a particular prior state, they are not substitutes for backup and should not be considered as such.

Although Windows 2008 Server is generally considered a server operating system, many developers and people who demonstrate software use Windows Server 2008 so that they can use Hyper-V. For these use cases, performance is usually less of an issue than minimizing physical disk space usage; therefore dynamically expanding virtual hard disks are a good compromise on minimizing space while maintaining good performance.

Virtual hard disks can be attached to either IDE or SCSI buses. Hyper-V virtual machines must boot from a VHD attached to an IDE bus. A virtual SCSI bus supports more devices than a virtual IDE bus. If you need more than four VHDs, you'll have to use a virtual SCSI bus.

Virtual machines and physical machines are more alike than not. The same principles of maximizing disk performance that apply to physical machines also apply to virtual machines. When there is concurrent disk access, separate spindles or logical unit numbers (LUNs) should be used to avoid disk contention. On a physical machine, to maximize performance by minimizing contention, you might put tempdb on a spindle or LUN by itself. Translating this to the virtual world, tempdb would exist by itself in its own VHD. This VHD containing tempdb would in turn be placed on its own spindle or LUN to avoid I/O contention. If other VHDs were stored on the same physical device, I/O contention could occur.

CPU configuration

Hyper-V allows up to four processor cores to be allocated to a virtual machine and refers to them as logical processors. If your SQL Server workload requires more than four processors, it is not a suitable candidate for virtualization with Hyper-V.

If you have two SQL Server instances running on identical hardware, you might want to consolidate them onto one physical machine by migrating both of them into virtual machines. If they typically run at under 40 percent of the available CPU resources on the physical machines, having two of these running as virtual machines on the same hardware will not overtax the available physical resources. If a third SQL Server instance is added to the physical machine, and it uses as much CPU as the other virtual machines, the total CPU demand from all three virtual machines exceeds the physical CPU available. In this example, with three virtual machines each needing 40 percent of the available CPU, they will all perform suboptimally because there isn't enough physical resource available.

Conventional approaches to performance monitoring are not adequate for identifying all performance problems in virtualized SQL Server instances. Task Manager shows the CPU usage within the virtual machine in isolation. An individual SQL Server may show only minimal CPU usage but actually be starved for CPU. If the running virtual machines collectively are overtaxing the physical machine, all virtual machines will suffer.

In figure 4, Task Manager in the child partition (shown on the right side of the screen capture) gives the appearance of ample CPU resource availability, which is clearly not the case. The child partition has no visibility of the load in other partitions.

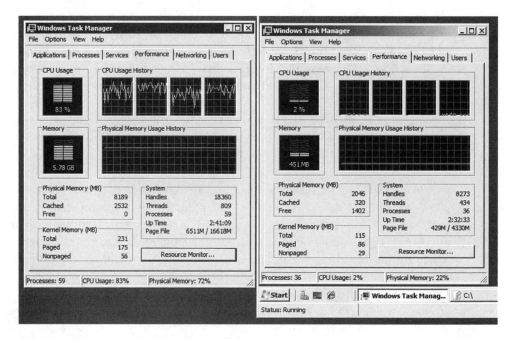

Figure 4   Task Manager results are local to the partition in which it runs.

As you can see, the parent partition is using 83 percent of the available CPU resources. If a process running in the child increases to take 40 percent of the available CPU, competition for the overtaxed CPU resources occurs. The child takes resources from the parent, reducing the resources for the parent. There isn't an overall Task Manager for the entire physical machine that shows the sum of all of the individual Task Managers. Hyper-V provides its own set of Perfmon counters to provide a view of both what is happening at the overall physical server level as well as within the Hyper-V environment. These Hyper-V counters are exposed in the parent partition (that is, physical machine). You may choose from many different categories of Hyper-V counters. Refer to the Hyper-V documentation and product team blogs to determine which counters are most useful to you. Tony Voellm's blog at http://blogs.msdn.com/tvoellm/ is an excellent source of in-depth information on Hyper-V performance monitoring. Use the Hyper-V counters to make sure that the total physical CPU resources on your Hyper-V server are adequate to service all of your running virtual machines.

Configuring networking

Hyper-V offers both legacy network adapters and synthetic network adapters. Legacy network adapters are emulated devices and as such offer lower performance than synthetic adapters, but offer greater compatibility with older operating systems. Synthetic adapters provide near-native performance and require that Integration Services be installed in the virtual machine, which is not possible in all cases. When Integration

Services is installed, it installs drivers that enable synthetic (virtual) devices to work. A legacy network driver is slower because it emulates a physical device instead of being an outright substitute like a synthetic device. Integration Services cannot be installed in Windows Server operating systems prior to Windows Server 2003 R2 Service Pack 2. For example, a SQL Server 6.5 instance running in an NT 4 virtual machine must use a legacy network adapter.

The minimum number of recommended physical network adapters for a Hyper-V physical machine is two (although it is possible to run with a single network adapter). One should be reserved for use only for administering the physical machine. The other is used for the virtual machines. If there is substantial network traffic, it may be necessary to have one or more physical network adapters for each virtual machine. To ensure optimal network performance, check with your hardware vendor to ensure that you have all of the latest drivers. Network-intensive workloads use more CPU in a virtual machine than on a physical machine. For deeper technical information and best practices, see Microsoft's whitepaper *Running SQL Server 2008 in a Hyper-V Environment,* downloadable from http://download.microsoft.com/download/d/9/4/ d948f981-926e-40fa-a026-5bfcf076d9b9/SQL2008inHyperV2008.docx.

Memory configuration

Hyper-V does not allow memory to be overallocated. If 2 GB of memory is allocated to a virtual machine, but only 1 GB is ever actually used, the 1 GB of unused RAM is not available for use by other virtual machines. This imposes a limit on how many virtual machines can be running at any given time. The sum of the memory allocation for all running virtual machines should be 1-2 GB less than the server's physical memory. Enough memory has to be left available so that the hypervisor itself (and any antivirus software running in the parent partition) has enough RAM to avoid paging.

Addressing clock drift issues

It is common for database applications to need accurate timestamps for data. Operating systems employ various techniques to minimize clock drift where the time on the computer diverges from the time. Multiprocessor virtual machines can introduce additional clock drift because of how processor resources are shared. By default, Hyper-V Integration Services synchronize the virtual machines with the physical machine. If you want to treat the virtual machine more like a physical machine, you can disable the time synchronization in Integration Services and instead use synchronization with an external time source or a primary domain controller (PDC) emulator.

Backup considerations

SQL Server backup strategies have to consider both data loss as well as catastrophic loss of the server. The Hyper-V Volume Shadow Copy Service (VSS) Writer Integration Component enables virtual machines to be backed up so that VSS-aware applications running in virtual machines are backed up in an application-consistent manner.

When Integration Services are installed, VSS on the physical machine coordinates with VSS in the virtual machine. Having backups of virtual hard disk files and configuration files allows a virtual machine to be restored to a different physical machine.

When planning a data backup strategy, it is best to think of a virtual SQL Server instance as being like a physical SQL Server instance. The real value of SQL Server backups is the ability to do point-in-time recovery. This requires true SQL Server backup tools and strategies. Running SQL Server inside a virtual machine doesn't change that. Backups of the Hyper-V server do not eliminate the need for traditional SQL Server backups.

Advantages of physical to virtual migration

Existing physical machines can be converted to virtual machines and continue operating just as they did when they were physical machines. This also opens up new possibilities. When a physical or virtual machine isn't functioning properly, a virtual copy can be made. The problematic machine can be fixed or replaced and brought back online while preserving the problem condition in the virtual copy. The virtual machine can be debugged at length without disturbing the original environment from which it came.

System Center Virtual Machine Manager (SCVMM) 2008 has a tool for converting physical machines to virtual machines, which is known as P2V. It can also do virtual-to-virtual or V2V conversions of Microsoft Virtual Server or VMware virtual machines. You may also use third-party conversion tools that can be purchased or even obtained for free.

System Center Virtual Machine Manager (SCVMM) conversion can be valuable in troubleshooting difficult-to-reproduce problems. Instead of telling your end user that a problem can't be reproduced, SCVMM 2008 can be used to do a P2V of the problem machine. You can provide the virtual machine to support personnel to analyze the problem at length without disrupting or inconveniencing the user.

Test environments and virtualization

Virtual machines are well suited for creating test environments. To obtain the maximum value of a test environment, it must be valid and complete. Although a successful P2V provides a valid representation of a physical machine, it may not by itself comprise a complete test environment. For example, to test a global deployment of a SQL Server distributed database application, you would probably need a complete environment consisting of many virtual machines. Multiple virtual SQL Servers would be utilized. Each would be configured to the time zones used at corporate datacenters around the world. End user client experience testing requires multiple client virtual machines. Regional and language settings would be different in the various client VMs to match the corporate environment.

Test environments are generally much more dynamic than production environments. To enable agility, templates and prebuilt building blocks such as virtual hard disks and ISO files are needed. ISO files are image copies of physical optical media such as DVDs and CDs. Although Hyper-V supports installing from physical optical media, ISO image files are a better choice because they are read at the speed of the hard drive they reside on. Optical drives are much slower than hard drives. SCVMM 2008 provides an organized framework for managing virtual building blocks and assets such as ISO files and virtual machine templates. Visual Studio Team System 2010 has the Microsoft Test and Lab Manager which builds upon SCVMM 2008 and provides a comprehensive test environment.

Summary

Although this is the end of our discussion of running SQL Server in a virtual machine, it is also the beginning of planning an effective virtualization strategy. Remember that a virtual machine is still a machine. The same design patterns for physical machines apply to virtual machines and effective management policies are as applicable (perhaps more so) than in a physical environment. Extend your design patterns by taking into consideration the unique characteristics of virtual machines to ensure success.

About the author

John Paul Cook is a SQL Server application DBA based in Houston, Texas. In addition to writing about database application development and virtualization, he speaks about SQL Server at conferences and user group meetings. John is particularly interested in using version control and virtualization to bring agility and reliability to the systems development lifecycle. His interests also include database performance tuning and deployment. You can read his blog at http://sqlblog.com/blogs/john_paul_cook/default.aspx.

Performance Tuning and Optimization

Edited by Kalen Delaney

There are many different aspects to performance tuning for SQL Server, including tracking down hardware and network issues, monitoring the SQL Server service's use of memory and processor resources, analyzing the causes of blocking, and investigating suboptimal index usage and query plans, to name only a few areas. Performance problems can result in a general slowdown of SQL Server and the applications running against it, or can just impact individual queries or processes, or even individual users.

Because there are so many areas that could be the source of performance problems, there is no one best way to troubleshoot poor performance. Most SQL Server professionals have a few areas of the product where they tend to focus, so those people might start their troubleshooting efforts in one of those areas.

Microsoft provides a host of tools to help you track down the source of performance problems. The earliest versions of SQL Server enabled you to see your query plans (albeit, not graphically) through an option called SHOWPLAN or to examine the system's behavior using Performance Monitor. Slightly later versions started including the ability to trace the activities your SQL Server was involved in, starting with the basic ability to monitor the client-to-server communication and progressing to the ability to see every action of SQL Server, either internal or external. The most recent version includes the amazing ability to set up a data warehouse of performance data that can easily be analyzed using a set of built-in reports. The tool even provides recommendations for how to remedy the problems encountered. So does this mean we don't need to understand how to troubleshoot on our own, because SQL Server can now do everything for us? Of course not. The tools have always given you a head start, and made things easier when starting on your SQL Server journey. But the more you know, the better you'll be able to determine which tool can give you the information you need, and what you need to do to solve the problems, including problems that are not detectable by the tools.

This section includes a wonderful selection of articles from 10 different experts, each describing one area of performance troubleshooting. There is a focus on indexes because that's an area where you can see immediate and drastic performance improvements. But the section doesn't just cover indexing options; it includes articles on deadlocking, using metadata to diagnose system resource problems, examining disk I/O behavior, and using SQL Server's ability to correlate the tracing tool with Performance Monitor.

I wish to thank all the SQL Server MVPs for their ongoing generosity in providing support to the SQL Server community, and especially to the authors for helping to make this book a reality.

About the editor

Kalen Delaney has been working with SQL Server for almost 22 years, and writing about it for almost 20. In addition to writing deep technical books such as *Inside SQL Server* and *SQL Server 2008 Internals,* she writes courseware and delivers advanced SQL Server training around the world.

Kalen has been invited by Microsoft to present special internal training on many occasions. She has spoken at Microsoft Technical Education Conference (TechEd) and presented at every PASS (Professional Association for SQL Server) Summit since the organization's inception. She is delighted that her love for SQL Server can be put to such good use in the publication of this book.

40 When is an unused index not an unused index?

Rob Farley

Indexes can help you access your data quickly and effectively, but index overhead can sometimes be costly. Keeping an index updated when data is changing is one cost, but there is also the cost of extra storage space and the increased size of backups. So if an index isn't being used, you should remove it, right?

In this chapter, I'll show you ways to find out if an index is used. Then I'll show you a type of index that may appear to be unused even although it really is used. Hopefully this won't leave you too disheartened about the idea of researching your indexes but instead convince you of the power of SQL Server.

Overview of indexing

My favorite analogy for indexes is telephone directories. I'm not sure whether I heard this analogy or came up with it—I just know that it's a way of describing indexes that everyone grasps easily. Like most analogies, it doesn't fit completely, but on the whole it's fairly good.

In Australia, the company Sensis publishes two phone books: the Yellow Pages (which lists entries according to business type) and the White Pages (which lists telephone entries by surname or business name). I assume that somewhere there is a list of all the information about the telephone numbers in Australia. Nowadays it would be electronic, but for the purpose of the analogy, we're going to consider a paper-based system. Suppose that the master list of the telephone number information is a massive folder stored at the telecommunication provider's head office. Suppose also that it's sorted by telephone number.

This folder would not be useful if I wanted to look up the phone number of my friend Andrew. His number could be on any page of the folder, so I'd have to hunt through the lot—starting on page one and continuing until I found him. If he had two numbers, I would have to keep looking to the end, even if it turned out he was on page one. If the folder contains millions of phone numbers, this would not be feasible. The folder is analogous to a clustered index in SQL Server. The folder contains all the information that is available, and the phone number acts as the key to unlock it—providing order to the information and a way of identifying each individual record.

The White Pages is useful for finding Andrew's phone number, though. I know Andrew's surname, so I can find him very quickly. As it's sorted by surname, I can turn straight to his record (almost—I might have to jump around a little) and see his phone number there.

As I only need his phone number, the White Pages (but I'd rather call it a nonclustered index) is the only resource I need. I can say that it covers my query. But if I wanted to get another piece of information, such as his billing number, I'd have to use his phone number to look him up in the master folder. In SQL Server land, this is known as a key lookup.

I won't go further into indexes now. Entire chapters could be written about best practices for indexes, and I want to make a point about unused indexes.

Unused indexes

If I never used the White Pages, there would be no point in having it in that small cupboard on which the phone sits. I could put other, more useful stuff there. What's more, whenever someone moves or changes his name or phone number, the White Pages must be updated. Although I get a new physical copy only once a year, the online version is updated much more often. Perhaps if I were eager, I could keep my eye out for changes to the underlying data and keep my copy of the White Pages up to date. But that would be arduous.

The same principle applies to indexes in databases. If we don't use an index, there's little point in having it around. Learning how to find the indexes that aren't used is a fairly useful skill for a database administrator to pick up, and SQL Server 2005 makes this easier.

SQL Server 2005 introduced Dynamic Management Views (DMVs) that are useful for providing dynamic metadata in the form of queryable views. There are other types of system views, such as catalog views like the useful `sys.indexes`, but for finding out which indexes are used, the most useful view is the DMV `sys.dm_db_index_usage_stats`. Let's look at the structure of this view, by expanding the relevant part of the Object Explorer in SQL Server Management Studio (SSMS), which is in the System Views section under the database of interest. Figure 1 comes from SQL Server 2008 Management Studio, even though my queries are running against SQL Server 2005. I'm also using administrator access, although you only need `VIEW DATABASE STATE` permission to read from the DMV.

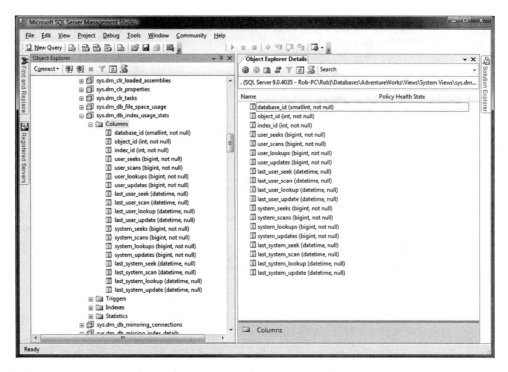

Figure 1   The structure of sys.dm_db_index_usage_stats

You'll notice that the DMV lists the number of seeks, scans, lookups, and updates that users and the system perform, including when the latest of each type was done. The DMV is reset when the SQL Server service starts, but that's just a warning to people who might have thought that data remained there from long ago. An index that isn't used won't have an entry in this view. If no seeks, scans, lookups, or updates have been performed on an index, this view simply won't list the index. Incidentally, bear in mind that to get the name of the index, you may want to join this view to sys.indexes.

You can also find out which indexes are used by looking at the execution plans that are being used by the queries issued against the database. This is even more useful, as the impact of an index can be easily evaluated by its impact on individual queries. If you consider the performance gain on an individual query, and examine how often this query is executed, you have a fantastic metric for the impact of an index. Query plans make it clear which indexes are being used, as an icon is shown for each index scan or seek. SQL Server 2008 Management Studio has significantly improved the readability of execution plans by displaying only the table name and index name, rather than using the three-part naming convention for the table and the index name. Figure 2 is a screen shot of an execution plan from SSMS 2005. Compare it with figure 3, which is a screen shot of an execution plan from SSMS 2008.

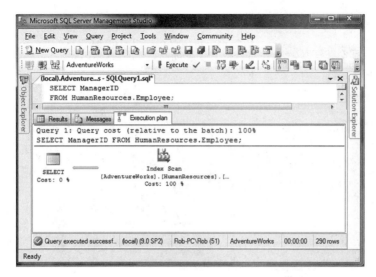

**Figure 2 Execution
plan in SSMS 2005**

As you can see in figure 3, the query plan is not different; it's just displayed in a more readable way. This is the main reason I opted to use SQL Server 2008 Management Studio throughout this chapter.

Although you could use a SQL trace to collect the query plan for every query that runs, this is not practical. The impact on performance of this type of trace can be significant, and processing the plans can also be painful. Using the `sys.dm_db_index_usage_stats` DMV to evaluate index usage is far easier. Querying the DMV every so often (particularly prior to any maintenance windows that might involve a service restart) can allow the information to be collected and analyzed, giving a strong indication of which indexes are used, and which are needlessly clogging up the system.

After the unused indexes have been identified, it is simple to drop them and free up the space in the data files.

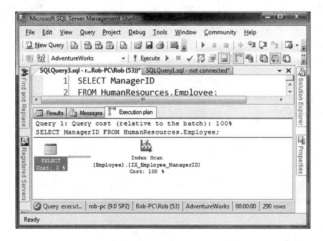

**Figure 3   Execution plan in
SSMS 2008**

Unused indexes that are actually used

Let's consider a couple of different queries, looking at which indexes are being used and which aren't. We'll look at the queries themselves, and also look at the execution plans and the metadata stored within sys.indexes and sys.dm_db_index_usage_stats. To avoid distractions I'll use my local server, which has just had its service restarted, thereby resetting sys.dm_db_index_usage_stats. I will also use a fresh copy of the AdventureWorks sample database on SQL Server 2005. You can find Adventure-Works on the CodePlex website, with all the other samples that Microsoft makes available. It's also found on the installation DVD for SQL Server 2005 Developer Edition.

I'll use the Production.Product and Production.ProductSubcategory tables. The Production.Product table has a field called ProductSubcategoryID, which acts as a foreign key to the Production.ProductSubcategory table. The ProductSubcategoryID field in Production.Product allows NULLs, to cater for those products which are not allocated to a SubCategory.

Let's consider the following query:

```
SELECT DISTINCT color FROM Production.Product;
```

This gives us ten rows, each containing a different color that is used in the Product table. The word DISTINCT ensures that no two rows are identical. If we consider its execution plan, shown in figure 4, we can clearly see how the DISTINCT operator is applied—through the use of a distinct sort.

We don't have an index that starts with the Color field, so the system has no better way of finding different colors than to scan through the whole table (on the Clustered Index) and then perform a distinct sort.

But what if we also needed the ProductNumber of each one? Let's run the query, and look at the execution plan, shown in figure 5.

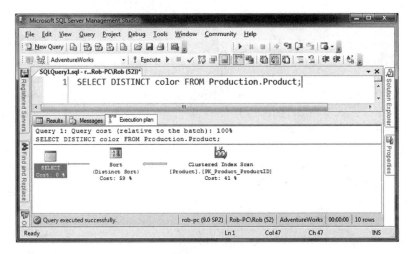

Figure 4   Execution plan for simple DISTINCT query

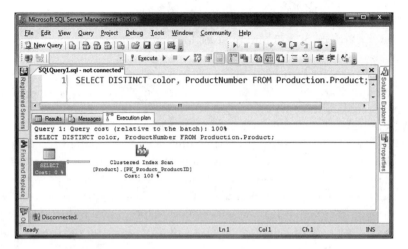

Figure 5   Execution plan for second simple `DISTINCT` query

We see that the `Distinct Sort` operator is no longer visible. We see from the execution plan (or by querying `sys.dm_db_index_usage_stats`) that the only index being used is the `Clustered Index`, and yet another index is playing an important role. We'll examine this in the next section.

For now, let's consider the query in listing 1.

```
SELECT s.Name, COUNT(*)
FROM Production.ProductSubcategory s
    JOIN
    Production.Product p
    ON p.ProductSubCategoryID = s.ProductSubCategoryID
GROUP BY s.Name;
```

If the server instance is restarted, the DMV is reset. Now we can run this query knowing that it's not being tainted by earlier queries and can see which indexes are being used by the query, as shown in figure 6. We can also look in the execution plan to see what's being used, as shown in figure 7. Both of these methods of reviewing indexes show us that the only indexes being used are the clustered indexes (all clustered indexes have an index_id of 1). In particular, we're not using a nonclustered index which exists on the table, called AK_ProductSubcategory_Name.

So, clearly, we should be able to drop the index AK_ProductSubcategory_Name, as it's not being used. We can use the following statement to drop it:

```
DROP INDEX AK_ProductSubcategory_Name
ON Production.ProductSubcategory;
```

And if we want to re-create it later, we do this:

```
CREATE UNIQUE NONCLUSTERED INDEX AK_ProductSubcategory_Name
ON Production.ProductSubcategory (Name);
```

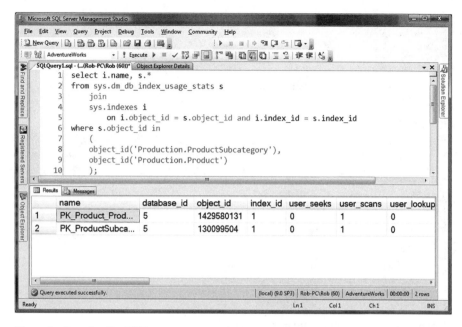

Figure 6   Querying the DMV

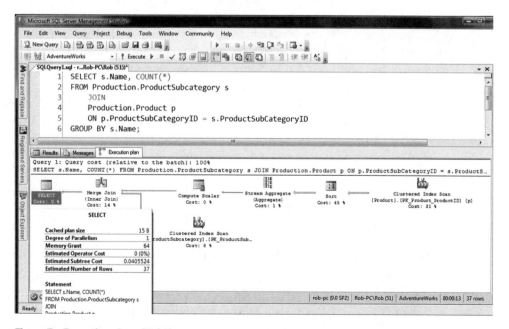

Figure 7   Execution plan with index

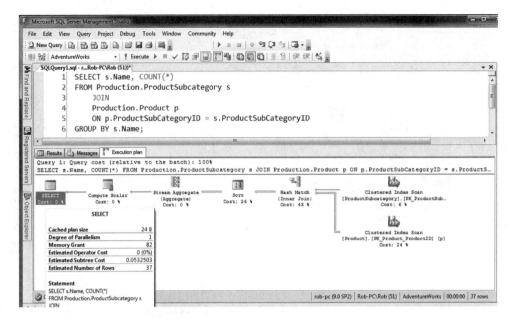

Figure 8   Execution plan without index

But when we drop the index, the execution plan of this query changes. It now appears as in figure 8. In fact, looking at the estimated cost of the query as reported in the plan, we see that it's approximately 30 percent higher (estimated cost of 0.05325 on my machine, compared to 0.04055 earlier). It seems our index is being used after all. Compare the execution plan in figure 8 with the one in figure 7; you can clearly see differences in the ways they are being used.

Note in particular the fact that the query is the same in both cases. Assuming the data has not changed, the results will be identical. Adding or removing indexes will not affect the rows that are returned by a query.

I'm not suggesting that our indexing strategy for this index is perfect. There are indexes that could make the query run better. The point is simply that the index called AK_ProductSubcategory_Name is actually being used, despite the fact that neither of the traditional methods (examining the execution plan or examining the DMV) is showing its use. Let's look at what's going on in more detail.

How is the unused index being used?

The DMV tells us that the index isn't being used, and this is wrong. But actually, it's my statement *the DMV tells us that the index isn't being used* that's wrong. The DMV is saying nothing of the sort. It correctly tells us that the index isn't being used for scans, seeks, lookups, and updates. The execution plan is also correct, because it indicates the indexes (or heaps) from which the data is being fetched.

What neither of these tells us is that the existence of the index is being used by the optimizer. The optimizer sees that we're grouping by a field which has a unique index on it, and realizes that this is somewhat redundant. That's right—AK_Product Subcategory_Name is a UNIQUE index, ensuring that every entry in the Name column is different from all the rest. Therefore, the optimizer can treat the query as if it's grouping by the field from the other table (the field that we're joining to) without changing the logic of the query at all. Without the unique index, the optimizer considers that there may be nondistinct values in the field, so it must perform the grouping on that field explicitly. We see this in our first, simpler queries as well. When the unique field ProductNumber was introduced to the mix, the optimizer realized that no Distinct Sort was required, and treated the query as a simple index scan.

In figure 7, we see that the Production.ProductSubcategory table is accessed only after the grouping has been completed. The Sort operator is sorting the Production. Product table by the ProductSubcategoryID field and aggregating its data on that field. Even though we request the grouping to be done on s.Name, the system has completed the grouping before s.Name becomes available. The optimizer is clearly using the existence of the unique index when deciding how to execute the query, even though the index isn't being used in other ways.

How does this affect me?

If you are tempted to investigate the index usage in your system, please bear in mind that unique indexes may be in use even if they are not being used in a way that is reflected in sys.dm_db_index_usage_stats or in the execution plan. If you remove one of these indexes, you may have queries which perform worse than before.

You may also want to consider introducing unique indexes. Even if you have logic in your application's business layer that ensures the uniqueness of a particular field, you could improve the performance of some queries by creating a unique index on them. Don't create additional indexes without giving appropriate thought to the matter, but don't disregard indexes simply because they're not being *used*. The optimizer is powerful and can take advantage of these indexes in ways you might not have considered.

Summary

Indexes are incredibly useful in databases. They not only help you get to your data quickly and effectively, but they let the optimizer make good decisions so that your queries can run faster. By all means, take advantage of methods to evaluate whether or not indexes are being used, but also try to consider if the optimizer might be using some indexes behind the scenes.

About the author

Rob Farley is a Microsoft MVP (SQL) based in Adelaide, Australia, where he runs a SQL and BI consultancy called LobsterPot Solutions. He also runs the Adelaide SQL Server User Group, and regularly trains and presents at user groups around Australia. He holds many certifications and has made several trips to Microsoft in Redmond to help create exams for Microsoft Learning in SQL and .NET. His passions include the Arsenal Football Club, his church, his wife, and three amazing children. The address of his blog is http://msmvps.com/blogs/robfarley and his company website is at http://www.lobsterpot.com.au.

41 Speeding up your queries with index covering

Alex Kuznetsov

When a nonclustered index contains all the columns from one table needed to satisfy a query, that index is called *covering* with respect to that query, and that query is *covered* by that index. In many cases, creating a covering index is a quick and easy way to boost the performance of a query. But covering indexes aren't free—they use additional storage, slow down most updates, and may cause concurrency issues such as lock contention and deadlocks. This means that speeding up some selects may and usually will cause some modifications to run slower. Usually, you don't need to optimize standalone queries; in most cases, you should aim to improve the system's overall productivity. To accomplish that, you need to find some balance to provide a system with selects that run faster and updates that still perform reasonably well. You'll see several examples demonstrating these concepts in this chapter. The first example will demonstrate how a covering index speeds up selects.

Index covering speeds up selects

First, we need to discuss the difference between clustered and nonclustered indexes. Clustered indexes store key columns on their root and intermediate pages, and all columns on their leaf pages. In fact, the leaf level of a clustered index is the table's data. Nonclustered indexes also store key columns on their root and intermediate pages, but on their leaf-level pages they store all the index key column values, plus bookmarks that allow the database engine to find the corresponding rows in the table.

Also, nonclustered indexes may store other columns listed in the INCLUDE clause, which will be discussed later. For example, the table [AdventureWorks].[Production].[WorkOrder] has a nonclustered index on column ScrapReasonID. (I'm using the SQL Server 2005 version of the AdventureWorks database.) This index stores ScrapReasonID on all its levels as well as WorkOrderID on its leaf

541

level. For this index, WorkOrderID column is a bookmark—it uniquely identifies rows in the table. Consider the following query:

```
SELECT [DueDate],SUM([OrderQty]) AS SumQty
  FROM [AdventureWorks].[Production].[WorkOrder]
GROUP BY [DueDate]
```

The optimizer can choose to scan the whole clustering index (the whole table [AdventureWorks].[Production].[WorkOrder]) to satisfy this query, unless there's an index that would allow the query to run faster. You can create a covering index as follows:

```
CREATE NONCLUSTERED INDEX [IX_WorkOrder_DueDate] ON [Production].[WorkOrder]
(
    [DueDate], [OrderQty]
)
```

The index IX_WorkOrder_DueDate is several times smaller than the table [AdventureWorks].[Production].[WorkOrder]. Clearly, scanning this index will require fewer reads. The optimizer will choose to scan the index rather than a significantly bigger table that the index is created on.

NOTE   Starting with SQL Server 2005, you can also use an INCLUDE clause for further optimization, as follows:

```
CREATE NONCLUSTERED INDEX [IX_WorkOrder_DueDate_with_INCLUDE] ON
[Production].[WorkOrder]
(
    [DueDate]
) INCLUDE([OrderQty])
```

All the tables in the AdventureWorks database are smallish, so you won't notice much difference between IX_WorkOrder_DueDate and IX_WorkOrder_DueDate_with_ INCLUDE. For really big tables, the index IX_WorkOrder_DueDate_with_ INCLUDE may give noticeably better performance. The INCLUDE clause will be discussed in more detail at the end of this chapter.

NOTE   For such comparisons, it's convenient to use two copies of the same database—the original database exactly as it exists in production and the modified one with a covering index.

Back up your AdventureWorks database, create a new database named Adventure-Works_Copy, and restore the backup of AdventureWorks against Adventure-Works_Copy. You can either do it all via SSMS or you can run the script in listing 1, changing the folder from C:\Temp if necessary.

Listing 1   Restore the AdventureWorks database to AdventureWorks_Copy

```
USE master
GO
BACKUP DATABASE AdventureWorks TO
    DISK=N'C:\Temp\AdventureWorksFullBackup.bak'
GO
```

```
RESTORE DATABASE AdventureWorks_Copy FROM
    DISK=N'C:\Temp\AdventureWorksFullBackup.bak'
  WITH REPLACE, MOVE 'AdventureWorks_Data' TO
    'C:\Temp\AdventureWorks_Copy_Data.mdf',
    MOVE 'AdventureWorks_Log' TO 'C:\Temp\AdventureWorks_Copy_Log.mdf'
```

Highlight the following query in Management Studio:

```
SELECT [DueDate],SUM([OrderQty]) AS SumQty
  FROM [AdventureWorks].[Production].[WorkOrder]
GROUP BY [DueDate]

SELECT [DueDate],SUM([OrderQty]) AS SumQty
  FROM [AdventureWorks_Copy].[Production].[WorkOrder]
GROUP BY [DueDate]
```

Press Ctrl-L to see the execution plans. Note that the optimizer expects the covered query to run several times faster, because the covered query is expected to perform several times fewer reads. Is the optimizer correct in its estimate? Compare real execution costs and see for yourself. Run the following commands:

```
SET STATISTICS IO ON
SET STATISTICS TIME ON
```

Run both selects and see the difference in reads and CPU cycles—with a covering index, the database engine performs several times fewer reads and uses less CPU. Note that, to satisfy a query, the database engine not only reads data, it also acquires locks to implement the current isolation level, unless you run the query under READ UNCOMMITTED isolation level.

NOTE   Understanding isolation levels is essential. Because a good description of isolation levels would be substantially bigger than this chapter, it's beyond the scope of this discussion. I encourage you to read about isolation levels in Books Online or on the MSDN web site: http://msdn.microsoft.com/en-us/library/ms189122.aspx.

Acquiring the locks necessary to implement an isolation level uses up CPU cycles, more locks, and more CPU for higher isolation levels. Usually the covered query needs to acquire fewer locks, because it needs to read fewer pages. You can increase the isolation level to SERIALIZABLE, rerun both selects, and see for yourself that for this query, the advantages of the covering index are more pronounced for higher isolation levels.

Let's discuss range queries and compare a covering index versus a noncovering one. Let's create a noncovering index, as shown in listing 2.

Listing 2   Creating a noncovering index

```
USE [AdventureWorks]
GO
CREATE NONCLUSTERED INDEX [IX_WorkOrder_DueDate] ON
[Production].[WorkOrder]
(
    [DueDate]
)
```

Let's run two range queries as in listing 3, and then see the execution plans.

Listing 3   Running two range queries

```
SELECT [DueDate],[OrderQty]
  FROM [AdventureWorks].[Production].[WorkOrder]
WHERE [DueDate] = '20040630'

SELECT [DueDate],[OrderQty]
  FROM [AdventureWorks_Copy].[Production].[WorkOrder]
WHERE [DueDate] = '20040630'
```

To satisfy the first query, the optimizer uses index seeks and bookmark lookups (bookmark lookups are also known as *clustered key lookups*). The second query uses index seeks only—this is a much simpler and cheaper plan. This is why the optimizer expects the cost of the first query to be approximately 99 times more than the cost of the second one, as shown in figure 1.

Don't expect to get exactly 99 percent when you run the queries on your server—your mileage may vary, depending on your version of SQL Server. For example, I'm sometimes getting different benchmark results running the same query against the same data on SQL Server 2000 and SQL Server 2005. Yet you should get similar numbers—the second query is dramatically more efficient. The optimizer thinks so, and the real execution costs confirm that the optimizer is right.

If the range is wide enough, the noncovering index is no longer used for the range query—the whole clustering index (the whole table) is scanned instead. But only a portion of a covering index is scanned even if the range is wide. You can run the two queries in listing 4 and see for yourself.

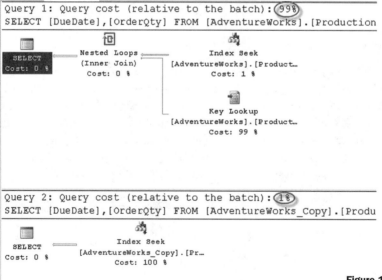

Figure 1   Index seek plan

Listing 4 Comparing covering and noncovering index performance

```
SELECT [DueDate],[OrderQty]
  FROM [AdventureWorks].[Production].[WorkOrder]
WHERE [DueDate] BETWEEN '20040630' AND '20040830'

SELECT [DueDate],[OrderQty]
  FROM [AdventureWorks_Copy].[Production].[WorkOrder]
WHERE [DueDate] BETWEEN '20040630' AND '20040830'
```

As you have seen, a covered query runs faster, because

- It may be satisfied by a simpler plan (this is true for many but not all queries).
- It needs to perform fewer reads.
- It may need to acquire less locks (this is true for many but not all queries).

Some rules of thumb about indexes aren't true for covering indexes

In general, blanket statements are rarely true in database programming. In particular, some rules of thumb are true for noncovering indexes, but not true for covering indexes. For instance, the rule "an index can only be used if the condition in the WHERE clause is index friendly" doesn't apply to covering indexes—although the following condition isn't index friendly:

```
SELECT DISTINCT [LastName],[FirstName]
  FROM [Person].[Contact]
WHERE [LastName] LIKE '%quist'
```

A covering index on (LastName, FirstName) can still be used to satisfy this query, although it'll require an index scan, not an index seek, and as such will take longer and more page reads than a query that can seek. You don't even have to use the left-most column of your covering index in your WHERE clause—a covering index on (First-Name, LastName) can also be used to satisfy this select just as well.

The rule that you need to have the most selective column first in your index isn't true for covering indexes, either. For instance, even though ContactID is more selective than FirstName, the following query runs faster against an index on (FirstName, ContactID) than against an index on (ContactID, FirstName):

```
SELECT DISTINCT [ContactID]
  FROM [Person].[Contact]
WHERE [FirstName] = N'Jane'
```

Covering indexes usually slow down modifications

Covering indexes usually slow down modifications. This is a no-brainer. All indexes usually slow down modifications, including covering indexes. The one word I feel that I need to explain is *usually*—I added it to the title of this section automatically, because blanket statements are rarely true in database programming. In the example in listing 5, a covering index speeds up a modification.

Listing 5   Update statement performance improved with a covering index

```
BEGIN TRANSACTION

UPDATE [AdventureWorks].[Production].[WorkOrder]
SET [OrderQty] = [OrderQty]+1
WHERE [DueDate] = '20040630' AND [OrderQty] = 12345678

UPDATE [AdventureWorks_Copy].[Production].[WorkOrder]
SET [OrderQty] = [OrderQty]+1
WHERE [DueDate] = '20040630' AND [OrderQty] = 12345678

ROLLBACK
```

As you've seen, in some rare cases a covering index may speed up an update, if it makes it easier to locate the rows being modified.

One index should cover many queries

Suppose that you have a table with a clustered index and two nonclustered indexes. Inserting one row into such a table means that at least three pages need to be modified or added (maybe more than three if there's a page split). The more nonclustered indexes you add on a table, the more pages a single-row insert must modify or insert. Similar reasoning is true for multi-row modifications, including updates and deletes—their real execution costs increase as the number of indexes grows. This is why it's important to keep the number of indexes low for tables that are frequently modified.

For example, consider two separate indexes on the [Person].[Contact] table, each covering a different SELECT statement as described in listing 6.

Listing 6   Creating two covering indexes

```
CREATE NONCLUSTERED INDEX [IX_Contact_Covering1] ON [Person].[Contact]
(
    [LastName], [FirstName], [EmailAddress]
)
GO
-- covers the following query:
SELECT [LastName], [FirstName], [EmailAddress] FROM [Person].[Contact]
WHERE [LastName] LIKE 'Lars%'
GO

CREATE NONCLUSTERED INDEX [IX_Contact_Covering2] ON [Person].[Contact]
(
    [LastName], [FirstName], [Phone]
)
GO
-- covers the following query:
SELECT [LastName], [FirstName], [EmailAddress] FROM [Person].[Contact]
WHERE [LastName] LIKE 'Lars%'
GO
```

You might instead consider creating only one index, as follows:

```
CREATE NONCLUSTERED INDEX [IX_Contact_Covering] ON [Person].[Contact]
(
    [LastName], [FirstName], [Phone], [EmailAddress]
)
```

This index will cover both selects and will slow down modifications less severely than the two previous indexes would.

One index can both cover queries and implement uniqueness

If you create a primary key or unique constraint, SQL Server automatically creates a unique index to implement the constraint. Note, though, that you don't have to create a constraint to enforce uniqueness. You can manually create a unique index, and this index is just as good as a constraint for most practical purposes—you can even have a foreign key constraint refer to a unique index instead of a primary key or unique constraint. Why is this relevant? Because you can have one index to both enforce uniqueness of a smaller set of columns and to cover a query involving a bigger set of columns.

For example, suppose that the EmailAddress column in Person.Contact isn't nullable (which at the time of this writing isn't true in AdventureWorks), and that you want to enforce the uniqueness of EmailAddress. Suppose that you also need an index to cover the following query:

```
SELECT [LastName], [FirstName], [EmailAddress]
FROM [Person].[Contact] WHERE [EmailAddress] LIKE 'lars%'
```

One index can be used to accomplish both goals, as follows:

```
CREATE UNIQUE NONCLUSTERED INDEX [IX_Contact_Unique_Covering] ON
[Person].[Contact]
(
    [EmailAddress]
)
INCLUDE([LastName], [FirstName])
```

Note that this index is different from a unique index on all three columns (Email-Address, LastName, FirstName). A unique index on all three columns would allow two persons with different names to have the same EmailAddress.

Keeping the number of indexes small is essential in most cases—it allows for quick selects without slowing modifications too much. Having one index serve many purposes allows you to keep the number of indexes small.

Summary

As you've seen, index covering is a simple and powerful way to speed up selects, because it allows the database engine to satisfy queries with fewer reads and locks. Although covering indexes may slow down modifications, in most cases this impact isn't prohibitively high. Usually you can manage to utilize index covering to keep your selects fast and your modifications reasonably performant too.

About the author

Alex Kuznetsov has been working with databases for more than a decade. He leads a team of database developers and optimizes database performance for a proprietary trading firm. Also he enjoys blogging on http://sqlblog.com and is currently writing a book on defensive database programming.

42 Tracing the deadlock

Gail Shaw

```
Msg 1205, Level 13, State 45, Line 5
Transaction (Process ID 53) was deadlocked on lock resources with another
process and has been chosen as the deadlock victim. Rerun the transaction.
```

A *deadlock* has to be one of the most frustrating error messages that SQL Server can produce. Little information is given as to what went wrong, and the only advice the error message gives is "Rerun the transaction." It appears that there's no way to find the root cause and to prevent the mysterious error from occurring.

In truth, there are ways to find information on exactly what happened to cause a deadlock and, with that information, in most cases it's possible to fix the root cause and prevent the error completely.

What's a deadlock?

At its simplest, a deadlock refers to a locking situation that, if no outside action is taken, will never resolve itself. It occurs when two or more processes have a lock on a resource and then try to acquire a lock on the resource held by the other process, or when two or more processes hold shared locks on a resource and attempt to convert them to exclusive locks. Figure 1 illustrates an example of a deadlock scenario.

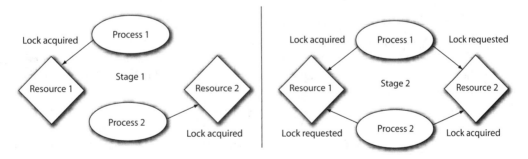

Figure 1   The first and second stages of a deadlock

Without intervention, the two processes will wait forever for the resource and they'll never complete. In order to resolve the situation, one of the processes must be killed and any modifications it made must be rolled back, so that the locks it held are released, allowing the other process to continue. This is the job of SQL Server's *deadlock detector*. It evaluates the locks held and locks requested and, if it finds an existing deadlock condition, it picks one of the deadlocked processes and kills it. The process killed by the deadlock detector is known as the *deadlock victim*.

The selection of the deadlock victim is based on a number of conditions:

- The deadlock priority, if set
- The number of data modifications that will need to be rolled back
- Whether the processes are system processes or user processes

In general, the process with the lowest deadlock priority or the one that's least expensive to roll back is the one that will be picked as the deadlock victim.

Causes of deadlocks

Deadlocks are typically caused by long-running transactions, or different transactions accessing the same objects in an inconsistent order.

A lack of useful indexes, poorly written code, and hardware bottlenecks can all cause transactions to run longer than they should, resulting in locks held for longer than necessary.

If statements in different stored procedures access tables in different orders (for example, one procedure first updates Table1 and then updates Table2, whereas another procedure first updates Table2 and then Table1), it's possible for two transactions to be holding a lock on the one object and wanting a lock on the other, resulting in a deadlock.

Isolation levels higher than the default (Read Committed) can also cause frequent deadlocks, as the locks are held longer, or more intrusive locks are held. This is true with the Serializable isolation level.

Deadlock graph

A *deadlock graph* is a representation of the processes involved in a deadlock, the locks that they held, and the resources that they were using. Deadlock graphs contain all the information needed to diagnose the cause of the deadlock, though not necessarily in a form that's easy to understand.

You may get a deadlock graph on SQL Server 2005 and SQL Server 2008 in three main ways. SQL Profiler includes a deadlock graph event, and there are two trace flags: 1204 and 1222. Of these, only trace flag 1204 was available on SQL Server 2000.

Trace flag 1204

Trace flag 1204 is one of the oldest ways to view a deadlock graph, and is the only method available on SQL Server 2000 or earlier.

To produce the deadlock graph, the trace flag needs to be enabled server-wide either using the DBCC TRACEON command (DBCC TRACEON (1204,-1)), or by adding the trace flag to SQL Server's startup parameters (-T1204).

Trace flag 1222

Trace flag 1222 works much the same as 1204 does, in that it writes deadlock information into the error log. The results produced by 1222 are far more detailed and easier to read than those produced by 1204. As such, it's preferred over 1204 for producing deadlock information on SQL Server 2005 or 2008.

Trace flag 1222 is enabled the same way as 1204 is, by using the TRACEON command (DBCC TRACEON (1222,-1)), or by adding the trace flag to the startup parameters (-T1222).

NOTE Despite popular belief, trace flag 3605 doesn't have to be enabled with 1204 or 1222 to write a deadlock graph into the error log.

SQL Profiler

In SQL Server 2005, the deadlock graph event was added to SQL Profiler. This event produces a graphical view of a deadlock graph that shows the processes, resources, and locks involved in a deadlock. The graph is saved in XML format and can be viewed in Management Studio.

This option requires that a trace be running against the target server. If deadlocks happen frequently, or can be reproduced on demand, this is a good way of getting the deadlock graph. If the deadlocks happen infrequently, it may not be feasible to run the profiler for long periods of time. In that case, trace flags may be a more appropriate option.

NOTE The Profiler GUI can cause an undesirable performance impact on a busy server. As such, server-side trace procedures should be used on production servers, and Profiler itself should be limited to development or test environments. Details of the server-side trace procedures are beyond the scope of this chapter. Full details on the sp_trace procedures can be found in Books Online.

Reading the deadlock graph

At a first glance, the deadlock graph produced by trace flag 1222 seems impossibly obtuse and near-impossible to read. In truth, much of the information given can be ignored, and it's mostly a case of knowing where to look and how to interpret the information given.

In this section, I'm going to walk through a deadlock graph, line by line, pointing out what sections are important and what they mean. Listing 1 shows an example of a deadlock graph (trimmed slightly so that it doesn't take three pages).

Listing 1   A sample deadlock graph

```
deadlock-list
 deadlock victim=process803294c8
  process-list
   process id=process803294c8 taskpriority=0 logused=316   ←──❶ First process
        waitresource=KEY: 6:72057594038845440 (1900f638aaf3) spid=53
   executionStack
     frame procname=WF.dbo.ViewThread line=20
             stmtstart=1090 stmtend=1362
  sqlhandle=0x03000600b15244168cf9db002b9b00000100000000000000

SELECT UserName, UserID FROM Users...
    inputbuf
Proc [Database Id = 6 Object Id = 373576369]

   process id=process809f8748 taskpriority=0 logused=316   ←──❷ Second process
        waitresource=PAGE: 6:1:351 spid=55
   executionStack
     frame procname=WF.dbo.ViewForum line=9
             stmtstart=416 stmtend=1734
   sqlhandle=0x03000600ea7638177375ae00379b00000100000000000000
SELECT * FROM
       (Select ForumName, Forums.Descr,...
    inputbuf
Proc [Database Id = 6 Object Id = 389576426]

   resource-list                      ←──❸ Resource list
   keylock hobtid=72057594038845440 dbid=6 objectname=WF.dbo.Users
        indexname=PK__Users mode=X associatedObjectId=72057594038845440
    owner-list
     owner id=process809f8748 mode=X
    waiter-list
     waiter id=process803294c8 mode=S requestType=wait
   pagelock fileid=1 pageid=351 dbid=6 objectname=WF.dbo.Threads
      id=lock83255f80 mode=IX associatedObjectId=72057594038910976
    owner-list
     owner id=process803294c8 mode=IX
    waiter-list
     waiter id=process809f8748 mode=S requestType=wait
```

The first thing to notice about the deadlock graph is that it's in two sections. First are the processes involved in the deadlock (indicated by ❶ and ❷) followed by a list of resources involved in the deadlock (starting at ❸). The resource list includes information on which process owns the lock and in what mode, and which process is waiting for the lock and in what mode.

The process list

In this section, each of the processes involved in the deadlock is listed, along with details about what procedures and queries the process was running at the time of the deadlock.

The line that identifies the process contains a great deal of information of value:

```
process id=process803294c8 taskpriority=0 logused=316
➥ waitresource=KEY: 6:72057594038845440 (1900f638aaf3)
➥ waittime=395 ownerId=29943 transactionname=user_transaction
➥ lasttranstarted=2008-10-17T14:25:26.013 XDES=0xa209b3d0
➥ lockMode=S schedulerid=2 kpid=2400 status=suspended spid=53
➥ sbid=0 ecid=0 priority=0 trancount=1
➥ lastbatchstarted=2008-10-17T14:25:26.013
➥ lastbatchcompleted=2008-10-17T14:25:26.013 clientapp=App
➥ hostname=S1 hostpid=3476 loginname=S1\U1 isolationlevel=read
➥ committed (2) xactid=29943 currentdb=6 lockTimeout=4294967295
➥ clientoption1=671088672 clientoption2=128056
```

The `waitresource` identifies exactly which lock the process is waiting for. In this case, it's an index key. The format of the resource for keys is `Database_ID:Partition_ID` and the value in the brackets is a hash of the index key values. The partition ID is important, in that it can be used to identify the table and schema using a query based on some of the metadata views:

```
SELECT OBJECT_NAME(o.object_id), SCHEMA_NAME(o.schema_id)
  FROM sys.partitions p
  INNER JOIN sys.objects o on p.object_id=o.object_id
  WHERE partition_id = 72057594038845440
```

This returns `Users` in the `dbo` schema, identifying one of the tables involved in the deadlock.

The *lock mode* identifies what type of lock was requested. In this process, it's `S`, indicating the lock was requested as a shared lock. Typical values here would be `S`, `X` (exclusive), `U` (update), `Sch-S` (schema stability), and `Sch-M` (schema modification).

Other useful information includes the `spid`, `clientapp`, `hostname`, and `loginname`. The `spid`, or session ID, identifies the session within the SQL Server instance. The `clientapp`, `hostname`, and `loginname` together identify where the query came from and who called it. The `hostname` is the name of the client machine that issues the request, and the `appname` is the application that issued the request. If the application is a querying tool (Management Studio or Query Analyzer), solving the deadlock may be as simple as asking the person who ran the query to not do so again.

The `isolationlevel` indicates what transaction isolation level the query ran under. The higher isolation levels (Repeatable Read and Serializable) have a greater chance of causing deadlocks than the default of read committed, whereas the read uncommitted isolation level is much less likely to cause a deadlock.

The last thing to notice is the `transactionname`. It reads `user_transaction`, which indicates that this select was running as part of an explicit transaction. This is important in understanding how and when the locks were taken. An exclusive lock is always held until the transaction is either committed or rolled back.

The most useful section of the graph lists the procedure (if applicable) and the statement start and end offsets for that procedure:

```
frame procname=WF.dbo.ViewThread line=20 stmtstart=1090
➥ stmtend=1362
➥ sqlhandle=0x03000600b15244168cf9db002b9b00000100000000000000
```

This section lists the full three-part name of the procedure that the process was running. If the call was ad hoc SQL, rather than a stored procedure, then the `procname` will read `adhoc`. The line number indicates on which line of the procedure the specific SQL statement starts. If the line number is 1, it's a strong indication that the specific SQL statement is a piece of dynamic SQL.

The statement start and statement end values specify the offsets within the procedure where the query starts and ends. The `sql_handle` can be used with the `sys.dm_exec_sql_text` DMF to get the SQL statement from the server's procedure cache. This usually isn't necessary, as most of the time the statement is reproduced in full in the deadlock graph right below this line.

The input buffer lists either the entire query (for ad hoc SQL) or the database ID and object ID for a stored procedure:

```
inputbuf Proc [Database Id = 6 Object Id = 373576369]
```

The object ID can be translated back to an object name using the object name function:

```
SELECT OBJECT_NAME(373576369, 6)
```

In this case it returns `ViewThread`, matching what was shown for the process name earlier in the deadlock graph.

NOTE   The `Object_Name` function took only one parameter, the object ID, prior to SQL Server 2005 SP2. From SP2 onward, it accepts an optional second parameter, the database ID.

The second process listed in the deadlock graph contains the same information and can be read in much the same way. I won't go through it all in detail, as many of the explanations given for the first process apply to the second as well.

The second process has a different `waitresource` than the first one did. In the case of the key lock, it was trivial to identify the table involved. The second process was waiting on a page lock.

```
process id=process809f8748 waitresource=PAGE: 6:1:351 spid=55
```

The numbers listed for the page indicate database ID (6), file ID (1), and page ID (351). The object that owns the page can be identified using DBCC PAGE, but in this case, it's not necessary, as the name of the table is given later in the deadlock graph in the list of resources. If DBCC Page were to be used, it would show that the page 6:1:351 belongs to a table with the ID 85575343. Using the `Object_Name` function reveals that the table's name is `Threads`.

The procedure that the second process was running is `WF.dbo.ViewForum` and the statement began on line 9.

DBCC PAGE

DBCC Page is an undocumented but well-known command that shows the contents of database pages. The command takes four parameters, the last being optional. The first three are the database ID or database name, the file ID, and the page ID. The last parameter indicates the print options.

Among the information that can be retrieved from the file header is the object and index that the page belongs to (if it's a data or index page).

To return the results to a query window, trace flag 3604 has to be enabled. An example use of DBCC Page would be

```
DBCC TRACEON (3604)
DBCC PAGE (1,1,215,0)
DBCC TRACEOFF(3604)
```

By this point, we have a fairly clear idea as to what was happening when the deadlock occurred.

The process with a session ID of 53 requested a shared lock on the index key 6:72057594038845440 (1900f638aaf3), in the Users table, so that it could run a select that starts on line 20 of the procedure ViewThread. The second process, with a session ID of 55, requested a shared lock on the page 6:1:351 belonging to the Threads table so that it could run a select that starts on line 9 of the procedure ViewForum.

The resource list

What we don't know yet is what locks these two processes were holding when the deadlock occurred. That's where the third part of the deadlock graph—the resource list—comes in. The resource list lists all of the locks involved in the deadlock, along with which process had them and which process wanted them.

The first entry in the resource list refers to the key lock on the primary key of the Users table. We know, from the first section of the deadlock graph, that this is what session ID 53 was waiting for:

```
keylock hobtid=72057594038845440 dbid=6
⮕ objectname=WF.dbo.Users indexname=PK__Users
⮕ id=lock800c0f00 mode=X associatedObjectId=72057594038845440
    owner-list
    owner id=process809f8748 mode=X
    waiter-list
    waiter id=process803294c8 mode=S requestType=wait
```

Process process809f8748, which is session ID 55, owned that lock in exclusive mode. Process process803294c8 requested the lock in shared mode and had to wait.

The second entry in the resource list refers to the page lock on the Threads table. We know from the first section that this is what session ID 55 was waiting for:

```
pagelock fileid=1 pageid=351 dbid=6 objectname=WF.dbo.Threads
   id=lock83255f80 mode=IX associatedObjectId=72057594038910976
   owner-list
    owner id=process803294c8 mode=IX
   waiter-list
    waiter id=process809f8748 mode=S requestType=wait
```

The process process803294c8, which is session ID 53, owned that resource in intent-exclusive mode and hence process process809f8748 (session ID 55) had to wait.

NOTE   An *intent-exclusive (IX)* lock is taken by a process before an exclusive lock and at a lower level of lock granularity, and is taken to signal the intention to take an exclusive lock; hence the name.

The two most common values for requestType are wait and convert. A value of wait indicates that a new lock has been requested; convert indicates that the process already has a lock on that resource in one mode and requested to convert the lock into a different mode. A typical example would be when a process has a shared lock and wishes to convert it to exclusive. The conversion can only occur if there are no locks on the resource that are incompatible with the new lock mode—for example in the repeatable read isolation level, where a row is selected and then updated within a transaction.

The big picture

Now the full picture of the events that lead up to and resulted in the deadlock is clear.

The process with a session ID of 53, while running the procedure ViewThread, began an explicit transaction and did a data modification on the Threads table. Later in the same transaction, it tried to do a select on the Users table, which was blocked. The second process, session ID 55, ran the procedure ViewForum. Within the procedure, it began an explicit transaction and did a data modification on the Users table. Following that, it attempted to run a select on the Threads table, which was blocked.

This deadlock turns out to be a case of objects accessed in different orders from different places. Although fixing the code is beyond the scope of this chapter, it turns out that reordering the queries in one of those procedures, so that the objects are accessed in the same order in both, prevents the deadlock completely.

Changing the isolation level to Snapshot or Read Committed Snapshot will also prevent the deadlock, because in the optimistic concurrency model, writers don't block readers. Again, a discussion on snapshot isolation is beyond the scope of this chapter.

Summary

The deadlock graph is the key to understanding and resolving deadlocks. The list of resources locked shows the state of events before the deadlock. The information provided about the process's state at the time of the deadlock, including locks requested and the process's input buffers, shows the cause of the deadlock clearly.

About the author

Gail is a database consultant from Johannesburg, South Africa, specializing in performance tuning and database optimization. Before moving to consulting, she worked at a large South African investment bank and was responsible for the performance of the major systems there.

She was awarded MVP for SQL Server in July 2008 and spoke at both TechEd South Africa and the PASS Community Summit in Seattle in the same year. She's a frequent poster on the SQLServerCentral forums and has written a number of articles for the same site.

43 How to optimize tempdb performance

Brad M. McGehee

Although most DBAs know about the tempdb database, many seem to think of it as a black box that takes care of itself with no involvement required from the DBA. Although this may be true on smaller, less active SQL Server instances, tempdb can significantly affect SQL Server's performance. DBAs can act to ensure that tempdb performance is optimized and to optimize the overall performance of SQL Server.

What is tempdb used for?

The tempdb database is one of SQL Server's included system databases and is used as a shared temporary workspace for many different kinds of activities, such as the following:

- Storing user objects, such as temporary local and global tables and indexes, temporary stored procedures, table variables, and the cursor.
- Storing temporary work tables used for hash joins, aggregations, cursors, and spool operations, and temporarily storing large objects; storing intermediate sort results from many different internal operations, such as creating or rebuilding indexes, in addition to some GROUP BY, ORDER BY, and UNION queries.
- Storing objects used when using AFTER triggers and INSTEAD OF triggers.
- Storing large XML objects.
- Storing the SQL Server version store (SQL Server 2005/2008), which includes the common version store and the online-index-build version store (Enterprise Edition).
- Storing intermediate results and sorting activity used during DBCC CHECKDB operations.
- Storing temporary objects for Service Broker.

If your SQL Server instance is not busy, and it doesn't employ many of the activities described previously, then tempdb performance may not be a problem for you. On the other hand, if any of your SQL Server instances are busy, and are heavily involved in many, if not most, of the previously described activities, then you may find that tempdb can become a significant bottleneck for your entire SQL Server instance.

Tempdb internals

Unlike other SQL Server databases, the tempdb database is dropped and re-created every time the SQL Server service is stopped and restarted. Here's what happens. When the SQL Server service is started, by default, SQL Server makes a copy of the model database to create a new 8 MB tempdb database, inheriting customizations made to the model database. In addition, a transaction log file of 1 MB is created. For both the MDF and the LDF files, autogrowth is set to grow by 10 percent with unrestricted growth. Each SQL Server instance may have only one tempdb database.

In addition, tempdb exhibits many behaviors that don't occur with other SQL Server databases. For example, tempdb is configured to run using the simple recovery model, and this setting cannot be changed. In addition, many database options, such as `Online`, `Read Write`, `Auto Close`, `Auto Shrink`, and others are preset and cannot be modified. The tempdb database has many other restrictions including the following: it can't be dropped; it can't be captured in a database snapshot; it can't participate in mirroring; and it can't allow `DBCC CHECKDB` to be run on it. And as you would expect, neither the tempdb database nor its transaction log file can be backed up. This makes sense, as tempdb is designed for temporary objects only, and is re-created each time SQL Server restarts.

After tempdb has been created, DBAs can create objects in it just as in other databases. As user-created or internal objects are added to tempdb, it will automatically grow as necessary to whatever size is required to hold the objects. On servers with heavy tempdb activity, tempdb can grow considerably.

As activity transpires in tempdb, transaction logging occurs, but somewhat differently than with other SQL Server databases. Operations performed within tempdb are minimally logged, which means that only enough information is logged so that temporary objects can be rolled back, if necessary. Minimal logging helps to reduce the overhead put on the SQL Server instance. Because the database is set to the simple recovery mode, the transaction log is truncated constantly.

How DBAs can help optimize tempdb

As I mentioned previously, if your SQL Server instance doesn't use tempdb much, then tempdb performance may not be an issue for you. On the other hand, you should keep one important thing in mind about tempdb: there is only one tempdb database per SQL Server instance, and it can become a major bottleneck that can affect the entire performance of your SQL Server. Keep in mind that even if most of your applications and databases behave well, a single misbehaving application and database can affect the performance of all the other databases running on the same server.

When building a new SQL Server instance, it is often difficult to determine how busy the tempdb database will be in production. Because of this, you may want to consider implementing many of the following suggestions when you build a new instance, as in many cases it is much easier to implement these recommendations when the server is first built, rather than trying to implement them after a problem has developed. Consider this as an ounce of prevention to avoid potential and unforeseen problems in the future.

In the following section, we take a look at many different practices you can employ to help optimize the performance of tempdb. Because each SQL Server instance is different, I am not suggesting that you employ every one of these recommendations on each of your SQL Servers. Instead, you must evaluate the kinds of problems you are having (or may have, if you are building a new SQL Server) and consider the available options (for example, you may not have the option to reconfigure your storage array or purchase new hardware). You implement only those recommendations that best meet your needs.

Minimizing the use of tempdb

As we discussed earlier, a lot of activity can occur in tempdb. In some cases, you can take steps to reduce SQL Server use of tempdb, helping to boost overall SQL Server performance. Although this is not a comprehensive list, here are some actions you may want to avoid:

- Using user-created temp tables. Often, I have seen T-SQL code that creates temp tables unnecessarily when the code could have been written to perform the same task without using temp tables. If you have to use a temp table, and the table has several thousand rows and is accessed frequently, consider adding an index to the table to boost performance of queries that are run against it. You may have to experiment with indexing to see if it helps or hurts overall performance.

- Scheduling jobs, such as DBCC CHECKDB, that use tempdb heavily, at times of the day when the SQL Server instance is busy.

- Using static- and keyset-driven cursors. In many cases, cursors can be avoided by rewriting the code.

- Using recursive common table expression queries. If the execution plan for such a query shows a spool operator, then you know that tempdb is being used to execute it.

- Using the SORT_IN_TEMPDB option when creating or rebuilding an index. Or if you decide to use this option, schedule the job to run during a less busy time of the day.

- Using online index rebuilding (Enterprise Edition), which uses row versioning and, in turn, uses tempdb.

- Using large object data types.

- Using table variables.

- Returning and sorting excessive amounts of data. Smaller sorts can be done in memory, but larger sorts spill over into tempdb.
- Returning and aggregating excessive amounts of data.
- Using joins that indicate a hash-type join in the query's execution plan.
- Using `AFTER` and `INSTEAD OF` triggers.
- Using row-versioning-based transaction isolation levels.

You may know that you can't avoid using the features in the previous list. If that's the case, then use them. Be aware that each of the choices in the list directly impact tempdb's performance. If you are having tempdb bottleneck issues and can't reduce the activity occurring in tempdb, you will have to resort to using some of the other tempdb optimization suggestions in this chapter instead.

Preallocating tempdb space and avoiding use of autogrowth

Every time SQL Server restarts using its default settings, a new 8 MB copy of tempdb is created (regardless of the model database's size), and autogrowth is set to 10 percent with unrestricted growth. Other than for the smallest SQL Server instances, 8 MB is rarely large enough, and because of this, tempdb must grow on demand to whatever size is necessary for your SQL Server instance to continue functioning. As you might expect, allowing autogrowth to size tempdb can often be problematic.

For example, let's say that the average size for tempdb for a particular SQL Server instance is 1 GB. In this case, when SQL Server is restarted, the initial size of tempdb is 8 MB. Soon thereafter, autogrowth kicks in and grows tempdb 10 percent, over and over again, until it reaches its optimal size of about 1 GB. This can result in autogrowth kicking in at busy times of the day, using up valuable server resources; and delaying transactions from completing because autogrowth has to complete before the transaction can complete. In addition, the use of autogrowth contributes to physical file fragmentation on disk, which can put extra stress on your disk I/O subsystem.

Instead of using autogrowth to manage tempdb sizing, use `ALTER DATABASE` to change the tempdb's MDF and LDF files to their optimal size. This way, when the SQL Server service is restarted, tempdb will be sized correctly right away. Additional performance gains can be achieved if you are using instant file initialization for your SQL Server instance, as this feature can dramatically decrease the time it takes for tempdb to be created when SQL Server is restarted, or when autogrowth events occur.

The difficult part is determining the optimal size of tempdb for a particular SQL Server instance. Although Books Online offers a way to estimate the normal size of tempdb, in practice, this is difficult to do. Personally, I start with an initial guess for the size (based on similar servers I am managing) and then watch the tempdb size over time. At some point, you should notice that tempdb is not growing, or that the amount of space you have allocated is not being fully used. Based on this information, I round this number up (the maximum amount of tempdb space actually used) to the nearest GB and use that figure as the optimal size for my tempdb database. This applies to both the MDF and LDF files. I still leave autogrowth on, as something unexpected may come up, and I want tempdb to grow if it needs to.

After a particular SQL Server instance's tempdb has been set, every time SQL Server is restarted, an optimum-sized tempdb will be created in one fell swoop, and you won't have to worry about the potential downsides of using autogrowth to size tempdb.

Don't shrink tempdb if you don't need to

After you have established the optimal size of tempdb, you may notice that the actual space used within tempdb varies considerably. Sometimes it may be less than half used, and other times it may be virtually full. For example, your tempdb database may be set to 1 GB (its optimal size), but sometimes only 250 MB of the allocated space is used, whereas at other times 950 MB of the allocated space is used. This is normal behavior, as the amount of space used in tempdb varies depending on what is happening on the SQL Server instance.

Don't let this varying amount of space trick you into considering shrinking tempdb when space usage drops. If you do, you will be using SQL Server resources unnecessarily and contribute to worse overall performance. For example, let's say that on a Friday you notice that your 1 GB of tempdb database is only using 250 MB, so you decide to shrink the tempdb database from 1 GB to 250 MB to recover disk space. But on Saturday, a series of weekly jobs runs that causes the now-250-MB-tempdb database to grow back to 1 GB using the autogrowth feature. In this case, all the resources required to shrink the tempdb database, and the resources to autogrow the database, will have been wasted.

In some cases, a wild-running query will cause tempdb to grow much larger than its normal size. If you are short on disk space and want to reclaim this empty space, and you are fairly confident that the wild-running query won't repeat itself, you have two choices:

- Shrink the database and log files manually using DBCC SHRINKFILE. This option may not work as expected, as internal objects or the version store aren't moved during this process, often resulting in less than expected shrinkage.
- Restart the SQL Server instance. This will re-create tempdb at the size it was as specified by the ALTER DATABASE statement. This option is more effective, but you must have downtime available for it to work.

Think of a tempdb's optimum size as its maximum size. If you keep this in mind, then you won't be tempted to shrink it when it is less than full.

Dividing tempdb among multiple physical files

Although there can only be one tempdb database per SQL Server instance, the tempdb database can be split into multiple physical files. If your tempdb is not active, then splitting it into multiple files may not buy you much additional performance. But if your tempdb is active, splitting it into multiple files can potentially boost your server's overall performance.

Unfortunately, selecting the ideal number of physical files needed to optimize tempdb's performance is not an exact science. As a starting point, you should consider creating as many physical files as there are CPU cores available to your SQL Server instance. For example, if your server has 8 CPU cores available to it, then divide the tempdb database into 8 physical files.

NOTE   If you decide to use multiple files for tempdb, it is important that each of them be exactly the same size (for example, if your tempdb's normal size is 1 GB, then you should have 8 physical files of 125 MB each). This is because SQL Server uses a proportional fill strategy to fill the physical files. In addition, the autogrowth settings should be identical for each physical file in order to ensure that each physical file grows identically.

Multiple files can boost disk I/O performance and reduce contention by spreading I/O activity over multiple files. This is beneficial even if the multiple files reside on a single disk volume, although locating each physical tempdb file on its own disk volume would generally provide an even greater benefit (at a much greater cost).

On the other hand, using more physical disk files can increase switching costs and file management overhead because each object created in tempdb will have to have IAM pages created in each of the physical files. This and other unknowns about your SQL Server instance complicate providing an exact recommendation for the optimum number of physical files to use for your tempdb. I recommend that you perform tests in your own environment to determine the number of physical files that optimize the tempdb for your particular needs. After testing, you may find that more or fewer tempdb physical files are needed for optimum performance.

Although the tempdb MDF file should generally be split into multiple physical files, this is not the case with the tempdb LDF file. Because tempdb uses the simple recovery model, and because it uses it own optimized logging method, dividing the LDF file into multiple physical files rarely provides any benefit.

Moving tempdb to a disk separate from your other databases

By default, when installing SQL Server, tempdb is stored in the same location as the rest of your databases. Although this may work for smaller, less busy SQL Servers, it can cause a lot of I/O contention problems on busy SQL Servers. Ideally, tempdb should be located on its own disk volume(s), separate from other disk activity.

Locating tempdb on a fast I/O subsystem

No matter where tempdb is located, it should be located on the fastest I/O subsystem available to your SQL Server instance. Your hardware will limit what you can do, but you might want to consider the following options, assuming your hardware (and budget) permits:

- Avoid putting tempdb on a RAID 5 I/O subsystem, because tempdb is subject to heavy writes, and RAID 5 often offers poor write performance.
- Instead, locate tempdb on a RAID 1 or RAID 10 I/O subsystem, which offer better write performance.
- If your SQL Server instance is storing data on a storage area network (SAN), consult with your SAN engineer to determine the best location for optimal performance. As a general rule of thumb on SANs, tempdb should be located on its own logical unit number (LUN) with its own dedicated drives.

Adding RAM to your SQL server instance

Depending on the operation, SQL Server often tries to perform the action in the buffer cache. If the space is insufficient, then the operation may be forced to use tempdb. For example, whenever a sort is performed, SQL Server tries to perform it in the buffer cache because that is the fastest way to perform a sort. But if the sort data is large, or if the buffer cache does not have enough space, then the sorting is done in tempdb. This not only slows down the sort; it also places additional overhead on tempdb.

One way to avoid this and similar problems is to add additional RAM to your SQL Server instance, so that these activities can be completed in the buffer cache without using tempdb.

Using SQL Server 2008 transparent data encryption

In SQL Server 2008, if you turn on transparent data encryption (TDE) for any one database on a SQL Server instance, then tempdb automatically becomes encrypted, which can negatively affect the performance of all the databases on the server, whether they are encrypted or not. Because TDE encrypts and decrypts data pages as they are being moved between the buffer pool and disk, CPU utilization increases as encryption and decryption occur. On a busy server with an active tempdb, this can significantly boost CPU utilization, potentially hurting the overall performance of your SQL Server. If your tempdb database is busy, avoid using TDE. If you must use TDE for security purposes, consider limiting the load on the instance, or consider using beefed-up hardware—CPU, memory, and faster disk access—to help overcome the encryption and decryption performance penalty.

Leaving auto create statistics and auto update statistics on

By default, the auto create statistics and auto update statistics database options are turned on for tempdb. In most cases, don't turn these options off, as SQL Server will automatically create and update statistics as needed in temporary tables and indexes, helping to boost performance of many operations performed on them.

Verifying CHECKSUM for SQL Server 2008

Although this is not a performance optimization suggestion, it is an important consideration for tempdb integrity. Starting with SQL Server 2008, the CHECKSUM database option is turned on by default for tempdb during a new install. This feature helps to ensure the integrity of the tempdb database. On the other hand, if you perform an in-place upgrade from an older SQL Server instance to SQL Server 2008, the CHECKSUM database option will not be automatically enabled for you on tempdb. To be on the safe side, you should manually enable the CHECKSUM database option on tempdb for added data protection.

Summary

As a DBA, it is a good idea to learn about the tempdb database and how it affects your SQL Server instances' performance. You may quickly learn that you have a tempdb bottleneck and not even know it. If tempdb has become a bottleneck for your SQL Server, consider all your options and implement one at a time, beginning with the easiest ones, and if they don't resolve the bottleneck, consider the more difficult ones until you have resolved the problem. And, before you implement any of the suggestions in this chapter, it is a good idea to test them on a test platform.

About the author

Brad M. McGehee is an MCSE+I, MCSD, and MCT (former) with a bachelor's degree in Economics and a master's in Business Administration. Involved in the industry since 1982, Brad is currently the Director of DBA Education for Red Gate Software, and is an accomplished Microsoft SQL Server MVP with over 14 years of experience with SQL Server and over 6 years of training experience. Brad is a frequent speaker at SQL PASS, European PASS, SQL Connections, SQLTeach, SQLBits, SQL Saturdays, TechFests, Code Camps, SQL Server user groups, and other industry seminars. He blogs at www.bradmcgehee.com.

44 Does the order of columns in an index matter?

Joe Webb

A single column index is straightforward. You may have heard it compared to the index in the back of a technical book. To find information in the book, say you want to learn more about how DBCC INPUTBUFFER is used, you look up DBCC INPUT-BUFFER in the index. The index doesn't contain the information on DBCC INPUT-BUFFER; it has a pointer to the page where the command is described. You turn to that page and read about it. This is a good analogy for a single column, nonclustered index.

In Microsoft SQL Server, you can also create an index that contains more than one column. This is known as a composite index. A good analogy for a composite index is the telephone book.

Understanding the basics of composite indexes

A telephone book lists every individual in the local area who has a publicly available telephone number. It's organized not by one column, but by two: last name and first name (ignoring the middle name that is sometimes listed but most often treated as an extension of the person's first name).

To look up someone in the telephone book, you first navigate to the last name and then the first name. For example, to find Jake Smith, you first locate the Smiths. Then within the Smiths, you find Jake.

SQL Server can use composite indexes in a similar manner. Composite indexes contain more than 1 column and can reference up to 16 columns from a single table or view. The columns that compose a composite index can contain up to a combined 900 bytes.

Let's consider some examples. Assume you have a Customers table as described in listing 1.

Listing 1   A sample Customers table

```
CREATE TABLE Customers
       (
        Customer_ID INT NOT NULL IDENTITY(1,1)
       ,Last_Name VARCHAR(20) NOT NULL
       ,First_Name VARCHAR(20) NOT NULL
       ,Email_Address VARCHAR(50) NULL
       );
```

The Customers table has a clustered index on Customer_ID and a nonclustered composite index on the Last_Name, First_Name. These are expressed in listing 2.

Listing 2   Creating indexes for the Customers table

```
CREATE CLUSTERED INDEX ix_Customer_ID
   ON Customers(Customer_ID);

CREATE INDEX ix_Customer_Name
   ON Customers(Last_Name, First_Name);
```

Finding a specific row

When we issue a query to SQL Server that retrieves data from the Customers table, the SQL Server query optimizer will consider the various retrieval methods at its disposal and select the one it deems most appropriate. Listing 3 provides a query in which we ask SQL Server to find a Customer named Jake Smith.

Listing 3   Finding a specific Customer row by Last_Name, First_Name

```
SELECT
   Last_Name
   ,First_Name
   ,Email_Address
FROM
   Customers
WHERE
   Last_Name = 'Smith' AND
   First_Name = 'Jake';
```

In the absence of an index, SQL Server would have to search through the entire table looking for the rows that satisfy this query. Because we have created a nonclustered index on the Last_Name and First_Name columns, SQL Server can use that index to quickly navigate to the selected rows. Figure 1 shows the query execution plan for the query.

In the figure, we can see that SQL Server used an Index Seek operation on the nonclustered index named ix_Customer_Name to locate the rows selected by the query. To retrieve the additional non-indexed columns (Email_Address), a Key Lookup was used for each row. The results were put together in a nested Loop join and returned to the client.

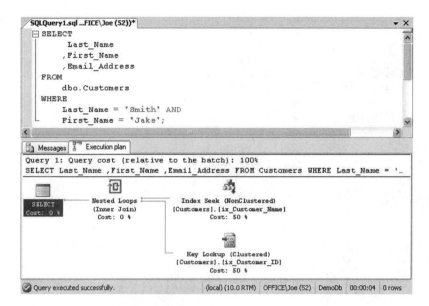

Figure 1   Query execution plan for listing 1

You may have noticed that the WHERE clause in listing 1 provides the columns in the order that they appear in the ix_Customer_Name index. This is not a requirement in order for SQL Server to be able to use the index. If we reversed the order of the columns in the WHERE clause, SQL Server would still be able to use the index. But don't take my word for it. Let's look at another example to prove that this is indeed the case. Listing 4 shows the newly rewritten query that reverses the order of the columns in the WHERE clause.

Listing 4   Finding a specific Customer row by First_Name, Last_Name

```
SELECT
    *
FROM
    Customers
WHERE
    First_Name = 'Jake' AND
    Last_Name = 'Smith';
```

Issuing the query produces the query execution plan found in the figure 2 query execution plan for listing 4. The plan is identical to the prior example in which the WHERE clause listed the columns in order.

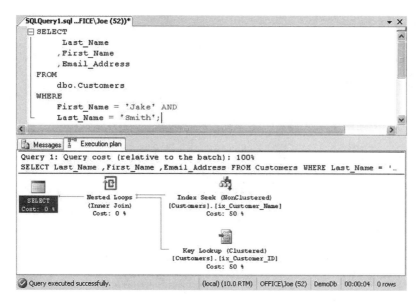

Figure 2   Query execution plan for listing 4

Finding a last name

In the prior example, we supplied values in the WHERE clause for both columns defined in the ix_Customer_Name index. The index is based on Last_Name, First_Name, and our query limited the results by providing a value for the Last_Name column and for the First_Name column.

Although this makes intuitive sense, a composite index's usefulness is not limited to only those instances where this is true. SQL Server can use a composite index when only some of the index's columns are provided. For example, consider the query depicted in listing 5.

Listing 5   Finding customers by Last_Name

```
SELECT
    Last_Name
    ,First_Name
    ,Email_Address
FROM
    Customers
WHERE
    Last_Name = 'Smith';
```

This query is similar to our prior example; however, notice that the WHERE clause now specifies only a Last_Name of Smith. We want to find all Smiths in our Customers table.

Looking at the query execution plan in figure 3 for the query specified in listing 5, we see that SQL Server did indeed use the ix_Customer_Name composite index. It

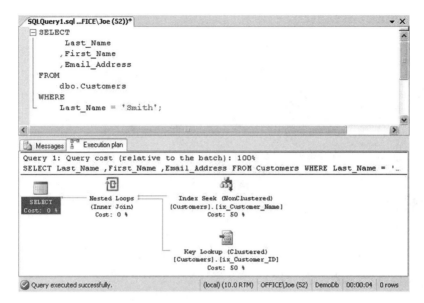

Figure 3   Query execution plan for listing 5

performed an Index Seek operation to find the rows that satisfied the query. Then a Key Lookup operation was used to retrieve the non-indexed column information for each row that satisfied the query.

Returning to our telephone book analogy, we can see why this index was deemed efficient by the Query Optimizer. To find all of the Smiths in the telephone book, we'd navigate to the page that contains the first Smith and keep moving forward until we found the entry after Smith. SQL Server resolved the query in a similar manner using the ix_Customer_Name index.

Finding a first name

The prior demonstration proved that SQL Server can use a composite index even though only some of the columns of the index are specified in the WHERE clause. But does it matter which columns are specified? To find out, let's consider another example.

In this example, we'll change what we are specifying in our search criteria. We'll no longer look for all Customers with a last name of Smith. Instead, we'll search for all Customers with a first name of Jake. Listing 6 shows our new query.

Listing 6   Finding Customers with a first name of Jake

```
SELECT
    Last_Name
    ,First_Name
    ,Email_Address
FROM
```

```
    Customers
WHERE
    First_Name = 'Jake';
```

When we run this query in SQL Server Management Studio and examine the query execution plan shown in figure 4, we can see that SQL Server no longer is able to use an `Index Seek` operation to specifically locate the rows that satisfy the query. Instead it must resort to an `Index Scan` operation.

Why is that? Let's consider our telephone book analogy again. How useful would the telephone book be if you need to find everyone with a first name of Jake? Not very. You'd have to start on the first page of the book and look through every entry to see if the person's first name is Jake. Why? Because the telephone book is not organized by first name; it's organized by last name, first name.

The same holds true for SQL Server. An index cannot be used to seek rows of data when the first column of the index is not specified in the WHERE clause.

That's not to say that the index is completely worthless for queries such as the one defined in listing 6. One the contrary, it can still improve performance significantly. Looking again at figure 4, we see that a nonclustered index scan on ix_Customer_ Name was used to resolve the query. In an index scan SQL Server examines every entry in the index to see if it matches the specified criteria. This may sound like an expensive operation, but it's much better than the alternative, a clustered index scan, also known as a table scan.

To see that this is the case, let's look again at the properties of the nonclustered index scan from our last example. Let's run the query again. This time we'll turn on STATISTICS IO so that we can measure the logical and physical reads required to satisfy the query. Listing 7 shows how to turn the setting on.

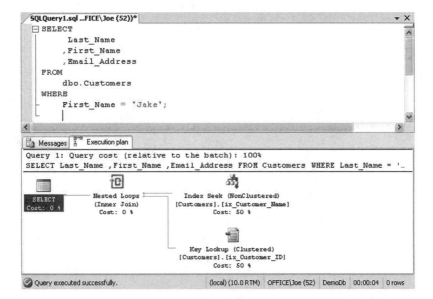

Figure 4   Query execution plan for listing 6

Listing 7   Turning STATISTICS IO on

```
SET STATISTICS IO ON
```

Before issuing our query, let's make sure we are starting with a clean state by clearing the procedure cache and freeing up memory. This is shown in listing 8.

Listing 8   Using DBCC to drop the procedure cache and free memory

```
DBCC DROPCLEANBUFFERS
DBCC FREEPROCCACHE
```

Now, let's rerun the query and look at the logical and physical reads required to retrieve the results. This is shown in figure 5.

Notice that the query required one pass through the index. That's the Scan Count of 1. It's also required 6,223 logical reads and 3 physical reads to retrieve the information from the ix_Customer_Name index pages. A logical read occurs when SQL Server requests a page from the buffer cache. A physical read occurs when SQL Server must go to disk to retrieve the page.

Let's compare these figures to that which would occur if the ix_Customer_Name nonclustered index were not there. To do this, we'll drop the index, as shown in listing 9.

Listing 9   Dropping the ix_Customer_Name index

```
DROP INDEX ix_Customer_Name ON dbo.Customers
```

Figure 5   Reads required for listing 6

Figure 6   Reads required for listing 6 without the `ix_Customer_Name` index

With the index gone, let's re-issue the query in listing 6. The results are shown in figure 6.

Without the benefit of the ix_Customer_Name index, SQL Server still required only one pass through the table to resolve the query. But the logical reads exploded to 14,982 and the physical reads ballooned to 109! Why? Let's look at the query execution plan to see; it's shown in figure 7.

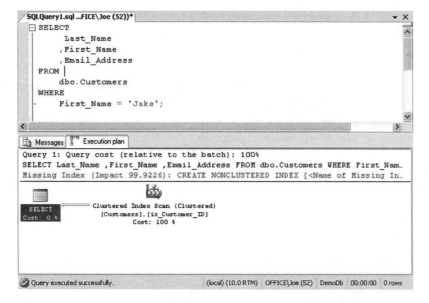

Figure 7   Query execution plan for listing 6 without the `ix_Customer_Name` index

The figure shows that a clustered index scan, or a table scan, was required to resolve the query. That means that each row of the table had to be read.

Compared to the table, a nonclustered index typically is contained on far fewer data pages and therefore requires far fewer reads. And as we know, disk I/O is a major contributing factor to poor performance. So a nonclustered index scan is still far more efficient than scanning the entire table.

Summary

Indexes that include multiple columns, known as composite indexes, allow SQL Server to efficiently search for rows in a table or view. Understanding how the query optimizer can use these indexes allows you to create queries that can improve performance and reduce resource contention.

About the author

Joe Webb, a Microsoft SQL Server MVP, serves as Chief Operating Manager for WebbTech Solutions, a Nashville-based IT consulting company. He has over 15 years of industry experience and has consulted extensively with companies in the areas of business process analysis and improvements, database design and architecture, software development, and technical training.

In addition to helping his consulting clients, Joe enjoys writing and speaking at technical conferences. He has delivered over 50 sessions at conferences in Europe and North America and has authored two other books.

Joe served for six years on the Board of Directors for the Professional Association for SQL Server (PASS), an international user group with 30,000 members worldwide. He culminated his tenure on the board by serving as the Executive Vice President of Finance for the organization. Joe also volunteers his time by serving on the MBA Advisory Board for Auburn University and the Computer Science Advisory Committee for Nashville State Community College.

When he's not consulting, Joe enjoys spending time with his family and tending to the animals and garden on his small farm in middle Tennessee. He may be reached at joew@webbtechsolutions.com.

45 Correlating SQL Profiler with PerfMon

Kevin Kline

If you've been working with SQL Server for a long time, as I have, you've seen Microsoft's flagship relational database product go through many transformations and expansions. As Microsoft has developed new features and capabilities for SQL Server, the product has grown enormously in size and scope. For example, the entirety of SQL Server version 7.0 was as large, in terms of its code base and development team, as a single major component of SQL Server 2008, such as SQL Server Integration Services (SSIS). Wow! That means with each major new addition of functionality, many of us have to decide whether we have the time and energy to invest in learning what's new.

You can draw a parallel to the expansion of the troubleshooting and performance tuning tools that ship with SQL Server. For many releases over a number of years, SQL Server has added newer performance monitoring tools and technologies like DMVs, wait state analysis, extended events (XEvents), the Performance Dashboard, and most recently the Management Data Warehouse (MDW). Each of these new tools and technologies is forward-looking, and you can install each of them on an older installation of SQL Server. If you ever have to support both old and newer versions of SQL Server, the only toolkits that you can rely on being present in nearly all versions of SQL Server are the Windows Performance Monitor (PerfMon, also known as Windows System Monitor or SysMon) and some form of SQL tracing tool like SQL Profiler. When you're competent with PerfMon and Profiler, you can be effective at troubleshooting and performance monitoring on many releases of SQL Server.

This chapter shows you how to use PerfMon and Profiler to find the root cause of poor performance in a SQL Server application by correlating PerfMon's resource consumption information with Profiler's specific event information.

What vexes you?

I've always enjoyed my grandparents' use of old-timey words and phrases. When my great-uncle wanted to know what was troubling me, he'd always ask "What vexes you?"

When it comes to database problems, Gartner Research has already answered that question for us. Their research shows that about 80 percent of database performance problems comes from poorly or improperly coded SQL statements, 15 percent from database design, and 5 percent from poor or inadequate hardware configurations.

Contrary to Gartner's wisdom, most attempted remedies to performance problems with database applications are *exactly the opposite* of what research shows us is the source of the problem. We've all heard product managers who, when encountering a performance problem with their applications, declare, "Let's put in more RAM or another CPU!" But if you've been around for a while, you know that a poorly coded SQL Server application can suck up all the hardware you give it, and still want more. When adding hardware doesn't work, the product manager usually says, "Let's try to throw a few more indexes in there. That ought to fix it!" But more indexes can't help a query or transaction that doesn't utilize the indexes. By implementing a few simple processes to check your code using PerfMon and Profiler, you can help ensure that all the SQL and T-SQL code used in your application performs optimally.

Getting started with PerfMon and Profiler

To get useful information about your SQL Server's behavior, you need to combine the use of both PerfMon and Profiler (server-side traces are a good alternative to Profiler). That's because of the fundamental nature of each tool. PerfMon is great at showing the overall resource consumption of most every area of Windows and of SQL Server. Profiler, on the other hand, shows you specific events as they occur (or fire) inside the SQL Server. By combining the output of both tools, we get a great view of overall resource consumption and the individual SQL Server events that are causing that resource consumption. When resource consumption, say CPU or Disk I/O, gets unacceptably high, we can tell exactly what statement, batch, or job caused it. That way, we know exactly where to focus our attention when rewriting or tuning a particular SQL Server activity.

Best practices using PerfMon

Methods for invoking and using PerfMon are well documented in the Microsoft help system, so I won't cover all of the basics of PerfMon here. For example, http://support.microsoft.com/kb/175658/EN-US/ tells you how to create a new PerfMon log of a given SQL Server's activity. However, keep some best practices in mind.

Just in case you've never seen or used PerfMon before, figure 1 shows you what it looks like in action.

When using PerfMon, remember that PerfMon helps you identify the bottleneck on resources, not the exact problem. Because of that behavior, we need to get PerfMon to give us a good overview of what's happening across our SQL Server as well as

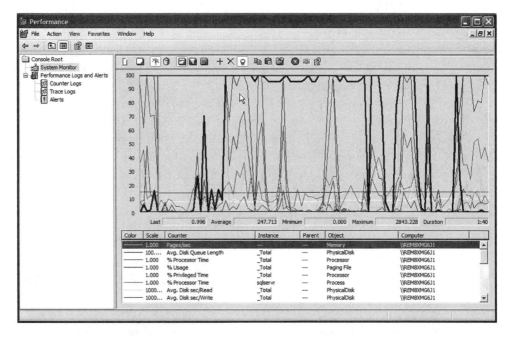

Figure 1   Windows PerfMon in action

insight into where, specifically, SQL Server is spending its time. Here is a short list of best practices:

- Always start with the Big Four PerfMon counters—Memory, CPU, I/O, and Network.
- Don't wing it when figuring out which PerfMon counters to use with SQL Server. Use the accumulated decades of experience of other SQL Server experts (like myself, Jimmy May, Brent Ozar, and the SQL Server CSS team) to guide you in choosing from the literally thousands of PerfMon counters that apply to SQL Server. Resources are identified at the end of the chapter.
- To reduce overhead, monitor only the counters that you need. The more you monitor, the more the overhead. (When in doubt, monitor more counters and then cut back one at a time rather than monitoring too few counters and not getting enough actionable information.)
- You can further reduce PerfMon overhead by reducing the polling frequency of your logging activity from 15 seconds to 30 seconds (or more) when the system is under a great deal of strain.
- The longer the polling interval, the smaller the log file. You can also cap the size of the log file, where disk space is scarce, by setting the file type to binary circular file and giving it a specific file size. When the log file reaches its maximum size, it continues to record PerfMon information, overwriting data at the start of the circular file.

- Unless you're really good at SELECT queries, resist the temptation of logging PerfMon data directly to a SQL Server table rather than to a binary flat file. The flat file technique is simple and straightforward. However, go ahead and log directly to a database table when you want to do extensive analysis, data manipulation, or automation.

- Unless there's an emergency, don't use PerfMon directly on the computer you intend to monitor, especially when recording PerfMon data to a log file. (Writing to a log file, in particular, can add considerable overhead.)

- PerfMon stops recording data when you log off. Instead of logging off, minimize PerfMon and lock the workstation. Alternately, you can run PerfMon as a service or set it to run at a scheduled time.

- Use the System Monitor view to see what is happening in real time, but remember that logging is an activity separate from the visual charting activity, which you must stop and start yourself.

- When in doubt, ask questions at the Windows Perfmon and Diagnostic Tools forum at http://social.technet.microsoft.com/Forums/en/perfmon/threads.

Warnings for older versions of Windows

Older operating systems, particularly Windows Server NT 4.0 and earlier, require the DISKPERF -Y switch to reveal true physical disk I/O information in PerfMon instead of logical disk I/O information. For some reason, Windows Server 2000 switched this around and automatically disabled the logical discounters, which must be manually enabled by typing DISKPERF -YV from the command prompt. Newer operating systems automatically reveal both physical and logical disk I/O activity. Further, PerfMon used the SQL Server: SQL Statistics: Transactions/sec counter for many early versions to indicate how many SQL Server operations were being performed per second. Obviously, this is an important PerfMon counter to monitor. This changed, rather dramatically in my opinion, with SQL Server 2005. Starting with SQL Server 2005, SQL Server: SQL Statistics: Batch Request/sec replaced the older transactions/sec as the counter that accurately measured overall SQL Server transactions performed per second. Despite this major change, transactions/sec still exists in PerfMon but it now measures a different set of values than it did in SQL Server 2000 and earlier versions. So remember, when measuring SQL Server transactional activities, use transactions/sec with SQL Server 2000 and earlier, but use batch requests/sec with SQL Server 2005 and later.

Best practices using Profiler

SQL Profiler is also well documented in the SQL Server Books Online. You can find the details for SQL Server 2008's implementation at http://technet.microsoft.com/en-us/library/ms187929.aspx, although it has been around since SQL Server 7.0 (and in slightly different forms even before that). Because it is based on recording an entry every time a specific event fires, SQL Profiler tracing is useful for determining the

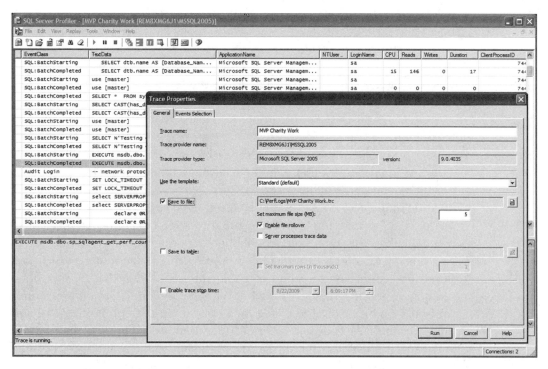

Figure 2   Profiler trace while starting a new trace

granular, specific operations of a SQL Server database over a specific chronological period. Figure 2 shows an instance Profiler that is running a trace in the background, while the user is about to start a new trace.

Many of the best practices that applied to PerfMon also apply to Profiler. For example, the less you monitor with Profiler, the less overhead it will consume on the monitored server. Therefore, to further the example, you'll probably want to create *filters* on your Profiler trace to restrict tracing to the production databases that you're concerned about (plus tempdb). Here are a few SQL Profiler best practices to consider:

- Reuse the existing Profiler *templates* to quickly get a trace up and running, choosing the one that sounds closest to your particular needs. For example, the Standard template is a good place to start, but you might use the TSQL-Locks template if you think locking is the main issue. You can find details at this website: http://technet.microsoft.com/en-us/library/ms190176.aspx.

- Reduce overhead by *filtering* your trace events. For example, you can track events fired only by a specific application or user, or only fired in specific databases. If you filter by database, be sure to capture tempdb as well as any production database you monitor. You can find details at this website: http://technet.microsoft.com/en-us/library/ms175520.aspx.

- Create your own traces by modifying the templates (or by starting with a blank trace) and selecting the events you want to trace. However, *always* capture the *start time* and *end time* of the events, so that you can correlate the results with PerfMon.

- When analyzing Profiler trace data, group the results by using the `Find` command to quickly locate the command you're searching for or group by `Client-ProcessID`, `DatabaseName`, or `ApplicationName` to quickly find what you're looking for.

- Reduce overhead on the monitored server by recording the Profiler log file on a workstation or server other than the one you're monitoring. The trace file, by default, will be stored in the temp directory.

- Record Profiler data to a SQL Server table only after you're experienced. Recording to a flat file is so simple and direct that you don't need the advanced techniques like those used for most troubleshooting or performance monitoring.

- You can invoke Profiler's functionality through a *server-side trace*, which is a stored procedure-based method of doing the same thing that Profiler does. Although you can certainly learn all of the server-side trace stored procedures yourself, I find it's easiest to configure a trace using the SQL Profiler GUI and then selecting File > Export > Script Trace Definite > For SQL Server 2008. Voila! You've got all the stored procedures (including filters and special configurations) scripted for you.

A correlated view of performance

So far, I've briefly described how to invoke SQL Profiler and Windows PerfMon, and presented a handful of best practices so that you can monitor SQL Server performance most effectively. How do you go about pulling both sets of data, the granular and event-driven data of Profiler along with the overall resource consumption data of PerfMon, into a single view? Here are simple step-by-step instructions for bringing the two data sets together into one cohesive view:

1 Start a Windows PerfMon counter log and record to a file.
2 Start a SQL Profiler event trace and record to a file.
3 When you're ready for analysis, stop recording to both files.
4 Open SQL Profiler and select File > Open > Trace File > my_tracefile.trc.
5 In SQL Profiler, select File > Import Performance Data > my_perfmon_ logfile.blg.
6 Select the PerfMon counters that you want to correlate against Profiler trace events. (The system may warn you if you specify a bunch of PerfMon counters.)

At this point, you should have a magical overlay showing the SQL Server Profiler event data in the top pane and the Windows PerfMon resource consumption data in the middle pane as shown in figure 3. And because the data for both PerfMon and Profiler are correlated, if you click on a Profiler entry on the top pane, the red marker bar in the

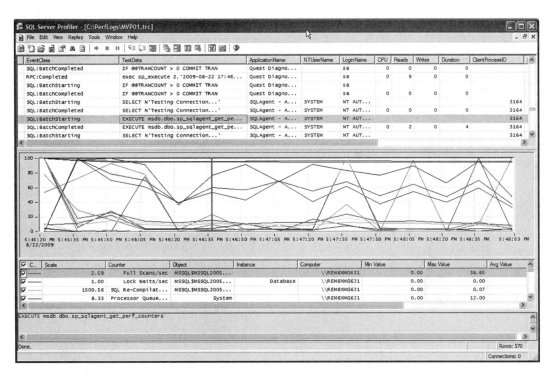

Figure 3 Overlay of PerfMon and Profiler data

PerfMon window jumps to the point in time for that Profiler entry. Conversely, if you click on a particular point on the PerfMon chart (say, just before disk I/O activity begins to crest upwards), the Profiler event in the top pane is highlighted. Finally, the exact SQL or T-SQL statement issued by that Profiler event is shown in the bottom pane.

This three-part correlation of data provides a powerful means of monitoring performance and troubleshooting problems: the middle-pane graph of PerfMon-derived resource consumption enables you to see one (or more) bottlenecks; the top-pane table of Profiler-derived events enables you to see the exact batch (or batches) that precipitated the bottleneck; and the bottom pane shows you the exact SQL or T-SQL code that needs to be examined, tuned, or replaced.

Summary

Although Microsoft has continued to implement new and innovative means of troubleshooting problems and monitoring performance, only SQL Profiler and Windows Performance Monitor are available on every version of SQL Server since SQL Server 7.0. To get the maximum value from the two tools, be sure to follow the simple best practices, such as monitoring a problem SQL Server from a different workstation. When you've collected logs from both PerfMon and Profiler, you can load both log files into SQL Profiler where you can review the correlated information from both data sets. Application performance in a Microsoft SQL Server environment is directly related to the efficiency of the SQL statements involved. By reviewing the bottlenecks in SQL Server resources as revealed by PerfMon, and correlating those bottlenecks with Profiler data, you can see exactly which SQL statements have hindered performance. Such statements are obvious tuning targets.

About the author

Kevin Kline is the Technical Strategy Manager for SQL Server Solutions at Quest Software. A Microsoft SQL Server MVP, Kevin is a founding board member of PASS (www.sqlpass.org) and the author of several books, including the best selling *SQL in a Nutshell* (O'Reilly). Kevin is a top-rated blogger, writer, and speaker at industry trade shows and has been active in the IT industry since 1986.

46 Using correlation to improve query performance

Gert-Jan Strik

SQL Server doesn't keep statistics on the correlation between nonclustered indexes and the clustered index (with the exception of correlation information between datetime columns, if the DATE_CORRELATION_OPTIMIZATION setting is turned on). Instead, the optimizer assumes it has a low correlation; it assumes that a range of nonclustered index values is scattered all over the clustered index.

This assumption affects the optimizer's decision whether or not to use the nonclustered index. If there is a high correlation, the optimizer will overestimate the cost of using the nonclustered index, which can cause it to disqualify the index from the query plan evaluation, resulting in a suboptimal query plan. The performance difference can be big, even by orders of magnitude.

This chapter explains what it means to have a high correlation with the clustered index, why the optimizer can misjudge such situations, how to determine the correlation for your situation, and how to optimize your queries accordingly.

NOTE In this chapter, I'll assume that you're familiar with indexes, and more specifically with the differences between clustered and nonclustered indexes. I'll also assume that you have some experience with query tuning.

The purpose of the optimizer

It's the optimizer's job to find the best query plan for a query. What is best? For the optimizer, it's the one that results in the shortest execution time.

In most cases, the performance of a typical query will be determined by the number of physical reads that are needed to satisfy the query. In a worst-case scenario, you have a *cold* cache, which means that no data or index pages are in cache. In a best-case scenario, you have a *hot* cache, and all relevant data is in memory.

If the page is cached, the data can be returned immediately. Otherwise, a physical read has to be issued to retrieve the page from disk. The duration of such a physical read depends on your storage subsystem. A physical read is typically several orders of magnitude slower than a read satisfied by the cache.

Physical reads come in two flavors: *sequential* reads and *random* reads. Although it depends on your storage subsystem and other factors like fragmentation, sequential reads are assumed to be significantly faster than random reads. Because of this, behind the scenes, the optimizer's primary objective is to minimize the number of physical reads and writes, and to favor sequential reads over random reads.

This chapter has the same goal: to help you minimize the number of physical reads. If you want to optimize your queries for a hot cache, then this chapter won't help you because the storage engine's performance characteristics are different for cached data.

Correlation with the clustered index

The term *correlation* is used loosely here. We're trying to determine the chance that two consecutive nonclustered index keys refer to the same data page. And we're only considering tables that have a clustered index, although the same theory would also hold for heaps.

Low correlation

Most nonclustered indexes have a low correlation with the clustered index. Figure 1 shows such a situation for the Product table. It has a nonclustered index on Product Name and a clustered index on Product ID.

The top row shows the nonclustered index values (the first 32 values). The letters in a block indicate the *range* of values. The number above a block indicates the number of values in that range. The bottom row shows the clustered index pages on which the row data is stored.

You can see that the first nine values in the nonclustered index refer to seven different pages in the clustered index, most of which are not shown. You can also see that if the storage engine would follow the nonclustered index, it would have to jump back and forth in the clustered index to retrieve the corresponding data.

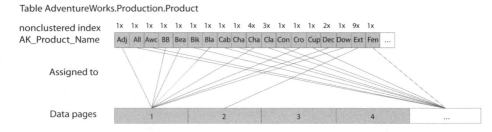

Figure 1   Low correlation index

Table AdventureWorks.Production.WorkOrder

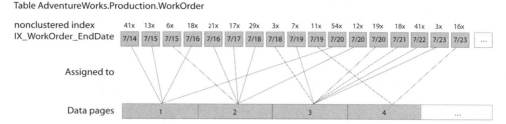

Figure 2   High correlation index

If a range of nonclustered index values does not relate to a significantly smaller range of consecutive data pages, then for the intent and purpose of this chapter, it has a low correlation.

Figure 2 depicts a nonclustered index that has a high correlation with the clustered index. The clustered index is on WorkOrderID, the nonclustered index is on EndDate. WorkOrders with a later EndDate typically have a higher WorkOrderID, meaning they are correlated.

The figure shows that many of the days, each with tens of rows, are stored on just one or two pages. If a range of nonclustered index values relates to a significantly smaller number of consecutive data pages, then it has a high correlation.

When the optimizer does it right

Let's look at an example. Listing 1 uses the AdventureWorks database on SQL Server 2005. It selects 88 rows (0.12 percent) of table WorkOrder. The table has 523 data pages, a clustered index on WorkOrderID, and it's assumed that there's a nonclustered index on EndDate.

NOTE   When you install the AdventureWorks database, there might not be an index on EndDate. I'll assume you created it like this: `CREATE INDEX IX_WorkOrder_EndDate ON Production.WorkOrder (EndDate)`.

Listing 1   Query to select WorkOrders for a 2-day date range

```
SELECT WorkOrderID, OrderQty, EndDate
FROM   Production.WorkOrder
WHERE  EndDate >= '20031101'
AND    EndDate <  '20031102'
```

The choice that the optimizer has to make is whether or not to use the nonclustered index. The optimizer has to choose one of the following options:

1 Use the index on EndDate to locate the desired rows and then look up the corresponding rows through the clustered index.
2 Scan the entire clustered index and filter out the unwanted rows.

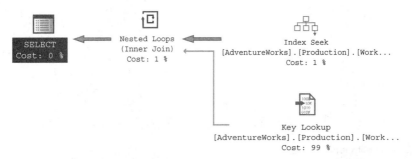

Figure 3   Query plan that uses the nonclustered index

Figure 3 shows the graphical query plan for listing 1. If you inspect the query plan, you will see that the optimizer estimates that 59 rows will be selected. If it uses the non-clustered index and clustered index seeks to look up the corresponding rows, it is estimated to cost a little over 59 reads, one read per row. If it had to scan the entire clustered index, it would cost a little over 523 reads, one read per page of the table. The optimizer makes the right choice, as displayed below.

To determine the number of physical reads, you can use SET STATISTICS IO ON before running the query, or use SQL Profiler. If SQL Server's cache is empty and you run this example, you will see only three physical reads and four read-ahead reads, a total of seven reads (you could get slightly different results if you have worked with the AdventureWorks database before).

When the optimizer does it right again

Let's change our example to select everything except this range of EndDates, as shown in listing 2. That would select 72,503 rows (99.88 percent).

Listing 2   Query to select all WorkOrders except for 2 days

```
SELECT WorkOrderID, OrderQty, EndDate
FROM   Production.WorkOrder
WHERE  EndDate <  '20031101'
OR     EndDate >= '20031102'
```

Because the number of selected rows exceeds the number of pages in the table—which was only 523—all potential query plans are estimated to require a little over 523 reads. In such a situation, the optimizer will always favor a clustered index scan, because that will use sequential reads, instead of random reads. Also, this avoids the risk of having to read the same page more than once.

Again the optimizer comes up with the optimal query plan, as displayed in figure 4.

If SQL Server's cache is empty and you run this example, you will see 1 physical read and 523 read-ahead reads, a total of 524 reads.

Figure 4 Query plan that scans the entire clustered index

When the optimizer gets it wrong

Listing 3 shows a third example. This time, the range is limited to 2,844 rows (3.9 percent).

Listing 3   Query to select WorkOrders for a one-month date range

```
SELECT WorkOrderID, OrderQty, EndDate
FROM   Production.WorkOrder
WHERE  EndDate >= '20031101'
AND    EndDate < '20031201'
```

The optimizer comes up with the same query plan as in listing 2, a clustered index scan (see figure 4). It assumes that all 523 data pages are needed to retrieve the data for these 2,844 rows. In other words, it assumes a low correlation between the nonclustered index and the clustered index.

If SQL Server's cache is empty and you run this example, you will see the same 1 + 523 reads as in listing 2. The reality is that this range of 2,844 rows does not cover 523 pages, but only a fraction of that. Figure 2 visualizes this, you can use the accompanying T-SQL script to determine it, and the next chapter will prove it: the optimizer selected a suboptimal query plan, and the optimizer got it wrong! It should have chosen the query plan of figure 3, using the nonclustered index.

Correcting the optimizer

You can influence the optimizer's behavior in several ways. The topics "Query Hint" and "Table Hint" in Books Online cover them.

The simplest method is to use the table hint INDEX. You use it in the FROM clause of the SELECT statement to specify the nonclustered index that should be used when accessing that table. The name of the nonclustered index on EndDate is called IX_WorkOrder_EndDate. Listing 4 shows the same query with the appropriate table hint.

Listing 4   Using an index hint

```
SELECT WorkOrderID, OrderQty, EndDate
FROM   Production.WorkOrder WITH (INDEX=IX_WorkOrder_EndDate)
WHERE  EndDate >= '20031101'
AND    EndDate < '20031201'
```

If SQL Server's cache is empty and you run this example, you will see 25 physical reads and 13 read-ahead reads, totaling 38 reads. The 13 read-ahead reads will be sequential reads, and the 25 physical reads might be random reads. Obviously, this is much faster than the 524 sequential reads of the optimizer's original plan.

When to expect correlation

You might expect correlation in some common scenarios:

- Both the clustered index and the nonclustered index use ever-increasing key values; for example, an Orders table with a clustered index on an Identity Order-ID, and a nonclustered index on the OrderDate. For a new order, both the OrderDate and the OrderID will have a higher value than the previous order. Other examples are the relation between an OrderDate and a DateDue, the relation between a name and its SoundEx value, and so on.

- When you use an Identity as a clustered index key, and you have imported a large percentage of the table data, and the import file was in sorted order; for example, if you have a Cities table with an Identity OrderID, and you import the city names in sorted order.

Determining correlation

You can use the accompanying T-SQL script to determine the correlation between index IX_WorkOrder_EndDate and the clustered index. You can modify the script to fit your needs, and test your own indexes for correlation.

Here is a short description of what the script does:

1. Retrieves the distribution statistics of the clustered index (one row per value range).
2. Determines the number of pages in the table, and uses that to estimate the number of pages per value range.
3. Retrieves the distribution statistics of the nonclustered index (one row per value range).
4. Determines the minimum and maximum clustered index key per nonclustered value range (a time-consuming step).
5. Interpolates the number of consecutive clustered index pages per nonclustered value range, based on the minimum and maximum clustered index key within the range.

If the estimated number of pages for a range (the result of step 5) is lower than its number of rows, then there is a high correlation. For example, if there is a range with 100 values that is estimated to cover 25 consecutive pages, then reading those 100 rows through the nonclustered index could not result in 100 physical reads, but (if none of the pages are cached) would result in a maximum of (a little over) 25 physical reads.

If the number of pages for your query's value range is lower than the total number of pages minus the number of nonclustered index pages, then it makes sense to correct the optimizer.

In other words, correct the optimizer if

```
consecutive pages covering your range  <  table pages - index pages
```

Summary

It's quite common to have tables with a high correlation between a nonclustered index and the clustered index. In these situations, the optimizer tends to overestimate the cost of using the nonclustered index, which can lead to suboptimal query plans. The accompanying T-SQL script shows you how to determine if there is a strong correlation, and predicts whether adding an index hint could help your queries' performance. As the examples have shown, such intervention can massively boost performance.

About the author

 Gert-Jan Strik is an IT Architect in the Netherlands who has been working with SQL Server ever since Version 6.5, and in recent years has developed a particular interest in performance optimization and the inner workings of the optimizer and storage engine.

47 How to use Dynamic Management Views

Glenn Berry

This chapter covers how to use Dynamic Management Views (DMVs) to easily uncover detailed information about your SQL Server workload that can help you diagnose and correct many common SQL Server performance issues. This type of information is extremely valuable, especially in a high-volume production online transaction processing (OLTP) situation, where poor database performance can have a severe impact on your business.

Why should I use DMV queries?

Dynamic Management Views (and Dynamic Management Functions) were introduced in SQL Server 2005, and enhanced in SQL Server 2008. Back in the pre–SQL Server 2005 days, it was much more difficult to find out what was happening inside of SQL Server when you encountered performance issues. Older versions of SQL Server were more like a "black box," which made you work much harder to find bottlenecks. Fortunately, tracking down bottlenecks is much easier now.

In the past, many DBAs would use SQL Server Profiler to capture performance information, or they'd use tools such as Performance Monitor to get a high-level view of what was happening on a particular database server. One problem with using SQL Server Profiler was the significant load that it could add to an already busy system (although this could be minimized if you used some care in how you configured and captured the trace). Performance Monitor is useful, but it doesn't let you drill down to the same level of SQL Server–specific detail that's possible with DMV queries.

Setting up security to run DMV queries

In order to run most DMV queries that are server-scoped, you'll need VIEW SERVER STATE permission on the server, whereas database-specific DMV queries require VIEW

DATABASE STATE permission for the database. It's useful to remember that VIEW DATA-BASE STATE permission for all databases is implied by VIEW SERVER STATE permission.

A common best practice is to create a specific login that you use only for monitoring, add that login as a database user, and then grant VIEW SERVER STATE permission to that login. For example, listing 1 creates a login called SystemMonitor.

Listing 1   Creating a monitoring login with view server state permission

```
USE master
      GO

      CREATE LOGIN SystemMonitor WITH PASSWORD=N'RubyRoxy456#',
      DEFAULT_DATABASE=[master], CHECK_EXPIRATION=OFF,
                              CHECK_POLICY=ON;
      GO

      USE AdventureWorks
      GO

      CREATE USER SystemMonitor FOR LOGIN SystemMonitor;
      GO

      USE master
      GO

      GRANT VIEW SERVER STATE TO SystemMonitor;
      GO
```

This approach is preferable to using a higher-permission login (such as sa) for this purpose. Once you're set up to monitor SQL Server 2005/2008 with DMVs, what should you be looking at?

Looking at top waits at the instance level

One of the first DMV queries that I like to run on a busy or unfamiliar database server looks at top waits for the server instance. This gives me a much better idea where to focus the rest of my information gathering, because I'd run different sets of DMV queries to further investigate CPU pressure, I/O pressure, memory pressure, index usage, and so on. The top waits DMV query is shown in listing 2.

Listing 2   Top waits query

```
  -- Isolate top waits for server instance
WITH Waits AS
(SELECT wait_type, wait_time_ms / 1000. AS wait_time_s,
    100. * wait_time_ms / SUM(wait_time_ms) OVER() AS pct,
    ROW_NUMBER() OVER(ORDER BY wait_time_ms DESC) AS rn
 FROM sys.dm_os_wait_stats
 WHERE wait_type NOT IN( 'SLEEP_TASK', 'BROKER_TASK_STOP',
  'SQLTRACE_BUFFER_FLUSH', 'CLR_AUTO_EVENT', 'CLR_MANUAL_EVENT',
  'LAZYWRITER_SLEEP')) -- filter out additional irrelevant waits
SELECT W1.wait_type,
  CAST(W1.wait_time_s AS DECIMAL(12, 2)) AS wait_time_s,
  CAST(W1.pct AS DECIMAL(12, 2)) AS pct,
```

```
    CAST(SUM(W2.pct) AS DECIMAL(12, 2)) AS running_pct
FROM Waits AS W1
INNER JOIN Waits AS W2
ON W2.rn <= W1.rn
GROUP BY W1.rn, W1.wait_type, W1.wait_time_s, W1.pct
HAVING SUM(W2.pct) - W1.pct < 95; -- percentage threshold
```

This query rolls up the top 95 percent of cumulative waits, grouped by wait type since SQL Server 2005/2008 was last restarted, unless you've manually cleared the wait stats since then. The wait types that show up at the top of this query give you a good idea what to look at in more detail. For example, if you saw WRITELOG and ASYNCH_IO_ COMPLETION as your top wait types, this would be a definite clue that you're seeing I/O bottlenecks. If you see a top wait type of SOS_SCHEDULER_YIELD, that indicates CPU pressure.

SQL Server 2005 has more than 200 different wait types, whereas SQL Server 2008 has more than 400 different wait types. You can get a fairly complete list of the wait types and what they mean by searching for sys.dm_os_wait_stats in SQL Server Books Online (BOL).

You can clear the wait stats by running this command:

```
DBCC SQLPERF('sys.dm_os_wait_stats', CLEAR);
```

I wish you could just as easily reset other DMV measurements with a simple command, but unfortunately that's not the case. Perhaps Microsoft will add that functionality in a future release of SQL Server. In the meantime, many DBAs like to capture DMV metrics in permanent tables or use the new Performance Data Warehouse feature in SQL Server 2008.

Looking for CPU pressure and what's causing it

One common performance issue you might run into with SQL Server is CPU pressure. Even with modern, multi-core CPUs, this can still be a problem. How can you detect whether your SQL Server is under CPU pressure? An initial quick and dirty method is to look at the Performance tab in Task Manager, and look for sustained periods above 95 percent CPU utilization.

Going a little deeper, I like to monitor Processor\%Processor Time and System\Context Switches/sec in Performance Monitor to get a more complete high-level impression of CPU pressure.

Finally, drilling into SQL Server itself, here are two DMV queries that you can run to get a feel for what's going on with the server, CPU-wise. The query in listing 3 is a good measure of CPU pressure. If the signal waits are above 20 percent, that's a strong indicator of CPU pressure.

> **Listing 3 Checking CPU pressure**

```
-- Total waits are wait_time_ms
-- (high signal waits indicates CPU pressure)
SELECT SUM(signal_wait_time_ms) AS 'signal_wait_time_ms',
```

```
CAST(100.0 * SUM(signal_wait_time_ms)/
SUM (wait_time_ms)AS NUMERIC(20,2)) AS '%signal (cpu) waits',
SUM(wait_time_ms - signal_wait_time_ms) AS 'resource_wait_time_ms',
CAST(100.0 * SUM(wait_time_ms - signal_wait_time_ms) /
SUM (wait_time_ms) AS NUMERIC(20,2)) AS '%resource waits'
FROM sys.dm_os_wait_stats
```

You should be aware that the results of this query are cumulative since SQL Server was started or since the statistics were cleared using this command:

```
DBCC SQLPERF('sys.dm_os_wait_stats', CLEAR);
```

The query in listing 4 is another confirmation of CPU pressure. If the runnable_ tasks_count is above single digits, you're likely seeing some CPU pressure (although it could be something else, such as severe blocking).

Listing 4 Checking the runnable tasks count

```
-- Check SQL Server Schedulers to see if they are waiting on CPU
SELECT scheduler_id, current_tasks_count, runnable_tasks_count
FROM sys.dm_os_schedulers
WHERE scheduler_id < 255
```

Once you have some solid evidence that you're experiencing CPU pressure, you'll want to start narrowing your focus to see what part of your work load is causing the most CPU pressure. The query in listing 5 will show you the cached stored procedures that are the most expensive from a CPU perspective.

Listing 5 Finding the most expensive stored procedures

```
-- Get Top 20 executed SP's ordered by total worker time
-- (CPU pressure)
SELECT TOP 20 qt.text AS 'SP Name',
     qs.total_worker_time AS 'TotalWorkerTime',
qs.total_worker_time/qs.execution_count AS 'AvgWorkerTime',
qs.execution_count AS 'Execution Count',
ISNULL(qs.execution_count/DATEDIFF(Second, qs.creation_time,
     GetDate()), 0) AS 'Calls/Second',
ISNULL(qs.total_elapsed_time/qs.execution_count, 0)
     AS 'AvgElapsedTime',
qs.max_logical_reads, qs.max_logical_writes,
DATEDIFF(Minute, qs.creation_time, GetDate()) AS 'Age in Cache'
FROM sys.dm_exec_query_stats AS qs
CROSS APPLY sys.dm_exec_sql_text(qs.sql_handle) AS qt
WHERE qt.dbid = db_id() -- Filter by current database
ORDER BY qs.total_worker_time DESC
```

One thing to pay attention to when you look at the results from the total worker time query is the Age in Cache column, which shows how long the plan for that stored procedure has been in the cache. If the query has recently been recompiled for any reason, it'll clear the plan out of cache, which will obviously affect the total worker time and skew the query results. Total worker time is the overall CPU cost of a particular query since it has been in cache. Depending on your workload, you might have queries that are relatively inexpensive for individual executions but are called very frequently (which makes them expensive in aggregate), or you may have individual queries that are more expensive CPU-wise, but are not called as often. Looking at total worker time is a reliable method for finding the most expensive queries from an overall CPU perspective.

Another similar DMV query, shown in listing 6, sorts by average worker time. This will let you find expensive CPU queries that may be easier to improve at the database level with standard database tuning techniques.

Listing 6   Finding expensive stored procedures, sorted by average worker time

```
-- Get Top 20 executed SP's ordered by Avg worker time (CPU pressure)
SELECT TOP 20
qt.text AS 'SP Name', qs.total_worker_time/qs.execution_count
    AS 'AvgWorkerTime',
qs.total_worker_time AS 'TotalWorkerTime', qs.execution_count
    AS 'Execution Count',
ISNULL(qs.execution_count/
    DATEDIFF(Second, qs.creation_time, GetDate())), 0)
    AS 'Calls/Second',
ISNULL(qs.total_elapsed_time/qs.execution_count, 0)
      AS 'AvgElapsedTime',
qs.max_logical_reads, qs.max_logical_writes,
DATEDIFF(Minute, qs.creation_time, GetDate())
      AS 'Age in Cache'
FROM sys.dm_exec_query_stats AS qs
CROSS APPLY sys.dm_exec_sql_text(qs.sql_handle) AS qt
WHERE qt.dbid = db_id() -- Filter by current database
ORDER BY qs.total_worker_time/qs.execution_count DESC
```

Finding I/O pressure in SQL Server

Most large-scale SQL Server 2005/2008 deployments sooner or later run into I/O bottlenecks. This happens for several reasons. First, systems engineers often just think about CPU and RAM when sizing "big" database servers, and neglect the I/O subsystem.

Second, many DBAs are unable to completely tune the SQL Server workload to minimize excessive I/O requirements. Finally, there are often budgetary issues that prevent the acquisition of enough I/O capacity to support a large workload.

Whatever your situation, it helps if you know how recognize and measure signs of I/O pressure on SQL Server 2005/2008. One thing you can do to help reduce I/O pressure in general is to make sure you're not under memory pressure, which will cause added I/O pressure. We'll look at how to detect memory pressure a little later.

For large SQL Server 2005/2008 deployments, you should make sure you're running a 64-bit edition of SQL Server (so you can better use the RAM that you have), and you should try to get as much RAM as you can afford or will fit into the database server. Having sufficient RAM installed will reduce I/O pressure for reads, and will allow SQL Server to issue checkpoints less frequently (which will tend to minimize write I/O pressure).

The DMV queries in listings 7 through 11 are useful for measuring signs of I/O pressure.

You'll want to run the query in listing 7 multiple times, because the results will rapidly change on a busy system. Don't get too excited by a single high number. If you see consistently high numbers over time, then you have evidence of I/O pressure.

Listing 7   Checking for I/O pressure

```
-- Check for Pending I/O (lower is better)
   SELECT pending_disk_io_count
   FROM sys.dm_os_schedulers
```

The query in listing 8 can help you identify which data and log files are causing the highest I/O waits. For example, perhaps you have a transaction log file on a slower RAID 5 array or LUN (which isn't a good idea). This query will help prove that the log file is causing user waits.

Listing 8   Identifying the highest I/O waits

```
-- Avg I/O Stalls (Lower is better)
SELECT database_id, file_id , io_stall_read_ms, num_of_reads,
CAST(io_stall_read_ms/(1.0 + num_of_reads)
   AS NUMERIC(10,1)) AS 'avg_read_stall_ms',
io_stall_write_ms, num_of_writes,
    CAST(io_stall_write_ms/(1.0 + num_of_writes) AS NUMERIC(10,1))
   AS 'avg_write_stall_ms',
io_stall_read_ms + io_stall_write_ms
   AS io_stalls, num_of_reads + num_of_writes AS total_io,
CAST((io_stall_read_ms + io_stall_write_ms)
   /(1.0 + num_of_reads + num_of_writes) AS NUMERIC(10,1))
   AS 'avg_io_stall_ms'
FROM sys.dm_io_virtual_file_stats(null,null)
-- This can be filtered by database and file id
ORDER BY avg_io_stall_ms DESC
```

The query in listing 9 lets you focus on the read/write activity for each file in a particular database. It shows you the percentage of reads and writes, both in number of reads and writes and in actual bytes read and written. This can help you analyze and size your disk I/O subsystem.

Listing 9   Checking I/O statistics for a database

```
-- I/O Statistics for a single database
SELECT
   file_id
 , num_of_reads
 , num_of_writes
 , (num_of_reads + num_of_writes) AS 'Writes + Reads'
 , num_of_bytes_read
 , num_of_bytes_written
 , CAST(100. * num_of_reads/(num_of_reads + num_of_writes)
   AS DECIMAL(10,4)) AS '# Reads Pct'
```

```
    , CAST(100. * num_of_writes/(num_of_reads + num_of_writes)
        AS DECIMAL(10,4)) AS '# Write Pct'
    , CAST(100. * num_of_bytes_read
        /(num_of_bytes_read + num_of_bytes_written)
        AS DECIMAL(10,4)) AS 'Read Bytes Pct'
    , CAST(100. * num_of_bytes_written
        /(num_of_bytes_read + num_of_bytes_written)
        AS DECIMAL(10,4)) AS 'Written Bytes Pct'
FROM sys.dm_io_virtual_file_stats(DB_ID(N'yourdatabasename'), NULL);
```

The query in listing 10 will help you find the stored procedures that are causing the most physical read I/O pressure (which means that the data has to be read from your disk subsystem instead of being found in memory). Obviously, adding more RAM to the server will help here, but standard query and index tuning can make a big difference also.

Listing 10   Locating physical read I/O pressure

```
-- Get Top 20 executed SP's ordered by physical reads (read I/O pressure)
SELECT TOP 20 qt.text AS 'SP Name', qs.total_physical_reads,
➥qs.total_physical_reads/qs.execution_count AS 'Avg Physical Reads',
qs.execution_count AS 'Execution Count',
qs.execution_count/DATEDIFF(Second, qs.creation_time, GetDate()) AS
➥'Calls/Second',
qs.total_worker_time/qs.execution_count AS 'AvgWorkerTime',
qs.total_worker_time AS 'TotalWorkerTime',
qs.total_elapsed_time/qs.execution_count AS 'AvgElapsedTime',
qs.max_logical_reads, qs.max_logical_writes,
DATEDIFF(Minute, qs.creation_time, GetDate()) AS 'Age in Cache'
FROM sys.dm_exec_query_stats AS qs
CROSS APPLY sys.dm_exec_sql_text(qs.sql_handle) AS qt
WHERE qt.dbid = db_id() -- Filter by current database
ORDER BY qs.total_physical_reads DESC
```

The query in listing 11 will help you find the stored procedures that are causing the most write activity. Query and index tuning can help here. You can also talk to your developers about middle-tier write caching or other application changes to reduce writes if possible.

Listing 11   Finding stored procedures with the most write activity

```
-- Get Top 20 executed SP's ordered by logical writes/minute (write I/O
➥pressure)
SELECT TOP 20 qt.text AS 'SP Name', qs.total_logical_writes,
➥qs.total_logical_writes/qs.execution_count AS 'AvgLogicalWrites',
qs.total_logical_writes/DATEDIFF(Minute, qs.creation_time, GetDate())
➥AS 'Logical Writes/Min',
qs.execution_count AS 'Execution Count',
qs.execution_count/DATEDIFF(Second, qs.creation_time, GetDate()) AS
➥'Calls/Second',
qs.total_worker_time/qs.execution_count AS 'AvgWorkerTime',
qs.total_worker_time AS 'TotalWorkerTime',
qs.total_elapsed_time/qs.execution_count AS 'AvgElapsedTime',
```

```
qs.max_logical_reads, qs.max_logical_writes, qs.total_physical_reads,
DATEDIFF(Minute, qs.creation_time, GetDate()) AS 'Age in Cache',
qs.total_physical_reads/qs.execution_count AS 'Avg Physical Reads'
FROM sys.dm_exec_query_stats AS qs
CROSS APPLY sys.dm_exec_sql_text(qs.sql_handle) AS qt
WHERE qt.dbid = db_id() -- Filter by current database
ORDER BY qs.total_logical_writes DESC
```

SQL Server memory pressure

SQL Server 2005/2008 loves memory, the more the better. If you're running on a 64-bit version of Windows Server 2003 or newer, with a 64-bit Enterprise Edition version of SQL Server 2005/2008, you can and should take advantage of as much memory as will fit in your server. In the commodity-level server space, the sweet spot for installed memory has moved up from 32 GB to 64 GB to 128 GB over the past several years, which makes it even more important to make sure you're running a 64-bit version of SQL Server.

Once you've loaded up your 64-bit database server with as much memory as possible, it's important that you do two things to make sure that SQL Server 2005/2008 will play nicely with all of the available memory. First, you should grant the Lock Pages in Memory Windows right (using gpedit.msc) to the SQL Server Service account. Second, you should set the Max Server Memory setting in SQL Server to a value that will leave sufficient available memory for the operating system (and anything else that's running on the server) while SQL Server is under a load. This is typically anywhere from about 2 GB to 4 GB available, depending on how much RAM you have installed and what else is running on the server.

After you have SQL Server properly configured for memory, you'll want to monitor how SQL Server is handling the memory that it has to work with. With Performance Monitor, I like to keep track of these three counters:

- SQL Server\Memory Manager\Memory Grants Pending (lower is better)
- SQL Server\Buffer Manager\Buffer Cache Hit Ratio (higher is better)
- SQL Server\Buffer Manager\Page Life Expectancy (higher is better)

The trend for these values is more important than their absolute value at any given time. If the average Page Life Expectancy is dropping over time, that's significant (and not in a good way). Still, people typically want to know what values are "good" and what values are "bad" for these counters, so here's what I look for:

- Memory Grants Pending above 1 is bad
- Buffer Cache Hit Ratio below 95 percent is bad
- Page Life Expectancy below 300 is bad

There are many good DMV queries that give you much more detail about how SQL Server 2005/2008 is using memory. We'll cover some of the more useful ones. Listing 12 lists the top 10 memory consumers in your buffer pool.

Listing 12   Top 10 consumers of memory from buffer pool

```
SELECT TOP (10) type, SUM(single_pages_kb) AS [SPA Mem, KB]
FROM sys.dm_os_memory_clerks
GROUP BY type
ORDER BY SUM(single_pages_kb) DESC
```

Here are some of the common types you'll see when you run the query in listing 12:

- CACHESTORE_SQLCP—SQL plans (dynamic or prepared SQL)
- CACHESTORE_OBJCP—Object plans (stored procedures, functions, and triggers)
- CACHESTORE_PHDR—Bound Trees
- USERSTORE_TOKENPERM—The User and Token permissions cache that caused so many performance issues with early builds of SQL Server 2005

In listing 13, we'll obtain the use counts for each query plan.

Listing 13   Getting query mix and use counts for each plan

```
SELECT usecounts, cacheobjtype, objtype, bucketid
FROM sys.dm_exec_cached_plans AS cp
WHERE cacheobjtype = 'Compiled Plan'
ORDER BY objtype, usecounts DESC
```

You want to see plans with high use counts. Avoiding ad hoc queries with concatenated WHERE clauses can help here. You can also take advantage of table valued parameters in SQL Server 2008. Using the new Optimize for Ad Hoc Workloads instance setting in SQL Server 2008 is also beneficial here.

The query in listing 14 will tell you which tables and indexes are taking up the most buffer space.

Listing 14   Finding indexes and tables that use the most buffer space

```
-- Breaks down buffers by object (table, index) in the buffer cache
SELECT OBJECT_NAME(p.object_id) AS 'ObjectName', p.object_id,
p.index_id, COUNT(*)/128 AS 'buffer size(MB)',  COUNT(*)
    AS 'buffer_count'
FROM sys.allocation_units AS a
INNER JOIN sys.dm_os_buffer_descriptors AS b
ON a.allocation_unit_id = b.allocation_unit_id
INNER JOIN sys.partitions AS p
ON a.container_id = p.hobt_id
WHERE b.database_id = db_id()
GROUP BY p.object_id, p.index_id
ORDER BY buffer_count DESC
```

In listing 15, we'll find the largest ad hoc queries sitting in the plan cache.

Listing 15   Finding ad hoc queries that are bloating the plan cache

```
SELECT TOP(100) [text], size_in_bytes
FROM sys.dm_Exec_cached_plans
CROSS APPLY sys.dm_exec_sql_text(plan_handle)
```

```
WHERE cacheobjtype = 'Compiled Plan'
AND objtype = 'Adhoc' AND usecounts = 1
ORDER BY size_in_bytes DESC
```

Again, using the new Optimize for Ad Hoc Workloads instance setting in SQL Server 2008 can really help if you have problems here.

The query in listing 16 will show you your 25 most expensive queries from a logical reads perspective (which equates to memory pressure).

Listing 16   Finding your 25 most expensive queries

```
-- Get Top 25 executed SP's ordered by logical reads (memory pressure)
SELECT TOP 25 qt.text AS 'SP Name', total_logical_reads,
qs.execution_count AS 'Execution Count',
total_logical_reads/qs.execution_count AS 'AvgLogicalReads',
qs.execution_count/DATEDIFF(Second, qs.creation_time, GetDate()) AS
'Calls/Second',
qs.total_worker_time/qs.execution_count AS 'AvgWorkerTime',
qs.total_worker_time AS 'TotalWorkerTime',
qs.total_elapsed_time/qs.execution_count AS 'AvgElapsedTime',
qs.total_logical_writes,
qs.max_logical_reads, qs.max_logical_writes, qs.total_physical_reads,
DATEDIFF(Minute, qs.creation_time, GetDate()) AS 'Age in Cache'
FROM sys.dm_exec_query_stats AS qs
CROSS APPLY sys.dm_exec_sql_text(qs.sql_handle) AS qt
WHERE qt.dbid = db_id() -- Filter by current database
ORDER BY total_logical_reads DESC
```

The query in listing 17 will help you find tables with the most reads. (User scans are much more expensive than user seeks or lookups.)

Listing 17   Finding tables with the most reads

```
SELECT object_name(s.object_id) AS 'Tablename',
SUM(user_seeks) AS 'User Seeks', SUM(user_scans) AS 'User Scans',
SUM(user_lookups)AS 'User Lookups',
SUM(user_seeks + user_scans + user_lookups)AS 'Total Reads',
SUM(user_updates) AS 'Total Writes'
FROM sys.dm_db_index_usage_stats AS s
INNER JOIN sys.indexes AS i
ON s.object_id = i.object_id
AND i.index_id = s.index_id
WHERE objectproperty(s.object_id,'IsUserTable') = 1
AND s.database_id = db_id()
GROUP BY object_name(s.object_id)
ORDER BY 'Total Reads' DESC
```

The query in listing 18 will help you find tables with the most writes.

Listing 18   Finding tables with the most writes

```
SELECT object_name(s.object_id) AS 'Tablename',
SUM(user_updates) AS 'Total Writes',
SUM(user_seeks) AS 'User Seeks', SUM(user_scans) AS 'User Scans',
```

```
SUM(user_lookups)AS 'User Lookups',
SUM(user_seeks + user_scans + user_lookups)AS 'Total Reads'
FROM sys.dm_db_index_usage_stats AS s
INNER JOIN sys.indexes AS i
ON s.object_id = i.object_id
AND i.index_id = s.index_id
WHERE objectproperty(s.object_id,'IsUserTable') = 1
AND s.database_id = db_id()
GROUP BY object_name(s.object_id)
ORDER BY 'Total Writes' DESC
```

SQL Server index usage

As you're probably aware, having proper indexes in place to support your workload is critical with SQL Server 2005/2008 (as with any relational database). Generally speaking, you'll want more indexes with a reporting or DSS workload, and fewer indexes with an OLTP workload. Regardless of your workload type, you should be aware of whether your indexes are being used and whether you're missing any indexes that would be useful for SQL Server.

In the dark ages before SQL Server 2005, it was difficult to discover this critical information, but with DMV queries, you can easily discover what's going on with your indexes. You can find indexes that aren't being used and you can find missing indexes. As Microsoft's Rico Mariani says, "If you aren't measuring, you're not engineering."

The DMV queries that you see in this section will tell you this information. If you see an index that has millions of writes, with zero or very few reads, then that means that you're getting little to no benefit from maintaining the index, and you should strongly consider dropping that index. As the number of reads goes up, it becomes more of a judgment call. That's why being familiar with your workload is important.

One caveat with the "missing index" query is that it can return results based on ad hoc queries or maintenance job–related work that can make it harder to interpret. You always want to look at the last_user_seek and the user_seeks columns to see the last time and how often SQL Server thinks it wants the index that it thinks is "missing." If you see a row with a high index advantage with a last_user_seek from a few seconds or minutes ago, it's probably from your regular workload, so you probably want to seriously consider adding that index. You should also be aware that this query won't recommend adding any clustered indexes.

One feature I've discovered over time is that if you add a new index of any sort to a table, or if you delete an index, it will clear out all of the missing index stats for that table. This may lead you to believe that there are no more missing indexes on the table, which is probably not true. Wait a little while, and then run the missing index query again to confirm whether there are any more missing indexes for the table.

The DMV queries in listings 19 through 21 will show bad indexes and missing indexes, and then let you concentrate on an individual table to determine whether you should make any index changes for that table based on your workload.

Listing 19 Finding bad indexes

```
-- Possible Bad Indexes (writes > reads)
SELECT object_name(s.object_id) AS 'Table Name',
i.name AS 'Index Name', i.index_id,
user_updates AS 'Total Writes',
user_seeks + user_scans +  user_lookups AS 'Total Reads',
user_updates - (user_seeks + user_scans + user_lookups) AS 'Difference'
FROM sys.dm_db_index_usage_stats AS s
INNER JOIN sys.indexes AS i
ON s.object_id = i.object_id
AND i.index_id = s.index_id
WHERE objectproperty(s.object_id,'IsUserTable') = 1
AND s.database_id = db_id() -- Filter for current database
AND user_updates > (user_seeks + user_scans + user_lookups )
ORDER BY 'Difference' DESC, 'Total Writes' DESC, 'Total Reads' ASC;
```

Indexes that have many more writes than reads are possible candidates for elimination. You should be aware that user scans are much more expensive than user seeks or user lookups. If you see lots of user scans, you may be missing some important indexes or you could be doing lots of aggregate queries or have small tables.

Listing 20 Looking at Index Advantage to find missing indexes

```
-- Missing Indexes by Index Advantage (make sure to also look at last user
➥seek time)
SELECT user_seeks * avg_total_user_cost * (avg_user_impact * 0.01) AS
➥index_advantage, migs.last_user_seek,
mid.statement AS 'Database.Schema.Table',
mid.equality_columns, mid.inequality_columns, mid.included_columns,
migs.unique_compiles, migs.user_seeks, migs.avg_total_user_cost,
➥migs.avg_user_impact
FROM sys.dm_db_missing_index_group_stats AS migs WITH (NOLOCK)
INNER JOIN sys.dm_db_missing_index_groups AS mig WITH (NOLOCK)
ON migs.group_handle = mig.index_group_handle
INNER JOIN sys.dm_db_missing_index_details AS mid WITH (NOLOCK)
ON mig.index_handle = mid.index_handle
ORDER BY index_advantage DESC;
```

Listing 21 Looking at Last User Seek to find missing indexes

```
-- Missing Indexes by Last User Seek
SELECT user_seeks * avg_total_user_cost * (avg_user_impact * 0.01) AS
➥index_advantage,
migs.last_user_seek, mid.statement AS 'Database.Schema.Table',
mid.equality_columns, mid.inequality_columns, mid.included_columns,
migs.unique_compiles, migs.user_seeks, migs.avg_total_user_cost,
➥migs.avg_user_impact
FROM sys.dm_db_missing_index_group_stats AS migs WITH (NOLOCK)
INNER JOIN sys.dm_db_missing_index_groups AS mig WITH (NOLOCK)
ON migs.group_handle = mig.index_group_handle
INNER JOIN sys.dm_db_missing_index_details AS mid WITH (NOLOCK)
ON mig.index_handle = mid.index_handle
ORDER BY migs.last_user_seek DESC;
```

After running the DMV queries in listings 20 and 21, you may see the same table showing up with multiple missing indexes. If I see this, I start to examine that table more closely.

Once you've narrowed your focus to a particular table, you can gather more specific index information about that table with the queries in listings 22 and 23.

Listing 22   Getting statistics for a table

```
-- Index Read/Write stats for a single table
SELECT object_name(s.object_id) AS 'TableName',
i.name AS 'IndexName', i.index_id,
SUM(user_seeks) AS 'User Seeks', SUM(user_scans) AS 'User Scans',
SUM(user_lookups)AS 'User Lookups',
SUM(user_seeks + user_scans + user_lookups)AS 'Total Reads',
SUM(user_updates) AS 'Total Writes'
FROM sys.dm_db_index_usage_stats AS s
INNER JOIN sys.indexes AS i
ON s.object_id = i.object_id
AND i.index_id = s.index_id
WHERE objectproperty(s.object_id,'IsUserTable') = 1
AND s.database_id = db_id()
AND object_name(s.object_id) = 'YourTableName'
GROUP BY object_name(s.object_id), i.name, i.index_id
ORDER BY 'Total Writes' DESC, 'Total Reads' DESC;
```

Listing 23   Missing indexes for a single table

```
SELECT user_seeks * avg_total_user_cost * (avg_user_impact * 0.01) AS
⇒index_advantage, migs.last_user_seek,
mid.statement AS 'Database.Schema.Table',
mid.equality_columns, mid.inequality_columns, mid.included_columns,
migs.unique_compiles, migs.user_seeks, migs.avg_total_user_cost,
⇒migs.avg_user_impact
FROM sys.dm_db_missing_index_group_stats AS migs WITH (NOLOCK)
INNER JOIN sys.dm_db_missing_index_groups AS mig WITH (NOLOCK)
ON migs.group_handle = mig.index_group_handle
INNER JOIN sys.dm_db_missing_index_details AS mid WITH (NOLOCK)
ON mig.index_handle = mid.index_handle
WHERE statement = '[databasename].[dbo].[yourtablename]' -- Specify one
⇒table
ORDER BY index_advantage DESC;
-- Show existing indexes for this table (does not show included columns)
EXEC sp_HelpIndex 'yourtablename';
```

As you consider making index changes to a large, busy table, you need to consider your workload characteristics. You should be more reluctant to add additional indexes if you have an OLTP workload. You should take advantage of online index operations whenever possible if you're running Enterprise Edition in order to avoid locking and blocking issues during index builds. You also should consider using the MAXDOP option during index builds to prevent SQL Server from using all of the CPU cores for an index build. This may mean that the index takes longer to build, but the rest of your workload won't be starved for CPU during the index-creation process.

Detecting blocking in SQL Server

Especially with OLTP workloads, you may run into blocking issues with SQL Server. Listing 24 shows one quick DMV query that's a good, indirect early warning signal of blocking.

Listing 24 Checking SQL Server schedulers to see if you may have blocking

```
SELECT scheduler_id, current_tasks_count, runnable_tasks_count
FROM sys.dm_os_schedulers
WHERE scheduler_id < 255
```

If you see the `current_tasks_count` above 10 for a sustained period, it's likely that you have blocking. When you have severe blocking, the `current_tasks_count` for each scheduler tends to go up quickly. The two DMV queries in listings 25 and 26 will give you more direct confirmation of blocking.

Listing 25 Detecting blocking

```
SELECT blocked_query.session_id AS blocked_session_id,
    blocking_query.session_id AS blocking_session_id,
    sql_text.text AS blocked_text, sql_btext.text AS blocking_text,
    waits.wait_type AS blocking_resource
FROM sys.dm_exec_requests AS blocked_query
INNER JOIN sys.dm_exec_requests AS blocking_query
    ON blocked_query.blocking_session_id = blocking_query.session_id
CROSS APPLY
(SELECT * FROM sys.dm_exec_sql_text(blocking_query.sql_handle))
    AS sql_btext
CROSS APPLY
(SELECT * FROM sys.dm_exec_sql_text(blocked_query.sql_handle)) AS sql_text
INNER JOIN sys.dm_os_waiting_tasks AS waits
ON waits.session_id = blocking_query.session_id
```

Listing 26 Detecting blocking (a more accurate and complete version)

```
SELECT t1.resource_type AS 'lock type',db_name(resource_database_id) AS
➥'database',
  t1.resource_associated_entity_id AS 'blk object',t1.request_mode AS 'lock
➥req',                              --- lock requested
  t1.request_session_id AS 'waiter sid', t2.wait_duration_ms AS 'wait time',
(SELECT [text] FROM sys.dm_exec_requests AS r
 CROSS APPLY sys.dm_exec_sql_text(r.sql_handle)
 WHERE r.session_id = t1.request_session_id) AS 'waiter_batch',
(SELECT substring(qt.text,r.statement_start_offset/2,
     (CASE WHEN r.statement_end_offset = -1
     THEN LEN(CONVERT(nvarchar(max), qt.text)) * 2
     ELSE r.statement_end_offset END - r.statement_start_offset)/2)
 FROM sys.dm_exec_requests AS r
 CROSS APPLY sys.dm_exec_sql_text(r.sql_handle) AS qt
 WHERE r.session_id = t1.request_session_id) AS 'waiter_stmt',
  t2.blocking_session_id AS 'blocker sid',
 (SELECT [text] FROM sys.sysprocesses AS p
```

```
       CROSS APPLY sys.dm_exec_sql_text(p.sql_handle)
       WHERE p.spid = t2.blocking_session_id) AS 'blocker_stmt'
       FROM sys.dm_tran_locks AS t1
       INNER JOIN sys.dm_os_waiting_tasks AS t2
    ON t1.lock_owner_address = t2.resource_address
```

The query in listing 27 will give you additional useful information about locks and blocking.

Listing 27   Looking at locks that are causing problems

```
SELECT t1.resource_type, t1.resource_database_id,
       t1.resource_associated_entity_id,t1.request_mode,
       t1.request_session_id,t2.blocking_session_id
FROM sys.dm_tran_locks AS t1
INNER JOIN sys.dm_os_waiting_tasks AS t2
ON t1.lock_owner_address = t2.resource_address;
```

Summary

The queries that I've shown you in this chapter are just the beginning. If you have responsibility for production database servers and databases, you really should be putting together a library of these types of DMV queries that you can use, both in normal usage and during a crisis. I have an extensive and growing collection of DMV queries that I've written and found over the past several years, and they've been extremely valuable for detecting and correcting performance problems.

DMV queries have much less server impact than SQL Profiler traces, and they provide much more granular SQL Server–specific detail than Performance Monitor traces. They also give you more control and detail than SQL Server Activity Monitor. DMV queries are oriented toward gathering snapshot-type information about current activity and aggregate activity since SQL Server was last started. As such, they're less useful for historical reporting and trend analysis unless you take steps to write their output to permanent tables.

You can easily set up a dedicated SQL Server login that your operations staff can use to run these queries to do first-level troubleshooting on a database server or database. It's easy to convert any of these queries to stored procedures, and then call them from an application. DMV queries were one of the more useful features added in SQL Server 2005. If you use them wisely, you can quickly and easily detect and diagnose many SQL Server ailments, truly becoming Dr. DMV.

About the author

Glenn works as a database architect at NewsGator Technologies in Denver, Colorado. He's a SQL Server MVP, and he has a whole collection of Microsoft certifications, including MCITP, MCDBA, MCSE, MCSD, MCAD, and MCTS, which proves that he likes to take tests.

He is also an adjunct faculty member at University College, University of Denver, where he's been teaching since 2000.

48 Query performance and disk I/O counters

Linchi Shea

SQL Server provides an excellent set of tools for troubleshooting query performance problems. At the top of the list, you have tools for capturing and analyzing query plans, tools for checking whether statistics are up to date or an index is useful, tools for capturing the time and resource cost of processing a query, and tools to help optimize SQL queries.

What you do not typically find in the toolset recommended for troubleshooting SQL Server query performance problems are the disk I/O performance counters. This is understandable because the disk I/O counters are the statistics at the operating system drive level. Although they can help you determine whether your disk subsystem is a bottleneck in the overall resource consumption of your SQL Server system, they do not generally reveal useful information on processing a particular query.

In some scenarios you can use the disk I/O performance counters in troubleshooting query performance problems. To completely ignore the disk I/O performance counters is to miss out on a powerful tool for troubleshooting SQL Server query problems.

Before diving into the query performance scenarios, let us first highlight the basics of disk I/Os, and review some salient disk I/O considerations in SQL Server query processing.

Expensive I/Os and very expensive I/Os

Disk I/Os are expensive and random disk I/Os are very expensive.

Accessing a piece of data on a disk drive is much slower than accessing the same piece of data in memory. How much slower? A conventional disk drive is an electro-mechanical device with a spinning spindle and one or more magnetic platters. No matter how fast the platters may spin, moving data through mechanical parts is inherently slower than moving data through electronic circuitry. In fact, disk access speed is measured in milliseconds (for example, 5 ms), whereas memory access speed is measured in nanoseconds (for example 100 ns).

What is important to recognize is that not all disk I/Os are equal in their performance. More specifically, random I/Os are far slower, or more expensive, than sequential I/Os.

Whether I/Os are random or sequential can be defined by the relative data locations of two consecutive I/O requests. If the next I/O request is for data at a random location, the I/O requests are random, whereas if the next I/O request is for data residing next to the currently requested data, the I/O requests are sequential. On a conventional disk, the time it takes to complete the operation of a random I/O typically includes moving the disk drive head to the right track on the platter and then waiting for the disk sector to rotate to the disk drive head. The time it takes to complete the operation of a sequential I/O typically involves moving the disk head between adjacent tracks and waiting for the right sector to rotate to the disk head.

Relatively speaking, the performance of a sequential I/O depends on the track-to-track seek time, whereas the performance of a random I/O depends on the average seek time. Why does this matter? Take a typical 15,000 rpm disk drive as an example. Its track-to-track seek time is 0.2 ms, whereas its average seek time is 2 ms. The performance difference has an order of magnitude!

SQL Server recognizes the performance difference between sequential I/Os and random I/Os, and its database engine employs many techniques to optimize for sequential I/Os. For example, in addition to being a technique for crash recovery, transaction logging can be viewed as an optimization that converts random writes to sequential writes. Read-ahead is another optimization that attempts to take advantage of sequential reads.

Disk performance counters

Windows exposes a large number of disk performance counters. You can use the following counters under the `LogicalDisk` object as the key performance indicators to evaluate disk I/O performance:

- `Avg. Disk sec/Read`—The number of seconds to complete a read operation on the disk drive, averaged over the polling interval
- `Avg. Disk sec/Write`—The number of seconds to complete a write operation on the disk drive, averaged over the polling interval
- `Avg. Disk Bytes/Read`—The number of bytes transferred from the disk drive per read operation, averaged over the polling interval
- `Avg. Disk Bytes/Write`—The number of bytes transferred to the disk drive per write operation, averaged over the polling interval
- `Disk Reads/sec`—The number of read operations on the disk drive per second
- `Disk Writes/sec`—The number of write operations on the disk drive per second

- `Disk Read Bytes/sec`—The number of bytes transferred from the disk drive per second
- `Disk Write Bytes/sec`—The number of bytes transferred to the disk drive per second
- `Current Disk Queue Length`—The number of requests outstanding on the disk drive

These counters measure five key I/O metrics:

- *Disk I/O latency*—For example, `Avg. Disk sec/Read`
- *Disk I/O size*—For example, `Avg. Disk Bytes/Read`
- *I/O operations per second*—For example, `Disk Reads/sec`
- *I/O throughput*—For example, `Disk Read Bytes/sec`
- *I/O queue length*—For example, `Current Disk Queue Length`

> ### I/O latency
>
> The latency of an I/O request is also known as I/O response time. It is measured by taking the difference between the time the I/O request is submitted and the time the completion acknowledgement is received. I/O latency can be measured at different levels of the I/O stack. The `Avg. Disk sec/Read` counter is a measure taken in the Windows logical disk driver.

It is critical, but often forgotten, that all the preceding disk I/O performance counters be collected and evaluated as a whole in order to see the complete picture of the disk I/O activities. In particular, if you focus on the disk latency counters without also checking the I/O size counters, you may end up drawing a wrong conclusion. For instance, a commonly accepted threshold for judging whether a disk I/O is taking too long is 10 ms. In practice, you need to make sure that this threshold applies only to smaller I/Os. When a system is doing large I/Os, the threshold of 10 ms may be too low, and can lead to false alarms.

Random or sequential I/Os and disk performance counters

By now, hopefully you agree that to gain better I/O throughput, sequential disk I/Os are much preferred over random disk I/Os. But how do you identify whether SQL Server is doing sequential I/Os as opposed to random I/Os? None of the disk performance counters tells you whether I/Os are sequential or random. What good does it do to talk about random I/Os versus sequential I/Os if you can't tell them apart?

The good news is that there is often a strong correlation between I/O sizes and I/O sequentiality. Generally speaking, small I/Os tend to be random in that their performance depends on the average seek time, and large I/Os tend to be sequential in that their performance depends on the track-to-track seek time.

Note that there is no hard and fast threshold that separates a small I/O from a large I/O. With that in mind, in the context of SQL Server, if an I/O is smaller than 64 KB, such as a single-page I/O, you can safely consider it a small I/O, and if an I/O is much larger than 64 KB, you can consider it a large I/O.

You may argue that small sequential I/Os, such as 2 KB sequential I/Os, are perfectly legitimate I/O patterns, and you would be right if you are looking at the disk I/O subsystem in isolation. After all, if you use an I/O benchmark tool such as SQLIO or Iometer, you can easily generate 2 KB sequential reads and writes.

SQLIO and Iometer

SQLIO is a Windows command-line tool for generating I/O workloads and measuring their performance. It is a free download from Microsoft. SQLIO is often used for benchmarking a disk subsystem. Iometer is a widely used multi-platform I/O benchmarking tool. Originally developed at Intel, Iometer is now distributed as an open source project. Google for SQLIO and Iometer to find their respective current download links.

Keep in mind that, as a SQL Server professional, you are interested in disk I/Os generated by SQL Server. And with the exception of database transaction logging, SQL Server is coded to avoid making small sequential I/O requests when it can issue large sequential I/Os. Whenever possible, SQL Server combines otherwise multiple sequential I/Os into a single larger I/O request. As described in Bob Dorr's excellent white papers, "SQL Server 2000 I/O Basics" and "SQL Server I/O Basics Chapter 2," checkpoints, lazy writes, eager writes, and read-ahead all use similar optimization to flush or read multiple contiguous pages, and as a result, heavily favor large I/Os.

For small sequential I/Os, the overhead with each I/O request is a significant factor in the overall I/O performance. In addition, because multiple concurrent I/O requests are often outstanding and the disk storage is often shared by different hosts or different applications in practice, it is difficult to limit small sequential I/Os to track-to-track seek time. For instance, if the disk head is being moved away because of other I/O requests taking place in between these small sequential I/O requests, the average seek time may become a determinant factor in the performance of these small sequential I/Os, therefore effectively turning them into random I/Os.

Although life is made difficult by not having any disk performance counters to distinguish random I/Os from sequential I/Os, it is easy to tell small I/Os from large I/Os using the following performance counters under the LogicalDisk object:

- Avg. Disk Bytes/Read
- Avg. Disk Bytes/Write

If you don't care about separating reads from writes, Avg. Disk Bytes/Transfer is a convenient counter to measure the I/O size.

SQL Server operations and I/O sizes

Before you can effectively take advantage of the I/O performance counters in trouble-shooting query performance problems, you need to understand how some of the key SQL Server operations manage their disk I/O sizes. It is beyond the scope of this chapter to discuss the I/O implications of every SQL Server operation. Instead, let's review the following key SQL Server operations with respect to how their performance is related to I/O sizes:

- Checkpoints
- Lazy writes
- Read-ahead reads
- Table scans and index scans
- Index seeks and bookmark lookups

Checkpoints and lazy writes use essentially the same algorithm to control the sizes of their disk I/O requests. SQL Server 2000 tries to bundle up to 16 pages (up to 128 KB) in a single write request, whereas SQL Server 2005 and 2008 can bundle up to 32 pages (up to 256 KB) in a single write request. Obviously, if dirty pages are not contiguous with respect to the page numbers in a data file, checkpoints and lazy writes will have to issue smaller I/Os.

Similarly, read-ahead reads will attempt to issue large I/O requests, whenever possible. In practice, it is common to see SQL Server read-ahead reads posting I/O requests that are greater than 128 KB in size. SQL Server 2005 and SQL Server 2008 are more aggressive than SQL Server 2000 when they post read-ahead reads. Like-to-like empirical tests found that the sizes of read-ahead requests issued by SQL Server 2005 and SQL Server 2008 are often larger than those by SQL Server 2000.

When SQL Server decides to use a table scan or an index scan to process a query, the access methods are often accompanied by large I/O requests. It should be noted that a table scan or an index scan will not necessarily result in large I/O requests. If SQL Server cannot make use of read-ahead reads, a table scan or an index scan may have to resort to 8 KB I/O requests. When you have a large table to scan, reading one 8 KB page at a time is inefficient.

Index seeks and bookmark lookups involve traversing and inspecting linked individual pages. The I/O pattern is typically 8 KB random reads; 64 KB reads may also be observed. Hopefully, the preceding discussion on random I/Os being very expensive has not led you to reject 8 KB random reads as universally inefficient. They are indeed inefficient if they have to be issued in large numbers, for instance, when processing a query that touches a large number of pages. That being said, if you are looking for a specific piece of data (for instance, an individual order or a customer address), small random I/Os are exactly what you need to quickly locate the data.

How expensive are small random I/Os, anyway?

Random I/Os are expensive because they depend on the average seek time, whereas sequential I/Os depend on the track-to-track seek time, and there can be more than an order of magnitude difference in the performance between the average seek time and the track-to-track seek time.

As a database professional, you probably would feel more comfortable if you see concrete performance numbers that are related to SQL Server query processing than you would with the disk geometry. Let's conduct a little experiment.

First, create a database with at least 6 GB for the data file and 2 GB for the log file. Then, run the script as shown in listing 1 to create a test table and populate it with 4 million rows.

Listing 1   Creating a test table and populating it with 4 million rows

```
EXEC sp_configure 'max degree of parallelism', 1;
go
Reconfigure with override;
go
CREATE TABLE test(
  c1 int,
  c2 int,
  dt datetime,
  filler CHAR(1000) NOT NULL
);
go

SET NOCOUNT ON;
go
DECLARE @i int;
SET @i = 1;

BEGIN TRAN
WHILE @i < 4000000
BEGIN
    INSERT test(c1, c2, dt, filler)
    SELECT @i,
           CASE WHEN @i%2 = 0 THEN @i ELSE 4000000-@i END,
           GETDATE(),
           'abc';

    IF (@i % 100000 = 0)
    BEGIN
       COMMIT TRAN;
       BEGIN TRAN;
    END

    SELECT @i = @i + 1;
END
COMMIT TRAN;
go
CREATE INDEX cx_test ON test(c2);
go
```

When this script completes, launch Performance Monitor and add the following two `LogicalDisk` counters to monitor the I/O size and the I/O throughput for the drives where the data file of the test database is created:

- `Avg. Disk Bytes/Read`
- `Disk Read Bytes/sec`

Then, run the two test scripts in table 1, one at a time.

Table 1   Test scripts to see the impact of small random I/Os

Test	Script

Test 1	`-- table scan and large sequential I/Os`
	`DBCC DROPCLEANBUFFERS;`
	`go`
	`SELECT MAX(dt) FROM test;`

Test 2	`-- bookmark lookups and small random I/Os`
	`DBCC DROPCLEANBUFFERS;`
	`go`
	`SELECT MAX(dt) FROM test WITH (INDEX=2);`

In test 1, you will see that SQL Server chooses to process the `SELECT` query with a table scan. In test 2, SQL Server is forced to use the nonclustered index to retrieve the data pages through bookmark lookups.

NOTE   In each test script, `DBCC DROPCLEANBUFFERS` is run first to remove all the clean pages from the SQL Server buffer pool. This ensures that all pages are retrieved from disk by the subsequent `SELECT` query. Do not run this statement on a production server.

Table 2 summarizes the performance statistics of the two tests in terms of query elapsed time, I/O size, and I/O throughput.

Table 2   Performance impact of small random I/Os

Test	Query elapsed time	I/O size	I/O throughput
Test 1	12	~ 256 KB	~ 340 MB/sec
Test 2	44	~ 8 KB	~ 80 MB/sec

Although the numbers may vary when you execute the tests in different environments, the following pattern should hold:

- SQL Server issues large I/Os (~256 KB per read) in test 1, and small I/Os (8 KB ~ 64 KB per read) in test 2.
- Depending on the storage capability, SQL Server should achieve much higher I/O throughput in test 1 than in test 2: a direct consequence of using large I/Os.

- The query performs significantly better in terms of elapsed time in test 1 than in test 2 because of the higher disk I/O throughput in test 1.

In this experiment, the same query ran almost four times as fast in test 1 as it did in test 2. On a lower end disk subsystem that has lower throughput capacity, the difference will not be so pronounced. For instance, on a disk subsystem whose maximum throughput capacity is 120 MB/sec, the 256 KB sequential scan was seen to achieve 100 MB/sec and the 8 KB random lookups reached 60 MB/sec. Although the gain was less than 100 percent, the difference was still significant.

Performance scenarios

These are the key messages in this chapter so far:

- Random I/Os are expensive.
- SQL Server is programmed to take advantage of sequential I/Os.
- You cannot directly observe whether I/Os are sequential or random. That being said, because sequential I/Os are associated with large I/Os and random I/Os with small I/Os, you can instead observe I/O sizes with the disk performance counters.
- Processing a large query with small I/Os is not efficient.

This is interesting information in itself. But how does it help you in practice? Let's explore four query performance scenarios where you can put this information to good use.

Scenario 1: constant checkpoints

This was a real-world case encountered by a database administrator (DBA).

When reviewing the logged SQL Server performance counter values, the DBA discovered that checkpoints were taking place almost continuously on one of their busiest databases. At the same time, it was found that lazy writes were kept constantly active as well. Both checkpoints and lazy writes were working hard to flush out dirty pages and make room for free pages that are needed in the buffer pool, but they could barely keep up with the changes.

Is there anything we could do to improve the situation? The DBA was asked to provide an analysis and recommend a course of action for better performance. Fortunately, the disk performance counters were also logged along with the SQL Server counters. Correlating the disk performance counters with the SQL Server buffer manager counters led to the observation that SQL Server was doing small I/Os during checkpoints (Avg. Disk Bytes/Write <= ~16 KB). The performance capacity of the disk storage subsystem was not being fully utilized by the checkpoint I/O requests.

The DBA realized that if the checkpoints could be done quicker, more free pages would be readily available, with the result of alleviating pressure on the lazy writer, keeping the pages in the buffer pool longer, and therefore improving the overall performance of the server. The solution in this case was to re-organize several key tables on different clustered indexes so that updates took place on pages that were more contiguous. This solution was evaluated against the potential increase in the lock contention, and in this case the I/O performance gain outweighed the downside risk of increased contention.

Scenario 2: NOLOCK and faster query processing

You probably know that using the NOLOCK hint in a table scan not only reduces—or even eliminates—the potential for blocking other user processes, it may also improve—sometimes significantly—the performance of your query. The often-stated reason is that with the NOLOCK hint, SQL Server can choose to perform the table scan via the allocation order instead of the index order. This is a fine explanation, but it says nothing about why an allocation order scan may be more efficient than an index order scan.

Looking from a disk I/O perspective, the efficiency of an allocation order scan lies in the fact that it generally issues larger I/Os than does an index order scan.

Let's again look at some empirical evidence. Modify the script in listing 1 so that it creates a clustered index on the c1 column instead of a nonclustered index on the c2 column. Run the following SQL statement after the test table is populated with data:

```
CREATE CLUSTERED INDEX cix_test ON test(c1);
```

Then, run the two scripts in table 3 separately to observe their respective I/O sizes and I/O throughputs with the performance counters Avg. Disk Bytes/Read and Disk Read Bytes/sec.

Table 3   Test scripts to see the impact of the NOLOCK hint

Test	Script
Test 1	DBCC DROPCLEANBUFFERS; go SELECT MAX(dt) FROM test;
Test 2	DBCC DROPCLEANBUFFERS; go SELECT MAX(dt) FROM test WITH (NOLOCK);

Table 4 summarizes the performance statistics from running the scripts on a test server.

Table 4   Performance impact of the NOLOCK hint

Test	Elapsed time	I/O size	I/O throughput
Test 1	70	~ 350 KB	~ 85 MB/sec
Test 2	36	~ 500 KB	~ 125 MB/sec

The query with the hint was nearly twice as fast as the query without the NOLOCK hint. Note also that with NOLOCK, the query was able to achieve much higher disk read throughput than when NOLOCK was not specified. And with the NOLOCK hint, the average I/O size of reading the pages from disk was much larger than without NOLOCK, although both were doing large I/Os.

WARNING The NOLOCK hint should not be used injudiciously just to help improve performance because your query may return inconsistent data. Where potential data inconsistency is acceptable or where not blocking the main process is paramount, the NOLOCK hint can be an effective tool.

Scenario 3: read-ahead reads

When it comes to processing large queries (queries that touch a large number of pages), read-ahead reads are central to their performance. If for whatever reason the read-ahead operation can't grab a sufficient number of pages to issue large I/O requests, your query performance will degrade dramatically.

To highlight the importance of the read-ahead operation, let's look at an extreme case where it is disabled entirely.

Again, modify the script in listing 1 so that it creates a clustered index on the c1 column instead of a nonclustered index on the c2 column. Run the following SQL statement after the test table is populated with data:

```
CREATE CLUSTERED INDEX cix_test ON test(c1);
```

Then, run the following two scripts, shown in table 5, separately to observe their respective I/O sizes with the performance counter Avg. Disk Bytes/Read. The script in test 1 runs the SELECT query with the read-ahead operation enabled, which is the default SQL Server behavior, and the script in test 2 runs the SELECT query with the read-ahead operation disabled via trace flag 652.

Table 5 Test scripts to see the impact of the read-ahead operation

Test	Script
Test 1	```DBCC DROPCLEANBUFFERS; go DBCC TRACEOFF(-1, 652); --it is off by default go SELECT MAX(dt) FROM test;```
Test 2	```DBCC DROPCLEANBUFFERS; go DBCC TRACEON(-1, 652); -- this disables readahead go SELECT MAX(dt) FROM test;```

Table 6 summarizes the performance statistics when the tests were run on one of my servers.

Table 6   Performance impact of the NOLOCK hint

Test	Elapsed time	I/O size	I/O throughput
Test 1	12 sec	~ 512 KB	~ 300 MB/sec
Test 2	50 sec	~ 64 KB	~ 80 MB/sec

On this particular test server, the impact of the read-ahead operation is dramatic. With the read-ahead operation, SQL Server was able to issue large I/O requests (~512 KB per read) and pushed the disk read throughput to ~300 MB per second. Without the read-ahead operation, SQL Server had to resort to relatively small I/O requests (~64 KB per read, and 8 KB per read was also observed on a different test server), and the read throughput was significantly lower at about 80 MB per second. The end result is that SQL Server was able to complete processing the query four times faster with read-ahead reads than without read-ahead reads on this test server.

Scenario 4: index fragmentation

You probably know, or have read, that index fragmentation is bad for the performance of large queries. In particular, logical scan fragmentation can have a detrimental impact on the performance of queries that are processed with index ordered scans. Why? The most common explanation is that when logical order doesn't match the physical order, SQL Server has to do more work in following the index page chain.

Instead of trying to understand how SQL Server navigates through logical scan fragmentation internally, you can gain a solid understanding of its performance impact by looking at the disk performance counters—more specifically, Avg. Disk Bytes/Read and Disk Read Bytes/sec.

Let's again use the script in listing 1. To introduce logical scan fragmentation, first remove the CREATE INDEX statement from the script, and then insert the following SQL statement immediately after the test table is created and before the test table is populated with data:

```
CREATE CLUSTERED INDEX cix_test ON test(c2);
```

After the test table is populated with data using the script in listing 1, run DBCC SHOW-CONTIG('test') to confirm the presence of significant logical scan fragmentation. The output should look like listing 2.

Listing 2   Output from running DBCC SHOWCONTIG on the test table

```
DBCC SHOWCONTIG scanning 'test' table...
Table: 'test' (69575286); index ID: 1, database ID: 8
TABLE level scan performed.
- Pages Scanned................................: 933333
```

```
- Extents Scanned.............................: 117019
- Extent Switches.............................: 600276
- Avg. Pages per Extent.......................: 8.0
- Scan Density [Best Count:Actual Count].......: 19.44% [116667:600277]
- Logical Scan Fragmentation .................: 85.33%
- Extent Scan Fragmentation ..................: 0.01%
- Avg. Bytes Free per Page....................: 3703.1
- Avg. Page Density (full)....................: 54.25%
```

Now, run the following script, and observe the disk I/O size with the `Avg. Disk Bytes/ Read` counter and the disk I/O throughput with the `Disk Read Bytes/sec` counter.

```
DBCC DROPCLEANBUFFERS;
go
SELECT MAX(dt) FROM test;
```

For comparison, defragment the clustered index by dropping and re-creating it, and then rerun the preceding script.

NOTE   Because the average page density from the DBCC SHOWCONTIG output is 54.25 percent, when you re-create the clustered index you need to set the fill factor to about 50 percent so that the re-created index has the same page density, and most importantly, the same number of pages. Otherwise, the comparison is not valid.

Table 7 summarizes the results from a test server with a directly attached disk drive.

Table 7   Performance impact of index fragmentation

Test	Elapsed time	I/O size	I/O throughput
Logical Scan Fragmentation = 0	43	~ 400 KB	~ 100 MB/sec
Logical Scan Fragmentation = 85%	275	~ 16 KB	~ 30 MB/sec

On this test server, the `SELECT` query ran more than six times faster without logical scan fragmentation.

The test result shows that logical scan fragmentation seriously hampered SQL Server's ability to perform read-ahead reads. Whereas it was able to do about 12000 read-ahead pages per second when there was no logical scan fragmentation, it could only do about 3000 read-ahead pages per second when logical scan fragmentation was at 85 percent. In addition, fragmentation caused SQL Server to issue small I/O requests; compare the `Avg. Disk Bytes/Read` of 16 KB with fragmentation to that of about 400 KB without fragmentation, and this resulted in SQL Server not being able to take full advantage of the I/O throughput capacity of the disk subsystem.

A note of caution is in order before you extrapolate this too far. If you run the same tests on a higher-end disk subsystem, you may not find the performance difference to be this dramatic.

Summary

The key message of this chapter is that the disk I/O performance counters can reveal a significant amount of information on query processing, and you can effectively use the disk I/O counter values to help analyze query performance issues in scenarios where SQL Server must incur significant physical I/Os, such as when processing large queries.

Despite much talk about preferring sequential I/Os to random I/Os, you cannot directly observe whether I/Os are sequential or random. For processing large SQL queries, you can instead choose to observe their I/O sizes and I/O throughputs. The key observation is that large I/Os are much more efficient than small I/Os, and large I/Os are often sequential I/Os, and SQL Server is optimized to take advantage of large I/Os.

In practice, you need to exercise caution when observing disk I/O sizes as there is often a multitude of activities on a server, and it may be difficult to attribute the values of the disk I/O performance counters to any specific queries.

About the author

Linchi Shea has been working with SQL Server since Version 4.21a. He works in the financial services sector in and around New York City. Linchi is passionate about creating robust and automated infrastructures for managing SQL Server in an enterprise environment. He has written many tools and utilities to simplify deploying, operating, and testing SQL Server. You can find him blogging about SQL Server enterprise issues at www.sqlblog.com. Linchi is a co-founder and co-lead of the NYC SQL Server users group, and has been a Microsoft MVP since 2002.

49 XEVENT: the next event infrastructure

Cristian Lefter

SQL Server gives many options for monitoring and troubleshooting, such as SQL Server Profiler and SQL Trace, Dynamic Management Views and Functions, the default trace, trace flags, performance counters, deadlock graphs, ring buffers, blocked process reports, DBCC commands, various logs, and others. So you may wonder why anyone would need a new event infrastructure such as Extended Events. It may sound shocking, but the diversity of the tools is the main reason. Having so many techniques available makes it difficult to maintain the code for each new release of SQL Server. That's from a developer's point of view. For the rest of us—customers, consultants, users, and even for Microsoft support—it's challenging to obtain relevant performance or troubleshooting information. Why? Because the information needed usually comes from multiple sources. Furthermore, each of the tools available before SQL Server 2008 has its own strengths and weaknesses.

Think about monitoring SQL Server using SQL Server Profiler: it's graphical, easy to use, and can be used in correlation with PerfMon logs, but the performance overhead can be pretty serious.

Extended Events is *the* potential event infrastructure for the next releases of SQL Server. This is my personal opinion, and the role of this chapter is to support this opinion with facts.

Extended Events infrastructure characteristics

The following are some of the characteristics of Extended Events that I consider to be important:

- XEVENT is a general event-handling infrastructure for servers.
- It allows defining events to be monitored and provides a variety of ways to consume the events.
- It can be synchronous or asynchronous (events are fired synchronously).
- It can trigger actions when an event fires.

- It uses predicates to filter events from consumers.
- It has causality tracking (through inherited IDs).
- It has high performance and good scalability.
- The cost of firing a single event is extremely small (approximately 2 µs CPU time on a 2 GHz processor). But keep in mind that when consuming the events, it's a different story—depending on how the event is consumed, the overhead can become significant.
- ETW (Event Tracing for Windows) is enabled (integration of Extended Events and ETW is supported).
- It's controlled through T-SQL DDL statements (such as CREATE and ALTER).
- It exposes rich metadata through a complete set of catalog views, Dynamic Management Views, and functions.

Listing 1 uses Extended Events to monitor long-running queries. We'll use the example to understand some of the concepts introduced by Extended Events.

Listing 1   Using Extended Events to monitor long-running queries

```
USE master;
GO
-- Create Event Session
CREATE EVENT SESSION GetLongRunningQueries ON SERVER
ADD EVENT sqlserver.sql_statement_completed(
ACTION (sqlserver.sql_text)
WHERE sqlserver.database_id=1 AND duration > 20000);
GO
-- Add Event Bucketing target
-- source_type = {0|1}, 0 = event 1 = action
ALTER EVENT SESSION GetLongRunningQueries ON SERVER
ADD TARGET package0.synchronous_bucketizer (set
➥filtering_event_name='sqlserver.sql_statement_completed', source_type=1,
➥source='sqlserver.sql_text');
GO
-- Start the Event Session
ALTER EVENT SESSION GetLongRunningQueries
ON SERVER STATE=START;
GO

-- For testing purpose we will create a stored procedure that will run
-- longer than 20 seconds
CREATE PROCEDURE usp_WaitForATime AS
BEGIN
DECLARE @D DATETIME=GETDATE(),@S VARCHAR(128);
WHILE (DATEDIFF(ss,@D,GETDATE())<22)
SET @S = @@VERSION;
END;
GO

-- Execute the procedure 5 times
-- This works in SQL Server Management Studio
EXEC usp_WaitForATime;
GO 5
```

```
-- Getting the information
DECLARE @MyXML XML;
SELECT @MyXML = CAST(T.target_data AS XML)
FROM sys.dm_xe_session_targets T
JOIN sys.dm_xe_sessions S
    ON S.address = T.event_session_address
JOIN sys.server_event_sessions ES
    ON S.name = ES.name
WHERE T.target_name = 'synchronous_bucketizer'
    AND S.name = 'GetLongRunningQueries';

-- Display the information as raw XML
SELECT @MyXML AS XML_Representation;

-- Display the information using XQuery for a better output
SELECT
T.Slot.value('@count', 'int') [NbmOfExecutions],
T.Slot.value('value[1]', 'varchar(MAX)') [QueryText]
FROM @MyXML.nodes('/BucketizerTarget/Slot') AS  T(Slot)

-- Clean-Up
DROP PROCEDURE usp_WaitForATime;
GO
ALTER EVENT SESSION GetLongRunningQueries
ON SERVER STATE=STOP;
GO
DROP EVENT SESSION GetLongRunningQueries
ON SERVER;
GO
```

Running the code produces the output shown in listing 2.

Listing 2 Output from running listing 1

```
XML_Representation
-----------------------------------------------
<BucketizerTarget truncated="0" buckets="256">
  <Slot count="5" trunc="1">
    <value>EXEC usp_WaitForATime;</value>
  </Slot>
</BucketizerTarget>


NbmOfExecutions QueryText
--------------- ----------------------
5               EXEC usp_WaitForATime;
```

In this chapter, I'll use the code from listing 1 to explain the following concepts:

- *Events*—Points of interests in the code of an application such as SQL Server. In the example, we're interested in the event fired when a T-SQL statement is finished (sqlserver.sql_statement_completed).
- *Packages*—Containers for Extended Events objects (events, targets, actions, types, predicates, and maps). In our example we use package0, which contains Extended Events system objects.

- *Targets*—The event consumers. In the case of our example, we use the `Event Bucketing Target`, which retains data (the `sql_text`) for the `sql_statement_completed` event.

- *Actions*—Programmatic responses or a series of responses to an event (such as capturing the T-SQL stack collection or generating a user dump). For the previous example, the action is collecting the `sql_text` column for the `sql_statement_completed` event. Other possible actions include capturing a stack dump, aggregating event data, appending information to event data, or storing state information.

- *Predicates*—Boolean expressions that filter the events. In our example, the `sqlserver.database_id` predicate filters the events that occurred in the database with the ID of 1 (the `master` database).

- *Types*—Encapsulate the characteristics of collected data. For example, the type of the `sqlserver.database_id` predicate is `pred_source`.

- *Maps*—Associate internal values to more meaningful descriptions. For example, the internal value 3 for `lock_resource_type` is mapped to the string `FILE` (which is self explanatory). The complete mappings can be obtained by running the following code:

```
SELECT name, map_key, map_value FROM sys.dm_xe_map_values
```

- *Sessions*—Contain targets and the enabled events.

The next section of the chapter goes deeper in explaining the XEVENT elements.

XEVENT architecture

If you need more details about the Extended Events architecture, this section is for you. I also encourage you to use Books Online for additional information.

SQL Server Extended Events engine

The SQL Server Extended Events engine is a collection of services and objects that enables you to define events, process event data, and manage the XEVENT sessions, services, and objects. One characteristic that makes XEVENT a general event infrastructure is that the events engine is event-agnostic. The processes that use the engine define the interaction with the engine and supply event points and actions to take when an event fires. Thus any event can be bound to any target.

Figure 1 represents the high-level architecture of the SQL Server Extended Events engine:

- The *SQL Server Extended Events engine* is integrated in the SQL Server database engine. A host process contains only one instance of the Extended Events engine. It handles session management, dispatching, and memory buffers for events.

- A *session* can contain *enabled events, targets,* and *buffers*.

- Instances of targets may be created and added to a session.

- The memory buffers for the events are dispatched to targets when they're filled.
- *Dispatchers* are worker threads.
- Each Windows process can have one or more modules (a Win32 process or Win32 module). Each of the Windows process modules can contain one or more Extended Events *packages*, which contain one or more Extended Events objects (types, targets, actions, maps, predicates, and events).

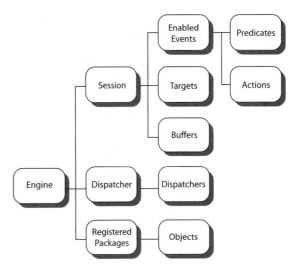

Figure 1   SQL Server Extended Events engine

Packages

Packages are containers for Extended Events objects such as events, targets, actions, types, predicates, and maps. As already mentioned, a Windows process can have one or more modules (a Win32 process or Win32 module), also known as *binaries* or *executable modules*. Each binary can contain one or more Extended Events packages.

Packages are identified by a name, a GUID, and the binary module that contains the package. Figure 2 gives a high-level representation for the architecture of a package.

SQL Server 2008 has three public packages (package0, sqlos, sqlserver) and a private one for the Security Audit feature (SecAudit). The code in listing 3 uses the

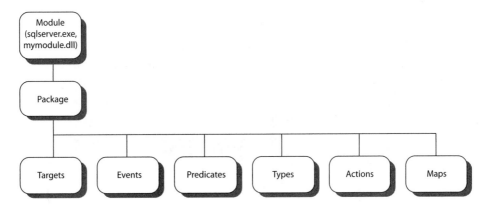

Figure 2   Extended Events packages

`sys.dm_xe_packages` Dynamic Management View (DMV) to list the names and the description of packages present on a SQL Server instance.

Listing 3   Using `sys.dm_xe_packages` to list packages

```
SELECT name, description FROM sys.dm_xe_packages
```

The output is shown in listing 4.

Listing 4   Output from running listing 3

```
name        description
----------  -----------------------------------------------------------
package0    Default package. Contains all standard types, maps, compare
            operators, actions and targets
sqlos       Extended events for SQL Operating System
sqlserver   Extended events for Microsoft SQL Server
SecAudit    Security Audit Events
```

Another DMV, `sys.dm_xe_objects`, allows you to get all objects contained by a package.

Events

Events are specific points of interest in the code of an application. In the case of SQL Server, they can be the start of a broker activation task, a lock timeout, a cache hit, and so on.

When an event fires, it signals that the point of interest was reached. The firing of an event can be used for tracing purposes or triggering actions. The actions (or the consumption of the event) can be synchronous or asynchronous.

Each event has a versioned schema that defines its payload (content). This schema is represented by event columns with well-defined types.

Event classification follows the ETW model (channel, keyword) to facilitate the integration of Extended Events with ETW and its tools.

Targets

The event consumers are the targets. The events are separated from consumers, a fact that allows any target to receive any event. Targets can process single events or full buffers of events, and can do so synchronously or asynchronously. They can start a task, write to a trace file, or aggregate event data.

The targets included in the three public packages of SQL Server 2008 are listed in listing 5. Listing 6 shows the output.

Listing 5   Enumerating Extended Events targets

```
SELECT
 o.name,
 o.description
FROM sys.dm_xe_objects o
JOIN sys.dm_xe_packages p
```

```
ON p.guid = o.package_guid
WHERE p.name in ('package0','sqlos','sqlserver')
AND o.object_type='target'
```

Listing 6   Output from running listing 5

```
name                         description
----------------------       ----------------------------------------------
etw_classic_sync_target      Event Tracing for Windows (ETW) Synchronous
                             Target
synchronous_bucketizer       Synchronous bucketizing target
asynchronous_bucketizer      Asynchronous bucketizing target
asynchronous_file_target     Asynchronous file target
pair_matching                Pairing target
synchronous_event_counter    Synchronous Counter target
ring_buffer                  Asynchronous ring buffer target.
```

Without going into too much detail for each target (as they're well documented in Books Online), their main usage is as follows:

- *Event Tracing for Windows (ETW) Synchronous Target*—Allows correlation between SQL Server and Windows
- *Synchronous bucketizing target and Asynchronous bucketizing target*—Allows creation of a histogram over event data in order to find the hot spots
- *Asynchronous file target*—Saves event data to a file for later analysis
- *Pairing target*—Allows identification of resource misuse (such as acquiring a lock and not releasing it)
- *Synchronous Counter target*—Keeps statistics about how often events are fired
- *Asynchronous ring buffer target*—In-memory ring buffer for saving event history

Actions

Actions are defined as programmatic responses or a series of responses to an event. Actions happen before the event is available for targets to consume, and are invoked synchronously on the thread firing the event.

Events are distinct from actions, and can add data to an event's payload. An example of an action is collecting the T-SQL stack.

Predicates

Predicates allow you to filter the events before they're published. They can maintain state, for example firing every *n*th time an event occurs or storing the maximum value reached for an event. They can operate on global or local event payload data.

Types and maps

Types define the characteristics of collected data and can be events, actions, targets, or predicates. To get an idea of the existing objects and their types, you can use SELECT name, object_type, description FROM sys.dm_xe_objects. As a simple example, the deprecation_announcement has the type event and has the following description:

"Occurs when you use a feature that will be removed from a future version of SQL Server, but will not be removed from the next major release of SQL Server."

Maps allow you to associate internal values to more meaningful descriptions. If you understand the principles behind database normalization, it would make sense to you to store locking modes as byte data types rather than strings. But then, you'd have to know that *lock mode 18* means *RangeI-X*. That's exactly what maps allow you to do by using the `sys.dm_xe_map_values` DMV.

Sessions

Sessions contain targets and the enabled events. The same event can be enabled in multiple sessions. The binding of actions and predicates is done per session level.

Sessions provide policy support for buffering (how the event data is stored) and dispatch (the time the data is retained in the buffers). Sessions are also a security boundary (the user-level permissions are checked per session when the session is created or altered).

The mapping between package objects and sessions is many-to-many. The event sessions can be created and managed through the DDL statements `CREATE EVENT SESSION` and `ALTER EVENT SESSION`. The event session DDL statements allow you to add targets, events, predicates, actions, and event session level options; set an event session to autostart at server startup; and add or remove targets and events from running event sessions.

XEVENT in action

The final section of this chapter is dedicated to real-life XEVENT usage scenarios as well as to some performance considerations.

Usage scenarios

Extended Events are likely to become the preferred method of monitoring and troubleshooting; therefore, the following are some possible usage scenarios:

- Monitoring system activity using Extended Events and Event Tracing for Windows (ETW)
- Determining which queries are holding locks
- Finding objects with the most locks taken on them
- Determining which queries are exceeding certain thresholds (such as a specified duration)
- Tracking waits
- Tracking spinlock contention (spinlocks are low-level synchronization objects used to protect access to resources for short periods of time)
- Investigating latch contention
- Generating a user dump

The number of usage scenarios is quite large and beyond the scope of this chapter. But, to give you another example of using XEVENT, listing 7 shows how to generate a user dump when an error occurs.

Listing 7 Generating a user dump

```
USE master;
GO
-- trigger a user dump for the error 208
-- 'Invalid object name'
CREATE EVENT SESSION GenerateUserDump ON SERVER
ADD EVENT sqlos.exception_ring_buffer_recorded (
        ACTION (sqlserver.create_dump_single_thread)
        WHERE (error = 208 and state=1 and package0.counter < 2));
GO
ALTER EVENT SESSION GenerateUserDump ON SERVER
STATE=START;
GO
-- Generate the 208 error
SELECT *
FROM NonExistentTable;
-- Cleanup
DROP EVENT SESSION GenerateUserDump ON SERVER;
GO
```

After generating the error, if you inspect the SQL Server error log, you'll find something similar to listing 8.

Listing 8 Output from running listing 7

```
Source Message
------ -------------------------------------------------------------------
spid51 External dump process return code 0x20000001.<nl/>External dump
       process returned no errors.
spid51 Stack Signature for the dump is 0xC0D2B2AE
spid51 Short Stack Dump
spid51 * ----------------------------------------------------------------
spid51 * ****************************************************************
spid51 *
spid51 *              SELECT * FROM NonExistentTable;
spid51 * Input Buffer 92 bytes -
spid51 *
spid51 * Dump triggered by event 'exception_ring_buffer_recorded'.
spid51 *
spid51 * BEGIN STACK DUMP:
spid51 *
spid51 ****************************************************************
spid51 ***Stack Dump being sent to C:\Program Files\Microsoft SQL
       Server\MSSQL10.MSSQLSERVER\MSSQL\LOG\SQLDump0002.txt
spid51 *
spid51 * User initiated stack dump.  This is not a server exception dump.
```

System health session

One feature based on Extended Events is the SQL Server Audit feature that allows you to monitor server-level and database-level groups of events or individual events.

Whereas the SQL Server Audit is known and well documented, the system health session, another feature based on XEVENT, is quite unheard of.

The system health session is an always-on session that captures events considered unhealthy. The events are captured using the ring buffer target. To convince yourself, run the statement shown in listing 9.

Listing 9   Querying `sys.dm_xe_sessions` to determine oldest session

```
SELECT TOP 1 name, total_buffer_size FROM sys.dm_xe_sessions
ORDER BY create_time;
```

The result should look like the following table.

```
name            total_buffer_size
------------    ---------------------------------------------------------------
system_health   4324761
```

How do we interpret the results? The name of the session is self explanatory, and the other column reveals that the ring buffer stores 4 MB worth of information.

To go further, we can see what events are captured by this session by running the code presented in listing 10.

Listing 10   Getting the system health session active events and filters

```
SELECT
    e.event_name,
    e.event_predicate
FROM sys.dm_xe_sessions s
JOIN sys.dm_xe_session_events e
    ON s.address = e.event_session_address
WHERE s.name = 'system_health';
```

From the output, we can conclude that system health records the following events:

- error_reported
- xml_deadlock_report
- scheduler_monitor_non_yielding_ring_buffer_recorded
- wait_info
- wait_info_external

Complex predicates limit the events that fire to out-of-memory errors, severe errors, lock waits exceeding 30 seconds, latches exceeding 15 seconds, and deadlocks.

The following is a partial example of the predicates used to limit the number of the events:

```
<or>
 <leaf>
```

```
<comparator name="greater_than_equal_int64" package="package0"></
   comparator>
<event name="error_reported" package="sqlserver" field="severity">
</event>
<value>20</value>
</leaf>
...
```

To get the information recorded by the system health session, you can use the code in listing 11.

Listing 11 Obtaining information from the system health session

```
-- Getting the information
DECLARE @MyXML XML;
SELECT @MyXML = CAST(T.target_data AS XML)
FROM sys.dm_xe_session_targets T
JOIN sys.dm_xe_sessions S
   ON S.address = T.event_session_address
JOIN sys.server_event_sessions ES
   ON S.name = ES.name
WHERE S.name = 'system_health';

-- Display the information as raw XML
SELECT @MyXML AS XML_Representation;
```

Performance considerations

Before we conclude this chapter and before using XEVENT, you should keep in mind the following facts:

- Though the performance cost for a single event firing is light—just 2 μs CPU time on a 2 GHz processor—consuming the event is a different story. So you may consider asynchronous targets instead of synchronous targets, as the former have less effect on runtime performance.

- You can partition session buffers to improve scalability. As the number of CPUs grows, event session buffers can be partitioned to keep overhead low.

- Examine event retention needs—XEVENT allows you to specify the event retention by configuring the EVENT_RETENTION_MODE event session option (ALLOW_SINGLE_EVENT_LOSS—an event can be lost from the session; ALLOW_MULTIPLE_EVENT_LOSS—full event buffers containing multiple events can be lost from the session; NO_EVENT_LOSS–no event loss is allowed).

- Retaining every event may have a much larger impact from a performance point of view because firing threads will stall waiting on a free buffer.

- Many events can't be added to an event session with NO_EVENT_LOSS.

- Choose ALLOW_SINGLE_EVENT_LOSS or ALLOW_MULTIPLE_EVENT_LOSS whenever possible.

Summary

Extended Events is a vast subject. You could probably fill a book and still just touch it. Yet I hope that this chapter convinced you to take a look at this new event infrastructure.

About the author

Cristian Lefter is a SQL Server MVP and a former SQL Server developer, currently working as a consultant at Micro Training, a consulting and training company. Cristian is a writer, blogger, SQL expert, and frequent reviewer for Manning, Apress, Wiley, and other publishers, as well as for ASPToday, Simple-Talk, Microsoft E-Learning, Asentus, Content Master, GrandMasters, and so forth. He is based in Bucharest, Romania.

You can reach him at his blog, http://sqlserver.ro/blogs/ cristians_blog/default.aspx, or his email address, Cristian-Lefter@hotmail.com.

PART 5

Business intelligence

Edited by Greg Low

The introduction of OLAP Services in SQL Server 7 started a revolution within the product. While SQL Server has for a long time been a great store for relational data and still is a great relational store, organizations are realizing more than ever that what really counts is the ability to derive information from their data.

The key contribution of business intelligence (BI) systems has been to convert mountains of data, often transactional in nature, into *actionable* information. In the end, it's all about making better business decisions and in ever-shorter timeframes.

The Microsoft BI toolkit has often been regarded as comprising SQL Server Integration Services, SQL Server Reporting Services, and SQL Server Analysis Services. Now an even-richer ecosystem has been created, and we need to expand that definition to include other tools, including Excel Services, PerformancePoint Services, and dashboards in SharePoint.

BI systems were once the province of only the largest organizations. Today they are an essential component of enterprises of all sizes. Surveys of CIOs show time and time again that BI is now a very high priority for organizations. I often tell people that I feel one of the greatest contributions Microsoft makes as a company is in taking complex technologies and making them available to a wide audience, often almost as commodities. The Microsoft BI platform does this in so many ways. An outstanding example is the range of complex technologies underpinning the data mining capabilities in SQL Server Analysis Services or the inclusion of advanced fuzzy logic concepts in SQL Server Integration Services.

I particularly wish to thank the authors for kindly giving of their time and talents to be involved with this book, my wife Mai for endlessly providing support for (and understanding) my workload, and Paul Nielsen for organizing and driving the book to completion. Whether you are a seasoned BI practitioner or a newcomer to BI, I know you'll find material in this section that will help you.

About the editor

Greg is an internationally recognized consultant, developer, and trainer. He has been working in development since 1978, holds a PhD in Computer Science, and is a Microsoft Regional Director. Greg is the country lead for Solid Quality Mentors in Australia (www.solidq.com.au). He hosts the popular SQL Down Under podcast (www.sqldownunder.com) and is a board member of the Professional Association of SQL Server (PASS), responsible for their global chapter program. Greg is one of a handful of people to have achieved a Microsoft Certified Master certification for SQL Server 2008 and regularly teaches SQL Server internals on campus in Redmond for Microsoft.

50 BI for the relational guy

Erin Welker

I have frequently been asked by database administrators (DBAs) how they can learn more about business intelligence (BI) and data warehousing. A skill set in database administration is a good base for data warehouse administration and business intelligence, which is why so many data warehouse administrators you meet are either ex-DBAs or perform double duty at their place of employment (I include myself in this category). The approaches have many differences, though. You could even say that the approach to OLTP database design and administration is completely at odds with the approach to designing a business intelligence solution. In this chapter, I will introduce some of the key terminology and give you some tips on starting down the path to business intelligence.

Business intelligence overview

Two general high-level methodologies are adopted in data warehousing. I have found Ralph Kimball's methodology of using dimensional modeling for data warehousing to be the most widely adopted approach in Microsoft shops. Bill Inmon suggests a more traditional relational design to data warehouses, which feeds one or more subject-specific data marts. I will admit my unfamiliarity with the Inmon approach, which is not to suggest that it is in any way inferior. I will simply say that business intelligence solutions that utilize the Microsoft BI stack tend to also adopt the Kimball methodology. As such, I will only discuss the Kimball methodology in this chapter.

Business intelligence results from an evolution of reporting, shown in figure 1. Some organizations still only utilize operational reporting, but some have implemented sophisticated data mining solutions.

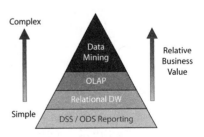

Figure 1   Reporting evolution

Terminology

Certain basic terms, many of which are defined differently by different people, are used in business intelligence. I will submit my definitions, which are based on my background, to serve as a reference for this chapter.

- *Data warehouse*—Aa relational store of data that serves as a basis for reporting queries and/or a source for OLAP cubes. It consists of tables that support multiple subject areas in the organization. It is often designed using dimensional modeling techniques and, in most Microsoft shops, is housed in SQL Server.

   This term is often interchanged with *data mart*, and in most cases data mart is more accurate. Data warehouse just sounds so much more substantial. I tend to use *data warehouse* even when referring to a data mart, because it tends to be used generically to cover both, and so that is the term used throughout this chapter.

- *Data mart*—Can be thought of as a mini data warehouse that is specific to a particular subject area. Subject areas tend to align themselves with organizational departments, such as Sales, Finance, or Human Resources.

- *Dimensional model*—Represents business data in terms of dimensions and facts. Dimensional models are represented as star or snowflake schema. (The section "Dimensional modeling" later in this chapter will cover this topic in more detail.)

- *Business intelligence (BI)*—Generally, a process and infrastructure that facilitates decision-making based on business data. BI is too often thought of in technical terms; it is far more driven by business.

- *Data mining*—The process of discovering valuable trends in historical data that can provide insight into future events, based on a predetermined set of factors. A well-known example is on Amazon.com, where books are recommended to you based on your past buying patterns compared to those of other customers who have purchased the same books.

- *ETL (extract, transform, and load)*—The process of moving data from a source system, usually online transactional processing (OLTP), transforming it into the data schema represented in the data warehouse, and loading it into data warehouse tables. ETL will usually also initiate cube loading. The transformation stage can include various processes, such as converting codes, cleansing the data, and looking up surrogate keys from dimension tables.

- *OLAP (online analytical processing)*—A process that allows a user to quickly analyze data using common techniques known as slicing, dicing, and drillthrough. In the Microsoft world, OLAP is provided via Analysis Services cubes.

Really, what is so different?

If you've had any exposure to operational reporting, you'll already know many of the differences between reporting systems and traditional OLTP systems. Some of the these are shown in table 1.

Table 1 OLTP versus reporting environment characteristics

	OLTP	Reporting
Queries	Few rows (1–50)	Many rows (millions, billions, or more)
Indexes	Few	Many
Query volume	Medium to high	Low
Updates	Small, frequent, dynamic	Large, infrequent, scheduled

The difference is even more fundamental. OLTP applications are designed based on a discreet set of specifications. Specific data is to be collected, and there are clear patterns about who will enter the data, at what point in the business process, and using what method. The first step to designing a business intelligence solution is to take several steps back to understand the business at its core: Why does it exist? What is its mission? How does the business plan to achieve its mission? What key performance indicators (KPIs) need to be measured to assess success? A business intelligence solution needs to be able to address not just the needs of today, but those of the future, and that can only be accomplished by obtaining a core understanding of the underlying business processes.

I remember a past client who had chosen to implement a replicated OLTP data scheme for all of their reporting needs. They were suffering from numerous repercussions of this decision, including tempdb capacity issues, slow query times, and the inability to scale. When asked why they were not open to discussion about a business intelligence solution that provided more efficient analysis via OLAP cubes, they cited a prior attempt at a BI application that only addressed the queries for which it was designed. When the questions (queries) changed, the cube did not contain the information necessary to respond, and the whole project was aborted. This is why it is so critical to model the data warehouse based on the business, not on the specific reporting needs of the day.

NOTE One of the hardest things for a relational DBA to come to grips with is the redundancy involved in data warehousing. It's disk intensive, to be sure. Often, a copy of a subset of the data is made for staging prior to loading the data warehouse, then there is the data warehouse itself, plus the cube store. This redundancy can be mitigated somewhat in the data warehouse design, but it's best to come to terms with the idea of redundancy as soon as possible. One exciting benefit is the potential to archive data from the operational system as it is loaded into the data warehouse, making the OLTP system more lean.

Approach

The following is a high-level view of how a business intelligence project should be approached. This is intended to provide an overview to contrast with the approach taken in typical OLTP development projects.

1 *Determine overall strategy*—The general approach to a business solution is to develop an overall strategy to the data warehouse, determining how departments interact with each other and developing a high-level plan for how each subject area will be built out. In practice, I find that most companies skip this step. Departments in an organization tend to vary in their readiness for data warehousing, and cooperation from all departments is critical for making this step possible.

2 *Address a subject area*—Each subject area should be addressed in great detail, fleshing out the relevant dimensions and developing one or more star schemas to represent the business segment. This is done by conducting interviews with business subject-matter experts.

TIP   One common pitfall I have found is clients insisting that the IT staff knows all there is to know about the business. It is true that they are intimate with the business rules that underlie the technology solutions that run much of the business, but that should not be confused with a core understanding of the business, including insights into where the business is heading. IT personnel are a valuable resource for knowing where data is housed and how to best get it into the data warehouse. The data model should be based on interviews with stakeholders within the departments represented in the subject area.

3 *Develop the dimensional model*—Developing a dimensional model that represents the business based on the information gathered in the preceding step is paramount in a successful business intelligence solution. It's important to get this step right. An indication of a well-designed model is its ability to accommodate changes easily.

4 *Extract, transform, and load*—When the dimensional model has been established, it is time to determine data sourcing, or how to best populate the model. ETL processes need to be designed to accommodate the initial loading of the data warehouse, as well as ongoing incremental loads, which will, hopefully, be able to isolate new data in the source system from data that has been previously loaded.

5 *Develop the cube*—Cube design usually closely follows the dimensional design, which is one reason for the focus on the dimensional design. Analysis Services provides easy mechanisms for understanding the dimensional model and building dimensions and measure groups.

The remaining steps involve data validation, the automation of remaining processes, and more. This is a simplified, high-level description of the approach to building a business intelligence solution. For more information, the best text I have found on the topic is *The Data Warehouse Lifecycle Toolkit* by Ralph Kimball and others (Wiley Publishing, 2008). Note that this book will only take you through the implementation of the relational data warehouse. For information regarding the implementation of Analysis Services cubes, as well as other things to consider when using the Kimball approach in a Microsoft BI implementation, check out *The Microsoft Data Warehouse Toolkit* by Joy Mundy and Warren Thornthwaite (Wiley Publishing, 2006).

Dimensional modeling

I'd like to spend some more time on dimensional modeling, because it is core to the implementation of a quality data warehouse. It can also be difficult to grasp for those used to modeling tables in third normal form. Why build a dimensional model in the first place? What's wrong with duplicating the source tables?

First of all, end users have a difficult time navigating tables in third normal form. A normalized model is intended to support the fast and accurate input of data, with minimal redundancy. OLTP table and column names are usually cryptic, and several tables may have to be joined together in order to create a query. The application has also built-in cryptic business rules that a user would have to know about, such as `WHERE ActiveInd = 'A'`, or `WHERE EntityCode = 'XYZ'`. Dimensional models make more sense to users because they more closely match how they view the business. They provide a flexible means of accessing the data. On top of all that, dimensional designs respond more quickly to queries that span large amounts of data. SQL Server often recognizes star schemas and optimizes accordingly.

Dimensional models are implemented as star or snowflake schemas. I will only address the star schema, because the snowflake schema can be considered a variation on the star schema. A star schema consists of from one to many dimensions (one dimension would be highly unlikely) that are related to a single fact table. The dimensions represent ways of looking at the data—the *who, what, where, when,* and *why*. The fact table has implicit foreign keys to each of these dimensions, as well as a collection of facts that are numerical. For example, a fact table may represent sales in terms of amount, quantity, tax, discount, and so on. The numbers in a fact table can then be aggregated, usually summed, across aspects of the dimensions to answer queries about what has happened in the past.

Let's take an example of a star schema that represents retail sales. The dimensions would be things like customer (who), product (what), sales territory (where), date (when), and promotion (why). The star schema might look something like figure 2.

An important thing to note is that the fact table joins to the dimension tables on surrogate keys, which are usually `IDENTITY` columns in SQL Server, intended to abstract the row from the business key. Always use surrogate keys (except on the Date dimension), even if you don't think you need one right now. Surrogate keys are useful in slowly changing dimensions and when a dimension spans multiple entities, each of which may assign distinct business keys. For example, Human Resources may use one

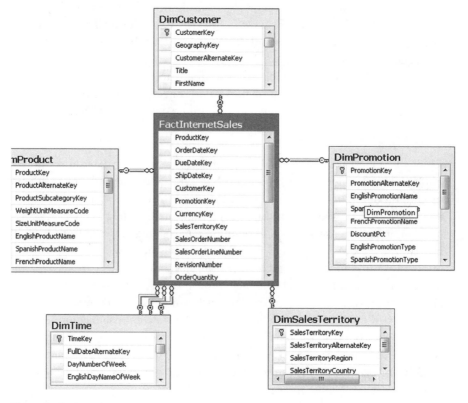

Figure 2   A star schema

key for an employee, such as a social security number, and a Sales system may assign its own business key to an employee. Using a surrogate key will tie the two together across applications, facilitating richer analysis.

TIP   Even if you are developing a dimensional model that currently supports a single department in the organization, be sure to keep the entire organization in mind to facilitate future enhancements. Shared, or conformed, dimensions facilitate analysis across departmental fact tables. For example, an Employee dimension might include employee salary, manager, and hire dates (Human Resource information) as well as sales region assignments (Sales information). Storing both sets of data enables the analysis of hiring programs and manager-mentoring effectiveness on sales performance.

Cubes, anyone?

You could stop after creating the data warehouse. Some do. Analysis Services, or any OLAP technology, requires a new skill set to develop and maintain cubes. But a cube solution vastly improves the analytical and usability factor in the resulting solution.

Users no longer have to know how to write T-SQL or be constrained by static reports. There are also a number of tools that consume OLAP data sources—Excel (shown in figure 3), PerformancePoint, Reporting Services, and Panorama, just to name a few. And the query response speed can go from many minutes (or hours) for a SQL query to seconds from a cube. The power of online analysis is the ability to quickly ask a question, get an answer, and then ask another question based on the first result.

Analysis Services cubes are specifically designed to retrieve thousands or millions of data points and aggregate them quickly. Some of this performance is accomplished through aggregations, which precalculate the data at predefined intersections of dimensions. Think of it as building several indexed views to provide summarized information in SQL Server. The difference in query time often differs in orders of magnitude.

There is a common misconception regarding where cube data is stored. Cubes have their own separate data store in addition to the data warehouse. This can be greatly minimized using ROLAP (relational OLAP) partitions, but this is universally considered a bad idea except for small real-time partitions, due to performance. MOLAP (multidimensional OLAP) is the preferred storage option, which results in a redundant data store that is specifically tuned for OLAP query performance. Cube processing is the activity that loads data into the cube from the data source.

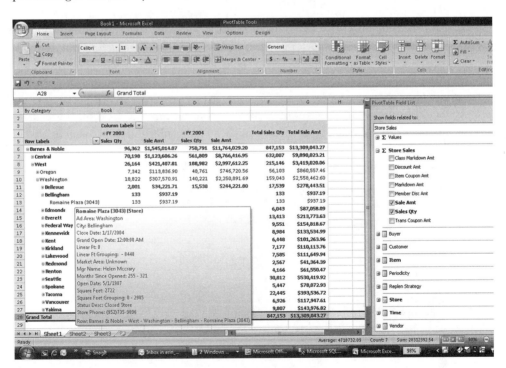

Figure 3   MS Excel 2007 Pivot Table sourcing Analysis Services cube

Resist cutting corners in regard to storing data in the data warehouse. It might be tempting to prune data from the data warehouse once it is contained in the cube, but this would remove your ability to reprocess the associated cube partitions, and that data would eventually be lost, because cubes must be reprocessed if associated dimension structures change. Again, the relational DBA approach is all about economizing on disk usage, but that mindset is at odds with the data warehouse implementation.

Microsoft BI stack

Microsoft provides all the tools required to implement a business intelligence solution, from the relational data warehouse store to the front-end analytics.

Microsoft's initial approach was to provide only the back-end tools, up to the delivery of OLAP cubes. They relied upon partners, such as Proclarity and Panorama, to deliver the front-end functionality. Over the last few years, Microsoft has completed the stack with the development of Business Scorecard Manager and the acquisition of Proclarity. Both of these products are now released in a single product called PerformancePoint.

The Microsoft BI stack is represented in figure 4.

How do I get started?

This chapter was intended to give you a basic introduction to business intelligence and to explain why it differs so dramatically from the traditional OLTP approach. From here, my best recommendation is to start the way I started, with a book I cannot recommend enough: *The Data Warehouse Lifecycle Toolkit* by Ralph Kimball and others. One of the things that I like about it is that it not only explains the *what*, but it also explains the *why*. I occasionally deviate from the approaches recommended in the book, but only after reading the *why* to be sure there was nothing I was missing. This book is not technical; it is more specific to the methodology, which is what is most

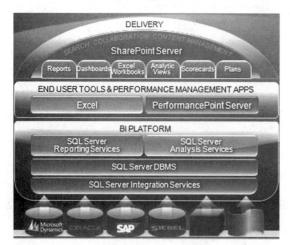

Figure 4   The Microsoft BI stack

lacking in technicians coming from an OLTP environment. It does contain some great information on dimensional modeling, including techniques for handling common scenarios that arise when trying to represent business data in a dimensional model.

It is difficult to make a universal recommendation about how to get your feet wet. One option is to develop your own cube to represent a solution to a problem. One of my favorite projects was to build a cube to analyze how disk space was being used on my computer. I have a difficult time identifying files that are duplicated in several folders, and building such a cube helped me identify where most of my space was going (I freed up about 30 percent of my disk space based on this analysis!). Another implementation could analyze server resource consumption. In fact, such a solution is available for download as a PerformancePoint sample (see "Scorecards and Dashboards for your IT Department" at http://www.microsoft.com/bi/department/department. aspx?id=tab1), so you can validate your approach.

If there is a data warehouse project in development or already implemented at your company, you may be able to find a way to become a team member and learn from other practitioners with more experience. And there are courses available from the major training vendors to get you started.

Summary

I hope you have gained some insight into the various aspects of business intelligence and learned how it differs from legacy OLTP applications. This should give you the fundamentals, so you can decide if this is something you want to pursue. I have found business intelligence projects to be some of the most rewarding in my professional career. Historically, IT projects have typically been about getting information entered into computer systems, so there is no greater reward than to see the excitement on a business user's face when they see how easy it can be to make some actionable knowledge out of years of stored data.

About the author

Erin Welker has spent 25 years in information technology development, management, database administration, and business intelligence. She began working with SQL Server in version 1.11, and Analysis Services, SSIS, DTS, and Reporting Services since their inception. Erin has consulted at several Fortune 500 and other well-known companies, developing business intelligence solutions with a specialization in performance. She loves to share her passion for SQL Server and BI through authoring and speaking.

51 Unlocking the secrets of SQL Server 2008 Reporting Services

William Vaughn

I want to share some of the Reporting Services technology implemented in SQL Server 2008—at least those features that make a difference to application developers. Thanks to your (and my) suggestions, Reporting Services is better this time. Thankfully, they left in almost all of the good features and added a few more. That said, there are still a number of things I would like improved—but I'll get to that. Yes, there are a few Reporting Services features that are still under development. These include the *real* MicrosoftReportViewer control that can process the second-generation Report Definition Language (RDL) produced by the Reporting Services 2008 Report Designers.

Why should developers care about Reporting Services?

Over the last 35 years I've written lots of programs and taught many developers how to build best practice applications. Many of these programs were simply ways to present data to ordinary end users or extraordinary corporate executives, so they could better understand, assimilate, and leverage the information being presented. Initially these reports were heavily processed and formatted data dumps to paper, which were often discarded as fast as the systems could print them. Later, reports were implemented as programs—often as Windows Forms applications, but more recently they might be based on ASP, Windows Presentation Foundation (WPF), or Silverlight platforms. Yes, sometimes developers were forced to use one of the early Microsoft and third-party Visual Studio report development tools, but after a period of frustration, some decided it was easier to take up a career in coal mining than to face the rigors of one of these troublesome reporting paradigms. All that has changed—mostly due to innovations in Microsoft Reporting Services.

Let's get started with an overview of Reporting Services in terms that anyone can understand. Later on I'll show how Visual Studio in one of its many manifestations can serve as a powerful tool to create your reports, get them deployed to the Reporting Services server, or include them in your ASP, Windows Forms, or other projects.

What is Reporting Services?

Reporting Services is just that: a service that runs (starting with SQL Server 2008) as a self-hosted service on a network server, as illustrated in figure 1. The SQL Server 2000 and 2005 versions of Reporting Services run as a web service hosted by Internet Information Services (IIS).

NOTE It's best if Reporting Services runs on a dedicated system because in high-stress production environments it can consume considerable resources that can hobble the performance of a DBMS engine sharing the same resources.

When a report is deployed to a Reporting Services service instance, its RDL file is compressed into a binary large object (BLOB) and stored in the SQL Server Reporting Services Catalog, where it waits to be rendered by a SOAP request from your application, the Report Manager, SharePoint Services, or by referencing the right URL.

Now let's look more closely at the Report Server. Reporting Services processes requests for reports as follows:

- *The Report Server* extracts the RDL by virtual directory path and name from the SQL Server Reporting Services report catalog. It's then decompressed (and decrypted) and passed to the Report Processor.
- *The Report Processor* works like a language interpreter—the RDL is the script that drives its operations. Its job begins by extracting the connection strings from

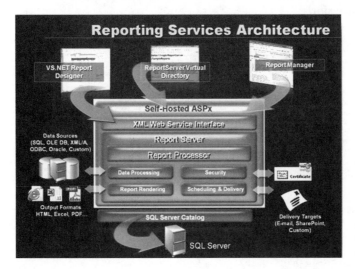

Figure 1   SQL Server Reporting Services architecture

the SQL Server report catalog tables and passing them, along with the queries and report parameters to the Data Processing Extension. Yes, a report can reference many data sources and can contain many queries—some of which might require input parameters.

- *The Data Processing Extension* opens the connection(s), passing in the appropriate credentials, and executes the report queries using any parameters specified in the RDL. Yes, the SELECT statements used to fetch report data or to populate parameter pick-lists are imbedded in the report RDL. The Report Processor subsequently merges data from the named columns extracted from the query rowsets with the RDL-defined report elements and passes the results to the Report Rendering extension.

- *The Report Rendering extension* works like a printer but with a number of specifically targeted output devices; the default is HTML so reports can be shown in Internet Explorer. (No, Reporting Services reports don't render consistently in Firefox or Chrome browsers.) In addition, in SQL Server 2008 the Report Rendering extension can also output the report to PDF, TIFF, Excel, CSV, and to Windows Word as well.

When an application or a user requests a report, the RDL might require the user or the Report Processor to supply the values for one or more report parameters. These parameters are often used to focus the report data on a specific subset or set display options as managed by RDL-resident expressions. Capturing parameters requires Reporting Services to render appropriate dialog boxes in the browser to capture these parameters as shown in figure 2.

NOTE   When starting the Report Manager for the first time (or after a period of inactivity), be prepared for a wait. It can take 30 to 90 seconds to get the Reporting Services functionality compiled and to render the initial menu of available reports.

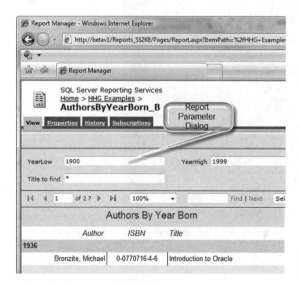

Figure 2   Report parameters as generated by the Report Processor

As I discuss later, when you set up your report with the Visual Studio Business Intelligence (BI) tools, you can specify as many query and report parameters as needed, as well as default values to use in place of user-provided values. After all required parameters are supplied, the user can click the View Report button to render the report—and repeat this as many times as needed. It's up to your code to make that process efficient—in some cases, the Report Processor might not need to re-run the query which can save considerable time.

Using Visual Studio to create an RDL report

SQL Server Reporting Services is available with all editions of SQL Server including the SQL Server 2008 Express with Advanced Services edition. Included with SQL Server is a version of Visual Studio used to create CLR executables and Reporting Services reports (among other tasks). I'll use this pared down business intelligence development toolkit to create, preview, and deploy a sample report. If you have any version of Visual Studio above Express, you'll be able to create and preview reports as well—even without Reporting Services, but I'll talk about that option a bit later.

NOTE   SQL Server Compact editions do not support Reporting Services. For more info, see http://www.microsoft.com/express/sql/download/default.aspx.

Setting up Reporting Services is an important step but we don't have enough room to devote a dozen pages to this process. Thankfully, it's easier than ever, so I don't anticipate that you'll have significant problems.

In this example, I'll be using Visual Studio 2008 SP1 that includes the ability to create Reporting Services reports. Nope, without SP1, you won't be able to do so, as SP1 activates all of the Reporting Services BI functionality. In Visual Studio 2005 you could build, test, and deploy reports. However, you can't open Visual Studio 2005 BI report projects in Visual Studio 2008 without SP1.

So follow along and I'll walk you through the process of creating your own report. Relax, it will be fun—I promise.

1   Start Visual Studio 2008 (SP1) and choose New Project.

2   Choose Business Intelligence Projects from the New Project dialog box.

3   Choose Report Server Project Wizard. This launches a wizard that I expect you'll use once. After that you'll reuse the RDL file it generates to create other reports.

4   Before clicking OK, point to an appropriate project save path and name the project. I'm calling mine SQL Bible Report. Click OK.

5   After the initial Welcome screen (where you clicked Next) you're ready to start defining where the data for your report is sourced. Sure, the data can come from anywhere—anywhere that can be seen with a .NET provider including the object linking and embedding (OLE) DB and Open Database Connectivity (ODBC). This means data can come from SQL Server, Analysis Services, SAP,

Oracle, a flat file, a third-party database visible with a custom ODBC driver or OLE DB provider, or even a JET/Access database.

6 Name your data source so you'll recognize it later. No, I don't recommend DataSource1. Next, choose the Type from the drop-down list. I chose SQL Server.

7 Fill in the Connection string by clicking on the Edit... button or type it in yourself if you're sure how to code it. I'm connecting to AdventureWorks2008.

8 Set the Credentials default to the Security Support Provider Interface (SSPI), which is fine for development. Peter (my coauthor of *Hitchhiker's Guide to SQL Server 2000 Reporting Services*) and I do not recommend using *trusted* authentication for production reports for many good reasons.

9 If you plan to have several reports in the Visual Studio project that use the same ConnectionString, go ahead and click Make This a Shared Data Source. Remember, the data source name you use here might be shared by other reports in other projects so check with your report DBA.

10 Click Next to open the Report Wizard's Design the Query dialog box. Enter the data source–specific SQL to return the rowset (just one) used to populate your report or click the Query Builder to get the wizard to help build it. This launches the ever-familiar Query Designer we've used for years. However, this time you're creating a report, not an updatable TableAdapter. This means you might not need nearly all of the columns or even the Primary Key columns.

> **NOTE** To make your report run faster and keep your DBA happy, be sure to choose only the columns needed and include a WHERE clause in your query to focus the rowset on only the data needed by the report.

11 For my report, I chose a few columns from the AdventureWorks2008 Production.Products table. I also set up a WHERE clause that returns rows where the SellStartDate is between a given range of dates as shown in figure 3.

12 After the query is done, click Next to proceed to the report layout dialog boxes. These give you the option to specify a Tabular or Matrix report.

Figure 3 Specifying the report query with a WHERE clause

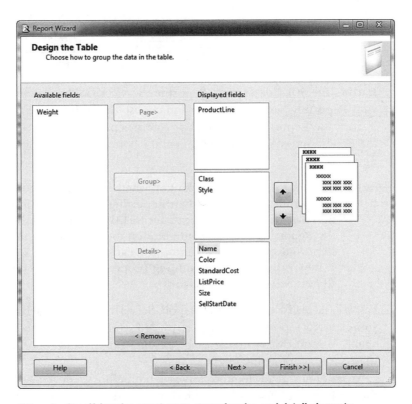

Figure 4 Specifying the report page, group breaks, and detail elements

13 Click Next to specify which column values are to be used to specify report page and group breaks as shown in figure 4. Note that I chose not to include the Weight in this report. This means the query will fetch data that's not needed—not a good idea. Click Next to continue.

14 Choose the Table layout mode (stepped or blocked) and whether you want sub-totals. Click Next to continue.

15 Choose the Table style (the color used as accents in the report) and click Next.

16 Stop. This is a critical point and if you don't get this right, nothing will work correctly. For some reason, the wizard has not detected that I installed a named instance during SQL Server setup and chose to use SSL web traffic encryption. This means you must change the Report Server path in the Choose the Deployment Location dialog box to point to the correct Reporting Services instance. In my case, I installed SQL Server 2008 on my BETAV1 system with the instance name of SS2K8. Note that the virtual directory (VD) is named ReportServer (the default VD name) followed by an underscore and the instance name as follows: BETAV1/ReportServer_SS2K8.

But before you jump in and change the Report server name, I suggest you see how Reporting Services Setup initialized the virtual directory name by

ReportServer Web Service URLs

URLs: http://BETAV1:80/ReportServer SS2K8
https://betav61:443/ReportServer SS...
https://betav1:443/ReprotServer SS2...

**Figure 5   Reporting Services
Configuration Manager Web
Service URLs report**

starting the SQL Server 2008 Reporting Services Configuration tool. Log into
your Reporting Services instance and choose the Web Service URL tab (on the
left). If the Report Server virtual directory is properly installed, it will provide
the Report Server Web Service URLs at the bottom of the dialog box as shown in
figure 5.

> **NOTE**   These settings are dependent on whether or not you had a proper
> SSL certificate in place when Reporting Services was installed. In
> my case, I created a certificate for BETAV1 beforehand. Notice that
> the Reporting Services configuration tool can also see my laptop's
> Reporting Services installation. You can click on these URLs to test
> if Reporting Services is running properly and to be taken to the
> Report Server virtual directory.

Yes, you'll need to change the Report Server name URL each and every time
you create a report from the Wizard. No, you won't want to run the wizard
again. In most cases you'll leverage existing reports and report projects where
these settings are maintained.

We're almost ready to move forward, but before we do, consider the name of
the deployment folder—this is where Visual Studio will deploy the report. Consider that anyone with access to an explorer might be able to see your Reporting Services Virtual Directory (VD) and the Report Manager, so as you start
creating reports, others will be able to see your unfinished reports as you learn
to use Reporting Services.

You can deal with this problem in a couple of ways. First, you should work
with Report Manager and your DBA to prevent access to reports under development. Next, it makes sense to create a directory to place the work in progress
reports, and use rights management to hide these from casual viewers. This
makes sure that unauthorized people don't run reports they shouldn't. More
importantly, it prevents people from bringing the system to its knees by running
reports that consume all of the available resources or those that are not ready
for use.

17   Now we're ready to click Next, which brings us to the last dialog box. Here you
can name the report, view the Report Summary, and choose to preview the
report after the wizard is done. Name the report, check the Preview checkbox,
and click Finish.

> **WARNING**   After you click Finish, you're done. You won't be able to rerun the wiz-
> ard to alter the report later.

Figure 6   Visual Studio BI project with the newly generated report

18   At this point you're taken back to Visual Studio where your report layout is shown in the Design Window, the Report Data window is exposed, and the (report) Preview tab is exposed. You are ready to execute the report and render it locally (as shown in figure 6).

No, you don't need to have Reporting Services up and running at this point—that won't be necessary until you're ready to deploy the report.

Sure, the Visual Studio BI tools include a Report Designer that helps developers (or trained end users) build reports by hand. No, this does not involve setting type and getting ink all over your clothes (been there, done that). It means working with a drag-and-drop paradigm to add appropriate report control elements to a report and drag columns from pre-built `DataSet` objects exposed in the Report Data window.

Using the Visual Studio 2008 Report Designer

If you're familiar with SQL Server 2005 Reporting Services, you'll see a number of important differences in the Visual Studio 2008 BI toolset. Note that there is no Data tab—it's been replaced by the far more sophisticated Report Data window, which is used to manage Built-in Fields (something new for Reporting Services 2008), Parameters, Images, and the data sources created for the report. Sure, you can pull in data from any number of data sources for a single report. There are other changes as well like the incorporation of the Tablix report element that combines functionality of the Table and Matrix report elements. This permits you to group by rows and columns as well as manage RichText data in your reports.

Dundas offerings

Microsoft Partners like Dundas have also helped Microsoft add new functionality to the BI tools. As you develop your reports you'll find an improved Chart report element as well as a Gauge element. Dundas also provides a host of data visualization products to enrich your reports that are exposed through the Reporting Services extensibility model.

After you're ready to see your report rendered and populated with data, click the Preview tab on the Report Design window. At this point, the local renderer in Visual Studio processes the RDL just as would be done by the Reporting Services service. It displays the report just as the user would see it (well, almost).

Managing report parameters

If your report requires any query (or report) parameters, the report is rendered with UI prompting dialog boxes to capture these values from the user as shown in figure 7. Where did these parameters come from? Well, remember that the query WHERE clause called for two dates to be provided before the query can run. When the Report Processor finds parameters imbedded in the report, it automatically generates the UI elements to capture the parameters—even if it means building an interactive drop-down list for acceptable parameter values.

NOTE   Report parameters don't initially have a preset default value. Wouldn't it make sense to provide default values or even a drop-down list of acceptable values? Unfortunately, the wizard has not evolved to the point of capturing default values for parameters. Thankfully, this is fairly easy to configure here in the Visual Studio BI tools or in the Report Manager.

You can configure how parameters are displayed, managed, populated, and validated through a Report Parameter Properties window. Figure 8 illustrates the dialog box exposed by drilling into the Report Data window and a specific Report Parameter. Here you're given the option to set default values, provide a hard-coded list of permissible values, define an expression to compute the default value, or specify a query to populate a list of permissible values (and more).

If you define default values for all your report parameters, the Report Processor does not wait to capture parameters before rendering the report. This means it's

Figure 7   The report rendered in the Preview tab

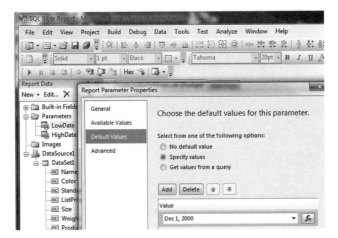

Figure 8 Setting a default value for report parameters

important to provide default values that don't return all available rows. Let users decide which part of the data they need to see.

NOTE Report performance is directly tied to the amount of work the Report Processor needs to perform to build and render the report. This means that parameters that focus the report query on specific, relevant rows are critical to a best-practice design.

Deploying your report

When you're happy with how the report behaves and appears to the user, you're ready to deploy it to a specific Reporting Services instance. Yes, you chose that instance name when you ran the Report Wizard, but let's assume that you did not use the Report Wizard to create your report (and I don't expect you will after you have built your first report). In any case, it does not hurt to double-check these settings in the report project property page as shown in figure 9.

Notice that you're able to set whether or not Visual Studio overwrites existing server-side data sources when deploying the report. This should be left as False as it permits your DBA to properly reset the data souce when it comes time to bring your report into a production directory.

Verify the TargetServerURL to make sure it correctly addresses your Reporting Services Server instance as I discussed earlier.

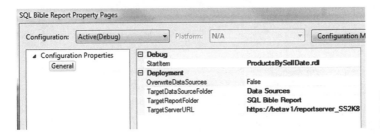

Figure 9 Setting the report deployment properties

Assuming the Reporting Services instance is started and accessible from your development system, you're ready to deploy the report. From the Solution Explorer window, right-click an individual report (.RDL) or the report project and choose Deploy. If the TargetServerURL is set correctly and the Reporting Services server instance is running and properly initialized, your report should deploy in a few seconds.

Using the Report Manager

After your report is deployed, you're ready to see how it is rendered in a browser by invoking it from Report Manager.

WARNING   If you plan to use Report Manager, it assumes you have not installed the SharePoint Services extensions. This configuration option is an either/or deal—you can use one or the other, but not both.

Again, I suggest using the SQL Server Reporting Services Configuration utility to verify that your Report Manager URL is correctly configured as shown in figure 10.

Figure 10   Verifying the Report Manager URL

I find it's easiest to click on the appropriate URL and save it in my IE favorites. Doing so launches the Report Manager as shown in figure 11—eventually (it can take 90 seconds to launch).

NOTE   I like to think of the Report Manager as two tools, one to view directories and launch selected reports and another to manage the reports and Reporting Services configuration.

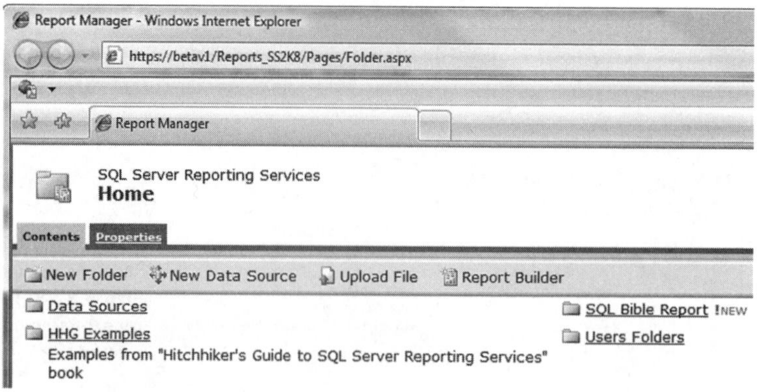

Figure 11   The Report Manager home directory

In this case we'll be navigating to the new SQL Bible Report path and launching the new report we just deployed. Click on the SQL Bible Report icon and choose Products by Sell Date (or the path and report name you choose for your report). This instructs the Reporting Services service to start the Report Processor, which processes the report and sends the rendered HTML back to the browser. The report that's shown in the browser should appear to be similar to the report previewed in the Visual Studio BI project but because these are two different rendering engines (one client-side and one server-side), you can expect some subtle differences—especially on complex reports.

In the 2008 version of Reporting Services, you can now render reports to Microsoft Word as well as the previously supported XML, CSV, PDF, MHTML, Excel, and TIFF formats. You can also navigate to a specific page, zoom in, find specific items, and print the report.

Using the Visual Studio MicrosoftReportViewer control

No discussion of Reporting Services would be complete without mentioning the latest implementation of the (still evolving) Visual Studio ReportViewer (MRV) control. Unfortunately, Visual Studio SP1 does not include an update for this control despite its name change. It's expected that the real version of the MicrosoftReportViewer control won't appear until Visual Studio 2010 ships. Be that as it may, it's still an important technology first introduced in Visual Studio 2005.

The MRV control was made possible by leveraging the innovative work done by the Microsoft engineers working on the Visual Studio BI tools. Because they had to create a stand-alone Report Processor that previewed the report on the developer's system, all they had to do was expose the reporting interface as a class (not to minimize the work required to accomplish this). The end result is the MicrosoftReportViewer control that developers can use to leverage some RDL reports. Visual Studio also contains report-authoring tools that create local client-side reports and persist them as Report Definition Language Client-side (RDLC) files. But there's a hitch. First, consider that there are three types of RDL report file formats:

- First-generation RDL as implemented by Reporting Services 2005
- First-generation RDLC as implemented by Visual Studio 2005 BI tools
- Second-generation RDL as implemented by Reporting Services 2008

Because there are few significant differences between first-generation RDL and RDLC report files, they are easily transmogrified. Unfortunately, there is no support for second-generation RDL local reports in the Visual Studio 2008 MRV control. However, you can display server-hosted second-generation reports. We expect this to be updated with the next major revision of Visual Studio or as a separate release from the SQL Server team sometime in 2010.

Let's see how the MRV control works. Consider that the MRV Report Processor does not attempt to run any queries. It assumes that you pass in the following (basic) items to the control before you can expect it to render the report:

- An RDLC file containing the report definition. Although an RDLC file contains information about the data source, the query and the columns it returns, and how these are mapped to report elements, the MRV control only uses this information to map columns of the data provided by the host application to the report elements.
- A data structure that implements IBindingList. This includes any .NET Data Table and custom data arrays.
- Any report parameters used in expressions imbedded in the RDLC.
- A pointer to the named data souce referenced in the RDLC.

These items are set via properties in the `ReportViewer.Local` report class exposed by the MRV control and are set and managed by your code. This means it's up to your client-side code to take on many of the tasks that Reporting Services would perform server-side. These include the following:

- Building a project (Windows Forms or ASP) that includes a MRV control bound to a specific RDLC report file. Yes, this can be assigned at runtime.
- Building the UI elements to capture user-provided or code-generated query and report parameters, capturing and validating the parameter values.
- When the report is to be displayed, establishing a client-side connection to the appropriate data providers—one for each unique data source.
- Executing data queries for each dataset defined by the report including passing in any query parameters and (typically) constructing one or more `DataTable` objects.
- Passing the `DataTable` object (or objects) to the MRV `Local` report class via binding interfaces.

Visual Studio makes the process of setting up a locally rendered report easy. After you create a local RDLC report (using the same Report Wizard as discussed previously), linking it up to a MRV control is a matter of choosing it from a configuration menu. If you use the Visual Studio Table Adapter Configuration Wizard to build the data souce (report data query), Visual Studio automatically saves the appropriate code to the `Form_Load` event handler in your project to fill the bound data table. This means you don't have to write any code at all—except the code needed to manage any input parameters.

There is a lot more to the MRV control and how to implement it in a variety of application scenarios than I have space to present here.

What's in Reporting Services 2008 for developers?

Let's visit some of the refined features that should make your job as a developer easier and a few unfinished features that will stick out on the road like a dead moose hit by that cement truck that passed you a minute ago.

Virtual directory changes

Reporting Services 2008 no longer needs IIS—at least not to host the virtual directories. This makes it faster (as IIS does not add an additional layer). You'll still want to set up a certificate to be able to access your reports via Secure Sockets Layer (SSL). Running a production report without SSL is like mentioning your big sister's phone number on the local country-western radio station.

Reporting Services 2008 has also changed the default virtual directory name used to reference the Report Manager and Report Server. For the two people in Cleveland that didn't set up SQL Server with a named instance, you can skip on down to the next tip. For the rest of you, when it comes time to address the Report Manager, or to deploy your Visual Studio BI Report Project, you'll discover the syntax shown in figure 12. Note that the deployment TargetServerURL name appends the instance name after `reportserver` with an underscore (_) instead of a dollar sign ($) which probably offended someone in the Ural Mountains and all IIS purists.

Notice that this dialog box is still not sizeable so if the server name or instance name is a bit longer, you'll have to figure out how to squirrel around with the arrow keys to inspect the current setting. This also means that when it comes time to get to the Report Manager (and you'll want to), you'll need to use this URL: https://<system name>/Reports_<instance name>.

Using SQL Server Reporting Services Configuration Manager

This is not a new tool, but it's had a facelift and its functionality polished up. This is where you bind the SSL port to the certificate you created with IIS manager. Anyone installing Reporting Services (any version post 2000) needs to visit this tool and walk through the icons to make sure everything is not only hooked up correctly, but to configure SSL, set up the email links and, most importantly, set and back up your

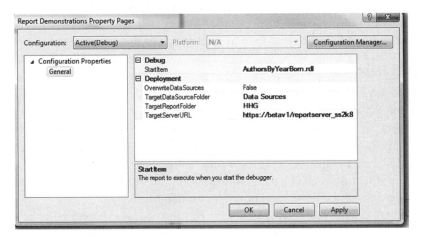

Figure 12   Setting the TargetServerURL

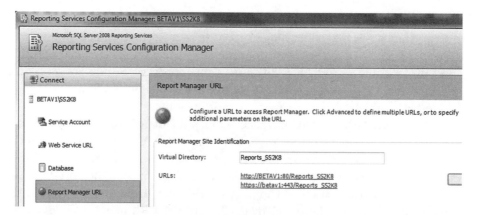

Figure 13   The Reporting Services Configuration Manager—setting the Report Manager URL

encryption keys. It's going to be pretty tough to get your reports back without these keys. I visited the Report Manager URL link and saw the page as shown in figure 13.

Exporting reports

Reporting Services still does not have an easy way to export your reports, so you can protect your work outside the scope of the scheduled SQL Server backup. Frankly, I would find it hardly worth the effort if I had to restore a single report, and my only option was to restore the entire Reporting Services database.

Thankfully, Jasper Smith has (apparently) mastered SOAP and the programmatic interfaces to Reporting Services and invented a (free) utility[1] to suck out the RDL and data sources and all of the other catalog items from the database. I tried this utility and although it initially did not seem to support SQL Server 2008 (2.0.0.0.11), I was able to get it to connect to my SS2K8 instance and script out the reports as well as create a Visual Studio BI project for each directory. This saved me a lot of worry and trouble to propagate my test reports to another system. The Reporting Services team tells me that this is on their radar and might appear in a future release.

Enabling My Reports

Not all of you will expose the Report Manager utility to your users, but those of you who do might also want to enable the My Reports feature to help users maintain a personal directory of reports based on their domain login name. For example, after I enabled My Reports, Reporting Services included a new directory tree for my reports that I could use to help catalog specific reports that I use on a regular basis. However, enabling this feature is a bit tricky. Unfortunately, the documentation is a bit sketchy, but it's not that hard after you know the secret handshake.

Start SQL Server Management Studio but instead of connecting to a Database Engine, choose Reporting Services from the initial Connect to Server dialog box. The

---

[1] Jasper's utility can be found at http://www.sqldbatips.com/showarticle.asp?ID=62.

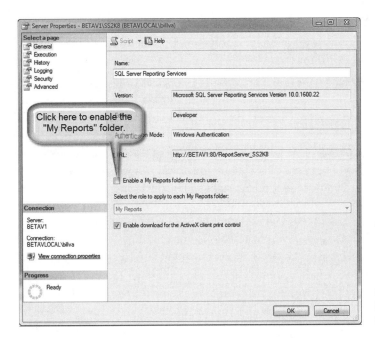

Figure 14   Setting Reporting Services properties

Reporting Services Object Explorer is one way to create specific Reporting Services Roles to which you can assign specific rights. This prevents all or groups of users from accessing reports that they should not see. But that's not why we're here—we want to enable the My Reports functionality. Right-click on the base connection and choose Properties. The dialog box shown in figure 14 should appear (except if you're a member of Congress, in which case seven identical copies will appear).

When enabled, you'll be able to set the role applied to each of the My Reports directories created on the server. Yes, that's right. As Windows users open the Report Manager URL, shown in figure 15, they will each have a new path created in the Reporting Services catalog for domain name.

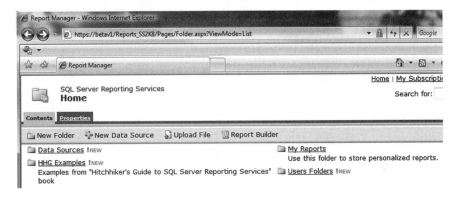

Figure 15   The Report Manager with My Reports enabled

Working with the Report Designer

Many report designers are available to Reporting Services developers. The Microsoft designers include the following:

- *The Report Designer used in Visual Studio 2003*—This designer has the Reporting Services add-in tacked on with binary duct tape. The designer can only work with Reporting Services 2000 RDL reports. This version of Visual Studio does not support the ReportViewer control.

- *The Report Designer used in Visual Studio 2005*—This designer cannot see or work with Reporting Services 2008 (at all) but it can import Reporting Services 2003 (SQL Server 2000) Reporting Services RDL reports and interface with Reporting Services 2005. It supports the first-generation ReportViewer control, which can cross pollinate with SQL Server 2005 Reporting Services RDL reports.

- *The Report Designer used in Visual Studio 2008*—This designer still cannot see or work with Reporting Services 2008 (at all) or even open Reporting Services 2005 projects. It still supports the first-generation ReportViewer control and can cross pollinate with SQL Server 2005 Reporting Services RDL reports.

- *The Report Designer used in Visual Studio 2008 SP1*—This designer can now work with Reporting Services 2008 and even open Reporting Services 2005 projects, which it converts to the Visual Studio 2008 format. It supports only first-generation ReportViewer control projects and can cross pollinate with SQL Server 2005 Reporting Services RDL reports but not Reporting Services 2008 RDL.

- *The Report Designer launched by the Reporting Services BI Tools*—This (Visual Studio) BI designer is specifically designed to work with Reporting Services 2008 and also Reporting Services 2005 projects and converts them to the Visual Studio 2008 BI format. It does not support Windows Forms or ASP development at all so the ReportViewer control is not an issue here.

Confused? Join the club. Yes, there are at least four people over in Building 35 on the Microsoft campus who understand the reasoning behind these evolutionary trends that keep breaking compatibility between versions, but that does not help us understand why we can't do what we've been told to do when creating Reporting Services reports.

The real story is, there is a SQL Server Reporting Services 2008 RDL rendering engine that solves many ugly problems seen in the first-generation RDL renderers (yes, there are several). SQL Server Reporting Services 2008's rendering engine supports the Tablix control (which isn't a report control at all), and lots of Rich Text functionality. That's good. The fact that the engine is faster and more flexible is also good. The problem is that the 2008 rendering engine and the Report Designers who build RDL to feed it create new and incompatible RDL files that can't be consumed by the old engine. That's bad—at least for the people who want to use the easy-to-develop-your-report BI tools to build these new reports and leverage the ReportViewer control in Windows, WPF, and ASP applications to deploy them. You see, behind the scenes, the Visual Studio 2008 SP1 ReportViewer control only knows how to render the old (first-generation) RDL-style reports. Sigh.

Thankfully, another upgrade to Visual Studio and the ReportViewer control to incorporate the next-generation RDL renderer is underway. I hope it ships before the new Boeing 787 rolls off the line and given that the machinists are on strike, it might have a chance.

Summary

Consider that reporting is a way of life for any serious (and many not-so-serious) application developers. Given how easy it is to create server-hosted or even client-hosted reports, it's easy to see how developers are leveraging these evolving technologies to reduce the amount of code needed to present data (and graphics) to end users. Consider as well that the Report Processor is designed to take on the responsibility of dealing with complex hierarchies and aggregates as well as parent-child relationships with little code to implement it. That's why I like it. It generates more solutions with less code that I have to write, debug, and deploy.

About the author

William (Bill) Vaughn is an industry-recognized author, mentor, and subject matter expert on Visual Studio, SQL Server, Reporting Services, and data access technologies. He's worked in the computer industry for over 37 years. In 2000, after 14 years at Microsoft, Bill stepped away to work on his books, consulting, mentoring, and independent training seminars. He's written over a dozen books, including *Hitchhiker's Guide to Visual Studio and SQL Server*, seventh edition, and *Hitchhiker's Guide to SQL Server Compact Edition*. He and Peter Blackburn also wrote the critically acclaimed *Hitchhiker's Guide to SQL Server 2000 Reporting Services*.

52 Reporting Services tips and tricks

Bruce Loehle-Conger

This chapter covers performance and design tips and tricks that I've picked up over the years. When you're through with the chapter, you'll not only know how to design reports with the best possible performance, but you'll also come away with new ways of solving problems. I guarantee that no matter how expert you are in Reporting Services (RS), you'll find something new in this chapter.

Performance tips

The first three topics all approach optimizing performance in the same manner: limiting the amount of data that the rendering engine is working on. For good performance, limit the amount of data processed by RS. Let the database engine do what it does best and use it to retrieve the smallest set of data that the report needs to render to the final state.

Filters versus query parameters

Filters can be handy, but whenever possible, stay away from using them. Filters require RS to first retrieve all of the data, and then RS applies the filter. Query parameters follow the opposite processing path: query parameters let the database engine first apply the parameters to the data, then RS performs rendering tasks only on the subset of data specified by the parameters.

Filters are useful when developing snapshot reports. In this case, it still makes sense to limit the data as much as possible, but filters will be necessary to allow users to apply report parameters at runtime to focus the report on the data they want to see.

Linked servers

Linked servers allow you to treat data that resides on a different server as if it's on the same server. But it's easy to lose track of the fact that the data isn't all on the same server. You may perform a query against a linked server in two ways. You can use four-part naming or you can use the OPENQUERY syntax.

The issue is how the database engine performs the processing. For the best performance, you want to build a pass-through query—the whole query should be passed on to the remote server for processing and have it return the result. Just like normal query processing, SQL Server has to make decisions on how to process the linked server data. The danger with the four-part nomenclature is that it's easy to create a query that causes the entire remote server table to be brought over the wire to SQL Server. If the table is large, you're in for a rude awakening. In SQL Server 2000, four-part naming was almost unusable. In SQL Server 2005, it improved dramatically. If in doubt, examine the query plan—it should show the processing being done remotely and should say "Remote Query" or "Remote Scan" and 100 percent. My testing has shown that even when the query plan shows 100 percent of the query being executed remotely, OPENQUERY still exhibits better performance. The code in listing 1 was executed against a table with 500K records. The OPENQUERY ran in .1 seconds and the four-part naming ran in 3 seconds.

Listing 1 Queries to compare performance of OPENQUERY and four-part naming

```
declare @MAXDATE datetime, @SQL nvarchar(255)

set @SQL = N'select @DATE = theDate from openquery(emerald,''select
➥ max(datestamp) as theDate from billing_recharge'')'

select getdate()as startdate

exec sp_executesql @SQL, N'@DATE datetime OUT',@MAXDATE out

select getdate()as afteropenquery

select @MAXDATE = max(datestamp) from emerald.iwts.dbo.billing_recharge

select getdate()as after4partnaming
```

Drillthrough instead of drill-down

This is a design choice that makes a big performance difference. *Drill-down* would be a wonderful UI choice if it weren't for the problem of performance. The issue here is similar to filters. All the data is brought over from the database. Even though the user might never drill down into the data, all of the data is still retrieved. Imagine your query returns an entire year of sales data. You show the per-week totals that can be expanded to show by day and the by-day expanded to show the detail information. This type of report would mean that all the year's sale data is being processed by the RS engine, which puts a large burden on your server.

A better way of handling this is to design a *drillthrough* report instead, because RS is optimized for this type of report. Plus, I've found that users find the interface quite easy and intuitive. Taking the same example as before, I'd create a report that summarizes the sales per week. Next, I'd add a column and put in a text box report item that says *By Day*, add an underline, and make it blue. Then I'd use Jump To Report to open up the By Day report.

Another advantage of drillthrough reports is that the reports you design are more likely to be useful when brought into Excel. In my experience, it's best to always keep in mind the efficacy of exporting the data to Excel. Using drillthrough reports accomplishes both tasks.

Data export

I've seen people try to use RS as a data extraction tool like SSIS or BCP. This isn't a good idea. But Excel is a powerful tool, and power users will always come up with new ways of looking at and analyzing the data. Invariably, users will want to pull large amounts of data into their spreadsheets for further analysis. What you want to do is make this as quick and easy as possible for them. This was a particular issue with SQL Server 2000, which was extremely slow at rendering in Excel format. Even with later versions of RS, if the data is large enough, you'll want the fastest way possible to get the underlying data from the report into Excel. The absolute fastest way to do this is to export in CSV format.

The problem is that RS 2000 and RS 2005 export CSV in Unicode format. When Excel imports Unicode format, the data is all put into a single field instead of splitting it into individual cells. The solution is to configure RS to render CSV in ASCII format instead of Unicode by editing rsreportserver.config as shown in listing 2. You'll need to stop and restart RS for the change to take effect. Note that this isn't a problem in RS 2008, because it defaults to ASCII.

Listing 2   Editing rsreportserver.config to render CSV in ASCII

```
<!--
  <Extension Name="CSV"
    Type="Microsoft.ReportingServices.Rendering.CsvRenderer.CsvReport,
➥ Microsoft.ReportingServices.CsvRendering"/>
-->
  <Extension Name="CSV"
    Type="Microsoft.ReportingServices.Rendering.CsvRenderer.CsvReport,
➥ Microsoft.ReportingServices.CsvRendering">
      <Configuration>
          <DeviceInfo>
              <Encoding>ASCII</Encoding>
          </DeviceInfo>
      </Configuration>
  </Extension>
```

Connection pooling

Creating the connection to the database is a resource-intensive task. *Connection pooling* reuses connections instead of creating a new connection each time. In order for connection pooling to work its performance magic, the connection string must match exactly. This includes the login. In order to benefit from connection pooling with your reports, you need to do two things.

First, your data source must be configured to use a specified user and password. Although this could be a domain user (Integrated Security=SSPI), I prefer to configure SQL Server to run in mixed mode, which allows me to use a SQL login. When I configure the data sources to use the same login, connection pooling kicks in. I give the special login read-only access and execute rights to whatever stored procedures I use for the report. This allows me to eliminate the step of granting rights to the database for every new user.

Second, depending on the protocol, you might have to enable connection pooling. If you're using ODBC, you'll need to enable connection pooling. Open up the ODBC Administrator. Go to the Connection Pooling tab, find the driver, and enable it. The ADO.Net OLE DB and SqlClient .NET data providers automatically use connection pooling.

Design tips

In the second part of this chapter, let's cover a number of design issues, beginning with a common one: the use of stored procedures and temp tables.

Stored procedures and temp tables

Using stored procedures and temp tables is the number one problem I address on the newsgroups. I use temp tables successfully and extensively with both SQL Server and Sybase. If you follow these guidelines, it'll work for you:

- If your field list isn't showing up, then in RS 2000 and RS 2005, go to the Data tab and click on the Refresh Fields button, which is to the right of the dataset drop-down box. If you're in RS 2008, pull up the dataset properties by double-clicking on the dataset and click on the Refresh Fields command button.
- Don't explicitly drop the temp tables. Let the temp tables fall out of scope. It's not necessary to explicitly drop the tables, as SQL Server will properly dispose of them when they're no longer needed. If you do explicitly drop them, the stored procedure won't work with RS.
- Have your last statement be a SELECT.
- If none of these work, then add SET FMTONLY OFF. Simon Sabin, a SQL Server MVP, provided me with this tip a long time ago. Here's his explanation: "The issue with RS is that the rowset of the SP is defined by calling the SP with SET FMTONLY ON because temp tables don't get created if you select from the temp table—the metadata from the rowset can't be returned. Turning FMTONLY OFF in the SP bypasses this issue." I've found this to only be an issue when you create a temp table in your stored procedure that's then filled with data from another stored procedure.

Excel merged cell solution

You create this beautiful report that your users export to Excel. They want to sort the data, but they bump up against the dreaded merged cell problem and they can't sort the data. What happens is that when RS renders to Excel, it tries to make the Excel spreadsheet look as close as possible to the original report. In doing this, Reporting Services ends up creating merged cells, which prevents Excel from allowing the sorting of the data. Two design solutions are available. One has to do with lining up free-standing text boxes so that the Reporting Services renderer doesn't create a spreadsheet with merged cells. I have a much easier solution: remove any freestanding text boxes such as those put in by the report wizard. I then add additional header lines to the table control, and put my report titles, parameter information, and so forth in these additional headers. You can merge cells together and this won't cause a problem on export to Excel.

RS 2008 renders reports to Excel more completely than previous versions. On one hand, this is good. Previously, if you had a subreport in a cell of a table object when you exported it, RS would put an error message in the cell of the spreadsheet. RS 2008 now renders the subreport correctly by putting the subreport into the appropriate spreadsheet cell. Unfortunately, this can cause the merged cell problem discussed previously. I haven't found a workaround for this.

Excel web queries and reports

Exporting to Excel is one of RS's strengths. It allows users to build on the data in the report by performing additional analysis or building their own charts. Eventually, a lot of work gets put into these spreadsheets and users want to share them with others on a wider scale. You have several options at this point. One possibility is to use the spreadsheet as the specification for designing a report that does the same thing. Another option is to pull the report data into Excel. Excel has a couple of ways to do this.

One way is to create a connection to the database and execute the query or stored procedure from within Excel. This can be done by either using Excel's support for creating the query or writing VBA code to pull in the data. Neither was what I was looking for. Creating the query required creating a database source name (DSN) on each computer. Writing VBA code required either embedding a username and password or using integrated security. As I said earlier, I try to touch the database as little as possible where it comes to security. I have only a single read-only user that's used by RS. That brings us to the possibility of using web queries.

Web queries are an Excel feature that allows you to enter a URL during the design process of the web query; then Excel presents the web page and you pick the part you want to bring in. I put in a URL in the same format as used for the Jump to URL field and pick the table of data I'm interested in. The first problem is that it only brings in the first page of data. This is resolved by setting the interactive height for the report to 0, which includes all the data returned with no paging. It works great. If all you want to do is perform a one-off data load when the spreadsheet is open, you have a URL that will work for your purposes. But if you want to allow refreshing the data, this solution won't work. What happens is the link being used by Excel is tied to the session being maintained by RS. Once enough time has passed that the session has timed out, Excel can no longer refresh the data.

The final piece of the puzzle falls into place when you add the `Format=MHTML` switch to the URL, telling it to render in MHTML format. Now everything works automagically, using no VBA code and without having to touch each desktop. Deploy the spreadsheet to Reporting Services and you now have a spreadsheet that all your users can benefit from.

Let's go over the steps one by one. First, when using web queries, you should create the URL with all your parameters hard-coded:

```
http://Servername/ReportServer?/Folder/
ReportName&rs:Format=MHTML&Parameter 1=ParameterValue
```

You can take some additional configuration steps in Excel. When creating the web query, you have the option to have it run automatically at startup. Instead of doing that, I prefer to create a macro with the name Auto_Open. This macro automatically runs at startup. You can also tie the macro to a shortcut. When data is brought into Excel, you have the option of how you want Excel to bring in the data. It can come in as straight text or full HTML. Right-click anywhere on the data in the spreadsheet and select Edit Web Query. Click on Options. Other configuration changes are available by right-clicking again and selecting Data Range Properties.

If your report can take a static parameter or no parameters, you're done. But if you want to have a parameter tied to a cell in the spreadsheet, this is also possible. Edit the web query and change the URL to

```
http://Servername/ReportServer?/Folder/
ReportName&rs:Format=MHTML&Parameter 1= ["SomeParamName"]
```

At this point, you get an error about a missing parameter. This is because of how Excel tries to refresh the data during the design process. Just ignore the error.

Next, right-click the spreadsheet again and you'll see a new menu option for Parameters. Click to configure the parameters. You can configure the parameter to prompt the user, put in a constant value, or tie the parameter to a cell. You can also have the data refresh automatically when the cell value changes. You can now get as fancy as you want with the spreadsheet—if the value of the cell is either a string or a number. Unfortunately, if it's a date, you have a problem.

When tying a parameter to a cell that contains a date, Excel passes the internal representation of the date, not a date format that RS will recognize. To resolve this issue, I've come up with two Excel macros that significantly help with adding parameters to the web query. The first is a macro I use to correct the URL. After the hard-coded URL string is working, I run the fix-up script shown in listing 3 to change the URL to include the parameters.

Listing 3   Script to change URL to include parameters

```
Sub FixupURL()
Dim strURL As String
Dim strT As String
Dim oQuery As QueryTable
    Set oQuery = Sheets("Sheetname").QueryTables(1)
```

```
    strURL =      "URL;http://Servername/ReportServer?/Folder/
ReportName&rs:Format=MHTML&Parameter1= [""SomeParamName""]"
    oQuery.Connection = strURL
    strT = oQuery.Connection
    MsgBox (strT)
End Sub
```

Next, use the macro shown in listing 4 to put in the date parameters and refresh the query.

Listing 4   Macro to add date parameters and refresh the query

```
Sub RefreshData()
Dim strQueryTableName As String
Dim strParam1Name As String
Dim strParam2Name As String
Dim oQuery As QueryTable
Dim strFromDate As String
Dim strToDate As String

    strFromDate = Sheets("Sheetname").Range("FromDateCellName")
    strToDate = Sheets("Sheetname").Range("ToDateCellName")
    Set oQuery = Sheets("Sheetname").QueryTables.Item(1)
    oQuery.Parameters.Item(1).SetParam xlConstant, strFromDate
    oQuery.Parameters.Item(2).SetParam xlConstant, strToDate
    oQuery.Refresh

End Sub
```

If you don't want to use the web query wizards, you can use CSV format, which is the fastest way to get data into your spreadsheet. As before, first get your URL string perfected. Next, use the macro shown in listing 5.

Listing 5   CSV alternative to web query wizards

```
Sub CreateWebQuery()
Dim strURL As String
Dim strFromDate As String
Dim strToDate As String
Dim strT As String
Dim oQuery As QueryTable
Dim i As Integer
Dim strSheetname As String

strSheetname = "Test"
Sheets(strSheetname).Select

For i = 1 To ActiveSheet.QueryTables.Count
    ActiveSheet.QueryTables(1).Delete
Next i

strURL =
➥ "URL;http://Servername/ReportServer/Pages/ReportViewer.aspx?/Foldername/
➥ Reportname&FROMDATE=[""FROMDATE""]&TODATE=[""TODATE""]&rs:Format=CSV"
'This code assumes a sheet called DateRange that has the two necessary
➥ dates
```

```
strFromDate = Sheets("DateRange").Range("FromDate")
strToDate = Sheets("DateRange").Range("ToDate")

Set oQuery = ActiveSheet.QueryTables.Add(Destination:=Range("A1"),
➥ Connection:="URL;")
With oQuery
    .Connection = strURL
    .Name = strSheetname 'Naming webquery the same as sheet
    .EnableRefresh = False
    .FieldNames = True
    .RowNumbers = False
    .FillAdjacentFormulas = True
    .PreserveFormatting = True
    .RefreshOnFileOpen = False
    .BackgroundQuery = False
    .RefreshStyle = xlOverwriteCells
    .SaveData = False
    .AdjustColumnWidth = False
    .RefreshPeriod = 0
    .Refresh BackgroundQuery:=False
    .Parameters.Item(1).SetParam xlConstant, strFromDate
    .Parameters.Item(2).SetParam xlConstant, strToDate
    .EnableRefresh = True
    .Refresh
End With
ActiveSheet.Columns("A:A").TextToColumns Destination:=Range("A1"),
➥ DataType:=xlDelimited, _
    TextQualifier:=xlDoubleQuote, ConsecutiveDelimiter:=False, Tab:=False, _
    Semicolon:=False, Comma:=True, Space:=False, Other:=False
ActiveSheet.Columns("A:A").EntireColumn.AutoFit

End Sub
```

HTML or Word documents

You might find it handy to have RS host file types other than reports. I've used Reporting Services to host both Word and HTML documents. To add a document to your project, right-click on Reports; choose Add, Existing Item; and point to an existing document file. Deploy the file just like you'd deploy a report. One little quirk has to do with deploying changes. In versions of Reporting Services prior to RS 2008, I found that I had to delete the document from Report Manager and then redeploy for any changes to make it to the server.

Server portability

At some point, you might need to roll out a new server. When that happens, you'll want to thoroughly test the new server and go live as easily as possible. Two steps are available that will greatly ease this chore. First, you need to design your reports for portability. The main culprit here has to be using Jump to URL. You don't want to embed the name of the server in the URL. Instead, use the global variable Globals!ReportServerUrl:

```
=Globals!ReportServerUrl & "?/SomeFolder/SomeReport&ParamName=" &
Parameters!ParamName.Value
```

I tend to use Jump to URL when I want the jump to render in a different format than the default HTML, or I want the report to be rendered to a different window. If the action you desire is the same as Jump to Report, and you want to reference a report that's not in the same project, you don't have to use Jump to URL. Instead, you can use Jump to Report. Normally, you enter the name of the report. Instead, enter the report folder and report name. This has two issues. You have to map the parameters manually, and you can't test it in the IDE. You have to deploy the report to test the link.

The other suggestion for making your site portable has nothing to do with report design. Instead, it's a systems suggestion. Register a virtual name for your server in the DNS. This name should have a different fixed IP address than your server. When you provide users with the link to Report Manager on your server or wherever you integrate RS into your solution, use this virtual server name.

Next, take advantage of the fact that you can configure TCP/IP for your network card to handle two IP addresses. To either add or remove IP addresses, first go to the properties of the TCP/IP stack. The General tab should have the fixed IP address of your server. Click on Advanced and then the Add button. Now, when you're ready to go live, you don't have to coordinate anything with any other group. Remove the address of your virtual server and add it to the new server. As an added benefit, this approach allows you to keep the old server around—just in case.

Embedding T-SQL in a report

Although it's possible to embed T-SQL in a report, this can be a source of trouble. The first step is to switch to the Generic Query Designer. In RS 2000 and RS 2005, you click on the Generic Query Designer button in the Data tab. In RS 2008, click on the Edit as Text button. If you want to write queries that can go against multiple databases, you have four choices:

- Use stored procedures
- Use an expression-based dataset
- Use an expression-based data source (RS 2008)
- Embed T-SQL in the report

I tend not to like to litter up the database with stored procedures when I'm doing a simple SELECT. Expression-based datasets are awkward. They don't return a list of fields, which makes developing a report a multistep process. Before I found out about embedding T-SQL, I created some expression-based reports. I'd first develop a report using static SQL and once the report was finished, I'd change it to an expression.

RS 2008 introduced expression-based data sources, which are a step forward. But I don't like to use report-based data sources—I prefer to use shared data sources, which brings me to embedded T-SQL. I used embedded T-SQL with RS 2005 because I could develop and test the T-SQL outside of the report. Embedded T-SQL has come into its own with RS 2008—where it now works with the Report Wizard, and where the report parameters are automatically created and all fields are recognized. Try the following T-SQL with the Report Wizard:

```
declare @SQL varchar(255)

select @SQL = 'select table_name from ' + @Database +
➡'.information_schema.tables order by table_name'

exec (@SQL)
```

User!UserID

Sometimes you might want to develop a report where you limit the data shown depending on the specific user requesting the report. Normally, I prefer to use security to determine who can run a report; therefore, anyone with the rights for the report can see all the data, but this isn't always what you want. I have some reports that anyone in our company can use as far as security is concerned. First, I create a table for the reports that lists the user, what reports they can run, and the parameter values for that report. The report dataset joins to this table. A key point here is that a query parameter doesn't have to be mapped to a report parameter. Instead, the query parameter is mapped to the User!UserID global parameter. This global parameter contains the user running the report. This means that you can't use this for subscriptions. Also, report snapshots can use the wrong UserID when accessed via web services or URL access. Report Snapshots work correctly with UserID only when the report is accessed via Report Manager. My advice is to only use UserID for on-demand reports. User!UserID includes the domain. If you don't want the domain, use the following expression when mapping the query parameter:

```
select RIGHT(@UserID, LEN(@UserID) - CHARINDEX('\', @UserID)) as UserName
```

Summary

Reporting Services is both a flexible and powerful tool, but there are a number of things we need to be aware of to derive maximum performance from our reports. Hopefully I've provided you with several ideas that you can use when building your next report.

About the author

Bruce Loehle-Conger works for a Fortune 100 company and works with data ranging from real-time control databases to SQL Server to Sybase. He has been working with Reporting Services since it was first in beta form and was one of the first two MVPs to be awarded for Reporting Services.

53 SQL Server Audit, change tracking, and change data capture

Aaron Bertrand

SQL Server 2008 introduces three new features for tracking data and object changes within the database: change tracking, change data capture, and SQL Server Audit. Based on the marketing information alone, it might be difficult to determine which, if any, would be useful for your specific scenario. In this chapter, I will compare the features, outline their pros and cons, and try to help you to decide which solution or solutions might work best in your environment.

What are these solutions used for?

Since shortly after the very first database was persisted to disk, database administrators everywhere have been asking questions like, "Who did what to my data, and when did they do it?" It is in our nature to be curious about the way users utilize our systems in general. In some specific cases, it is important to track down exactly when a piece of data was changed, and who was responsible for the change.

Before talking about the new features introduced in SQL Server 2008, it will be useful to briefly outline some of the key motivations for implementing an auditing or change tracking solution in the first place.

One reason is compliance enforcement. Depending on your industry, you may be required to adhere to regulations for data access and privacy, for example Sarbanes-Oxley, HIPAA, or PCI-CISP. Even if you are not required to do so by law, you may still have an interest in recording information about all of the activity on your server. (For example, you may be interested in identifying specific activity, such as a delete operation that nobody will take credit for, without resorting to a log reader utility.) In the past, this could be accomplished by placing the server in `C2 Audit Mode`, which is an all-or-nothing approach, or by using SQL Trace. Both of these solutions can be overkill if, for example, you only care about queries against the EmployeeSalary table, or updates to the OrgChart table. Although you could filter a SQL Trace to reduce the overhead, there are some scenarios that could lead you to miss events.

A related reason for implementing an auditing or change tracking solution is to answer the simple question, "Who is accessing which data in your system?" For a long time, users have been asking for a *SELECT trigger* that would allow them to log all (or selected) database access to a table or to a file. Auditing products can do this for you, but there is no universal way, with SQL Server alone (at least through SQL Server 2005), to pick and choose which table you want to audit for this purpose.

Another reason is to observe data trends, in the case where you don't have a nice big data warehouse to play with. Sometimes you will want to monitor values over time, for example the changing price of gasoline you are charging over the period of a week, so that you can correlate that with daily revenue during the same time frame. If your application is not currently set up to track values historically, then all you have at any given time is the current price. You can set this up manually with triggers, but it can be cumbersome to set up and maintain.

Yet another motivation for row-level auditing is for incremental data loading. You may want to mirror incremental changes to other environments, such as a data warehouse or a data cache server, without the overhead of database mirroring, replication, or needing to determine the deltas between large tables at runtime. In SQL Server 2005 you can accomplish this with database snapshots, but these place several limitations on the source database, such as requiring both source and snapshot to be online perpetually (and reside in the same instance), and reduced performance due to additional I/O operations to maintain the snapshot. Database snapshots also apply to the whole database and cannot be targeted at specific tables.

And finally, your semi-connected applications will often need to determine if potential updates are still valid, and can be applied without conflict. Ideally, your application should be able to ask the database a simple question like, "Has the row I'm working on been changed?" Currently, this is usually assisted by a ROWVERSION column, but this gives you an extra column in your table that can be difficult to work with. Some would suggest using merge replication for semi-connected applications, and although that is a valid alternative in some cases, it can be overbearing to set up and maintain for the average user.

What do people do now?

Before SQL Server 2008, people would use third-party tools, or write code themselves (usually with triggers), for auditing or change-tracking purposes. An article written several years ago, titled "How do I audit changes to SQL Server data?" shows how to use a simple trigger to maintain a log of user activity (INSERT, UPDATE, and DELETE statements only) against a specific table: http://sqlserver2000.databases.aspfaq.com/ how-do-i-audit-changes-to-sql-server-data.html. Here are some third-party tools that are commonly used for implementing change tracking and auditing:

- *ApexSQL Audit*—http://www.apexsql.com/sql_tools_audit.asp
- *Krell Software's OmniAudit*—http://www.krell-software.com/omniaudit/index.asp
- *Lumigent Audit DB*—http://www.lumigent.com/products/audit_db.html
- *Upscene Productions' MSSQL LogManager*—http://www.upscene.com/products.audit.mssqllm_main.php

Some of these are either not enough or overkill, depending on the purpose of the implementation. Over time, SQL Server customers have been clamoring for some of the functionality found in these tools to be included with the product. Microsoft has answered by providing these three new features with SQL Server 2008.

How does SQL Server 2008 solve these problems?

You can look at each of the three new features and determine which of the preceding issues it will help you solve. Assume you have a simple Employees table, which you want to make available to the payroll system, and which you want to monitor for changes by unauthorized individuals. Listing 1 shows how to prepare the schema and data.

Listing 1   Preparing Employees schema and data

```
USE [master];
GO

CREATE DATABASE [HR];
GO

USE [HR];
GO

CREATE TABLE dbo.Employees
(
    EmployeeID  INT PRIMARY KEY,
    FirstName   NVARCHAR(32),
    LastName    NVARCHAR(32),
    Salary      DECIMAL(13, 2)
);
GO

INSERT dbo.Employees
(
    EmployeeID,
    FirstName,
    LastName,
    Salary
)
VALUES
    (1,'John','Elway',300000),
    (2,'Sam','Adams',150000),
    (3,'Don','Mattingly',125000),
    (4,'Teemu','Selanne',113500),
    (5,'Aaron','Bertrand',62750);
GO
```

SQL Server Audit

SQL Server Audit adds a much easier and more flexible manner of auditing database engine events, compared to utilizing SQL Trace or the C2 Auditing feature available in previous versions of SQL Server. There is an underlying framework that allows you to configure audits at the server or database level, all using relatively straightforward T-SQL commands or the graphical user interface (GUI) components in SQL Server Management Studio. The auditing itself is built on top of the new Extended Events infrastructure, and can write audit records either to a file or to the Windows event log (Application or Security). The overhead of Extended Events is advertised as significantly lighter than the overhead of SQL Trace, but the impact of auditing on your system depends wholly on exactly what and how much you audit.

Reviewing the audited events is simple as well. For file targets, you can use the Log File Viewer utility inside Management Studio, or a new function included in SQL Server specifically for this purpose (fn_get_file_audit). If you target the Windows event log, you can access this programmatically through existing APIs, or through the event log viewer included in Windows. Note that this feature is available in Enterprise and Developer Editions only. (For a more thorough treatment of SQL Server Audit, you can start at the "Understanding SQL Server Audit" Books Online topic, located at http://msdn.microsoft.com/en-us/library/cc280386.aspx.)

The list of actions you can monitor with SQL Server Audit is expansive. At the server level, there are 36 action groups that are eligible for tracking with a SQL Server Audit, and at the database level, there are 15. (An action group is a set of actions.) An example of a server level action group is the DBCC_GROUP, which is raised any time a user executes any DBCC command. At the database level, an example of an action group is the SCHEMA_OBJECT_CHANGE_GROUP, which is raised whenever a user issues a CREATE, ALTER, or DROP operation against a schema. There are also seven individual actions at the database level: SELECT, UPDATE, INSERT, DELETE, EXECUTE, RECEIVE, and REFERENCES. And finally, you can audit an audit, using the audit-level action group AUDIT_CHANGE_GROUP. You can learn more about these actions and action groups in the Books Online topic, "SQL Server Audit Action Groups and Actions," located at http://msdn.microsoft.com/en-us/library/cc280663.aspx.

Now, for this table, if you wanted to monitor changes, you could do so by setting up an audit to the Application Log, and then set up a database audit specification for this table directly. Listing 2 shows the code to do this.

Listing 2 Creating a server and database audit

```
USE [master];
GO

CREATE SERVER AUDIT ServerAudit
    TO APPLICATION_LOG
    WITH ( QUEUE_DELAY = 1000, ON_FAILURE = CONTINUE );
GO
```

```
ALTER SERVER AUDIT ServerAudit
    WITH ( STATE = ON );
GO

USE [HR];
GO

CREATE DATABASE AUDIT SPECIFICATION HRAudit
FOR SERVER AUDIT ServerAudit
ADD ( SELECT, INSERT, UPDATE, DELETE ON dbo.Employees BY [public] )
WITH ( STATE = ON );
GO
```

When reviewing audit information (whether in a file, or in the event log), there is a variety of information available to you, including the time of the action, the session_id (SPID) of the user that performed the action, the database, server and object that was the target of the action, and whether or not the action succeeded. For a full listing of the columns written to an audit row, see the Books Online topic, "SQL Server Audit Records," located at http://msdn.microsoft.com/en-us/library/cc280545.aspx. I was disappointed to see that host name and/or IP address of the session_id is not recorded. This can be important information in some instances, and is difficult to determine after the session has disconnected from the server. For example, if SQL Authentication is enabled, and the sa (or another sysadmin) password is commonly known, then anyone can connect that way via their own machine, and be relatively untraceable.

Another important note here is that the type of action (for example, SELECT or ALTER) is recorded, but in the case of SELECT or DML queries, none of the data involved is included. For example, if you run the statement in listing 3, the event log entry will look like listing 4 (I've left out some of the columns).

Listing 3   Updating the Employees table

```
UPDATE dbo.Employees
    SET Salary = Salary * 1.8
    WHERE EmployeeID = 5;
```

Listing 4   Event log entry for the UPDATE command in listing 3

```
Log Name:      Application
User:          N/A
Event ID:      33205
Audit event:   event_time:2008-10-05 18:14:31.3784745
action_id: UP
session_id: 56
session_server_principal_name: sa
server_instance_name: SENTINEL\SQL2008
database_name: HR
schema_name: dbo
object_name: Employees
statement: UPDATE [dbo].[Employees] set [Salary] = [Salary]*@1  WHERE
    [EmployeeID]=@2
```

(Note that you may also see other events in the event log corresponding to the auditing activity itself.)

Because the literal values in the statement are replaced by parameter placeholders, and because the previous version of the data is not included, it is going to be difficult to find the entries where salaries were increased. Also, the information in the event log entry does not include the host name and/or IP address of the computer that issued the statement. So, if you are using SQL Authentication and your developers share a single login, it will be difficult with auditing alone to figure out who performed this update. You can work your way around this by adding the SUCCESSFUL_LOGIN_GROUP to the Server Audit Specification, as shown in listing 5.

Listing 5   Creating a Server Audit with the SUCCESSFUL_LOGIN_GROUP

```
USE [master];
GO

CREATE SERVER AUDIT SPECIFICATION CaptureLogins
FOR SERVER AUDIT ServerAudit
ADD ( SUCCESSFUL_LOGIN_GROUP )
WITH ( STATE = ON );
GO
```

Once you do this, you will have login records in the log or file that you can correlate with session_id and event_time to the relevant database audit activity. The successful login entry will have (in addition to session_id and other data observed above) host name information in the following form, under the Additional information field:

```
Additional information:<action_info...>...
<address>local machine / host name / IP</address>
```

If you are using Windows Authentication, on the other hand, then this seems like a reasonable way to capture exactly who executed the statement (without having to correlate to login events), but not necessarily what values they passed in. Take the case where you find that Employee 5's salary has been increased from $100,000 to $250,000. Three such events appear in the Application Log, from three different users, with the exact same UPDATE statement. The first could have updated the salary to $250,000, and the other two could have left it that way (by explicitly defining $250,000 in their UPDATE statement, even though it did not ultimately change the data in the table). Or, the increment could have been performed by the second or third person, or each person could have increased the salary by $50,000. There are millions of other possible permutations, and this is a simple case. Imagine trying to unravel this mystery on a busy system with thousands of simultaneous users all affecting the same table.

Before moving on to the next section, if you have created the sample code above, you can remove it using the code in listing 6.

Listing 6   Cleaning up the audit specification

```
USE [HR];
GO
IF EXISTS
(
    SELECT 1
        FROM sys.database_audit_specifications
        WHERE name = 'HRAudit'
)
BEGIN
    ALTER DATABASE AUDIT SPECIFICATION HRAudit
    WITH (STATE = OFF);

    DROP DATABASE AUDIT SPECIFICATION HRAudit;
END
GO
USE [master];
GO
IF EXISTS
(
    SELECT 1
        FROM sys.server_audit_specifications
        WHERE name = 'CaptureLogins'
)
BEGIN
    ALTER SERVER AUDIT SPECIFICATION 'CaptureLogins'
    WITH (STATE = OFF);

    DROP SERVER AUDIT SPECIFICATION 'CaptureLogins';
END
GO
IF EXISTS
(
    SELECT 1
        FROM sys.server_audits
        WHERE name = 'ServerAudit'
)
BEGIN
    ALTER SERVER AUDIT ServerAudit
    WITH (STATE = OFF);

    DROP SERVER AUDIT ServerAudit;
END
GO
```

Change tracking

Change tracking is a feature that adds the ability to determine, at a glance, which rows in a table have changed in a specified period of time. This can be useful for synchronizing data between the primary database and a middle-tier data cache, and for allowing semi-connected applications to detect conflicts when updates have been made on both sides. Change tracking is meant to allow you to identify the rows that changed, but does not keep any information about the values that were changed (for example, a previous version of the row). Change tracking occurs synchronously, so there is some overhead to the process. In general, the overhead is equivalent to the maintenance costs of adding an additional nonclustered index to the table.

The process assumes that you can always get the current version of the row directly from the table, and that you only care about knowing whether or not a row has changed. (Change tracking is described more in-depth in Books Online, starting at the topic, "Change Tracking," at http://msdn.microsoft.com/en-us/library/cc280462.aspx.)

To set up change tracking on a table, the table must have a primary key, and you must first enable the feature at the database level. (Books Online also suggests that the database must be at least at a compatibility level of 90, and that snapshot isolation is enabled.) Using the HR database and the dbo.Employees table created in the previous section, you can enable change tracking as shown in listing 7.

Listing 7   Enabling change tracking

```
ALTER DATABASE HR SET ALLOW_SNAPSHOT_ISOLATION ON;

ALTER DATABASE HR SET CHANGE_TRACKING = ON
(CHANGE_RETENTION = 3 DAYS, AUTO_CLEANUP = ON);
GO

USE HR;
GO

ALTER TABLE dbo.Employees
ENABLE CHANGE_TRACKING
WITH (TRACK_COLUMNS_UPDATED = OFF);
GO
```

At the database level, the option CHANGE_RETENTION indicates how long you keep information about rows that have changed. If the applications last checked for changed data before that period started, then they will need to proceed as if the entire table is brand new (so a caching application, for example, will need to reload the entire table and start from scratch). AUTO_CLEANUP is the option that specifies whether this periodic purging should take place, and it can be disabled for troubleshooting purposes. Although this sounds like something that requires SQL Server Agent, it is handled by an internal background task. It will work on all editions of SQL Server, including Express Edition, with or without SQL Server Agent enabled.

At the table level, the TRACK_COLUMNS_UPDATED option is used to specify whether the system should store information about which columns were changed, or store the fact that the row was changed. The former can be useful for an application that tries to synchronize or cache data from a table that contains both an INT column and a LOB column (for example, VARCHAR(MAX)). Instead of pulling an identical copy of the LOB column for a row that changed, it can ignore that column and keep its local copy if it knows that it was not a part of any update that has happened since it was last loaded.

Once change tracking is enabled, what an application can do is connect to the database, and determine the current baseline version of the table. This is a BIGINT value that is returned by calling the new function CHANGE_TRACKING_CURRENT_VERSION() (this represents the most recent committed transaction). Once the application knows this value, it can load all of the data from the table, and then can check for further updates later using the CHANGETABLE() function. This function will return a set of data representing any rows that have changed in the specified table since the baseline version retrieved above. The following is all in T-SQL, but you can envision how an application would use the same logic. Open two new query windows in Management Studio, connected to the HR database, and run the code in listing 8.

Listing 8   Determining (and updating) the baseline version of a table

```
SET TRANSACTION ISOLATION LEVEL SNAPSHOT;

-- Check the current baseline:
SELECT Baseline = CHANGE_TRACKING_CURRENT_VERSION();

-- Load the current version of the table:
SELECT EmployeeID, FirstName, LastName, Salary FROM dbo.Employees;

-- Now, switch to the second query window, and make some updates to the
    table:
UPDATE dbo.Employees SET LastName = 'Kinison' WHERE EmployeeID = 2;

DELETE dbo.Employees WHERE EmployeeID = 5;

INSERT dbo.Employees
(
    EmployeeID, FirstName, LastName, Salary
)
SELECT
    6, 'Kirby', 'Quigley', 62500;
```

Listing 9 shows the code to retrieve the changes made to the Employees table. Replace <x> with the result from the baseline query in listing 8.

Listing 9   Retrieving changes to the Employees table

```
SELECT
    NewBaseLine = CHANGE_TRACKING_CURRENT_VERSION(),
    cv = SYS_CHANGE_VERSION,
    ccv = SYS_CHANGE_CREATION_VERSION,
    op = SYS_CHANGE_OPERATION,
    EmployeeID
FROM CHANGETABLE(CHANGES dbo.Employees, <x>) AS ChT;
```

The results should look something like this:

```
NewBaseLine cv ccv   op EmployeeID
3            3  NULL  U  2
3            2  NULL  D  5
3            1  1     I  6
```

Now, the application can use this output to determine which of the following it needs to do:

- Reload the data from the row for EmployeeID 2, because it has been updated since the last time it was loaded.
- Load the new row for EmployeeID 6, because it has been created since the table was last loaded.
- Remove the row for EmployeeID 5 from its local cache, because it has been deleted.
- Record the new baseline value (3) as it will need to use this as the version to check against the next time it polls for changes.

Note that change tracking does not record any information about the user who made the change. It only records the fact that a row changed. But as with SQL Server Audit, there are ways around this limitation. SQL Server 2008 supports new syntax to allow change tracking to add some contextual information to the DML statement, allowing that data to be stored along with other details of the change. This was intended to provide an application the ability to differentiate between its own updates from those of other applications, but you can use it for whatever other devious purposes you can dream up. For example, as shown in listing 10, you can easily add information such as host name and user name using an INSTEAD OF UPDATE TRIGGER, by utilizing the new WITH CHANGE_TRACKING_CONTEXT() construct, in order to store information about users performing updates to your table.

Listing 10 Using WITH CHANGE_TRACKING_CONTEXT() in an INSTEAD OF trigger

```
CREATE TRIGGER dbo.AppendEmployeeUpdates
ON dbo.Employees
INSTEAD OF UPDATE
AS
BEGIN
    SET NOCOUNT ON;

    DECLARE @i VARBINARY(128);

    SET @i = CONVERT
    (
        VARBINARY(128), SUSER_SNAME() + '|' + HOST_NAME()
    );

    WITH CHANGE_TRACKING_CONTEXT (@i)
    UPDATE e
        SET e.FirstName = i.FirstName,
            e.LastName  = i.LastName,
            e.Salary    = i.Salary
        FROM dbo.Employees e
        INNER JOIN inserted i
        ON e.EmployeeID = i.EmployeeID;
END
GO
```

In this case, because you are not tracking individual column updates, you don't have to worry about only updating those columns that have changed. If you do implement a solution where individual columns matter, you might want more complex logic such that the trigger only touches the base table columns that should now contain different values. And for an even more bulletproof trigger, you would also want to handle the case where the primary key might change (even though, in theory, this should never happen). You could do this in a stored procedure instead, if you can prevent direct updates to the table itself, and enforce all access via stored procedures. That is possible in some environments, but not all.

Once the trigger is in place, you can run the following UPDATE statement:

```
UPDATE dbo.Employees SET LastName = 'Malone' WHERE EmployeeID = 2;
```

And now when you call the CHANGETABLE function, as shown in listing 11, you can add a new column that will return that contextual information (assuming the existing baseline was 3 after the above statements).

Listing 11   Calling the CHANGETABLE function

```
SELECT
    NewBaseLine = CHANGE_TRACKING_CURRENT_VERSION(),
    [user|host] = CONVERT(NVARCHAR(128), SYS_CHANGE_CONTEXT),
    cv = SYS_CHANGE_VERSION,
    ccv = SYS_CHANGE_CREATION_VERSION,
    op = SYS_CHANGE_OPERATION,
    EmployeeID
FROM CHANGETABLE(CHANGES dbo.Employees, 3) AS ChT;

-- results:
NewBaseLine user|host                cv  ccv   op EmployeeID
4              SENTINEL\Aaron|SENTINEL 11  NULL  U  2
```

Arguably, you could also use the trigger to store the old and new values off in a table somewhere for deferred analysis. But that would require you to manually create tables to capture all of that information, and come up with your own cleanup mechanism. And, without spoiling any surprises, you would be duplicating the functionality of another feature added in SQL Server 2008.

Before proceeding, you can disable change tracking on the HR database and the dbo.Employees table using the code in listing 12.

Listing 12   Disabling change tracking

```
USE [HR];
GO

ALTER TABLE dbo.Employees
DISABLE CHANGE_TRACKING;

ALTER DATABASE HR
SET CHANGE_TRACKING = OFF;
```

Change data capture

Change data capture (CDC) is similar to change tracking in that it captures information about changes to data. But the information it captures (and how) is significantly different. Instead of capturing the primary key for each row that has changed, it records the data that has changed, for all columns, or for the subset of columns you specify. It records all of the data for INSERTs and DELETEs, and in the case of UPDATEs, it records both the before and after image of the row. And it does this by periodically retrieving data from the SQL transaction log, so the activity does not interfere directly with your OLTP processes. It does require that SQL Server Agent is enabled and running.

The primary motivation for including CDC in SQL Server 2008 was to facilitate an easier process for extract, transform, and load (ETL) applications. Making all of the changed data available separately allows the application to pull only the updated data, without having to go to the base tables for the data (or to verify timestamp columns or perform expensive joins to determine deltas). You can investigate CDC in much more depth starting with the Books Online topic, "Overview of Change Data Capture," located at http://msdn.microsoft.com/en-us/library/cc627397.aspx.

To set up CDC, you must be running Enterprise or Developer Edition, and you must enable it at the database level first, and then for each table you want to capture. Note that unlike SQL Server Audit and change tracking, CDC features are enabled and disabled via system stored procedure calls. Using the same HR database and dbo.Employees table as in previous sections, listing 13 shows the commands necessary to start capturing data changes.

Listing 13 Enabling a database and table for change tracking

```
USE HR;
GO

EXEC sys.sp_cdc_enable_db;
GO

EXEC sys.sp_cdc_enable_table
    @source_schema = N'dbo',
    @source_name   = N'Employees',
    @supports_net_changes = 1,
    @role_name = NULL;
GO
```

The first two parameters to the enable_table stored procedure are self-explanatory, but the last two are not. The @supports_net_changes parameter dictates whether the changed data can be retrieved as a data set that includes one row per key value, summarizing all of the changes that took place in the indicated timeframe (in this way, it works similarly to change tracking, but you will also see the data in each column in addition to the primary key value). Note that to support net changes, the source table must have a primary key or a unique index defined. You will still be able to investigate each individual change, but if you look at the net, this will allow you to perform one DML statement on the target instead of multiple, in the case where your extract, transform, and load (ETL) program is replicating changes to another system. The @role_name parameter is used to specify who can access the changed data table. This can be a fixed server role, a database role, or left as NULL (in which case, sysadmin and db_owner have full access, and other users inherit their permissions from the base table).

The sys.sp_cdc_enable_table stored procedure has five other optional parameters. One is called @captured_column_list, which allows you to capture only changes to a specific subset of the columns. For example, you may not want to capture VARCHAR(MAX) or VARBINARY(MAX) contents, when all that has changed is a BIT column. The other is @filegroup_name, which lets you place the captured data on a filegroup other than PRIMARY/DEFAULT. The other three are @capture_instance, which allows you to specify a name for your CDC instance (because you can have multiple captures on the same table); @index_name, allowing you to specify an unique index instead of the primary key; and @allow_partition_switch, which lets you dictate whether partition switches are allowed against the source table. The @capture_instance parameter can be particularly useful in preventing the system from trying to create conflicting names for the capture instance table. For example, if you have a table called dbo_foo.bar and another table called dbo.foo_bar, enabling both for CDC, without specifying a value for @capture_instance, will fail. This is because CDC tries to name both capture tables "dbo_foo_bar." Although this is a fairly contrived case, if in doubt, use the @capture_instance parameter to ensure you have unique names.

To retrieve information about data changes to a table, you use the new CDC functions cdc.fn_cdc_get_all_changes_<capture_instance> and, if you have enabled net changes, cdc.fn_cdc_get_net_changes_<capture_instance>. These procedures require from and to parameters, but they are not based on time; instead you must determine the range of log sequence numbers (LSNs) that you wish to query. To obtain this information, you can use the function sys.fn_cdc_map_time_to_lsn.

Now that CDC is enabled for the dbo.Employees table (make sure once again that SQL Server Agent is running), you can make some changes to the data, and see how you (or your applications) might query for the individual or net changes. Run the DML statements in listing 14.

Listing 14   Inserting data into the Employees table

```
SELECT CURRENT_TIMESTAMP;

INSERT dbo.Employees
(
   EmployeeID,
   FirstName,
   LastName,
   Salary
)
SELECT
   7,
   'Howard',
```

```
    'Jones',
    80000;

UPDATE dbo.Employees SET LastName = 'Donaldson' WHERE EmployeeID = 3;

UPDATE dbo.Employees SET Salary = Salary * 2 WHERE EmployeeID = 4;

DELETE dbo.Employees WHERE EmployeeID = 6;

UPDATE dbo.Employees SET LastName = 'Stern' WHERE EmployeeID = 7;

UPDATE dbo.Employees SET LastName = 'Malone' WHERE EmployeeID = 3;
```

Be sure to copy the result from the very first line in the query. You will need this to determine the range of LSNs you will need to pull from the CDC table. Now you can run the query in listing 15.

Listing 15   Query against (and results from) a change data capture function

```
DECLARE
    @start DATETIME,
    @end   DATETIME,
    @lsn_A BINARY(10),
    @lsn_B BINARY(10);

SELECT
    @start = '<plug in the value from above>',
    @end = CURRENT_TIMESTAMP,
    @lsn_A = sys.fn_cdc_map_time_to_lsn('smallest greater than', @start),
    @lsn_B = sys.fn_cdc_map_time_to_lsn('largest less than', @end);

SELECT operation = CASE __$operation
    WHEN 1 THEN 'D'
    WHEN 2 THEN 'I'
    WHEN 4 THEN 'U' ELSE NULL END,
    EmployeeID, FirstName, LastName, Salary
FROM cdc.fn_cdc_get_all_changes_dbo_Employees(@lsn_A, @lsn_B, 'all');

-- result:
Operation EmployeeID FirstName LastName    Salary
I         7          Howard    Jones        80000.00
U         3          Don       Donaldson   125000.00
U         4          Teemu     Selanne     227000.00
D         6          Kirby     Quigley      62500.00
U         7          Howard    Stern        80000.00
U         3          Don       Malone      125000.00
```

This result set does not include the before images of rows affected by UPDATE statements, because it is intended to be used to make a target data source look like the source. Hopefully you can see here that it would be easy to reconstruct all of the DML statements, in order to apply the same changes to another table that looked identical to this one before you made changes. If you change the final SELECT to use the get_net_changes function instead, as shown in listing 16, you can see that the set is compressed. Only the values necessary to make the target table look like the source (with one row per key) are included.

Listing 16   Using the `get_net_changes` function

```
SELECT operation = CASE __$operation
    WHEN 1 THEN 'D'
    WHEN 2 THEN 'I'
    WHEN 4 THEN 'U' ELSE NULL END,
    EmployeeID, FirstName, LastName, Salary
FROM cdc.fn_cdc_get_net_changes_dbo_Employees(@lsn_A, @lsn_B, 'all');

-- result:
Operation EmployeeID   FirstName LastName    Salary
U         4            Teemu     Selanne     227000.00
D         6            Kirby     Quigley      62500.00
I         7            Howard    Stern        80000.00
U         3            Don       Malone      125000.00
```

And finally, as per listing 17, you can see the before and after image of each key row throughout all updates by looking directly at the CDC table.

Listing 17   Viewing the before and after image of each key row

```
SELECT [image] = CASE __$operation
    WHEN 3 THEN 'BEFORE'
    WHEN 4 THEN 'AFTER' ELSE NULL END,
    EmployeeID, FirstName, LastName, Salary
FROM cdc.dbo_Employees_CT
WHERE __$operation IN (3,4)
ORDER BY __$start_lsn, __$operation;

-- result:
Image   EmployeeID FirstName  LastName    Salary
BEFORE  3          Don        Mattingly   125000.00
AFTER   3          Don        Donaldson   125000.00
BEFORE  4          Teemu      Selanne     113500.00
AFTER   4          Teemu      Selanne     227000.00
BEFORE  7          Howard     Jones        80000.00
AFTER   7          Howard     Stern        80000.00
BEFORE  3          Don        Donaldson   125000.00
AFTER   3          Don        Malone      125000.00
```

One challenge you might come across is when your schema changes. In this case you will need to disable CDC for the table and re-enable it when the change is complete. CDC will not break without this action, but if you add, remove, or rename columns, your captured data will be incomplete.

Also, because change tracking and SQL Server Audit are synchronous, and CDC polls the transaction log after the fact, it is not so straightforward to capture the user-name responsible for the change. If this is an important part of your solution, then you are probably better off sticking to one of the other features discussed in this chapter, or resorting to more traditional means (for example, triggers, log reading utilities).

To clean up the CDC settings, you can use the code in listing 18.

Listing 18 Cleaning up change data capture settings

```
USE HR;
GO
EXEC sys.sp_cdc_disable_table
    @source_schema = N'dbo',
    @source_name   = N'Employees',
    @capture_instance ='dbo_Employees';
GO
EXEC sys.sp_cdc_disable_db;
GO
```

Comparison of features

At first glance, these three new features in SQL Server 2008 seem quite similar. As demonstrated here, their functionality may overlap in some cases, but they are clearly different and serve unique purposes. This treatment should help equip you with much of the information you will need to decide which feature you will need to use. To wrap up, table 1 should help you decide whether to use SQL Server Audit, change tracking, or CDC.

Table 1 Comparing SQL Server Audit, change tracking, and change data capture

Criteria	SQL Server Audit	Change tracking	Change data capture
Capture DML statements	Yes[1]	No	No
Capture result of DML statements	No	Yes	Yes
Capture before and after values	No	No	Yes
Capture intermediate values	No	No	Yes
Capture SELECT statements	Yes	No	No
Capture user name / spid	Yes	Yes[4]	No
Capture host name	Yes[2]	Yes[4]	No
Should use specific isolation level	No	Yes[5]	No
Require SQL Server Agent	No	No	Yes
Available in all SKUs	No[3]	Yes	No[3]

1. You can see a tokenized copy of the DML statement, but the values in the statement are replaced by parameter placeholders.
2. You can capture host name in a separate login audit event, then correlate it manually with the event in question.
3. This feature is available in Enterprise, Evaluation, and Developer Editions only.
4. You can capture this information using a trigger to affect the context information included with the change tracking data.
5. Using snapshot isolation level can significantly impact tempdb usage and performance. Additionally, this may be a concern if you use distributed transactions, change schema frequently, disable constraints when bulk loading, or take databases offline (for example, detach or auto-close). You should read up on snapshot isolation level in Books Online: http://msdn.microsoft.com/en-us/library/ms177404(SQL.100).aspx

Summary

SQL Server 2008 provides a healthy offering of features that can assist you in tracking and dealing with changes to your data and schema. My goal for this chapter was to provide a useful and practical guide to help you decide how these features might help solve data management issues in your environment. Hopefully this will give you a good starting point on implementing one or more of these features where you need it most.

About the author

Aaron Bertrand is the Senior Data Architect at One to One Interactive, a global marketing agency headquartered in Boston, Massachusetts. At One to One, Aaron is responsible for database design and application architecture. Due to his commitment to the community, shown through blogging at http://www.sql-blog.com, peer-to-peer support on forums and newsgroups, and speaking at user group meetings and code camps, he has been awarded as a Microsoft MVP since 1998. Aaron recently published a technical white paper for Microsoft, detailing how to use the new Resource Governor feature in SQL Server 2008.

54 Introduction to SSAS 2008 data mining

Dejan Sarka

With SQL Server 2008, you get a complete business intelligence (BI) suite. You can use the SQL Server Database Engine to maintain a data warehouse (DW), SQL Server Reporting Services (RS) to create managed and ad hoc reports, SQL Server Integration Services (SSIS) to build and use extract, transform, and load (ETL) applications, and SQL Server Analysis Services (SSAS) to create Unified Dimensional Model (UDM) cubes.

Probably the easiest step into business intelligence is using reports created with RS. But this simplicity has a price. End users have limited dynamic capabilities when they view a report. You can extend the capabilities of RS with report models, but using report models to build reports is an advanced skill for end users. You also have to consider that the performance is limited; for example, aggregating two years of sales data from a production database could take hours. Therefore, RS reports aren't useful for analyses of large quantities of data over time directly from production systems.

In order to enable end users to do dynamic analysis—online analytical processing (OLAP)—you can implement a data warehouse and SSAS UDM cubes. In addition to dynamic change of view, end users also get lightning-speed analyses. End users can change the view of information in real time, drilling down to see more details or up to see summary information. But they're still limited with OLAP analyses. Typically, there are too many possible combinations of drilldown paths, and users don't have time to examine all possible graphs and pivot tables using all possible attributes and hierarchies. In addition, analysts are limited to searching only for patterns they anticipate. OLAP analysis is also usually limited to basic mathematical operations, such as comparing sums over different groups, operations that end users can solve graphically through client tool GUI.

Data mining (DM) addresses most of these limitations. In short, data mining is data-driven analysis. When you create a DM model, you don't anticipate results in advance. You examine data with advanced mathematical methods, using data mining algorithms, and then you examine patterns and rules that your algorithms find. The SSAS data mining engine runs the algorithms automatically after you set up all of the parameters you need; therefore, you can check millions of different pivoting options in a limited time. In this chapter, you're going to learn how to perform data mining analyses with SSAS 2008.

Data mining basics

The first question you may ask yourself is what the term *data mining* means. In short, data mining enables you to deduce hidden knowledge by examining, or training, your data with data mining algorithms. Algorithms express knowledge found in patterns and rules. Data mining algorithms are based mainly on statistics, although some are based on artificial intelligence and other branches of mathematics and information technology as well.

Nevertheless, the terminology comes mainly from statistics. What you're examining is called a *case*, which can be interpreted as one appearance of an entity, or a row in a table. The attributes of a case are called *variables*. After you find patterns and rules, you can use them to perform predictions. In SSAS 2008, the DM model is stored in the SSAS database as a kind of a table. It's not a table in a relational sense, as it can include nested tables in columns. In the model, the information about the variables, algorithms used, and the parameters of the algorithms are stored. Of course, after the training, the extracted knowledge is stored in the model as well. The data used for training isn't part of the model, but you can enable drillthrough on a model, and use drillthrough queries to browse the source data.

Most of the literature divides DM techniques into two main classes: directed algorithms and undirected algorithms. With a directed approach, you have a target variable that supervises the training in order to explain its values with selected input variables. Then the directed algorithms apply gleaned information to unknown examples to predict the value of the target variable. With the undirected approach, you're trying to discover new patterns inside the dataset as a whole, without any specific target variable. For example, you use a directed approach to find reasons why users purchased an article and an undirected approach to find out which articles are commonly purchased together.

You can answer many business questions with data mining. Some examples include the following:

- A bank might ask what the credit risk of a customer is.
- A customer relationship management (CRM) application can ask whether there are any interesting groups of customers based on similarity of values of their attributes.
- A retail store might be interested in which products appear in the same market basket.
- A business might be interested in forecasting sales.

- If you maintain a website, you might be interested in usage patterns.
- Credit card issuers would like to find fraudulent transactions.
- Advanced email spam filters use data mining.

And much, much more, depending on your imagination!

Data mining projects

The Cross-Industry Standard Process for Data Mining (CRISP-DM) defines four main distinct steps of a data mining project. The steps, also shown in figure 1, are as follows:

- Identifying the business problem
- Using DM techniques to transform the data into actionable information
- Acting on the information
- Measuring the result

In the first step, you need to contact business subject matter experts in order to identify business problems. The second step is where you use SQL Server BI suite to prepare the data and train the models on the data. This chapter is focused on the transform step. Acting means using patterns and rules learned in production.

You can use data mining models as UDM dimensions; you can use them for advanced SSIS transformations; you can use them in your applications to implement constraints and warnings; you can create RS reports based on mining models and predictions; and more. After deployment in production, you have to measure improvements of your business. You can use UDM cubes with mining model dimensions as a useful measurement tool. As you can see from figure 1, the project doesn't have to finish here: you can continue it or open a new project with identifying new business problems.

The second step, the transform step, has its own internal cycle. You need to understand your data; you need to make an overview. Then you have to prepare the data for data mining. Then you train your models. If your models don't give you desired results, you have to return to the data overview phase and learn more about your data, or to the data preparation phase and prepare the data differently.

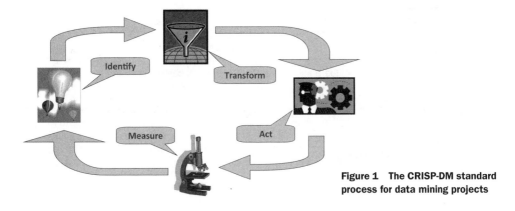

Figure 1   The CRISP-DM standard process for data mining projects

Data overview and preparation

Overviewing and preparing the data is probably the most exhaustive part of a data mining project. To get a comprehensive overview of your data, you can use many different techniques and tools. You can start with SQL queries and reports, or you can use UDM cubes. In addition, you can use descriptive statistics such as frequency distribution for discrete variables, and the mean value and the spread of the distribution for continuous variables. You can use Data Source View for a quick overview of your variables in table, pivot table, graph, or pivot graph format. Microsoft Office Excel statistical functions, pivot tables, and pivot graphs are useful tools for data overview as well.

After you understand your data, you have to prepare it for data mining. You have to decide what exactly your case is. Sometimes this is a simple task; sometimes it can get quite complex. For example, a bank might decide that a case for analysis is a family, whereas the transaction system tracks data about individual persons only. After you define your case, you prepare a table or a view that encapsulates everything you know about your case. You can also prepare child tables or views and use them as nested tables in a mining model. For example, you can use an "orders header" production table as the case table, and an "order details" table as a nested table if you want to analyze which products are purchased together in a single order. Usually, you also prepare some derived variables. In medicine, for example, the obesity index is much more important for analyses than a person's bare height and weight. You have to decide what to do with missing values, if there are too many. For example, you can decide to replace them with mean values. You should also check the outliers—rare and far out-of-bounds values—in a column. You can group or discretize a continuous variable in a limited number of bins and thus hide outliers in the first and the last bin.

SSAS 2008 data mining algorithms

SSAS 2008 supports all of the most popular data mining algorithms. In addition, SSIS includes two text mining transformations. Table 1 summarizes the SSAS algorithms and their usage.

Table 1 SSAS 2008 data mining algorithms and usage

Algorithm	Usage
Association Rules	The Association Rules algorithm is used for market basket analysis. It defines an itemset as a combination of items in a single transaction; then it scans the data and counts the number of times the itemsets appear together in transactions. Market basket analysis is useful to detect cross-selling opportunities.
Clustering	The Clustering algorithm groups cases from a dataset into clusters containing similar characteristics. You can use the Clustering method to group your customers for your CRM application to find distinguishable groups of customers. In addition, you can use it for finding anomalies in your data. If a case doesn't fit well in any cluster, it's an exception. For example, this might be a fraudulent transaction.

Table 1 SSAS 2008 data mining algorithms and usage *(continued)*

Algorithm	Usage
Decision Trees	Decision Trees is the most popular DM algorithm, used to predict discrete and continuous variables. The algorithm uses the discrete input variables to split the tree into nodes in such a way that each node is more pure in terms of target variable—each split leads to nodes where a single state of a target variable is represented better than other states. For continuous predictable variables, you get a piecewise multiple linear regression formula with a separate formula in each node of a tree. A tree that predicts continuous variables is a Regression Tree.
Linear Regression	Linear Regression predicts continuous variables, using a single multiple linear regression formula. The input variables must be continuous as well. Linear Regression is a simple case of a Regression Tree, a tree with no splits.
Logistic Regression	As Linear Regression is a simple Regression Tree, a Logistic Regression is a Neural Network without any hidden layers.
Naïve Bayes	The Naïve Bayes algorithm calculates probabilities for each possible state of the input attribute for every single state of predictable variable. These probabilities are used to predict the target attribute based on the known input attributes of new cases. The Naïve Bayes algorithm is quite simple; it builds the models quickly. Therefore, it's suitable as a starting point in your prediction project. The Naïve Bayes algorithm doesn't support continuous attributes.
Neural Network	The Neural Network algorithm is often associated with artificial intelligence. You can use this algorithm for predictions as well. Neural networks search for nonlinear functional dependencies by performing nonlinear transformations on the data in layers, from the input layer through hidden layers to the output layer. Because of the multiple nonlinear transformations, neural networks are harder to interpret compared to Decision Trees.
Sequence Clustering	Sequence Clustering searches for clusters based on a model, and not on similarity of cases as Clustering does. The models are defined on sequences of events by using Markov chains. Typical usage of Sequence Clustering would be an analysis of your company's website usage, although you can use this algorithm on any sequential data.
Time Series	You can use the Time Series algorithm to forecast continuous variables. Internally, the Time Series uses two different algorithms. For short-term forecasting, the Auto-Regression Trees (ART) algorithm is used. For long-term prediction, the Auto-Regressive Integrated Moving Average (ARIMA) algorithm is used. You can mix the blend of algorithms used by using the mining model parameters.

Creating mining models

After a lengthy introduction, it's time to start with probably the most exciting part of this chapter—creating mining models. By following the instructions, you can create predictive models. You're going to use Decision Trees, Naïve Bayes, and Neural Network algorithms on the same mining structure. The scenario for these models is based on the AdventureWorksDW2008 demo database. The fictitious Adventure Works company wants to boost bike sales by using a mailing campaign. The new potential customers are in the ProspectiveBuyer table. But the company wants to limit sending leaflets only to those potential customers who are likely to buy bikes. The company wants to use existing data to find out which customers tend to buy bikes. This data is already joined together in the vTargetMail view. Therefore, the data preparation task is already finished, and you can start creating mining models following these steps:

1 In Business Intelligence Development Studio (BIDS), create a new Analysis Services project and solution. Name the solution and the project *TargetMail*.

2 In Solution Explorer, right-click on the Data Sources folder and create a new data source. Use the Native OLE DB\SQL Server Native Client 10.0 provider. Connect to your SQL Server using Windows authentication and select the AdventureWorksDW2008 database. Use the Inherit option for the impersonation information and keep the default name, Adventure Works DW2008, for the data source.

3 Right-click on the Data Source Views folder, and create a new data source view. In the Data Source View Wizard, on the Select a Data Source page, select the data source you just created. In the Select Tables and View pane, select only the vTargetMail view and ProspectiveBuyer table. Keep the default name, Adventure Works DW2008, for the data source view.

4 Right-click the Mining Structures folder and select New Mining Structure. Walk through the wizard using the following options:

   - On the Welcome page of the Data Mining Wizard, click Next.
   - In the Select the Definition Method page, use the existing relational database or data warehouse (leave the first option checked).
   - In the Create the Data Mining Structure window, in the Which Data Mining Technique Do You Want to Use? drop-down list under the Create Mining Structure with a Mining Model option, select the Decision Trees algorithm from the drop-down list (the default).
   - Use Adventure Works DW2008 DSV in the Select Data Source View page.
   - In the Specify Table Types page, select vTargetMail as a case table by clicking the Case check box for this table.

5 By clicking on appropriate check boxes in the Specify the Training Data page, define CustomerKey as a key column (selected by default), BikeBuyer as predictable column, and CommuteDistance, EnglishEducation, EnglishOccupation, Gender, HouseOwnerFlag, MaritalStatus, NumberCarsOwned, NumberChildrenAtHome, Region, and TotalChildren as input columns.

6 In the Specify Columns' Content and Data Type page, click the Detect button. The wizard should detect that all columns, except CustomerKey, have discrete content. Note that if you want to use Age and YearlyIncome attributes in the model, you'd have to discretize them if you don't want a Regression Tree.

7 In the Create Test Set page, you can specify the percentage of the data or number of cases for the testing set—the holdout data. Use the default splitting,

using 30 percent of data as the test set. You'll use the test set to evaluate how well different models perform predictions.

8 Type TM as the name of the mining structure and TM_DT as the name of the model in the Completing the Wizard page.

9 Click Finish to leave the wizard and open the Data Mining Designer. Save the project.

You're going to add two models based on the same structure. In Data Mining Designer, select the Mining Models tab. To add a Naïve Bayes model, right-click on TM_DT, and then select the New Mining Model option. Type TM_NB as the name of the model and select the Microsoft Naive Bayes algorithm. Click OK.

To add a Neural Network model, right-click the TM_DT model and again select the New Mining Model option. Type TM_NN as the name of the model and select the Microsoft Neural Network algorithm. Click OK. Save, deploy, and process the complete project. Don't exit BIDS. Your complete project should look like the one in figure 2.

Harvesting the results

You created three models, yet you still don't know what additional information you got, or how you can use it. In this section, we'll start with examining mining models in BIDS, in the Data Mining Designer, with the help of built-in Data Mining Viewers. The viewers show you patterns and rules in an intuitive way. After the overview of the models, you have to decide which one you're going to deploy in production. We'll use the Lift Chart built-in tool to evaluate the models. Finally, we're going to simulate the

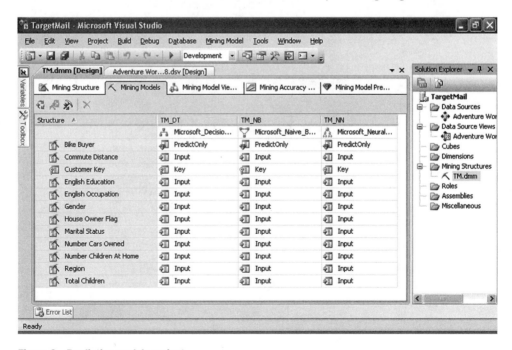

Figure 2 Predictive models project

deployment by creating a prediction query. We'll use the Data Mining Extensions (DMX) language with a special DMX prediction join to join the mining model with the ProspectiveBuyer table and predict which of the prospective customers is more likely to buy a bike.

Viewing the models

To make an overview of the mining models, follow these steps:

1 In BIDS, in the Data Mining Designer window, click the Mining Model Viewer tab. If the TM_DT model isn't selected by default in the Mining Model drop-down list on the top left of the window, select it.

2 Verify that you have the Decision Tree tab open. In the Background drop-down list, select value 1 of the Bike Buyer to check the potential buyers only. We're not interested in groups of customers that aren't going to buy a bike. Note the color of the nodes: the darker the color is, the more bike buyers appear in the node. For example, the node that groups people for whom the Number Cars Owned attribute is equal to 0 and Region is Pacific is quite dark in color. Therefore, the potential bike buyers are in that node. From the Mining Legend window, you can see more detailed information: more than 91 percent of people in this node have bought a bike in the past. You can see this information shown in figure 3.

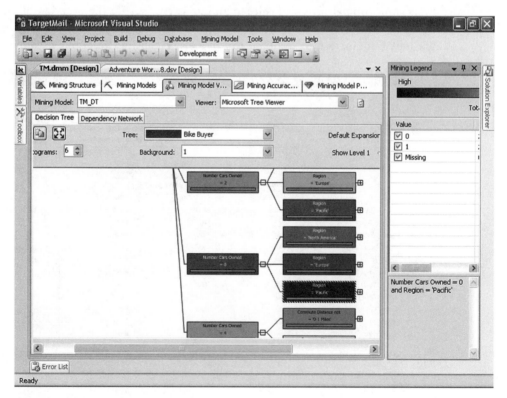

Figure 3   Decision tree

3 In the Dependency Network viewer, use the slider on the left side of the screen to show the strongest links only. Try to identify the two variables with the highest influence on the Bike Buyer attribute.

4 Navigate to the Mining Model Viewer tab and select the TM_NB model to view the model that uses the Naïve Bayes algorithm.

5 The first viewer is the Dependency Network viewer. Does the Naïve Bayes algorithm identify the same two variables as having the highest influence on the Bike Buyer attribute? Different algorithms make slightly different predictions.

6 Check other Naïve Bayes viewers as well. The Attribute Discrimination viewer is useful: it lets you see the values of input attributes that favor value 1 of the Bike Buyer attribute and the values that favor value 0.

7 Check the Neural Network model. The only viewer you'll see is the Attribute Discrimination viewer, in which you can again find the values of input attributes that favor value 1 of the Bike Buyer attribute and those values that favor value 0. In addition, you can filter the viewer to show the discrimination for specific states of input attributes only.

Evaluating the models

As you probably noticed, different models find slightly different reasons for customers' decisions whether to buy a bike. The question is how you can evaluate which model performs the best. The answer is quite simple in SQL Server 2008. Remember that when you created the models, you split the data into training and test sets. The model was trained on the training set only; you can make the predictions on the test set. Because you already know the outcome of the predictive variable in the test set, you can measure how accurate the predictions are. A standard way to show the accuracy is the Lift Chart. You can see a Lift Chart created using the data and models from this section in figure 4.

In figure 4, you'll notice five curves and lines on the chart; yet, you created only three models. The three curves show the performance of the predictive models you created, and the two lines represent the Ideal Model and the Random Guess Model. The x axis shows the percentage of population (all cases), and the y axis shows the percentage of the target population (bike buyers in this example). The Ideal Model line (the topmost line) shows that approximately 50 percent of the customers of Adventure Works buy bikes. If you want to know exactly who's going to buy a bike and who isn't, you'd need only 50 percent of the population to get all bike buyers. The lowest line is the Random Guess line. If you picked cases out of the population randomly, you'd need 100 percent of the cases for 100 percent of bike buyers. Likewise, you'd need 80 percent of the population for 80 percent of bike buyers, 60 percent of the population for 60 percent of bike buyers, and so on. The mining models you created give better results than the Random Guess Model, and of course worse results than the Ideal Model. In the Lift Chart, you can see the lift of the mining models from the Random Guess line; this is where the name *Lift Chart* comes from. Any model predicts the outcome with less than 100 percent of probability in all ranges of the population;

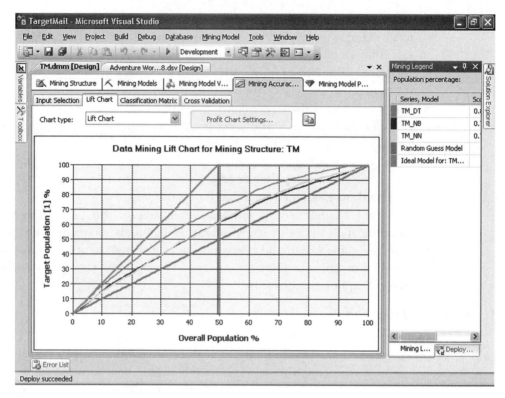

Figure 4   Lift Chart for models created in this section

therefore, to get 100 percent of bike buyers, you still need 100 percent of the population. But you get interesting results somewhere between 0 and 100 percent of the population. For example, with the best-performing model in this demo case, the line right below the Ideal Model line, you can see that if you select 70 percent of the population based on this model, you'd get nearly 90 percent of bike buyers. You can see in the Mining Legend window that this is the Decision Trees model. Therefore, in this case, you should decide to deploy the Decision Trees model into production.

In order to create a Lift Chart, follow these steps:

1 In BIDS, in the Data Mining Designer, click the Mining Accuracy Chart tab.

In the Input Selection window, make sure that all three mining models are selected in the Select Predictable Mining Model Columns to Show in the Lift Chart table and that the Synchronize Prediction Columns and Values check box is checked. Also make sure that in the Select Data Set to Be Used for Accuracy Chart option group, the Use Mining Model Test Cases option is selected. Leave the Filter expression box empty.

2 In the Predict Value column of the Select Predictable Mining Model Columns to Show in the Lift Chart table, select 1 in the drop-down list of any row. We're interested in showing the performance of the models when predicting positive outcome—when predicting buyers only.

3 Click the Lift Chart tab. Examine the Lift Chart. Don't exit BIDS.

Creating prediction queries

Finally, it's time to select probable buyers from the ProspectiveBuyer table. You can do this task with a DMX prediction join query. Detailed description of the DMX language is out of scope for this book. Fortunately, you can get a jump start with the Prediction Query builder in BIDS. A similar builder is included in the RS Report Designer when you're authoring a report based on a data mining model, and in SSIS Package Designer in the Data Mining Query task and Data Mining Query transformation. In order to create a DMX prediction query in BIDS, follow these steps:

1. In the Data Mining Designer, select the Mining Model Prediction tab.
2. In the Select Model window, select the best-performing model. In this case, this is the Decision Trees model, which should be selected by default, as it was the first model created.
3. In the Select Input Table(s) window, click on the Select Case table button. Select the ProspectiveBuyer table. Click OK.
4. Check the join between model and table; it's done automatically based on column names. You can change the join manually, though following a consistent naming convention is a good practice.
5. In the bottom pane, define the column list of your DMX Select statement.
6. In the Source and Field columns, select the following attributes: Prospective-BuyerKey, FirstName, and LastName, from the ProspectiveBuyer table, and Bike Buyer from the TM_DT mining model. Your selections in the Prediction Query builder should look like the selections in figure 5.

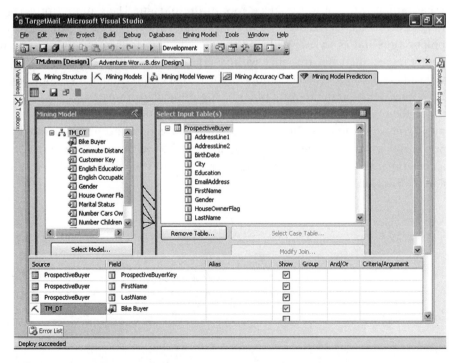

Figure 5 Prediction Query builder

7 In the Switch to Query Result drop-down list, accessed through the leftmost icon on the toolbar, select the Query option. Check the DMX query created.

8 In the Switch to Query Result drop-down list, select the Result option. In the result table, you can easily notice who's going to buy a bike and who isn't, according to the Decision Trees prediction.

9 Save the project and exit BIDS.

Sources for more information

You can learn more about data mining using SQL Server 2008 Books Online, SQL Server Analysis Services—Data Mining section (http://msdn.microsoft.com/en-us/library/bb510517.aspx).

For a complete overview of the SQL Server 2008 BI suite, refer to the MCTS Self-Paced Training Kit (Exam 70-448): Microsoft SQL Server 2008—Business Intelligence Development by Erik Veerman, Teo Lachev, and Dejan Sarka (MS Press, 2009).

An excellent guide to SSAS data mining is *Data Mining with Microsoft SQL Server 2008* by Jamie MacLennan, ZhaoHui Tang, and Bogdan Crivat (Wiley, 2008).

You can find a lot of additional information, tips, and tricks about SSAS data mining at the SQL Server Data Mining community site at http://www.sqlserverdatamining.com/ssdm/default.aspx.

If you're interested in Cross-Industry Standard Process for Data Mining (CRISP-DM), check the CRISP-DM site at http://www.crisp-dm.org/index.htm.

Summary

Data mining is the most advanced tool in the BI suite. Data mining projects have a well-defined lifecycle. Probably the most exhaustive part of the project is the data preparation and overview. With SSAS 2008, you can quickly create multiple models and compare their performance with standard tools such as Lift Chart. In addition, you can create DMX prediction queries through a graphical query builder. SQL Server 2008 includes all of the most popular data mining algorithms.

All elements of the SQL Server 2008 BI suite are interleaved; it's easy to use one element when creating another. For example, you can create mining models on SQL Server databases and Analysis Services UDM cubes; you can deploy a mining model as a new dimension in a SSAS UDM cube; and you can use mining models in RS reports and SSIS packages.

About the author

Dejan Sarka focuses on developing database and business intelligence applications. Besides projects, he spends about half of his time on training and mentoring. He's a frequent speaker at some of the most important international conferences. He's the founder of the Slovenian SQL Server and .NET Users Group. As lead author or coauthor, Dejan has written seven books about SQL Server. Dejan Sarka has also developed two courses for Solid Quality Mentors: Data Modeling Essentials and Data Mining with SQL Server.

55 To aggregate or not to aggregate—is there really a question?

Erin Welker

Aggregations have long been the key to gaining the best query performance from Analysis Services, yet they are commonly misunderstood. What, exactly, are aggregations? What is the best approach for designing aggregations? What tools are available to assist you with this task? What changes have occurred in the various releases of Analysis Services that affect your approach to aggregation design?

I hope to answer all of these questions and more in this chapter. Read on.

What are aggregations?

You can think of aggregations as precalculated answers to OLAP queries. Let's take the scenario of a query on a cube with three dimensions—Product, Customer, and Sales date—with the attributes listed in table 1.

A query might be issued that asks the question, "What were the total sales for nonfiction books (a category of books) in Texas for last month?" If an aggregation has been created on the cube to precalculate summed values of sales by state, month, and product category (indicated by the asterisk (*) next to the aggregated levels in table 1), this query will be extremely fast because all Analysis Services has to do is retrieve the appropriate aggregation from disk or cache.

Table 1 Aggregation example

Product	Customer	Sales date
Category*	Country	Fiscal year
Subcategory	State*	Fiscal month*
Product	City	Date

Aggregations don't have to exactly match the queried dimension attributes. If user-defined hierarchies exist that relate higher levels to lower levels in each dimension, queries at higher levels can leverage aggregations at the lower level. Let's assume the three user-defined hierarchies represented in table 1 and the same aggregation that was previously mentioned (summing values of sales by state, month, and product category). What happens if a follow-up query is issued to ask, "What is the percentage of total sales for nonfiction books in the state of Texas, compared to the total sales across all states in the U.S.?" This answer is also easy for Analysis Services to answer. Because the values for total sales by state per product category are precalculated, only 50 state-level aggregations are affected by this query. This compares to summing values down to the lowest level of granularity, which could include anywhere from thousands to millions, or even billions, of values!

If you come from a relational database background, you can loosely compare aggregations to indexes. In this comparison, you know that indexes provide an expeditious way of retrieving query results. Unlike indexes, though, aggregations provide the best benefit to queries that select data at higher levels, which would require accessing a very large number of cells.

Just as with indexes, the savings at query time come at a cost, and the goal is to design the right indexes and aggregations to match your query load. With aggregations, this results in an OLAP solution that responds well to a wide variety of queries with the minimum cube-processing overhead.

Analysis Services makes no assumptions when it comes to aggregations—no aggregations will be created unless you tell it to. Performance may even be acceptable on smaller cubes without them, but larger cubes will likely benefit greatly from a good set of aggregations.

Designing aggregations

The easiest way to design aggregations is to go into the Aggregation Design Wizard (ADW), shown in figure 1, through SQL Server Management Studio (SSMS) or Business Intelligence Development Studio (BIDS). Aggregations are designed at the partition level, so you can access the wizard by right-clicking on a partition in either of those tools (in SSMS, drill down from the server to the database, to a cube, to a measure group, then to a partition). The ADW lets you design aggregations based on the target size, the desired performance benefit, or until you tell it to stop.

By default, the ADW in Analysis Services knows nothing about your expected query patterns and gives equal weight when considering possible aggregations across dimension attribute candidates. Using the ADW, with no additional input, is like rolling the dice. Hopefully, some of the resulting aggregations will be useful in satisfying the queries that will be issued against the cube, but wouldn't it be better to give Analysis Services some hints as to which dimensions' attributes will be most queried by users of the cube? When you create indexes in SQL Server, don't you use your knowledge of the queries that will be issued?

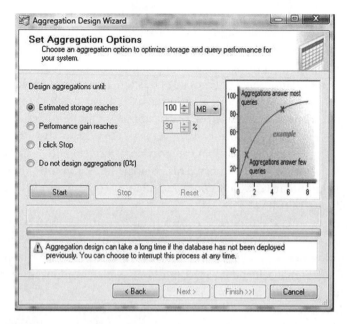

Figure 1   The Aggregation Design Wizard

Influencing aggregations

It is important to understand how Analysis Services makes its decisions so you can influence them appropriately. Keep in mind that the following information relates to indicating aggregation candidates. The ADW will ultimately determine what aggregations are worth designing based on the input that you provide. The better the input, the more efficient your resulting aggregation design will be. Fundamentally, you can provide Analysis Services with a list of candidate attributes for aggregation, their member counts in the cube data source, the performance target, and, optionally, a list of queries to optimize. I'll talk about the first topic in this section and the others later in the chapter.

There are several techniques for influencing the aggregation design. The first is to indicate to Analysis Services the attribute dimensions to consider for aggregation. By default, Analysis Services uses a number of conditions to determine which dimension attributes will be candidates. Attributes that are included in a natural hierarchy are automatically considered, unless you indicate that they should not be. Attributes that are not included in a natural hierarchy are usually not included.

NOTE A natural hierarchy is a user-defined hierarchy that contains two or more attributes that are related to each other by a one-to-many relationship from each level to the next. Excellent examples are calendar hierarchies (Year > Quarter > Month > Day) or geography hierarchies (Country > State > City).

The `AggregationUsage` property of a dimension attribute is an indication of which attributes the ADW will consider in the design.

- The default is `Default`. A number of conditions go into considering whether an attribute with this `AggregationUsage` value will be considered. For a good discussion on this, consult the "Microsoft SQL Server 2005 (or 2008) Analysis Services Performance Guide," available from http://www.microsoft.com. In most cases, all attributes in a natural hierarchy are considered, as well as the All level and the dimension key.
- `None` should be used for attributes that are rarely queried.
- Commonly queried attributes should be changed to `Unrestricted`. This tells the ADW to consider the attribute, but the wizard will ultimately determine if the attribute will be valuable in an aggregation design, based on the number of members, its relationship to other attributes, and the query load (for the usage-based optimizer).
- The final choice is `Full`, which forces all aggregations to use this attribute or an attribute lower in a hierarchy, if contained in a natural hierarchy. This property should seldom be used.

When you are not sure whether an attribute is flagged as a candidate for aggregation or not, open the ADW and go to the Specify Object Counts page. You can expand each dimension to view a list of attributes. The attributes displayed in bold are aggregation candidates. If you feel that one of the unbolded attributes should be a candidate, just change the `AggregationUsage` property to `Unrestricted` in the cube designer in BIDS.

Analysis Services 2008 includes some nifty wizards for aggregation design. Because these wizards are backwards compatible with Analysis Services 2005, you can install the SQL Server 2008 client tools to leverage these wizards even before you are ready to upgrade your cubes. Figure 2 shows a part of the updated ADW in 2008, which can be used to review and update the `AggregationUsage` property across all attributes in the cube at once.

Cube Objects	Default	Full	None	Unrestricted
⊟ Buyer	3	0	0	0
Buyer Name	⊙	○	○	○
Buyer Index	⊙	○	○	○
Buyer ID	⊙	○	○	○
⊟ Item	30	0	14	0
Item	⊙	○	○	○
EAN	⊙	○	○	○
ISBN	⊙	○	○	○
Retail Amt	⊙	○	○	○
Status Detail	○	○	⊙	○
Current Status	○	○	⊙	○
Publish Date	⊙	○	○	○
Publish Year	⊙	○	○	○
Subject	⊙	○	○	○

Set All to Default   < Back   Next >   Finish   Cancel

Figure 2   SQL Server 2008 Aggregation Usage designer

Attribute relationships

Analysis Services 2005 and 2008 have a core concept that I have yet to mention, though it is a critical one. If you read anything on performance in Analysis Services, you will likely read about the importance of indicating appropriate relationships between attributes in your user-defined hierarchies. Simply creating a user-defined hierarchy in a dimension does not perform this automatically because it cannot be assumed. You probably see a lot of visual tips about creating relationships when in the dimension designer. These tips provide feedback to let you know that something is potentially wrong with your design.

Attribute relationships tell Analysis Services how attributes relate to one another. By default, all attributes are directly related to the dimension key. For example, consider a Time dimension where we have a user-defined hierarchy named Calendar. This may consist of the levels Year, Qtr, Month, and Day. Even if you create a user-defined hierarchy with one below the other, no assumptions are made about the relationship from one to another. Because all attributes are directly related to the key, Analysis Services sees the user-defined hierarchy like the illustration on the right.

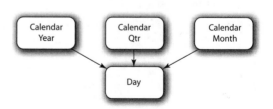

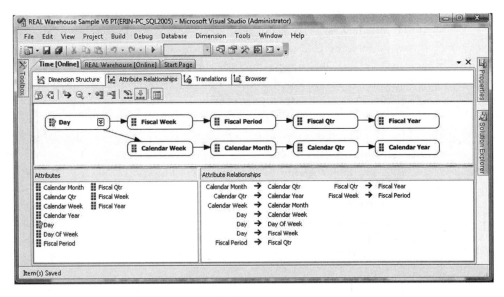

Figure 3   The SQL Server 2008 Attribute Relationships designer

The ADW will not recognize that queries that involve Calendar Year could benefit from aggregations that include the Calendar Qtr level, or that queries at the Calendar Qtr level could benefit from aggregations that include Calendar Month. This is just one of the many issues involved in not specifying attribute relationships. To design attribute relationships, simply drag and drop the appropriate attributes under their associated levels (Year under Quarter, Quarter under Month, and Month under Day).

SQL Server 2008 provides a visual designer to make this task even more intuitive, as well as feedback when something appears to be not quite right. After you create the aforementioned attribute relationships, the Attribute Relationships tab in BIDS 2008 gives a visual overview that looks like figure 3.

Usage-based optimization

The best aggregation design will focus on the set of queries that are expected to be executed. Analysis Services provides a means of collecting a log of queries that are submitted to the server so that they can be used as input to the usage-based optimizer (UBO). The UBO can be accessed in the same way as the ADW in SSMS or BIDS. The UBO Wizard will pull the information in the query log as input for determining aggregations that will benefit the queries in the log. You can then further filter the query log input by date range, user, or query frequency. You will usually want to save the query log in SQL Server, in which case you can manually prune the log entries to include only the queries you want to optimize, which are usually those of longer duration.

Running Profiler to analyze problem queries may reveal that aggregations are not used for a query, even though it seems like they should be. Look for the Get Data From

Aggregation event class to see if the query is leveraging aggregations. If not, you might need to manually design some aggregations to benefit one or more problem queries.

Analysis Services 2005 sample applications (http://msdn.microsoft.com/en-us/library/ms160876(SQL.90).aspx) include the Aggregation Manager, which is a sample tool that can be downloaded from CodePlex (http://sqlsrvanalysissrvcs.codeplex.com/Release/ProjectReleases.aspx?ReleaseId=13572). This tool allows you to view existing aggregations, design aggregations via UBO, and manually designate aggregations. I haven't found this tool to be very user-friendly, but it was invaluable for designing aggregations for Analysis Services 2005 cubes.

Another way to review and manually create aggregations is with SQL Server 2008 client tools, shown in figure 4. As previously mentioned, these tools can be used to update information on Analysis Services 2005 and are, in my opinion, more intuitive. Either way, manually creating aggregations should not be necessary in Analysis Services 2008, with its more evolved UBO engine. Note that UBO is part of the Analysis Services engine, so invoking UBO from SQL Server 2008 tools will still invoke the 2005 version of UBO.

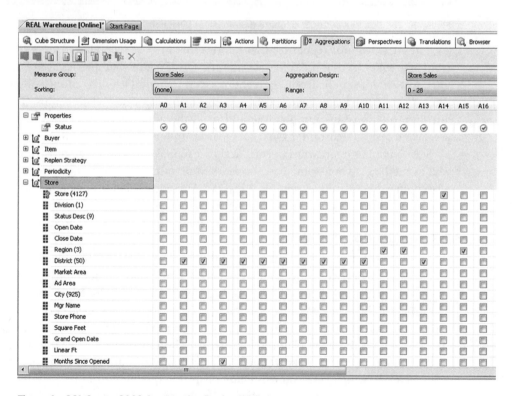

Figure 4   SQL Server 2008 Aggregation Design Wizard

High-level approach

The high-level approach to designing aggregations has remained the same from the earliest versions of Analysis Services to today. There are slight differences in the recommendations from industry experts, but there remains a common theme:

1   Use the Analysis Services ADW to create an aggregation design for a 5 to 20 percent improvement. In general, the larger the cube, the lower the aggregation design percentage because of the increased overhead of creating aggregations on large cubes during processing. Remember that aggregation design occurs at the partition level, so be sure to apply the design to all appropriate partitions.

2   Turn on query logging to capture a good representation of queries against the database. Preferably do this in a QA or test environment before end users initially start validating the cube, or for short intervals in production, if necessary. Logging has an overhead, so do not leave it on continually.

3   Use the Aggregation Management tool in Analysis Services 2005 or usage-based optimization (UBO) in Analysis Services 2008 to design aggregations that will benefit the lengthiest queries from the previous step. When using UBO, increase the design goal to roughly 70 percent and only include longer running queries.

4   Apply the aggregations designed in previous steps to all relevant partitions in the cube. This can be done in BIDS, the Aggregation Management tool, or via XML for Analysis (XMLA).

5   Reprocess the partitions, either individually or as a whole, noting the processing time. Remember, the tradeoff for more aggregations is increased processing time. If the processing time is not feasible for your production environment, you will need to back off some of the aggregations.

6   Repeat steps 2–5 periodically, perhaps monthly or quarterly, depending on your environment. Query patterns in an OLAP environment are prone to change over time, and revisiting the aggregation design compensates for this.

Other considerations

It might be tempting to go overboard on aggregation designs. Why not, if they are so powerful? In addition to the obvious drawback of increased cube-processing time, there is also the issue of Analysis Services leveraging many specific aggregations to address individual queries when only a few are really necessary. Aggregations take disk space and memory, so designing the most efficient set of aggregations results in the best resource utilization. The target number of aggregations should be in the hundreds, or even fewer in smaller cubes. Remember that Analysis Services can leverage aggregations that are not specific to a query—that has long been a differentiator between it and other OLAP products.

Be sure that member counts are accurately specified, as well. These are input to the ADW to calculate the cost of designing an aggregation at a dimension level. This count is often calculated early in the cube design and never updated as members are subsequently added. As a result, the ADW may underestimate the overhead of creating an aggregation at that level. Analysis Services will not design an aggregation that is larger than one third of the underlying fact table. It uses the member counts to determine how large an aggregation will be.

There are hierarchy types in Analysis Services that cannot adequately leverage aggregations. The most notable is parent-child, and this is one reason to limit parent-child hierarchies in your cube. If the number of levels is predictable, consider redesigning the dimension to create attributes for each level, and then create a standard user-defined hierarchy to designate each level and create attribute relationships from one to the other.

Summary

This should serve as an introduction to aggregations and effective aggregation designs. Aggregations are an important aspect of well-performing OLAP solutions in all but the smallest cubes. Knowing the underlying fundamentals of a solid aggregation design is critical for high-performance cubes.

About the author

Erin Welker has spent 25 years in information technology development, management, database administration, and business intelligence. She began working with SQL Server in version 1.11, and with Analysis Services, SSIS, DTS, and Reporting Services since their inception. Erin has consulted at several Fortune 500 and other well-known companies, developing business intelligence solutions with a specialization in performance. She loves to share her passion for SQL Server and BI through authoring and speaking.

56 Incorporating data profiling in the ETL process

John Welch

When you work with data on a regular basis, it's not uncommon to need to explore it. This is particularly true in the business intelligence and data warehousing field, because you may be dealing with new or changing data sources quite often. To work effectively with the data, you need to understand its profile—both what the data looks like at the detail level and from a higher aggregate level. In the case of small sets of data, you may be able to get a picture of the data profile by reviewing the detail rows. For larger sets of data, this isn't practical, as there is too much information to easily hold in your head. Fortunately, SQL Server 2008 includes new functionality that makes this easier.

The data profiling tools in SQL Server Integration Services (SSIS) 2008 include a Data Profiling task and a Data Profile Viewer. The Data Profiling task is a new task for SSIS 2008. It can help you understand large sets of data by offering a set of commonly needed data profiling options. The Data Profile Viewer is an application that can be used to review the output of the Data Profiling task. Over the course of this chapter, I'll introduce the Data Profiling task in the context of data warehousing and explain how it can be used to explore source data and how you can automate the use of the profile information in your extract, transform, and load (ETL) processes to make decisions about your data.

Why profile data?

Why should you be concerned with data profiling? In data warehousing, it is common to profile the data in advance to identify patterns in the data and determine if there are quality problems. Business intelligence applications often use data in new and interesting ways, which can highlight problems with the data simply because no one has looked at it in those ways before. The Data Profiling task helps identify these problems in advance by letting you determine what the data looks like statistically.

In many scenarios, the Data Profiling task will be used at the beginning of a data warehousing project to evaluate the source data prior to implementing ETL (or data integration) processes for it. When it is used this way, it can help identify problematic data in the sources. For example, perhaps the source database contains a Customer table with a State column, which should represent the U.S. state in which the customer resides. After profiling that table, you may discover that there are more than 50 distinct values in the column, indicating that you have either some incorrect states, some states have been entered in both their abbreviated form and spelled out, or possibly both. Once the problem data has been identified, you can design and incorporate the appropriate business rules in the ETL process to exclude or cleanse that data as it moves to the data warehouse, ensuring a higher quality of information in the warehouse. For the preceding example, this might be implemented by setting up a list of allowed values for the State column and matching incoming data against this list to validate it.

This upfront exploration of data and identification of problems is valuable, as it allows you to establish the rules that define what data can enter the data warehouse, and what data can be excluded, due to quality issues. Allowing bad data to enter the data warehouse can have a number of effects, all of them bad. For example, poor quality data in the warehouse will cause the users of the warehouse data to not trust it, or to potentially make bad decisions based on incorrect information. These rules are typically set up front, and may not be updated frequently (if at all) due to the complexities of changing production ETL processes. As data sources and business conditions change, these rules may become outdated. A better solution is to base some of the business rules on the current profile of the data, so that they remain dynamic and adjustable, even as the source data changes.

Changing production ETL processes

Why is modifying ETL processes so challenging? For one thing, any modifications usually require retesting the ETL. When you are dealing with hundreds of gigabytes—or terabytes—of data, that can be very time consuming. Also, any changes to the business rules in the ETL can impact historical data already in the warehouse. Determining whether to update historical information, or just change it moving forward, is a major decision in itself. If you do want to make changes to historical data, determining how to apply these updates can be complicated and typically involves multiple groups in the company (IT and any impacted business units) coming together to agree on an approach.

Now that we've discussed why data profiling is a good idea, let's move on to the data profiling capabilities in SQL Server 2008.

Introduction to the Data Profiling task

The Data Profiling task is new for SSIS 2008. It has the capability to create multiple types of data profiles across any target tables you specify. Using it can be as simple as adding it to a package, selecting a SQL Server table, and picking one or more profiles to run against that table. Each profile returns a different set of information about the data in the target table.

First, we'll cover the types of profiles that can be created, and then how you can work with them.

Types of profiles

The Data Profiling task supports eight different profiles. Five of these look at individual columns in a table, two of them look at multiple columns in the same table, and one looks at columns across two tables. A specific data profile works with specific data types (with some exceptions, which will be pointed out). In general, though, profiles work with some combination of string (`char`, `nchar`, `varchar`, `nvarchar`), integer (`bit`, `tinyint`, `smallint`, `int`, `bigint`), or date (`datetime`, `smalldatetime`, `timestamp`, `date`, `time`, `datetime2`, `datetimeoffset`) column data types. Most profiles do not work with binary types (such as text or image) or with non-integer numeric data.

THE COLUMN LENGTH DISTRIBUTION PROFILE

The Column Length Distribution profile provides the minimum and maximum lengths of values in a string column, along with a list of the distinct lengths of all values in the column and a count of rows that have that distinct length. For example, profiling a telephone number column (for U.S. domestic telephone numbers) where you expect numbers to be stored with no formatting should produce one value—a distinct length of 10. If any other values are reported, it indicates problems in the data.

THE COLUMN NULL RATIO PROFILE

The Column Null Ratio profile is one of the exceptions in that it works with any type of data, including binary information. It reports the number of null values in a particular column. For example, profiling a column that is believed to always have a value because of rules enforced in the user interface may reveal that the rule isn't always enforced.

THE COLUMN PATTERN PROFILE

The Column Pattern profile only works on string columns and returns a list of regular expressions that match the values in the column. It may return multiple regular expressions, along with the frequency that the pattern applies to the data. For example, using this profile against a telephone number column might return the values \d{10} (for numbers with no dashes—5555555555), \d{3}-\d{3}-\d{4} (for numbers with dashes—555-555-5555), and \d{3})\d{3}-\d{4} (for numbers with parentheses —(555)555-5555).

THE COLUMN VALUE DISTRIBUTION PROFILE

The Column Value Distribution profile works on string, date, and numeric types (including `money`, `decimal`, `float`, `real`, and `numeric`). It returns the count of distinct values in a column, the list of the distinct values in a column, and the number of times each item is used. For example, this could be used to profile the distribution of product sales by product category by referencing a table of product sales that contains a column with product categories.

THE COLUMN STATISTICS PROFILE

The Column Statistics profile works on date and numeric types (including `money`, `decimal`, `float`, `real`, and `numeric`), but not on string data. It returns statistical information about the column: minimum and maximum values for date columns, and minimum, maximum, average, and standard deviation for numeric columns. A potential use for this is to profile the sale price of products to determine whether the data falls into acceptable ranges.

THE CANDIDATE KEY PROFILE

The Candidate Key profile works with integer, string, and date data types. It evaluates a column or combination of columns to determine if they could be a key for the table. For example, this profile could be used against the combination of a name and telephone number column to determine if it could be used as key for the table. It is not uncommon to have primary keys that are generated values, using `IDENTITY` columns or the `NEWSEQUENTIALID` function, and you may need to determine whether there is a set of columns that represents the business or logical key for the data. You can use the Candidate Key profile to determine whether a proposed business key uniquely identifies each row in the table.

THE FUNCTIONAL DEPENDENCY PROFILE

The Functional Dependency profile works with `string`, `integer`, and `date` data types. It evaluates how much the values in one column are determined by the values in another column or set of columns. It returns the determinant columns, the dependent column, and the strength of the dependency. This is useful for evaluating the data quality in one column based on another column. For example, a State column should have a strong functional dependency on a Zip Code column. If it doesn't, it can indicate data-quality issues.

THE VALUE INCLUSION PROFILE

The Value Inclusion profile works with `string`, `integer`, and `date` data types. It determines whether a set of values in one table is present in another table. This can be used to determine whether a column is a good candidate to be a foreign key to another table, or to validate that all values present in one column exist in a reference table. For example, it can be used to validate that all state values in a table exist in a reference table of states.

Input to the task

Now that we've reviewed the available profiles, let's take a look at how the task can be configured. You can configure a single Data Profiling task to generate multiple data profiles. Each profile can have its own reference to a connection manager and can target a single table (with the exception of the Value Inclusion profile, which targets two tables). For columns, you can use a wildcard so that it runs the same profile across all the columns in the table. Fortunately, the task is smart enough to only run profiles across columns with compatible data types. For example, using the Column Pattern profile with a wildcard for columns will only profile string columns.

As with most tasks in SSIS, there is an editor in the Business Intelligence Development Studio (BIDS) environment that allows you to set the properties for each profile. The Profile Requests page of the editor is pictured in figure 1. You can use the Quick Profile button located on the General page of the editor to easily define multiple profiles, for either a specific table or an entire database.

The settings for the profiles are stored in the `ProfileRequests` property of the task, which is a collection of all the profile requests. Behind the scenes, the profile requests collection is converted to an XML document that conforms to the XML Schema located at http://schemas.microsoft.com/sqlserver/2008/DataDebugger/ DataProfile.xsd. We'll use this XML later in this chapter when we configure the task to be dynamic.

Output from the task

When the Data Profiling task is executed, it produces XML output that conforms to the DataProfile.xsd schema for the profile settings that are input. This XML can be directed to a file by using a file connection manager, or it can be stored in a variable

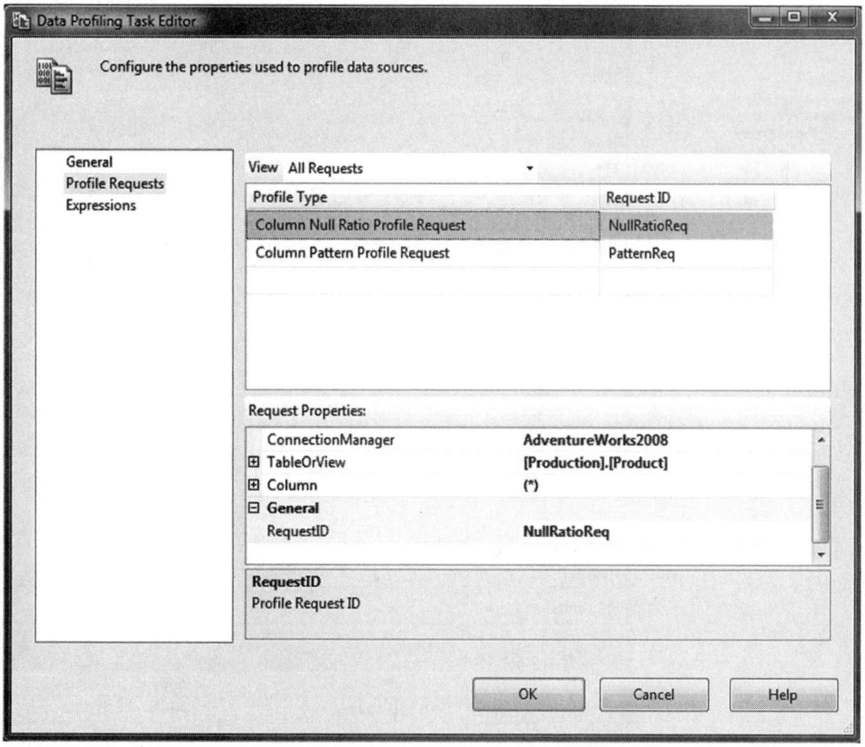

Figure 1   The Data Profiling Task Editor

inside the package. Typically, you will store the XML in a file if you are profiling data to be reviewed by a person at a later time, and plan on using the Data Profile Viewer application to review it. Storing the XML output in a variable is most often done when you want to use the profile information later in the same package, perhaps to make an automated decision about data quality.

The XML output includes both the profile requests (the input to the task) and the output from each profile requested. The format of the output varies depending on which profile generated it, so you will see different elements in the XML for a Column Null Ratio profile than you will for a Column Length Distribution profile. The XML contains a lot of information, and it can be difficult to sort through to find the information you are looking for. Fortunately, there is an easier user interface to use.

The Data Profile Viewer, shown in figure 2, provides a graphical interface to the data profile information. You can open XML files generated by the Data Profiling task in it and find specific information much more easily. In addition, the viewer represents some of the profile information graphically, which is useful when you are looking at large quantities of data. For example, the Column Length Distribution profile displays the count associated with specific lengths as a stacked bar chart, which means you can easily locate the most frequently used lengths.

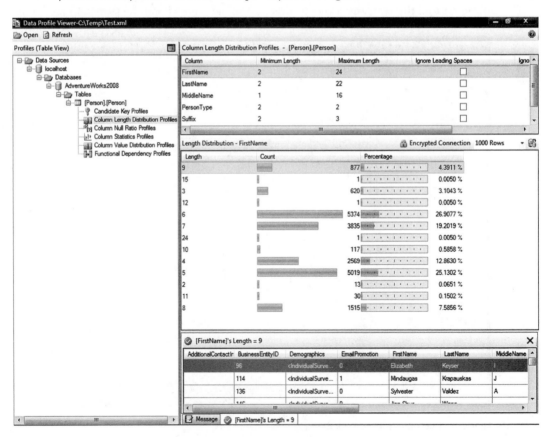

Figure 2   Data Profile Viewer

The Data Profile Viewer lets you sort most columns in the tables that it displays, which can aid you in exploring the data. It also allows you to drill down into the detail data in the source system. This is particularly useful when you have located some bad data in the profile, because you can see the source rows that contain the data. This can be valuable if, for example, the profile shows that several customer names are unusually long. You can drill into the detail data to see all the data associated with these outlier rows. This feature does require a live connection to the source database, though, because the source data is not directly included in the data profile output.

One thing to be aware of with the Data Profile Viewer: not all values it shows are directly included in the XML. It does some additional work on the data profiles before presenting them to you. For example, in many cases it calculates the percentage of rows that a specific value in the profile applies to. The raw XML for the data profile only stores the row counts, not the percentages. This means that if you want to use the XML directly, perhaps to display the information on a web page, you may need to calculate some values manually. This is usually a straightforward task.

Constraints of the Data Profiling task

As useful as the Data Profiling task is, there are still some constraints that you need to keep in mind when using it. The first one most people encounter is in the types of data sources it will work with. The Data Profiling task requires that the data to be profiled be in SQL Server 2000 or later. This means you can't use it to directly profile data in Oracle tables, Access databases, Excel spreadsheets, or flat files. You can work around this by importing the data you need into SQL Server prior to profiling it. In fact, there are other reasons why you may want the data in SQL Server in advance, which will be touched on in this section.

The Data Profiling task also requires that you use an ADO.NET connection manager. Typically, in SSIS, OLE DB connection managers are used, as they tend to perform better. This may mean creating two connection managers to the same database, if you need to both profile data and import it in the same package.

Using the Data Profile Viewer does require a SQL Server installation, because the viewer is not packaged or licensed as a redistributable component. It is possible to transform the XML output into a more user-friendly format by using XSL Transformations (XSLT) to translate it into HTML, or to write your own viewer for the information.

The task's performance can vary greatly, depending both on the volume of data you are profiling and on the types of profiles you have requested. Some profiles, such as the Column Pattern profile, are resource intensive and can take quite a while on a large table. One way to address this is to work with a subset of the data, rather than the entire table. It's important to get a representative sample of the data for these purposes, so that the data profile results aren't skewed. This is another reason that having the data in SQL Server can be valuable. You can copy a subset of the data to another table for profiling, using a SELECT that returns a random sampling of rows (as discussed in "Selecting Rows Randomly from a Large Table" from MSDN: http://msdn.microsoft.com/en-us/library/cc441928.aspx). If the data is coming from an external source, such as a flat file, you can use the Row Sampling or Percentage

Sampling components in an SSIS data flow to create a representative sample of the data to profile. Note that when sampling data, care must be taken to ensure the data is truly representative, or the results can be misleading. Generally it's better to profile the entire data set.

Making the Data Profiling task dynamic

Why would you want to make the Data Profiling task dynamic? Well, as an example, think about profiling a new database. You could create a new SSIS package, add a Data Profiling task, and use the Quick Profile option to create profile requests for all the tables in the database. You'd then have to repeat these steps for the next new database that you want to profile. Or what if you don't want to profile all the tables, but only a subset of them? To do this through the task's editor, you would need to add each table individually. Wouldn't it be easier to be able to dynamically update the task to profile different tables in your database?

Most tasks in SSIS can be made dynamic by using configurations and expressions. *Configurations* are used for settings that you wish to update each time a package is loaded, and *expressions* are used for settings that you want to update during the package execution. Both expressions and configurations operate on the properties of tasks in the package, but depending on what aspect of the Data Profiling task you want to change, it may require special handling to behave in a dynamic manner.

Changing the database

Because the Data Profiling task uses connection managers to control the connection to the database, it is relatively easy to change the database it points to. You update the connection manager, using one of the standard approaches in SSIS, such as an expression that sets the `ConnectionString` property, or a configuration that sets the same property. You can also accomplish this by overriding the connection manager's setting at runtime using the `/Connection` switch of `DTEXEC`.

Bear in mind that although you can switch databases this way, the task will only work if it is pointing to a SQL Server database. Also, connection managers only control the database that you are connecting to, and not the specific tables. The profile requests in the task will still be referencing the original tables, so if the new database does not contain tables with the same names, the task will fail. What is needed is a way to change the profile requests to reference new tables.

Altering the profile requests

As noted earlier, you can configure the Data Profiling task through the Data Profiling Task Editor, which configures and stores the profile requests in the task's `Profile-Requests` property. But this property is a collection object, and collection objects can't be set through expressions or configurations, so, at first glance, it appears that you can't update the profile requests.

Fortunately, there is an additional property that can be used for this on the Data Profiling task. This is the `ProfileInputXml` property, which stores the XML representation of the profile requests. The `ProfileInputXml` property is not visible in the Properties window in BIDS, but you can see it in the Property Expressions Editor dialog box, or in the Package Configuration Wizard's property browser. You can set an XML string into this property using either an expression or a configuration. For it to work properly, the XML must conform to the DataProfile.xsd schema mentioned earlier.

Setting the ProfileInputXml property

So how can you go about altering the `ProfileInputXml` property to profile a different table? One way that works well is to create a string variable in the SSIS package to hold the table name (named `TableName`) and a second variable to hold the schema name (named `SchemaName`). Create a third variable that will hold the XML for the profile requests (named `ProfileXML`), and set the `EvaluateAsVariable` property of the `ProfileXML` variable to `True`. In the `Expression` property, you'll need to enter the XML string for the profile, and concatenate in the table and schema variables.

To get the XML to use as a starting point, you can configure and run the Data Profile task with its output directed to a file. You'll then need to remove the output information from the file, which can be done by removing all of the elements between the `<DataProfileOutput>` and `<Profiles>` tags, so that the XML looks similar to listing 1. You may have more or less XML, depending on how many profiles you configured the task for initially.

Listing 1   Data profile XML prior to making it dynamic

```xml
<?xml version="1.0" encoding="utf-16"?>
<DataProfile xmlns:xsi="http://www.w3.org/2001/XMLSchema-instance"
       xmlns:xsd="http://www.w3.org/2001/XMLSchema"
       xmlns="http://schemas.microsoft.com/sqlserver/2008/DataDebugger/">
  <DataSources />
  <DataProfileInput>
    <ProfileMode>Exact</ProfileMode>
    <Timeout>0</Timeout>
    <Requests>
      <ColumnNullRatioProfileRequest ID="NullRatioReq">
        <DataSourceID>{8D7CF241-6773-464A-87C8-60E95F386FB2}</DataSourceID>
        <Table Schema="Production" Table="Product" />
        <Column IsWildCard="true" />
      </ColumnNullRatioProfileRequest>
      <ColumnStatisticsProfileRequest ID="StatisticsReq">
        <DataSourceID>{8D7CF241-6773-464A-87C8-60E95F386FB2}</DataSourceID>
        <Table Schema="Production" Table="Product" />
        <Column IsWildCard="true" />
      </ColumnStatisticsProfileRequest>
    </Requests>
  </DataProfileInput>
  <DataProfileOutput>            **No profile output**
    <Profiles />           ◁──┘  **should be included**
  </DataProfileOutput>
</DataProfile>
```

Once you have the XML, you need to change a few things to use it in an expression. First, the entire string needs to be put inside double quotes ("). Second, any existing double quotes need to be escaped, using a backslash (\). For example, the ID attribute ID="StatisticsReq" needs to be formatted as ID=\"StatisticsReq\". Finally, the profile requests need to be altered to include the table name variable created previously. These modifications are shown in listing 2.

Listing 2   Data profiling XML after converting to an expression

```
"<?xml version=\"1.0\" encoding=\"utf-16\"?>
<DataProfile xmlns:xsi=\"http://www.w3.org/2001/XMLSchema-instance\"
       xmlns:xsd=\"http://www.w3.org/2001/XMLSchema\"
       xmlns=\"http://schemas.microsoft.com/sqlserver/2008/DataDebugger/\">
  <DataSources />
  <DataProfileInput>
    <ProfileMode>Exact</ProfileMode>
    <Timeout>0</Timeout>
    <Requests>
      <ColumnNullRatioProfileRequest ID=\"NullRatioReq\">
        <DataSourceID>{8D7CF241-6773-464A-87C8-60E95F386FB2}</DataSourceID>
        <Table Schema=\"" + @[User::SchemaName] +      Use variables for
            "\" Table=\"" +                             schema and table name
            @[User::TableName] + "\" />
        <Column IsWildCard=\"true\" />
      </ColumnNullRatioProfileRequest>
      <ColumnStatisticsProfileRequest ID=\"StatisticsReq\">
        <DataSourceID>{8D7CF241-6773-464A-87C8-60E95F386FB2}</DataSourceID>
        <Table Schema=\"" + @[User::SchemaName] +
            "\" Table=\"" +
            @[User::TableName] + "\"/>
        <Column IsWildCard=\"true\" />
      </ColumnStatisticsProfileRequest>
    </Requests>
  </DataProfileInput>
  <DataProfileOutput>
    <Profiles />
  </DataProfileOutput>
</DataProfile>"
```

To apply this XML to the Data Profiling task, open the Property Expressions Editor by opening the Data Profiling Task Editor and going to the Expressions page. Select the ProfileInputXml property, and set the expression to be the ProfileXML variable. Now the task is set up so that you can change the target table by updating the SchemaName and TableName variables, with no modification to the task necessary.

Now that we've made the task dynamic, let's move on to making decisions based on the output of the task.

> ### Expressions in SSIS
>
> Expressions in SSIS are limited to producing output no longer than 4,000 characters. Although that is enough for the example in this chapter, you may need to take it into account when working with multiple profiles. You can work around the limitation by executing the Data Profiling task multiple times, with a subset of the profiles in each execution to keep the expression under the 4,000-character limit.

Making data-quality decisions in the ETL

The Data Profiling task output can be used to make decisions about the quality of your data, and by incorporating the task output into your ETL process, you can automate these decisions. By taking things a little further, you can make these decisions self-adjusting as your data changes over time. We'll take a look at both scenarios in the following sections.

Excluding data based on quality

Most commonly, the output of the Data Profiling task will change the flow of your ETL depending on the quality of the data being processed in your ETL. A simple example of this might be using the Column Null Ratio profile to evaluate a Customer table prior to extracting it from the source system. If the null ratio is greater than 30 percent for the Customer Name column, you might have your SSIS package set up to abort the processing and log an error message. This is an example of using data profiling information to prevent bad data from entering your data warehouse.

In situations like the preceding, though, a large percentage of rows that may have had acceptable data quality would also be excluded. For many data warehouses, that's not acceptable. It's more likely that these "hard" rules, such as not allowing null values in certain columns, will be implemented on a row-by-row basis, so that all acceptable data will be loaded into the warehouse, and only bad data will be excluded. In SSIS, this is often accomplished in the data flow by using Conditional Split transformations to send invalid data to error tables.

Adjusting rules dynamically

A more complex example involves using data profiling to establish what good data looks like, and then using this information to identify data of questionable quality. For example, if you are a retailer of products from multiple manufactures, your Product table will likely have the manufacturer's original part number, and each manufacturer may have its own format for part numbers. In this scenario, you might use the Column Pattern profile against a known good source of part numbers, such as your Product table or your Product master, to identify the regular expressions that match the part numbers. During the execution of your ETL process, you could compare new incoming part numbers with these regular expressions to determine if they match the known formats for part numbers. As new products are added to the known good source of part numbers, new patterns will be included in the profile, and the rule will be adjusted dynamically.

It's worth noting that this type of data-quality check is often implemented as a "soft" rule, so the row is not prohibited from entering the data warehouse. After all, the manufacturer may have implemented a new part-numbering scheme, or the part number could have come from a new manufacturer that is not in the Product dimension yet. Instead of redirecting the row to an error table, you might set a flag on the row indicating that there is a question as to the quality of the information, but allow it to enter the data warehouse anyway. This would allow the part number to be used for recording sales of that product, while still identifying a need for someone to follow up and verify that the part number is correct. Once they have validated the part number, and corrected it if necessary, the questionable data flag would be removed, and that product could become part of the known good set of products. The next time that you generate a Column Pattern profile against the part numbers, the new pattern will be included, and new rows that conform to it will no longer be flagged as questionable.

As mentioned earlier, implementing this type of logic in your ETL process can allow it to dynamically adjust data-quality rules over time, and as your data quality gets better, the ETL process will get better at flagging questionable data.

Now let's take a look at how to use the task output in the package.

Consuming the task output

As mentioned earlier, the Data Profiling task produces its output as XML, which can be stored in a variable or a file. This XML output will include both the profile requests and the output profiles for each request.

Capturing the output

If you are planning to use the output in the same package that the profiling task is in, you will usually want to store the output XML in a package variable. If the output will be used in another package, how you store it will depend on how the other package will be executed. If the second package will be executed directly from the package performing the profiling through an Execute Package task, you can store the output in a variable and use a Parent Package Variable configuration to pass it between the packages. On the other hand, if the second package will be executed in a separate process or at a different time, storing the output in a file is the best option.

Regardless of whether the output is stored in a variable or a file, it can be accessed in a few different ways. Because the output is stored as XML, you can make use of the XML task to use it in the control flow, or the XML source to use it in the data flow. You can also use the Script task or the Script component to manipulate the XML output directly using .NET code.

Using SSIS XML functionality

The XML task is provided in SSIS so that you can work with XML in the control flow. Because the Data Profiling task produces XML, it is a natural fit to use the XML task to process the data profile output. Primarily, the XSLT or XPATH operations can be used with the profile XML.

The XSLT operation can be used to transform the output into a format that's easier to use, such as filtering the profile output down to specific profiles that you are interested in, which is useful if you want to use the XML source to process it. The XSLT operation can also be used to remove the default namespace from the XML document, which makes using XPATH against it much easier.

XPATH operations can be used to retrieve a specific value or set of nodes from the profile. This option is illustrated by the Trim Namespaces XML task in the sample package that accompanies this chapter, showing how to retrieve the null count for a particular column using XPATH.

NOTE The sample package for this chapter can be found on the book's website at http://www.manning.com/SQLServerMVPDeepDives.

> #### New to XML?
> If you are new to XML, the preceding discussion may be a bit confusing, and the reasons for taking these steps may not be obvious. If you'd like to learn more about working with XML in SSIS, please review these online resources:
>
> - General XML information: http://msdn.microsoft.com/en-us/xml/default.aspx
> - Working with XML in SSIS: http://blogs.msdn.com/mattm/archive/tags/XML/default.aspx

In the data flow, the XML source component can be used to get information from the Data Profiling task output. You can do this in two ways, one of which is relatively straightforward if you are familiar with XSLT. The other is more complex to implement but has the benefit of not requiring in-depth XSLT knowledge.

If you know XSLT, you can use an XML task to transform and simplify the Data Profiling task output prior to using it in the XML source, as mentioned previously. This can help avoid having to join multiple outputs from the XML source, which is discussed shortly.

If you don't know XSLT, you can take a few additional steps and use the XML source directly against the Data Profiling task output. First, you must provide an .XSD file for the XML source, but the .XSD published by Microsoft at http://schemas.microsoft.com/sqlserver/2008/DataDebugger/DataProfile.xsd is too complex for the XML source. Instead, you will need to generate a schema using an existing data profile that you have saved to a file. Second, you have to identify the correct outputs from the XML source. The XML source creates a separate output for each distinct element type in the XML: the output from the Data Profiling task includes at least three distinct elements for each profile you include, and for most profiles it will have four or more. This can lead to some challenges in finding the appropriate output information from the XML source. Third, because the XML source does not flatten the XML output, you have to join the multiple outputs together to assemble meaningful information. The sample package on the book's website (http://www.manning.com/SQLServerMVP-DeepDives) has an example of doing this for the Column Pattern profile. The data flow is shown in figure 3.

In the data flow shown in figure 3, the results of the Column Pattern profile are being transformed from a hierarchical structure (typical for XML) to a flattened structure suitable for saving into a database table. The hierarchy for a Column Pattern profile has five levels that need to be used for the information we are interested in, and each output from the XML source includes one of these levels. Each level contains a column that ties it to the levels used below it. In the data flow, each output from the XML source is sorted, so that consistent ordering is ensured. Then, each output, which represents one level in the hierarchical structure, is joined to the output representing the next level down in the hierarchy. Most of the levels have a `ColumnPattern-Profile_ID`, which can be used in the Merge Join transformation to join the levels, but there is some special handling required for the level representing the patterns, as they need to be joined on the `TopRegexPatterns_ID` instead of the `ColumnPattern-Profile_ID`. This data flow is included in the sample package for this chapter, so you can review the logic if you wish.

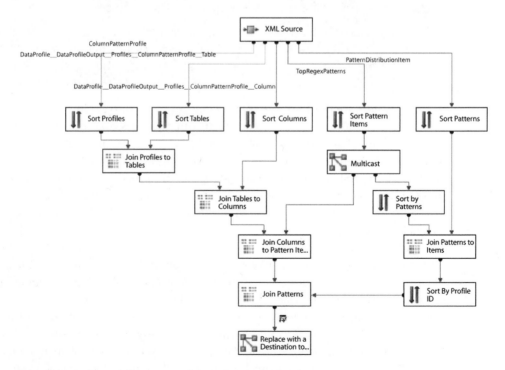

Figure 3 Data flow to reassemble a Column Pattern profile

Using scripts

Script tasks and components provide another means of accessing the information in the Data Profiling task output. By saving the output to a package variable, you make it accessible within a Script task. Once in the Script task, you have the choice of performing direct string manipulation to get the information you want, or you can use the XmlDocument class from the System.Xml namespace to load and process the output XML. Both of these approaches offer a tremendous amount of flexibility in working with the XML. As working with XML documents using .NET is well documented, we won't cover it in depth here.

Another approach that requires scripting is the use of the classes in the DataProfiler.dll assembly. These classes facilitate loading and interacting with the data profile through a custom API, and the approach works well, but this is an undocumented and unsupported API, so there are no guarantees when using it. If this doesn't scare you off, and you are comfortable working with unsupported features (that have a good chance of changing in new releases), take a look at "Accessing a data profile programmatically" on the SSIS Team Blog (http://blogs.msdn.com/mattm/archive/2008/03/12/accessing-a-data-profile-programmatically.aspx) for an example of using the API to load and retrieve information from a data profile.

Incorporating the values in the package

Once you have retrieved values from the data profile output, using one of the methods discussed in the previous sections, you need to incorporate it into the package logic. This is fairly standard SSIS work.

Most often, you will want to store specific values retrieved from the profile in a package variable, and use those variables to make dynamic decisions. For example, consider the Column Null Ratio profiling we discussed earlier. After retrieving the null count from the profile output, you could use an expression on a precedence constraint to have the package stop processing if the null count is too high.

In the data flow, you will often use Conditional Split or Derived Column transformations to implement the decision-making logic. For example, you might use the Data Profiling task to run a Column Length Distribution profile against the product description column in your Product table. You could use a Script task to process the profile output and determine that 95 percent of your product descriptions fall between 50 and 200 characters. By storing those boundary values in variables, you could check for new product descriptions that fall outside of this range in your ETL. You could use the Conditional Split transformation to redirect these rows to an error table, or the Derived Column transformation to set a flag on the row indicating that there might be a data-quality issue.

Some data-quality checking is going to require more sophisticated processing. For the Column Pattern checking scenario discussed earlier, you would need to implement a Script component in the data flow that can take a list of regular expressions and apply them against the column that you wanted to check. If the column value matched one or more of the regular expressions, it would be flagged as OK. If the column value didn't match any of the regular expressions, it would be flagged as questionable, or redirected to an error table. Listing 3 shows an example of the code that can perform this check. It takes in a delimited list of regular expression patterns, and then compares each of them to a specified column.

Listing 3   Script component to check column values against a list of patterns

```
public class ScriptMain : UserComponent
{
    List<Regex> regex = new List<Regex>();

    public override void PreExecute()
    {
        base.PreExecute();

        string[] regExPatterns;
        IDTSVariables100 vars = null;
        this.VariableDispenser.LockOneForRead("RegExPatterns", ref vars);
        regExPatterns =
        vars["RegExPatterns"].Value.ToString().Split("~".ToCharArray());
        vars.Unlock();

        foreach (string pattern in regExPatterns)
        {
            regex.Add(new Regex(pattern, RegexOptions.Compiled));
        }
    }

    public override void Input0_ProcessInputRow(Input0Buffer Row)
    {
        if (Row.Size_IsNull) return;

        foreach (Regex r in regex)
        {
            Match m = r.Match(Row.Size);
            if (m.Success)
            {
                Row.GoodRow = true;
            }
            else
            {
                Row.GoodRow = false;
            }
        }
    }
}
```

Summary

Over the course of this chapter, we've looked at a number of ways that the Data Profiling task can be used in SSIS, from using it to get a better initial understanding of your data to incorporating it into your ongoing ETL processes. Being able to make your ETL process dynamic and more resilient to change is important for ongoing maintenance and usability of the ETL system. As data volumes continue to grow, and more data is integrated into data warehouses, the importance of data quality increases as well. Establishing ETL processes that can adjust to new data and still provide valid feedback about the quality of that data is vital to keeping up with the volume of information we deal with today.

About the author

 John Welch is Chief Architect with Mariner, a consulting firm specializing in enterprise reporting and analytics, data warehousing, and performance management solutions. John has been working with business intelligence and data warehousing technologies for seven years, with a focus on Microsoft products in heterogeneous environments. He is an MVP and has presented at Professional Association for SQL Server (PASS) conferences, the Microsoft Business Intelligence conference, Software Development West (SD West), Software Management Conference (ASM/SM), and others. He has also contributed to two recent books on SQL Server 2008: *Microsoft SQL Server 2008 Management and Administration* (Sams, 2009) and *Smart Business Intelligence Solutions with Microsoft SQL Server 2008* (Microsoft Press, 2009).

57 Expressions in SQL Server Integration Services

Matthew Roche

SQL Server Integration Services (SSIS) is Microsoft's enterprise extract, transform, and load (ETL) platform, and is used in large-scale business intelligence projects and small-scale import/export jobs around the world. Although SSIS contains an impressive set of features for solving a range of data-centric problems, one feature—expressions—stands out as the most important for SSIS developers to master.

Expressions in SSIS are a mechanism to add dynamic functionality to SSIS packages; they are the primary tool that SSIS developers can use to build packages to solve complex real-world problems. This chapter examines SSIS expressions from the perspective of providing elegant solutions to common problems and presents a set of tested techniques that will allow you to take your SSIS packages to the next level.

SSIS packages: a brief review

Before we can dive into the deep end with expressions, we need to look at SSIS packages—the context in which expressions are used. Packages in SSIS are the units of development and deployment; they're what you build and execute, and have a few common components, including

- *Control flow*—The execution logic of the package, which is made up of tasks, containers, and precedence constraints. Each package has a single control flow.
- *Data flow*—The high-performance data pipeline that powers the core ETL functionality in SSIS, and is made up of sources, transformations, and destinations. The SSIS data flow is implemented as a task, which allows multiple data flow tasks to be added to a package's control flow.
- *Connection managers*—Shared components that allow the control flow and data flow to connect to databases, files, and other resources outside of the package.

- *Variables*—The sole mechanism for sharing information between components in an SSIS package; variables have deep integration with expressions as well.

SSIS packages include more than just these elements, but for the purposes of this chapter, that's enough review. Let's move on to the good stuff: expressions!

Expressions: a quick tour

Expressions add dynamic functionality to SSIS packages using a simple syntax based on a subset of the C language. Expression syntax does not include any control of flow (looping, branching, and so on) or data modification capabilities. Each expression evaluates to a single scalar value, and although this can often seem restrictive to developers who are new to SSIS, it allows expressions to be used in a variety of places within a package.

How can we use expressions in a package? The simplest way is to use property expressions. All containers in SSIS, including tasks and the package itself, have an `Expressions` property, which is a collection of expressions and the properties to which their values will be assigned. This allows SSIS package developers to specify their own code—the expression—that is evaluated whenever a property of a built-in or third-party component is accessed. How many other development tools let you do that?

Let's look at an example. Figure 1 shows the properties for an Execute SQL Task configured to execute a `DELETE` statement.

Although this Execute SQL Task is functional, it isn't particularly useful unless the package always needs to delete the order details for `[OrderID]=5`. This task would be much more useful if it instead deleted whatever order number was *current* for the package execution. To implement this dynamic behavior, we're going to take two steps. First, we're going to add a new variable, named `OrderID`, to the package. (If you

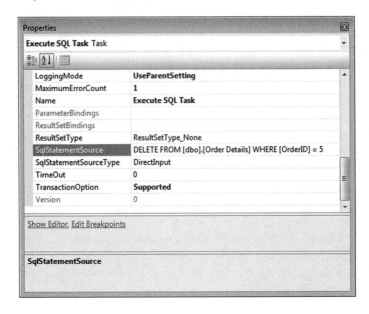

Figure 1
Static task properties

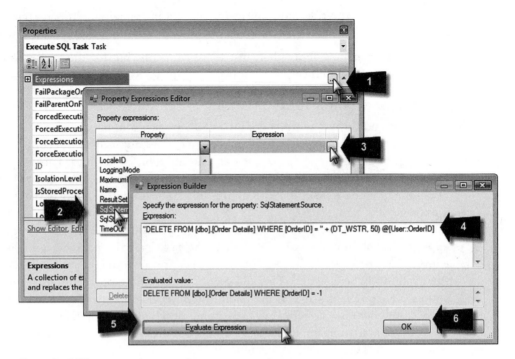

Figure 2   Adding a property expression

don't know how to do this already, consider it an exercise—we won't walk through adding a variable step by step.) Second, we're going to add a property expression to the SqlStatementSource property of the Execute SQL Task. To do this, we'll follow the steps illustrated in figure 2.

1 In the Properties window, select Execute SQL Task and then click on the ellipsis (...) button next to the Expressions property. This will cause the Property Expressions Editor dialog box to be displayed.

2 In the Property Expressions Editor dialog box, select the SqlStatementSource property from the drop-down list in the Property column.

3 Click on the ellipsis button in the Expression column. This will cause the Expression Builder dialog box to be displayed. (Please note that figure 2 shows only a subset of the Expression Builder dialog box to better fit on the printed page.)

4 Enter the following expression in the Expression text box:

```
"DELETE FROM [dbo].[Order Details] WHERE [OrderID] = " + (DT_WSTR, 50)
@[User::OrderID]
```

5 Click on the Evaluate Expression button to display the output of the expression in the Evaluated Value text box. (At this point it may be useful to copy and paste this value into a SQL Server Management Studio query window to ensure that the expression was constructed correctly.)

6 Click on the OK buttons to close the Expression Builder and Property Expressions Editor windows and save all changes.

7 Execute the package to ensure that the functionality added through the expression behaves as required.

Several important techniques are demonstrated in these steps:

- We started with a valid static value before we added the expression. Instead of starting off with a dynamic SQL statement, we started with a static statement which we tested to ensure that we had a *known good* starting point.
- We added a single piece of dynamic functionality at a time. Because our example was simple, we only added a single piece of dynamic functionality in total; but if we were adding both a dynamic WHERE clause and a dynamic table name, we would've added each dynamic expression element to the static SQL statement individually.
- We tested the expression after each change. This basic technique is often overlooked, but it's a vital timesaver. The Expression Editor has limited debugging capabilities, and locating errors in a complex expression can be painfully difficult. By testing the expression after each change, the scope of debugging can be significantly reduced.

With this example setting the stage, let's dive deeper into SSIS expressions by illustrating how they can be used to add dynamic functionality to our packages, and solve real-world problems.

Expressions in the control flow

We'll continue by looking at expressions in the SSIS control flow. Although the example in the previous section is technically a control flow example (because we applied a property expression to a property of a task, and tasks are control flow components) there are more interesting examples and techniques we can explore. One of the most important—and overlooked—techniques is using expressions with precedence constraints to conditionally execute tasks.

Consider the following requirements:

- If a specific table exists in the target database, execute a data flow task.
- If the table does not exist, execute an Execute SQL Task to create the table, and then execute the data flow task.

If this problem needed to be solved using a traditional programming language, the developer would add an if statement and that would be that. But SSIS does not include an if statement, a branching task, or the like, so the solution, although simple, is not always obvious.

An often-attempted approach to solve this problem is to add a property expression to the Disabled property of the Execute SQL Task. The rationale here is that if the Execute SQL Task is disabled then it won't execute, and only the data flow task will run. The main problem with this approach is that the Disabled property is designed to be used only at design time; setting `Disabled` to `True` is similar to *commenting out* a task so that it remains part of the control flow—but as far as the SSIS runtime is concerned, the task doesn't exist.

The preferred way to achieve this goal is to use expressions on the precedence constraints that connect the various tasks in the control flow. In addition to the three different constraints that can be used (success, failure, and completion), each precedence constraint can be edited to include an expression that determines whether or not this particular branch of the control flow logic will execute. The expression must have a Boolean return value—it must evaluate to true or false—and this value controls the conditional execution. Figure 3 illustrates the control flow configuration necessary to implement the required behavior using expressions.

Implementing this solution has three primary steps:

1. The results of the `SELECT` statement run by the Execute SQL Task are stored in a Boolean package variable named `TableExists`. To map the value into a Boolean variable, `CAST` the data type to `BIT` in the `SELECT` statement, returning 1 if the table exists, and 0 if not.

2. Each precedence constraint has been edited to apply the Expression and Constraint Evaluation operation option, with the appropriate expression (for one, `@TableExists`; for the other, `!@TableExists`) specified to enforce the required logic. Note that the two expressions are both mutually exclusive (they cannot both be true at the same time) and also inclusive—there is no condition that's not represented by one of the two expressions.

3. The `@TableExists` precedence constraint has been edited to specify the `Logical OR` option—this is why the constraints that reference the data flow task are displayed with dotted lines. This is required because, as you'll recall, the two

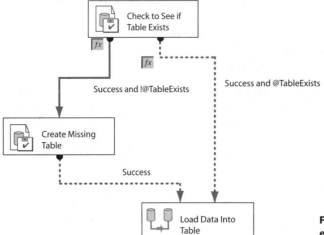

Figure 3   Conditional execution with expressions

paths from the first Execute SQL Task are mutually exclusive, but both paths end at the data flow task. Unless one of the two precedence constraints that end at the data flow task is so edited (you only need to edit one, because the change in operation will apply to all precedence constraints that end at the same task)—the data flow task will never execute.

Self-documenting precedence constraints

If you would like your precedence constraints to include the constraint options and expressions shown in figure 3, all you need to do is set the `ShowAnnotation` property for each precedence constraint. The default value for this property is `AsNeeded`, and does not cause this information to be displayed; but setting this property to `ConstraintOptions` for each precedence constraint will cause these annotations to be displayed. Unfortunately, SSIS does not support setting a default value for this property, but it is easy to select multiple precedence constraints and set this property for all of them at one time. Taking this step will make your packages self-documenting, and easier to debug and maintain.

The final settings for the `@TableExists` precedence constraint can be seen in figure 4.

One additional requirement for this approach is the need for a task from which the precedence constraints can originate. In this example, the need for the Execute SQL Task is obvious—the package uses this task to check to see if the target table

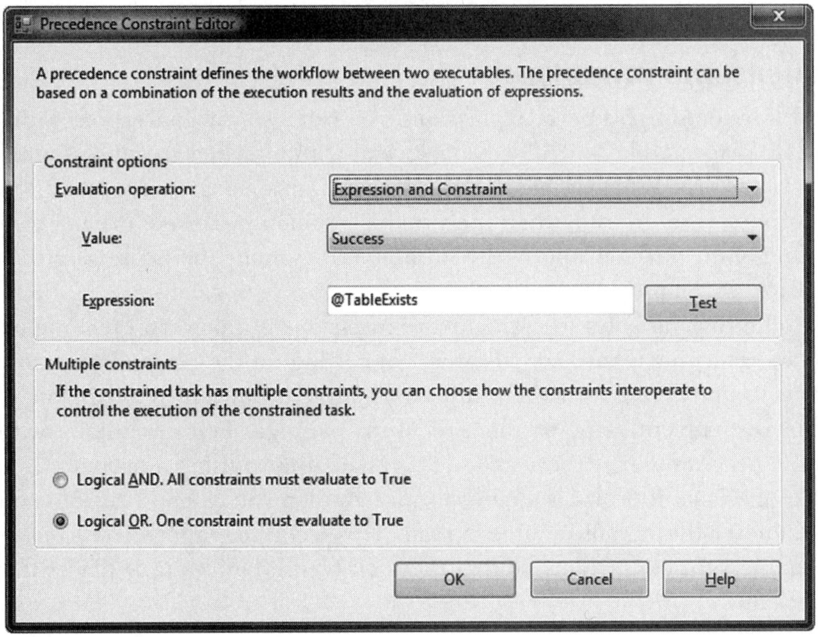

Figure 4   Precedence constraint with expression

exists. But there are other common scenarios, such as when the state upon which the conditional logic must be based is set via a package configuration, and the first task in the package must be executed or skipped based on this state, where the natural package logic does not include a task from which the expression-based precedence constraints should originate. This can pose a predicament, because precedence constraints must originate from a task or container, and this type of conditional logic is implemented in SSIS by using precedence constraints and expressions.

In situations such as these, a useful technique is to add a *placeholder* task—one that serves as the starting point for precedence constraints—to the control flow. Two obvious candidates for this placeholder role are the Script Task and the Sequence Container; each of these components will work without any configuration required, and won't alter the package logic.

Additional reading online

For more detailed examples on how to use expressions in the control flow, see these online resources:

- Expressions and precedence constraints: http://bi-polar23.blogspot.com/2008/02/expressions-and-precedence-constraints.html
- Using placeholder tasks: http://bi-polar23.blogspot.com/2007/05/conditional-task-execution.html
- Expressions and the Foreach Loop Container: http://bi-polar23.blogspot.com/2007/08/loading-multiple-excel-files-with-ssis.html

---

Expressions and variables

In addition to using property expressions, you can also use expressions with SSIS variables. In fact, variables in SSIS have a special ability related to expressions: they not only have a `Value` property, but also an `EvaluateAsExpression` property. If this `Boolean` property is set to true, when the variable's value is accessed, instead of returning the value of the `Value` property, the variable will evaluate the expression that's stored in its `Expression` property.

Configuring variables to evaluate as expressions is a powerful technique. Instead of always returning a hard-coded value—or relying on the Script Task or other components to update the variable's value—the variable can return a dynamic value that reflects the current state of the executing package. For developers with object-oriented programming experience, this is analogous to using a property get accessor instead of a field; it provides a mechanism by which you can add custom code that is run whenever the variable's value is read. This technique allows you to use variables as containers for expressions, so that they can be used in multiple places throughout the package.

One real-life example of this technique is managing the locations of filesystem resources. Consider a package that works with files in a folder structure, like the one shown in figure 5.

Figure 5
Deployment folders

As you can see, there is a DeploymentRoot folder that contains subfolders for the different types of files with which the package interacts. In the real world, the root folder could exist on different drives and in different locations in the filesystem structure, on the different machines to which the package may be deployed. To handle this eventuality, you'd use package configurations—or a similar mechanism—to inform the package where the files are located, probably by using the configuration to set the value of a @DeploymentRootPath variable. You could then use multiple configurations to set the values of multiple variables, one for each folder, but there is a better way. And as you have likely guessed—this better way uses expressions.

For the folder structure shown in figure 5, you could create four additional variables, one for each subfolder, configured to evaluate as the following expressions:

- `@ErrorFilePath - @DeploymentRootPath + "\\ErrorFiles"`
- `@ImportFilePath - @DeploymentRootPath + "\\ImportFiles"`
- `@LogFilePath - @DeploymentRootPath + "\\LogFiles"`
- `@OutputFilePath - @DeploymentRootPath + "\\LogFiles"`

And it doesn't stop there. It's not uncommon to see packages where a different subfolder must be used per client, or per year, or per day—and having a set of variables based on expressions that can in turn be used as the basis for more granular expressions is a great way to achieve reuse within a package. And, in this scenario, only one configuration is required—the value for the @DeploymentRootPath variable can be set via a configuration, and all other filesystem paths will be automatically updated because they're based on expressions that use this variable as their source.

Additional reading online

For more detailed examples on how to use expressions with package variables, see these online resources:

- Filesystem deployment: http://bi-polar23.blogspot.com/2007/05/flexible-file-system-deployment.html
- Dynamic filename expressions: http://bi-polar23.blogspot.com/2008/06/file-name-expressions.html
- Dynamic filenames and dates: http://bi-polar23.blogspot.com/2008/06/looking-for-date-what-in-name.html

Expressions in the data flow

As we've seen, expressions are pretty much everywhere in the SSIS control flow. You can assign them to task properties, to precedence constraints, to variables—you name it. But when we move into the SSIS data flow, support for expressions is very different and often limited. Several data flow transformations are explicitly designed to use expressions, but the ubiquitous expression support that the SSIS control flow delivers is missing in the data flow.

In fact, property expressions, as we saw them used earlier, are a feature of the control flow, and do not even exist in the data flow. If you look at the Properties window for a data flow component, you will see that there is no Expressions property like there is for control flow components. Fortunately, the control flow and data flow do work together to provide some property expression support through the data flow. Figure 6 illustrates how the SqlCommand and SqlCommandParam properties of a Lookup transformation in a data flow are exposed as properties of the data flow task itself. And because these Lookup transformation properties are now exposed as properties of the data flow task, property expressions can be applied to them just as they can to any other task property.

Unfortunately this approach has some limitations, as not all data flow component properties are exposed in this way. As figure 6 shows, only two properties of the Lookup transformation are exposed, and no other component properties are exposed for this particular data flow. Also, the set of exposed properties is smaller in earlier versions of SSIS. Figure 6 shows a package built using the SQL Server 2008 version of SSIS; if you look for these properties to be exposed in a SQL Server 2005 SSIS package, you'll be disappointed because this dynamic functionality is not available in SQL Server 2005.

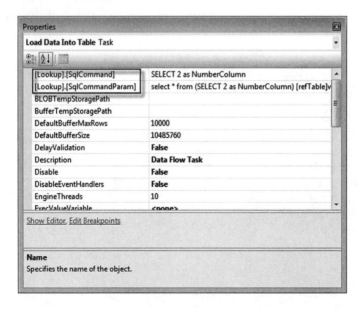

Figure 6   Exposed data flow
component properties

Despite these limitations, expressions are still powerful tools within the SSIS data flow. Two data flow components—the Derived Column transformation and the Conditional Split transformation—both have expressions at their core. The Derived Column allows developers to add new columns to the data flow pipeline, with those columns' values based on expressions set in the Transformation Editor. When working with data sources that do not allow calculations to be performed in the source query, such as text files, this ability is crucial to transforming the data before loading it into the destination database. The Conditional Split transformation allows developers to specify a set of `Boolean` expressions which are applied to each row passing through the data flow pipeline; it also allows developers to redirect rows to different transformation outputs based on these expressions, so that different processing can be applied to different rows. Figure 7 shows an example of the Conditional Split transformation at work, splitting data flow records into two outputs—one for new orders placed within the last 30 days, and one for old orders.

In addition to the expression-based functionality provided by the Conditional Split and Derived Column transformations, there are other, less obvious, opportunities to use expressions to add dynamic behavior to the SSIS data flow. But unlike the control flow where such opportunities are typically found with the label `Expression`, in the data flow these opportunities are usually found under the label `Variable`.

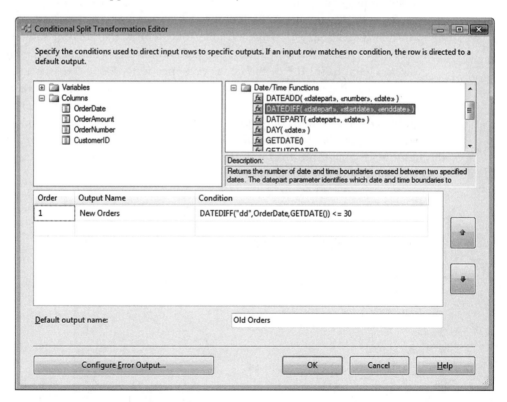

Figure 7   Conditional Split transformation

For example, the OLE DB Source component has a `Data Access Mode` property. This property must be set at design time, and cannot be set via an expression, but two of the four options—`Table Name or View Name Variable` and `SQL Command From Variable`—give you the ability to specify a variable name instead of a literal value. And because variables can be based on expressions, this means that the source query can be based on an expression as well.

For example, consider an SSIS data flow based on the following source query, but which needs to process orders for only a single salesperson per execution:

```
SELECT OrderDate
      ,OrderAmount
      ,OrderNumber
      ,CustomerID
      ,SalesPersonID
  FROM Orders
```

You could use the Conditional Split transformation to discard records that don't contain the current SalesPersonID value, but this is inefficient. A better solution would be to filter the records in the source query itself, so that only those records for the current salesperson are ever extracted from the source system. This approach is easy to implement, but not always obvious to SSIS developers who haven't seen it used.

To make this query dynamic, create a variable that evaluates as an expression that returns the `SELECT` statement filtered by the current salesperson. Assuming that there's a @SalesPersonID package variable that defines the current salesperson to process, figure 8 shows the expression that implements this dynamic source query.

Now you need to set the `Data Access Mode` property to `SQL Command From Variable`, and specify the name of the variable to use for the query—and the data source component will retrieve only those records that apply to the current salesperson. Even though the OLE DB Source component doesn't directly support expressions, the ability to specify a variable for the source query allows us to use expressions indirectly, through the variable. And this is not the only data flow component that supports this feature; several data flow components have similar variable-based options.

This technique implies some flexibility, as practically any query can be supplied by the variable that contains the SQL statement, but it's important to remember the

Figure 8   SQL script variable expression

metadata-bound nature of the SSIS data flow. When the package is built, the SSIS data flow uses the metadata—the column names, data types, and so on—to define the *signature* of the buffers used by the data flow pipeline; this metadata cannot change without the rest of the data flow also being updated. Whereas you can build many different kinds of queries using expressions, the SSIS data flow will only allow queries that have the same metadata signature to be used for any given data flow.

> **SSIS expressions and SQL injection attacks**
>
> The data source technique shown above, or any technique that uses string concatenation to build a SQL statement, is potentially vulnerable to SQL injection attack. Due to the typical execution context of SSIS packages (most packages are executing in a controlled server environment and do not accept input data from non-trusted sources), this technique is sometimes seen as acceptable even where it would not be allowed in a user-facing client application. As an SSIS developer you need to understand the specific details of your environment and decide if this technique is acceptable. SSIS does provide other techniques to deliver similar functionality, so there are options available if this technique cannot be used.

Expressions and connection managers

The final example we'll look at is using expressions with connection managers, which deserves dedicated coverage due to the capabilities that can be achieved. Connection managers play a unique role in SSIS packages: they define the gateway between the package and external resources, such as databases and files. One common and well-documented example of using expressions and connection managers is to loop over a set of input files (see the SSIS tutorials in SQL Server Books Online for step-by-step instructions). By using the Foreach Loop Container in the package's control flow to loop over a set of files, you can assign the file path of the current file to a package variable. Then, by using an expression on the ConnectionString property of a Flat File connection manager, you can work on the current file using any task (generally the data flow task, but it can be just about anything) within the Foreach Loop Container.

But this doesn't really demonstrate the degree of flexibility that can be achieved by using expressions with connection managers. Not only can this technique be used for non-file data sources (imagine looping over a set of databases instead of a set of files), but it can also be used for exporting data, as well as importing data. Let's look at an example.

Consider a database that tracks data, including products and product categories. The schema is shown in figure 9.

You could export product data to a text file, but real-world requirements aren't so straightforward. For example, what if the products in each product category needed to be exported into a different, category-specific text file? Given the fact that the set of product categories will change over time, this makes the problem much more interesting. But by using SSIS expressions in conjunction with the Flat File connection

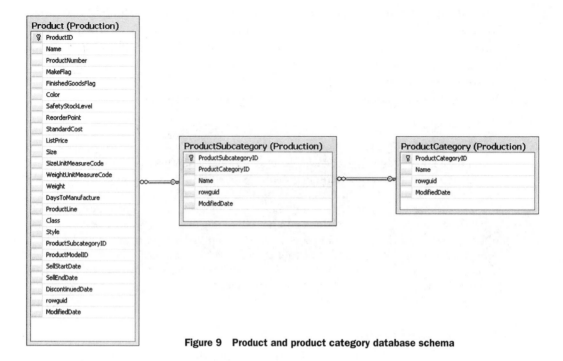

Figure 9   **Product and product category database schema**

manager for the exported text files, as well as applying a few of the techniques demonstrated earlier, the solution can easily be implemented.

To get started, and to follow the guidelines presented at the beginning of the chapter, we'll build a package that exports a single text file and provides the foundation needed for the required functionality. The *starter* package includes the following components:

- An OLE DB connection manager that references the source database.
- A Flat File connection manager that references the destination file location.
- A data flow task that performs the ETL processing.
- A set of string variables (some of which are based on expressions) to be used by the other components:

  - @CurrentCategoryName—This variable, assigned the value Bikes, is used to store the name of the product category for which product data will be exported. As we'll see later on, this variable will be used in many expressions in the package and is at the core of the dynamic behavior we're implementing.
  - @ExportFileName—This variable, based on the expression @[User:: CurrentCategoryName] + ".txt", is used to define the name of the file to which to export the product data.

- @ExportFolder—This variable, based on the expression @[User::Root Folder] + "TextFileExports\\", is used to define the folder in which the exported files will be created.
- @RootFolder—This variable, assigned a filesystem folder path, is used to define the root folder to which the SSIS package is deployed. (It's worth noting that the @RootFolder and @ExportFolder variables aren't technically necessary for this example, but they're useful in real-world packages that use the filesystem like the example does.)
- @SqlSelectProducts—This variable, based on an expression that uses the @CurrentCategoryName variable in a SQL SELECT statement's WHERE clause, is used by the OLE DB Source component in the data flow to SELECT the product records for the current product category.

Figure 10 shows these components in the starter package.

Remember—the whole point of getting the package to this starting point is to provide a functional and tested baseline on which to build the additional expression-based dynamic functionality. We skimmed over the details of getting to this point because there is nothing here that we haven't already seen earlier in the chapter.

The next step to take is to update the Flat File connection manager to use an expression based on the @ExportFileName variable for its ConnectionString property. This is as simple as using a property expression for the ConnectionString property, with the following expression: @[User::ExportFolder] + @[User::ExportFileName]. With this property expression in place, the Flat File connection manager will now reference a file in the @ExportFolder folder with the @ExportFileName name, and

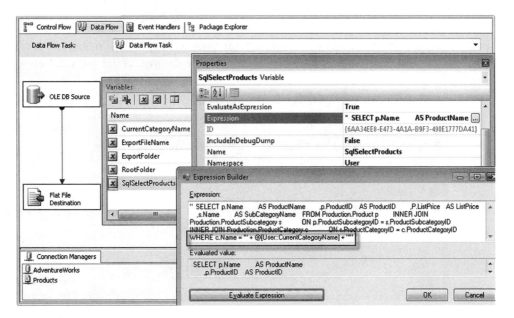

Figure 10   Flat File export starting point

because of the expression on the @ExportFileName variable, the file name will automatically reflect the name of the current product category being exported. Now all we need to do is to loop over the available product categories to put these package components to work.

The first step in setting up such a loop is to add a variable named @Product-Categories of type Object to the package. Then, add an Execute SQL Task configured with the Full result set ResultSetType to the package that executes the following SELECT statement, and stores the result set in the @ProductCategories variable.

```
SELECT Name AS CategoryName
  FROM Production.ProductCategory
```

Next, add a Foreach Loop Container to the package, and configure the container to use the Foreach ADO Enumerator to loop over the @ProductCategories variable, and to map the CategoryName field in the result set to the @CurrentCategoryName variable. The only step that remains is to move the existing data flow task into the Foreach Loop Container so that the finished package looks like the one shown in figure 11.

Now, when the package executes, the data flow task will execute once for each product category in the database, and a Flat File will be created with the name of each category, containing the list of the category's products, as shown in figure 12.

We started with a package that used a data flow task to export a single text file and then—without making changes to the data flow task—the same package exported a dynamic set of text files based on the product categories defined in the database. How did this happen?

Figure 11   The finished package

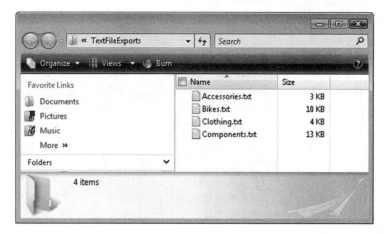

Figure 12   Exported files for each category

The answer is rooted in expressions:

- The @SqlSelectProducts variable, which is used as the source query of the OLE DB Source component in the data flow, is based on an expression that uses the @CurrentCategoryName variable in its WHERE clause.
- The @ExportFileName variable also uses the @CurrentCategoryName variable in its expression, so that the value of the @ExportFileName variable always includes the value of the @CurrentCategoryName variable.
- The ConnectionString property of the Flat File connection manager is based on the @ExportFileName variable, so that when the value of this variable changes, the name of the file referenced by the connection manager changes as well.

With all of these expressions in place, moving the data flow task inside the loop *lit up* the dynamic behavior in the expressions, because the loop changes the value of the @CurrentCategoryName variable for each iteration through the loop. This value then propagates to the components that need to be category-specific, including the connection manager and the OLE DB Source component in the data flow. All that is needed to put all the pieces together is to set the @CurrentCategoryName variable to the correct values, and the Foreach Loop Container is a perfect fit for the job.

Additional reading online

For more detailed examples on using expressions with connection managers, see these online resources:

- Loading multiple Excel files with SSIS: http://bi-polar23.blogspot.com/2007/08/loading-multiple-excel-files-with-ssis.html
- Connection string examples: http://bi-polar23.blogspot.com/2008/12/connection-strings.html

Summary

This chapter presented a set of techniques and approaches for using expressions in SSIS packages to solve real-world problems. Although a complete coverage of SSIS expressions would likely require a book of its own, the examples and techniques shown in this chapter should give you a great head start on applying expressions to your own challenges. Whether you're new to SSIS development or an experienced BI developer, there are always new ways to apply expressions to your packages which enable the dynamic behavior required to solve the problems that your projects send your way. By using the techniques presented here, you'll be well prepared to solve whatever SSIS problems the future has in store.

About the author

Matthew Roche is a Senior Program Manager with Microsoft Learning. Matthew has been a Microsoft Certified Trainer since 1996, and until joining Microsoft in late 2008, he was a SQL Server MVP with a focus on SQL Server Integration Services. When he is not working to improve the quality of Microsoft's training products or building ETL solutions by using SSIS, Matthew spends time with his amazing wife and two wonderful children, and listens to the world's loudest and most powerful heavy metal music. Look for Matthew in the front row on your favorite Manowar DVD.

58 SSIS performance tips

Phil Brammer

Managing performance in SQL Server Integration Services (SSIS) can be an ever-changing battle that depends on many factors, both inside and outside the control of the SSIS developer. In this chapter, we will discuss a few techniques that will enable you to tune the Control Flow and the Data Flow elements of a package to increase performance.

NOTE The following information is based on Integration Services in SQL Server 2005, Service Pack 2.

SSIS overview

SSIS packages are built around a *control flow* or a *work surface* to manage all activity within a package. The control flow is responsible for directing the execution path, as well as for managing predecessors, logging, and variables. The control flow also enables developers to use web services, interact with FTP sites, use custom scripts, and perform many more tasks that can all be linked together in serial or executed in parallel.

Data flow tasks are responsible for extracting, transforming, and loading data from a source to a destination. A source or a destination can be a database table, flat files, memory objects, custom objects, or other supported items. A generous list of components to transform data ships with SSIS and contains such items as row counters, aggregators, lookup transformations, and many more. Data flow tasks reside on the control flow and they can be the only task, or one of many.

Control flow performance

Tuning the control flow to perform as fast as possible depends on whether your tasks can run in parallel. If at all possible, set your control flow tasks to run parallel to each other to ensure that they start processing as soon as they can, and that they aren't waiting for upstream tasks to finish.

You can control how many tasks can run in parallel using the `MaxConcurrent-Executables` property of the control flow. This property defaults to -1, which means that the number of parallel tasks processing at the same time will be limited to the number of logical processors plus 2. For example, if you have four processors on your server, SSIS will limit the number of parallel tasks to six. If your package in this example has eight parallel tasks, two of them will wait until one of the six executable slots opens up. You can change the `MaxConcurrentExecutables` property to a value greater than the number of processors on your server, but it still doesn't mean that all tasks will process at the same time. Execution trees in a data flow task, for instance, can consume available executables, preventing other control flow tasks from executing.

Data flow performance

The data flow task is one of the core elements of SSIS. It is where data is extracted from one or more sources, possibly transformed, and then delivered to one or more destinations. As a result, this task has the most flexibility when it comes to tuning for performance. We will focus on five areas of the data flow that can be adjusted to maximize performance: source acquisition, transforming data, destination loading/updating, lookups, and the data flow in general.

Source acquisition performance

The data flow can work with data only as fast as it can acquire data from its source. If you can only select rows from a source database at a throughput of 10,000 rows per second, SSIS will be limited to processing no more than 10,000 rows per second as well. As shown in figure 1, the easiest way to determine how fast you can acquire data from a source is to hook the source component up to a Row Count transformation or a Copy Column transformation and execute the data flow task, taking note of the time it takes to extract your source data. I recommend repeating this

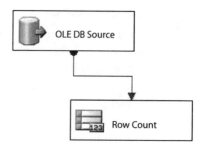

Figure 1   An OLE DB Source component hooked up to a Row Count transformation

process six or more times to establish an average baseline. To use the Row Count transformation, you'll have to set up an SSIS variable to use in the transformation's properties. The Copy Column transformation doesn't have this requirement, and can be hooked up to the source component with no configuration needed.

Once you have your extract average baseline, you'll know the fastest possible speed at which SSIS can process your data. To ensure that you have the source properties tuned to achieve maximum performance, follow these tips:

- Make sure you are using current drivers for your connection. If there are multiple drivers available, be sure to test each one for the best performance, and ensure your packages use the optimum driver.

- Use SQL Command or SQL Command from Variable when setting the data access mode property of an OLE DB Source component and your source is a SQL Server database. This will execute the procedure sp_executesql. If you use a data access mode of Table or View or Table Name or View Name from Variable, SSIS will use the OPENROWSET() method to generate your results.
- Only select the columns you need in your data flow. This serves two purposes: it limits the amount of memory SSIS requires to store the data in its buffers, and it potentially buffers the source extract from source metadata changes. If you were to issue SELECT * FROM myTable instead, any column data type changes, additions, or removals can cause SSIS to fail validation and cause the package execution to fail.
- Add a WHERE clause to your source extract query to filter rows, returning only those rows that are required for processing. Of course, this only works if you are working with a source that's queryable (such as SQL Server, Oracle, DB2, and Teradata) and not a flat file or other non-database source.
- Large sorts should be done in the source extract query if possible. This will cause the sort to run on the server and prevent SSIS from having to buffer all of the data to sort it, which on large datasets could result in swapping out to disk.

Data transformation performance

Transforming data is an extremely broad topic with a growing list of third-party components; I'll only cover some of the general guidelines that should work across most transformation scenarios.

The first thing I recommend is building your transformations to perform all of the work you need to accomplish. Then, instead of adding a destination component, add a Row Count or a Copy Column transformation to assess the slowdown of your transformations, much like I demonstrated in the previous section. If your numbers are similar to your source acquisition baseline, you likely will not gain much by way of tuning your transformations. But if your numbers are much slower than your source acquisition baseline, you know you may have room for improvement.

To ensure your transformations have the best performance, some of the things to consider are

- Avoid unnecessary data type casting. If possible, cast to an appropriate data type in your source query.
- Some components such as Aggregate and Sort require that they receive all input rows before they can begin processing the rows. These are known as *asynchronous components*, and will block the flow of data to downstream components. You may want to consider implementing this logic in the source query if possible.
- If you are using a single Aggregate transformation with multiple outputs and those outputs are going to separate destinations, consider creating an aggregate for each destination. This will ensure that each aggregate will not have to wait on the lowest-granular aggregation to process, as is the case when using a single Aggregate transformation with multiple outputs.

Destination performance

The fastest destination component is the Raw File destination. This component stores its data in a format specific to SSIS and is extremely fast, with the only bottleneck being the speed of the disk you are writing to. This component is especially useful for exchanging data between data flows, as the metadata is stored in the raw file itself, which eliminates the need to specify the file layout when using the file as a source. This component can't be configured to perform any faster than your disk allows.

Perhaps the most common destination component in SSIS is the OLE DB Destination. This component allows the flexibility of issuing bulk inserts or row-by-row inserts. As shown in figure 2, to use the bulk insert function of this destination, select *Table* or *view - fast* load from the drop-down box of the data access mode property. The fast load option issues a bulk insert command at the destination and allows you to specify the number of rows to commit as a batch. The Maximum Insert Commit Size property defaults to 0, which tells SSIS to commit all incoming rows as a single batch. Setting this property to something other than 0 ensures that after SSIS has processed the set number of rows, it will issue a commit. If an insert error happens in a batch of rows, all of the rows in the batch are rolled back and the component raises an error. If you have the component set to redirect errors, the entire batch will be redirected, not just the row causing the error.

Setting the commit size properly depends on what type of table you are inserting into and the number of rows being sent to the destination. If the number of rows is small, a commit size of 0 may work well for you. For a large number of rows, if the table doesn't have a clustered index (for example, a heap table), the default commit size of 0 will generate the best performance. For a table that has a clustered index defined, all rows in the batch must be sorted up front to be inserted, which can cause performance issues depending on your memory specifications on the server. For that reason, on a table with a clustered index, it is best to set the commit size to a value appropriate for your environment (for example, 100,000 rows).

You may also find, on a table with a clustered index, that it is more beneficial to drop the index before inserting the rows and then rebuild the index after successfully completing all inserts. You'll have to test this for each table to find the right solution.

The next component, OLE DB Command, is commonly used for updating destination tables. But, depending on your design, you may want to instead consider inserting your updates into a temporary table, and later, back on the control flow, issuing an Execute SQL task to perform a batch update. The OLE DB Command component executes each time a row passes through it, and for this reason it can become the slowest component in a data flow. Evaluate your options when considering using this component, and test them before making a decision that could negatively impact performance. This is unavoidable in some cases, such as when you are updating a table that you have a lookup selecting against in the same data flow, and you need the updated results to be reflected immediately.

The other commonly used destination is the flat file. Much like a raw file, its performance is dependent on the disk you are writing files to. This destination doesn't

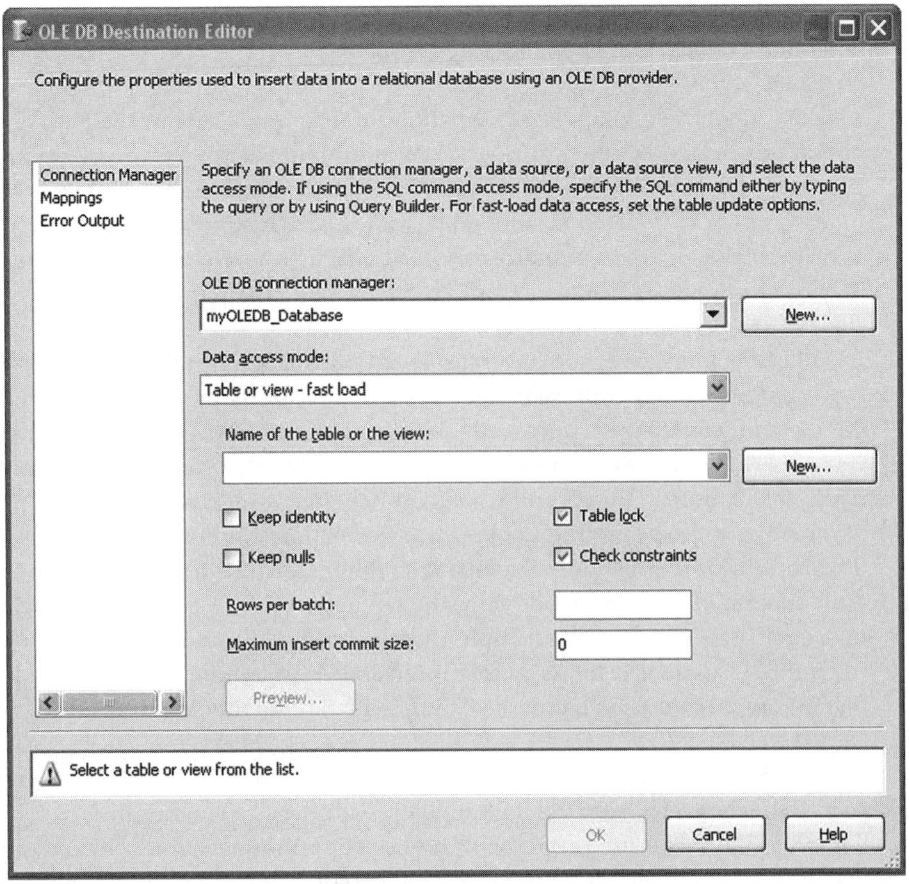

Figure 2   The OLE DB Destination fast load panel

store its metadata in the file, and as such, if you later want to read data from this file, you must define the column mappings in each package that uses the file as a source.

Perhaps the most effective destination component is the SQL Server destination. Use this component if your destination is SQL Server and the package resides on and is executed on the target SQL Server. This destination component bypasses the network layer when inserting into SQL Server, and is extremely fast as a result. The downside of using this destination is that it requires your data types to explicitly match the data types of the columns you are inserting into. Unlike the OLE DB destination, the SQL Server destination will not implicitly cast data types.

Lookup transformation performance

The Lookup transformation allows you to use a lookup table to achieve things such as checking to see whether a record exists and looking up a description of an item from a dimension table. It is a powerful transformation, and one that you'll most likely use at some point.

The Lookup transformation has three primary settings: no cache, partial cache, and full cache. Each has benefits and drawbacks.

NO CACHE

This setting of the Lookup transformation forces a query against the lookup table (or query) for each row passing through it. As a result, this setting is very slow performing. The only performance gain you can get here is to make sure your lookup columns are indexed properly so as to avoid a table scan. Comparisons with this cache mode are done in the lookup table's database, not SSIS. To use the no cache mode, select Enable Memory Restriction from the Advanced tab of the Lookup transformation.

FULL CACHE

In full cache mode, the Lookup transformation will attempt to store all lookup table rows in memory. SSIS will cache all rows before it starts processing data in the data flow. It is crucial that you select only the columns and rows that you need to perform your lookup, so that the memory storage is limited to the minimum amount possible. If you select more columns and rows than necessary, you risk causing SSIS to run out of memory, and because the Lookup transformation will not swap its memory out to disk, running out of memory is a fatal data flow error. The full cache mode is the fastest lookup mode; for this mode only, the equality rules are often different than those of a database engine. (For example, full cache mode uses case-sensitive rules even when the database may be set to case-insensitive.) To use the full cache mode, ensure that no options are selected on the Advanced tab of the Lookup transformation.

PARTIAL CACHE

The partial cache mode is a mix between no cache and full cache modes, in that it partially caches rows from the lookup table, with the size (in megabytes) of the cache limited to the cache size property of the Lookup transformation. Any rows that don't match the cached dataset are sent to the database to see if they physically exist in the lookup table. Use this mode when using full cache would otherwise take up too much memory and you want to limit the upper memory requirements of the cache, or when you want to force the database to perform the equality checks and not SSIS. To use partial caching, ensure that Enable Memory Restriction is selected, and also ensure that either Enable Caching, Modify the SQL Statement, or both are selected.

General data flow performance

Each data flow has a few properties that should be evaluated for each implementation. `DefaultBufferMaxRows` and `DefaultBufferSize` are two properties that can drastically increase data flow performance if adjusted correctly.

`DefaultBufferMaxRows` specifies the maximum number of rows SSIS will place in a buffer. `DefaultBufferSize` specifies the default buffer size that SSIS uses in its calculations to determine how many rows to place in a buffer. The maximum allowable buffer size is 100 megabytes.

Tuning these two parameters will ensure that your data flow is optimized for its specific dataset. To determine the optimum setting, turn on the custom data flow logging event `BufferSizeTuning`. This event, when reading the resulting log file, will tell you how many rows were placed in the buffer. If your `DefaultBufferMaxRows` is set to the default of 10,000, and the `BufferSizeTuning` logging event is reporting only 2,000 rows were placed in the buffer, you'll need to increase the `DefaultBufferSize` property to accommodate more rows or reduce the size of each row by eliminating unnecessary columns.

If your data flow has BLOB data in it, specifying a folder in the `BLOBTempStorage-Path` property will allow you to change where BLOB data is spooled out to disk. Choosing a faster disk, instead of the disk specified in the `TMP`/`TEMP` environment variables, you may be able to increase data flow performance when working with BLOB data.

NOTE   SSIS always spools BLOB data to disk. Ensure that `BLOBTempStoragePath` is set to a disk that's large enough to handle your BLOB data.

Summary

Tuning SSIS can be a time-consuming process and difficult to master. Each design situation will present unique challenges. To help you succeed in tuning your packages, be sure to

- Turn on package logging to help you understand what your packages are doing.
- Turn on the `BufferSizeTuning` custom event for your data flows in the logging provider to help you tune the `DefaultBufferMaxRows` and `DefaultBufferSize` properties.
- Always use SQL, if possible, to select from sources, and in your lookup transformations as well.
- Perform sort operations within the database if you can.
- Only select the columns you need in your data flow sources and lookup transformations.

About the author

Phil Brammer has more than nine years data warehousing experience in various technologies, including Red Brick, Teradata, and most recently, SQL Server. His specialty is in building extract, transform, and load (ETL) processes, using tools such as Informatica, and SQL Server Integration Services. He continues to play an active role in the Integration Services community via online resources as well as his technical blog site, http://ssistalk.com.

59 Incremental loads using T-SQL and SSIS

Andy Leonard

Back in the old days, when we used to walk to the card punch centers barefoot in the snow uphill both ways and carve our own computer chips out of wood, people performed incremental loads using the following steps:

1 Open the source and destination files.
2 Look at them.
3 Where you see new rows in the source file, copy and paste them into the destination file.
4 Where you see differences between rows that exist in both files, copy the source row and paste over the destination row.

Doubtless, some of you are thinking, "Andy, you nincompoop, no one cut and pasted production data—ever." Oh really? I'd wager that in some department in every Global 1000 company, someone somewhere regularly cuts and pastes data into an Excel spreadsheet—even now. Read on to discover two ways to perform incremental loads in SQL Server the right way—using T-SQL and SQL Server Integration Services.

Some definitions

What, exactly, is an *incremental load?* An incremental load is a process where new and updated data from some source is loaded into a destination, whereas matching data is ignored. That last part about matching data is the key. If the data is identical in both source and destination, the best thing we can do is leave it be.

The chief advantage of an incremental load is time: generally speaking, it takes less time to perform an incremental load. The chief risk is misidentification. It's possible to assign source rows to an incorrect status during the incremental load—the trickiest row status to identify is changed rows. Misidentified rows means a loss of data integrity. In the data warehouse field, less data integrity is often referred to as "bad."

Incremental loads aren't the only way to load data. Another popular method is called *destructive loads*. In a destructive load, the destination data is first removed—by deletion or, more often, truncation—before data is loaded from the source.

The chief advantage of a destructive load is data integrity. Think about it—if you're simply copying the source into the destination, the opportunity to err drops dramatically. The chief disadvantage of a destructive load is the length of time it takes. Generally speaking, it takes longer to load all of the data when compared to loading a subset.

A T-SQL incremental load

Let's look at a couple of ways to accomplish incremental loads. Our first example will be in Transact-SQL (T-SQL). Later, we'll see an example using SQL Server 2005 Integration Services (SSIS 2005). To set up the T-SQL demo, use the following code to create two databases: a source database and a destination database (optional, but recommended):

```
CREATE DATABASE [SSISIncrementalLoad_Source]
CREATE DATABASE [SSISIncrementalLoad_Dest]
```

Now we need to create source and destination tables. We'll start with creating the source table, as shown in listing 1.

Listing 1   Creating the tblSource source

```
USE SSISIncrementalLoad_Source
GO
CREATE TABLE dbo.tblSource
(ColID int NOT NULL
,ColA varchar(10) NULL
,ColB datetime NULL constraint df_ColB default (getDate())
,ColC int NULL
,constraint PK_tblSource primary key clustered (ColID))
```

The source table is named tblSource and contains the columns ColID, ColA, ColB, and ColC. For this example, make ColID the primary unique key. Next, we'll create the destination table, as shown in listing 2.

Listing 2   Creating the tblDest destination

```
USE SSISIncrementalLoad_Dest
GO
CREATE TABLE dbo.tblDest
(ColID int NOT NULL
,ColA varchar(10) NULL
,ColB datetime NULL
,ColC int NULL)
```

This listing creates a destination table named tblDest with the columns ColID, ColA, ColB, and ColC. Next, we'll load some test data into both tables for demonstration purposes, as shown in listing 3.

Listing 3   Loading data

```
USE SSISIncrementalLoad_Source
GO
INSERT INTO dbo.tblSource              ← Insert unchanged row
(ColID,ColA,ColB,ColC)
VALUES(0, 'A', '1/1/2007 12:01 AM', -1)
INSERT INTO dbo.tblSource              ← Insert changed row
(ColID,ColA,ColB,ColC)
VALUES(1, 'B', '1/1/2007 12:02 AM', -2)
INSERT INTO dbo.tblSource              ← Insert new row
(ColID,ColA,ColB,ColC)
VALUES(2, 'N', '1/1/2007 12:03 AM', -3)
USE SSISIncrementalLoad_Dest
GO
INSERT INTO dbo.tblDest                ← Insert unchanged row
(ColID,ColA,ColB,ColC)
VALUES(0, 'A', '1/1/2007 12:01 AM', -1)
INSERT INTO dbo.tblDest                ← Insert changed row
(ColID,ColA,ColB,ColC)
VALUES(1, 'C', '1/1/2007 12:02 AM', -2)
```

As you can see, this listing populates the tables with some generic time and date information we'll use in our query, shown in listing 4, to view the new rows.

Listing 4   Viewing new rows

```
SELECT s.ColID, s.ColA, s.ColB, s.ColC
FROM SSISIncrementalLoad_Source.dbo.tblSource s
LEFT JOIN SSISIncrementalLoad_Dest.dbo.tblDest d ON d.ColID = s.ColID
WHERE d.ColID IS NULL
```

This query should return the new row—the one loaded earlier with `ColID` = 2 and `ColA` = N. Why? The `LEFT JOIN` and `WHERE` clauses are the key. Left joins return all rows on the left side of the `JOIN` clause (`SSISIncrementalLoad_Source.dbo.tblSource` in this case) whether there's a match on the right side of the `JOIN` clause (`SSISIncrementalLoad_Dest.dbo.tblDest` in this case) or not. If there's no match on the right side, `NULL`s are returned. This is why the `WHERE` clause works: it goes after rows where the destination ColID is `NULL`. These rows have no match in the `LEFT JOIN`; therefore, they must be new.

Now we'll use the T-SQL statement in listing 5 to incrementally load the row or rows.

Listing 5   Incrementally loading new rows

```
INSERT INTO SSISIncrementalLoad_Dest.dbo.tblDest
(ColID, ColA, ColB, ColC)
SELECT s.ColID, s.ColA, s.ColB, s.ColC
FROM SSISIncrementalLoad_Source.dbo.tblSource s
LEFT JOIN SSISIncrementalLoad_Dest.dbo.tblDest d ON d.ColID = s.ColID
WHERE d.ColID IS NULL
```

Although occasionally database schemas are this easy to load, most of the time you have to include several columns in the JOIN ON clause to isolate truly new rows. Sometimes you have to add conditions in the WHERE clause to refine the definition of truly new rows.

It's equally crucial to identify changed rows. We'll view the changed rows using the T-SQL statement in listing 6.

Listing 6   Isolating changed rows

```
SELECT d.ColID, d.ColA, d.ColB, d.ColC
FROM SSISIncrementalLoad_Dest.dbo.tblDest d
INNER JOIN SSISIncrementalLoad_Source.dbo.tblSource s ON s.ColID = d.ColID
WHERE (
(d.ColA != s.ColA)
OR (d.ColB != s.ColB)
OR (d.ColC != s.ColC)
)
```

Theoretically, you can try to isolate changed rows in many ways. But the only sure-fire way to accomplish this is to compare each field as we've done here. This should return the changed row we loaded earlier with ColID = 1 and ColA = C. Why? The INNER JOIN and WHERE clauses are to blame—again. The INNER JOIN goes after rows with matching ColIDs because of the JOIN ON clause. The WHERE clause refines the result set, returning only rows where ColA, ColB, or ColC don't match and the ColIDs match.

This last bit is particularly important. If there's a difference in any, some, or all of the rows (except ColID), we want to update it. To update the data in our destination, use the T-SQL shown in listing 7.

Listing 7   Updating the data

```
UPDATE d
SET
d.ColA = s.ColA
,d.ColB = s.ColB
,d.ColC = s.ColC
FROM SSISIncrementalLoad_Dest.dbo.tblDest d
INNER JOIN SSISIncrementalLoad_Source.dbo.tblSource s ON s.ColID = d.ColID
WHERE (
(d.ColA != s.ColA)
OR (d.ColB != s.ColB)
OR (d.ColC != s.ColC)
)
```

Extract, transform, and load (ETL) theory has a lot to say about when and how to update changed data. You'll want to pick up a good book on the topic to learn more about the variations.

NOTE Using SQL Server 2008, the new MERGE command can figure out which rows need to be inserted and which only need updating, and then perform the insert and update—all within a single command. Also new in

SQL Server 2008 are the Change Tracking and Change Data Capture features which, as their names imply, automatically track which rows have been changed, making selecting from the source database much easier.

Now that we've looked at an incremental load using T-SQL, let's consider how SQL Server Integration Services can accomplish the same task without all the hand-coding.

Incremental loads in SSIS

SQL Server Integration Services (SSIS) is Microsoft's application bundled with SQL Server that simplifies data integration and transformations—and in this case, incremental loads. For this example, we'll use SSIS to execute the lookup transformation (for the join functionality) combined with the conditional split (for the WHERE clause conditions) transformations.

Before we begin, let's reset our database tables to their original state using the T-SQL code in listing 8.

Listing 8   Resetting the tables

```
USE SSISIncrementalLoad_Source
GO
TRUNCATE TABLE dbo.tblSource
INSERT INTO dbo.tblSource          <— Insert unchanged row
(ColID,ColA,ColB,ColC)
VALUES(0, 'A', '1/1/2007 12:01 AM', -1)
-- insert a "changed" row
INSERT INTO dbo.tblSource          <— Insert changed row
(ColID,ColA,ColB,ColC)
VALUES(1, 'B', '1/1/2007 12:02 AM', -2)
INSERT INTO dbo.tblSource          <— Insert new row
(ColID,ColA,ColB,ColC)
VALUES(2, 'N', '1/1/2007 12:03 AM', -3)
USE SSISIncrementalLoad_Dest
GO
TRUNCATE TABLE dbo.tblDest
INSERT INTO dbo.tblDest            <— Insert unchanged row
(ColID,ColA,ColB,ColC)
VALUES(0, 'A', '1/1/2007 12:01 AM', -1)
INSERT INTO dbo.tblDest            <— Insert changed row
(ColID,ColA,ColB,ColC)
VALUES(1, 'C', '1/1/2007 12:02 AM', -2)
```

With the tables back in their original state, we'll create a new project using Business Intelligence Development Studio (BIDS).

Creating the new BIDS project

To follow along with this example, first open BIDS and create a new project. We'll name the project SSISIncrementalLoad, as shown in figure 1. Once the project loads, open Solution Explorer, right-click the package, and rename Package1.dtsx to SSISIncrementalLoad.dtsx.

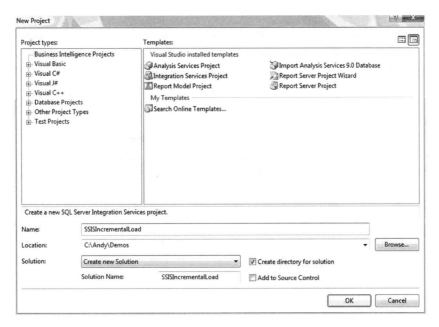

Figure 1   Creating a new BIDS project named SSISIncrementalLoad

When prompted to rename the package object, click the Yes button. From here, follow this straightforward series:

1 From the toolbox, drag a data flow onto the Control Flow canvas. Double-click the data flow task to edit it.

2 From the toolbox, drag and drop an OLE DB source onto the Data Flow canvas. Double-click the OLE DB Source connection adapter to edit it.

3 Click the New button beside the OLE DB Connection Manager drop-down. Click the New button here to create a new data connection. Enter or select your server name. Connect to the SSISIncrementalLoad_Source database you created earlier. Click the OK button to return to the Connection Manager configuration dialog box.

4 Click the OK button to accept your newly created data connection as the connection manager you want to define. Select dbo.tblSource from the Table drop-down.

5 Click the OK button to complete defining the OLE DB source adapter.

Defining the lookup transformation

Now that the source adapter is defined, let's move on to the lookup transformation that'll join the data from our two tables. Again, there's a standard series of steps in SSIS:

1 Drag and drop a lookup transformation from the toolbox onto the Data Flow canvas.

2   Connect the OLE DB connection adapter to the lookup transformation by clicking on the OLE DB Source, dragging the green arrow over the lookup, and
dropping it.

3   Right-click the lookup transformation and click Edit (or double-click the
lookup transformation) to edit. You should now see something like the example shown in figure 2.

When the editor opens, click the New button beside the OLE DB Connection Manager
drop-down (as you did earlier for the OLE DB source adapter). Define a new data connection—this time to the SSISIncrementalLoad_Dest database. After setting up the
new data connection and connection manager, configure the lookup transformation
to connect to dbo.tblDest. Click the Columns tab. On the left side are the columns
currently in the SSIS data flow pipeline (from SSISIncrementalLoad_Source.
dbo.tblSource). On the right side are columns available from the lookup destination
you just configured (from SSISIncrementalLoad_Dest.dbo.tblDest).

We'll need all the rows returned from the destination table, so check all the check
boxes beside the rows in the destination. We need these rows for our WHERE clauses
and our JOIN ON clauses.

We don't want to map all the rows between the source and destination—only the
columns named ColID between the database tables. The mappings drawn between
the Available Input columns and Available Lookup columns define the JOIN ON clause.
Multi-select the mappings between ColA, ColB, and ColC by clicking on them while
holding the Ctrl key. Right-click any of them and click Delete Selected Mappings to
delete these columns from our JOIN ON clause, as shown in figure 3.

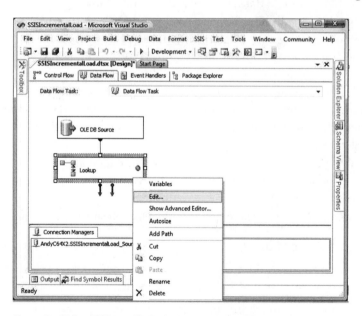

Figure 2   Using SSIS to edit the lookup transformation

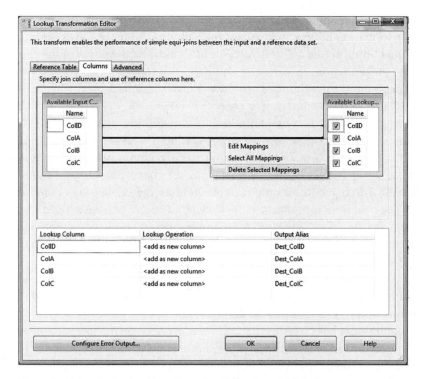

Figure 3   Using the Lookup Transformation Editor to establish the correct mappings

Add the text *Dest_* to each column's output alias. These rows are being appended to the data flow pipeline. This is so that we can distinguish between source and destination rows farther down the pipeline.

Setting the lookup transformation behavior

Next we need to modify our lookup transformation behavior. By default, the lookup operates similar to an INNER JOIN—but we need a LEFT (OUTER) JOIN. Click the Configure Error Output button to open the Configure Error Output screen. On the Lookup Output row, change the Error column from Fail Component to Ignore Failure. This tells the lookup transformation that if it doesn't find an INNER JOIN match in the destination table for the source table's ColID value, it shouldn't fail. This also effectively tells the lookup to behave like a LEFT JOIN instead of an INNER JOIN. Click OK to complete the lookup transformation configuration.

From the toolbox, drag and drop a conditional split transformation onto the Data Flow canvas. Connect the lookup to the conditional split as shown in figure 4. Right-click the conditional split and click Edit to open the Conditional Split Transformation Editor. The Editor is divided into three sections. The upper-left section contains a list of available variables and columns. The upper-right section contains a list of available operations you may perform on values in the conditional expression. The lower section contains a list of the outputs you can define using SSIS Expression Language.

Expand the NULL Functions folder in the upper-right section of the Conditional Split Transformation Editor, and expand the Columns folder in the upper-left section. Click in the Output Name column and enter New Rows as the name of the first output. From the NULL Functions folder, drag and drop the ISNULL(<<expression>>) function to the Condition column of the New Rows condition. Next, drag Dest_ColID from the Columns folder and drop it onto the *<<expression>>* text in the Condition column. New rows should now be defined by the condition ISNULL([Dest_ColID]). This defines the WHERE clause for new rows—setting it to WHERE Dest_ColID Is NULL.

Type Changed Rows into a second output name column. Add the expression (ColA != Dest_ColA) || (ColB != Dest_ColB) || (ColC != Dest_ColC) to the Condition column for the Changed Rows output. This defines our WHERE clause for detecting changed rows—setting it to WHERE ((Dest_ColA != ColA) OR (Dest_ColB != ColB) OR (Dest_ColC != ColC)). Note that || is the expression for OR in SSIS expressions. Change the default output name from Conditional Split Default Output to Unchanged Rows.

It's important to note here that the data flow task acts on rows. It can be used to manipulate (transform, create, or delete) data in columns in a row, but the sources, destinations, and transformations in the data flow task act on rows.

In a conditional split transformation, rows are sent to the output when the SSIS Expression Language condition for that output evaluates as true. A conditional split transformation behaves like a Switch statement in C# or Select Case in Visual Basic, in that the rows are sent to the first output for which the condition evaluates as true. This means that if two or more conditions are true for a given row, the row will be sent to the first output in the list for which the condition is true, and that the row will never be checked to see whether it meets the second condition. Click the OK button to complete configuration of the conditional split transformation.

Drag and drop an OLE DB destination connection adapter and an OLE DB command transformation onto the Data Flow canvas. Click on the conditional split and connect it to the OLE DB destination. A dialog box will display prompting you to select a conditional split output (those outputs you defined in the last step). Select the New Rows output. Next connect the OLE DB command transformation to the conditional split's Changed Rows output. Your Data Flow canvas should appear similar to the example in figure 4.

Configure the OLE DB destination by aiming at the SSISIncremental-Load_Dest.dbo.tblDest table. Click the Mappings item in the list to the left. Make sure the ColID, ColA, ColB, and ColC source columns are mapped to their matching destination columns (aren't you glad we prepended *Dest_* to the destination columns?). Click the OK button to complete configuring the OLE DB destination connection adapter. Double-click the OLE DB command to open the Advanced Editor for the OLE DB Command dialog box. Set the Connection Manager column to your SSISIncrementalLoad_Dest connection manager. Click on the Component Properties tab. Click the ellipsis (...) beside the SQLCommand property. The String Value

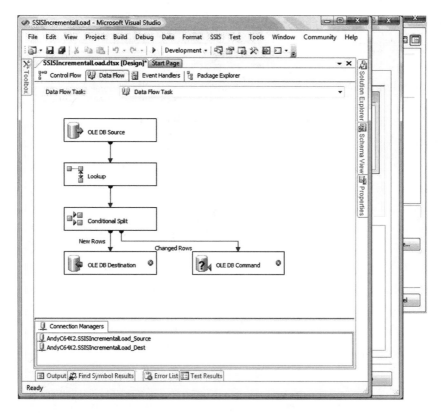

Figure 4   The Data Flow canvas shows a graphical view of the transformation.

Editor displays. Enter the following parameterized T-SQL statement into the String Value text box:

```
UPDATE dbo.tblDest
SET
ColA = ?
,ColB = ?
,ColC = ?
WHERE ColID = ?
```

The question marks in the previous parameterized T-SQL statement map by ordinal to columns named Param_0 through Param_3. Map them as shown here—effectively altering the UPDATE statement for each row:

```
UPDATE SSISIncrementalLoad_Dest.dbo.tblDest
SET
ColA = SSISIncrementalLoad_Source.dbo.ColA
,ColB = SSISIncrementalLoad_Source.dbo.ColB
,ColC = SSISIncrementalLoad_Source.dbo.ColC
WHERE ColID = SSISIncrementalLoad_Source.dbo.ColID
```

As you can see in figure 5, the query is executed on a row-by-row basis. For performance with large amounts of data, you'll want to employ set-based updates instead.

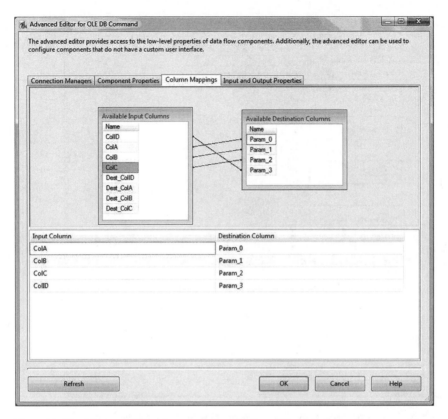

Figure 5   The Advanced Editor shows a representation of the data flow prior to execution.

Click the OK button when mapping is completed. If you execute the package with debugging (press F5), the package should succeed.

Note that one row takes the New Rows output from the conditional split, and one row takes the Changed Rows output from the conditional split transformation. Although not visible, our third source row doesn't change, and would be sent to the Unchanged Rows output—which is the default Conditional Split output renamed. Any row that doesn't meet any of the predefined conditions in the conditional split is sent to the default output.

Summary

The incremental load design pattern is a powerful way to leverage the strengths of the SSIS 2005 data flow task to transport data from a source to a destination. By using this method, you only insert or update rows that are new or have changed.

About the author

Andy Leonard is an architect with Unisys corporation, SQL Server database and integration services developer, SQL Server MVP, PASS regional mentor (Southeast US), and engineer. He's a coauthor of several books on SQL Server topics. Andy founded and manages VSTeamSystemCentral.com and maintains several blogs there—Applied Team System, Applied Database Development, and Applied Business Intelligence—and also blogs for SQLBlog.com. Andy's background includes web application architecture and development, VB, and ASP; SQL Server Integration Services (SSIS); data warehouse development using SQL Server 2000, 2005, and 2008; and test-driven database development.

index